# THE YOUNG HEGEL

STUDIES IN THE RELATIONS BETWEEN DIALECTICS AND ECONOMICS

# The Young Hegel

## Studies in the Relations between Dialectics and Economics

by

GEORG LUKÁCS

translated by Rodney Livingstone

The MIT Press
Cambridge, Massachusetts

# Translator's Note

Lukács' terminology presupposes an audience familiar with the language of German idealist philosophy and of the Hegelian–Marxist tradition. To provide a key to that language would be a daunting and perhaps unrewarding task in the present context. At all events I have preferred simply to take over the vocabulary already developed by earlier translators, in the hope that Lukács' own text and a few additional footnotes would suffice to render his argument comprehensible. It is for this reason that I have, wherever possible, made use of existing translations of the works of Kant, Hegel, Marx, Engels and Lenin, rather than compound the confusion by developing my own new language.

It may be of assistance to the reader to list here some of the key terms which recur throughout the book and indicate where explanations may be found, either in Lukács' text, or in editorial footnotes. Other important concepts will be found listed in the Index under Hegel:

1. *Aufheben* = annul, preserve, supersede or sublate. See p. 99.
2. *Bürgerliche Gesellschaft*: used by Hegel to mean 'civil society' as opposed to political society. As such it can refer to any post-classical society, in which the 'civil' and the 'political' became distinct. (See esp. p. 375.) However, Lukács tends to assimilate it to its modern meaning of 'bourgeois society'. I have tried to use the meaning that seemed right in the context.
3. *The categories* of Kantian philosophy, see p. 259.
4. *Entäusserung*: one of the words for 'alienation'. I have preferred to translate it as 'externalization', since in Hegel's usage it has a broader application than the current term. See pp. 532 ff.
5. *Erinnerung* = (1) memory & (2) internalization. See pp. 508, 515.
6. *Gestalten des Bewusstseins* = the forms or configurations of consciousness. See pp. 474–5.
7. *Infinite progress*: see pp. 223–4.
8. *Intellektuelle Anschauung* = intellectual intuition, see pp. 246–7.
9. *Reflexionsbestimmungen* = determinations of reflection. See p. 284.

Thanks are due to the following for permission to reprint material already translated: Lawrence & Wishart for quotations from the works of Marx, Engels and Lenin; George Allen & Unwin for quotations from J.B. Baillie's translation of *The Phenomenology of Mind*; The Clarendon Press for quotations from *Hegel's Political Writings*, edited by Z.A. Pelczynski and translated by T.M. Knox and from Hegel's *Philosophy of*

*Right* also translated by T.M. Knox; to University of Chicago Press, for quotations from T.M. Knox's translations of the early theological writings in *Friedrich Hegel on Christianity*, Harper & Row Torchbooks, New York 1961. I have occasionally modified these translations to adapt them to Lukács' argument (and once or twice, where Lukács uses a different text).

I should also like to record a debt of gratitude to Professor Tony Manser and the other members of the Hegel Seminar at Southampton University whose discussions of the *Phenomenology* and the *Logic* over a period of two years greatly increased my understanding of Hegel. It is my hope that thanks to them I have become better able to avoid the numerous pitfalls that await the unwary translator of philosophical German texts.

Southampton, August 1974                                       R.S.L.

*For Mikhail Alexandrovitch Lifschitz*
*in devotion and friendship*

# Contents

# Preface to the new edition (1954)

This book was completed in late Autumn 1938. The imminent outbreak of war delayed its appearance for many years. In 1947/8, when publication became possible I thoroughly revised the text but because of the many other claims on my time I could only take account of a very small part of the literature on Hegel that had appeared since 1938. The present new edition for the German Democratic Republic has again been revised, but apart from stylistic improvements almost no changes have been made.

In the Introduction the reader will find a full account of the methodological considerations that have guided the author throughout the work. On this point too I see no reason to modify the positions adopted sixteen years ago. The attempts made in France to 'modernize' Hegel in an existential, irrationalist sense—above all in the well-known book by Jean Hyppolyte—have not given me any cause to emend my arguments or even to supplement them. The fundamental critique given here of the picture of Hegel current in the Age of Imperialism* applies with equal force to these French efforts to provide a re-interpretation even though the conditions both internal and external for a 'Hegel Renaissance' in France must differ in many ways from those in Germany.

I will perhaps be permitted to make a few remarks for the benefit of the German readers of my other, often later, works. My account of the development of the young Hegel supplements in many respects the ideas I have attempted to formulate in my other studies of the history of German philosophy and literature. Above all the present work contains a positive vision to contrast with the 'classical' age of irrationalism as presented in my work *The Destruction of Reason*. In that book I examined the irrationalist tradition established by Schelling and his successors. Here I shall be concerned with the critique and overcoming of irrationalism as seen from Hegel's side, though this in its turn is just the negative, critical motif counterpointing the main theme: the foundation of the new idealist, dialectical method. The two books mutually complement each other in yet other ways. Only in the present studies of Hegel was it possible to provide a positive explanation of why it was above all his philosophy that became the great stumbling-block for the irrationalists of the period and why the latter rightly focused their attacks on him as the outstanding representative of the progressive bourgeois philosophy of the age. At the same time it becomes clear why the limitations and aberrations of

---

* G.L. uses this phrase to refer to the period following the foundation of the German Empire in 1870, and more specifically, the era of William II and the First World War.—*Trans.*

Hegel's idealism could provide them with a real pretext for their critique of the dialectics of historicism and enable them to mount a relatively accurate attack upon it. Hence, from the examination and critique of Hegel's early development, we can understand why irrationalism still possessed the vestiges of philosophical substance in Schelling's early period, and why it lost even this slight justification later on in Nietzsche, once scientific socialism had appeared on the scene to oppose it. And if we are to understand not only the direct impact of Marx on the development of German thought but also his sometimes extremely indirect influence, an exact knowledge of Hegel, of both his greatness and his limitations, is absolutely indispensable.

The same issue is equally crucial to the understanding of the golden age of German literature. I have pointed to the connections here from the standpoint of German literature in my studies of Hölderlin and Heine, and above all in my discussions of Goethe's *Faust*. Since an analysis of *The Phenomenology of Mind* constitutes the core of the present work I have naturally attempted to demonstrate its profound intellectual and philosophical affinities with *Faust* so that the attentive reader will discover a perhaps not wholly idle complement to my earlier studies of Goethe's masterpiece from the opposite perspective. This applies with equal force to almost all the problems of a progressive German literature. One of the central tasks of German literary history is to settle accounts with the reactionary elements of Romanticism. The more reactionary the representatives of Romanticism were, the more they were glorified, and under the German Empire German literary historians either strove to blur the distinction between German Classicism and Romanticism or simply proclaimed their reactionary views openly and aggressively. Hence the intellectual reconstruction of the true situation is an important task for scholarship.

At the same time it is a task inseparable from general issues of cultural politics. At a time when the people of Germany are feeling their way, when significant sections of the German intelligentsia have not made up their minds whether to move forwards or backwards, a correct view of the intellectual conflicts of the past can also act as a compass for the future. In my philosophical and literary studies I have always endeavoured to subordinate other aims to the great challenge posed by this fact. I believe that the elucidation of Hegel's own philosophy as well as of its connections with the progressive and reactionary currents of his age can likewise help to clarify this urgent and important problem.

In all such ideological decisions the question of one's attitude to Marx is crucial. And this is not merely a matter of Marx's importance as thinker and politician, as philosopher, economist and historian: what counts is an understanding of what Marx has meant and still means in the context of German culture. It is three decades since Thomas Mann wrote

'I said that the state of Germany will not give cause for satisfaction,
Germany will not be able to find its true self until Karl Marx has read
Friedrich Hölderlin—, an encounter which, by the way, is on the
point of taking place. I forgot to add that if the acquaintance remains
one-sided it will necessarily prove sterile.'

This is indeed a highly promising cultural programme, especially if the
attempt is made to recover the authentic Hölderlin—as the present
writer has done here and elsewhere. It would be a dangerous illusion,
however, to conclude that this programme has been even minimally realized by the mass of the German nation, and the disappearance of Marx
from the cultural horizon of broad sections of the German people
remains a source of weakness which can be seen daily and hourly in
every sphere of activity. The German people has objectively weaker revolutionary traditions than other nations and cannot afford the luxury of
renouncing this crucial asset.

The task of revitalizing the German tradition can be approached in a
number of ways. One of them is to demonstrate the roots of Marx's work
in Germany so as to show the extent of Marx's involvement with the
progressive German tradition from Lessing to Heine, from Leibniz to
Hegel and Feuerbach, and to prove how profoundly German his works
are from the structure of their thought down to his very style. A correct
historical analysis of Hegel which sets out from Marxian perspectives can
make a contribution to the solution of this problem.

Of course, the present work is primarily a scholarly exploration of
facts and relations in philosophy and the history of philosophy. Its value
is determined by the success with which it achieves a greater clarity in
these matters than had existed previously. However, no knowledge can
exist in isolation. A correct understanding of Hegel inevitably raises the
questions we have just outlined and the book is designed to clarify them
too. The author cannot pronounce on the success or failure of his enterprise but thinks it his duty to acquaint the reader frankly with his intentions.

BUDAPEST, January 1954

# Introduction

THE history of the origins and development of classical German philosophy is an important and as yet unsolved problem in the Marxist history of philosophy. Even though the Marxist classics have repeatedly drawn attention to the extraordinary importance of the problem, even though Engels included Kant, Fichte and Hegel among the precursors of the philosophy of the revolutionary workers' movement, even though Marx and Lenin have brilliantly illuminated the central issues in a number of profound studies this story has not yet been fully explored.

We have not even arrived at the point of concretely unravelling the historical points of departure, of a concrete analysis of the available facts and texts, of a radical critique of the most important, false and misleading bourgeois theories on the subject.

For a long time the bourgeois interpretation of the origins and growth of classical German philosophy was dominated by the brilliantly original though idealistically distorted and in many respects schematic view established by Hegel himself. Hegel's pioneering historical insight consisted in his discovery that the various philosophical systems were connected by inner dialectical bonds. He was the first man to conceive of the history of philosophy as something more than a mere collection of anecdotes and biographies, of metaphysical assertions about the validity or otherwise of particular views of particular philosophers and to elevate it to the status of an authentic historical science. Within the context of the history of classical German philosophy Hegel discerned the starting-point for the meteoric rise of the dialectical philosophy of idealism in the 'transcendental', 'critical' philosophy of Kant and he rightly regarded his own system as the consummation and conclusion of the movement Kant had initiated. With great penetration and with profound insight into the most vital problems of dialectics (the thing-in-itself and the dilemmas it posed, the antinomies and the theory of contradiction, etc.) he perceived how Fichte's central preoccupations sprang from the contradictions and inadequacies of the Kantian system, just as Fichte's own contradictions and faults led to Schelling and from there to himself.

There is much truth in all this and much of great importance for a Marxist history of philosophy. But since Hegel, as an objective idealist, sees philosophy in terms of the autonomous movement of the concept he gets everything upside-down here too. Engels shows repeatedly that the various philosophical systems do indeed begin with the problems left unsolved by their predecessors, but as a dialectical materialist he also shows again and again that this purely philosophical analysis is peripheral to the real analysis and that the historian of philosophy must make the descent to the real, underlying objective foundations of the movement of philosophy. Whenever, as is the case with Hegel, the immediate manifestations of the history of philosophy are turned into idealist absolutes and treated 'immanently', i.e. as if the 'problems' of one philosophy lead smoothly to those of the next without the need to consider the realities underlying them, then even the grain of truth contained in such a history becomes exaggerated and distorted. In Hegel's own work the adoption of this procedure causes him to disregard the unevenness and complexity of the real development of philosophy even in this particular period. In consequence the highly complicated reflections of actual historical events no less than the systematic efforts to incorporate developments in the natural sciences into a total dialectic are reduced to the 'immanent' combinations of a few—admittedly very important—categories.

This circumvention of the real world resulted in a schematic view of the history of philosophy and when bourgeois philosophy went into a decline it led to wholly unscientific distortions and misrepresentations of history.

During the Second International this schematic 'immanent' view even infected Marxists like Plekhanov and Mehring. The views of Menshevik idealism on the history of philosophy were powerfully reinforced by the errors and defects of Hegel's own interpretation. We can only establish a consistent Marxist–Leninist line on these problems if we overcome these errors, and thoroughly assimilate the philosophical advances made during the Leninist–Stalinist period of Marxism. Above all it is essential for us to study Lenin's philosophical works in depth. In any such history of classical German philosophy, in any such critical account of its development, the newly discovered and published works of Marx and Engels must also play a decisive role.

In bourgeois philosophy itself Hegel's conception of the history of philosophy did not long survive the defeat of the bourgeois revolution of 1848. Even before this period many other views emerged, more primitive than Hegel's and hostile to the real tendencies of history. The most important of these unhistorical views, that of Arthur Schopenhauer, only became widely influential after 1848. Schopenhauer's approach to philosophy is rooted in his conviction that the efforts of Fichte, Schelling and Hegel to resolve Kant's contradictions were nothing but *aberrations*. According to Schopenhauer, philosophy should revert to the only correct method, that of Kant; anything else was deception, idle talk, a swindle. On the one hand, then, Schopenhauer simply repudiates the entire dialectical development of classical German philosophy and calls for a return to a metaphysical conception of reality. On the other hand, he 'purifies' Kant of his hesitant steps towards materialism; he brings Kant and Berkeley together under one umbrella. (In many respects Herbart has a not dissimilar effect, different though he is in other ways.)

This view, which amounts to the total annihilation of the history of classical German philosophy, reappears later in the neo-Kantians in an even more philistine form. This can be seen most clearly in the works of Otto Liebmann (*Kant and his successors*, 1865, etc.). With Liebmann we witness the philosophical triumph of that German neo-Kantianism which succeeded in transforming Kant into a thorough-going subjectivist and agnostic and which repudiated as 'unscientific metaphysics' every attempt to know objective reality as it is, independently of consciousness. This signifies the victory in neo-Kantianism of the Schopenhauerian line of the history of philosophy with its interpretation of post-Kantian philosophy as a single great aberration from the uniquely true subjectivism of Kant. The main difference is that here it is done more prosily, without Schopenhauer's genius for picturesque abuse. Hegel is treated as a 'dead dog'.

This view dominates most of the histories of classical German philosophy dating from about the middle of the last century, above all in their treatment of Hegel. Undoubtedly, remnants of Hegelianism in a National Liberal and trivialized form still survive. This can be seen in the well-known histories of philosophy by Kuno Fischer and J. E. Erdmann. However, the most important book on Hegel in this period, the work of Rudolf Haym, is in the last analysis one long diatribe against Hegel's 'unscientific' treatment of objectivity and of dialectics.

The study of classical German philosophy was not resumed until the Age of Imperialism. By that time liberal neo-Kantianism was increasingly failing to satisfy the ideological needs of Germany's imperialist bourgeoisie. We see instead the emergence of doctrines which, while they leave the agnostic foundations of neo-Kantianism intact, nevertheless were searching for ways in which to bring about a reactionary revival of objective idealism. (Examples are the Romantic revival, '*Lebensphilosophie*', Husserl's 'phenomenology', Dilthey's 'realist psychology' etc.) Intimately bound up with these reactionary tendencies we find a revival of classical German philosophy, primarily of Hegel. At the same time there was a renewed interest in the problem of its origins and this attempted to advance beyond both the schematicism of the later Hegelians and the out-and-out rejection of Hegel by the orthodox neo-Kantians.

Evidently, the 'renaissance' of classical philosophy in the Age of Imperialism did not imply the renewal or extension of Hegelian dialectics, nor did it bring about the concretization of Hegel's historicism. Instead it represented the attempt to press Hegel's philosophy into the service of an imperialist, reactionary restructuring of neo-Kantianism. In line with this the theoreticians and historians at the start of the neo-Hegelian revival aimed their polemics above all against those arguments which set up Kant and Hegel as mutually exclusive opposites. The neo-Hegelianism of Imperialism turned a blind eye to the profound and annihilating criticism which Hegel levelled at Kant's subjectivism and agnosticism. Its basic tenet was the *unity* of classical German philosophy, and of Kant and Hegel above all. All these philosophers (Windelband, J. Ebbinghaus, Brunstäd, etc.) endeavoured to prove that *all* the problems of Hegel's philosophy could already be found in Kant and that Hegel only made conscious and explicit what had been present unconsciously and implicitly in Kant. This gave rise to a view of history in which the Hegelian scheme of the development of classical German philosophy was reiterated and renovated only in appearance, and which therefore contained all its idealist and schematicizing errors in an intensified form. In reality this view was wholly incompatible with Hegel's own. Hegel had severely criticized the errors of his predecessors from the standpoint of objective idealism and of dialectics while at the same time he singled out for particular praise and appreciation the historical significance of those incipient attempts to formulate and solve dialectical problems. The neo-Hegelians of Imperialism proceeded in the opposite direction. They deduced Hegel from Kant, i.e. they took notice only of those elements of Hegel that could readily be reconciled with Kantian agnosticism. They reduced the whole development of classical German philosophy to a Kantian level. This tendency can still be seen quite clearly in neo-Hegelianism after the (First) World War—when it is frequently accompanied by other and even more openly reactionary motifs. Hermann Glockner, the editor of the new edition of Hegel's works and one of the leaders of the post-war neo-Hegelians, put the matter clearly in his speech to the first Hegel Congress:

'In Germany today the problem of Hegel is primarily a problem of Kant.'

In this context we can only briefly refer to the general class foundations and political background to this changing picture of Hegel. A comparison will best put the new situation into perspective. When Haym in his day had attacked Hegel's objectivism and his dialectics he had done so in the service of liberalism, albeit a liberalism inclining towards National Liberalism. At any rate, while completely misunderstanding the dialectical character of Hegel's views he dismissed them as reactionary and believed that the growth of a liberal ideology would be greatly facilitated by the demise of Hegel's philosophy. By contrast, for Friedrich Meinecke, the well-known historian of the Age of Imperialism and the close associate of the neo-Kantians of south-west Germany

(Windelband and Rickert), Hegel's philosophy was essentially the precursor of Bismarck's politics and his view of the state. When Haym was
writing, the resistance of the German bourgeoisie to the foundation of
the Bismarckian Empire, to the pseudo-constitutional, reactionary
character of the German state was still alive, even though enfeebled by
liberal timidity and inconsequentiality. The later revival of Hegelianism
can be seen to be closely connected with the fact that all traces of this resistance had now vanished. Neo-Hegelianism set out to propagate an
ideology of concrete and positive, and in effect, total 'reconciliation'
with the political form of Germany. It is obvious, therefore, that the
reactionary elements of Hegel's philosophy necessarily receive the greatest prominence.

Such reactionary elements, however, are not confined to political history. The neo-Hegelians we have been discussing were striving to
extend and modernize neo-Kantianism to the point where it encompasses the entire history of classical German philosophy. But this was
far from being enough to satisfy the reactionary ideological requirements of the Age of Imperialism. We have already mentioned the growing influence of irrationalist 'Lebensphilosophie'. The great popularity
enjoyed by Dilthey's contribution to the revival of Hegel can be traced
back to the fact that here Hegel's dialectics are distorted so as to harmon-
ize with the emergence of philosophical irrationalism. In this sense
Dilthey's monograph of 1906 on the young Hegel betokens a turning-point in the history of Hegel-studies. The crux of the matter is that
Dilthey meets the imperialist and reactionary revival of Romanticism
halfway when—by ignoring or distorting the most vital historical facts
—he brings Hegel within the orbit of philosophical Romanticism.

In the post-war period neo-Hegelianism proceeded along the paths
laid down by Dilthey while also drawing on the philosophical results
of the other neo-Hegelian trends. Richard Kroner in his *From Kant to
Hegel*, a book of decisive importance for the later development of neo-
Hegelianism, argues that 'Dialectics is irrationalism made rational,
made into a method'. The general aim of neo-Hegelianism—clearly
reflected in the speeches of Glockner, Kroner, etc.,—is to make apparent use of Hegel's approach to the philosophy of history, to exploit his
concept of 'reconciliation', in order to achieve a 'synthesis' of all contemporary philosophical movements (including Fascism).

It is no accident that Dilthey's monograph which focuses its attention
on Hegel's *youth* should stand at the beginning of this whole development. Dilthey believed that he had discovered certain motifs in Hegel's
transitional phase, and especially in the moments of crisis during that
phase, which were susceptible to exploitation by an irrationalist, mystical interpretation of Hegel. Much earlier he had similarly falsified
Hölderlin, the friend and companion of Hegel in his youth. (I have

provided a detailed critique of this reactionary falsification of Hölderlin in my essay on his *Hyperion*—See *Goethe and His Age*, London 1968, pp. 136–57.) Dilthey's irrationalist view of Hegel's philosophy reintroduced into it certain tendencies derived from the German dissolution of Hegelianism. Thus late in life the famous Hegelian aesthetician, Friedrich Theodor Vischer, turned away from his own Hegelian beginnings and erected an irrationalist theory of myth to oppose Hegel's dialectics. Dilthey now injected this theory into the interpretation of Hegel himself. (On this subject see my essay *Karl Marx and Friedrich Theodor Vischer* in *Beiträge zur Geschichte der Ästhetik*, Aufbau Verlag, Berlin 1953.)

As we have seen, Dilthey's interpretation of Hegel played a decisive role in the later development of neo-Hegelianism. With his book the figure of the young Hegel, who had been peripheral for Kuno Fischer or Haym, now moved steadily into the forefront of attention. Increasing use was made of Hegel's sketches and notes, most of them not intended for publication, and they were interpreted in such a way as to give birth to a 'true German' philosopher, i.e. a mythical, irrationalist figure palatable to Fascism. This development reaches its pinnacle in Theodor Haering's monograph of which the first volume appeared in 1929.

Although the perversion of the history of philosophy in Germany reaches a climax here, at least as far as Hegel is concerned, the whole movement has had the positive effect of having made possible the publication of the scattered, concealed or forgotten manuscripts of Hegel's youth. We are now at a point where we can begin to chart Hegel's early development.

I append a list of the most important of these publications as constant reference to them will be necessary in the course of our concrete analysis of his youthful development.

1. *Hegel's Early Theological Writings*, ed. Hermann Nohl, Tübingen 1907 (cited here as 'Nohl').

2. *The German Constitution* and the *System of Ethics*, both published in *Schriften zur Politik und Rechtsphilosophie Hegels* by G. Lasson, Leipzig 1923 (cited here as 'Lasson').

3. *Hegel's Jena Logic, Metaphysics and Philosophy of Nature*, ed. G. Lasson, Leipzig 1923 (cited here as the *Jena Logic*).

4. Hegel's lectures from the period immediately prior to *The Phenomenology of Mind*, published under the title *Jenenser Realphilosophie*, Vols. I and II by J. Hoffmeister, Leipzig 1931 (cited here as *Realphilosophie*).

5. *Documents on Hegel's Development*, ed. J. Hoffmeister, Stuttgart 1936 (cited here as 'Hoffmeister').

Taken together, all these publications amount to a fairly sizable and as yet barely tapped mine of information about the emergence of the

Hegelian dialectic. In part, work on this topic has been rendered easier by the philological research that accompanied the publication and interpretation of these texts. With the aid of the letters and manuscripts that can be dated with certainty, Nohl, Hoffmeister, Haering, Rosenzweig and others have carried out a detailed investigation into the chronology of Hegel's manuscripts. They have established with precision the changes in Hegel's handwriting and with the help of such information they have managed to provide the individual manuscripts with exact or approximate dates. As we have been unable to test their results we shall have to accept their chronology except where the philosophical content forces us to deviate from it.

This should not be taken to mean that we now possess all the documents pertaining to Hegel's early development or that all those we do have are in a satisfactory state from the point of view of scholarship. The original editors of Hegel's literary remains dealt with the material entrusted to them in an amazingly high-handed and irresponsible manner. It appears that a number of the most important manuscripts have been irretrievably lost. Examples of this are the first economic manuscript from his period in Frankfurt and above all the extended commentary on Steuart's works. We shall see very clearly in Part II just what the loss of this particular manuscript has meant for any attempt to reconstruct the development of Hegel's views on economics. Rosenkranz, who still had it in his possession, had not the slightest idea of the part played by economics in Hegel's overall views. From his remarks alone we cannot come to any conclusion about them. This means that at a decisive turning point in Hegel's development we are reduced to hypotheses, constructions based on scattered comments, deductions from later writings, etc.

Moreover, even in the case of manuscripts published entirely or in part by Rosenkranz there is much to be desired from a scholarly point of view. For example, in his account of Hegel's life he has printed extracts from Hegel's historical notes from his period in Berne and philosophical comments from his time in Jena, but without stating when precisely in these periods the notes, etc., were made. As he possessed the manuscripts himself this would not have been too difficult a task. Today, however, with the manuscripts long since lost, we must again have recourse to ingenious guesswork. The importance of the published notes for our understanding of Hegel's development is very great, and sometimes even crucial. The Berne notes, for instance, contain a number of comments on the French Revolution. It would be of very great value if we could establish an exact chronology here, if we could determine the various phases of Hegel's attitude on this issue, and learn, for example, which events in the French Revolution provoked immediate reactions from him. In the case of the Jena philosophical notes an exact chronology would be even more desirable. It is well known that in Jena Hegel at first sided with Schelling against Kant and Fichte and it was only with the introduction to *The Phenomenology of Mind* that he turned against Schelling too. Now the Jena notes contain critical comments on Schelling's students and on Schelling himself. It is evident that if we knew exactly when Hegel turned against Schelling, undoubtedly some time before he published anything overtly critical of him, we would be able to establish a much more concrete view of Hegel's development than is possible today. Thus in making use of this material we can only establish the changes in Hegel's views in a very general way.

Nevertheless, despite all these defects and lacunae we still possess a relatively substantial body of material on Hegel's early development. And since Fascistoid neo-Hegelianism has settled on precisely this period as suitable for turning Hegel into an irrationalist consonant with their own views, the task of confronting their falsifications with the historical facts is by no means unimportant. All the more since the spirit of the 'new science' has now infected even Marxist writings, availing itself of the circumstance that Marxists have hitherto scarcely concerned them-selves at all with Hegel's youth. Thus during the Hegel Centenary of 1931 the pseudo-Marxists simply took over and disseminated word for word Dilthey's interpretation of his early development.

However, our interest in Hegel's early development goes beyond the polemical demolition of Fascist lies. Considered from a Marxist point of view it is obvious that we are faced with a very important stage in the *growth* of dialectics in Germany. A correct Marxist interpretation even of Hegel's later works cannot remain indifferent to the road which led Hegel to his later positions. We thus acquire a much more concrete knowledge of his point of view *vis-à-vis* his predecessors Kant, Fichte and Schelling. The legend of his connections with Romanticism is re-vealed to be wholly untenable. In a word—and as is self-evident to a Marxist—we can gain an incomparably better insight into Hegel if we follow the story of its genesis than if, following the method adopted by Hegel himself, we were to compare and contrast e.g. the mature works of Schelling with the mature works of Hegel without taking genetic questions into account.

The development of Hegel's philosophy also poses all the great histori-cal questions concerning the general foundations of classical German philosophy and the development of the dialectical method into the Hegelian form of dialectics. The present work makes no claim to deal with this extraordinarily large problem in the context of Hegel's own personal development. It prefers to confine itself to *one of its strands*, viz. its socio-historical roots.

For the growth of dialectics in classical German philosophy was also influenced to a decisive extent by the contemporary crisis in the natural

sciences, by the extremely important discoveries which upset the foundations of previous scientific thought, by the rise of the new science of
chemistry and the emergence of genetic problems in the most disparate
sciences. In his book on Feuerbach Engels gives a very detailed account
of the impact of these revolutions in the natural sciences upon the crisis in
metaphysics and the sudden surge of philosophy towards a dialectical
approach to reality.

This extremely important process has never been thoroughly investigated. Bourgeois historians of philosophy have for a long time looked
down their noses at the 'speculations into the philosophy of nature'
(*Naturphilosophie*) indulged in by the classical German philosophers. In
the middle and end of the nineteenth century Marx and Engels were the
only thinkers who were able to see clearly and to appreciate the real
problems of this period notwithstanding the idealist and even absurdly
mystical form in which they became manifest. On this point Engels
writes in the Preface to the *Anti-Dühring* as follows:

> 'It is much easier, along with the unthinking mob *à la* Karl Vogt, to
> assail the old natural philosophy than to appreciate its historical sig-
> nificance. It contains a great deal of nonsense and fantasy, but not
> more than the unphilosophical theories of the empirical natural scien-
> tists contemporary with that philosophy, and that there was also in it
> much that was sensible and rational began to be perceived after the
> theory of evolution became widespread . . . The natural philosophers
> stand in the same relation to consciously dialectical natural science as
> the utopians to modern communism.'

A Marxist approach to these problems would presuppose a broad and
thorough acquaintance with the detailed histories of all the natural
sciences. The present writer does not feel competent even to broach these
issues. The intention of these remarks is only to emphasize to the reader
that the present study is necessarily one-sided and stands in need of
further research from other quarters.

This additional research is necessary and urgent and not merely for the
reasons given above. We must add that contemporary reactionary philosophies of the Age of Imperialism have a much more positive attitude to
natural philosophy than their predecessors. But this only complicates and
distorts the issue even further. For in their search for weapons to use
against scientific interpretations of nature the modern students of natural
philosophy have fixed upon the nonsense, the mysticism, the elements
that are scientifically reactionary. Hence an investigation of the true relations between the developments in science and the origins of the dialectical method implies at the same time taking up arms against the anti-
scientific theories of Fascism and its precursors.

Our present study will concern itself with another, no less important complex of problems relating to the emergence of dialectics in classical German philosophy, namely with the effects of the great socio-political events of the period, and in particular with the French Revolution and its impact on the growth of dialectical modes of thought in Germany.

The impact of the French Revolution on Germany is another theme which stands in need of further study. Bourgeois historiography, above all after 1848, strove constantly to obliterate the memory of all democratic and revolutionary aspirations in Germany. Today we know extraordinarily little of the many Germans who directly supported the French Revolution. Georg Forster is the only one who has not sunk into total oblivion, doubtless because he already had a wide reputation as a scientist and journalist, although even in his case a genuine Marxist analysis of his works and his activity does not yet exist. But Forster is only one among many, and an overall view of the impact of the French Revolution would only be possible if all the facts were considered in their breadth and depth. A further important but neglected problem is that of assessing the opinions of the broad masses of the people, since it is clear from Goethe's various memoirs, for all his extreme caution in describing such matters, that public opinion was profoundly disturbed by the events in France.

Any such study would be forced to give due weight to the backwardness, both political and socio-economic, of Germany at that time. The individual utterances and attitudes of Germans on the subject of the French Revolution must constantly be judged with this in mind. Hence the categories which in France emerged and developed as the necessary consequence of actual class struggles cannot be applied mechanically to the ideological reflections of these struggles in a retrograde Germany. It should not be forgotten, for example, that in France even the Girondins took part in the meetings at the Jacobin Club for a long time and that clear differences between the parties only emerged as the class struggles became more acute. It would therefore be mechanical and mistaken to attach the political labels of the French Revolution to individual German attitudes and positions when comparable social differences only arose much later in Germany.

This brings us to yet another problem of enormous importance, the central problem of the bourgeois revolution in Germany. It is well known that Lenin singled out the creation of national unity in Germany as the crucial issue confronting that revolution. Now the enthusiasm for the French Revolution necessarily released a powerful wave of patriotism in Germany, a powerful desire to sweep away the atomized mass of petty feudal absolutist states, to put an end to the impotence of the nation as a whole. There was a profound longing for a free and united Germany. But the foundations of these tendencies in world history conceal an insoluble contradiction. Writing on the Spanish war of liberation against Napoleon, Marx states that as in every comparable liberation movement of the time 'reaction goes hand in hand with regeneration'. This profound observation fully applies to Germany as it was then. On the one hand, the revolutionary wars of the French Republic necessarily turned into wars of conquest. And if Napoleon's victories did away with the vestiges of feudalism, particularly in the Rhineland, thus satisfying the objective requirements of the bourgeois revolution, such conquests inevitably increased the fragmentation and impotence of the German people. On the other hand, as a consequence of Germany's backward social structure the national movements became permeated by reactionary mysticism. They were not strong enough to throw off the yoke of the petty princes by revolution and so they were unable to organize resistance to the Napoleonic invasion on a national and democratic footing. Indeed, they were so weak that they were unable even to see the problem in these terms and they attempted instead to organize resistance in league with, or rather under the leadership of, the reactionary monarchies of Prussia, Austria, etc. With historical inevitability they became the objective pillars of the reaction that dominated Germany after the fall of Napoleon.

These contradictions can be seen in the life, the thought and the deeds of all outstanding Germans of this period. Whether we look at generals and statesmen such as Baron vom Stein, Gneisenau or Scharnhorst, at poets like Goethe and Schiller, or at philosophers like Fichte and Hegel —in every case we find their lives dominated by these contradictions and the impossibility of resolving them.

Hence the historian of this period is faced by the complex, two-fold task of surveying both the great, world-historical event and also its distorted reflection in a retrograde Germany. Marx has described this situation in his remarks on Kant in *The German Ideology*. In Kant's thought he finds echoes of 'French liberalism with its basis in real class interests'. And he immediately adds that the problems become gravely distorted by the backward condition of Germany.

> 'Therefore, Kant [he continues] separated this theoretical expression from the interests it expressed, made the materially inspired determinations of the will of the French bourgeoisie into *pure* self-determination of the "free will", of will in and for itself, of human will as such, and so he transformed the will into a set of purely ideological concepts and moral postulates.'

Here Marx has discovered and brilliantly formulated one of the chief reasons why philosophy had to develop in the direction of idealism in Germany. And with this Marx points with equal precision to the inevitable deformation of philosophical problems necessarily arising from idealism.

However, the historical problems of this epoch in the history of philosophy are by no means all solved by pointing to the origins of idealism and energetically criticizing its failings. Marx himself, in his *Theses on Feuerbach*, underlines the positive contribution of classical idealism. After criticizing the merely contemplative character of the old materialism he goes on:

> 'Hence it happened that the *active* side, in contradistinction to materialism, was developed by idealism—but only abstractly, since, of course, idealism does not know real, sensuous activity as such.'

With these words Marx provides the essential lever with which to initiate a precise, profitable and genuinely historical critique of Hegelianism, the sort of critique that Lenin was to give many decades later in the brilliant commentaries on Hegel in his own early writings.

The task facing the historian of classical German philosophy can be defined as the need to provide a concrete account of the fruitful effects of this 'active side' for dialectics. He must show how the reflection of great, world-historical events in a backward Germany produces this idealist abstraction from real human activity and at the same time he must demonstrate that this abstract and partly distorted reflection of reality leads philosophers to their original insights into specific general principles of activity, movement, etc. The task of the historian would be all too simple if he could rest content with a demonstration of the negative consequences of Germany's backwardness. The world-historical role of classical German philosophy in the history of human thought is a fact that must itself be explained in Marxist terms from the concrete state of society at the time.

Thus Marx and Engels have provided us with a key to the critique of classical German philosophy. But here too the tradition they initiated evaporated during the Second International. The theme launched by Marx was dropped and not resumed and taken a step further until Lenin. Concerning his contemporaries' criticism of Kant he writes:

> '1. Plekhanov criticises Kantianism (and agnosticism in general) more from a vulgar materialist than from a dialectical-materialist standpoint: he tends only to *reject* their arguments *a limine*, instead of *correcting* them (as Hegel corrected Kant) by deepening, expanding and universalizing them and by showing the *connections* and *transitions* between all the different concepts. 2. The Marxists criticised the Kantians and the supporters of Hume (early in the twentieth century) more after the manner of Feuerbach or Ludwig Büchner than of Hegel.'

It is evident that these important remarks of Lenin's apply with equal force to the methodology of the historical and critical treatment of

Hegel's philosophy.

Engels has finely and convincingly shown in a letter how hegemony in philosophy passed in succession from England to France and from France to Germany and that the leading philosophical nation is not always the nation that is most advanced economically and socially; maturity in economic development does not always coincide with philosophical maturity and here too the law of unequal development applies.

The seminal and original insights of classical German philosophy are intimately bound up with the way in which they reflect the great political events of the period. In the same way the darker sides both of the method of idealism and of its elaboration of particular points are the mirror images of Germany's backwardness. Our task is to unravel the complicated workings of this process of interaction and to reveal the living dialectical core of the development of classical German philosophy.

We repeat: the central historical events whose intellectual reflections we have to investigate are the French Revolution and the resulting class struggles in France with their consequent impact on internal German problems. And in general it can be said that the greatness of the ideological representatives of this period stands in direct proportion to the strength of their interest in events of world-historical, international moment. Fichte's philosophy reached a dead-end because he could not resolve the contradictions of a national democratic revolution in Germany. By contrast, in Goethe's works and in Hegel's *The Phenomenology of Mind* and the *Logic* we have books which have exerted a decisive influence on the whole ideological development ever since.

However, there is a special feature of Hegel's position and of his preoccupation with the significant world-historical events of the day which sets him apart from all his contemporaries in philosophy. It is not only the case that he made the greatest and fairest German assessment of the French Revolution and the Napoleonic period. In addition, he is the only German thinker to have made a serious attempt to come to grips with the *industrial revolution* in England. He is the only man to have forged a link between the problems of classical English economics and those of philosophy and dialectics. Marx has shown in *The German Ideology* how the French materialists clothed economic ideas in an abstract philosophical form which corresponded to the needs of a bourgeoisie preparing itself for revolution. He shows further how these ideas returned to England to receive a more concrete economic form which, given the ideology of what was already a dominant bourgeoisie, inevitably led to a total philosophical trivialization (cf. Marx on Bentham). On the other hand, the multi-faceted opposition to the social and economic effects of the rise of capitalism constitutes one of the most important sources of Romanticism. In his dialectical grasp of these problems Hegel

is as far removed from Benthamite superficiality as he is from the false
and reactionary 'profundity' of Romanticism. His purpose is rather to
grasp the true inner structure, the real motive forces of the present and of
capitalism and to define the dialectic of its movement.

It would be an error to search for evidence of this tendency of Hegelian philosophy only in those comments which expressly and directly
refer to the problems of capitalist society. His preoccupation with this
theme in fact determines the structure of his system and the particular
character of the dialectic as well as the greatness of his achievement. It is
at this point that we find one of the chief sources of his superiority as
philosopher and dialectician over his contemporaries. Our study aims to
show at least in outline how this process of interaction informed the development of the young Hegel. It will demonstrate that during one crisis
in his life, at a time when he had become estranged from the ideals of the
great contemporary revolution, he found his way out of the labyrinth
and back to dialectics with the aid of a compass provided by political
economy and in particular the economic condition of England. We shall
attempt to show in detail at this point just how crucial was his understanding of economic problems for the emergence of a consciously dialectical mode of thought.

This interpretation of Hegelian philosophy is neither more nor less
than the attempt to apply to his early development the brilliant insight
formulated by Marx in his *Economic and Philosophic Manuscripts* of 1844:

> 'The greatness of Hegel's *Phenomenology* is then . . . that Hegel views
> the self-creation of man as a process . . . and therefore that he grasps
> the nature of *labour* and understands objective man, true, because real
> man as the product of *his own labour*.'

Marx shows here the extent to which Hegelian philosophy forms an
analogue of English classical economics. Of course, in England the concrete problems of bourgeois society appear in the form of concrete economic laws, while Hegel can do no more than supply the abstract
(idealist) reflection of their general principles. As against this it may be
observed that Hegel is the only person who grasps the dialectical character of this movement and can advance from there to a general theory of
dialectics. (I must remind the reader once again that even so we have
touched on only one aspect of the origins of Hegelian dialectics.)

From the foregoing it will be apparent to the reader that for all the
magnitude of this view of the dialectics of human society it still remains
an *idealist* dialectic with all the faults, limitations and distortions inevitable in an idealist interpretation. And the task of this study is indeed to
throw light on the vital interaction of the valuable and the weaker sides
of Hegel's dialectics at the various stages of his development. The present
writer hopes that his work will shortly be followed by others which will

correct and supplement the one-sidedness of his historical approach; works which will deal with the influence of the natural sciences upon dialectics. Not until we have such studies will it be possible to gain an overall view of Hegel's development. Such works will doubtless concretize and correct some of the conclusions of the present work. The present writer nevertheless entertains the hope that as far as is possible within the limitations of the source material available at present, his account of Hegel's development is correct in its *broad outlines*.

If we have achieved this goal then we shall have succeeded in establishing a methodological perspective in the history of philosophy which in importance goes beyond the mere understanding of Hegel's early development: we refer to the inner connections between economics and philosophy, economics and dialectics. In the course of time historians of philosophy have increasingly found themselves compelled to go beyond the confines of philosophical problems in the narrow sense and to direct their attention towards the historical development of human thought across the whole spectrum of the special sciences. Naturally enough, they have tended and still tend to concentrate above all on the natural sciences. A study of the interactions between science on the one hand, and philosophical method, epistemology and logic on the other has yielded not inconsiderable results, even though it has constantly suffered from its over-emphasis on the agnosticism of Kant or Berkeley and Hume as the criterion of its method and so has heedlessly neglected the complex interrelations between a philosophically conscious (albeit idealist) dialectic (German natural philosophy) and the dialectic which sprang—somewhat obscurely—from scientific practice (Lamarck, Darwin, etc.). In contrast to this the methodological connections between philosophy and the theoretical understanding of the phenomena of society have hitherto attracted scarcely any attention.

Not by chance, as we believe. The explanation is to be found in social factors and their development. In the early stages of bourgeois economics the great innovators of this novel science regarded it, on the one hand, as the basic science of society and, on the other hand, with true artlessness and frankness they thought of the categories of economics as the repositories of *relations between men*. At a later stage, however, the fetishism of economic categories which develops necessarily and increasingly with the advance of capitalism penetrated further and further into the methodology of the social sciences. These work to an increasing extent exclusively with fetishized categories without ever being able to reach the point where they can deal with the relations between men (and their relations with nature as mediated by these categories). Parallel to this development, and in great measure in consequence of it, economics has lost its place as the basic science of society and has become just one among many highly specialized sciences. Now since philosophy for the most part has also taken this road towards increased specialization it can easily be understood why it has not occurred to the philosophers to profit methodologically from a special study of the development of economic categories.

We repeat: the economists of former times had a very different approach to these matters. Galiani wrote, 'Value is a relation between persons'. And as late as the break-up of the school of Ricardo this theme was still very consciously emphasized, e.g. by Thomas Hodgskin. Important as this insight is, it remains only a half-truth. When citing the above-quoted words of Galiani Marx observed:

> 'He should have added "a relation concealed behind the husk of things"'.

And he went on to say:

> 'In other words, Hodgskin says that the effects of a certain social form of labour are ascribed to objects, to the products of labour; the relationship itself is imagined to exist in *material* form. We have already seen that this is a characteristic of labour based on commodity production, on exchange-value, and that this *quid pro quo* is revealed in the commodity, in money (Hodgskin does not see this), and, to a still higher degree, in capital. The effects of things as materialized aspects of the labour process are attributed to them in capital, in their personification, their independence in respect of labour. They would cease to have these effects if they were to cease to confront labour in this *alienated form*. The *capitalist*, as capitalist, is simply the personification of capital, that creation of labour endowed with its own will and personality which stands in opposition to labour. Hodgskin regards this as a purely subjective illusion behind which lurks deception and the interests of the exploiting classes. He does not see that the mode of perception itself springs from the actual relationship; the latter is not the expression of the former, but vice versa'.[1]

With this we find ourselves in the very centre of the interaction between the categories of philosophy and economics: the dialectical categories of the social sciences appear as intellectual reflections of the dialectical process being enacted objectively, in the lives of men, but independently of their will and their knowledge and this objectivity turns social reality into a 'second nature'. On further reflection we perceive that, rightly seen, it is in this very dialectic of economics that the most primary, fundamental and crucial relations between men find expression, and that here is the vantage-point from which the dialectics of society can be studied in their pure form. Hence it is surely no accident that the birth of dialectical materialism—as an epistemology—coincided with the discovery of this dialectic in economic life. Friedrich Engels' magisterial outline of economic categories in the *Deutsch–Französische Jahrbücher* and the *Economic and Philosophic Manuscripts* of Marx clearly mark this new departure. Nor is it a mere matter of chance that this last work proffers an analysis both of the dialectical nature of the views of the classical economists and of the economic bases of Hegel's *The Phenomenology of Mind*.

As the reader will observe, Marx's arguments here have been a decisive influence on the present work. But if we have discussed them at some length this is because we believe that they open doors to a fruitful development of the methods of the history of philosophy. Our studies concern themselves with the interrelations between the development of Hegel's views on economics and his purely philosophical dialectics, and it is our hope that with the aid of this novel point of view we may have succeeded in discovering new patterns or correcting current ones.

But is this approach to be confined to Hegel? Is he the only thinker in whose work economics has exerted such a powerful influence? Every connoisseur of English philosophy will at once reply in the negative. He will know of the links between Locke and Petty; he will know that Locke, Berkeley and Hume were also economists, that Adam Smith was also a philosopher, and that Mandeville's views on society are inseparable from his insights into economics, and so on. At the same time, however, he will be no less aware that the methodological connections between, say, Locke's economics and his theory of knowledge are *terra incognita* and that up to now scholars have limited themselves to the biographical observation that economics and philosophy have become united in this one man and they have then gone on to treat the two spheres of activity independently.

Needless to say, such connections are not limited to English philosophy. Ever since Plato and Aristotle, indeed as far back as Heraclitus, there has scarcely been a single universal thinker who has ignored such problems entirely. Of course, this does not mean that every thinker who has concerned himself with those relations between men which in the modern age have become the proper province of economics has necessarily conceived of them in terms of specifically economic problems: it suffices if he has found them problematical in one form or another.

Here, so I believe, we have an extraordinarily rich new field for the history of philosophy. I accordingly bring these remarks to a close with the hope that this field will soon be vigorously cultivated and that the present attempt to discover such interconnections will soon be superseded by other, more comprehensive studies

## NOTES

1    *Theories of Surplus Value*, Vol. III, London 1972, pp. 295–6.

# PART I

# Hegel's Early Republican Phase
## (Berne 1793–1796)

# CHAPTER ONE

# Hegel's 'theological' period: a reactionary legend

THE starting-point of Hegel's development, like that of almost every major figure in Germany at the time, was the *Enlightenment*. Here too we find ourselves confronted by a very large and largely unexplored aspect of the history of philosophy. For many years German historians of literature and philosophy were at pains to erect a Wall of China between the Enlightenment and the age of Classicism. In a wholly mistaken manner even the *Sturm und Drang* was set up as diametrically opposed to the Enlightenment. In more recent years, however, historians have come to enlist the Enlightenment itself in the service of reactionary apologetics and they were joined in this by scholars who began to use the Enlightenment so interpreted so as more easily to recast the important representatives of Classicism in the same reactionary mould.

A Marxist history of philosophy will be eager to look a little more closely at the class character of the German Enlightenment as well as the impact of the French and English Enlightenment on Germany. It will have to discover the dominant class antagonisms within the German Enlightenment. For it is immediately apparent that the ideology of the Enlightenment was made to serve the interests both of the feudal absolutism of the petty states and of the bourgeoisie preparing itself ideologically for revolution. Marx has already drawn attention to this dichotomy within the Enlightenment in *The German Ideology*. France was much more advanced and its classes were in consequence much more sharply differentiated; its class struggles had a greater clarity and definition. This meant that the important members of the Enlightenment were the natural ideologists of the approaching bourgeois revolution. Since there was no real prospect of a bourgeois revolution in Germany the influence of the French Enlightenment was correspondingly less clear-cut and unambivalent than in France itself.

Feudal absolutism and its ideologists have often endeavoured to turn certain aspects of the Enlightenment to their own purposes. Opposition to this on the part of the Gerean Enlightenment, and socio-political opposition in particular, was, by contrast, much feebler than it would have been in a more developed economy. And this feature of the German Enlightenment is reflected in every sphere of ideology. Whereas the French tended to an ever more definite form of materialism with Diderot, Holbach and Helvétius, the German Enlighteners were dominated

3

by nothing more bold than the idea of a 'religion of reason'. In Germany atheists and materialists were the exception; for the most part they were isolated outsiders (like J. Ch. Edelmann).[1] The limits of the radicalism of the vanguard of German Enlightenment were set by a Spinozistic pantheism. And even this, if made public, as in the case of the ageing Lessing or the young Goethe, was sufficient to arouse panic and cries of horror in the ranks of the average German Enlighteners. It is very characteristic that Lessing concealed his Spinozistic views from his close friend Moses Mendelssohn and that the latter was deeply scandalized when, after Lessing's death, his Spinozism became public knowledge with the publication of an account of his conversation with F. H. Jacobi.

The scope of the present study forbids a complete analysis of the German Enlightenment proper. It must suffice for our purposes to point out that the education received by Hegel in the Tübingen Seminary consisted of an Enlightenment adapted to aristocratic, courtly needs. We now have a series of notes (recently published by Hoffmeister) which make it perfectly clear that Hegel had a very intimate and comprehensive knowledge of the literature of the German, English and French Enlightenment. The later Berne essays also show him to have made a thorough study of the Enlightenment, one which extended beyond philosophy and historiography and included also imaginative literature. (Thus the Berne notes quote from one of Marivaux' novels.) His staple reading matter consisted initially of the German Enlighteners. In the Tübingen Notes already referred to we find an almost complete tally of the writers, of the German Enlightenment, even the minor ones, and they are not merely listed, but also treated in greater or lesser detail. Especially at the start of his stay in Berne he constantly comes back to Mendelssohn's then famous *Jerusalem*. Lessing's writings, in particular *Nathan the Wise*, are especially prominent.

But this is by no means the end of Hegel's reading-list in Tübingen. From his notes and studies we can see very clearly that he had a very thorough knowledge of the chief figures of the French Enlightenment: Montesquieu, Voltaire, Diderot, Holbach, Rousseau and others. We see also from the notes that he had closely studied the works of Hugo Grotius, Raynal's[2] *Indian History*, Hume's *History of England*, Gibbon's *Decline and Fall of the Roman Empire*. Furthermore, he had read Schiller's historical writings, a number of essays by Benjamin Constant and the works of the German revolutionary, Georg Forster.[3] It goes without saying that, given the orientation of education at that time, Hegel was thoroughly familiar with the philosophers and historians of antiquity. And—as we shall show in detail—the young Hegel already regarded the Greek *polis* not as a social phenomenon of the past that came into being and fell into decay as the result of definite concrete conditions, but as the eternal model, the unsurpassed paradigm for a contemporary revolution of state and society.

This is enough to suggest the main direction of Hegel's early reading very clearly. In the internal debates affecting the entire German Enlightenment Hegel finds himself increasingly on the democratic left-wing, criticizing and opposing those elements of the Enlightenment which came into being in the course of attempts to adapt the movement to the absolutism of the petty German princes. His development from Tübingen to Berne indicates a shift in which the English and French Enlightenment gradually displace German writers. And in so far as he does have recourse to German writers, these tend increasingly to belong to the radical wing of the German Enlightenment. It is both striking and significant how frequently at this time Hegel refers to what was for the Germany of the period the very radical criticism of religion in Lessing's *Nathan the Wise*. It is no less striking and typical that his comparison between the Ancients and the Moderns, specifically between classical art and Christian art, is based on views formulated in Georg Forster's *Views from the Lower Rhine*. Hegel made detailed excerpts from this work and it is very revealing of the·outlook of his modern publishers that Hermann Nohl, although compelled to admit the existence of these excerpts, declined to reprint them in his book, thus making it difficult for the modern reader to realize their importance for Hegel's development.

We shall have later to concern ourselves with the striking fact that in his youth Hegel was on the whole indifferent to philosophical problems in the strict sense. He did indeed read the ancient philosophers and Kant and Spinoza, but the only work by the latter which is attested with certainty is his *Theologico-Political Tractatus*. The study of this work may well have been connected with his interest in the history and criticism of theology.

In this connection we must refer to Hegel's reading of Mosheim's Ecclesiastical History;[4] for all modern editors and commentators attach enormous importance to his preoccupation with religion and theology. We shall discuss this question in detail later on. It is enough here if we point out that many of the works of the Enlightenment already alluded to also deal with religion and especially with Christianity. And whereas Hegel only makes excerpts of a factual nature from Mosheim, his notes on Gibbon, Forster, etc., show him coming down very definitely against Christianity. Nor is the fact that Hegel is also said to have shown interest in the German mystics (Meister Eckhart, Tauler, etc.) of any assistance to the constructions of Dilthey, Nohl and Co. For, as we shall see later on, the existence of Christian sects is of prime importance for Hegel's view of Christianity as a whole at this time. Just as he uncovered and criticized the sectarian nature of primitive Christianity, so too he will have had an historical and polemical interest in the problem of later sects.

However, to return to the question of his reading in philosophy, it is

clear that pride of place belongs to Kant whom he must certainly have
read at Tübingen. What is of importance, however, for the state of
philosophy at the time and for the mood of the younger generation of
philosophers, is that both Hegel and Schelling focused their attention on
*The Critique of Practical Reason*, Hegel more so than Schelling. From the
Berne period there is not a single remark that would suggest more than a
superficial interest in the problems of *The Critique of Pure Reason* and with
epistemology in the narrower sense. Furthermore, from his correspondence with Schelling we can see that it was only hesitantly and
without any great sense of urgency that Hegel read the first works of
Fichte, and when he did so he evidently reacted very critically. By contrast, it is very characteristic that he felt inspired by Schiller's *Letters on
Aesthetic Education*. And typically, as one would expect from his own
views at the time, this was due not so much to his sympathy with their
aesthetic and philosophical content as with their attacks on the modern
collapse of culture, and their comparison of modern decadence with the
grandeur of classical culture.

Of course, all this does not mean simply that Hegel's world-view can
be equated with that of the Enlightenment. Not even of the German Enlightenment. A rapprochement with the French and English Enlightenment was precluded by the fact that right from the start his point of
view was that of *idealism*. Hegel, unlike many of his distinguished contemporaries, never had any leanings towards philosophical materialism.
Lenin, in the *Empiriocriticism*, has noted such leanings in Kant; and in all
the early works of Schiller, at the time of his medical studies, we can also
observe definite tendencies towards materialism. Similarly, in our portrayal of Hegel's Jena period, we shall document how powerfully Schelling tended at moments towards materialism in the course of his work on
natural philosophy. Hegel is much more consistent than these thinkers
and remained a steadfast idealist throughout his life. Even the sporadic
signs of materialism which Lenin detects in the *Logic* are part of his
detour through objective idealism, through the encyclopaedic length
and breadth of his knowledge and his sober, unprejudiced respect for
facts. His conscious philosophical thought, however, was always that of
an idealist.

We have already asserted that in Tübingen and Berne Hegel did not
concern himself with philosophical problems in any intensive manner
and that at no time did he become involved with problems in the theory
of knowledge. Nevertheless, we can observe the emergence of a unified
view of social and historical phenomena. At the same time there is little
evidence of any sustained preoccupation with the problems of natural
philosophy in Berne. Hegel does not attempt to analyse philosophically
the premises of his coherent viewpoint. Like many of his contemporaries his aim is to apply Kant's analysis in *The Critique of Practical Reason* to

history and society. The Kantian influence takes two predominant forms: on the one hand, Hegel regards social problems primarily as problems of morality; on the other hand, the problem of praxis, i.e. the transformation of social reality by man himself, remains the constant focus of his thought.

However, on one crucial matter, Hegel, from very early on, went beyond Kant. Kant had investigated moral problems from the standpoint of the individual. In his view conscience was the fundamental moral fact. And if he seemed to be able to establish his idealism in objective reality, he could do so only by projecting the common features, the universal validity of the ethics he was attempting to discover into a fictitious apparently more than individual, but in reality mystified individual subject: the so-called 'intelligible self'. In Kant social problems are secondary, deriving from the subsequent interactions of the primary reality, namely the individual subjects.

In contrast to this, Hegel's early subjectivism has a practical bent which is social and collective right from the start. For Hegel activity, social praxis, was always both the starting-point and the central object of thought. This implies a methodology which has definite points of contact with Herder. Herder was the first thinker of the German Enlightenment to raise the question of the nature of collective social praxis —even though he was never able to arrive at a clear conceptual definition of the nature of the acting subject and the real laws governing his actions; above all on questions of method he leaves matters in an impenetrable half-light. It cannot be proven that Hegel was influenced by Herder's ideas at any given point, indeed there is nothing in the records to suggest that he was ever particularly impressed by Herder. Despite this, Herder's ideas were in the air at the time and it would be futile to seek for specific parallels in his work and in Hegel's early writings.

Crucial, however, for the entire development of Hegel is the fact that he proceeds from Herder's unclarified concept of the collective subject. In his Berne period he makes no attempt to clarify this concept epistemologically. He seeks instead to trace the fortunes of this collective subject, its deeds and its fate in the course of history, of the transformation of social reality. We shall see that the central theme of this process is the fragmentation of the collective subject into 'private individuals' of which society henceforth will be the mere 'aggregate'.

As we shall see, Hegel in his Berne period simply noted this fragmentation as an historical fact, without drawing any elaborate philosophical conclusions from it. His chief preoccupation at this time was practical: how was it possible for the collective subjectivity of the city-states of antiquity to fall into decay in the first place? This was the question that agitated him and it signals the appearance in his thought of the intellectual reflection of the world-historical illusions that guided the actions

of Robespierre, St. Just and the other Jacobin leaders of the French Revolution. Only after the defeat of Jacobinism, only after Thermidor, in
the midst of the philosophical crisis that overwhelmed him in Frankfurt
did he come to think of modern bourgeois society and the 'private' individual in more favourable terms. And we shall see how the twin themes
of political economy and a dialectical view of society began to preoccupy his mind as a result of that crisis.

For the moment, however, we are concerned with this conceptually
unanalysed collective subject of history. And we know too that Hegel
gave a moral slant to all the social and historical problems that confronted him. It follows inevitably that in these debates *religion* must have
played a decisive role. Here we have one of the points which the reactionary philosophy of the Age of Imperialism could turn to good
account in its falsification of Hegel. It is very symptomatic that Hermann
Nohl entitled his edition of the Berne and Frankfurt fragments *Hegel's
Early Theological Writings*. This was meant to suggest to the reader that
Hegel's interest in theology in the Tübingen seminary went beyond the
need to earn his bread and butter, and that theological problems constituted the foundation and the starting-point of his entire thought. This
insinuation is made even more explicit by Hegel's other modern editor,
Georg Lasson. In his eyes religion and theology are the central axis
around which the whole Hegelian system revolves; he attacks every
critic, however reactionary, who omits to put religion in the very centre
of his interpretation of Hegel. In this context it is relevant to consider the
basic thesis of the chief modern biographer of the young Hegel, Th. L.
Haering, who regards Hegel as a 'teacher of his nation' in the sense that
he re-interprets the practical starting-point we have been discussing in
terms of an attempt to impart religious instruction to the people.

What is the truth about the 'theological' character of Hegel's youthful works? The unprejudiced and attentive reader will find precious
little to do with theology in them, indeed as far as theology is concerned the tone is one of sustained hostility. Of course, we have already
agreed that the religious problem occupies an important place in his
historical analyses, and it never ceases to do so, as we can see from his
mature philosophy.

We need to ask two questions about this. First, what is the nature of
his concern with religion in this early phase? Second, what is the historical foundation underlying this concern, what are its historical conditions and determinants? Turning to the second question first we must
at once point out that the question of the historical content and the historical efficacy of the religions, and especially of Christianity, had
formed one of the perennial themes of the entire German Enlightenment up to Reimarus[5] and Lessing. And we must add that the problem continues to appear right up to the time of the dissolution of

Hegelianism in the writings of Strauss, Bruno Bauer and Feuerbach. Thus by asking such questions Hegel positions himself in the main-stream of the German Enlightenment. Engels has discovered the real reasons for this phenomenon in Feuerbach:

'At that time, however, politics was a very thorny field and hence the main fight came to be directed against religion; this fight, particularly after 1840, was indirectly also political.'[6]

This indirect political quality inherent in religion and the attack on re-ligion existed to the same extent in the period of Hegel's *Early Theological Writings*. Indeed, whereas in the period of preparation leading up to the revolution of 1848 philosophical radicalism soon came to dismiss the criticism of theology as a half-measure, as an inadequate form of ideo-logical opposition, any serious attempt to criticize theology in the German Enlightenment of the eighteenth century was inevitably felt, given the backward conditions of the time, to have a far greater revol-utionary force. This is the proper context in which to appraise Hegel's *Early Theological Writings*. Their main thrust is directed against the Chris-tian religion. We noted earlier that the pillar of Hegel's view of the philosophy of history at this period was the notion that the collapse of the city-states of antiquity meant the disappearance of the society of human freedom and greatness and the transformation of the heroic, republican *citoyen* of the *polis* into the bourgeois, the merely egoistic 'private indivi-dual' of modern society. We may anticipate our analysis of Hegel's dis-cussion of Christianity in this period and give our conclusion which is that in his youth Hegel conceives of Christianity as the religion of the 'private individual', of the bourgeois, as the religion of the loss of human liberty, of the millennia-long despotism and enslavement of mankind. Such ideas place Hegel firmly in the mainstream of Enlightenment thought.

This conclusion stands in need of the qualifying remark that Hegel, like the German Enlightenment, never took his attacks on Christianity as far as the great English and French thinkers. His critique of Christianity never reaches the point of materialist atheism. Quite the reverse, the core of his work here is religious. His aim is to discover the social prerequisites for a return from the religion of despotism and enslavement to a religion of freedom on the model of antiquity.

In the German context there is nothing surprising about his. Engels observed that even Feuerbach's attack on religion and his unmasking of religion occasionally turns into a demand for a new, 'purified' faith. And Engels shows further that the overestimation of the historical importance of religion, the belief that the great turning-points of history are deter-mined by religious changes, continues to colour Feuerbach's view of his-tory. All this applies with even greater truth to the German

Enlightenment before Hegel. We need only think of a man of Lessing's importance and integrity and remind ourselves that his struggles for Enlightenment never broke through the framework of religion. On the other hand, we must not overstate the matter: if it is true that the German Enlightenment never reached the resolute materialism and atheism of Diderot, Helvétius or Holbach, it is no less true that it went beyond them at certain points in its historical understanding of the origins of religion and the social roots of religious change. (This applies above all to Lessing and Herder.)

It is here that we have to look for the importance of Hegel's early writings. Hegel poses the very radical question of the social reasons for the rise of Christianity and places this in the very centre of his work. With that idealist overestimation of the role of religion in history, of which we have just spoken, he sees Christianity as the ultimately decisive cause of all the social and political events of the modern world which excite his greatest animosity. His chief practical aim, the revival of the democracy of the *polis* with all its freedom and greatness, stood in need of historical foundations, of an historical underpinning: he had to chart those social movements, that social and political decline, which led to the predominance of the Christian religion. His goal is to do away with the entire complex tradition: he researches into the causes of its origins in order to plot the trajectory of its decline and fall.

We can see from this how all these early views of Hegel's reflect the influence of the *French Revolution*. His early enthusiasm for the French Revolution is not in dispute. It is well known that while still boys in Tübingen the three friends Hegel, Hölderlin and Schelling planted a tree of liberty and danced around it singing revolutionary songs. There is likewise a tradition according to which they were the centre of a secret society devoted to the reading of forbidden writings about the French Revolution. Their enthusiasm was part of a more general mood that prevailed among the best members of the German intelligentsia of the day about whom we have spoken in earlier studies. We pointed out there that in many cases this enthusiasm was short-lived. Only very few contemporary German intellectuals were able to understand and make a just appraisal of the events of 1793/4. The majority were shocked and repelled by the plebeian dictatorship of the Paris Jacobins (Klopstock and Schiller were typical of many). Of course, it is one of the legends of bourgeois historians that their disappointment led them to become the confirmed enemies of the French Revolution in general and that they thenceforth renounced the principles of 1789. In most cases the truth is the very opposite of this and nowhere more so than with Hegel.

In a letter to Schelling at Christmas 1794 Hegel wrote:

'You will have heard that Carrière has gone to the guillotine. Do you still read *French* newspapers? If I remember rightly I have heard that they have been banned in Württemberg. This trial is very important and has uncovered the perfidious nature of the Robespierrites. [7]

This letter shows very clearly that even in his youth Hegel was hostile to Jacobinism. Hegel's special position among his German contemporaries does not lie in his political radicalism. Not only Forster went a lot further on this issue—in his life as well as in theory—the same is true of Fichte; and older members of the Enlightenment such as Wieland or Herder, retained feelings of sympathy even for the extremist aspects of the Revolution for a much longer time. The outstanding feature of Hegel's position was that even though he rejected the extreme left wing of the Revolution right from the beginning, he nevertheless retained his faith in its *historical necessity* and to the very end of his life he regarded it as the very *foundation of modern civil society*.

Of course, Hegel's view of modern civil society undergoes a number of radical changes. In Berne, despite his rejection of Robespierre's policies, Hegel still sees the Revolution as the foundation of the approaching renewal of society. Later, after his Frankfurt crisis, when he has deepened his knowledge of the economic nature of modern society, he no longer regards the Revolution as the impulse, the vehicle for a future renewal of society, but rather as the historically past, if historically necessary foundation of reality as it is in the contemporary world. This inspires in him an admittedly somewhat tempered enthusiasm even for the radical sides of the Revolution.

We shall later follow Hegel's development with the aid of his own statements through to the famous chapter (on Absolute Freedom and Terror) in *The Phenomenology of Mind*. For the present it is enough to acquaint ourselves more fully with Hegel's mood at the time. In a somewhat later letter to Schelling he writes (16 April 1795):

'I think that there is no better sign of our time than the fact that *mankind portrays itself as being so worthy of respect*. It is a proof that the aura surrounding the oppressors and the gods of this earth is fading. The philosopher will demonstrate this dignity and the peoples will learn to feel and not merely to demand the rights that have been so trampled under foot, but to receive them and take possession of them themselves. Religion and politics have conspired together. The former has *taught* what the latter *wanted*: contempt for mankind, man's inability to achieve good, to become something through his own efforts. With the propagation of the idea of how things *should* be, the indolence of people settled in their ways, their willingness to accept everything as it *is* for evermore, will disappear. [8]

This letter is interesting in a number of ways. In the first place, it shows the extent to which Hegel's premises derive from the *Critique of Practical Reason*. Quite in contrast to his later views where he insists on reality as the starting point and rejects the abstract Kantian 'Ought' as a foundation of social science, Hegel here follows Kant by opposing the revolutionary 'Ought' to the reactionary inertia of 'Is'. At the same time, however, he boldly re-interprets Kant without concerning himself too much about epistemological legitimations. The 'Ought' here has a purely political and social meaning, its moral character forms only the general idealist backcloth. Moreover, the antithesis between Is and Ought does not reside within the individual psyche as a contrast between the empirical and the intelligible self, as in Kant, It is an antithesis between progressive and reactionary tendencies in politics and society itself.

As to the socio-political content of the letter, it is evident that Hegel's struggle against the dominant forms of philosophy and religion was the ideological aspect of his struggle against despotism in general. Inasmuch as he regarded the critique of Christianity as a component of the general struggle against the despotism of feudal absolutism he placed himself alongside the Enlightenment and above all the great class struggles which centred on religion during the French Revolution. Engels very rightly emphasizes the fact that, unlike all previous bourgeois revolutions, a distinguishing feature of the French Revolution was its irreligious nature. Whereas earlier bourgeois revolutions, including the English Revolution of the seventeenth century, were fought under the banner of religion, the French Revolution

'appealed exclusively to juristic and political ideas, and troubled itself about religion only in so far as it stood in its way. But it never occurred to it to put a new religion in place of the old. Everyone knows how Robespierre failed in his attempt.'[9]

With these words Engels accurately sums up the main line of the French Revolution. However, if we turn to Hegel's relationship to these events we must remind ourselves of our earlier arguments about the distorted reflection of the revolution in Germany arising from the country's economic and political backwardness. For, even though the leading politicians of the French Revolution were impeded by all sorts of prejudices and illusions (partly of a religious nature), they nevertheless approached the issue as thinking politicians. The relation of the revolutionary state to Catholicism was determined in reality by two factors. On the one hand, the Catholic church was an ideological and organizational centre of the royalist counter-revolution. On the other hand, the leading politicians saw or, at any rate, felt that the influence of Catholicism on the mass of the peasantry could not simply be abolished by decree. If we examine the very chequered history o. this theme in all its details we find that they fully bear out Engels' account.[10]

The bourgeois historians of the religious movements during the Revolution are united on one point: they all vastly over-estimate their real significance. Thus Mathiez, for instance, places too much emphasis on the connections between the Babeuf conspiracy and the Theophilanthropists, even though from his own account it is very clear that Babeuf and his colleagues only made use of the religious and moral meetings of this sect to acquire a reasonably secure legality for their own meetings.[11] And from the information contained in Aulard and Mathiez it is quite obvious that the struggle of Danton and Robespierre against the religious views of Hébert and Chaumette, etc., was dictated by purely political considerations, namely the fear that the extremist agitation of the latter would drive the peasantry into the Royalist camp for good.

Indeed, even Robespierre's attempt, in the last phase of his rule, to found a new religion, the cult of the 'Supreme Being' was primarily a political and not a religious action, even though it was the action of a desperate politician in an objectively desperate situation. And this remains true despite its being coloured by Robespierre's Rousseauistic views, by the illusion he and his followers entertained about the perspectives and possibilities of the democratic bourgeois revolution. In the emphasis on morality which came for Robespierre to occupy the centre of the stage of the Jacobin revolutionary Terror, we see the reflection of his desperate struggle against the capitalist tendencies unleashed by the Revolution which were pushing the whole movement towards the liquidation of the plebeian dictatorship of the Jacobins, towards the open, unashamed dictatorship of the bourgeoisie, towards Thermidor. Terror in the name of republican virtue, the struggle against all forms of moral perversion and corruption was in Robespierre's case the ideological aspect of the defence of the plebeian version of the democratic, bourgeois revolution against both the royalist counter-revolution and even against the bourgeoisie itself. The fact that Robespierre's policy was based on illusion and that the Jacobin dictatorship simply had to collapse once it had carried out its task of saving the Revolution from foreign invasion by mobilizing the masses, does not detract in the least from the political character of Robespierre's actions in his last phase, even on the issue of religion.

Thus when Robespierre in his speech to the Convention of 5 February 1794[12] proclaimed that a moral counter-revolution, was being made which would prepare the way for a political counter-revolution, he was absolutely in the right from his point of view—discounting the necessary illusions, of course. And his endeavours to found a new religion, viz. the cult of a Supreme Being, were based on the need for a broad base in the moral attitudes of the people which would help to secure and further the revolution; what he needed was a counterweight both to the agitation of the Church and to the demoralizing and corrupting acts of the bourgeoisie.[13] Amid the fluctuations of the class struggles after Thermidor we witness the emergence of a number of sects which similarly attempted to prop up the spirit of republicanism by exerting a religious and moral influence over the masses. The 'Theophilanthropists' were the most important of them. This sect consisted chiefly of moderate republicans and for a time it had a certain influence over individual republican-minded members of the Directory. Its premise was the belief that the old religions were unsuited to the task of erecting a system of republican ethics and that without such a moral reform the republic would be deprived of any roots in the masses, in the morality of the people.

Robespierre had already come to regard the great popular festivals the republican customs of celebrating the salient events in daily life (birth, marriage, burial) as important instruments in the religious and moral edification of the people. In the speech to the Convention already cited he spoke at length of the significance of popular festivals among the Greeks, in particular of the important role assigned to the independent activity of the people. He concludes that all this could be revived in France on a much greater scale:

'A system of such festivals would constitute the gentlest bond of fraternity and the most potent instrument of regeneration.'[14]

Naturally enough, these somewhat external means of 'religious revival' played a much greater part in the sectarianism after Thermidor than in the actions of a politician like Robespierre.

We have already argued that historians like Aulard and Mathiez attached far too much importance to these religious movements. From our point of view, however, it is less important to consider the significance of these movements in France itself than to see how they were received in the retrograde society of Germany, and above all how they affected Hegel.

We have no direct proof that Hegel concerned himself to any great extent with these religious phenomena. Nevertheless, it is extremely probable that he was acquainted with them. Mathiez[15] gives a detailed bibliography of the journals which published articles for or against the Theophilanthropists. Among these we find Wieland's Teutsche Mercur, one of the most widely read periodicals, as well as the Minerva of Archenholz. We have precise knowledge that Hegel both knew and read the latter publication.[16] Since we also know that in Switzerland he followed a large variety of French journals it would be extremely surprising, in view of his interest in the religious and moral regeneration of mankind, if he had no no knowledge of the French religious movements at all.

But of greater weight than these circumstantial arguments is the internal evidence. In the course of our discussion of Hegel's views on antiquity in the following chapters we shall talk at length of the great importance he attached to the popular festivals of Greece and the active participation of the people in Greek religious rites. His attitudes here come very close to those of Robespierre in the speech from which we have already quoted. And as for the general elevation of morals with the aid of a new religion to be based on a regeneration of antiquity, it is evident that this lay at the heart of his interests at this time.

Like most German idealists Hegel regarded the moral regeneration of the people less as the product than as the prerequisite of revolution. Schiller had already put forward a similar view in the *Aesthetic Letters* which, as we have seen, made a great impression on Hegel. Schiller's attitude, however, is pessimistic. Just because he held the moral regeneration of the people to be the indispensable prerequisite of a successful revolution, he despaired that the latter would ever come about, even though he thought of the abolition of feudal absolutism as an historical and moral necessity. Even so it is noteworthy that Schiller dismissed the idea that the state could bring about the regeneration of the people through education.

The young Hegel parts company with Schiller here since he is much more sanguine about the prospects for the regeneration of mankind and the onset of a revolutionary period in which humanity and freedom celebrate their rebirth. It is for this reason that religion plays such a major role in his early idealism. Still within the framework of Kant's ethics and social theory, he realizes that the state can do no more than compel its citizens to obey the law: it can enforce legality but not morality. But since he also believes that the stability of a government depends on its roots in the moral principles of the people he casts around him in history to discover the factors that determine these moral principles. And he finds in religion the most efficacious of all such factors. Thus in *The Positivity of the Christian Religion*, his most important treatise from the Berne period, he has this to say about the relations between the state and its citizens:

> 'The state can only induce its citizens to make use of these institutions by inspiring confidence in them. Religion is the pre-eminent instrument for this purpose, and whether or not it can fulfil this task depends on the use made of it by the state. This purpose is clearly in evidence in the religions of all people. One thing they all have in common is that they all aspire to create that moral climate which no application of civil laws can bring about . . .'[17]

Here, we believe, the character of Hegel's early writings is plain for all to see. He believes that what he regards as the crucial turning-points of history, namely the transition from Greek freedom to medieval and modern despotism, and the hoped-for transition from this despotism to a new freedom, are intimately connected with religious movements. Both democracy and despotism require religions adapted to their needs if they are to survive. And it is apparent from what we have said already that the way in which Hegel poses the question of a religion of the future and its role in the revival of classical antiquity has very close parallels with the illusions of the French revolutionaries and with religious and moral aspirations within the Revolution. One of the inevitable consequences of Hegel's Germanness was that in his youth he reacted so powerfully to the least significant aspect of the French Revolution. In our further discussions, however, we shall see that even from this remote point of view he contrives to grasp a number of the objectively central moments of the socio-historical development.

Of course, an essential part of idealism is its vast over-estimation of the historical role of religion. And this over-estimation is maintained throughout Hegel's career. As we shall see, Hegel later revised his early opinions very thoroughly on almost every important issue. But as late as his Berlin lectures on the philosophy of history, even in the midst of arguments dealing with the July Revolution of 1830, he still returns to the same problem. In the course of a diatribe against the liberalism of the countries of Western Europe he says:

> 'For it is a false principle which maintains that the shackles of law and freedom can be cast off without a liberation of conscience, or that there can be a revolution without a reformation.'[18]

It is evident that Hegel's youthful assumption of the historical efficacy of religion accompanied him—admittedly with great modifications of substance—throughout his life. This is the heritage of philosophical idealism that he never shook off. But for all that the belief in Hegel's 'theological' early period remains a legend created and fostered by the reactionary apologists of imperialism.

## NOTES

1   J. Ch. Edelmann (1698–1767) was a freethinker who was greatly persecuted for his hostility to Christianity. His autobiography was published posthumously in 1847—*Trans.*

2   Guillaume Thomas Francois Raynal (1713–96) was an important precursor of the French Revolution. His most celebrated work, the *Histoire philosophique et politique des établissements et du commerce des Européens dans les deux Indes* appeared in 1770 in 6 volumes. It is a compendium of information and ideas with an advanced anti-clerical bias and includes contributions by Diderot. It fell foul of the Holy See in 1774 and was placed on the Index. In 1781 it was condemned and burned in Paris, its author being forced into exile

—*Trans.*

3  Georg Forster (1754–94), traveller, scientist, writer and politician, became world-famous at the age of twenty-four when he published his account of Captain Cook's second voyage (1772–75) on which he had accompanied his father, the naturalist Johann Reinhold Forster. Later he became a professor at Cassel and Vilna and librarian at Mainz. Here, when the French invaded in 1792, Forster joined the revolutionaries and became one of the leaders of the German Jacobins. He died in Paris where he had gone in 1793 to convey to the National Convention the offer of a union of the 'liberated' Rhineland with the French Republic—*Trans.*

4  Johann Lorenz von Mosheim (1693–1755) was the founder of pragmatic church history in Germany. His chief work was the *Institutiones Historiae Ecclesiastica* which appeared in 1755 in Latin and from 1769 to 1778 in German.—*Trans.*

5  Hermann Samuel Reimarus (1694–1768) was a prominent German deist. His chief work, the *Apology for or Defence of the rational Worshippers of God*, was published in fragmentary form by Lessing in 1774–77. Since Lessing did not indicate the identity of the author he was suspected of having written the work himself and came under attack for the hostility towards supernatural religion expressed in it.—*Trans.*

6  Fr. Engels, *Ludwig Feuerbach and the End of Classical German Philosophy*, in Marx/Engels, *Selected Works*, Vol. II, Moscow and London 1950, p. 332. Referred to henceforth as *Feuerbach*.

7  K. Rosenkranz, *Life of Hegel*, Berlin 1844, p. 66. Cited here as 'Rosenkranz'.

8  Rosenkranz, p. 70.

9  Fr. Engels, op. cit., Vol. II, p. 332.

10  The main monographs on this topic are:
Aulard, *Le culte de raison et le culte de l'être suprême*, Paris 1909.
Mathiez, *Les origines des cultes révolutionaires*, Paris 1904.
Mathiez, *La théophilanthropie et le culte décadère 1796–1801*, Paris 1904.

11  Mathiez, *Théophilanthropie*, pp. 40ff

12  *Oeuvres de Robespierre*, ed. A. Vermorel, Paris 1867, p. 302.

13  Speech of 7 May 1794, ibid., pp. 308ff.

14  Ibid., pp. 329ff.

15  Ibid., pp. 390ffff

16  Letter to Schelling, Christmas 1794, in Rosenkranz, p. 65.

17  Nohl, p. 175.

18  Hegel, *Werke*, Berlin 1840, Vol. IX, p. 542.

# CHAPTER TWO

# What is the meaning of 'positivity' in Hegel's early works?

THE real issue of central importance in the works of Hegel's Berne period was that of 'positive' religion, especially of 'positive' Christianity. To present our conclusions first, we must assert that the heart of the matter is that for Hegel the positive religion of Christianity was a pillar of despotism and oppression, whereas the non-positive religions of antiquity were religions of freedom and human dignity. To revive these was the revolutionary challenge facing his generation.

We must begin by clarifying Hegel's conception of positivity. He employs the concept in a number of places in his Berne writings and, in what follows, we shall allow Hegel to state the matter as far as possible in his own words.

'A positive faith is a system of religious propositions which are true for us because they have been presented to us by an authority which we cannot flout. In the first instance the concept implies a system of religious propositions or truths which must be held to be truths independently of our own opinions, and which even if no man has ever perceived them and even if no man has ever considered them to be truths, nevertheless remain truths. These truths are often said to be objective truths and what is required of them is that they should now become subjective truths, truths for us.'[1]

The main point here is the independence of such propositions together with the demand that the subject should regard them as binding on himself even though he has not created them. Positivity, then, means primarily the suspension of the moral autonomy of the subject. To this extent it seems very close to Kantian ethics and does in fact contain a number of similar features. However, what Hegel means by the subject is something different from Kant's moral subject; for Hegel it is something social and historical. Admittedly, its definition is extraordinarily vague and unclear. What it amounts to—inasmuch as it is more than a shorthand for the world view of the Greeks, i.e. the historical and moral ideal —is the identity of the moral autonomy of the individual with the democratic collective embracing the entire people. The contradiction between the subjectivity of the individual and the social activity of the totality arises in Hegel's view only with the break-up of the democracy of the *polis* and the intervention of the Christian religion. Thenceforth the Christian religion stands opposed to the individual as something objective, 'positive', and the need to obey its commandments is, on the one hand, a consequence of the loss of freedom and, on the other, a continuously self-reproducing process of oppression and despotism.

In Hegel's view this period of despotism extends to the present day and pervades every aspect of social life and ideology. He judges the moral degradation of men according to the degree to which they have come to accept their loss of freedom and according to whether they solve the problems of ideology by orienting themselves towards freedom or towards submission to the positive authority. A passage from Hegel's Travel Journal (July to August 1796) reflects his mood precisely and illustrates even more clearly the general definition of positivity given above. At around this time he made a small tour of the Bernese Oberland and observed the poverty of nature there, and the great problems facing men who were trying to wrest a living from unfavourable conditions through their own labour. As might be expected from his interests at this time, he speculates about the religion, the world view that would arise under such circumstances and comes to the following, highly characteristic conclusion:

'In these barren wastes cultivated men might well have invented all other theories and sciences; but one can scarcely believe that they could have thought of that part of the physico-theological argument which would demonstrate to man's pride that nature had prepared everything for his enjoyment and well-being; *a pride which is characteristic of our* age in which man finds more satisfaction in the contemplation of all that has been done for him by an alien being, than in the consciousness that it is he who has furnished nature with all these purposes.'[2]

Here we see the radical subjectivity of the early Hegel very clearly. Kant, too, had attacked the crude and dogmatic arguments from design in the so-called physico-theological proof of the existence of God. But Kant's method had been to demonstrate the internal contradictions in such teleological views by showing the antinomies which spring from them. None of this interests Hegel. He is fascinated by the question of what sort of man is attracted by the physico-theological proof, what sort of man will reject it. Is a man proud of what he has made himself, or does he derive pleasure from the belief that an alien power (God) cares for him? Thus Hegel aims to purge morality of all theological—positive—elements, but unlike Kant, he does not do this because the objects of theology are unknowable, but because he holds faith to be incompatible with freedom and the dignity of man. Thus Hegel energetically repudiates the process by which Kant, who had dissolved theological entities in *The Critique of Pure Reason*, declaring them to be unknowable, later reinstated the very same entities, with the aid of the 'postulates of practical reason' and restored them to their place in his view of life.[3]

In this struggle against the revival of theology with the aid of Kantian ethics Hegel was not alone, his views were shared by his young friend Schelling. In a letter of 1795 Schelling complains to Hegel that in Tübingen, where he was studying, *The Critique of Practical Reason* had infused new life into reactionary, orthodox theology.

> 'Every dogma imaginable has been converted into a postulate of practical reason and where the theoretical and historical proofs are wanting, the practical reason (*à la* Tübingen) simply cuts the Gordian knot. It is blissful to be able to witness the triumph of these heroes of philosophy. The lean years of philosophy that have been foretold, are now a thing of the past!'[4]

In this battle Schelling based himself to a considerable degree on the philosophy of Fichte.

Hegel was wholly in accord with Schelling in his attack on this new Kantian theology. His reply, however, contains a number of very characteristic features on which we must dwell a little. Above all he shows very little interest in the strictly philosophical problems involved. At the same time he is revealed to be highly critical of Fichte. Having expressed his agreement with Schelling, he goes on:

> 'It is undeniable that *Fichte*, with his *Critique of Revelation* has flung open the gate to the kind of nonsense you describe and whose last act I can easily imagine. He has made only moderate use of it himself, but once his principles have become firmly established it will not be possible to stem the tide of theological logic. Starting with the sanctity of God he deduces what his moral nature impells him to do and so re-introduces the old style of dogmatic reasoning. Now that moral faith has been re-established, it would perhaps be worth the effort to discover how far we may argue backwards from the newly *legitimated idea of God*; e.g. whether by way of justifying teleological arguments we may proceed from ethical theology to physico-theology and there hold sway unopposed.'[5]

Looking back to the earlier passage on the physico-theological proof it is clear that Hegel makes a much more thorough-going attempt than any of his contemporaries to liberate Kant's practical reason, the moral autonomy of man, from all elements of theology; and that he regards all the efforts of Kant and Fichte in this direction as no more than a continuation of Christian positivity in a new guise.

His reply to Schelling contains yet another passage of such absorbing interest that we cannot forbear to quote it. Even though he remains fairly indifferent to the epistemological implications of positive religion and theology, he goes right to the heart of the social foundations of the debate and gives a very blunt, naturalist view of the social underpinning of this theological renaissance:

'What you tell me of the -si Diis placet- theological, Kantian trends in philosophy in Tübingen is not at all surprising. Orthodoxy will never be budged as long as it is bound up with worldly advantage and so closely intertwined with the state as a whole. This interest is too poweful to be easily surrendered and it has its effect without our ever quite realizing how widespread it is.'[6]

We can see from this that Hegel has a much larger and more social understanding of the concept of the practical than did Kant, Fichte and even the early Schelling. Hegel does, it is true, make Kant's practical concept of freedom the philosophical premise of his own demands for freedom and human dignity, but his idea of how to realize these demands is at once transferred to the social plane. And at this period he is not in the least concerned about the difficulties of combining this subjective, idealist premise with the real social and historical conclusions he draws from it. It is well known that, later on, Hegel both severely criticized the subjective nature of Kant's ethics and attempted to resolve the social problems implicit in this ethics on the basis of objective idealism, of an idealist dialectics of social development.

In Berne, however, Hegel attempts an interesting socio-historical extension of the dualism of Kant and Fichte, which for him too necessarily arises from a subjective, idealist view of the nature of morality. Kant held that there are two utterly separate worlds with no mediating transitions: the world of ethics, of the intelligible self (the noumenon) in which the categories of the manifest world (causality, etc.) have no validity, and the world of knowledge, of the empirical self (the phenomenon) where these categories hold sway. With his theory of the 'non-Ego' (i.e. the entire external world) posited by the 'Ego', Fichte shifts the whole problem into the realm of general philosophy, where he converts Kant's explanation of ethics into the foundation and starting-point of the theory of knowledge. As we shall see, this view in its turn has a profound effect on the early philosophy of Schelling.

Hegel has a quite different approach to the problem of relating the free moral consciousness to objective reality. For him, too, objective reality is a 'dead', objective world of externals alien to the moral consciousness in all its living subjectivity. However, this antithesis is not 'eternal', it is no philosophical, epistemological antithesis as it is for Kant and his successors: it is instead an *historical* growth. It is the defining feature of the Middle Ages and the modern world. However, in the

city-states of antiquity it did not exist and the idea that it could be abolished lies at the heart of Hegel's deepest hopes for the future.

   Only if we keep this in mind will we be able to grasp the full implications of the crucial issue of the Berne period, namely the meaning of
'positive' Christianity. In Hegel's view this positivity is the actual social
reality corresponding to Kant's ethical dualism. Only when we realize
this will we be able to appreciate that Hegel's indifference towards
Fichte's reform of Kantianism does not spring from an antipathy towards
philosophy. It is important to avoid the impression that the early Hegel
had no real philosophical problems and that his biography consists of the
*awakening of his philosophical instincts.* On the contrary, we shall see later
on that most of the elements peculiar to his thought grow organically
from this conception of the antithesis between positivity and moral subjectivity. But problems of epistemology only become acute for Hegel
and move to the forefront of his attention when the contradictions in his
original view appear as the objective contradictions of social reality, i.e.
when epistemology becomes the dialectics of reality itself.

   It is for this reason that this alien, dead, 'givenness' of the laws of morality is the salient characteristic of positivity. An essential part of every
moral law, he insists, is that the moral subject should legislate for himself.

> 'The Christian religion, however, proclaims the moral law as some-
> thing external to us, as something "given" and must therefore strive
> to win respect for it on other grounds. We may therefore regard it as a
> defining feature of a positive religion that it posits the moral law as
> something given to mankind.[7]

This gives rise to a complex ethical casuistry within Christianity as
contrasted with the free workings of an unspoilt moral sense in societies
with a non-positive religion. The Christian religion possesses a code
which prescribes

> 'partly . . . what man ought to do, partly what he ought to know and
> believe, and partly what he ought to feel. On the possession and
> manipulation of this code rests the entire legislative and judicial
> power of the church, and if the rights of human reason are imcompa-
> tible with submission to an alien code of this sort, then the entire
> power of the church, and if the rights of human reason are incompa-
> rights to legislate for himself and to account to himself for the man-
> agement of that law, since with that alienation he would cease to be a
> human being.[8]

Here we have a clear statement of the insoluble contradiction between
positive religion and human freedom. In his most important work of this
period in Berne, in *The Positivity of the Christian Religion* from which we
have already quoted, and from which we shall now cite further passages,

Hegel charts this antagonism through a number of spheres of moral life and for important aspects of the problems of society. Positive religion, so depicted, is in Hegel's view the determining moment of the whole of life in the Middle Ages and modern times. Obviously its ramifications are felt even in the realms of knowledge, the understanding and reason. According to Hegel the loss of moral freedom necessarily entails the loss of the independent use of one's reason. The alien, lifeless, given and yet dominant object of positive religion destroys the harmonious and coherent life which man had earlier enjoyed in the age of freedom; it transforms the crucial issues of life into transcendental, unknowable problems inaccessible to reason.

The emergence of such problems is likewise the consequence of positive religion in Hegel's view. Its power lies precisely in the fact that in every sphere of his thought and his being man acknowledges this alien authority; once he has renounced his moral freedom he can no longer resist the superior force of positive religion. So the tentacles of the latter reach out into every sphere of life and stifle every attempt to make free use of human reason.

'The capacity for this [positive faith] necessarily presupposes the loss of the freedom, the autonomy of one's reason which henceforth stands helpless before a superior power. This is the point at which all belief or disbelief in a positive religion begins. At the same time, it is the centre around which all disputes revolve and even if it never rises to the surface of consciousness it is nevertheless the deciding factor between submissiveness and rebellion. The orthodox must stand fast at this point and make no concessions . . .'[9]

This dominance extends even into the realm of knowledge. The judgment of reason concerning the so-called historical truths of religion, to say nothing of miracles, must be that they are merely products of the imagination, 'fictions', etc. Positive religion cannot tolerate this.

'Recourse must be had, therefore, to a higher faculty before which reason must fall silent. Faith is erected into a duty and removed into a supernatural world to which the understanding has no access—and in this context faith means a configuration of events presented to the imagination while the understanding constantly searches for a different explanation. And what prevents the understanding from entering this world is duty, i.e. fear of a mighty ruler which compels the understanding to collude in activities abhorrent to it.'[10]

There can be no doubt: these ostensibly theological writings are one long indictment of Christianity. Every connoisseur of the literature of the Enlightenment will have been reminded by our quotations of the wider anti-religious struggles of that age. At the same time, however, it

is important to note not only the resemblances but also the methodological differences separating Hegel and the Enlightenment. We have
already stated that Hegel, unlike Diderot, Holbach or Helvétius, never
attacked religion as such, but contrasted positive religion polemically
with a non-positive religiosity. (In this respect he comes closest to Rousseau.) But there is a further point at which they diverge: the outstanding
members of the Enlightenment, like Hegel, speak frequently of the de-
grading effects of Christianity, of its destruction of freedom and human
dignity. But they never focus on this with the same exclusiveness as
Hegel. For them it is no less important to confront the Teachings of
Christianity and religion in general with the facts of reality as established
by science and so to unmask the inner hollowness and the contradictions
of religion.

This motif plays a very subordinate role in Hegel's early thought. As
we have noted, he mentions from time to time that the dogmas of Christianity are incompatible with reason and reality; however, this is of no
more than passing importance for him. Even when he comes expressly to
consider this question he is less disturbed by the discrepancies between
religious dogmas and the truths of science than by the immoral demands
of the church that human reason should accept such dogmas untested,
positively, and that they should be made the objects of faith and religious
feeling. This approach to the anti-religious struggle enables us to see just
how the great writers of the French Enlightenment towered above the
early Hegel. At the same time, we must admit that even though the subjectivism that led Hegel to this approach is itself the social and ideological product of the backward state of Germany, the German
Enlightenment and Kantian philosophy, etc., it likewise forms the foundations for his development both of the 'active side' and the historicism
of his method.

Later on in this chapter we shall have to return to the question of the
foundations and consequences of Hegel's view of positivity. We were
concerned here only in sketching its basic features, its chief contours,
with a view to clarifying his approach to the philosophy of history.

As we have seen, Hegel is the advocate of the 'primacy of practical
reason'. He simply equates the Absolute, the autonomous and the practical. This exclusive sovereignty of the practical reason is the feature
common to his early work and that of Schelling. In the context of the relation of practical reason to theology, we have already had occasion to
observe both the identity of views and the divergences between Hegel
and Schelling. Since the initial philosophical friendship and the later
breach between Schelling and Hegel both play an important role in the
emergence of the dialectic we must necessarily acquaint the reader with
his position at this period. In one of his earliest works, the *New Deduction
of Natural Law* (Spring 1796), Schelling declares, in agreement with

Fichte and in terms that show a definite parallel to Hegel's idea of 'positivity', that the Absolute, the Unconditional, can never be an object:

> 'As soon as I attempt to hold fast to it as an object it returns to within the confines of the contingent. Whatever is an *object* for me, can only appear; as soon as it becomes more than appearance, my freedom is destroyed . . . If I am to realize the Unconditional, it must cease to be an object for me.'

The Absolute is thus identical with the ego.[11]

Schelling's views with all their implications emerge even more clearly in a small essay not intended for publication and of which we possess a fragment in a copy by Hegel dating from 1796. The copy begins with the section on ethics. We do not know what preceded it. Perhaps some of it has been lost; perhaps, not untypically, he copied out only this one section. Schelling declares here that the whole of philosophy (he uses the term 'metaphysics') is identical with morality, an approach first developed by Kant but by no means exhausted by him. It is a view that must lead to quite original conceptions of nature and the natural sciences. We see here the seeds of Schelling's later visions of natural philosophy. What concerns us, however, is his view of society and the state. Schelling has this to say on the subject:

> 'From nature I come to the *works of man*. Guided by the idea of humanity, I intend to show that there can be no idea of the *state*, since the state is *mechanical*—just as there can be no such thing as the idea of a *machine*. Only that which is *free* can be called an *idea*. We must therefore transcend the state! For every state must treat free men as cogs in a machine; and this must be prevented. Hence the state must *cease to exist*.'

Proceeding from these considerations Schelling goes on to set out the principles for a history of mankind 'and to expose the entire wretched hotch-potch of the state, constitution, government and legislature.' This is to be followed by his ideas about morality and religion.

> 'The destruction of all false gods, the persecution of the priesthood with their new hypocritical adoption of reason—all this to be brought about by reason itself. The absolute freedom of all spirits who bear the intellectual world within themselves and who may seek neither God nor immortality *outside themselves*.'

The fragment closes with the proclamation of aesthetics as the pinnacle of the philosophy of mind and with a call for the creation of a new, popular mythology.[12]

In these scattered remarks it is not hard to discern the important themes of his famous period in Jena when he developed his speculations in natural philosophy. Nor is it any more difficult to perceive how close Schelling's application and extension of 'practical reason' comes to Hegel's concept of 'positivity'. It is easily comprehensible, therefore, why in their youth Schelling and Hegel should have regarded each other as allies. But it is no less important to see that even at this early stage there were profound—as yet unavowed—differences between the two men. As we have observed, Schelling's rejection of 'positivity' goes far beyond anything contemplated by Hegel. In principle and right from the start he regards the state and all its works as 'positive' in Hegel's sense; the liberation of mankind is identical for him with liberation from the state. This shows that at this early stage Schelling does not share, or has ceased to share, Hegel's revolutionary hopes for a radical regener-ation of society and the state, a regeneration that will result in the aboli-tion of their 'positive' qualities. He thus transforms Hegel's revolutionary utopia in which mankind is liberated from the state. And it is equally evident that such a view is very closely connected—whether as cause or effect is of little moment—with Schelling's energetic defence of Fichteanism at this time.

Hegel differs from his philosophical ally above all by virtue of his much more *historical* approach. He does not imagine every state to be 'positive', only the despotic state from Imperial Rome to the present day. The state of antiquity stands in sharp contrast to this: it is the product and expression of the free self-activity of man, of democratic society. Hence his goal and his perspective on the future is not the destruction of the state in general, but the reconstruction of the—non-positive—city-states of antiquity, of their free, spontaneous democracies.

In appearance and by comparison with the methodological practices of the age Hegel's approach is far less philosophical than Schelling's. Schelling operates with pairs of opposites derived from Kant and Fichte—freedom and necessity, essence and appearance—(opposites that coincide much more directly in Fichte's thought and his own, than they do in Kant); and he uses them in such a way as to turn epistemology wholly into ethics. And in this ethics anything which is not the subject of praxis, becomes a mere object (or in Hegel's terminology, is merely 'positive'). This world of lifeless objectivity is identical with the Kantian world of 'appearances'. Only through praxis does man come into contact with true reality, with essence. We can now clearly see the connection between Schelling's use of Kantian epistemo-logy and his own anti-historical standpoint. At the same time we can see why Hegel, for whom positivity was essentially an historical problem, could find little to interest him in the extension of Kant's theory of knowledge at the hands of Fichte and Schelling.

Hegel's indifference to his friend's ethical–epistemological constructions does not imply the absence of philosophical interests. In reality, we can see here the seeds of Hegel's later method of combining philosophical and conceptual problems with the historical development of objective reality. When he takes the concept of positivity, which in theology and jurisprudence had been a general, unhistorical concept operating as the polar opposite to the natural religion of the deists or alternatively to natural law, and when he puts it at the very centre of his thought he takes the first, unconscious step in the direction of his later dialectical view of history. Of course, we must emphasize once more that at this time Hegel not only did not see the full philosophical implications of his approach; he scarcely concerned himself with his own philosophical premises.

The historical aspect of Hegel's method developed only gradually. Definite signs of it, in particular the distinction he makes between classical antiquity and Christianity, are in evidence from the start as far as we can see from the available sources. But his historical method matured only slowly; we shall see, in our discussion of his Frankfurt period in Part II, how the historical concept of positivity gains in flexibility and depth.

In his student days in Tübingen his methods still have a marked tendency towards anthropology and psychology. We have already mentioned that we possess a relatively rich harvest of notes and excerpts dealing with the 'anthropological' treatment of mental faculties, of the various physical and mental qualities of man, a collection which has drawn on almost the entire literature of the German Enlightenment. These extracts which have only appeared in the last few decades (first in the journal *Logos*, then in Hoffmeister's book) have not been exploited by students of Hegel. In particular, no research has been carried out on the question of the extent to which they were incorporated into the 'anthropological' sections of the *Phenomenology* and the *Encyclopaedia*.

This question naturally goes beyond the framework of the present study. We should only like to make the general methodological remark that the historicization of 'anthropology' forms part of the general pattern of Hegel's overall development. This is not just confined to the *Phenomenology* where he attempted to integrate the problems of 'anthropology' in an historical, dialectical process; it also forms an integral part of his entire later system. Thus concepts like 'intuition' [*Anschauung*], 'idea' [*Vorstellung*], 'concept' [*Begriff*], all of which appear in the original notes as 'anthropological' problems, reappear in the later works as systematic principles (intuition: aesthetics; idea: religion; concept: philosophy). Furthermore they provide the foundation for his system of periodization (aesthetics: antiquity; religion: Middle Ages; philosophy: the modern world).

What interests us here is the original 'anthropological' contrast of memory and imagination. At this time Hegel made a distinction between objective and subjective religion. For objective religion

'the understanding and memory ... are the effective forces at work ... Practical knowledge may be a part of objective religion, but if so it is no more than dead capital—objective religion can be organized in the mind, it can be systematized and put into a book or presented to others in the form of a speech. Subjective religion finds expression only in feelings and actions ... Subjective religion is alive; inwardly, in essence, it is sheer efficacy; and outwardly it is activity.'

He goes on to compare subjective religion to the living organisms of nature and objective religion to the stuffed animals in scientific collections.[13] This contrast is typical throughout the whole Berne period and the reader will have observed that the objective religion of the Tübingen notes represents an early form of the positive Christianity of Berne. I need cite only one further sentence from the Berne historical studies to illustrate the continuity of thought:

'memory is the gallows, on which the Greek gods have been hanged ... Memory is the grave, the repository of the dead. The dead dwell in it as dead matter. They are exhibited there like a collection of stones.'

This is followed by a sharp attack on Christian ceremony:

This is the activity of the dead. Man strives to make himself into an object, submit entirely to the rule of an alien force. Such service is called worship.'[14]

Hegel's position in Tübingen centres on a very sharp, Enlightened polemic against objective religion. In his eyes only subjective religion has any value. Admittedly, the latter still retains an unhistorical inflection, derived from the 'natural religion' or 'religion of reason' typical of the Enlightenment. Lessing is clearly the most potent influence here:

'Subjective religion is found among good men, objective religion can be of whatever colour you please, it hardly matters which—what makes me a Christian in your eyes, makes you a Jew in mine, Nathan says (Nathan the Wise, Act IV, sc. 7). For religion comes from the heart which is often unfaithful to the dogmas accepted by the understanding or the memory.'[15]

In the Tübingen period the antithesis of objective and subjective religion often cuts across the other antithesis of public and private religion. A synthesis of the two pairs of opposites is only achieved in Berne. But even in Tübingen Hegel makes a distinct parallel between the subjective and the public on the one hand, and the objective and the private on the other.

Here we have palpable evidence of Hegel's dialectical method, long before dialectics as such became a conscious problem for him. For any formal, metaphysical approach would undoubtedly connect the subjective with the private rather than the public. If Hegel now spontaneously bursts the confines of metaphysical thought this is due partly to the growing effect of his historical awareness, and partly to the irresistible longing for freedom released by the impact on him of the French Revolution. In his view subjective religion is a genuinely 'popular religion'. And the requirements which such a religion must satisfy are formulated as follows:

'1. Its teachings must be based on universal reason. 2. The imagination, the heart and the senses should not go away empty-handed. 3. It must be designed so that all the needs of life—the public acts of the state—combine with it.'

And in the negative, polemical section that follows Hegel repudiates every faith based on fetishism, including that of the pseudo-Enlightened apologists of Christianity.[16]

Hegel's language here is perfectly unambiguous. We need only add that he explicitly assumes the *rationality* of subjective and public religion. Thus the reactionary interpretations that regard Hegel's contrast between memory and the imagination as the sign of his 'irrationalism' can be seen to be nothing more than slanders and distortions. As for the social content of his requirements, Hegel does not leave his view in doubt. He emphasizes that public religion should not just contain commandments and prohibitions, such as 'thou shalt not steal', but it

'must above all include less obvious factors which are indeed often the most important. Chief among these are the improvement, the ennobling of a nation's spirit—so that its sense of dignity, so often dormant, should be aroused in its soul, so that the people should not throw itself away, nor permit itself to be thrown away.'[17]

Thus even the Tübingen student already conceives of subjective, public religion as the religion of the self-liberation of the people.

NOTES
1   Nohl, p. 233.
2   Rosenkranz, p. 482. The physico-theological proof of the existence of God is more familiar as the argument from design. God's existence is inferred from the 'clear signs we everywhere find of an order in accordance with a determinate purpose'. Since 'this purposive order is quite alien to the things of the world and only belongs to

them contingently' there must exist 'a sublime and wise cause' beyond the world itself. Although Kant thinks that the proof always deserves to be mentioned with respect, he exposes its inadequacies, arguing that 'the utmost . . . that it can prove is an architect of the world, . . . not a creator' and that the proof therefore needs to be supplemented by the cosmological proof which rests in turn on the ontological proof. *Critique of Pure Reason*, trans. Kemp Smith, London 1950, pp. 518–24.—*Trans*.

3    Freedom, the immortality of the soul and God are the three postulates of practical reason defended by Kant in the second Critique.

4    Plitt, *Schelling's Life in his Letters*, Leipzig 1869, Vol. I, p. 72. Referred to henceforth as Plitt.

5    Rosenkranz, pp. 67ff.

6    Ibid., p. 67.

7    Nohl, p. 212.

8    Ibid.

9    Ibid., p. 234.

10    Ibid., p. 236.

11    Schelling, *Werke*, ed. Manfred Schröter, Jena 1926, Vol. I, p. 108.

12    Published in Hoffmeister, pp. 219ff.

13    Nohl, p. 6f.

14    Rosenkranz, p. 518f.

15    Nohl, p. 10.

16    Nohl, p. 20f.

17    Nohl, p. 5.

# CHAPTER THREE

# Historical perspectives and the present

Hegel, we may say, attempted to turn subjective, public religion into the foundation, the chief support of the freedom movement in Germany. We have already seen that these endeavours led to a strange mixture of historical objectivity and radical, philosophical subjectivism. Hegel's historical programme in Berne was to trace the democratic subjectivism of society in its highest and most developed form in antiquity; he went on to depict in darker colours the decay of that world and the emergence of the lifeless, anti-human, despotic period of positive religion, and from a contrast of these two he tried to gain a perspective on the future emancipation. Thus the contrast between antiquity and Christianity, subjective and positive religion was the foundation of Hegel's political philosophy in Berne.

The practical character of his philosophy has naturally been noticed even by his reactionary interpreters. Haering goes so far as to place this problem in the centre of his study when he describes Hegel's 'popular pedagogic' leanings as the most significant elements of his development. There is nothing to object to in that, of course. But Haering and other reactionary apologists make a point of interpreting Hegel's early views from the reactionary features of his later political position, implying that these constituted the ever-present 'essence' of Hegel's philosophy and making every possible use of the many, inevitable confusions in his early thought, especially in the realm of religious thought, to prove the existence of reactionary tendencies at the very heart of his philosophy.

Of course, Hegel's early republican leanings cannot be entirely ignored. They are indeed obscured or overlooked wherever possible, but they cannot be wholly disregarded. The imperialist apologists find their way out of the impasse by dismissing his republicanism as an 'infantile disorder'. Franz Rosenzweig, for example, regards Hegel as a precursor of Bismarckian politics. Distorting and suppressing the available evidence in a completely anti-historical fashion, he firstly obscures the fact that even in his old age Hegel was never a precursor of Bismarck and that even his reactionary views were quite different from those of Bismarck. Secondly, he suppresses all the great historical crises (Thermidor, the fall of Napoleon) which had such a great influence on Hegel's political development and ended up by inducing that mood of profound resignation so characteristic of so many important Germans who had

hoped that the Napoleonic age would bring about a regeneration of
their own country. (One thinks here of the later Goethe.) By discovering Hegel's similarity to Bismarck 'prefigured' in his soul from
youth onwards, it becomes easy to represent his republicanism and his
whole relationship with the French Revolution as something superficial
that is gradually discarded with increasing 'maturity'.

Such writers remain quite unmoved by the fact that even the writings
of the old Hegel state unambiguously his view that the French Revolution was historically inevitable and that it forms the basis of modern
culture, etc. We need give only one example of this ingenious mixture of
quotation and omission. Rosenzweig, in his discussion of one of Hegel's
early political writings, quotes all sorts of statements implying an anti-
republican position, hostility to the Enlightenment etc. Then, with apparent objectivity but in effect blurring the truth, he adds contemptuous-
ly:

> 'But of course at this time Hegel's admiration for monarchy was only
> skin-deep.'[1]

We already know how closely the practical character of Hegel's
philosophy was connected with his political dreams. We must now go
on to show, with the aid of quotations, just how he saw the contemporary state of Germany as the product of that development whose chief
characteristic he described as positive religion. This will help us to see
why the emphasis on the freedom and democracy of antiquity implied a
revolutionary contrast with the state of Germany at the time.

After what we have said it will come as no surprise to see that Hegel's
views here too begin with religion and the religious tradition. Thus,
speaking of the German tradition, he says:

> 'Our tradition—folk songs and such like. There is no Harmodius, no
> Aristogeiton to merit undying fame because they defeated their
> tyrants and gave equal rights and laws to their people, men whose
> names live on in the mouths of the people, in their songs. What does
> the historical knowledge of our people amount to? We lack a specific,
> national tradition; our memory and imagination are filled with the
> pre-history of another people, with the deeds and misdeeds of kings
> who do not concern us.'[2]

In this context, Hegel compares German and Greek architecture; his interest here is not primarily aesthetic. He is much more concerned with
the different ways of life: the free, beautiful life of the Greeks, and the
narrow, petty, philistine life of the Germans, a life punctuated only by
uproarious and stupid drunkenness. The difference in architecture is
merely an expression of the different life-contents of the two peoples.
(Here too we find an approach that will later reappear in the *Aesthetics*

—albeit at a quite different level of dialectical argument and historical concretization.)

We must turn once again to the principal writings of the Berne period, *The Positivity of the Christian Religion* to discover Hegel's most important observations about contemporary Germany. He talks there of the way in which first the Roman conquest and later Christianity destroyed the primitive national religions, including those of the Germans. And the development of Germany was of the sort that could provide no sustenance for a national, religious imagination.

> 'With the possible exception of Luther among the Protestants, who could be our heroes, when we have never formed a nation? Who could be our Theseus, to found our state and provide us with laws? Where are the Harmodiuses and Aristogeitons, the liberators whom we would celebrate in our skolia? The wars which have devoured millions of Germans were wars fought for the glory or independence of our princes—the nation was no more than a tool and even though the people fought bitterly they would not have been able to say at the end why or what they had gained by it?'

And Hegel goes on to give a sceptical account of the living heritage of Protestant historical traditions making the point that the German powers-that-be were not interested in ensuring the survival of the liberating aspect of Protestant tradition among the people.[3]

This analysis leads Hegel to the conclusion that the German people, which suffers from the absence of an indigenous religious imagination organically growing up alongside and interwoven with its history, is in addition 'entirely lacking in political imagination'.[4] And this absence of a national life of the imagination pervades the whole of German culture. Typically, what interests him primarily is not the great achievements of German culture, although he was intimately aware of them, but the absence of a popular German culture, with real roots in the people. This lack is the chief target of his complaints against contemporary German culture:

> 'The charming *jeux d'esprit* of Hölty, Bürger and Musäus in this sphere are quite lost on our people whose general level of culture is too low for it to be receptive to the pleasures they offer; similarly the imagination of the more educated classes of the nation inhabits a realm quite different from that of the lower classes, and the latter simply do not understand the characters and scenes of those authors and artists who cater for the former.'

Here too he makes a comparison with antiquity, pointing out that in Greece it was precisely the greatest art, that of Socrates and Phidias, that was of the people and could move the entire nation.[5]

In this context Hegel defends the idea of a future German culture built on classical foundations. The growing influence of classical culture was the *sine qua non* of true progress and, in particular, he combats the views of Klopstock whose poetry has its sources partly in the early history of the German people (e.g. the battle in the Teutoburger Forest, [where Hermann or Arminius defeated the Roman Legions under Varus in AD 108—*Trans.*]), and partly in the Judaeo-Christian tradition (the latter as a belated and enfeebled echo of the ideological traditions of the English Revolution as mediated by Milton). To Klopstock's anti-classical: 'Is Achaia the fatherland of the Tuiscones?'[6] Hegel replies firstly with a lengthy argument to the effect that the artistic regeneration of the ancient German tradition was a task as hopeless as Julian's attempt to revive classical religion.

'That dream of ancient Germany finds nothing to correspond to it in our age; in the world of our ideas, opinions and beliefs it is as isolated and as alien as the Ossianic or Indian traditions . . .'

And on the issue of a Judaeo-Christian revival he retorts:

'And what the poet says of Greek mythology we could say with equal justice of Judaeic myths and ask: Is Judaea the fatherland of the Tuiscones?[7]

Here, too, especially on the issue of the Old German tradition we find Hegel putting a point of view he will retain his whole life long. He does not only have political objections to the wars of Liberation [i.e. the war against Napoleon—*Trans.*], he also regards with hostility all the neo-Germanic aspirations of the Romantics. This too has been ignored or 're-interpreted' by the imperialist critics who endeavour to make Hegel into a Romantic.

This image of the pettiness and the lack of freedom of modern Germany, of the absence of a true popular culture, is closely linked with Hegel's overall democratic outlook at this period. During his stay in Berne, a city ruled at the time by a patrician oligarchy, Hegel reaches the same negative conclusions about this Swiss city as about Germany. And his judgement is even more explicitly political since he can speak more freely in a letter than in writings intended for publication, where he would have to keep the German censors in mind. Writing to Schelling on 16 April 1795, he says:

'Every ten years the conseil souverain increases its membership by roughly the numbers that have been lost during this period. You can have no idea of how human the whole business is. The intrigues among cousins and aunts at our princely courts are as nothing compared to the combinations here. The father nominates his son, or the son-in-law who brings in the greatest marriage portion, etc. To get to know an aristocratic constitution you just have to spend a winter here before the Easter selection.[8]

This letter needs no commentary. His Berne experience evidently inspired in him an undying contempt for such aristocratic oligarchies. His dislike does not even abate when his other political opinions of the Berne period have been long since revised.

Hegel considers such political and cultural conditions to be the product of a development inspired above all by the hegemony of positive Christianity. And if he could refer to the 'glorious dawn' of the French Revolution even in his old age we can form some conception of the impatience with which he had awaited the regeneration of the world. This regeneration underlies his critique of Christianity and its positive content is the revival of the classical tradition. Hence, his analysis and praise of Greek democracy has a great *immediate, political* significance.

Here too Hegel's views have many precedents. In the great class struggles surrounding the liquidation of feudalism the model of Greek democracy played a leading role in the writings of the ideological vanguard from the Renaissance on. One of the greatest failures of the historiography of ideology is that the relationship between the classical revival and the struggles of the bourgeoisie for emancipation has never been adequately explored. Indeed, bourgeois historians have been at pains to obliterate the traces of this relationship, preferring to interpret the classical revival as an immanent concern of art or philosophy, etc. Nevertheless, a true history of these ideological conflicts would show the intimate connections in every sphere from the plastic arts right through to politics and history. Furthermore, to make the point negatively it would show how the reverence for antiquity at once lost its progressive significance and degenerated into empty academicism as soon as this socio-political content disappeared in the course of the nineteenth century. Naturally, we cannot attempt even an outline of the development from Macchiavelli, via Montesquieu, Gibbon, etc., to Rousseau, in whose work, as Engels has emphasized, we find the first beginnings of a dialectical approach to the study of society.

It is apparent from the foregoing that Hegel was thoroughly conversant with the larger part of this literature. (The exception is Macchiavelli, whose works he appears to have read later, probably towards the end of his stay in Frankfurt.) But even discounting these literary influences we can see that Hegel's admiration for the classical tradition was closely connected with this development, since it was on that tradition that the political philosophy of the French Revolution, and the systematization of its heroic illusions, was based. The leading Jacobins were the immediate pupils of Rousseau.

Even though the Jacobin ideology of the revival of the classical democracies was the heroic illusion of plebeian revolutionaries, it was by no
means entirely arbitrary. Its exponents based their views on very real
socio-economic premises. The distinction between them and the less radical supporters of a revolutionary democracy was itself economic: the
radical Jacobins believed that the *relative equality of wealth* forms the foundation of real democracy, that the growth of inequalities among the citizens of a state leads inexorably to the destruction of democracy and to a
new despotism. This doctrine appears in the radical parts of the literature
on the classical revival referred to above and the idea that the relative
equality of wealth is the premise of a democratic society reaches its peak
in Rousseau's Social Contract.

The importance of the debates on this issue during the Revolution
itself can be seen in any scrupulous history of the period. We need cite
only a few instances. Thus in a frequently quoted essay by Rabaut St.
Etienne in the *Chronique de Paris* of 1793 we find the following demands:

> '1. The most equitable division of wealth possible, 2. Laws to preserve
> these and to prevent future inequalities from arising.'[9]

Rabaut generally went along with the Gironde. However this proposal
naturally met with no response from them.[10] Similarly, in the same year
we find in the *Révolution de Paris*:

> 'In order to prevent great inequalities from arising in the wealth of the
> universally equal republicans an upper limit must be established
> above which acquisitions will not be permitted even assuming the
> payment of the appropriate taxes.'[11]

Likewise, a resolution of the People's Club of Castres determined:

> 'Never to deviate from our true principles and never to admit as a
> member any man with great wealth unless he is known as a pure and
> ardent patriot who has made every effort in his power to eliminate
> this inequality.'[12]

Finally, in the debate on progressive taxes and forced loans in 1793
Cambon stated:

> 'This system is the most rational and the one best in harmony with our
> principles, for such measures will bring about that very equality
> which some people would consign to the realm of fiction.'[13]

Such illustrations could be multiplied at will.

Marx has ruthlessly unmasked the illusory character of the Jacobin
aspiration to revive the classical tradition, by analysing the very different
economic circumstances underlying the two movements. In *The Holy
Family* he writes:

'Robespierre, Saint-Just and their party perished because they confused the *realistic, democratic republic* of antiquity based on *actual slavery*,
with the *spiritualist, representative democratic state of modern times*, with its
basis in *emancipated slavery* in *bourgeois society*. What a colossal illusion
to have to acknowledge and to sanction in the *Rights of Man* our
modern bourgeois society, the society of industry, of universal competition, of private interests freely pursuing their own ends, of
anarchy, of individuality alienated from its nature and its spirit
—while at the same time, having been forced subsequently to annul
the manifestations of the life of that society in separate individuals,
they strive to model the *political head* of the society in classical form!'[14]

However, in France itself these illusions were the heroic illusions of
plebeian revolutionary politicians, i.e. notwithstanding their illusory
character they were closely bound up with particular elements of the
political actions of the plebeian party in the years 1793–94. Hence it was
possible to carry out certain political measures essential in real terms,
even with the aid of such a misconceived rationale. It is enough if we cite
two instances. First, at a time when France was threatened by the coalition of European powers the exigencies of the war made it necessary
to pass a series of compulsory measures both to counteract counter-
revolutionary tendencies (even in the bourgeoisie) and to ensure the
maintenance of supplies to the army and the poorer sections of the population of the cities, the social basis of radical Jacobinism. Second, the radical prosecution of the democratic revolution involved the confiscation
and distribution of a large number of feudal estates and so in intention
and, for a time at least, in reality it brought about a partial scaling-down
of landed property to the level of small peasant holdings.

Thus in line with Marx's criticisms we see that the actions of the Jacobins were based on illusions in the sense that they failed to understand the
real socio-political grounds for their revolutionary measures and they
entertained utterly false ideas about their effects. However, their misconceptions do not negate the democratic, revolutionary essence of their
actions. On the contrary, the living dialectical contradiction characteristic of this period of the revolution is the product of this indissoluble
mixture of correct, plebeian revolutionary policies and fantastic illusions
about the general direction of the forces of bourgeois society unleashed
by the revolution.

It is from this standpoint that we must examine the relation of the ideological forerunners of the revolution to the Jacobins themselves. Marx
has pointed out, very rightly, that the Jacobins entirely neglected the real
basis of the society of antiquity in slavery, because they were incapable of
integrating the position and role of the proletariat in their picture of
bourgeois society. This fundamental error does not, however, invalidate

what was within certain definite limits a correct feeling that there was a
genuine parallel between Greek society.and a modern society based on
roughly equal small-holdings. Marx clearly established this parallel:

> 'This independent ownership of free small-holdings as the dominant,
> normal form of ownership constitutes on the one hand the economic
> foundation of society in the greatest periods of classical antiquity, and
> on the other hand we also find it recurring in the modern world as one
> of the forms resulting from the dissolution of feudal landed property.
> Thus we find the yeomanry in England, the peasantry in Sweden and
> the French and West German peasants. . . . For the fullest develop-
> ment of this mode of production the ownership of land is as indis-
> pensable as the ownership of tools is necessary for the free
> development of handicraft. It forms the basis for the growth of per-
> sonal independence.'[15]

These observations are of outstanding importance for our discussion.
Above all, Marx dryly points to the economic connection between the
golden age of the ancient democracies and the relative equality of
peasant ownership. For just as the emancipated freeholders formed the
backbone of the army in the French revolutionary and Napoleonic wars
so too in the English Revolution the yeomanry were the backbone of the
armies that freed the nation from the yoke of the Stuarts.

To this extent, then, the illusions of the Jacobins had real economic
substance. The illusory side of their views is shown in their conviction
that what was a transitional stage on the way to an advanced capitalism
was a permanent condition of an emancipated humanity, i.e. they
attempted to perpetuate what could be no more than a passing phase.
The historical studies of Marx and Engels have produced voluminous
evidence of the falsity and insubstantiality of these illusions. Engels, for
example, points out that a century after the yeomanry had fought
Cromwell's battles that same yeomanry had vanished almost without
trace amid the storms of primitive accumulation, of Enclosures, etc. And
Marx in his historical works on the French Revolution of 1848 has shown
that the French smallholders were liberated from the yoke of feudalism
only to find themselves beneath the much heavier yoke of capitalist
money-lenders. The illusion of the Jacobin revolutionaries, then, consists
'merely' in their failure to note the fact that their revolutionary measures
actively unleashed the forces of capitalist development.

This idea and this reality exerted an extraordinarily profound influence on contemporary German philosophy. But as we come to look at
this influence in greater detail we must again remind ourselves that even
though German philosophy echoes the events of the French Revolution
these echoes are distorted by the economic and political backwardness of
the country. We have already asserted that the idealist character of

German philosophy is to be attributed to this backwardness. Now we must go further and note as the effect of this idealism the fact that the philosophers tended to concentrate on those aspects of the Revolution which expressed the most wayward illusions of those participating in it. That is to say, the German philosophers of the 1790s seized hold of these illusions and systematized them, thus strengthening their illusory nature. These illusions were in themselves idealist distortions of objective reality; in their German form they became even more distorted: what we find are illusions of illusions.

Of all the German philosophers, Fichte was the one who came down most emphatically in favour of the French Revolution. His first books, published anonymously, were open pamphlets in defence of the Revolution and in opposition to its enemies, the absolutist feudal monarchies of Europe. And as late as 1796, when he began to systematize his views on practical philosophy in the narrower sense, in his *Foundations of Natural Law*, he drew the most radical conclusions from the illusions of the Jacobins. Like the traditions of jurisprudence of the seventeenth and eighteenth centuries Fichte's natural law was based on the idea of a social contract. However, it was modified on the one hand by the subjectivism of Kant and on the other by the social views of the Jacobins. Hence for Fichte the social contract implied the obligation of society to provide for the existence of its members—within the framework of a relative equality of wealth. He writes:

> 'All rights to property rest on the contract of all with all. This contract states: we all retain our property on the condition that we leave you in possession of yours. As soon as a man cannot live from his work, i.e. as soon as he is not left in possession of his own, then as far as he is concerned the contract is null and void, and from that moment on he is no longer bound by law to recognize the property of any man.'[16]

These views of Fichte come close to those of the extreme left wing of the Jacobins. And interestingly, of all the German philosophers it was Fichte who adhered to them longest. Referring to *The Closed Commercial State*, Benjamin Constant noted scornfully at one point that Fichte was still writing in 1800 about a utopia whose principles were largely identical with the socio-economic policies of the last period of Robespierre's regime. Of course, we must at once add the qualification that through his systematization Fichte became part of the trend that exacerbated these idealist illusions. (Fichte's later development, the internal conflicts arising in his thought in consequence of his joining the national liberation movement, do not fall within the scope of this work. A brief indication, however, was necessary since in Fichte's case, too, bourgeois historiography has ignored or distorted the real problems and conflicts.)

Even in his Berne period Hegel never went as far as Fichte. We have already seen from his letter to Schelling how hostile he felt towards the radical, plebeian wing of Jacobinism. Despite this it cannot be denied that the Rousseauesque and Jacobin idea of the relative equality of wealth supplies the economic underpinning for his philosophy of the Revolution. But his position has one peculiarity which we must take note of here, even though we shall defer our analysis of it until our discussion of his views on Christianity and antiquity. Briefly, it is the curious fact that in Hegel's eyes antiquity appears as an age almost without an economy. Hegel starts with the dogmatic assumption of a relative equality of wealth in the Greek city-states and then goes on to analyse only the political, cultural and religious features in which their specific nature is revealed. In contrast to this, his observations on Christianity are full of remarks—however naive—about economics. For his view here is that this age is the age of the private individual who is *exclusively* concerned with his own property. Thus for the early Hegel the decline of the public life of antiquity and the emergence of the age of despotism constitute the period of economic life as he understands it. Only after his Jacobin illusions have come into conflict with reality does he feel the need for a greater grasp of economic problems. It is very characteristic, therefore, that it is not until relatively late, in his Jena period in fact, that he comes to appreciate the role of slavery in classical Greece.

This should not be taken to mean that Hegel was blind to social problems at this time. On the contrary, the problem of the division of labour plays a very important role in his analysis of the difference between antiquity and Christianity. That his analysis is not free from illusions, however, can be seen from his idealized views of antiquity as an age notable for the absence of a division of labour and from his hope that a democratic revolution would mean the return of that happy state.

In itself, of course, the critique of the capitalist division of labour was a highly progressive element in humanist philosophy at this period. Schiller in particular deserves praise for having made the whole problem of such central importance. And we have already seen that Hegel read the relevant work, namely the *Letters on Aesthetic Education*, with real enthusiasm. In a study of Schiller's aesthetics I have shown at length that his critique of the division of labour under capitalism was not the product of the anti-capitalism of the Romantics, but represented the continuation of the best traditions of the Enlightenment, above all the work of Ferguson.[17] It cannot be discovered with any certainty just how much Hegel was influenced here by Schiller or indeed how much is to be traced back to Ferguson whose works he undoubtedly knew. What is important here is the similarity of Schiller and Hegel *vis-à-vis* Ferguson. In the writings of both men the economic basis of the division of labour is very much underplayed and they are much more concerned about its ideological and cultural implications. Of course, Hegel's special emphasis is on political action rather than art as the chief path from fragmentation back to the humanistic ideal of wholeness. For Schiller the greatness of classical art as the manifestation of man in an unfragmented state was a central theme. The same ideal reappears in Hegel in the form of the fully human, fundamentally political existence of the classical democracies. His interest in classical art is sporadic and when it does occur it is mainly by way of illustrating this central theme.

Even more important is the distinction between the views of the two men in respect to the philosophy of history. Schiller's book was written at a time when he had already turned away from the French Revolution. It is consequently filled with pessimism about the future and, equally naturally, antiquity has become magnified into a glorious age providing an eternal model for all mankind. At the same time this golden age now forms part of an absolutely irretrievable past. The Hegel of the Berne period finds himself at virtually the opposite standpoint. Antiquity survives as an actual, living example to mankind. It may have passed away but we must revive it; in fact, this revival constitutes the central practical, cultural and religious task of the modern age.

## NOTES

1  Rosenzweig, *Hegel and the State*, Munich and Berlin 1920, Vol. I, p. 51.
2  Nohl, p. 359. Harmodius and Aristogeiton were renowned for their murder of Hipparchus, the son of Pisistratus, who enjoyed sole power in Athens. See Herodotus, *The Histories*, Bk. 5 and 6, Penguin Books 1971, pp. 331 and 404.—*Trans.*
3  Nohl, p. 215.
4  Ibid.
5  Ibid., p. 216.
6  Tuisco or Tuisto: mentioned by Tacitus as the presiding deity of the Germans—*Trans.*
7  Nohl, p. 217.
8  Rosenkranz, p. 69.
9  Cited by Aulard, *Political History of the French Revolution*, Munich –Leipzig 1924, Vol. I, p. 364.
10  Ibid., p. 365.
11  Ibid., p. 366.
12  Ibid., Vol. II, p. 723.
13  Ibid., Vol. I, pp. 367ff.
14  Marx/Engels, *The Holy Family*, Moscow and London 1956, pp. 163–4.
15  Marx, *Capital*, Vol. III, Moscow and London 1962, p. 787.
16  Fichte, *Werke*, Leipzig 1908, Vol. II, p. 217.

17  Cf. the essay entitled 'Schiller's Theory of Modern Literature' in my book, *Goethe and his Age*, London 1968, pp. 101–36.

# CHAPTER FOUR

# The republics of Greece and Rome

FOR the early Hegel, then, classical antiquity constituted a utopian political contrast to the present. The fragmentary works of the Berne period published by Nohl give us a very clear idea of the way he saw classical culture at this time. However, to grasp its full political implications we must refer to some fragmentary historical studies which illustrate its relation to the present much more vividly than Nohl's publications. Because of the importance of these fragments and because of the systematic falsifications of Hegel's development by bourgeois scholars we must ask for the reader's indulgence if we quote these passages at length.

'In the *states of the modern world, security of property* is the axis around which all legislation revolves and to which most of the rights of the citizenry pertain. In many of the free republics of antiquity, the constitution itself often encroached upon the strict rights of property, the concern of all our authorities and the pride of all our states. In the Spartan constitution security of property and industry was almost entirely disregarded, indeed one can almost say that it was forgotten. In Athens affluent citizens were usually robbed of a part of their wealth. However, this was normally done under an honourable pretext: the person whom the state wished to rob was given an office which required enormous expenses. The citizens were divided into tribes and any member of a tribe who was elected to an expensive office could look around among the members of his tribe to see if he could not find someone wealthier than himself. If he succeeded in finding one and the latter claimed to be poorer, the first man could propose a mutual exchange of their possessions—a proposal which could not be refused. History shows in the cases of Pericles in Athens, of the patricians in Rome whose ruin the threatening power of the Gracchi and others vainly strove to avert by means of agrarian laws, and of the Medici in Florence, just how very dangerous the disproportionate wealth of a few citizens can become to even the freest form of constitution. It can even destroy freedom itself. It would be important to study how many of the strict rights of property would have to be sacrificed if a republic were to be introduced permanently. Perhaps the system of the Sansculottes has been done a grave injustice by those who see rapacity as the sole motive underlying their wish for a greater equality of wealth.'[1]

These remarks require no commentary from us since we intend to cite further passages from the Berne studies that will illuminate them in a variety of ways. It was necessary to begin with this fragment because the connection between equality of wealth in antiquity and in the French Revolution, the problem of the equality of wealth as a foundation of republican freedom, emerges more clearly here than in most of Hegel's other Berne notes.

More interesting perhaps is the following fragment written in French on the subject of the army and the conduct of war under a monarchy and a republic. The question of whether the fragment is the work of Hegel himself or only an excerpt has been the subject of fierce philological debate among his imperialist apologists. When Rosenkranz first published it he described it as Hegel's own independent work and indicated that it was the concluding section of an essay dealing with the changes necessary within the armed forces when a state changes from a monarchical to a republican form of government. (At this point we must again note that we have cause to regret the amazing negligence shown by Hegel's immediate disciples as the custodians of his posthumous papers. The manuscript of the essay whose conclusion Rosenkranz has published has been lost in the meantime.) For their part more recent representatives of 'modern scholarship', Lasson, Rosenzweig, Hoffmeister & Co. dispute the claim that the fragment could be Hegel's own work. 'The text reads more like demagogic speech by a French general than an essay by Hegel', Hoffmeister observes.[2] Of course, the substantive value of this 'criticism' is more or less nil. For, in the first place, when it suits them, these neo-Hegelian gentleman always appeal to the fact that Rosenkranz was a direct disciple of Hegel and enjoyed the benefit of still living traditions in his editorial labours—and only in instances such as this one do they realize that 'suddenly' Rosenkranz, the first and most conscientious biographer of Hegel, is no longer reliable. In the second place, even if Hoffmeister & Co. were right and the fragment were no more than an extract from a French manifesto, it would still prove nothing. For it would still leave us with the question of why Hegel had chosen this manifesto to copy and in what context he had used it in the—now lost —essay. And since every unprejudiced reader of the Berne notes can see how well the fragment fits in with his entire philosophy of history and society, it becomes clear that the neo-Hegelians have done nothing to advance their cause with their 'sharp-witted philology'.

Here is the text of the fragment:

'Under the monarchy the people became an active force only for the duration of armed conflict. Like a paid army it had to keep its ranks in the heat of battle. But no sooner was the victory won than it had to return to a state of perfect obedience. Our experience accustoms us to seeing how at a word of command a mass of soldiers will enter into an organised fury of carnage and into the lottery of life and death, and how at another command they will again become peaceful. The same thing is required of a people that has armed itself. Here the word of command is liberty, the enemy tyranny, the commander-in-chief the constitution, subordination obedience to the representatives of the people. But there is a great difference between the passivity of ordinary military obedience and the ardour of an insurrection; between obedience to the order of a general and the flame of enthusiasm which liberty pours into the veins of every living creature. This is the sacred flame that tunes every nerve and it is for its sake, for the sake of enjoying this flame of liberty, that every nerve is keyed up. These efforts are the enjoyment of liberty, and you wish it to be renounced; these occupations, this activity for the public cause, this interest is the *driving force*, and you want the people to sink into inertia and boredom once more?'[3]

Both these passages speak a very clear language. They show how profoundly and intimately Hegel's enthusiasm for the classical democracies was interwoven with his attitude to the French Revolution. Our immediate task is to give a comprehensive picture of the classical ideal as cherished by Hegel in this period and to do so as far as possible in his own words since these are extremely telling and should not be weakened by paraphrase. We must begin our presentation with a lengthy general quotation from the chief work of this period, on positive Christianity, to which we have several times referred, before proceeding to his views on specific aspects of classical culture.

'The Greek and Roman religions were religions only for free peoples, and with the loss of freedom the strength they provided, their sense and their appropriateness for man disappeared also. What is the use of an army of cannons that has run out of ammunition? It must go in search of other weapons. What is the use of a fisherman's net if the river has dried up?

'As free men they obeyed laws they had given themselves, they obeyed men they had installed in positions of authority, they waged wars they had themselves resolved upon, gave up their property and their passions and sacrificed thousands of lives for a cause that was their own. They neither learnt nor taught, but lived in accordance with maxims, performing actions they could call their own; in public, private and domestic life every man was free, each lived according to his own laws. The idea of his country, of the state was the invisible higher thing for which he laboured and which spurred him on; this was the ultimate purpose of the world, or at any rate of his world—a purpose he found enacted in reality, or which he helped to enact and to maintain. His individuality bowed to his idea, he required subsistence, life and permanence for it alone and could himself provide for his needs. It would not ever, or only seldom, occur to him to want or to implore permanence or eternal life for himself; only in passive, inert moments would he feel a strong desire for something merely for himself.—Cato only turned to Plato's Phaedo when his republic, his world, when what had been the highest order of things was destroyed; only then did he seek refuge in an even higher order.

'Their gods reigned supreme in the realm of nature, ruling over everything which makes man happy or unhappy. High passions were their work, as were great gifts of wisdom, eloquence and of counsel. Their advice was sought about the successful or unsuccessful outcome of an enterprise, men implored their blessing and gave thanks for gifts of every kind—when man came into open conflict with these rulers over nature he could oppose them with his own freedom. Man's will was free, it obeyed its own laws; men knew no divine ordinances or if they called the moral law divine, it was not handed down to them on any tablets: it ruled invisibly (Antigone). At the same time, they acknowledged every man's right to have his own will, be it good or bad. The good recognized their own duty to be good, but also respected the rights of others not to be able to achieve the same ideal. For this reason they proclaimed neither a divine morality, nor one invented or abstracted by themselves for others to cleave to.

'Victorious wars, the growth of wealth and an increased familiarity with several comforts of life, with luxury, produced an aristocracy of wealth and military glory. This aristocracy acquired influence and power over many men who, corrupted by the sight of their deeds and even more by the use they made of their wealth, gladly and willingly granted them power and authority in the state. . . . Soon the freely granted authority was maintained by force and this in itself presupposes the loss of that feeling, that consciousness which Montesquieu calls virtue and makes into the essential principle of a republic; its character is the ability to sacrifice an individual in order to save an idea that has been realized in a republic for its citizens.

'The image of the state as a product of his own activity faded from the soul of the citizen; understanding and concern for society as a whole became the province of a single man, or a few men; each man was assigned a more or less limited place, different from that of his fellows; the government of the machine of state was entrusted to a small number of citizens and they served as individual cogs whose value lay in their association with each other. The part assigned to each man in the fragmented totality was so minute in comparison to the size of the whole that the individual did not need to see or understand it. Usefulness to the state was instilled in its subjects by the state and the aim they all set themselves was acquisition and self-subsistence and perhaps also vanity. All activity, all purposes hence-forth referred to individuals. There was no longer any activity for the whole, for an idea—each man either laboured for himself or was forced to work for another. The freedom to obey self-imposed laws, to follow self-imposed authorities in peace and in war to obey generals who were implementing plans which all had resolved upon—all this died out. All political freedom faded away; the law only gave the citizen a right to the security of property, the pursuit of which now filled his entire life. The phenomenon that tore to shreds the whole web of his intentions, the activity of his whole life, namely death, became something terrible for him: for nothing survived him, unlike the republican whose republic lived on after him and so he began to conceive the vague idea that his soul must be immortal.[4]

The main outlines of Hegel's view of the democracies of Greece and Rome stand out very clearly. The implicit reference to the present, to the French Revolution can hardly escape the unprejudiced reader and this impression is strengthened by comparison with the passages cited earlier. It is revealing, for instance, how often Hegel departs from the objective tone of the narrative historian and speaks simply of republicans and re-publican virtue, quoting Montesquieu admittedly, but the reader cannot help thinking of the republican virtues proclaimed by Robespierre.

The parallel is reinforced by the argument that the crucial factor in the decline of the republics of antiquity was the abolition of equality of wealth. Moreover, the reader cannot fail to be struck by the naive and ideological manner in which Hegel construes the transition from free-dom to unfreedom. He sees the importance of the economic factors diagnosed first by Rousseau, but only abstractly and without being able to supply the concrete mediating links from them to the ideological problems that interest him primarily.

Hegel's central ideological problem here is, once again, what he calls subjectivity in contrast to positivity. In the sphere of pure politics this can be expressed relatively clearly: men obey self-created laws, self-chosen authorities, the state is continually produced by their activity. And it is characteristic of Hegel's position at this stage that he rejects the idea of class, whether spiritual or secular, for this state of society. We have already seen how he disregarded the existence and signifi-cance of slavery in classical antiquity. His conception of classical so-ciety was essentially classless. As soon as class distinctions became economically and politically fixed, real freedom was at an end.

We must emphasize that here too his account of the processes at work is extraordinarily abstract and very ideological. Thus in one of the earliest Berne studies he writes:

> 'But when a class—either the ruling class or the priests, or both to-
> gether—loses that spirit of simplicity which had brought into being
> and hitherto inspired their laws and ordinances, then not only is it
> irreparably lost but also the oppression and dishonouring of the
> people is certain. (For this reason, the mere division into classes is
> already dangerous to freedom since it can foster an *esprit de corps*
> which can become a threat to the spirit of the whole.)[5]

This rejection of the classes in a democracy is as determined as it is
naive. Nevertheless, we should not overlook the fact that here in Hegel
we see the first faint glimmerings of an understanding of gentile society.
Of course, even the later Hegel never acquired a definite conception of
gentile society—Bachofen was the first to develop any real understanding of that, despite the presence of idealist and mystical distortions
in his work. But it is beyond dispute that the analysis of the tragic conflict of the `Antigone` in *The Phenomenology of Mind*, or the much later aesthetic conception of the 'heroic age' (in the *Aesthetics*) contain strong
suggestions of this state of society in a mystified form. In the early writings Hegel's understanding of this issue is still highly abstract: on the one
hand, there is abstract equality (classless society), on the other hand, the
complete self-government, self-activity of the people. However, the
sober and realistic appraisal of the facts of daily life, which we have
already seen in his letter to Schelling about the material basis of orthodoxy, is never far from the surface. Thus it is not without interest to
observe him speaking of the festivals of antiquity with the greatest enthusiasm, but without failing to point out that an essential feature of these
festivals was that they were not merely arranged by the people but that
the people also administered all the religious donations.[6]

The freedom and independence of the people is the source of the non-
positive, non-fetishized, non-objective character of classical religion.
Now Hegel is, of course, perfectly aware, despite his extreme subjective
and idealist interpretation of 'practical reason', that a world wholly
without objectivity, without any objectification of thoughts and feelings, is quite impossible. He therefore strives to define in a series of complex arguments and analyses the specific character of the 'objectless'
objectivity of antiquity.

I shall give an extreme and for that reason very revealing example
from his numerous analyses of this issue. In the course of his historical
studies Hegel has occasion to speak of the role of women mourners at the
public funerals in Athens. He comes to regard even tears as an objectification of grief.

> 'But since grief is essentially subjective, it only externalizes itself with

reluctance. Only the gravest exigency can induce it to do so. . . . This cannot take place through the agency of something alien to it. Only if it is given to itself will it possess itself as itself and as something partly outside itself. . . . Speech is the purest form of objectivity in the eyes of subjectivity. It is not yet anything objective, but it is the movement towards objectivity. Lament in the form of a song achieves the form of beauty to a higher degree since it moves in accordance with rules. The elegies of women mourners are therefore the most human expression of grief, of the need to lighten one's burden by developing it to its fullest extent and contemplating it in its true proportions. This contemplation alone is the balm.[7]

The decisive moment here for Hegel is that the object is not fixed, not established for ever; there should never be an ultimately defined object but only a progress towards objectivity and then a return to a modified purified subjectivity.

This line of reasoning is very closely connected with his purely political, republican image of antiquity. The life of man in Greece or Rome had its centre in the realm of the public. At the same time, men are free, autonomous individuals with their own fates. Their private thoughts, feelings and passions must be so constructed that they never remain fixed at this one point: they must always be able to flow smoothly back into the stream of public life.

In this period Hegel frequently draws comparisons between Jesus and Socrates. He notes in passing the fetish involved in fixing the number of Jesus' disciples at twelve, but his main point is that Jesus took his disciples out of society, out of life, cutting them off and turning them into men whose chief characteristic was precisely their disciplehood. In the case of Socrates, his disciples remain social, they stay as they are, their individuality is not remoulded artificially. They return therefore into public life enriched;

'each of his disciples was himself a master; many founded schools, several were great generals, statesmen, heroes of all kinds'.

Jesus, however, created a narrow-minded, closed sect; 'among the Greeks he would have been an object of laughter'.[8]

In Hegel's view, then, the ever-open road back into public life is the foundation for normal existence in the classical world and this stands in sharp contrast to the deformed and deforming pathology of man under Christianity.

Once again we can best throw light on Hegel's position by citing one of his more extreme examples. He repeatedly comes back to the distinction between the Bacchantes of antiquity and the witches of the Middle Ages.

'In the bacchanalia, Greek women were given room to express their pent-up passions. Their physical and emotional exhaustion was succeeded by their peaceful return to the realm of their normal feelings and their accustomed lives. Outside the festivals the savage Maenad was a rational woman.'

Thus the main point about the Greeks was 'the return to ordinary life', whereas in the witchcraft of the Christian age we find

'the advance from isolated outbreaks of madness to a thorough-going and permanent derangement of the mind.'⁹

We are less concerned here with the accuracy of Hegel's interpretation of the classical Bacchanalia, than with his general interpretation of life in antiquity, with the living interaction between public and private, with the free, creative suspensions of the private in public life that prove to be valid even where, as here, the more pathological sides of human nature are involved.

The precise definition of this interaction is important for our understanding of Hegel because it enables us to see just how remote his republican subjectivism is from individualism in the modern sense. Indeed, we might argue that Hegel's position is the antipole of modern individualism. Hegel was of course perfectly familiar with the latter phenomenon, which, however, he thought of as the product of decadence, of positive religion and of the Christian era. It is highly indicative of Hegel's historical perceptiveness that for all the mystification and tortuousness of his subjective idealism, he nevertheless had a very clear insight into the connection between modern individualism as an ideology and a life-style, and the actual fragmentation and impoverishment of human personality in the course of the medieval and post-medieval periods. At the same time, he is equally aware of the fact that man can only develop a many-sided, mature personality if and when social conditions permit and encourage this sort of harmony, and if they promote a vital interaction between a man's public and private life.

Hence the impoverishment and mutilation of man's life is one of the persistent themes of Hegel's critique of the modern world. He made excerpts from the great travel-book by the Mainz Jacobin Georg Forster and was particularly impressed by the latter's contrast between the art and culture of antiquity and the modern world which in Forster's case, too, stems from a republican spirit. Hegel's extracts are followed by this contrasting picture of life in modern and classical times:

'In a republic one lives for an idea, in a monarchy only for specific things—even in a monarchy, men cannot dispense with ideas, they fix on a particular idea, an ideal—in a republic they live according to ideas as they ought to be; in a monarchy, they have an ideal, i.e. rarely something they have made themselves, a deity.—In a republic, a great mind expends his entire physical and moral energies in the service of his idea; the sphere of his activity has unity. The pious Christian who dedicates himself to his ideal is a mystical fanatic. If his ideal fills him to the exclusion of all else, if he cannot divide his energies between this and his secular life, if all his strength goes in this one direction, a Mme de Guyon[10] will be the result—The need to contemplate the ideal will satisfy the over-stimulated imagination, and even the senses will assert their rights; examples are the countless nuns and monks who dallied with Jesus and dreamed of embracing him. The idea of the Republican is of the sort that enables his noblest energies to find satisfaction in true labour, while that of the fanatic is a mere figment of the imagination.'

Hegel follows this up with a comparison, still based on Forster, of classical and Christian art (architecture in particular) which, as might be expected, comes down firmly on the side of classical art. But here too we must note that art is not considered for its own intrinsic value but as the expression of the different social life-styles of the two great epochs.[11]

We can see how radically Hegel criticizes the whole modern tradition from a polemic directed against Schiller whom he nevertheless greatly venerated even at this early period. In his *On Naive and Sentimental Poetry* of 1795–96, an essay of absolutely fundamental importance for the definition of modern literature, Schiller had indeed acknowledged the incomparable and undying greatness of classical poetry. At the same time, however, he attempted to provide an historical and philosophical justification of modern literature. Schiller's efforts in this direction—no less than the similar tendencies in Goethe—had a profound influence on Hegel's later views on modern art. In this period, however, Hegel ignores these historical and philosophical discoveries. Indeed, without mentioning Schiller by name, he conducts a vigorous attack on one section of his treatise.

*On Naive and Sentimental Poetry* contains a passage in which Schiller praises modern poets at the expense of classical ones for their superior representation of love.

'Without wishing to encourage sentimentality [*Schwärmerei*] which indeed does not enhance nature but abandons it, we may still believe, I hope, that in regard to the relations between the sexes and the emotion of love, nature can possess a nobler character than has been given it by the Ancients.'

He supports his arguments with references to Fielding and Shakespeare. We must remind ourselves of the history of individual love and its reflection in poetry in Friedrich Engels' key work *The Origins of the Family* to appreciate the accuracy of Schiller's assessment of the historical factors, even though he could have no idea of their underlying causes. Hegel's polemic, however, is directed precisely at Schiller's genuine insight. In the modern over-estimation of love, and its lower place in the scale of values of antiquity, he sees yet another instance of the socio-political contrast he discusses so frequently. He asks,

'Does this phenomenon have nothing to do with the spirit of their [i.e. the Greeks'] free life!'

He imagines a situation in which a knight regales Aristides, the Athenian statesman, with an account of all the deeds he had performed out of passion, without mentioning the object of these deeds. In this situation, Hegel remarks,

'would not Aristides who did not know to whom or what this entire expenditure of feeling, action and enthusiasm was devoted, exclaim in wonder: I have dedicated my life to my country; I have laboured for it without expecting any distinction, or power or wealth as reward. But I am aware that I would not have done so much for it, I could not have held it in the same unique and profound veneration as you have displayed. I know of Greeks who have done more, who were more greatly inspired, but I know of none who had ever attained the same heights of self-denial as yourself. And what was the object of your noble life? It must be infinitely greater and worthier than anything I can imagine, greater even than freedom and my country!'[12]

Here, in Hegel's ironical repudiation of the entire modern cult of individual love, we find an inspired paean to the normative life of antiquity. Hegel rejects the sentimental culture of the modern world because it is exaggerated, because it squanders lofty feelings on merely individual, merely private and hence unworthy objects. The only objects worthy of heroic deeds are freedom and one's country.

These views contain a certain admixture of republican asceticism which likewise forms part of the armoury of the Jacobin followers of Rousseau and which Hegel had been prepared for philosophically by the idealist asceticism of *The Critique of Practical Reason*. However, his radicalism goes far beyond that of Kant whom he criticizes for his inconsistent application of ascetic principles in morality.

It is well known that in his ethics Kant refused to permit any connection between the imperatives of duty and sensuality, or any suggestion that their form and content could be modified by men's claims to sensual happiness. Hegel is in agreement with this. Where he demurs is when, in drawing out the religious implications of his ethic, Kant introduces the idea that we may become *worthy* of happiness, an idea which is closely connected to the sudden appearance of God as a 'postulate of practical reason'.[13] In this Hegel sees above all a renewal of positive religion. In his view the Kantian ethic calls for

'an alien being, in whom the control over nature resides, a control which nature misses and which it can no longer afford to despise. In this philosophy faith means a lack of awareness that reason is absolute, complete unto itself—that its infinite idea must be created from itself alone, free from the admixture of anything alien to it, and that this can be achieved only through the removal of that intruder [i.e. the Kantian God—G.L.] and not through his presence.—The so-conditioned ultimate purpose of reason provides a moral faith in the existence of God which cannot be practical . . .'[14]

Hegel here shows Kant's ethics to be inconsistent with its own premises. In the process he frees it from the proofs of the existence of God that Kant had smuggled back in at the cost of intensifying the asceticism of *The Critique of Practical Reason*.

However, this is not the decisive motif of Hegel's criticism. He does indeed believe that Kant's God is infected by the 'positivity' he rejects so emphatically in his Berne period, but his ultimate objection to Kant's arguments is that he sees them as an obstacle to the creation of an heroic, republican morality, as an expression of modern philistinism. Thus he observes scathingly:

'In our age all we can say of a man who has just died honourably for his country or virtue, is that he deserved a better fate.'

And in the course of his attack on the 'positive' character of Kant's synthesis of happiness and morality in his postulated God, he adds:

'Anyone, e.g. a republican or a soldier who is fighting not perhaps for his country, but at any rate for his honour, who has set himself a certain goal and does not manage to achieve that other goal, viz. happiness, nevertheless has a goal whose fulfilment depends entirely on himself and he does therefore not stand in need of any help from outside.'[15]

It is evident that Hegel reserves his praise here for the ascetic heroism of the French Revolution and in consequence imports a number of features into his portrait of antiquity which have nothing to do with antiquity itself. But in all these arguments we see how Hegel saw the complete fulfilment of human aspirations, the real development of the essential forces of human personality exclusively in an absolute service to one's country, to the interests of public life and to the republic. And conversely, in every aspiration aimed solely at the private life of the individual, he saw only philistinism.

Here too, in his ironic treatment of philistinism, it is important to take the precise historical circumstances into account. Bourgeois historians in Germany are accustomed to classify every attack on philistinism as part of Romanticism. In Hegel's case, however, this would be quite misleading. Bourgeois literary historians have been accustomed to classify Hölderlin as a Romantic and Hölderlin stands ideologically very close to Hegel's early philosophy; and now it is fashionable to classify Hegel along with the Romantics also. That this is wrong in principle can be seen if we point out that the Romantic critique of philistinism was aimed at its modern, prosaic elements to which they opposed an aesthetic ideal. Hence the Romantic critique tends on the one hand to slip into an apology for Bohemian or anarchistic leanings, and on the other hand it glorifies the moral and spiritual narrow-mindedness of a pre-capitalist society of craftsmen which has not yet experienced the division of labour.

With all this Hegel and his colleagues have little in common. For Hegel, philistinism is in fact the survival of medieval narrowness in the life and thought of modern times. And he never attacks philistinism in the name of an aesthetic ideal. What characterizes philistinism in his view is imprisonment in the problems of purely private interests, and hence the counter-ideal is, as we have seen, the complete identity of the citizen with the affairs of public life so typical of the Greek city-state. Marx, too, has given a penetrating definition of the specific features of the Jacobin position:

> '*The whole of French terrorism* was nothing but a *plebeian method* of dealing with the enemies of the *bourgeoisie*, with absolutism, feudalism and *philistinism*.'[16]

It is evident then that Hegel's critique of philistinism belongs in the general framework of his campaign for the aims of democratic revolution.

Thus Hegel confronts the Christian, philistine ethics of the 'private man' with the heroic ethics of public life. He takes this confrontation so far as to defend the right to suicide, conducting his defence with classical examples and Stoic arguments. This line of reasoning is by no means unique in the eighteenth century. Goethe's *Werther* contains a passionate vindication of the right to commit suicide and here too Goethe's position is connected with the struggle for democratic freedom. However, Hegel goes beyond this in the direction of the exclusive predominance of public life, of the interests of the republic and freedom. Only in such a context does he find suicide morally defensible. He quotes from a number of Christian, philistine condemnations of suicide and concludes:

> 'Cato, Cleomenes and others who took their own lives after the free

constitutions of their countries had been abolished did so because they found it impossible to return to private life; their souls had embraced an idea which they could no longer work for; once their soul had been exiled from its greater sphere of activity it longed to be rid of the fetters of the body so as to return to the world of eternal ideas.'[17]

The problem of death, of dying, is an integral part of Hegel's confrontation of the greatness of classical republicanism with the pettiness and debasement of modern Christianity. Hegel wants no part of the Christian view of the utter contrast of life and death; he regards dying as necessary and organic continuation of the way a man has conducted his life.

'The heroes of all nations die in the same manner, for they have lived and in the course of their lives they have learnt to recognize the power of nature. The failure to suffer its lesser evils disables a man from enduring its greater tests. How could it otherwise come about that the peoples in whose religion the preparation for death forms a corner-stone should on the whole die so unmanfully, while other nations approach this moment undaunted.'

This is followed by an account of the beauty of death among the Greeks, an account influenced in important ways by Schiller's philosophical poems. And Hegel goes on to compare this beauty with the narrow pettiness of positive religion, of Christianity:

'For this reason we see how the beds of the ailing are surrounded by friends and priests who overwhelm the anguished soul of the dying with their half-suppressed, prescribed groans and sighs.'[18]

And elsewhere he even aims his mockery at the death of Jesus, speaking ironically of the way the entire world is expected to feel gratitude to Jesus for his self-sacrifice,

'just as if many millions had not given their lives in a lesser cause, without the sweat of fear, but with a smile, with joy even, for their king, their country, their loved one—how would *they* have died then for humanity—.'[19]

These are the essential features of classical antiquity as compared with Christianity. Once the reader has familiarized himself with this material he will require no further proof, I believe, that Hegel projected this image of antiquity into the utopian picture of a republic of the future, and that each constantly influenced the other. From the standpoint of Hegel's later development it is particularly important to underscore this view of antiquity, above all the fact that antiquity was in his eyes not just part of history, but a living model for the present, and 'centuries will pass before the spirit of Europeans will make them realize and teach them how to implement in their daily life and their legislation those things which the Greeks' own feelings naturally taught them.'

The exemplary status of the Greeks has, as we have seen, democratic republicanism as its political content. Its philosophical manifestation is the radical subjective idealism of the early Hegel, his energetic, passionate repudiation of the positive religion of Christianity with its anti-human despotism.

## NOTES

1   Rosenkranz, p. 525.
2   Hoffmeister, p. 466. Similar remarks can be found in Lasson, pp. vii –xii, and Rosenzweig, op. cit., Vol. I, p. 239.
3   Rosenkranz, p. 352; for the original French text see the Appendix.
4   Nohl, pp. 221ff.
5   Ibid., p. 38.
6   Ibid., p. 39.
7   Rosenkranz, p. 519f.
8   Nohl, p. 33. Cf. also ibid., p. 162f.
9   Rosenkranz, p. 524. Cf. also Nohl, p. 54f.
10  Mme. de Guyon (1648–1717) was a mystical advocate of Quietism with a special emphasis on prayer, passivity and indifference even to eternal salvation. She taught at St. Cyr, thanks to the influence of Mme. de Maintenon, and corresponded with Fénelon. When Quietism was condemned at Isay in 1695 and then by the Pope in 1699 she was imprisoned and not released until 1703. Her chief work is the *Moyen court et très facile de faire oraison* of 1685.—*Trans.*
11  Nohl, p. 366f.
12  Rosenkranz, p. 523f.
13  The conclusion of Kant's argument is as follows:

'The moral law commands me to make the highest possible good in a world the ultimate object of all my conduct. But I cannot hope to effect this otherwise than by the harmony of my will with that of a holy and good Author of the world; and although the conception of the *summum bonum* as a whole, in which the greatest happiness is conceived, as combined in the most exact proportion with the highest degree of moral perfection (possible in creatures), includes *my own happiness*, yet it is not this that is the determining principle of the will which is enjoined to promote the *summum bonum*, but the moral law, which, on the contrary, limits by strict conditions my unbounded desire of happiness.

'Hence also morality is not properly the doctrine how we should *make* ourselves happy, but how we should become *worthy* of happiness. It is only when religion is added that there also comes in the hope of participating some day in happiness in proportion as we have endeavoured to be not unworthy of it.' (*Critique of Practical Reason*, trans. T. K. Abbott, London 1963, p. 227.—*Trans.*)

14 Nohl, p. 238.
15 Ibid., p. 239.
16 Marx, Article in the *Neue Rheinische Zeitung*, 15 December 1848. MEGA 1, Vol. 7, p. 493. G.L.'s italics.
17 Nohl, p. 362.
18 Ibid., p. 46.
19 Ibid., p. 59.

# CHAPTER FIVE

# Christianity: despotism and the enslavement of man

WHEN we come to Hegel's treatment of Christianity, that hated and despised incarnation of philosophical positivity, of political despotism, we shall not only find a completely different tone—that is very plain to see—but also a much more *historical* approach, though even here it does not go beyond the limits set to Hegel's insight into historicity in his Berne period.

We have seen how Hegel established a close connection between the economic foundations of antiquity—as viewed through Rousseauesque spectacles—and its republican heroism and greatness. But we have also observed that the problem of the *origins* of such a society never came to the surface. For the early Hegel classical antiquity was a purely utopian ideal. His unhistoricity here was not simply the result of his extreme philosophical subjectivism; for we have seen that this by no means needs preclude a very realistic appraisal of specific concrete social factors. We believe instead that his failure to develop an historical view of classical antiquity was closely related to the economic and political backwardness of Germany. However illusory the dream of a revival of classical republicanism had been, even in France, it nevertheless stood in a real relationship to the real goals of an actual revolution and its ideological preparation. In France, the possibility and necessity of relating these ideals and illusions to social realities brought about a much more genuinely historical view of classical antiquity. In Germany, however, the state of society did not yet allow the possibility of a democratic revolution. Hegel's enthusiasm, therefore, was purely ideological. For this reason it is nothing more than a wish-fulfilment and inevitably the question of how to bring about such a revolution remains the weakest, vaguest and least concrete aspect of his argument. (We shall see that this weakness persists unchanged for a long time and is never fully overcome.) Hegel's Berne period not only represents the culmination of his revolutionary enthusiasm, but also—in consequence of the gulf between ideology and social reality in Germany—it is the period of his greatest abstraction. This abstraction, this remoteness from a real purchase on future possibilities, is reflected in his unhistorical approach to the question of how the classical civilization of his ideal ever came into being.

When we come to his interpretation of Christianity, the situation is quite different. Here an historical approach follows directly from his revolutionary enthusiasm. The greater his enthusiasm for Greece, the more extreme the contrast between that and the wretchedness of life in the succeeding era became; whereas the more he suffered under modern, Christian society, the more energetically, historically and concretely he was forced to put the question: how could such a beautiful and human society perish and give way to such a wretched one? Thus he writes:

'The ousting of heathen religion by Christianity is one of those miraculous revolutions the causes of which must be sought by the reflective historian. The great, public revolution must have been preceded by a silent, secret revolution in the spirit of the age, a revolution not visible to anyone, least of all to living contemporaries and one which is as difficult to describe as to comprehend. Ignorance of these revolutions in the world of the spirit results in amazement at the end-product; a revolution such as the ousting of an age-old, indigenous faith by a strange one is inevitably fought out much more immediately in the realm of the spirit and so its causes must be sought directly in the spirit of the age.—How can a religion be supplanted which has been established in a state for centuries and which is intimately bound up with the constitution, how can people cease to believe in gods to whom cities and empires ascribe their origins, to whom the peoples daily offered up sacrifices, whose blessings they invoked for all their affairs, beneath whose banner their armies were alone victorious, to whom they had expressed thanks for their victories, to whom they dedicated their songs when happy, and their prayers when downcast, whose temples and altars, treasures and statues had been the pride of entire peoples, the renown of the arts, and whose worship and festivals were the occasion for universal joy—how was it possible for the myriad threads binding faith in the gods to the texture of human life to be torn asunder and broken?'[1]

Hegel's basic historical explanation is the one we have already seen in the essay, *The Positivity of the Christian Religion*: it is explained by the development of inequalities of wealth which according to Hegel, and indeed to his French and English predecessors, inevitably brings despotism in its wake. Here too Hegel does not achieve the historical concreteness of Gibbon or Ferguson, Montesquieu or Rousseau. It should be remembered, therefore, that when we speak of a more historical approach here we are only speaking relatively, bearing in mind the limited possibilities available to him.

But this greater historicity shows itself above all in the fact that Hegel attempts to explain the dominance of Christianity with reference not to the rise of Christianity in the first instance, but to the decline of the states of classical antiquity. His premise, therefore, is that there was a social need for a religion to fill the gap left by the loss of freedom, and he explains that Christianity was the victor because it was suited to this end.

'In this situation, without faith in anything stable or in an absolute, accustomed to obey an alien will and alien laws, without a country, in a state which promised no happiness . . . in this situation a religion presented itself to men which either was adapted to the requirements of the age (for it had its roots in a people equally, if differently, corrupt, vapid and sterile)—or else it was a religion from which men could mould or fashion whatever their needs dictated.'[2]

The primary factor for Hegel, then, is the erosion of the old democratic freedom, the old free activity of the people, through the emergence of inequality of wealth. Corresponding to the old state of affairs is that nonpositive religion which in reality was nothing but the spur, the incentive to heroic action in the midst of a natural life lived close to nature. The destruction of these forms of life is the most important process studied here by Hegel. He repeatedly returns to the fact that the extension of the Roman Empire meant the levelling out of the various nations and the destruction of their national religions. Probing further he discerns a link between the destruction of the old relations between man and nature, and the fall of the Roman Republic.

'Through the establishment of the Roman Empire which deprived almost the entire known world of its freedom, nature was subjected to a law alien to man and cut off from him. Its life became stone and wood; the gods became created and servile beings. Wherever force came to life, benevolence was revealed or greatness ruled, there the heart and character of man was to be found. Theseus only became a hero to the Athenians after his death . . . The Roman Caesars were deified. Apollonios of Tyana[3] performed miracles. The great was no longer divine, and therefore no longer beautiful or free. In this *separation of the natural and the divine* a man came to join them together, as conciliator and redeemer.'[4]

Hegel goes on to examine the various spiritual trends prevalent during the decline of Rome in order to discover just how the process led inexorably to the acceptance of Christianity.

'After the destruction of Greek and Roman freedom, when men's ideas lost control over the objects, the genius of mankind split in two. The spirit of the *corrupt mob* said to the objects: I am yours, take me! and hurled itself into the river of objects, let itself be swept along by them and perished in the flood.'

There follows an analysis of the various spiritual currents which opposed this process, and with an historical insight that is quite amazing for the time, he concludes that for all their opposition they were unable to change the basic tendency. Thus he refers to this general pattern to explain the fact that the late Roman Stoics turned away from life. (It is revealing that at this period he says nothing either about the Epicureans or the Sceptics. In Jena we find him preoccupied with the Sceptics and he shows great understanding of them. He was never able, however, to get his bearings properly with Epicurus.) Hegel goes on to show how the feeling of impotence led to the assumption of objects imperceptible by the senses, to the worship of these objects and thence to the various theurgic movements. He shows further that there is a straight line from here to Christianity. In conclusion, he states:

'In its maturity the church combined the desire of the Stoics with that of these inwardly broken spirits. It permits men to live amidst the whirl of objects and opens up the prospect of elevating men above them by means of easy exercises, sleight of hand, trembling of the lips, etc.'[5]

In Hegel's view, then, the essential factor that produced the need for a new religion in the Roman world, a need satisfied by Christianity, was the withering of republican virtue and freedom, the increasingly private nature of all aspects of life. This was the climate so favourable to the development of individualism in the modern sense of the individual who cares exclusively for his own narrow, material or at best spiritual needs and who thinks of himself as an isolated 'atom'; the social activity of such a man can only be that of a small wheel in an enormous machine, whose overall purposes he neither can nor wishes to comprehend. Thus according to Hegel modern individualism is also the product of the division of labour within society. In such a society the need naturally springs up for a private religion, a religion of private life.

We have seen already from the Tübingen Notes that Hegel regarded the private nature of Christianity as its most important characteristic. In contrast to the religions of the Greeks and Romans which always address themselves to the entire people, Christianity refers primarily to the individual and to his salvation, the redemption of his soul.

Hegel also turned his attention to a further historical question. The Christianity adopted by Imperial Rome was not identical in all respects with the faith originally founded by Jesus as this has been handed down to us in certain parts of the New Testament.

This issue is an age-old subject of debate and fills the pages of the history of religion. As early as the Middle Ages, the revolutionary sects made a polemical contrast between the practices of the Church and the original teachings of Jesus, and in the decline of the latter they discerned the reasons for the decline of Christianity and for its falling into the hands of exploiters and oppressors. These ideas were very influential among the supporters of Thomas Münzer and the radical wing of the Puritans during the English Revolution. After the latter event the practice of making particular dogmas and stories from the Old and New Testaments serve as ideological ammunition gradually died out among radical political movements. The preparatory stages of the bourgeois, democratic revolution in France evince an increasing hostility towards all the manifestations of Christianity: towards both the Church and the religion itself. This does not mean, however, that the confrontation between the moral precepts of Jesus and the immoral praxis of the Church ceased to play a part in the anti-clerical polemics of the Enlightenment. Even in the French Revolution itself, we find the sporadic appearance of 'Jesus the good Sansculotte' as a counter-weight to monarchical and counter-revolutionary priests. In a more backward Germany, where as we have seen there was neither a definite trend towards atheistic materialism, nor a radical attack on religion in general and where even in the camp of the Enlightenment the 'religion of reason' could be of paramount ideological importance, the incorporation of many of Jesus' sayings and teachings (such as The Sermon on the Mount) within 'rational religion' was only to be expected.

Naturally enough, views as prevalent as these could not fail to influence Hegel. As we shall see in Part II, in the course of his crisis in Frankfurt, this German approach even strengthens his own historical perspectives and leads him to conceive of the founder of Christianity as a world-historical tragic figure. In Berne he had much less sympathy for the figure of Jesus or insight into him. He did indeed warm to him as the teacher of a pure morality. But even here, as we pointed out in the previous chapter, he placed him beneath Socrates. This comparison, so unfavourable to Jesus, sprang originally from Hegel's overall view at this time. Jesus as teacher educates his disciples away from the life of society, each is encapsulated in his individuality, whereas Socrates leads his disciples back into activity in public life.

However great the differences between the Christianity of Jesus himself and Christianity as it later developed they nevertheless both remain private religions. It is for this reason that the original band of disciples has such a definitely 'positive' character in Hegel's eyes. This is expressed even in the number of disciples which Hegel regards as itself a symptom of fetishism.[6]

The source of the 'positivity' inherent in the teachings and activity of Jesus himself was to be found, according to Hegel, in the circumstance that Jesus always and as a matter of principle addressed to himself to the *individual* and, equally as a matter of principle, ignored the problems of society as such. This can be seen precisely in his attacks on wealth, inequality, etc., where he puts forward views that one would expect Hegel to approve of, but which he—quite consistently—rejects on account of their asocial character. He speaks, for instance, of the famous incident of the rich youth:

> ' "If thou wouldst be perfect, go, sell that thou hast and give it to the poor", Christ says to the youth. This image of perfection which Christ proposes contains the proof that his teachings were concerned primarily with the education and perfection of the individual man and they make it very clear how little such teachings are capable of being extended to society as a whole—.[7]

This brings us to the second historical question posed by Hegel. What had forced Christianity to become 'positive' in Hegel's sense? It was the process by which moral precepts intended only for the individual and envisaging only his perfection were extended in the course of time to entire societies. Hegel distinguishes three phases in this development. There is, firstly, the teaching of Jesus and his relation to his immediate disciples. Secondly, we find the Christian sect that grew up after his execution and in which the seeds of the 'positivity' already implanted began to germinate, turning what was intended as the moral union of the first community of Christians into a religious sect with pronounced 'positive' elements. Finally, we see these doctrines spreading throughout society, Christianity as a dominant church in which the forces of 'positivity' so alien and inimical to life acquire that fateful importance that will determine the entire history of the Middle Ages and modern times.

It is obvious that this scheme is incomparably more historical than Hegel's conception of the Greek *polis*. It is of interest to note that Hegel relied heavily here on Rousseau's idea of the qualitative changes produced in democracies by a quantitative increase. In the section on democracy (*Le Contrat Social*, Bk. 3, chapter IV) Rousseau points out that mere quantitative expansion can prove dangerous and even fatal to a democracy. It is very characteristic that although these remarks refer directly to the democracies of antiquity in Rousseau, they are applied only to Christianity by Hegel. Moreover, we should note the far from insignificant shift in emphasis whereby the cause of the decline is no longer an internal dialectic within the democracies themselves, as in Rousseau, but the growth of private morality, and the application to a larger society of the ethical precepts binding upon individuals. The increase in the size of society, then, produces in the wake of quantitative change, qualitatively different forms of positivity. (We witness here the first, as yet very primitive, schematic and unconscious form of the transition from quantity into quality in Hegel. It is also of interest to note that this Rousseauan idea reappears, in a generalized, modified form, in the context of political and constitutional problems, e.g., in *The Encyclopaedia* 108, Addition.)

Thus Hegel proceeds from the assumption that the later, terrible sides of Christianity were

> 'already implicit in its earliest, undeveloped scheme—and were then exploited and extended by autocrats and hypocrites'.

And generalizing from this he adds that the Christian religion

> 'provides us with yet another instance of the many which go to show that when the institutions and laws of a small society, where every citizen has the right to belong or not to belong, are extended to civil society at large, then they are always inappropriate and incompatible with civic freedom.'[8]

Hegel then goes on to discuss in great detail the various modifications to the particular doctrines and precepts of Jesus in the original community, and to show how in the fully-grown Christian church they developed into a consummate positivity and a hypocritical despotism. The detail of his analysis is explicable in terms of the state of Germany at the time; we are well aware from Hegel's letters of the use to which a reactionary orthodoxy put Kant's philosophy. Of course, even these studies do not make Hegel's early writings 'theological'—since their main thrust is anti-theological. Nevertheless, the history of the corruption of particular Christian doctrines has no very great interest for us today. We shall confine ourselves therefore to a description of the main line of the historical development. And here we must again emphasize that for Hegel the quantitative expansion of the Christian community was bound up with the emergence of social and economic distinctions within it, i.e. that here too Hegel's central historical preoccupation, the inequality of wealth, plays a crucial role. Thus with the growth of the community, the original close union and brotherly feelings evaporated. In the same way the fact that the community comes increasingly to be formed from a number of socially and economically divergent strata spells the end of communal property. The original rule that property should be held only in common with others

> 'ceases to be the condition for admission . . . all the greater is the emphasis on voluntary contributions to the communal treasury as a way of buying one's way into heaven. . . . The clergy could only gain by this since it recommended generosity to the laymen while taking good care not to throw away its own possessions, and so in order to enrich the poor and needy, i.e. itself, it reduced the other half of mankind to beggary.'

In a similar fashion, the original emphasis on equality became transformed into a 'positive' religious dogma:

'This theory was indeed retained undiminished—except for the prudent corollary that equality existed in the eyes of heaven and so no further notice need be taken of it on earth.'

All the customs and ceremonies of Christianity became 'positive', i.e. inhuman comedies which hypocritically disregarded the real condition of the people entangled in them. Thus Holy Communion originally represented the departure of the teacher from his disciples and then became transformed into a celebration in memory of the beloved teacher, now dead, a ceremony in which the equality and fraternity of the disciples was the decisive moral and religious factor.

'But as Christianity became more widespread, a greater inequality among the Christians became prevalent, which although repudiated in theory was retained in practice, so that a fraternity in any real sense soon ceased to exist.'⁹

Thus in every sphere Christianity developed into a 'positive' church and transformed the original private morality of its progenitor into that dogmatic sanctimoniousness which in Hegel's view is the form of religion necessary for and appropriate to a society based on private interests, to a bourgeois society.

There is only one way out of this impasse: the revival of the freedom and self-activation of man characteristic of the Greeks. We have already referred to the way the imperialist interpreters of Hegel's early work triumphantly point to his thorough study of Mosheim's Ecclesiastical History. But even this cannot be twisted into an argument supporting the thesis of an early theological phase. For Hegel steadfastly refused to contemplate any religious, Christian, solution to the problem of Christian 'positivity', dismissing such hopes as doomed from the outset. He had obviously read the history of the later sectarian movements, and it was this that led him to his negative conclusions. In fact, it is with reference to Mosheim's work that we find him discussing the fate of those men who appear from time to time and endeavour to put an end to the dead 'positivity' of Christianity by reverting to its original morality. Of the fate that awaits such endeavours he remarks:

'If they did not keep their faith to themselves, then they became the founders of a sect which, where it was not condemned by the Church, gained a following and as it flowed further and further from its original source nothing but the rules and laws of its founders survived. These rules then ceased to be laws inspired by freedom and degenerated into mere ecclesiastial statutes—and this in turn brought about the foundation of yet other sects . . .'¹⁰

Thus the positivity of Christianity with all its catastrophic effects cannot be overcome so long as it rests on that form of human society to which Christianity owes its diffusion and its hegemony.

Hegel's early writings contain very detailed descriptions of the way all moral problems are distorted by Christianity and are transformed into hypocrisy and subservience to despotism. We shall not concern ourselves here with his discussions of purely individual moral problems, but shall address ourselves instead to his critique of the effects of Christianity upon public life, the state and history.

The most revealing and the most incisive comments are to be found in the passages immediately following his extracts from Gibbon's *Decline and Fall*. Hegel says there:

'The first Christians found consolation and the hope of future rewards for themselves and retribution for their enemies—their oppressors who worshipped idols. But the subject of a monastery, or indeed of any autocratic state cannot appeal to his religion to avenge him on a gluttonous prelate or a financier getting fat on the sweat of the poor, since such men too hear the same mass, and indeed read it themselves, etc.—Instead he derives so much solace, so much compensation for the utter loss of his human rights in a mechanical religion that in his animality he loses all sense of his own humanity . . .

'Under the Roman Emperors the Christian religion was incapable of hindering the decay of every virtue, the suppression of the freedoms and rights of the Romans, the tyranny and cruelty of the governors, the decline of genius and of all the arts and all the basic sciences. Nor was it able to bring new life to the melancholy mind, to the withered branches of national happiness and national virtue. But eroded and poisoned by the universal plague, and with its own servants deformed into the instruments of despotism, it made the decadence of the arts and sciences, obedience to despotism and a passive tolerance of the destruction of every fine flower of humanity and freedom, into a veritable system: it became the advocate, the most passionate glorifier of the most scandalous iniquities of despotism and, what is even worse than any individual crimes, it went so far as to adulate despotism which drained all human energies dry and undermined humanity with its slow secret poison.'[11]

This gloomy picture of the historical impact of Christianity is meant to refer not only to Rome in its decline, but also the entire span of medieval and modern history. Discussing the historical achievements of the Christian religion elsewhere, he says:

'How unsuccessful it was in mastering the corruption of all classes, the barbarity of the ages and the coarse prejudices of peoples. When opponents of the Christian religion who, their hearts full of human feelings, contemplate the history of the Crusades, the discovery of America, the contemporary slave-trade—and not merely these outstanding episodes in which Christianity in part performed greatly to its credit, but the whole chain of princely corruption and popular depravity—their hearts will certainly bleed at the sight. And when they compare this with the claims of the teachers and servants of religion to excellence, general utility and so forth—they must surely be filled with bitterness and hatred of the Christian religion . . .'[12]

In like fashion Hegel discusses the influence of the Christian religion through every period of history and in every sphere of its activity. He repeatedly shows, e.g., that it is just those countries where the influence of the Church is greatest (such as the Papal States or Naples) that are the most corrupt, socially and politically, in the whole of Europe. His recurrent accusation against the Church is summed up in the following lapidary sentence:

'The Church has taught men to scorn civic and political freedom as filth in comparison with the rewards of heaven and the enjoyment of life.'[13]

Thus throughout its long period of rule, Christianity has procured the debasement of all real humanity. It has become the chief pillar of all autocratic caprice, of every sinister reaction. And Hegel is not thinking of isolated abuses, of the excesses of corrupt lay or spiritual rulers. The effects of Christianity spring directly from its very heart: from its positivity.

We have already seen from Hegel's earlier comparison of the wretchedness of Christian morality with the heroic ethic of classical antiquity how Christianity as the religion of private life, of private interests, concerned exclusively with individuals, must necessarily destroy all the high virtues of the Greeks and Romans. It creates a view of life in which all heroism or self-sacrifice appears ridiculous. A man preoccupied only with his own property will inevitably think that self-sacrifice for the commonweal is mere folly.[14] And even the more subtle, spiritual satisfactions of individualism are dismissed by Hegel as the expressions of philistine egoism. A good instance of this is his view of all belief in the immortality of the soul, of eternal bliss. We may remind the reader that Hegel argued that since the republicans of antiquity thought of their lives as merging entirely with the fortunes of the community, they neither needed nor sought after personal immortality.

The foundation of such heroism was, as we have seen, the self-activation of the people in the city-state. We have already pointed out that Hegel thought of these republics as classless societies. In contrast to this he discerns a close connection between Christianity and the class-

stratification of society. In particular, he thinks of the priesthood as a particular class. This stratification—Hegel occasionally compares the priesthood to the guilds—is connected in its turn to all the material and
spiritual interests of society. We have seen that Hegel believed that the
change from property owned in common to the egoistic enrichment of
the monasteries was part of an inexorable process. Elsewhere he explains
in detail about the self-activation of a people not yet divided into classes,
contrasting this with the Christian priesthood whom he regards as the
'repository of myths'[15] and the monopolists of religious truth. This monopoly is a means by which the priesthood maintains its own hegemony
and lends its support to the secular rules of the world. And the fact that
the myths and legends of Christianity are alien to the peoples of Europe
increases both the power of their monopoly and also its illiberal character in Hegel's eyes.

Thus men live beneath the yoke of the positive religion of Christianity
in a society that confronts them as something unalterably 'given' and
wholly alien. We may sum up Hegel's view of the historic mission of
positive Christianity by saying that it breaks man's will to live a creative
life in a society of free men. For this reason he expresses his opinion of the
social function of Christianity in these terms:

'It was revealed in the very divinity proclaimed by the Christian religion, a divinity beyond the reach of our power and our will, though
not of our pleas and our prayers—the realization of a moral idea
could henceforth *only be desired* (for what we desire, we cannot
achieve ourselves, we wait to receive it without our own intervention)—it could *no longer be willed*. It was this hope of a revolution
to be brought about by a divine Being, while men are reduced to the
role of passive onlookers, that inspired the first Christian mission-
aries—and when this hope finally faded people were content to wait
for a revolution at the end of the world.'[16]

The young Hegel's hatred and contempt for positive religion and for
Christianity evidently have their roots in his enthusiasm for the Revolution. Since he puts an idealistic interpretation on the Revolution,
regarding it as the realization of the 'practical reason' conceived as a
social theory, the question of will must inevitably become of the first
importance for him. For the will is, as we have seen, not merely the principle of praxis, it is the Absolute itself. Everything depends on will. As
long as men had willed freely, the classical republics had survived in all
their glory. When Christianity transformed the free, active will into
humble, passive desire, it opened the door to despotism. Of course,
Hegel realized that there were socio-historical reasons for the change
from will to wish, to desire. But since he was a German—and in Germany (even if there had been far fewer idealist illusions and prejudices)

there were no visible objective forces that might have brought about a democratic revolution—his utopian revolutionary hopes were forced to narrow themselves down to an over-enthusiastic, over-exaggerated emphasis on the will.

From this idealist perspective the prime mover of the historical process could only be religion. It is for this reason that Hegel sees positive religion as the most important obstacle to the liberation of man. It becomes a monster which makes him cry out, like Voltaire, 'Écrasez l'infâme!'. And it is this that enables him to sum up his views on religion and its role in history as follows:

'In this way the despotism of the Roman rulers had banished the spirit of man from the earth, the rape of freedom had forced man's eternal, absolute spirit, to seek refuge in God—the misery it spread forced him to seek and to expect to find his happiness in heaven. The objectivity of the Deity increased in direct proportion to the increase in the corruption and slavery of man, and this objectivity is in reality no more than a 'revelation, a manifestation of this spirit of the age . . . The spirit of the age was revealed in the objectivity of its God when . . . it was introduced into a world alien to us, in a realm in which we had no share, where we could not acquire a place through our activity, but at most by begging or conjuring our way in; it was an age when man was a Non-ego and his God was another Non-ego. . . . In such an age the Deity sheds all its subjectivity and becomes nothing but object; and the inversion of all moral precepts is easily and logically justified by theory. . . . This is the system of every Church. . . .'[17]

At this decisive point of his attack on Christianity the influence of Georg Forster is at its greatest, being perceptible even in points of style. Thus Hegel had copied the expression 'begging one's way in' (hineinbetteln) and used it in a similar context to Forster himself.

We shall now, in conclusion, draw attention to one further aspect of Hegel's critique of Christianity: the question of *reconciliation with reality*. This is important above all because it reveals the contrast between the early and the later Hegel in an extreme fashion. Hegel repeatedly returns to the subject and in the most scathing tones. We shall cite only a few of the most characteristic passages.

'In the womb of a mankind so corrupt that it must surely condemn itself by any moral criteria . . ., it was only natural to conceive and to welcome the doctrine of the corruptness of human nature. This doctrine . . . satisfied pride by placing blame elsewhere and by providing a reason for pride even in the feeling of degradation itself; it gave honour to what is shameful, and by turning everything that

might give us cause to believe in any active force into a sin, it sanctified and perpetuated every sort of weakness.'[18]

And elsewhere:

'But when Christianity found a way into the increasingly degenerate
upper classes, when great distinctions between the noble and the
mean began to arise within it, when despotism poisoned all the wells
of life and existence, then the age revealed the whole vapidity of its
nature by the turn it gave to its conceptions of the divinity of God and
its disputes about it; and it revealed its shame all the more clearly for
attempting to conceal it beneath an aura of sanctity and exalting it as
the greatest glory of mankind.'[19]

And finally:

'A people in this mood must welcome a religion which exalts the
dominant spirit of the age, its moral impotence, the dishonour it
endures through being trodden underfoot; such a religion is sanctified
in the name of "passive obedience" which makes it appear as honour
and the lóftiest virtue,—an operation by means of which men might
gaze in wonder and pleasure at the transformation of the contempt of
others and their own sense of disgrace into pride and peace of
mind.—'[20]

It was necessary to document these views so thoroughly to enable readers conversant with his later development to see the great divergence
from his earlier position on this issue. We are aware that 'reconciliation'
with reality is one of the cruxes of his later philosophy of history, even
though we must of course interpret it in the dialectical sense outlined by
Engels in his essay on Feuerbach. No doubt, Hegel's mature position
in relation to historical reality is full of internal contradictions, and
we shall have occasion to discuss them later when we come to examine the origins of his later view during his crisis in Frankfurt and
after that in Jena. But the dialectical core of this view is always the
recognition of social reality as it actually is; this remains true even
though this reality is, naturally, no more than a stage, a moment in
the historical process, a reality which, no less naturally, is destined to
be transformed into non-reality, non-being, to be abolished and preserved [aufgehoben]. Accordingly, for the later Hegel, the various
philosophical systems must inevitably appear as historically necessary
summations of the age in thought. This later conception is premised
on a view of history in which there is a continuous dialectical process from the beginnings of mankind down to the present.

For the later Hegel 'reconciliation' is a category expressing the
idea that the objective course of history is independent of the moral

aspirations and evaluations of the men active within it. The various philosophies, ideologies, religions, etc., appear correspondingly as intellectual syntheses of a particular historical era. For this reason, Hegel rejects all purely moral evaluations of them. This is not to say that he abstains from any point of view. But his chief criterion is the progressive or reactionary nature of a particular period and not, as earlier on, its relation to an eternal, supra-historical morality. To this extent 'reconciliation' is an index of the great development in Hegel's historical sense.

But the development is highly contradictory. For his use of the category also points to a real reconciliation with the most retrograde tendencies of the past and present. In particular, it tacitly accepts the reactionary institutions of contemporary Germany and this leads to the abandonment of all conflict, and of all real criticism, especially with regard to Christianity. Hence, the historical and scientific advance on the moral indignation of his Berne Period exacts a great price in terms of his progressive outlook.

As yet Hegel can see no objective historically necessary road leading to the 'real' present. The real present for him is the great miracle of the French Revolution, the apparent revival of the democratic freedom of antiquity. And between antiquity itself and its revival in the future, there stretches the corrupt, decadent age of despotism, oppression and 'positive' religion. Hegel does indeed perceive the historical necessity that gave birth to positive religion, but he does not discern any real historical forces active in it which might lead by an internal dialectic to a revival of classical civilization. (It is revealing that we do not possess a single note dating from Hegel's early period which attempts to come to grips with the *real causes* of the French Revolution.)

His exaggerated expectations and longings for a revolutionary regeneration of mankind do not permit him to develop a satisfactory methodological basis for his philosophy of history, one which could explain the road from the past to the present and future in terms of its own dialectic. For this reason, the regeneration of classical freedom remains a mere postulate, an abstraction of which his passionate hatred of Christianity whose manifestations we have already seen, was the necessary, organic complement. This hatred has its source in Hegel's view of freedom and other moral concepts as *eternal*, supra-historical categories. In his opinion, Christianity violates these eternal truths, perverts them, and invests what is base and eternally iniquitous with an aura of false sanctity. It is at this perversion of moral concepts that Hegel directs his entire revolutionary hatred.

It would be an error to interpret Hegel's increasing maturity simply in terms of an advance in his opinions. It goes without saying that there is a tremendous progress in that respect, above all in the philosophy of history. His very abandonment of the revolutionary ideals of his youth enabled him to develop into the leading exponent of German idealism; it enabled him to achieve such a profound and true insight into the necessity of the historical process and the methodology of history that he even went beyond what was possible within the framework of idealism. But a price had to be paid, and the fact that this maturity could only be achieved at the cost of renouncing the goals of a democratic revolution is a grim indication of the tragic conflict imposed on Hegel by the backward socio-economic state of Germany. Marx and Engels have repeatedly pointed out how the greatest Germans of this period succumbed in this constant battle against the German 'misère', and how even a giant such as Goethe could alternate 'between the colossal and the petty'.[20] Nor was Hegel more successful at avoiding this fate. And when we pursue the further development of his views to the point where his idealist dialectic culminates in a magnificent unified method, we cannot avoid reflecting upon the disharmony of German history which force Hegel also to alternate 'between the colossal and the petty'.

## NOTES

1 Nohl, p. 220.
2 Ibid., p. 224.
3 Apollonius of Tyana lived in the first century AD. He was a neo-Phythagorean sage whose fame as a wandering ascetic and wonder-worker is largely due to the biography written by Philostratus who was perhaps attempting to build him up as a kind of pagan counterpart to Christ.—*Trans*.
4 Rosenkranz, p. 522.
5 Ibid., p. 521f.
6 Nohl, p. 33.
7 Ibid., p. 360.
8 Ibid., p. 44.
9 Ibid., pp. 167ff.
10 Ibid., p. 210f.
11 Ibid., p. 365f.
12 Ibid., p. 39.
13 Ibid., p. 207.
14 Ibid., p. 230.
15 Ibid., p. 65.
16 Ibid., p. 244—G.L.'s italics.
17 Ibid., p. 227f.
18 Ibid., p. 225.
19 Ibid., p. 225.

20 Engels: *Deutscher Sozialismus in Versen und Prosa* II, MEGA 1, Vol. 6, p. 57. Cf. also Marx and Engels, *Über Kunst und Literatur*, Berlin 1950, p. 218.

# CHAPTER SIX

# The place of 'positivity' in the development of Hegel's thought

Our previous deliberations have endeavoured to map out the frontiers of Hegel's early philosophy of history. Our present task is to establish briefly the philosophical significance of Hegel's central concepts at this period. We shall not attempt at this stage to subject them to any thorough-going criticism. For the time being we shall be content to trace the main lines of his development up to the point where they first crystallize out in a historically significant form in *The Phenomenology of Mind*. Only then will it be possible, necessary and instructive to make an assessment of the intrinsic value of the dialectics developed by Hegel. Only then will it be worth our while to compare it with materialist dialectics and try to reach any judgment about the historical contribution and philosophical limitations of this climactic point of idealist dialectics. Until then we shall keep our study for the most part within the limits laid down by Hegel itself, i.e. we shall endeavour to establish what sorts of questions and answers were influential at subsequent, more mature stages in the development of the Hegelian dialectic. It would no doubt be relatively simple to subject all the concepts prominent even at this stage to an exhaustive materialist critique. But on the one hand, Hegel himself overcomes certain errors and extremes, certain undialectical features in his early thought, and on the other hand there are a number of idealist weaknesses that are never overcome and survive throughout all the phases of his development. In either case, to plunge straight into detailed criticisms would inevitably involve us in wearisome repetitions.

We have observed that the philosophically and historically crucial concept of Hegel's thought in this period is that of positivity. In the highest form yet established by Hegel, in the confrontation between subjective self-activation and freedom on the one hand, and dead objectivity on the other, positivity contains the seeds of a problem that will prove central to the later development of the dialectic: viz. the problem he was later to designate by the term 'externalization' (*Entäusserung*) and which, in the context of his later, much more comprehensive and systematic ideas, contains the entire problem of the nature of objects (*Gegenständlichkeit*) in thought, nature and in history. We need only remind ourselves that in his later philosophy the whole of nature is conceived as an externalization of mind, of spirit.

74

At this point, however, Hegel has not conceived the problem in epistemological terms. Even though he occasionally makes use of Fichte's terminology and applies the expression 'non-ego' to men and the God of Christianity, this should not be taken to imply that he simply accepts Fichte's theory of knowledge. He merely uses the expression as an image for a social and moral condition of man. And he is just as casual in the use he makes of Kantian categories. What interests him chiefly, one might almost say, exclusively, at this period, is the mtual interaction between social praxis and moral and religious ideologies. What is very characteristic of this phase, however, is the way he always treats the subject of this social praxis as collective, but without making any attempt to clarify the nature of this subject or to define it more precisely. Anyone familiar with his later thought will realize at once that this subject turns into 'spirit' (*Geist*) and that his system, founded on logic and the philosophy of nature, advances from subjective spirit through objective spirit to its crowning pinnacle in absolute spirit. In Berne and even in Frankfurt there is no real sign of such an elaborate system. The first version of this line of development does not make its appearance until *The Phenomenology of Mind*. In Berne his immediate interest is historical: he wishes to trace the actual historical path, the real fate of this collective subject (i.e. of the incarnation of the continuity of the development of society as it appears in an idealist, mystified form). The fact that the resulting historical account is an abstract idealist construct is by the way; what is more important, indeed of the very highest significance, is that in the course of his studies he arrives at the concept of positivity, of objectivity.

The insight he gained was the idea that the actual objectivity, the independent existence of objects apart from human reason, could be conceived as the product of the development and activity of that very same reason. He comes close here to the motifs that will be fully developed in his mature dialectics and at the same time, he firmly erects the frontiers of his own idealism, frontiers he will never be able to transcend. This second moment is at once comprehensible to any materialist and in Part IV we shall discuss at length the profound criticisms which Marx levelled at the idealist limitations of Hegel's whole philosophy. For the origins of the Hegelian dialectic, however, it is the first moment that is decisive, although it is of course inextricably intertwined with the limitations implied by the second. It contains the idea that the entire development of society together with all the ideological formations which it creates in the course of history are the product of human activity itself, a manifestation of the self-production and reproduction of society. With the aid of this idea German idealism succeeds in transcending certain—no less idealist—limitations of the historical approach found in mechanical materialism. Essentially, the latter was able to incorporate only the ever-present natural conditions of any society (the climate, etc) into its view

of history, while, on the other hand, it confined its study of human praxis
to the scrutiny of those visible or palpable reasons that determine the
actions of individual men. Engels emphasized the great superiority of
Hegel's philosophy of history over his predecessors (with reference to its
later formulation):

> 'On the other hand, the philosophy of history, particularly as repre-
> sented by Hegel, recognizes that the ostensible and also the really oper-
> ating motives of men who act in history are by no means the ultimate
> causes of historical events; that behind these motives are other motive
> powers, which have to be discovered. But it does not seek these
> powers in history itself, it imports them rather from outside, from
> philosophical ideology, into history.'[1]

This critical insight into Hegel's philosophy of history must be modified
to apply to his early thought by pointing out that there the idealist errors
bulk even larger while only the first signs of his later momentous discoveries are in evidence.

But the first signs are indubitably there. On the one hand, in his emphasis on the social character of the motive forces of history (however
much he mystifies them idealistically), and on the other hand, in the circumstance that even for the early Hegel the heart of history was the history of human freedom. The positivity of religion contained what was
no doubt a very general conception of objectivity; but at the same time it
was essentially the result of an historical development, with an historical
beginning and presumably a conceivable end, and so it was the starting-
point for an historical dialectic of freedom—an authentic discovery
despite its highly abstract and idealist form. In the thought of the Berne
period, Hegel saw the historical process as possessing a single great triadic structure: 1) the original freedom and self-activation of human society—2) the loss of this freedom under the hegemony of positivity—3)
the recovery of the lost freedom. The similarity to the idealist dialectics
of Rousseau's interpretation of history is evident.

Hegel focuses his analysis of the loss and recovery of freedom on the
workings of the process in religion. The lifeless inhuman and anti-human
character of objectivity, of positivity obtains its highest expression in the
Christian religion. On the other hand, despite all Hegel's efforts to provide social and economic explanations, religion remains in his view the
ultimate cause of a state of society and of a relationship between man and
his environment which is unworthy of man himself. Hence to comprehend and shake off the yoke of despotism means primarily to rid oneself
of this positivity. It means liberating man from a religion whose objects
are transcendental, other-worldly for him. For this reason Hegel requires
philosophy to provide a theory that will expose and destroy the other-
worldly objectivity of positivity and will reconvert all objectivity into

self-activating subjectivity.

> 'Setting aside a few earlier attempts, it has become the privilege of our age at least in theory to reclaim as the property of man all the treasures previously thrown away on heaven . . .'[2]

In this and similar statements we see a philosophical tendency emerging that has a definite affinity with Feuerbach. This affinity was first observed in the 1850's by the Liberal Hegel scholar, Rudolf Haym, who also drew attention to one difference between the two men, in the course of which he nevertheless failed to remark on the great superiority of Feuerbach's materialism over Hegel's early thought. He says:

> 'According to Feuerbach, the true essence of God is the essence of man; according to Hegel, the true essence of God is the essence of perfected politics.'[3]

Haym's own philosophical development belongs to the period before 1848; in his youth he experienced the dissolution of Hegelianism and the powerful influence of Feuerbach. For this reason he had at least a glimmering of insight into the real situation and, unlike the neo-Hegelians of the Age of Imperialism, he did not consciously strive to distort and falsify history. Of course, it is true that he only emphasized the strong side of Hegelian philosophy in his comparison with Feuerbach and neglected to mention the other, materialist side which would redress the balance. It is also true that Feuerbach's critique of religion is not without its weak, idealist elements to which Engels has drawn attention in no uncertain manner. According to Engels,

> 'Feuerbach by no means wishes to abolish religion; he wants to perfect it. Philosophy itself must be absorbed into religion.'[4]

However, Feuerbach's ideological failings must not be allowed to blind us to the superiority of his mechanical materialism in the crucial questions of epistemology which exercised an important influence on the critique of religion. This remains true even though Feuerbach himself may not have taken his theories to their logical conclusion.

The superiority of materialism can be seen in the very concept of positivity so crucial for the early Hegel. It is no accident that it should have been Feuerbach who aimed his annihilating attacks at Hegel's later, much more developed and thought-out view of positivity, viz. against his concept of 'externalization'. The early Marx always acknowledged Feuerbach's achievements here and he continued and extended what was valuable in Feuerbach. This is a question that we shall have to return to in detail in Part IV. Here it must suffice to point out that in Feuerbach the objects of nature are held to be independent of human consciousness. Therefore, when Feuerbach dissolves the concept of God into anthropology, when he declares that the God of the religions was made by man in his own image, this does not cause him to abandon objectivity (as it does Hegel), but instead it leads him to reaffirm real objectivity, the existence of the external world independently of human consciousness. Such a view will alone be capable of really dissolving the ideas of religion. For only this will clearly reveal their self-appointed, illusory, false objectivity for what it really is. Only the clear contrast with the real objectivity of the external world can expose the falsity, the hollowness and emptiness of the objects of religion. And if, as Engels has so rightly observed, Feuerbach was unable to take his materialist abolition of religion to its logical conclusion, his materialist approach nevertheless suggests a method for the philosophical demolition of religious ideas.

It follows that the so-called anthropological approach to the criticism of religion, viz. the demonstration that religious conceptions are only projections, apparent objectifications of what man thinks, feels and wishes, can never be more than one constituent of an authentic materialist critique. Lenin saw this weakness very clearly:

> 'This is why the term the "anthropological principle" in philosophy used by Feuerbach and Chernyshevsky is so *narrow*. Both the anthropological principle and naturalism are only inexact, weak descriptions of *materialism*.'[5]

With this Lenin draws attention to the weaknesses of Feuerbach's philosophy and criticizes them with his wonted incisiveness. Over and above that he provides a larger framework for the critique of the anthropological principle wherever it makes its appearance in the context of idealist philosophy.

This is what happens in Hegel's early works. Haym makes the serious error of completely abstracting the anthropological principle from materialism and idealism, whereas in the context of idealism it would gain a whole new dimension. For idealism there is no world of objects independent of consciousness. For the idealist the true objectivity of the objects of the external world and the false pseudo-objects of religious ideas all move on the same plane. Both are the product of an idealistically mystified subject—and it is of very little importance whether the idealist thinks in terms of the real consciousness of the individual, or of a mystified collective of 'universal', 'supra-human' consciousness. It follows, then, that if the idealist wishes to attribute reality to an object in the external world, he cannot deny the same reality to the objects of religion. Conversely, if, like Hegel in his dealings with positive religion, he should attempt to dissolve the objects of religion, he thereby does away entirely with the real objectivity of the real world and reintegrates it in a 'creative subjectivity'. This is the fate that befell not only the early philosophy of Hegel, but also the entire late phase of classical German philosophy. Both Schelling and Hegel—each in his own way—strove to escape from the impasse of mystical solipsism, of the subjective idealism of Fichte, by positing a mystical identical subject–object which would externalize the objective world and then reintegrate it in itself.

In Hegel's early work this method was not yet fully developed, but the nucleus, the tendency, was already present. And this basic assumption defines the idealist limitations and misconceptions inherent in his application of the anthropological principle to the critique of religion. This principle has long existed in rudimentary form. It can be found in the Greek philosophers and occurs frequently in the writings of the French Enlightenment. Therefore, when Hegel attempts to analyse the religious ideas of a period as the projections of the modes of existence prevalent in them, when he attempts to establish a close correlation between religious forms and forms of life, his achievement can have no claim to originality. So far from that being the case, we may even believe the anthropological principle to be weakened by his idealist assumptions, weakened to a much greater extent than by the old-style materialists whom Lenin rightly criticized. The distinction may be summarized in this way: for all the weaknesses that may occur in the use of the anthropological principle by materialists of whatever persuasion, they always adhere to the idea of clear and unambiguous causality: it is man who creates his God (or idea of God). In Hegel's philosophy, however, we discover a strange, confused interaction. On the one hand, a causal view is to be found in rudimentary form: the freedom and self-activation of the democratic Greek people gave birth to the serene world of the Olympian gods; the indignity and debasement of life under late Roman despotism gave birth to the positive religion of Christianity, etc. At the same time, however, we also find the opposite: the gods enter the arena of world history as real actors, freedom is not merely the origin of the Olympian gods, but also their gift to mankind; Christianity not only springs from the moral decadence of a people governed by tyrants, but equally tyranny is an effect brought about by the Christian religion.

Hegel is never able to free himself from the half-light of this position on the philosophy of religion. Not only in *The Phenomenology of Mind*, but also in his discussions of religious problems in his very last writings we come across this same confused ambiguity, which as he grows older leads to an even more willing acceptance of the pseudo-objective status of religion. In his youth Hegel desired passionately to destroy the Christian religion. But his anti-religious struggles were at all times vitiated by the quite central failing that he wished to replace one faith with another, to substitute for positive Christianity the non-positive religion of the Greeks.

Thus religion is made into an indispensable element of human life, and of the entire course of history. History is not for Hegel a process in which man emancipates himself from religious conceptions which he had taken over from primeval times and which for thousands of years have undergone various transformations corresponding to the changes in society. History is rather the process of religious change, or, to put it in the language of objective idealism: it is the history of God's metamorphoses. And once idealism has arrived at this point—which in the case of the young Hegel is true only to a very limited extent—the history of God will necessarily become one of the most important moments of history itself. In that event, all counter-tendencies flowing from the anthropological criticism of religious ideas, however correct in themselves, will be obscured if not wholly overwhelmed by this idealist theological principle. Thus we can see the emergence in the young Hegel of a whole series of idealist tendencies which will prove fatal for the later consolidation of the Hegelian system. This realization, however, should not blind us to those principles in which the potent and true aspects of his historical dialectic also begin to stir in his early period. For, however misguided Hegel's confused conception of the interaction between man and God may be, it nevertheless represents an attempt to grapple with a very real problem, albeit one that can only be properly solved by dialectical materialism. This problem, which completely baffled Feuerbach and the other mechanical materialists, is that of the historical origins and historical impact of religious ideas. And there can be no doubt—and every reader of the passages we have quoted from Hegel's early writings can easily convince himself of this—that Hegel both asked this question and struggled earnestly with it, even though it was not possible for him to arrive at a real solution or even a satisfactory statement of it.

While Marx was still in his youthful idealist phase, he paid some attention to this problem in his Dissertation—at an incomparably higher level of clarity than Hegel—but he too was unable to solve it. He states:

> 'The proofs of the existence of God are either nothing but *empty tautologies*—for instance, the ontological proof asserts only: "what I really (realiter) conceive, is a real conception for me", i.e. it has an effect on me, and in this sense *all* gods whether heathen or Christian have possessed a real existence. Did not old Moloch really rule? Was not the Delphic Apollo a real power in the lives of the Greeks? Kant's criticism is irrelevant here.'[6]

Marx could only put forward a satisfactory solution to this problem when he had gained a clear insight into dialectical materialism. Not until then could he expose the senselessness of religious ideas with a precision far greater than that of the most important mechanical materialists who preceded him. At the same time, he could also show in concrete terms how the growth of the forces of production and the resulting changes in the relations of production led to the emergence of particular religious ideas in particular periods and how they then dominated the emotional and intellectual life of men.

What is important and interesting in the philosophically so confused position of the early Hegel is that he poses the question of the concrete historical effects of religion. The Enlightenment attacked Christianity and did so in a more radical and intelligent manner than Hegel. But it was hardly able to pose this question, let alone answer it. And even Feuerbach does not really, in all seriousness, enquire why of all religions it was Christianity that became dominant in the West. Feuerbach accepts this fact just as a fact, and then goes on to deduce Christianity from the abstract 'nature' of an equally abstract man, simply from the nature 'of man'. Now such an argument can do no more than explain the birth of religious ideas in general, but it cannot explain the birth let alone the historical development of specific religious ideas.

Hegel intervenes at just this point. The quotation from Haym, reproduced earlier on, touches on Hegel's main achievement here: he sees the problem of the origins of religion as not merely historical, but also, and inseparably from this, as social. History for Hegel is the history of human social activity. His social analysis is no doubt very primitive, the socioeconomic categories he applies are doubtless naive, misconceived and artificial, and his explanations are still full of prejudices derived from Kant and the Enlightenment. (Examples are the belief that the state of society depends on whether the government is good or bad, after the manner of the Enlightenment, or the over-estimation of the social importance of purely moral problems typical of Kant.) Nevertheless, his view signals a real advance in the methodology of the study of the rise and fall of the religions. We see here how right Marx was in the *Theses on Feuerbach* when he argued that there was a connection between the old materialism and classical idealism in Germany. For Hegel's preoccupation with the social factors at work in religion is a striking instance of the 'active side' emphasized by Marx. And our earlier analysis also provides evidence for the other aspect of Marx's account of idealism, viz. the idea that in it this 'active side' can never be more than an abstract, ideological activity.

We have already pointed to one consequence of this inevitable abstractness: Hegel's inability to direct his attack at religion per se. In the unconscious dialectic of his view of history there is a tendency to claim that only the positive religions are religions in the strict sense and so neither the religion of the Greeks nor the religious revival he expected really came within the definition. His polemic against the inhuman character of positive religion has in this context a much more definite anti-religious bias than is usual in Hegel. Of course, he is prevented by his idealism from taking it further. Thus positivity becomes an unstable, ambivalent concept. On the one hand, it expresses an extreme idealist repudiation of all objectivity; on the other hand, it contains faint indications of those sorts of objectification which Marx was later to call 'fetishism'. Of course, all this remains extremely confused and obscure in Hegel. Even his much later, more mature formulation of the problem, his conception of social objectification as 'externalization' fails to eliminate the obscurities. The reason for this lies, as we have suggested, in idealism itself. For if Marx is able clearly to isolate the fetish-character of the commodity in all its 'ghostly objectivity', this is only possible because dialectical materialism was able to establish a clear definition of the real objective nature of objects and so eliminated all possible confusion between true objectivity and the objectivity of fetish objects. (The point here is to establish the philosophical distinction between idealism and materialism—it is obvious that Hegel, especially in his youth, did not have the information about economics at his disposal which would have enabled him to relate the fetish forms back to the concrete economic structure of society.)

If it is true that what we discover in the early Hegel is only a highly confused intuition, enveloped in a mystical fog, of certain important social and philosophical connections, it is no less true that this fact is of enduring historical importance. The point is that there are two closely related impulses which will play a significant role in the later development of Hegel's dialectic. These impulses are firstly, the belief that the whole of human history together with all the social formations that are born and pass away, are the product of human activity; [secondly,] that all these formations get out of the control of man and become autonomous powers with an objectivity of their own. We may remind ourselves of the way in which, in Hegel's view, Christianity develops into something essentially different from its founder's intentions. Moreover, this dialectic functions throughout the entire history of Christianity. From our previous discussions it is very apparent that this second impulse is very prominent in Hegel's concept of positivity. Positivity is by no means something introduced into human history from outside. On the contrary, Hegel's historical sense is at its most developed precisely in his elaboration of this concept. The elements of Christianity which have the greatest pretensions to transcendence (an omnipotent God, revelation, miracles, etc.) are the very things which Hegel passionately reclaims as the products of an internal social process, admittedly one of break-up and decay. Positivity, the historical climax of man's social inactivity, of the abandonment of human dignity is, according to Hegel, the result of a necessary development of man's social activity.

We must not proceed further in our discussion without drawing attention once more to the idealist limitation of Hegel's world-view. We have seen that his efforts to translate his correct but indistinct intuitions into a real knowledge of society all fail because his view of positivity becomes entangled with a general theory of objectivity. We shall argue at length in Part IV that this tendency is disastrous for the entire Hegelian dialectic. But it must not be forgotten that the great discoveries of the dialectic are inextricably intertwined with these weaknesses and that an historical study of the genesis of his dialectic has to try and disentangle the confusion. In the present case, the problem is that Hegel transforms the lifeless objectivity of positive religion into a social movement, into a product of the social activity of human beings. This is the first step on the road to the dialectic with its underlying idea of the transformation of all inert existence into movement. Of course, he still has a long way to go before this end is reached. For, in the first place, in his Berne period such tendencies are confined entirely to social problems. There is as yet no hint of a more general application, to movement as such—which we find in the *Logic*. Our research into Hegel's development of this theme will necessarily be imperfect. We must confine ourselves to his social attitudes and it would be very relevant to consider his scientific studies at this point since recent advances in science played a great role in his attempt to formulate more general laws of movement. At this point then a real understanding of Hegel's development will only become possible when the development of his scientific views is better known and can be integrated into the picture as a whole.

But even in the realm of societal categories Hegel is very far from developing his intuitions of a dialectical nexus, of the intellectual reproduction of social objects as the products of human activity, and of their dissolution in the movement of society, into a genuine philosophical method. The contrast between the periods he analyses is far too rigid and metaphysical for that: in Greece all is self-activating and public, in Christianity all is passive and private. The world of the classical *citoyen* is starkly contrasted with that of the modern *bourgeois*. And we can hardly find any awareness of the dialectic which perceives that the passivity of men in the Christian era is also a form of social activity. To say nothing of the fact that in every society the particular interests of individuals and individual classes (Hegel speaks always of 'Estates' [*Stände*]) are intertwined in a dialectical, contradictory manner with public interests. In subsequent chapters we shall attempt to trace in detail the changes in Hegel's understanding of the dialectics of society brought about by his study of political economy. We shall also have to establish the inevitable limitations of his thought in this respect. We may anticipate our conclusions with the general observation that the inadequacies of his understanding of the dialectics of society and history spring not only from the general limitations of his idealism, but also from the metaphysical tradition that he had inherited and which had marked him for life.

However, in these confused intuitions there are a number of themes that are important both intrinsically and also for his later development. Chief among these is the idea that a religion can only gain widespread control of men's minds if it is appropriate to the social conditions which gave birth to it or facilitated its rise to power. Hegel thereby discredits theories which see religion as no more than the conscious deception of a people, and regards the impact of a religion as simply the consequence of the original act of deception: in short he dispenses with the merely ideological interpretations of the Enlightenment. We have observed how this new standpoint does not make Hegel any more tolerant of Christianity. On the contrary, his discussions of the various kinds of hypocrisy and deception, which, in his view, derived necessarily from the nature of Christianity are indignant and satirical in tone. The advance here is to be seen precisely in the weight given to the idea that religions have a necessary existence and in his attempts to concretize his diagnosis of this fact. Thus he gives a number of examples of the way the original Christian communities, where a certain fraternal feeling and social equality had prevailed, gradually but inevitably gave way to hypocrisy with the rise of the universal church, the emergence of social and economic distinctions and the sanctioning of these distinctions by the church. On the other hand, Hegel constantly returns to the point that although the religious and moral tenets of Christianity conflict radically with truth, reason and the dignity of man, they are by that very fact in harmony with the social and moral climate of the age. He thus exposes the deception and hypocrisy in a much more historical, social and concrete manner than the abstract ideologists of the Enlightenment. Hegel does not deny that men were deceived by the priests, but this was only possible because the disruption of the society in which they lived and the moral degradation this brought in its train demanded just such a deception as the Christian priests were able to provide.

A further attempt at greater socio-historical concretization can be found in the central role assigned to the non-positive, non-objective character of the religion of the Greeks. Here, indeed, we can glimpse the strikingly contradictory character of his subjectivism and if its absurd implications do not come fully into the open this is due solely to his failure to develop his ideas to their logical conclusion. We are referring, of course, to the non-objectivity of the Greek world, the idea of a free, self-activating subjectivity which only creates objects till further notice so to speak; objects have no opportunity to attain true independence of the subject, but are instead transformed back into subjectivity, recalled into the active subject, the people.

This conception of subjectivity will later play a crucial role in the Hegelian system. After all, one of the chief dialectical problems in *The Phenomenology of Mind* involves the transformation of substance into subject. His youthful conception of the Greeks contains the first germ of this idea. This is particularly true of its revolutionary application to the present, to the dream of a classical revival, of the rediscovery of the free, creative activity of the people, the non-objectivity of the world of objects in the epoch inaugurated by the French revolution. To use the language of the *Phenomenology* we arrive at this scheme: (a) the period of the subject that has not yet transformed itself into substance—(b) subjectivity devoured by substance (positivity)—(c) reintegration of substance in the newly-awakened subject. Needless to say, this scheme is never stated so baldly in his early writings, but it is certainly implicit in his reconstructions of history.

Of course, Hegel's later philosophy is by no means confined to the greater systematization, the dialectical clarification of the course of history: it also sets out to change our view of it radically. For the later Hegel, history no longer begins with the Greeks. This does not only refer to the fact that the history of the Orient comes within his purview (a trend which already begins in Frankfurt); it is also true philosophically. The course of history increasingly departs from its origins in a Rousseauesque triad: freedom—loss of freedom—recovery of freedom. It is replaced by a much more evolutionary conception of the general growth of the idea of freedom in the course of history: freedom for one man (oriental despotism)—freedom for a few (classical antiquity)—freedom for all (Christianity and modern times). It would be a mistake to believe that Hegel's youthful view vanishes without a trace. On the contrary, highly modified and de-historicized, it underlies the system as it appears in the *Encyclopaedia*. The basic schema here is: logic (the self-activation of spirit)—natural philosophy (the externalization of spirit)—philosophy of mind (the path of spirit to perfect freedom, to the identical subject—object, logic as the culmination of the philosophy of spirit).

But even apart from these far-reaching consequences, even apart from this subterranean existence of his first, not finally thought-out schema, his contradictory interpretation of classical Greece has other more concrete and historically more important consequences. In our critique of the weaknesses of Hegel's philosophy of religion, we pointed to the crucial defect that he does not repudiate or attack religion in itself, he merely confronts positive religion with a non-positive one. It was this factor that led to the great popularity of his early writings in the Age of Imperialism. We need hardly add that this popularity did not go beyond the frequent quotation of a number of particularly confused passages and certainly did not extend to the study of his whole early development. There can be no doubt, however, that alongside the so-called irrationalism of the early Hegel, this ethereal, aesthetic religion without either substance or dogma has played a very definite role. The reactionary ideologists of the Age of Imperialism, particularly before the First World

War, very often did not venture openly to defend actual religions; yet at the same time they were eager to preserve and lend support to religion in general. Lenin had a clear insight into the great idealogical danger implicit in this trend. In a letter to Maxim Gorki, he wrote:

> 'A Catholic priest who rapes a girl . . . is far less of a threat to democracy than a priest without a surplice, a priest without any crude religion, an ideal and democratic priest who preaches the creation of a new god. For it is easy to expose the first priest, it is not hard to have him condemned and thrown out. But the second priest is not so easily dealt with—it is a thousand times harder to expose him and no "fragile and irresolute" petty-bourgeois will come forward to condemn him.[7]

However, this central failing of Hegel's early conception of religion has one historical aspect of great importance for his later development. This is the idea that Greek religion is not a religion in the same sense as the later positive religion of Christianity. This belief leads Hegel to a concrete historical analysis of the nature of Greek civilization. And the more his interpretation of Greece frees itself from parallels with the present, and perspectives on the future, the more historical it becomes. That is to say, he comes increasingly to regard classical antiquity as something finally dead and buried, as a stage in the history of the spirit that has been definitely overcome. In the coming chapters, we shall show in detail how this change of view is connected to changes in his attitude towards the present, the historical actuality of the Revolution and of a democratic republic in Germany. And so we shall see how these changes in their turn modified his entire philosophical system.

Here, it is enough to say that this particular view of Greece contains the seeds of his later arguments in the *Aesthetics* concerning the fate of the beautiful in the course of human history. It is well known that in the later system Greek art is seen as the authentic objectification of the aesthetic principle. This is by no means a conclusion based on formal artistic considerations, but is organically deduced from the analysis of Greek life as a whole. In all subsequent periods, as early as the age of Romanticism (which for Hegel means the Middle Ages and Renaissance) the aesthetic ceases to manifest itself in a pure form. The dominant principle of this era is religion, Christianity. And the march of the dialectic of mind beyond this latter stage no longer involves a return to the Greeks, but on the contrary, it heralds the dawn of spirit in its conceptual phase, and aesthetically, this means: the age of prose. Needless to say, the theoretical bases of this periodization are strongly ideological and highly idealistic. The most valuable of Hegel's aesthetic analyses are those which go beyond questions of principle and focus on the actual manifestations, the true objectifications of Greek life in art. But we must not forget that for Hegel himself the idea that Greek religion was not truly religious provided a sort of key to an understanding of the special quality of Greek civilization, even though the discoveries he made went far beyond his idealist schema.

The tragic contradiction in Hegel's development becomes visible at this point too. As a German thinker at the turn of the nineteenth century he could only choose between utopian illusions and the resigned acceptance of the miserable reality of Germany as it then was. For Hegel Greek civilization could only be either, as in Berne, a Jacobin dream of the democratic regeneration of man, or else it had to be a golden age of beauty, now irrevocably lost, an organic human culture which could only be succeeded by the arid age of prose, a prose from which there is no escape. Hence man must simply accommodate himself to it and to gain an accurate conceptual understanding of it becomes the loftiest task of philosophy. We know how Hegel's thought moved from one of these alternatives to the other, and in subsequent chapters we shall have the opportunity to study some of the main stages in his journey. We shall also come to understand that his dialectics were made possible only because he travelled along this road. The heroic Jacobins among his predecessors or contemporaries, men like Georg Forster or Hölderlin, were destined to remain on the margins of the ideological development of Germany.

It is very instructive in this context to glance briefly at the differences between Hegel's idealist dialectics and the materialist dialectics of Marx and Engels. Marx too places the Greeks in the very centre of his views on aesthetics; for him also Greek civilization represents the purest and most noble manifestation of human aesthetic activity hitherto. Marx is perfectly explicit about the normative character of classical art. After referring to the concrete historical conditions that made it possible, he goes on to say:

> 'But the difficulty is not that of understanding how Greek art and the epic poetry are associated with certain forms of social development. The difficulty is that they still give us aesthetic pleasure and are in certain respects regarded as a standard and an unattainable ideal.'[8]

Marx, too, places Greek beauty in sharp contrast to the prose of capitalism. And since he understands the nature of capitalism much more thoroughly than Hegel does even at the point of his greatest maturity, since his opposition to the capitalist system was much more entrenched and more solidly based scientifically, his condemnation of capitalist culture was much more profound, more comprehensive and annihilating than Hegel's ever could be. And it follows that in Marx's case there could be no question of a resigned acceptance of the actual state of human culture such as we find in the later Hegel. The contemplation of the past and immortal beauty of Greece never becomes a reason for melancholy. His profound and comprehensive grasp of human history, of its true motive forces, of the real economic and social structure of capitalism led Marx beyond utopias to the scientific view of the regeneration of man through socialism. In this perspective, the normative status of Greek art becomes a unique inheritance; in the era of liberation, at the end of man's 'pre-history', it will spur mankind on to build a culture that will surpass by far all the cultures of the past. Thus in his resolution of the Hegelian dilemma of utopia and resignation, Marx not only proves the superiority of materialist over idealist dialectics, but also, even where he has learnt from Hegel, even where he salvages important elements of his thought, such ideas as he does take become completely remodelled in the course of their integration into a materialist dialectic.

For Hegel himself there could be no escape from this dilemma. Had he continued to think along the lines of his early essays the fate of a Forster or Hölderlin would have been unavoidable. The brilliant but sporadic insights of his early writings in Berne could only mark a significant stage in the development of human thought because Hegel managed to go beyond the republican illusions of his first period. We have seen that all these beginnings, rudimentary and confused as they were, nevertheless pointed towards the dialectical approach to history. In Berne there could be no question of a thorough-going dialectical analysis of history—even within the limits of idealism. We can convince ourselves of this most easily by observing that at this stage there is absolutely no sign of the most important dialectical categories of his later method: immediacy and mediation, the dialectical interaction of the particular and the general, etc.,—all these are absent. There is only a rudimentary dialectical schema of the course of history, and even this is shot through with metaphysical concepts. And if Hegel does succeed for the most part in avoiding a rigid metaphysical position, this is only because he fails to argue consistently from his own premises, leaving many of his conclusions in a confused state of semi-darkness. But this of course is only a pseudo-solution and no thinker of Hegel's stature could possibly rest content with it in the long run. However, we have been able to observe on a number of occasions that his confusion and obscurity are not essentially intellectual or methodological. On the contrary, we have seen again and again that they spring from the utopian illusions he brought to the consideration of the present. The truth of the Marxist belief that a correct understanding of later historical developments provides a key to earlier ones, and that the present must be comprehended if the past is to be rightly understood, proves its worth in the case of Hegel himself. The decisive crisis in his thought—and we shall describe it in detail in the next chapter—focused on his change of attitude towards the present, towards the reality of capitalism.

## NOTES

1 Engels, *Feuerbach*, in *Selected Works*, Vol. II, p. 355.
2 Nohl, p. 225.
3 Haym, *Hegel und seine Zeit*, 1887. 2nd edition, Leipzig 1927, p. 164.
4 Engels, *Feuerbach*, in *Selected Works*, Vol. II, p. 342.
5 Lenin, *Philosophical Notebooks*, in *Collected Works*, Vol. 38, London and Moscow 1963, p. 82.
6 Marx, *The difference between the nature philosophy of Democritus and Epicurus*, MEGA 1, Vol. I, Part I p. 80.
7 Lenin, letter of 14 November 1913 to Gorki. On a number of issues affecting the ideological development of Germany see my essay 'Feuerbach and German Literature' in *Literaturtheorien des 19. Jahrhunderts und des Marxismus*, Moscow 1937.
8 Marx, *A Critique of Political Economy*, London and Moscow 1971, p. 217.

# PART II

# The Crisis in Hegel's views on Society and the Earliest Beginnings of his Dialectical Method (Frankfurt 1797–1800)

# CHAPTER ONE

# General description of the Frankfurt period

THERE was no path leading from the views Hegel had formed in Berne to the social reality of his situation in Germany. Any attempt to turn such views to practical account was rendered futile from the outset by the untimeliness, indeed the objective impossibility, of a bourgeois revolution in Germany. Yet Hegel had been passionately concerned with practice right from the start. He had always hoped to take an active part in the political life of his time. It is quite typical of him that he had no sooner completed *The Phenomenology of Mind* than he eagerly accepted the post of editor offered to him in Bamberg. It is true that he later became disillusioned by his experiences in Bamberg but this was due chiefly to a censorship which severely restricted the scope of the newspaper.

There can be no doubt that a considerable section of the German bourgeois intelligentsia sympathized with the ideas of the French Revolution. In all probability the number of sympathizers has been underplayed by the tendentious descriptions of bourgeois historiography. However, it was never sufficiently large or influential either materially or morally to ensure the wide dissemination of the ideas of the French Revolution in the press or through literature and philosophy. This is clearly borne out by the tragic fate of Hegel's friend Hölderlin.

The gulf between Hegel's Berne views and the state of society was widened still further by the course of the French Revolution itself. This had two causes: on the one hand, the internal logic of the class struggles in France itself and, on the other hand, the effects of the wars waged by the French Republic in response to the intervention of the absolutist feudal powers.

The great turning-point of the French Revolution, the events of Thermidor (1794), came while Hegel was still in Berne. It appears not to have made any decisive immediate impression on him. We have seen how he welcomed the reprisals directed against the followers of Robespierre, but this does no more than confirm the distance separating him from the radical, plebeian wing of the French Revolution. But we cannot detect any change in his republican and revolutionary views after Thermidor. At first glance this is a surprising fact, but it can be explained both by the course of the Revolution itself and by the young Hegel's own standpoint. The internal history of France under the Directory was a constant balancing act by the bourgeois republicans who desired to preserve and consolidate their gains, gains essential for the bourgeoisie, and who were caught between royalist attempts to turn the clock back and efforts by the rump of the radical parties to advance the plebeian side of the Revolution. The leaders of the bourgeois republicans were repeatedly forced into a temporary alliance with one or other of these extremes and the resulting instability eventually expressed itself in a need for military dictatorship. Hence Napoleon Bonaparte's *coup d'état* on 9 November 1799.

Even more important for an understanding of the period is an analysis of the social implications of Thermidor itself. In contrast to the liberal historians and the Trotskyites, their counter-revolutionary parrots, Marx defines the social content of Thermidor with extraordinary clarity:

> 'After the fall of Robespierre the *political* Enlightenment . . . which had been *rhapsodic* hitherto, began to transform itself into a *prosaic* reality. Under the government of the *Directory, bourgeois society*, freed by the Revolution from the trammels of feudalism and officially recognized in spite of the *Terror's* wish to sacrifice it to an ancient form of political life, broke out in powerful streams of life. The storm and stress of commercial enterprise, the craze for wealth, the frenzy of the new bourgeois life, whose first self-enjoyment is still audacious, heedless, frivolous and intoxicating; a real enlightenment of French *landed property* whose feudal forms had been smashed by the hammer of revolution and which had become the object of all-round cultivation thanks to the feverish energy of its many new owners; the first stirrings of an emancipated industry—these are some of the manifestations of the new-born bourgeois society. *Bourgeois society* is represented *positively* by the *bourgeoisie*. The bourgeoisie thus *begins* its reign.'[1]

Naturally enough, in a backward Germany the echo of this new phase in the history of the French bourgeoisie is even more distorted, indirect and ideological than the heroic events of the Revolution itself. There could be no question of an economic boom in Germany corresponding to developments in France. Very few German observers understood or were even able to understand the economic implications of post-Thermidorean France. But this only reinforced the ideological consequences. The very fact that the majority of bourgeois humanists in Germany misunderstood and rejected the plebeian asceticism of the extreme left in France necessarily gave rise to a feeling of sympathy for a life-loving and life-affirming bourgeois regime that rejected both feudalism and reaction while also proceeding energetically against revolutionary 'extremes'. This sympathy which at a later stage became focused on the person of Napoleon contained elements of a humanist idealization and romanticization of post-Thermidorean developments.

Thus we witness the birth of a naive belief that it might be possible to realize the humanist ideal of an all-round, fully developed, life-affirming mankind in the context of existing bourgeois society. It goes without saying that the important spokesmen of bourgeois humanism were aware of the contradictions in this society and above all of the obstacles and impediments which capitalism places in the path of the individual seeking to develop his personality. Getting to grips with these problems constitutes one of the chief themes of German classical literature. In the course of our discussion of Hegel's views in this period we shall see again and again the many parallels between his thought and that of the outstanding representatives of classical humanism in Germany, the thought of Goethe and Schiller. Here too the imperialist neo-Hegelians, who have pounced on the intellectual and terminological confusion, obscurity and mysticism of Hegel's Frankfurt period in order to represent him as the forerunner or supporter of reactionary Romanticism, have turned the truth upside down.

At this stage of French history, then, the debates surrounding bourgeois society stand in the foreground. In line with the backwardness of Germany on the social, economic and political planes these debates take place in an almost pure ideological realm. There is no political analysis of bourgeois society as there is in France, no scientific investigation of the underlying laws of the economy as in England. Instead we find a probing into the situation of man, of personality and its development within bourgeois society from a humanist standpoint. Ideological this analysis may be, but for all that it is undoubtedly a reflection of French developments after Thermidor and in the literary products of the period, above all in those of Goethe, an extraordinary degree of realism is achieved.

In Hegel's early philosophy idealistic elements are incomparably more prominent and influential. But it must be emphasized—and here we anticipate a fundamental tendency in his development—that Hegel, alone among German thinkers of his day, was impelled by the logic of his analysis of bourgeois society to undertake a serious examination of the *problems of economics*. And this is reflected not just in the circumstance that he, alone among the leading German thinkers, made a thorough study of the classical English economists; his interest went beyond that and extended, as we shall see, to an examination of the concrete economic problems of England. Thus in the Frankfurt period we see an extraordinary widening of Hegel's intellectual horizons. In Berne his views on the philosophy of history had been founded on the world-historical fact of the French Revolution. From now on the economic development of England likewise becomes a basic component of his view of history and his understanding of society. But for all this it remains true that Hegel was still a German philosopher whose fundamental vision was determined in every respect by the backwardness of Germany.

Indeed it was precisely this which became more marked during the Frankfurt period, and this was a direct consequence of the French Revolution itself. After an absence of three years Hegel returned to Germany, spent a few months in his native land, Württemberg, and went from there to live in Frankfurt, one of the commercial centres of Germany. He was in a good position, therefore, to inspect the effects of the French Revolution on life in Germany. In Württemberg these effects were quite powerful and—within the framework of Germany's general backwardness—they were the cause of a government crisis which lasted for a number of years. Hence the problem of how the absolutist feudal structure of Germany would have to be modified because of the French Revolution appeared to Hegel not just as a general historical issue but in concrete political terms.

But by this time the impact of the French Revolution in Germany was no longer confined to this ideological aspect, to the growing awareness that the feudal governments had become untenable. This was the very period in which the campaigns which had started as wars to defend the French Republic now went over to an almost continuous offensive. In the first instance this meant that Germany and Italy had to provide the battlefields, instead of France itself. More importantly, however, developments after Thermidor meant that the mixture of a defensive war and an international propaganda war which had prevailed in the first years of the Revolution increasingly gave way to what was predominantly a war of conquest. Elements of the propaganda war did survive throughout the entire period, even under the Empire. Every French government found itself compelled to sweep away the vestiges of feudalism in the conquered territories as far as possible, and to bring such areas into line with the political and economic state of France. But increasingly this tendency became subordinated to the self-aggrandizement of the bourgeois republic, and later of the Empire.

Thus the wars with France intervened directly and profoundly in the lives of Germans. As we shall see later in detail this intervention was full of contradictions. On the one hand, the best and most progressive ideologists of Germany placed their hopes for the rejuvenation of Germany in the influence of the French Revolution, and this sometimes went as far as welcoming armed intervention. We are not thinking here only of the setting up of a republic in Mainz and the connection between this and the temporarily victorious campaign of Custine; for even later, at the time of the Confederation of the Rhine, this mood had not vanished completely. On the other hand, the French invasions increased the fragmentation of the German nation. National unity, the emergence of a unified nation-state seemed to become even more remote, the possibility of achieving it ever more dubious.

In the course of our detailed discussion of Hegel's Frankfurt period we shall see how far he was from a political and philosophical resolution of the contradictions arising from this situation. But we shall also be able to see how his greater proximity to the concrete problems of bourgeois society and of the political and social fate of Germany led him to place the phenomenon of contradictoriness in the forefront of his own thought: we see how he comes to *experience* contradiction as the foundation and the driving force of life. We emphasize the word 'experience', since Hegel's development, unlike that of Schelling, does not involve a progress from one philosophical system to the next. We must recall what we said about Hegel's Berne period, above all the fact that he showed a remarkable lack of interest in philosophical problems, especially those of epistemology and logic. His aim was to probe certain social and historical interconnections and he had recourse to philosophy only as a basis for the generalizations indispensable to that task. Initially and in general terms this remains his procedure in Frankfurt. But we shall see that over and above the increasing concretization of the social and political problems he tackles, there is also a growing tendency consciously to concern himself directly with philosophical questions so that social and political issues become increasingly translated into philosophical problems. And interestingly enough, this happens all the more abruptly and directly when the philosophical core of the problem under discussion hinges on the nature of contradiction.

The difficulty facing the interpreter of Hegel's notes and fragmentary writings can be located in the extraordinarily abrupt, unmediated, unprepared transition to the philosophical plane. In glaring contrast to both his earlier and his later writings Hegel's thought in Frankfurt proceeds almost always from his own personal experiences and his style bears the marks of both the passion and the confusion, the unresolved nature of personal experience. Moreover, his first attempts to articulate philosophically the contradictions he has experienced himself rarely achieves genuine clarity and definition either in form or content. Hegel's earliest philosophical pronouncements often peter out in mystical abstractions. An additional factor is that to start with he evidently feels hardly any need to grasp particular ideas in a systematic fashion. In the first instance he is concerned to solve specific concrete historical and also political problems. At the same time philosophical views tend to grow out of his analyses of particular phenomena and the connections between them become increasingly intimate. Finally, at the end of the Frankfurt period he makes the first attempt in his life to gather his philosophical views together into a single system.

Thus the first appearance of the dialectical method in Hegel is highly confused. His contradictory experiences of the particular manifestations

of life are welded together in a highly mystified totality which Hegel repeatedly designates with the word 'life'. As yet he has made no systematic reckoning with logic or with the epistemology of metaphysical
thought. Thus the opposition between dialectics and metaphysics
appears to him as a contrast between thought, idea, concept, etc., on the
one hand, and 'life' on the other. This contrast already gives an indication of the profundity of the dialectics of Hegel's maturity, with their
passionate grasp of the contradictions contained in the concrete phenomena of existence. As Lenin has convincingly shown, this often brings him
within reach of true, materialist dialectics. In the Frankfurt period,
however, his conception of 'life' is not only confused in itself, but its content is essentially mystical. For at this stage the opposition between ideas
and life drives him to regard religion as the highest consummation of
'life' and thus as the apex of his philosophical system.

This represents an extraordinary change when we compare it to his
Berne period. As we shall show in detail this change reflects the fact that
Hegel's prime concern from now on is with the place of the individual,
*of man in civil society*. In Berne Hegel had, to a certain extent, still looked
at the society of his day from outside. That is to say, he had regarded the
entire course of history from the fall of the Roman republic to the present
as a unified process of decline, as a stage embracing the whole of history
which was merely provisional, even though it might last for centuries,
and which would be succeeded in the end by a revival of the republics of
classical antiquity. Consistently with this he had eyes only for the negative sides of this process. We might say in short that he regarded the
entire history of civil society as a single process of decay.

The change that now takes place in his thought can be indicated by the
fact that he begins to see in civil society a fundamental, incontrovertible
fact with whose existence and nature he has to come to terms both intellectually and practically. This process begins in a highly *subjective*
manner, i.e. Hegel is not yet able to inquire into the objective nature of
civil society, as he will do later at Jena. His present problem is to discover
how the individual has to proceed in order to come to terms with civil
society, how the moral and humanist postulates of personal development
come into conflict with the laws and the nature of civil society and how
these contradictions can be ironed out and the opposites *reconciled*.

This development entails a fundamental change in Hegel's attitude to
the present. To indicate his attitude we have employed what was to
become the celebrated and notorious category of 'reconciliation'. This is
no accident, for this category which, as we recall, he had attacked so violently in Berne (see p. 69–71), re-emerges in this period as a crucial problem. It is not that he fails to explore contradictions in the relations
between the individual and society, or, more accurately, that in the
course of his analysis of concrete problems, ever new contradictions fail

to come to light. It is that the goal of his thought is to annul contradictions, to reconcile them whenever they appear. (The term 'annul' [*aufheben*], so vital for his later thought, likewise makes its first appearance in Frankfurt and gradually becomes a dominant category in his writings.)

This new form of Hegelian subjectivism must be sharply distinguished from the subjective idealism of his Berne period. The latter has been fully discussed in Part I and we need here only remind the reader of our conclusion that at that stage the subject of the socio-historical process was always a collective one. The separation of the individual from the immediately social nature of life in the city-state of antiquity, the emergence of 'private human beings' appeared to Hegel as the clearest possible symptom of decadence. Hegel's Frankfurt subjectivism, however, is subjectivism in a literal sense. He really does begin immediately with the individual, with his experiences and fate and goes on to study the specific forms of society and their influence on this individual fate, their interaction with each other.

Only slowly and gradually does the study of the individual's objective environment, of civil society, gain the upper hand. From the standpoint of the individual destiny of the individual human being, of the 'private human being' he had formerly so despised, Hegel now attempts to trace the general laws of society and to press forward to an objective understanding of them. The old problem of 'positivity' makes its reappearance as a central problem, but is given a much more complex, contradictory and historical treatment than in Berne. And this very issue now leads Hegel to a far more penetrating study of the dominant forces active in civil society: it leads to a study of economic problems. His ‹efforts to discover a philosophical reconciliation between the humanist ideals of the development of personality and the objective, immutable facts of society leads him to an increasingly profound understanding, firstly of the problems of private property and later of labour as the fundamental mode of interaction between individual and society.

Hegel's changed attitude to the present is associated with an equally radical change in his view of *Christianity*. After what we have said up to now this can scarcely come as a surprise. It is a commonplace that the major turning-points in every idealist view of history are closely bound up with religious changes. Even Feuerbach fails to diverge from this pattern. In the case of Hegel the negative evaluation placed on civil society, the society of 'private human beings' had been intimately connected with his views of Christianity. Notwithstanding his efforts to discover the social causes for the decline of the city-states of antiquity he was left essentially with Christianity as the driving force of the modern world. Given such a conception of history it is hardly surprising that any modification of his view of the present should at once carry over to his judgment of Christianity. Since his early idealist position remained intact in

Frankfurt, and even took a definite turn towards religious mysticism, Christianity was the obvious source for the ideological and moral foundations for the modern world.

That such a position is idealistic is too obvious to require any discussion. At the same time we must point out that it is not accidental or without roots. Hence its persistence and even indestructibility. These roots whose effects make their appearance in such distorted and mystical forms in the various idealist systems of history are in fact the objective historical bond connecting Christianity to the entire history of the modern world. In a number of profound and detailed studies Marx and Engels have explained why Christianity alone, rather than any of the other sects which proliferated at the time of the collapse of the Roman Empire, was able to expand into a world religion. They have shown how Christianity was able to adapt itself to prevailing needs in the different phases of the economic development of Europe and how the various stages of the class struggle in Europe were accompanied by novel forms of Christianity (medieval sects, Lutheranism, Calvinism etc). And they have shown that even modern bourgeois society must continue to give birth to a superstructure of Christianity modified in certain definite ways. In his polemic against Bruno Bauer, the Young Hegelian idealist, Marx states:

> 'In fact the perfect Christian state is not the so-called *Christian* state which proclaims Christianity as its foundation, as state-religion, and which consequently tends to exclude other religions. It is rather the *atheistic* state, the *democratic* state, the state which relegates the Christian religion to a place on a par with the other elements of civil society . . . This state is able to abstract from religion because the human basis of religion is incorporated in itself in a secular form . . . The foundation of this state is not Christianity, but the *human ground* of Christianity. Religion remains the ideal, unworldly consciousness of its members because it is the ideal form of that stage of *human development* which is realized in the democratic state.'[2]

In idealist theories of history, not excluding that of the young Hegel, these real historical connections appear upside-down and in a distorted form. Christianity, the necessary product of social developments in the Middle Ages and in modern times, appears as the primary driving force of history. In these general terms there is no decisive shift in Hegel's philosophy in Frankfurt from his earlier position in Berne. Whether he rejects Christianity in Berne or seeks a reconciliation with it in Frankfurt amounts to much the same thing, for in both cases religion retains the dominant position in his typically idealistic view of history. Of course, since Hegel starts from the problems of life facing the individual and since he is in search of a reconciliation with the present, this gives rise to a much more intimate relationship with Christianity than he had enjoyed hitherto. In this sense his attitude in Frankfurt reverses that of Berne.

The choice of the problems of the individual as a starting-point is something that we only find in Hegel during the transitional period of crisis in Frankfurt. Both in his earliest works and in his maturity the individual interests him only as a member of society. The incisive criticism directed later at the moral positions of Kant and Fichte, Schleiermacher and the Romantics generally focuses on their failure, expressed in a variety of ways, to see that apparently pure individual actions have a social component and that even individual ethical categories are socially conditioned and determined. Thus Hegel's own concern with the individual, his own use of the individual's needs and aspirations as a base point for his thought, is no more than an episode in his career, even though it is an episode fraught with consequences which persist in later years. We shall see again and again that the first seeds of the method of *The Phenomenology of Mind* can be traced back to Hegel's approach in Frankfurt: to the journey from individual consciousness to the objective problems of society, to his attempts to discover specific dialectical stages of thought and feeling, i.e. to demonstrate that a higher stage results from eliminating the contradictions of lower stages.

The Frankfurt writings only disclose this message, however, when one looks at them with the later works in mind. Considered on their own, or after the Berne writings, their opacity and confusion is astonishing. Never again will such unclarified concepts buried in a haze of unspoken meanings play such a prominent role in Hegel's thought as in Frankfurt. The experience that contradictoriness is the foundation of life breaks through with increasing intensity but at this stage the contradictions seem to be tragically incapable of resolution. It is no accident that for a time categories such as fate become the fulcra of his efforts to comprehend the world in philosophical concepts and that only in this period does a mystical conception of the religious life form the climax of his thought. For his life and thought are going through a period of crisis whose social and historical origins we have briefly indicated in our introductory remarks: the crisis in his republican, revolutionary views, a crisis which found a provisional solution in Jena when he came to accept the existing social order in its specifically Napoleonic form. In his Frankfurt period Hegel gropes towards something new and slowly but steadily dismantles the old; there is uncertainty, a quest—a genuine crisis.

Hegel was fully conscious of this himself, and both at the time and in his later writings he makes reference to his experience of crisis. It is typical of his later writings that Hegel speaks with the utmost frankness of the unhappy state of hypochondria, self-laceration and disintegration which he experienced. In the description in the *Encyclopaedia* of the different ages of man Hegel gives an account of adolescence and of the approach to manhood which draws heavily on the Frankfurt period. He says that the ideals of youth have a more or less subjective quality.

> 'The subjectivity of the substantive content of such an ideal implies not only an opposition to the world as it is, but also the urge to do away with this opposition by realizing the ideal.'

The transition of the youth from his ideal life into civil society involves a painful process of adaptation punctuated by crises.

> 'There is no easy escape . . . from this hypochondria. The later one is infected by it, the more serious its symptoms are. [Hegel's Frankfurt period fell between the ages of 27 and 30.] . . . In this morbid mood a man is reluctant to surrender his subjectivity, he is unable to overcome his antipathy for reality and so finds himself in a state of relative impotence which can easily turn into true impotence. Therefore, if a man wishes to survive, he must acknowledge that the world is independent and essentially *complete* . . .'[3]

Even more revealing, because it is more personal, is this description of the Frankfurt period in a letter of 1810:

> 'I know from my own experience this state of the mind or rather the moral reason once it has ventured with its interest and its fears into the chaotic realm of the phenomenal world . . . inwardly certain of its goal but as yet unclear and unspecific about it as a whole. I suffered from this hypochondria for a number of years to the point of total exhaustion; no doubt every man experiences such a turning-point in his life, the nocturnal point where his whole being contracts and he must force himself through the narrows until he becomes secure and certain of himself, secure in ordinary daily life, and if he has already made himself incapable of being fulfilled by that, then secure in a more inward, more noble existence.'[4]

The Frankfurt documents are even more explicit. The concrete human and social factors that triggered off the crisis are revealed much more clearly than in the more general reminiscences of later years. Thus a fragment of Hegel's pamphlet on *The German Constitution* begins with a description of the spiritual climate of the modern world.

> 'They [human beings] cannot live alone and man is always alone. . . . The state of a man whom the age has driven into an inner world will either be no more than a living death, if he confines himself to that world, or, if nature urges him back into life, there will be a sustained endeavour to annul the negative elements of the world as it is so as to enable him to discover and enjoy himself in it and to survive.'[5]

Hegel's most intimate confessions can be found in some letters that he wrote at the beginning of his stay in Frankfurt to Nanette Endel, a friend of his sister whom he had got to know in Stuttgart after leaving Berne. In a letter of 9 February 1797 he writes:

'. . . and since I find that it would be an utterly ungrateful task to set an example to people here and it is certain that St Anthony of Padua had greater success preaching to the fish than I would achieve by such a life here, I have resolved after lengthy meditation to make no attempt to improve these people but instead to follow the crowd . . .'

Other documents reveal that Hegel was on much better terms with the Frankfurt family where he was employed as a tutor than he had enjoyed with his pupils and their family in Berne. We have seen his brusque rejection of the Berne patriciate in his letter to Schelling. The present letter shows how profoundly Hegel had changed his external attitudes towards the people around him. It might be thought that the above quotation points to the purely tactical nature or even the outright hypocrisy of Hegel's relations with the people around him. However, such motives are quite alien to his character. A passage from another letter dated 2 July 1797 in which he talks to Nanette Endel of the change in his view of nature shows quite clearly that we are dealing with a much more fundamental change in his outlook as a whole:

'. . . and just as in Berne I fled into the arms of nature to reconcile myself with myself and with mankind so here I often seek refuge in the bosom of this ever-loyal mother so as to fall out with the people with whom I live here peaceably, and so that under her aegis I may become immune from their influence and frustrate any alliance with them.'[6]

These letters, particularly the latter, reveal the change in Hegel's attitude to the society of his day. At the same time we notice that this change contains an internal contradiction, or rather, an entire complex of contradictions from the very outset. Hegel himself only gradually became conscious of the character and the objective basis of these contradictions. Hence the tortured, hypochondriacal crisis-ridden mood of the Frankfurt period despite the fact that his personal circumstances were much more congenial than in Berne. I am not thinking here just of his external circumstances: intellectually he was far less isolated in Frankfurt than he had been in Berne; in the initial period he was in close contact with his friend Hölderlin and through him he made the acquaintance of other far from insignificant representatives of the younger literary and philosophical generation in Germany, such as Sinclair.[7]

On the other hand, the fact that these contradictions are essentially experienced and bound up with his personal fate rather than systematic and conceptual in nature leads to the preoccupation with philosophical problems already mentioned in which he advances from an individual experience to a conceptual generalization but in such a manner that the final conclusions reveal the entire process that led to them including the original experience that gave rise to them. In the fragment from *The German Constitution* already referred to we have seen an illustration of this approach. The reason for it is that Hegel is still on the road to becoming a dialectical philosopher. He does not yet regard the personal experience that triggers his thought as he will do later in Jena, as something whose objective origins and laws need to be examined. He sees it as an integral part of the problem under discussion. This is perfectly understandable since the problem he is tackling is his personal debate with society, his attempt to discover a place for himself within society.

Obviously, this is not just a personal problem. If it had merely belonged to Hegel's own biography it would not hold the great interest for us which it in fact possesses. But the contradiction with which Hegel is struggling in Frankfurt is objectively the same as that which engaged all the important thinkers and writers of the age in Germany. The solution to it constitutes the premise on which the classical literature and philosophy of the period is based and since this literature and philosophy have achieved international recognition it follows that the social contradiction at their roots must be more than a local German affair, even though its specific manifestations were determined by the actual conditions in Germany at the time.

What is at issue is the attitude of the great German humanists towards the bourgeois society that had triumphed in the French Revolution and in the Industrial Revolution in England, but which simultaneously had begun to reveal its horrifying, anti-cultural and prosaic aspects with a clarity very different from the period of heroic illusions before and during the French Revolution. The major bourgeois humanists in Germany now found themselves confronted by the complex and contradictory necessity of having both to recognize this bourgeois society, of accepting it as the only possible necessary and progressive reality, and at the same time to expose and denounce its contradictions critically and freely, rather than to capitulate and apologize for the inhumanity they entailed. In Goethe's *Wilhelm Meister* and *Faust*, in Schiller's *Wallenstein* and his aesthetic writings and in Hegel's *The Phenomenology of Mind* as well as his later works we see how German literary and philosophical classicism came to grips with these contradictions and proposed various solutions; the way in which they did so is proof of their world-historical stature—and at the same time it shows the limitations imposed on them by the horizons of the bourgeoisie in general and the backwardness of Germany in particular.

When Hegel, in the letter we have quoted, seeks refuge in nature so as to avoid being assimilated into his social environment we may regard this as a primitive, immediate expression of just this contradiction. On the one hand, his aim is thoroughly to understand and to function within the civil society of his day; on the other hand, he recoils from its inhuman, lifeless and life-denying aspects, refusing to see them as vital and life-giving. The contradiction that emerges in his earliest experiences in Frankfurt is therefore both a passionately grasped and experienced contradiction in his personal life and also, and inseparably from this, an important objective contradiction of his age.

The Frankfurt crisis, then, in Hegel's life and thought expresses itself in the difficulties of raising this contradiction to the plane of philosophical objectivity. Hegel's philosophical genius, his intellectual superiority over his contemporaries enable him to go further than the mere statement of a contradiction in his own personal experience; they enable him to recognize not just the contradictoriness of bourgeois society (within the bounds imposed on him by the general limitations of the bourgeois mind and the barriers of philosophical idealism), but beyond that to see in such contradictoriness the dialectical nature of all life, of all being and thought. The Frankfurt crisis ends with Hegel's earliest formulations of the dialectical method, albeit in a highly mystical version. It ends also —and not by chance—in a dialectical 'reconciliation' with the society of his age which fully acknowledges the underlying contradictions of that society. In a brief poem written either at the end of his stay in Frankfurt or shortly after he moved to Jena Hegel gives a very clear statement of the mood that enabled him to overcome the crisis:

'Kühn mag der Götter Sohn der Vollendung Kampf sich vertrauen,
Brich den Frieden mit dir, brich mit dem Werke der Welt!
Strebe, versuche du mehr als das Heut und das Gestern, so wirst du
Besseres nicht, als die Zeit, aber aufs Beste sie sein.'
[Boldly the son of the gods may join the battle for perfection
Break your peace with yourself, break with the works of the world!
Strive for, aspire to more than today and yesterday
Then you will be not better than the age, but the age at its best.][8]

NOTES
1  Marx/Engels, *The Holy Family*, p. 165f.
2  Marx, *The Jewish Question*. See Marx/Engels, *Die Heilige Familie*, Berlin 1953, pp. 41, 42, 45.
3  *Encyclopaedia*, p. 396 Addendum. *Werke*, Berlin 1845, VIII. Abt. Band II, p. 98.
4  Published in Rosenzweig, op. cit., Vol. I, p. 102. Rosenzweig has also published an extract from the manuscript reminiscences of the Hegelian scholar Gabler which recalls a conversation with Hegel that took place in 1805 and in which he expresses himself in a very

similar way. Ibid., p. 236.

5  Lasson, p. 139. We shall postpone our discussion of our reasons for assigning this fragment from *The German Constitution* to the Frankfurt period until we come to analyse these fragments in detail.

6  *Beiträge zur Hegelforschung*, ed. Lasson. Second issue, Berlin 1920, pp. 2, 7 and 11.

7  Isaac von Sinclair (1775–1815) was a poet and diplomat, known chiefly nowadays for his friendship with Hölderlin whom he cared for during the period of the latter's mental breakdown. He was also friendly with Hegel and wrote philosophical essays which attempted to mediate between Hegel and Fichte.—*Trans.*

8  Hoffmeister, p. 388.

# CHAPTER TWO

# Old and new in the first years in Frankfurt

ONE of the outstanding features of Hegel's character as a philosopher was his slow and gradual development. In the preceding chapter we emphasized the radical change in his outlook in order to give the reader a clear idea of the intellectual mood of his years in Frankfurt. In reality, however, this process was a gradual one, though he sometimes advanced in fits and starts. Many attitudes of his Berne period remained unaltered for a long time or were subject to only minor changes. Sometimes we find him modifying old ideas, old historical constructs without realizing clearly how far he has departed from the original pattern. An instance can be seen in his last work in Frankfurt: he wrote a new introduction to his principal essay in Berne, *The Positivity of the Christian Religion*, even though, as we shall see, his conception of positivity had undergone a complete transformation in the meantime. And what happened here is typical of his general development.

In particular, we must bear in mind that throughout this period Hegel kept faith with his republican convictions. Indeed, it can be asserted that Hegel did not 'reconcile' himself to a monarchy in the German style until confronted with the stability of the Restoration after the defeat of Napoleon. Until then we find a highly complex series of transitions which are not entirely reconstructible because of the loss of the most vital manuscripts. In general, however, we may say that his development proceeded along the lines of political developments in France, though with certain inevitable delays. The only reservation to be made here is that Hegel increasingly takes the theoretical and practical implications of the situation in Germany into account. This means that his political analyses gain in concreteness and immediacy, but also that the utopian character of his objectives and aspirations—given the backwardness of German conditions—constantly undermines his arguments or makes them disappear in a fog of speculation.

When Hegel left Berne for Frankfurt he took his republican convictions with him. His mood at that time is well conveyed by the poem *Eleusis* which he wrote to Hölderlin from Berne and which expresses his feelings about the prospect of their reunion. A few lines will suffice to give the reader the flavour of Hegel's mood:

'. . . der Gewissheit Wonne
des alten Bundes Treue fester, reifer noch zu finden,
des Bundes, den kein Eid besiegelte,
der freien Wahrheit nur zu leben, Frieden mit der Satzung,
die Meinung und Empfindung regelt, nie, nie einzugehen'.

[The certain bliss
of finding the old pact firmer, riper,
the pact sealed by no oath,
to live for the free truth alone
and never, never to make peace with laws
that prescribe thought and feeling.][1]

The very beginning of Hegel's stay in Frankfurt is marked by the appearance of his first printed work, one which on the whole still reflects his Berne attitudes. It was an annotated translation of a pamphlet by J. J. Cart, a Swiss lawyer, which waˢ concerned with a defence of the rights of the Vaudois against the Berne oligarchy. The canton of Vaud had been oppressed by Berne for centuries. An attempted uprising in the wake of the French Revolution had failed and had only brought sterner reactionary measures from the Berne oligarchy. The liberation of the canton came only in the course of the revolutionary wars at around the time when Hegel was engaged on his translation and commentary. In his preface Hegel makes explicit reference to this turn of events and evidently published his pamphlet with the intention of providing the arrogant forces of reaction in Germany with an image of the instability of their power. At the conclusion of his preface he writes:

> 'From a comparison of the contents of these letters with the latest events in the Vaud, from a contrast between the appearance of peace enforced in 1792 and the pride of the government in its victory with its real weakness in this land and its sudden downfall there, a whole host of practical lessons might be learnt; however, the events speak plainly enough for themselves: all that remains to be done is to appreciate them fully. Their cry echoes above the whole world: *Discite justitiam moniti*. But fate will smite hard those who are deaf.'[2]

These remarks show that Hegel's outlook had not changed since he left Berne. But Falkenheim, who discovered the pamphlet, has already attempted to exploit certain elements in it to disprove Hegel's revolutionary tendencies. He bases his argument on the fact that in the preface Hegel defends the 'ancient rights' of the Vaudois against the Bernese oligarchy. He declares that no revolutionary would do that. A further symptom of the non-revolutionary character of the pamphlet follows from this, namely the historical method of presentation. This argument is based on the old reactionary prejudice widespread among German professors to the effect that historicism is an invention of the reaction, that it began with Burke and the French philosophers of the Restoration in contrast to the preceding age which was essentially anti-historical. There is no point in pursuing this theory, especially as the reader can see from Part I the extent of Hegel's historical orientation in his early revolutionary and republican views and the Cart translation is no exception to this.

No less untrue is the deduction made from Hegel's defence of 'ancient rights'. The very great importance of such struggles for 'ancient rights' can be seen in the events leading up to the French Revolution itself. Of course, the entire development is highly ambivalent. In part it involves the defence of feudal privileges against the levelling down by absolutism in the name of economic and social progress; in part it concerns the struggle to protect the rights of working people jeopardized by the process of primitive accumulation as initiated by feudalism and capitalism in league together. A further aspect of such traditional privileges is that they can provide a certain protection against the arbitrary encroachments of the absolute monarchy. The French parliaments, for example, were essentially reactionary institutions who sternly resisted every attempt to reform taxation or abolish even the most iniquitous feudal privileges and in consequence they attracted the fiercest criticism from all the important members of the French Enlightenment. But at the same time, since they were the only organized foci of resistance to the encroachments of absolutism they enjoyed tremendous popularity in the years leading up to the French Revolution.[3] Marx and Engels even go so far in their polemic against Guizot as to single out this 'conservative' element of France in the period leading up to the Revolution as its most characteristic feature.[4]

It is evident that in countries more backward than Switzerland or Germany the defence of 'ancient rights' plays an even greater if also more ambivalent role. But however that may be there can be do doubt that when Hegel takes up the defence of the Vaudois against the Bernese oligarchy he is not doing so from an anti-revolutionary position. No doubt his defence of 'ancient rights' is not undertaken from an explicit and consistent democratic point of view. He does not make that distinction here any more than Schiller does a few years later when he dramatizes the defence of the 'ancient rights' of the people in *Wilhelm Tell*. It is only when we come to the young Marx's important articles in the *Rheinische Zeitung* that we find a consistent revolutionary and democratic line which distinguishes between the 'ancient rights' of the working people and the privileges of exploiters.

Although we have seen that this pamphlet heralds no change in Hegel's position this does not detract from the importance of his notes for an understanding of his development. We should just mention briefly here that his hatred of the aristocratic regime in Berne is just as fierce as in the letter to Schelling previously quoted, but is much more firmly founded on factual evidence. The diligence with which Hegel has assembled information about the Bernese economy, system of taxation etc. is quite remarkable. We obtain here a glimpse into his workshop and can gain some idea of the prodigious effort that later went into acquiring his encyclopaedic knowledge of almost every field. These economic studies also have an additional, negative significance: it is notable that they are still no more than purely empirical collections of factual information together with political commentaries. The idea of generalizations about economic problems clearly has not yet occurred to Hegel.[5] There is also a further feature of biographical importance in that we find Hegel occupying himself for the first time with conditions in England. At this stage he does so purely in the context of the politics of the French Revolution. He comments on a statement by Cart who attacks the notion that a low rate of taxation provides an index of the happiness of a people. Cart points out that in England, which he greatly admired, taxation was heavy but the people freely administered their own affairs. Hegel concurred in this view and even reinforced it by pointing to the significance of the tax on tea as a cause in the outbreak of the American War of Independence. The point here was that in his view the tax was unimportant in itself but that the struggle for independence was sufficient to launch the revolution. He diverges from Cart only in his estimate of English liberty. He mentions the acts of repression in England following the French Revolution, the weakness of Parliament vis-à-vis the government, the suspension of constitutional safeguards and the abrogation of personal freedoms and the rights of citizens. He says in conclusion:

'Thanks to these measures the prestige of the English nation has declined even among many of her greatest admirers.'[6]

We may regard this work then as a late echo of Hegel's Berne period.

All the more striking is the change in his thought, his style and his approach to philosophical problems in the fragments dating from the same period or a little later which have been published by Nohl.[7] In all of them signs of the Frankfurt crisis are clearly visible. We have already suggested that Hegel's terminology was never so fluid and confused as during this period. He takes up concepts, experiments with them, modifies them and drops them again. Just because his thought begins to concern itself with the contradictoriness of life his notes seem at first glance to contain nothing but a confused tangle of contradictions. The source of the confusion lies in the predominantly personal nature of his approach to reality. It is easy to understand how the opacity of the Frankfurt fragments has proved to be a regular hunting-ground for reactionary interpretations and for attempts to assimilate Hegel to the reactionary mysticism of the Romantics. Dilthey's celebrated book has provided the model for the entire literature on Hegel in the Age of Imperialism. These critics managed to remove almost all reference to contemporary events and social problems even from the Berne writings so it will not come as a surprise to see the Frankfurt fragments described as 'mystical pantheism' (Dilthey). This makes it all the more pressing to isolate the—admittedly meagre and confused—core of rationality they do possess, their bearing on reality and the real problems of bourgeois society.

When Hegel now comes to examine the relationship between modern civil society and the individual he finds his old Berne problem of positivity standing in his way. In their struggle against the social order of feudal absolutism the humanists came to conceive of civil society as the world freely created and owned by men themselves. Undoubtedly they had many illusions about this world. The actual emergence of a developed bourgeois society in France and England gave a new twist to both these convictions and to the illusions accompanying them. Society appeared even more strongly as the product and moreover the constantly re-created product of mankind's own activity. At the same time, society engendered a whole series of manifestations, forms of life and institutions that confronted the individual with a dead objectivity which inhibited his personal development and killed off everything that the humanists postulated as essential for the individual and for relations between individuals. As bourgeois ideologists the outstanding German humanists of the age found themselves compelled to accept the general foundations of the society that had come into being. But at the same time they were implacably opposed to all that was dead and deadening in it. However, their opposition, their criticism never went beyond the horizon of bourgeois society itself, at least it never did so directly. On the contrary, their efforts were directed towards the discovery of forms of subjective activity, the creation of types of human beings and forms of life with whose aid all that was dead and deadening could be annulled *within* the framework of bourgeois society. Goethe's great novel *Wilhelm Meister's Apprenticeship* is the greatest poetic expression of these aspirations. And the appearance of *Faust* thirty years later testifies to Goethe's life-long struggle with this antagonism between humanism and bourgeois society in the context of the solutions available at that stage of history. It is not by chance that Pushkin described *Faust* as the 'Iliad of our age'.

In Frankfurt we see how Hegel's view of the problem of positivity shifted in this direction. In Berne the problem had been dealt with entirely in the context of the philosophy of society and history: positivity had appeared to Hegel to be the product of the decline of mankind symbolized by the emergence of Christianity and civil society. In his view only the revolutionary rebirth of the republics of antiquity could lead to the abolition of positivity. Such a revolution would be sudden and its success total, for in his view the ancient city-states in their prime were completely free of anything resembling positivity.

The question now presents itself differently. His new starting-point is the life of the individual. The individual lives in a society which abounds in positive institutions, positive relations between men and indeed men who have been deadened by positivity and transformed into objects. Hence the question has ceased to be: how can this positive society be smashed and replaced by a radically different type of society? On the contrary, the question he now poses is this: how can the individual in this society lead a human life, i.e. how can the positivity in himself, in other people and in his relations to people and things be eliminated? Thus the social problem is transformed into one of individual morality, into the problem of what shall we do? How shall we live? And the underlying aim here is to bring about a reconciliation with bourgeois society and a (perhaps partial) abolition of its positive character. (This seemingly brings Hegel closer to the Kantian ethic than he had been in Berne. But we shall see later that this greater proximity only serves to bring the actual philosophical disagreements between Kant and Hegel out into the open.)

The category which provided a focus for Hegel's philosophical interests throughout this period was *love*. Here, once again, we find a category which seems to establish a certain link between the young Hegel and Feuerbach (even though Feuerbach could have had no knowledge of these early works of Hegel's which had not yet been published). Since a number of modern philosophers (such as Löwith) attach great importance to the alleged similarities between Feuerbach and the young Hegel, it is necessary to establish their *opposition* on this point. For however vague and dubious Feuerbach's ethics of love may be, however much it tends to lapse into idealism (as Engels has convincingly demonstrated) it yet remains true that, epistemologically, the relationship between I and Thou on which it is based is conceived in the spirit of materialism. What counts for Feuerbach is that the Thou is independent of the consciousness of the I. His ethics of love does indeed lapse into idealist excesses, it does obscure the contradictions of bourgeois society, but for all that it does stand firmly on a materialist base: its recognition that all objects (and hence all other people) are independent of *my* consciousness. By contrast, for Hegel the entire meaning of love is that through it just this independence is overcome. The fundamental idealistic flaw in Hegel's conception of positivity is that it can be overcome only by overcoming objectivity itself and from this it follows that every objectivity not directly produced by consciousness must contain an element of positivity. This defect is particularly in evidence in his rhapsodically mystical conception of love and makes the transition into religion inevitable.

'Religion is one with love. The beloved is not opposed to us, he is at
one with out very being; in him we see only ourselves—and then he
is again not us—he is a miracle beyond our comprehension.'[8]

We can see that the two conceptions of love rest on diametrically
opposed theories of knowledge. But this must not blind us to the fact that
the concept of love is in neither case an accidental phenomenon and that
its social foundations are similar in both thinkers. However, its social significance is different and this is because of the 40-years' interval separating the two and the consequent differences in the state of the economy
and the class struggle. In both instances love is a vague idealistic concept
embodying the humanistic, bourgeois and revolutionary demand for a
many-sided, fully developed human being who enjoys correspondingly
rich, developed, many-sided and human relations with his fellow
humans. On the other hand, the vagueness, the idealistic extravagance of
the notion is a symptom of their mistaken belief that these aspirations can
be realized within bourgeois society. In the 1840s, however, when the
proletarian movement was already gathering momentum and the era of
scientific socialism was being born such a delusion meant something
quite different from what it meant at the turn of the nineteenth century.
When the followers of Feuerbach among the 'True' socialists attempted
to make his ethics of love yield socialist conclusions they inadvertently
revealed the narrow reactionary illusions implicit in the category.

But at the time when Hegel was concerned with the problem there
was no such sharp conflict with the progressive tendencies of the age. As
we shall see, in the course of his later development Hegel came to adopt a
much more comprehensive and realistic attitude towards bourgeois society. But at this stage the mysticism and muddle of his Frankfurt writings was an essential step towards grasping its contradictory nature. And
just because the concept of love has such a *transitional character* we must
regard it in a different light.

Furthermore, we must bear in mind that in the Germany of the time it
simply was not possible to see through the illusory nature of the categories that clothed universal human aspirations in the language of idealism.
Economically backward as Germany was it was not possible to define
the progressive nature of capitalism in purely economic terms as the
classical English economists did. The realization that progress lay in the
development of the material forces of production could only be attained
in England itself, and even there it had to wait some decades for its supreme formulation from a bourgeois standpoint, in the works of
Ricardo.

But if the advanced development of the English economy could give
birth to the supreme achievements of classical economic theory, it also
prevented the conscious dialectical formulation of the contradictions and

antagonisms in capitalism. It is true that Smith and Ricardo did not shrink from giving expression to all the contradictions that they perceived and they present their views with the unhesitating love of truth typical of all major thinkers; they are unperturbed if one perceived fact conflicts with another equally well-established one. Hence Marx is quite right when he writes of Ricardo:

> 'With the master what is new and significant develops vigorously amid the "manure" of contradictions, out of the contradictory phenomena. The underlying contradictions themselves testify to the richness of the living foundation from which the theory itself developed.'[9]

But contradictoriness is only present materially, as it were *de facto*, and nothing could be further from the minds of the classical English economists than to fix on contradiction as the fundamental fact of economic life and hence of the methodology of political economy.

But the awareness that life is based on contradictions is the fundamental problem faced by classical German literature and philosophy. Since their starting-point is the contradiction between their humanist ideals and a bourgeois reality full of the vestiges of feudalism it is true of them too that the 'manure of contradictions' forms the basis of their problems and solutions. The entire range of human existence becomes their theme; they can experience, shape and think through all the contradictions that arise within this great complex. Since the economic basis of these contradictions does not and cannot become visible to them they lose themselves in idealist speculations. But by the same token, since the intellectual side of this movement is consciously lived through, i.e. since their starting-point is the living experience of contradictoriness, of one contradiction arising from the solution of its predecessor, their path leads them to the first, if idealistic, formulation of dialectics.

The antithesis between truly living human beings developing all their talents and human beings in bourgeois society who are deformed into the automata of the world of commodities and reduced to one-sided 'specialists' performing a single narrow function within the capitalist division of labour—this antithesis forms the ground theme of Goethe's *Wilhelm Meister*. It is not just exemplified in the contrast between Wilhelm and Werner, his boyhood friend and a businessman. It can be seen also in Goethe's presentation of art and in particular of the theatre where he brilliantly depicts the destructive effects of the division of labour on a wide range of people. Moreover, it is typical of the state of Germany at the time that Goethe does not entirely reject religious solutions to these contradictions. The life of the canoness described in the *Confessions of a Beautiful Soul* gives a moving account of such a solution in which a sensitive woman holds herself aloof from ordinary life with the aid of religion while through love she sustains a living human relationship with her fellow human beings. Of course, the religious solution is by no means Goethe's final word. On the contrary, the canoness is compared unfavourably with those who enter into the ordinary life of the capitalist world. The ideal figures in the novel are Lothario and Nathalie who succeed in sustaining the human vitality of love whilst actively participating in the ordinary life of bourgeois society.

While in Frankfurt Hegel could not achieve anything comparable to this. The religious solution played a far more prominent part in his thought during this transitional phase: it was accepted much more uncritically and a higher historical and human value was placed on it. But we shall see that even here the contrast is not as great as it first seems.

With a forthrightness more typical of his Berne writings Hegel begins by opposing the subjective, the human and the living to the objective, the dead and the positive. But his new approach now increasingly dissolves these rigid opposites into flexible and elastic contradictions. On the one hand, this increases the opaque mysticism of his thought; throughout the entire period in Frankfurt religion remains the authentic sphere of real life, of true vitality and of the genuine negation of what is dead and 'positive'. On the other hand, the concrete oppositions of the subjective and the objective give rise to a series of increasingly complex contradictions which point in a quite different direction from the religious sphere.

What we have here in fact is the discrepancy noted by Engels between Hegel's system and his method. More precisely this discrepancy can be located in the critique, which long remained unconscious and, as it were, dormant, of the religious solution to contradictions. As we shall see, what Hegel is seeking in religion is the highest form of love, i.e. a reality permeated with human subjectivity and cleansed of all social positivity. But the very process of giving up his earlier hostility to Christianity leads to a situation in which those features of Christianity and of religion in general which are hostile to life and which preach escape from life present themselves with increasing vividness to his mind. And since his foremost aim is to reconcile the individual with the concrete reality of society as it is, he must inevitably become more and more aware of the weaknesses in the religious attitude. The trouble with it is that it does nothing to mitigate, let alone eliminate, the positivity of the world as it is, and that in consequence it is simply a complement of that positivity. Hence seen in this light religious subjectivity is merely another way of surrendering one's full humanity.

'If dependence on an object constitutes one pole, then the other extreme is fear of the objects, flight from them, fear of union with them, extreme subjectivity.'[10]

The view that pure subjectivity, flight from the objects into religion, is on the same plane as positivity is a view destined to play a crucial role in Hegel's Frankfurt period. As we shall see, it introduces a contradiction into Hegel's view of Christianity and, in particular, of the life and teaching of Jesus. And looking beyond Frankfurt we shall find Hegel arguing in Jena that Fichte's subjective idealism and French materialism are two false extremes which nevertheless represent equally important tendencies of the age.

For the time being, however, he draws no significant conclusions. His chief interest is to give a highly critical picture of those men who have fallen victim to the forces of positivity and conversely to praise the redemptive power of love.

'Since something dead here forms part of the love relationship, love is girt by matter alone, and this matter is quite indifferent to it . . . and while the objects by which he is confronted change, they are never absent . . . this is the ground of his tranquillity in the face of loss and his sure confidence that his loss will be made good because it can be made good. This attitude makes matter something absolute in man's eyes; but, of course, if he never existed, then nothing would exist for him, and what necessity was there for his existence? That he might wish to exist is intelligible enough, because beyond that collection of restricted experiences which make up his consciousness there is nothing whatever . . . but a bleak void and man cannot bear to think himself in that nullity.'[11]

This rather ponderous and confused account of the state of mind of the average man in bourgeois society is now followed by a statement of Hegel's ideal of love. For man in bourgeois society the entire world consists of impenetrable, incomprehensible objects mechanically separated from men and from each other; he drifts among them in empty, unsatisfying activity. He has no real, substantial relationship with the objects, with his fellow-men or even with himself. Love, on the other hand, is in Hegel's eyes the principle that transcends these dead barriers and creates living relationships between men and this in turn serves to transform men into living things for themselves.

'True union, or love proper, exists only between living beings who are alike in power and thus in one another's eyes living beings from every point of view; in no respect is either dead for the other. . . . In love the separate does still remain, but as something united and no longer as something separate and the living senses the living.'[12]

It is indicative of the continuity in Hegel's development that a number of expressions in these extracts go back not just to Berne but, more specifically, to the excerpts from Forster. Instances are the emphasis on the necessity for equality between lovers, the assertion in the passage following our quotation that man in bourgeois society is subject to an alien power from whom he implores mercy in fear and trembling. However, such expressions have undergone a change of meaning. Equality for Forster and for Hegel at the time when he made the excerpts meant above all political equality. Now, however, Hegel is much more concerned about equality of behaviour or attitude towards society. The social content of equality, namely equal power, acquires, as we shall see at once, a new, problematical dimension: it depends on the material, economic position of the lovers. But for the moment Hegel only poses this question in order to sweep it aside once more before advancing towards the unity that abolishes all separateness between men and creates a truly unified life for them.

It is easy to understand why the reactionary neo-Hegelians of the Age of Imperialism should have attempted to make capital from the emphasis Hegel gave to such categories as love, life, etc. Eager to transform Hegel into a Romantic philosopher of life (*Lebensphilosoph*) they ignore the transitional phase of crisis in Frankfurt and seize upon the categories which arise from it, but which later disappear from his writings, in order to give a Romantic, vitalist interpretation to his entire oeuvre. But quite apart from the inadmissibility of this extrapolation such an interpretation does not even fit the Frankfurt period properly. Even in Frankfurt Hegel was no Romantic. It is not for nothing that we have stressed the similarities between the humanism of his approach and that of Goethe and Schiller; the existence of these parallels should suffice to show the untenability of the legend.

When we come to speak of Hegel's stay in Jena we shall see how remote Hegel remained from the aspirations of the Romantics even though Jena was at the time the focal point of the Romantic movement.

As for vitalism, the so-called philosophy of life, Hegel's own later writings make his hostility towards it quite clear. As early as Jena he vigorously criticized Friedrich Heinrich Jacobi, the most typical representative of this tendency at the time, and he never abandoned his dislike of it. And even in Frankfurt, as a careful scrutiny of the fragments will show, he never really accepted the basic assumption of *Lebensphilosophie*, viz. the idea of 'immediate knowledge'. It is true, of course, that Hegel was engaged in a conflict with the rationalist 'philosophy of reflection' of the day and the Frankfurt period in particular is full of the first great debate with the philosophy of Kant. In like fashion at the end of the Frankfurt period when his conception of positivity had become more historical and dialectical, Hegel directed his criticism at the rationalism of the Enlightenment. But this is not to say that he ever embraced the contemporary 'philosophy of life'. We must not allow ourselves to

be led astray here by concepts such as 'love' and 'life'. Hegel's first biographer, Rosenkranz, was often guilty of over-simplification in his
efforts to approximate Hegel's philosophy to the subjective idealism of
Kant, but since he was necessarily unfamiliar with recent philosophical
movements he was able to see more clearly than the later neo-Hegelians
that what Hegel meant, in Frankfurt, by 'life' was basically the same as
what, in Jena, he designated 'Sittlichkeit' (ethical life), i.e. the concrete
totality of man's actions in society.[13]

It is quite true that Hegel does oppose love to reflection in Frankfurt.
However, he does not follow the contemporary fashion of setting up
'immediate knowledge' as an absolute negation of reflection. Instead he
proposes love as a dialectical annulment of the reflective stage. Obviously it would be wrong to imply that Hegel had consciously and consistently worked out this dialectical relationship at the beginning of his
stay in Frankfurt. But his notes make it quite clear that in his account of
the relations between love and reflection he has a glimmering of his later
definition of 'Aufheben' as both 'annul' and 'preserve'.

> 'This unity is therefore perfect life because in it even reflection gets its
> due; in the original, undeveloped unity the possibility of reflection, of
> cleavage, still stood over against it; in this unity, however, unity and
> cleavage are united, they are a simple living thing that had been
> opposed to itself (and still feels itself so opposed), but has not rendered
> this opposition absolute. In love one living being senses another living
> being. Thus in love all tasks, the self-destructive one-sidedness of
> reflection and the infinite opposition of an unconscious, undeveloped
> unity, are resolved.[14]

Such passages are significant not just as refutations of the distortions of
the reactionary neo-Hegelians but because they give a clear indication of
the stage Hegel had reached in his development. They show how rapidly
the experienced contradiction with bourgeois society and the internal
conflict with himself arising from it led Hegel to a dialectical understanding of contradiction. For him to emerge 'suddenly' as a fully-
fledged dialectician all that he needed was to achieve self-consciousness
about the ideas that had fought their way confusedly to the surface in the
course of these arguments. It is this situation that explains why many
bourgeois historians have greeted Hegel's 'sudden' maturity in Jena with
such astonishment.

But, of course, Hegel's development into a dialectician proceeded
very unevenly. The internal contradictions in his philosophical position
can be seen most clearly on the issue of reflection. As we have seen, his
conception of love is designed to bring about the dialectical supersession
of reflection, i.e. love is thought of as existing on a higher plane than the
original 'unconscious, undeveloped unity' precisely because it contains

reflection within it. But at the same time we find that Hegel's religious mysticism often gains the upper hand and at such times love appears as a total, ultimate 'union' from which every last trace of cleavage, of reflection has been eliminated. Such diametrically opposed solutions are in evidence not only in the earlier part of the Frankfurt period but also right at the very end, in the *Fragment of a System* which concludes this phase of his development. And such contradictions can be found not only in his view of love but also in his view of the religious life even though the latter was supposed to resolve the contradictions in the former.

Hegel's efforts in the quoted passage to secure a dialectical resolution of the relationship between reflection and love is important in yet another respect, since it throws light on the social implications of the profound gulf separating him from the Romantics and vitalists of the day. When Hegel refuses to accept life as something immediately given and chooses to see it instead as an objective which can only be achieved after the annulment and subsequent preservation of reflection, what he is after is a philosophical rescue action to preserve humanist ideals *within* capitalist society, a development or transfiguration of capitalist society which would make fully human relations a possibility. His emphasis on the need to preserve reflection while annulling it shows that unlike the reactionary Romantics he did not yearn for a primitive pre-capitalist society, and unlike Schelling with his concept of 'intellectual intuition', he did not imagine that any genuine fulfilment or understanding of life could be achieved outside social relations, 'independently' of them, as it were, shaking them off and leaving them behind one. It is evident, and the subsequent history of German philosophy confirms it, that although each of these two tendencies frequently inveighed against the other they yet aspired to one and the same goal: to solve the contradictions of bourgeois society by reverting to a more primitive, pre-capitalist form of social organization (the philosophy of the post-1815 Restoration). We have repeatedly drawn attention to the illusions cherished by Hegel and we shall later have occasion to criticize them when their social implications manifest themselves more concretely. But all these illusions are not enough to justify the establishment of a bond between Hegel and the reactionary Restoration of his day. For all his illusions Hegel went in an entirely opposed direction, socially and hence also philosophically.

Hegel's attitude to bourgeois society is most clearly expressed where he abandons his extravagant religious generalizations and his vague language of experience and investigates the problem of love finding fulfilment in the world of reality. This brings him at once to the problem of possessions and property. We should remind ourselves here that in Berne he had taken up a very general historical view of such matters: he held that the relatively equitable distribution of property formed the

economic basis of republican liberty in antiquity, and that the growing
inequality of the later classical period was the basis of its decline, of the
corruption of the *citoyen* of antiquity into the modern *bourgeois* and the
private individual. Hegel now finds himself compelled to scrutinize
the problem of property in a more concrete fashion. At first he does so
primitively in terms of mere experience. We know that in the course of
his historical and political studies Hegel had collected economic data,
too, but at this stage this was a mere heap of empirical information from
which he made direct political inferences. In harmony with this his first
interest in property was to discover its immediate effects on the psychological and moral life of man. That is to say, he regarded property as
something dead and 'positive', something incapable of an organic connection with any living, subjective activity. The bond between property
and labour was something that did not enter into his thoughts during
these years. He thought of property only as a means of enjoyment or, at
best, of personal power.

Obviously it was not really possible to establish a really living relationship between such a notion of property and the highly abstract subjectivity of his conception of love. More interesting is the fact that Hegel
was at pains to establish such a relationship. He was aware that love must
be realized in society as it is, i.e. by people who either do or do not own
property and who for the most part own different amounts of it. And
although he sees property as the home of death and positivity, i.e. as
something diametrically opposed to love he does make the attempt to
study their interrelations.

> 'Yet the lovers are connected with much that is dead; external objects
> belong to each of them. This means that a lover stands in relation to
> things that are opposed to him in his own eyes as objects and oppo-
> sites; this is why lovers are capable of a multiplex opposition in the
> course of their multiplex acquisition and possession of property and
> rights. . . . Since possession and property make up such an important
> part of men's life, cares and thoughts, even lovers cannot refrain from
> reflection on this aspect of their relations.'[15]

Given the primitive nature of these economic concepts and the
psychological interpretation of the relations between men and property
Hegel could not get beyond a superficial compromise. What is important is that he saw that the problem itself could not be side-stepped. The
solution he fixes on here is that lovers should own property jointly.

But no less typical of Hegel's sober realism is his presentiment that this
solution is illusory. In a marginal note on the passage just quoted he adds:

> 'By pooling their property . . . the joint owners create the illusion
> that their particular rights have been annulled; at bottom, however, a

right is retained to the part of the property that is not directly used; only this right is not asserted. Where property is held in common things are not the property of any one person, but ownership, the right to a portion is concealed in the relationship.'[16]

Thus Hegel perceives that the annulment of the positivity of property through joint-ownership on the part of lovers is no true annulment.

Hegel's realism, his uninhibited criticism and demolition of his own extravagant and tortuous conclusions is evident also in his occasional realization of the transitory, momentary nature of love.

'This unity, (the child) however, is only a point; a seed; the lovers cannot so contribute to it as to make it a manifold in itself from the start. Their union is free from all inner division; in it there is no working on an opposite. Everything which gives the newly begotten child a manifold life and a specific existence, it must draw into itself, set over against itself, and unify with itself.'[16]

The point is clear enough: even though Hegel places love in the very centre of his thought at this stage he is very far from glorifying it in the Romantic style. He regards it as the highest point of existence; it alone can overcome all that is dead and 'positive' in the world. At the same time he perceives that no higher reality can be based on it which would provide a real counter-weight to the positivity of bourgeois society. In the course of his later development in Frankfurt he treats the absence of love as an absence of objectivity. He desires to confront the dead positivity of the world with a non-positive, living objectivity. His old contrast of the two ages now becomes an internal contrast within bourgeois society. This leads to an attempt to elevate the non-positive objectivity of religion above the merely living subjectivity of love. We shall return later to the contradictions that result from this procedure. Here we need only mention that at this point he looks for and discovers another solution for the inadequacy of purely subjective love, a solution that remains decisive for his later socio-philosophical writings: love as the basis of marriage and the family. Immediately after the lines we have just quoted he adds:

'Thus the process is: unity, separated opposites, reunion. After their union the lovers separate again, but in the child their union has become unseparated.'

And to the word 'reunion' he appended this note:

'The child is the parents themselves.'[17]

Here, then, is the germ of Hegel's theory of the family as the nucleus of bourgeois society.

Thus through the confusion and the contradictions of these early fragments it is possible to discern the first outlines of his view of society.
More precisely, they enable us to glimpse the pressures and tendencies
that led to his later conception of civil society. We shall see that the constant theme in his development is the search for a dialectical connection
between the apparently lifeless objects and institutions of society, a connection that would divest objectivity of its deadness and allow it to
become manifest as the premise and product of the activity of the subject,
i.e. that would conceive of society and history as mankind's own world,
the product of man's own activity. Up to now only the first, very modest
and rather obscure steps have been taken, and this applies both to the
content and the method. Hegel's knowledge of the structure of modern
civil society is still very vague, very empirical and far removed from any
grasp of its underlying laws. And parallel with this his method is scarcely
more than a vague search for the living connections between the subject
and the objective world of society. Presentiments of the dialectical interconnections occur from time to time and are then lost in the mystical
haze of religion.

His ruling principle at this time was still the rigid opposition of subject
and object; though there was too the passionate desire to overcome its
dualism. Right from the start of his stay in Frankfurt Hegel looked for a
mode of activity in bourgeois society that would satisfy his humanist
ideals and would nevertheless lead to activity *within* bourgeois society.
His philosophical formula was to lead to a revitalization of society from
within and not by importing any extraneous principle into society; the
dead machinery was to be brought to life. The road from death to life,
however, turns out to be the road which leads to the discovery of all the
contradictions in bourgeois society, albeit with the intention of resolving
them within that society itself. This is the road on which Hegel seeks the
reconciliation of mankind, of the ideals of humanity with bourgeois society, and right from the start, as soon as these problems emerge, we are
in a position to perceive both the strengths and weaknesses of Hegel's
view of society.

Given its rather confused basis in emotion and experience, Hegel's
present emphasis on vitality must inevitably lead him straight into the
arms of religion. We have already noted his greater affinity with Christianity during this period as contrasted with his brisk rejection of it in
Berne. If, as we have argued, love is now identical with religion, or, as
he will soon formulate the matter, if love is the road to religion, then it is
clear that reconciliation with Christianity is the goal he is making for.
Here too we find him taking a direction that he will adhere to his whole
life long. It would be going too far, however, to take all too literally the
reactionary interpretations, which derive ultimately from the right-

Hegelians among his own pupils, to the effect that Hegel was, or became, the philosopher of Protestantism. (In recent years Georg Lasson has taken up this theme with great enthusiasm and has criticized even the most reactionary neo-Hegelians if they ventured to 'underestimate' the strength of Hegel's Protestantism.)

Hegel's relations with Christianity were never unambiguous or free from contradictions or reservations. In the course of our study of the Frankfurt period we shall see that he was forced to get to grips with Christianity and above all with the personality of its founder, and that the religious categories of Christianity are of the highest importance for his entire philosophy. But we shall also see that his analysis culminates in the discovery of an insoluble tragic contradiction in the life and teaching of Jesus, and further, that the climax of Hegel's religious thought at this time is not by any means to be equated with Christianity. On the contrary, as late as Jena we shall still encounter fragments on the development of the various religions which go beyond Christianity and look forward to the birth of a new third faith. When we come to look at these later writings we shall have occasion to point out the ambiguities in his view of Christianity and religion in general, ambiguities that characterize even his very last statements on this problem. But for an understanding of the present phase it is enough if we establish that Hegel has abandoned his earlier rejection of Christianity and if, on the other hand, we maintain that what Hegel was looking for in religion in Frankfurt was that living unity of contradictions which represented the highest form of life to him at a time when his thought was rapidly maturing. The contradictory nature of this view inspired his basic line at the time: the tendency to absorb philosophy into religion. (The reversal of this process is one of the outstanding changes that took place in his thought in Jena.)

The new view of Christianity is not without its effect on his general philosophical and historical position. We shall just indicate briefly the most important changes. In Berne the historical scheme he had favoured was one in which the collapse of freedom in the city-states of antiquity had led to the decadent age of Christianity. In this process the Jewish origins of Christianity had been given the subordinate role of an immediate cause. The decisive factor was the political, economic and moral decay of the Roman Empire. As the progenitor of the religion of the new epoch in world history the Jews were treated only as a nation of equal degeneracy, able therefore to bring into being a religion that would supply the needs of a degenerate mankind. Now, however, Hegel begins to take a greater interest in the origins of Judaism and he devotes more attention to the similarities and differences between Judaism and Christianity. This extension of his historical interests is the first step towards his later philosophy of history in which the history of classical antiquity is preceded by a lengthy analysis of the Orient.

In the early years of his stay in Frankfurt his treatment of the Orient has relatively little to do with history. It involves little more than an historico-philosophical analysis of Jewish traditions as contained in the Bible. Nevertheless, a number of points emerge that will be important for his later historical views. For example, his analysis proceeds from the premise that the Jews differ from the Greeks primarily because of their 'estrangement from nature'. We have here the germ of his later view of the East, but even apart from that there is the very remarkable, if rather elliptical aphorism that this estrangement (*Entzweiung*)

'necessarily results in the birth of the state etc'.[18]

What is important for Hegel's later development is the perception that the state *comes into being* when the contradictions in society reach a certain point. In Berne the state of antiquity appeared to him to be the product of an age without internal social contradictions; it was the emergence and intensification of contradictions that led to the downfall of the state. Here we see the seeds of his later more dialectical and historical view, albeit in an inflexible and highly mystified form.

We can see the change in his views of the historical role of the state and the relationship of the citizen to the state even more clearly in another passage from the same fragment, *The Spirit of Judaism*. In order to understand it fully we must remind ourselves of Hegel's view in Berne. He had held then that people can only be said to have a relation to the state in a democratic republic in which the *citoyen* freely gives himself to it. The state may be said to be in decay when despotism rules and the citizens are purely private individuals incapable of any relation to it. Now, too, he emphasizes the utter contrast between the republics of antiquity and the Jewish theocracy. But at the same time he talks of the establishment of the kingdoms of Judah and Israel in these terms:

'The individual was entirely excluded from an active interest in the state; the political equality of the citizens was the reverse of republican equality, it was only the equality of insignificance. Not until the Kings do we find, together with the inequality that they introduced, a definite relation to the state on the part of many subordinates; many acquired a significance with respect to those beneath them and for some there was at least the possibility of acquiring such a significance.'[19]

This passage, too, is very confused, but so much is clear that Hegel now believed that the greater inequality under the monarchy did create stronger bonds with the state than the earlier, abstract equality of the primitive theocracy.

In other words, Hegel now begins to see that the classes and estates that arise in the course of history have an essential, determining influence on the relations between people and the state. In Berne he had regarded all class differentiations as symptoms of fragmentation and the decline of the state. Now, when he is striving to understand the nature of modern civil society he must obviously realize that the real links joining the various classes and estates in a simple whole are a constitutive part of modern society. He does not grasp this fully until the Jena period and this view does not receive its final definition until much later, in the *Philosophy of Right* in 1821. But it is important to see the germ of this idea in these early discussions of civil society.

Our last quotation shows that Hegel held fast to the evaluation of political life of antiquity that he had worked out in Berne. Nor was he to modify it later on; the only thing that does change is the place of antiquity in his historical scheme. He comes increasingly to regard classical civilization as something irretrievably lost, and this goes hand in hand with his growing understanding of the necessary origins and determinants of modern society.

In Frankfurt, however, his dominant religious bias creeps into his view of antiquity. In the search for a religious, non-positive objectivity Hegel harks back to Greek religion and sees in its animism a model for his own aspirations. But more interesting than that is his advance from that line of thought to a consideration of the problems of necessity and contingency, of subject and object.

'Where subject and object—or freedom and nature are thought of as unified, so that nature is freedom and subject and object are inseparable, there is the divine; such an ideal is the goal of every religion. A deity is at once subject and object; one may not say of it that it is a subject in contrast to the objects, or that it has objects. Theoretical systems become entirely objective, opposed to the subject; practical activity destroys the object and is entirely subjective—in love alone is one at one with the object; it neither exercises mastery, nor is it mastered. This love, transformed by the imagination into essence, is the deity. . . . Every union can be called the union of subject and object, of freedom and nature, of the real and possible.'[20]

We see here how Hegel's first attempts to formulate dialectical problems at once result in his deployment of the form of objective idealism current in German philosophy: the identical subject–object. His terminology, too, brings him close to Schelling and Fichte's theory of knowledge, both of which he retains in their essentials, while pressing forward to a more objective dialectics than theirs. It is not very important to establish here the extent to which Hegel was influenced by Schelling or whether it is simply the case that he spontaneously went in the same direction. For, given the kinds of questions that led to absolute idealism in Germany the idea of the identical subject–object was unavoidable. What is vital is the way in which different thinkers annul and preserve the subject and the object in a higher unity. Depending on how this is done absolute idealism either loses itself completely in religious mysticism (as with Schelling), or else it elaborates and maintains the living contradictions with enough vigour to force the idealist mysticism to yield up a significant understanding of reality. The struggle between these two tendencies occupies the whole of Hegel's development. From time to time Schelling's influence strengthens the retrograde tendency. His polemics against Schelling and the eventual parting of the ways point to the triumph of the other, even though in the framework of absolute idealism the victory can never be final.

However that may be, the fact remains that these fragments reveal an intense preoccupation with philosophical problems that was wholly absent in Berne. It is very characteristic of his present state that the notion of objectivity had become highly volatile and that he struggles with various formulations without reaching a satisfactory conclusion. For instance, it is interesting to see in the passage just quoted how he gives a subjective interpretation of the religiosity which in his view is destined to abolish the antagonism between subject and object. What he does is, as it were, to import subjectivity into the objects by means of the imagination, i.e. a procedure which, taken to its logical conclusion, can have no real impact on objectivity. His uncertainty at this stage is expressed above all in his wish to find a form of being in life, in religion that is higher than all ideas and concepts, a form of being that will do away with all the limitations and rigidities of reflection.

In the course of his investigation of these concepts Hegel stumbles on the idea that existence is independent of consciousness, but since he holds fast to his idealist theory of knowledge, the insight cannot be profitably exploited.

'This independence, this absoluteness of being is the stumbling-block; it must no doubt exist, but its mere existence does not mean that it exists for us. Thus the independence of being means that it just is, whether for us or not; being must be simply something separate from us, something in which a relationship with us is not necessarily implied.'

Hegel deduces various conclusions from this. Earlier on he says: 'Faith presupposes being', and he evidently wishes to establish the priority of being over thought. At the same time, he wants to discover in faith that higher religious principle with whose aid the objective ideal unity may be established. Hence he concludes:

'what is, *must* not be believed, but whatever is believed, *must* exist.'

These arguments are extraordinarily confused, but one thing does emerge from them, namely that the problems of the theory of knowledge, of objectivity are all in flux. And it is of great interest to see that it is in this context that we can discover the germs of the later dialectical distinctions within being (*Sein*, being, *Dasein*, being-in-the-world or determinate being, *Existenz*, existence). Of course, the distinctions have not been properly worked out. But it is of the greatest importance that these problems all emerge in the context of the central problem of Berne, the problem of positivity. The connection between the social problem of positivity and the philosophical problem of objectivity had been unconscious and instinctive in Berne, but it now starts to preoccupy Hegel actively. And it is no coincidence that at the same time the old conception of positivity now becomes unstable and that contradictions begin to arise within it.

Hegel's definition of positivity in Frankfurt corresponds exactly to the definition he had given in Berne.[21] But in the course of his studies it becomes more concrete, the definition is now more consciously philosophical and hence more flexible. Throughout this period Hegel was concerned, as we have seen, to achieve an existing, living union of the opposites, the antagonisms of life. In this context positivity now appears to him as a *false* union.

'Wherever there is eternal cleavage in nature and the irreconcilable is united, there is positivity.'

And elaborating on the ideas about faith and being already cited, he now defines positivity in this way:

'A positive faith is one which, instead of the only possible union, posits another; instead of the only possible being it posits a different one. Thus it unites that which is opposed in such a way that the union it achieves is incomplete, i.e. things are not united in the way they should be.'[23]

It is interesting to note how here, as earlier on with the distinction between being and consciousness, Hegel is driven to the outer edge of idealism, but at once turns around and hurls himself into the arms of subjectivity. For if we read the above quotations carefully, bearing in mind that by 'life' Hegel means the union of opposites in being, it is evident that positivity means more or less what a materialist would call the false reflections of objective reality. At the decisive moment, however, he reverses his direction and introduces the word 'should' without making it clear with what the syntheses of positive faith would or should not agree. And the same uncertainty makes itself felt when he goes on to say:

'Positive faith requires faith in something that does not exist.'[24]

And he strengthens this formulation by turning the contrast of positive and non-positive faith into a contrast between idea and being.

'In positive religion being, union is only an idea, something thought —I believe that it exists means: I believe the idea, I believe that I can imagine something, I believe in something believed (Kant, deity). Kantian philosophy—positive religion (deity a holy will, man an absolute negation; in the idea is united, ideas are united—an idea is a thought, but thoughts do not exist—).[25]

As he develops the concept more concretely he will abandon this view of positivity as mere idea. But the importance of these first attempts to formulate the concept of positivity is that they show Hegel's thought in a state of flux and that, as we have seen, the various gradations of being are making their appearance on the horizon. One final factor of interest is that this interpretation of positivity has suddenly brought the differences between Kant and Hegel to the surface and this in turn provides the first stimulus to Hegel's critique of Kantian philosophy.

NOTES

1  Hoffmeister, p. 380f.
2  Hoffmeister, p. 248. At the time the pamphlet passed almost unnoticed and has now become a bibliographical rarity. Hoffmeister maintains that only three German libraries possess a copy. Our quotation comes from Hoffmeister's reprint of the preface and the notes. The pamphlet itself appeared anonymously but bibliographical notices from the next few years point clearly to Hegel's authorship. Despite this the pamphlet was entirely forgotten until Hugo Falkenheim drew attention to it in an essay in the *Preussische Jahrbücher*, Berlin 1909, p. 193ff. The reader can find the most important bibliographical references in Hoffmeister, p. 457f.
3  D. Mornet, *Les origines intellectuelles de la révolution française*, Paris 1933, p. 434.
4  *Aus dem literarischen Nachlass von Karl Marx, Friedrich Engels*, ed. by Franz Mehring, Stuttgart 1913, Vol III, p. 410f.—Guizot had argued that because of its conservative nature the English Revolution of 1688 had succeeded where the French Revolution failed. Marx replied in his review that 'M. Guizot completely overlooks the fact that initially the French Revolution was just as conservative as the English, indeed far more so' and pointed out that the French wished to replace the novelty of absolute monarchy with *états généraux* going back to Henri IV and Louis XIII.—*Trans.*
5  Hoffmeister, pp. 459ff.

6   Ibid., p. 249. Habeas Corpus was suspended by annual Acts of Parliament from 1794 to 1801 and again in 1817.—*Trans.*

7   Unfortunately these fragments cannot be dated precisely. This applies particularly to No. 7 (*Drafts on the Spirit of Judaism*) and No. 8 (*Morality, Love and Religion*) in the appendix to Nohl. No. 9 (*Love and Religion*) dates from early in 1797, No. 10 (*Love*) was written late in 1797. No. 11 (*Faith and Being*) dates from 1798. Cf. Nohl, p 403f.

8   Nohl, p. 377.

9   Marx, *Theories of Surplus Value*, Part III, London 1972, p. 84.

10  Nohl, p. 376.

11  Ibid., p. 378. Trans. T. M. Knox in *Friedrich Hegel on Christianity*, New York 1948, pp. 303–4.

12  Nohl, p. 379. Knox, pp. 304–5.

13  Rosenkranz, p. 87.

14  Nohl, p. 379.

15  Nohl, p. 381f. Knox, p. 308.

16  Nohl, p. 382. Knox, p. 307.

17  Nohl, p. 381. Knox, pp. 307–8.

18  Nohl, p 368. We should mention here that these fragments are anticipated by a brief historical sketch from the Berne period published by Rosenkranz, p. 515f. But the views outlined there on the nature of the Orient were not taken up into Hegel's view of history at the time and so required no analysis from us.

19  Nohl, p. 370.

20  Ibid., p. 376.

21  Ibid., p. 364.

22  Ibid., p. 377.

23  Ibid., p. 383.

24  Ibid., p. 384.

25  Ibid., p. 385.

# CHAPTER THREE

# Fragments of two pamphlets on current German problems

*That the municipal authorities of Württemberg should be elected by its citizens* and *The German Constitution*.

THE contradictions in Hegel's position at this period are well illustrated by two fragmentary pamphlets written in 1798/9.

The first pamphlet was concerned with constitutional conflicts in Hegel's own land of Württemberg. It must have been written in the first half of 1798 since Rosenkranz has published a letter by a friend of Hegel's replying to it and this is dated 17 August 1798; clearly the pamphlet must have been completed by then.[1]

Hegel wrote his pamphlet in the course of the constitutional struggles that raged at the end of the century between the Duke of Württemberg and his Estates. They fell out on the issue of what attitude to adopt towards France. The Duke supported the Austrian intervention while the Estates sympathized with the French. After the Duke had attempted to subject the country to absolute rule without the Estates he had to summon them again in 1796 to elect a new Council (*Landesausschuss*) which the Duke hoped would be more tractable. But he was disappointed and the conflict just became more acute. In the course of the struggle a large number of pamphlets were published criticizing the obsolete feudal conditions still obtaining in Württemberg and also the antiquated constitution and they even went as far as to demand a representative assembly to be elected by the entire population. There were even said to be republican tendencies and there were calls for a Swabian republic.

Hegel's pamphlet was his contribution to the debate. The surviving fragments show very clearly his hesitant attitude on issues of the moment. Not that he was guilty of any compromise with feudal and absolute conditions in Germany, let alone of capitulation to them. Where he can remain at the level of criticism or philosophical generalization he shows great resoluteness in attacking conditions in Germany. And in this sense it cannot be said that his political opinions reveal any significant change. His intention is to intervene in the urgent questions of the day but wherever he attempts to tackle a concrete issue he displays the greatest uncertainty, his judgment falters and he finally comes up with surprisingly moderate proposals given his premises. The great critical run-up ends with relatively tame proposals for reform, as indeed Haym pointed out long ago.[2]

This uncertainty can be seen clearly in the changes made in the title of the pamphlet. Originally it read *That the municipal authorities of Württemberg should be elected by its people.* 'People' was later changed in favour of 'citizens'. The final version, however, ran as follows: *On the most recent domestic affairs of Württemberg and on the municipal constitution in particular.* The pamphlet originally bore a dedication 'To the people of Württemberg', but this was later deleted.[3] We can no longer determine whether these emendations were made to forestall censorship or because Hegel had changed his views; nor do we know whether and to what extent they are bound up with changes in the text. All we can do is analyse the rather meagre fragments that have survived.

Hegel's starting-point is very close to the republicanism he had adhered to in Berne and also in the Cart translation. The fragments published by Haym contain extremely derogatory statements about absolutism. For instance, he says that in an absolutist state

> 'all turns ultimately around one man who unites all powers within himself *ex providentia majorum* and there is no guarantee that he will recognize and respect the rights of man'.

And in harmony with this he states:

> 'The whole representative system of Württemberg is faulty and in need of thorough-going reform.'[4]

His criticism here has its basis in an appeal to justice and to the rights of man.

> 'In this view justice is the only measure. The courage to enforce justice is the only power that can clear away the tottering structure honourably and calmly, and bring about a secure state of affairs.'[5]

Only this striving for justice, only an attempt to raise oneself onto the plane of the universal will overcome the petty, particular interests of the philistines.

In his introductory remarks to the fragments Hegel gives a vivid picture of the growing desire for reform in Württemberg. He describes the mood as irresistible and argues that each delay will only increase it.

> 'It is no accidental vertigo that will pass. Call it delirium, but it can end only with death or the expulsion of the disease. It is the travail of the health that remains to drive out the evil.'[6]

Hegel then reasserts that conditions in Württemberg have reached breaking-point and are in need of complete revision.

He turns scornfully on the people who concede that reforms are necessary but who are prevented by class-interest from lending support to any
concrete proposal.

> 'All too often such desires and the zeal for the common good conceal
> the reservation "insofar as it coincides with our own interest". Their
> willingness to give their consent to all improvements takes fright and
> fades away as soon as a demand is made upon them.'

And his satirical comments on the necessity for political reforms are
summed up with the words:

> 'If there is to be a change, then something must be changed. We must
> assert this bald truth simply because the fear that is forced to act differs
> from the courage that wills to act in that, when the time to act arrives,
> people who are driven by fear are so weak that they wish to retain all
> they happen to possess. They are like the spendthrift who is forced to
> regulate his expenditure; every item that he is advised to give up now
> appears indispensable and he refuses to deprive himself of any, until
> the moment comes when both his necessities and luxuries are taken
> away from him.[7]

Why has the situation in Württemberg become untenable? Hegel's
answer is clear and simple. Because its institutions are the inheritance of
an earlier age now past and are socially and politically obsolete; they can
no longer satisfy the needs or the spirit of the modern world. We may
regard this as the typical progressive bourgeois attitude towards the institutions of feudal absolutism in Germany. At the same time they are not
without significance, since they point to a great advance in Hegel's own
historical and philosophical thought. For the first time Hegel employs
the idea of historical development in the defence of social progress.

In Berne he had looked to the resurrection of the republics of antiquity
in the midst of a world made degenerate by Christian positivity and the
inequality of wealth; this resurrection was to come about by a Cuvier-
like catastrophe. Now, tentatively and abstractly as yet, he begins to realize that the development of society is itself the impetus to progress. In
consequence he starts to consider the various institutions of politics and
society from a more historical perspective. That is to say, he no longer
regards an institution as good or bad in itself, as he had done in Berne,
but he realizes that an institution that was originally good may come to
impede progress in the course of time. Thus Hegel accounts for the obsolescence of institutions in Württemberg in this way:

> 'They are blind who would believe that institutions, constitutions

and laws from which the spirit has flown and which no longer accord with the customs, the needs and opinions of men, can continue to survive, and that forms which have ceased to exert any hold over feeling and reason can be powerful enough to bind a nation together![8]

Here we can see the great importance of his complex and unresolved ideas about his new definition of positivity which we discussed in the previous chapter. At that stage we could only show that Hegel's original rigid definition was now in a state of flux, that the inflexible antinomies of positivity and non-positivity had begun to break down into dialectical transitions. What Hegel had formulated shortly before in terms of true or false union now gains in historical concreteness: he now calls positive 'that from which the spirit has flown'. He is no longer content to ask what is or is not positive. He is now concerned with the question: *how* does an institution *become* positive? We shall see how this novel, consciously historical and philosophical version of positivity has been deepened by the end of the Frankfurt period and how it becomes the foundation for Hegel's mature philosophy of history. The present truncated state of the fragments does not permit us to draw any conclusions about the stage he had reached when he wrote the pamphlet and whether he had made any definite connection between the ideas quoted above and the problem of positivity. The most that can be said is that a few small extracts in Haym do suggest that there was a connection of some sort. But apart from a few words Hegel's original text Haym only gives his own highly abbreviated version. Thus he says:

'With hard-hitting words he describes and rebukes the officialdom that "has lost all sense of the innate rights of man and, trotting in the rear of the advancing age, caught between the claims of office and conscience, it can think of nothing but the need to find historical justification for positive institutions" '.[9]

Thus there does seem to have been a connection of a sort between positivity and historical obsoleteness in the original pamphlet, but the surviving texts do not permit us to determine how conscious and clear it was.

This quotation from Haym also points to another important, practical aspect of the pamphlet: the vigorous attack on the absolute bureaucracy of Württemberg. In a further fragment Hegel also speaks witheringly of the bureaucratic apparatus of the petty absolutist state. He perceives indignantly that this apparatus is in fact much more powerful than the Estates.

'Thus the officials . . . led the Council and with it the nation by the nose.'[10]

These comments are important because they show that Hegel was not just sharply critical of the feudal elements in the Württemberg constitution, but that he was no less hostile to the absolutist state which was at that moment in conflict with the feudal Estates. It is evident then that Hegel's objective could only be something radically different, viz. the bourgeois democratic transformation of the country.

All the more disappointing, therefore, are the vague and timorous concrete proposals that he puts forward. After his scathing attack on conditions in Württemberg, after his historical and philosophical justification of the need for radical change it is something of an anti-climax to hear him ask the question 'whether in a country which has had an hereditary monarchy for centuries it is advisable suddenly to allow an unenlightened mob accustomed to blind obedience and dependent on the impression of the moment to choose its own representatives.' And his concrete proposals follow the tenor of these remarks rather than the sharp tone of his criticism of Württemberg.

> 'As long as everything else remains unchanged, as long as the people does not know its rights, as long as there is no public spirit, as long as the power of the officials remains unrestrained, popular elections would only result in the complete overthrow of our constitution. The best solution would be to entrust the franchise to a body of enlightened and upright men independent of the court. But I do not see how an electoral system could be devised that would result in such an assembly, however carefully the active and passive franchise were determined.'[11]

The gulf between his critique of the existing situation and his timid and vague reforms is perfectly clear. We have seen how in Berne Hegel dissociated himself from the radical and plebeian wing of the French Revolution, but this is not enough to explain his reluctance to demand 'an independent' assembly of notables, even when we take into account the fact that he was writing in full knowledge of the experiences of the French Revolution and that he might have been afraid that an elected assembly would turn into a radical convention. For both in France and later even in Germany there were many moderate liberals who believed that an elected representative body would be the suitable vehicle for the reforms that had become necessary.

The true explanation lies in the general state of Germany and the ideological attitude arising from it which never ceased to determine Hegel's position (as well as that of such important contemporaries as Goethe). Looking at Germany from a cosmopolitan point of view he could get a pretty clear idea both of its backwardness and of the constitution that it ought to have. But he had no idea how his critical insights were to be transformed into political action. In consequence of his vagueness and uncertainty there arose in his mind a great variety of socially necessary but more or less reactionary illusions which were to determine his thought throughout his life. The more concrete his approach to a problem, the wider the gulf between his vision and his political proposals appeared and the more illusory the purely ideological attempts to bridge it. Marx has analysed the social origins and character of these illusions in a brilliant section of *The German Ideology*. He characterizes the political and economic fragmentation of Germany at the end of the eighteenth century in these words:

'The impotence of each separate sphere of life (one cannot speak here of estates or classes, but at the most only of former estates and classes not yet born) did not allow any one of them to gain exclusive domination. The inevitable consequence was that during the epoch of absolute monarchy, which was seen here in its most stunted, semi-patriarchal form, the special sphere which, owing to the division of labour, was responsible for the work of administration of public interests acquired an abnormal independence, which became still greater in the bureaucracy of modern times. Thus, the State built itself up into an apparently independent force, and this position, which in other countries was only transitory—a transition stage—has been maintained in Germany until the present day. It is this position of the State which explains both the honesty of the civil servant that is found nowhere else, and all the illusions about the State which are current in Germany, as well as the apparent independence of German theoreticians in relation to the burghers—the seeming contradiction between the form in which these theoreticians express the interests of the burghers and these interests themselves.[12]

Even a superficial glance at Hegel's arguments reveals that he exhibits all the attributes of the German ideology of his age as described by Marx. No doubt, the illusions about the 'honesty of the civil servant' and about the state will only make their appearance later on, but the state's apparent independence of the real interests of the up-and-coming bourgeois class is already the central pillar of his political and social methodology. This is the source both of the vagueness and timidity in his concrete proposals and of his illusions about an 'independent' body that would determine the constitution of Württemberg. What is important here is his relationship with liberalism. As far as his social *objectives* are concerned, Hegel is largely in agreement with the liberals. It is apparent that he had made a thorough study of notable advocates of liberalism like Benjamin Constant and Charles James Fox.[13] Nevertheless, right up to the end of his life we see an increasingly explicit rejection of the political *methods* of liberalism, above all of the German liberals. In particular, he refuses to share their faith in elections, parliaments, parliamentary reforms, etc.

This paradox is a reflection of Germany's economic and social backwardness and the resulting development of political ideology which is divided, retarded, petty and philistine, rather than just uneven. *Both* of its principal currents are tainted by its philistinism as well as its vague utopianism. The German liberals of the day put their demands forward dogmatically for the most part, without any real attempt to take the actual balance of power within society into account. (To avoid any misunderstanding here when I speak of the ideologists of liberalism I explicitly exclude the few revolutionary democrats such as George Forster.) Wherever the French intervention had given rise to a form of pseudo-constitutionalism this dogmatic approach was combined with petty-bourgeois opportunism and with a very bigoted church policy (in South Germany). Like Goethe, Hegel is fully aware of the narrow-mindedness of German liberalism. He does not share their mistaken assessment of the German situation nor of the socio-economic preconditions of bourgeois society. But his correct criticism of them is often accompanied by different illusions of his own, illusions which later lead him to increasingly reactionary positions on particular issues.

Thus the prejudices and illusions of *both* points of view available at the time reflect the German *misère*. Even the ablest minds of Germany with the widest, most cosmopolitan horizon are defeated by the petty, philistine provincialism of German society. Not until just before and especially just after the July Revolution of 1830 in France do we witness the emergence of a definite democratic *movement* in Germany and with it the first efforts to overcome this provincialism (Georg Büchner, Heine). But we need only think of the battles that the young Marx fought with the radical Young Hegelians to realize how deeply these provincial ideologies were rooted in Germany.

Since Hegel's ideological assumptions were dictated ultimately by the class structure of Germany at the time he was unable ever to overcome them. It is true that he does acquire a much greater understanding of the forces that move society, and his knowledge of the underlying laws becomes ever more profound. But only up to a certain point. There is always a point at which his concrete and clear grasp of class antagonisms comes to a halt and quite without any objective social justification turns into abstract generalizations which feed on illusions about the nature of the state and, later on, the bureaucracy. For all his life-long efforts to investigate the dialectical connections between the 'particularity' of private and class interests and their social product, the 'universal' is never logically developed from the real, particular social conditions; on the contrary, it is always imposed 'from above', idealistically, from a position apparently independent of class allegiances. It is evident that this fundamental contradiction is much less obvious here than in his later development. We shall also see great fluctuations in his political attitudes and his philosophical approach. But this fundamental contradiction is a persistent and indeed permanent feature of all his thought.

Hegel's pamphlet never appeared. A partial explanation is provided by a letter, published by Rosenkranz, from a friend of Hegel's in Stuttgart. In this letter the friend argues that publication at the present time would do more harm than good. Of the arguments he presents one is directed against Hegel's projected assembly of notables which the writer describes as 'arbitrary'. More important, perhaps, was the disappointment felt by progressive and even revolutionary Germans with the outcome of the war with France. The Congress at Rastatt which sat from December 1797 to April 1798 and which brought the war of the first Coalition against France to an end resulted only in loss of territory for Germany. German patriots had cherished hopes that the wars of the French Republic would lead to the international spread of democratic institutions and were bitterly disappointed when the peace negotiations resulted in no more than petty haggling for various territories. This disappointment is reflected in the concluding lines of the letter to Hegel:

'Of course, my dear friend, our reputation has suffered greatly. The rulers of the *grande nation* have sacrificed the most sacred rights of mankind to the mockery and derision of our enemies. I know of no vengeance that would fit their crimes. In these circumstances the publication of your essay would be just one evil the more.'[14]

The contradiction which comes emotionally to the surface here is one we have already discussed. It lies at the roots of all the theoretical and practical attempts of the age to achieve the unification of Germany. Hegel gives his own solution to this question in his next pamphlet which he drafted but did not complete. But it is interesting and very typical of Hegel that his notes do not show the least trace of bitterness towards the French. He approaches the problem of German unity from the internal contradictions in German national history and his later detailed discussions of this issue and of world history in general show that he never abandoned his sympathy for the developments in France; indeed, with the advent of Napoleon these sympathies only become more pronounced and he tended more and more to regard the Napoleonic solution to the problems of the French Revolution as paradigmatic. Of course, the gulf between his socio-historical analysis and his intended solution still remains unbridgeable.

This gulf can be seen in the surviving fragments of *The German Constitution* in the way in which the manuscript breaks off wherever a concrete proposal becomes inevitable. Hegel took up work on the pamphlet once more in Jena and greatly expanded both the critical and historical parts as well as those concerned with concrete proposals. But this just shifted the difficulty elsewhere and the gap between the theoretical and practical parts remained wider than ever. Thus when dealing with the past Hegel shows very clearly that all changes in political constitutions come about only because of the existence of real historical forces. But the Jena version of *The German Constitution* preserves a total silence on the subject of the historical forces that might bring about the reforms Hegel wishes to see introduced into Germany, and whenever he does allude to such forces he does so in a vague and mystificatory way.[15]

As to the first fragment, we are at once struck by the sharpness of his criticism and the boldness of his analysis in contrast to the absence of any concrete perspective. His study of the situation in Germany leads him to see the demise of Germany as a nation, its final fragmentation, as a very real threat. He does indeed hint at another, opposite solution, but the manuscript breaks off just as he is about to discuss it. For after an incisive critique of the autonomy of the different parts of Germany, Hegel goes on to say:

'If the tendency to become isolated is the only moving principle in the German Empire, then Germany is in the process of sinking inexorably into the abyss of its dissolution, and to utter a warning of this would indeed be evidence of zeal, but also of folly since it would be wasted labour. Is Germany not standing at the cross-roads between the fate of Italy and unification in a single state? There are above all two factors that enable us to hope for the latter, two factors that we may regard as a counter to the principle of disintegration.'[16]

But the manuscript has nothing further to say about these two principles.

We have already shown that Hegel's analysis reached this conclusion entirely from a consideration of the internal situation in Germany and he did not blame the French wars for the plight of the German Empire. Like all progressive Germans of the day Hegel saw the source of Germany's ills in the sovereignty of the greater and lesser principalities, in the fragmentation of Germany into a whole host of states of varying sizes. This leads him to the following very radical conclusion:

'Apart from despotisms, i.e. states with no constitution, no state has a more wretched constitution than Germany.'

And he adds:

'Voltaire went so far as to call its constitution an anarchy; this is the best description if Germany is considered as a state; but even this name is no longer valid since Germany can no longer be regarded as a state in any sense.'[17]

The arguments Hegel adduces in support of this harsh judgment are interesting and characteristic. They show how his view of the facts comes into conflict with his original opinions and how he advances through the 'manure' of these contradictions with the aid of very bold idealist constructs and ends up with greatly enriched knowledge. He locates the fundamental contradiction of the German constitution in the fact that it is not based on constitutional law at all, but on private law. This view still owes a lot to old-fashioned views of the state which are founded partly on natural law and partly on his view of Greece and Rome. Hence, he finds fault with the principles of German public law because their 'principles are not derived from concepts based on reason', but are merely 'abstractions of reality'. Thus Hegel is able to see how legal codes have arisen in the course of actual social conflicts and he acknowledges this fact where he finds it, but regards it as hostile to reason and as something in contradiction with reality as it should be.[18]

His position here is strongly idealistic and metaphysical and this becomes even clearer when we consider his explanation of the origins of these 'abstractions of reality'. In the course of his critical account of this aspect of German history he argues:

'For possession came earlier than law and did not spring from law; on the contrary, whatever was taken by force was made into legal right.'

When we follow his concrete analyses further we find that his objections to the foundations of the Empire in private law are connected with the fact that in the social conflict which effected the transition from the Middle Ages to the modern world the victors in Germany were the forces of feudalism.

'The function of the state was always just to confirm what was taken from its control . . . in Germany the individual member of the body politic owes his power in the state, his rights and his duties to his family, his estate or his guild.[19]

It is evident that in Hegel's eyes the victory of feudal principles are sufficient to explain why Germany has ceased to be a state. And he goes on to show that these public laws founded on private rights have an internal tendency to make themselves autonomous, to emancipate themselves from the state and the nation as a whole and that this leads to a chaos of conflicting rights and claims. Of course, law now appears to Hegel, even more now than later, not as the product but as the supreme principle of society and the state. But within the framework of this idealist distortion of reality he provides a vivid satirical picture of the situation in Germany where a single system gives one man as much right to resolve matters of war and peace for the entire nation as it gives another to possess so and so many fields or vineyards.[20]

These passages where he so sharply condemns German conditions give a much clearer illustration of the more historical attitude towards positivity, obsolescence and the need for reform than we had seen in the Württemberg article. He gives an extremely vivid picture of the once progressive forces that had been effective in the past and had indeed built up the imposing edifice of German Empire, and he also gives eloquent expression to the sense of tradition and loyalty that Germans feel for their past. But, on the other hand, he shows quite uncompromisingly that this entire historical structure is utterly divorced from the problems of the present and that, as he had formulated it in the Württemberg pamphlet, the spirit had flown from it.

> 'The building of the German constitution is the work of past centuries; it is not upheld by the life of the present; the entire fate of more than one century is imprinted in its forms and the justice and violence, courage and cowardice, the honour, the blood, the misery and the well-being of times long since dead and generations long since mouldering, still live on in it. The life and the forces whose development and activity are the pride of the generation now living have no share in it, no interest in it and derive no nourishment from it. This building with its pillars and archaic ornaments stands isolated from the spirit of the age.'[21]

Hegel does not use the word positivity here but this analysis undoubtedly contains an historical elaboration of positivity.

Of particular significance for the development of his philosophy of history is the section where he deals with the 'saga of German freedom'. For the first time he presents an account of a primitive, stateless society, the kind of society that he later called the 'heroic age'. Later on, of course, it was the development of antiquity before the founding of the state that was so crucial for his thought, but there is also evidence to suggest (e.g. in the *Aesthetics*) that he thought of the end of the Middle Ages as such a period, as the Vico-like recurrence of such a period. The present discussion is very characteristic of his developing dialectical sense of history. For his position here is just as far from a glorification of primitive societies, and from any desire to return to them, as it is from any vulgar materialist contempt for them, from any temptation to look down on them condescendingly from the 'height of the latest achievements' of civilization. He gives an interesting picture of the so-called age of German freedom, of a society

> 'in which ethical customs rather than laws transform a mass into a people and where equal interest rather than a universal command constitutes the state.'

And he concludes his discussion with the following general remarks:

'Just as it is cowardly and effete to describe the men of that society as loathsome, wretched and stupid, and to imagine ourselves to be infinitely more human, happy and clever, so too it is childish and silly to yearn for such a society—as if it alone were natural—or to fail to recognize that a society ruled by law is necessary—and that it alone is free.'[22]

A few years later, in the theses of his dissertation in Jena, Hegel expresses the same idea in a much more pithy, paradoxical way. Talking about Hobbes, and to some extent polemicizing against him, he writes:

'The state of nature is not unjust, and that is why man must emerge from it.'[23]

The other fragment deals with these questions in a more general philosophical manner. Rosenkranz who first published it goes so far as to call it a synthesis of Hegel's thoughts about the world crisis.[24]

Its starting-point and general mood are already familiar to us from Part II, Chapter 1. Following the description of the individual who finds himself in a state of crisis Hegel goes on to discuss the world-situation which he summarizes as follows:

'All the manifestations of the age show that the old life no longer provides satisfaction; in that life man was limited to the ordered control of his possessions, the contemplative enjoyment of his utterly subordinate little world, and then, to reconcile him to these limitations, self-destruction and elevation into heaven.'

The age has put an end to this philistine, religious complacency. Both impoverishment and luxury have abolished the old state of affairs. On the one hand, we see the pursuit of wealth, 'the bad conscience to turn one's property, things, into an absolute', and on the other hand, 'the spirit of a better life . . . has entered the age'. Hegel refers explicitly here to the French Revolution (and he may also have Napoleon in mind) and he also points to the great achievements of German literature and philosophy.

'Its onward impetus is fed by the deeds of individuals of great character, by the movements of entire peoples and by the depiction of nature and fate in the works of the poets; while metaphysics sets limits to the restrictions of existence and gives them their necessity in the context of the whole.'[25]

Hegel's notion of positivity is enriched here by a new element. The idea first became historicized—as we saw in the pamphlet on Württemberg—when he argued that institutions that had once corresponded to the customs of the people in the course of time became

divorced from their life and turned into positive institutions. Now he
suggests that a new spirit may begin to stir amidst the old, inflexible,
positive life, and the living antagonism and contrast between the old and
the new makes things that have been historically superseded into 'positive' phenomena.

How does Hegel imagine that change can be introduced into the
crumbling Empire? He gives a brief, very general, philosophical statement, which for that very reason is more radical and politically concrete
than elsewhere.

> 'Life which is full of limitations is a power which can only be over-
> come by something better if it too becomes a power. . . . Only as a
> particular against a particular can nature function in its actual life as
> an attack or refutation of the worse form of life. . . .'[25]

Hegel's realistic grasp of social conflict is undeniable here when he sees it
as the struggle of one power against another (one particular against
another). He is in no danger of embracing liberal illusions about 'the irresistible power of ideas' before which the fortresses of absolutism will
crumble like the walls of Jericho at the sound of Joshua's trumpets. At the
same time, he views the struggle against absolutism and the vestiges of
feudalism in the same way as the ideological protagonists of the revolutionary bourgeoisie. Hence when he comes to concretize his attack on
this calcified society he writes:

> 'This society does not base its rule on the power of particular against
> particular, but on its universality. The truth, the right that it claims
> for itself must be taken from it and given to those elements of the life
> that is required. . . . The positive aspects of the existing order, which
> is a negation of nature, should be left in possession of their truth: that
> right must exist.'[27]

When these very abstract and somewhat obscure statements are translated onto a philosophical plane they are seen to maintain the general
polemic of the bourgeois revolutionary class against the old feudal order.
They question the pretensions of the ruling classes, of feudalism, to be the
representatives and leaders of society as a whole, and dismiss these claims
as the arrogance of a small minority, of particular interest groups. On the
other hand, Hegel does not see the demands of the 'third estate' as the
demands of one class *vis-à-vis* other classes; what he sees is the hitherto
suppressed rights of the universal interest, the interests of society as a
whole. Thus in the shift to the plane of the universal and the particular,
the unmasking of the pretensions of a particular (feudal, absolutist) class
to universality, and the converse elevation of the particular demands of
the bourgeois class into a universality sanctioned by nature and history,
Hegel is simply providing an abstract philosophical statement of the

ideas which, without any philosophical ambitions, formed the essential stock-in-trade of progressive writers before and during the French Revolution. And once again it is of great interest for his development as a thinker that the very first appearance of the dialectic of the universal and particular should occur not in an abstract philosophical context but in an effort to clarify his thoughts about the real historical dialectics of the destruction of feudalism by the bourgeoisie both for himself and for others.

Hegel's further discussions show even more clearly how the philosophical approach sprang from political and historical problems. Immediately after the last passage quoted he goes on to say:

'In the German Empire a universal source of rights has ceased to exist, since it has isolated itself and turned itself into a particular. Hence universality exists now only as an idea and not as reality.'[28]

This latter idea provides further confirmation that Hegel's enemy here was the still surviving feudal, absolutist order. From the point of view of his philosophical development we must remind ourselves of those extracts from the Nohl fragments in which he attempted to find a new definition of positivity (see pp. 125–7 supra). We showed there that Hegel's new distinction between the positive and the non-positive was that while both were unions, syntheses, the positive was only an idea, a thought, while the non-positive was a being.

Let us remind ourselves further that connected with this distinction was Hegel's first attempt to distinguish between different levels of existence. His statements about this were extremely abstract and obscure. In the present, more historical discussion, however, they become much more concrete. The levels of existence, of existence which is more or less real, are linked to the historical question of the death or collapse of old social formations and the growth of new societies. And this brings us very close to the historical dialectic given by Engels:

'And so, in the course of development, all that was previously real becomes unreal, loses its necessity, its right of existence, its rationality. And in the place of moribund reality comes a new, viable reality . . .'[29]

Needless to say, Hegel is still far removed from that historical concreteness that he will achieve later in the *Philosophy of History*. What interests us here is to see how in these fragments he takes the first steps towards developing the dialectical method. It is typical of the state of his thought at the time that the fragment breaks off at the point where concrete conclusions had to be drawn from premises that were bold and progressive both philosophically and politically.

## NOTES

1   Rosenkranz, p. 91. The carelessness with which Hegel's literary
    remains have been treated is very much in evidence here. Rosen-
    kranz says that only a few fragments had survived. But Haym, op.
    cit., p. 489, claims that he had seen the whole pamphlet and in fact in
    his book on Hegel he includes some quotations missing from
    Rosenkranz and refers to a number of more or less important argu-
    ments without quoting Hegel verbatim. In the meantime, however,
    the manuscript has again vanished.

2   Haym, p. 67.

3   Rosenkranz, p. 91.

4   Lasson, pp. xiv and xv. Where possible we shall quote from Lasson's
    edition of the two pamphlets since this is the most accessible, and
    only where something is omitted or shortened will we refer to other
    editions.

5   Lasson, p. 151.

6   Ibid.

7   Lasson, p. 152.

8   Lasson, p. 151.

9   Haym, p. 67.

10  Lasson, p. 153.

11  Ibid., pp. xv and xvi.

12  Marx/Engels, *The German Ideology*, London 1965, pp. 211–12.

13  Rosenkranz, p. 62 and Haym, p. 67.

14  Rosenkranz, p. 91.

15  The two fragments of Hegel's pamphlet on the constitution that we
    shall examine were probably written late in 1798 and early 1799. At
    least Rosenzweig, Vol. 1, p. 88f. and Hoffmeister, p. 468 have made
    a convincing case for this date in the case of the first fragment. They
    have shown that where Hegel mentions the Congress of Rastatt the
    word 'become' has been crossed out and replaced by 'became', writ-
    ten in a different ink, i.e. the manuscript was presumably written at
    the time of the Congress but was taken up again and altered, prob-
    ably when Hegel was revising the entire article in Jena. There is dis-
    agreement about the dating of the second manuscript fragment
    among those scholars who were able to examine the original. Haer-
    ing, pp. 595 and 785, argues that it was written in Jena, i.e. he
    regards it as contemporaneous with the later version of the whole
    article. But Rosenzweig, Vol. I, pp. 92ff. and 235, and Hoffmeister,
    p. 469f., both believe it to have been written in Frankfurt. Rosen-
    zweig and Hoffmeister base their conclusions on purely philological
    arguments connected with the change in Hegel's handwriting,
    whereas Haering's view is founded on so-called 'internal evidence'.

This fact alone must incline one to accept the first view and this is strengthened by a consideration of Haering's internal evidence. The method and structure of the second fragment have the typical features of the Frankfurt period: they start from individual experiences and proceed from there to general historical and philosophical statements. This subjective approach is generally abandoned after he leaves Frankfurt. The reader can judge the mood, the intellectual atmosphere of the fragment from the extract from the introduction which we quoted in Chapter 1 (p. 102). That we should favour the date given above rests on the belief that, as the reader will see, it contains similar ideas to the article on Württemberg, but at a higher level of philosophical generalization, i.e. it was obviously written later. A further point is that in February 1799 Hegel commenced his study of economics and this fragment contains scarcely a trace of economic arguments. In all probability, then, it was written before Hegel read Steuart's economics. Of course, these comments are merely hypothetical, but given the present state of Hegel's literary remains we cannot dispense with hypotheses if our aim is to reconstruct the course of his development.

16  Lasson, p. 142.
17  Hoffmeister, p. 283.
18  Ibid., p. 285.
19  Ibid.
20  Ibid., p. 286.
21  Ibid., p. 283.
22  Ibid., p. 284.
23  Hegel, *Erste Druckschriften* (ed. Lasson), Leipzig 1898, p. 405.
24  Rosenkranz prints this fragment (pp. 88ff.) immediately after the criticism of Kant of 1798. As he was a personal student of Hegel's we may regard this as additional support for our view of its date.
25  Lasson, p. 140. By 'metaphysics' Hegel understands the philosophy that goes beyond the limits of subjective idealism.
26  Ibid.
27  Ibid.
28  Ibid., p. 141.
29  F. Engels, *Feuerbach*, in Marx/Engels, *Selected Works*, Vol. II, Moscow and London 1949 and 1950, p. 327.

# Critical engagement with Kant's ethics

THE internal crisis that marked Hegel's period in Frankfurt manifested itself not just in the way his manuscripts broke off, frequently at the decisive moment, but also in the abrupt changes of theme. We have seen how the studies of Christianity and Judaism were succeeded by the article on Württemberg. This was followed, though not at once, by the fragments on the German constitution. (We have taken them together only because of their thematic similarities and to avoid needless repetition.) In fact however the pamphlet on Württemberg was followed by an extensive analysis of Kant's ethical writings. We learn from Hegel's own diary that his study of Kant began on 10 August 1798, i.e. almost as soon as he had completed the Württemberg essay. If our hypothesis is correct, the work on Kant was followed by *The German Constitution* and from February 1799 we may date the beginning of his preoccupation with Steuart's economics. After that Hegel resumed his study of Christianity and wrote his largest essay of the Frankfurt period, *The Spirit of Christianity and its Fate*.

Throughout this transitional period one has the feeling that Hegel takes up problems with great passion because they affect him as immediate, personal problems, but that again and again he is forced to acknowledge that he has neither the socio-historical knowledge, nor the philosophical equipment to solve them in a way that would satisfy his own ambitions or do justice to the problems themselves. Of course, we can see that by increasing his knowledge and deepening his grasp of philosophy Hegel was attempting to bridge an unbridgeable chasm: we have pointed to the objective situation which *blocked* the *road* to a true historical and scientific understanding of bourgeois society. But the path he takes in search of this goal is the uninterrupted development of the dialectical method. The closer he imagines himself to be to the longed-for 'reconciliation', the more recalcitrant the contradictions in his material become, with the result that he temporarily abandons the project. But his constantly increasing knowledge of the dialectical structure of existence transforms each new stage into another step towards a definition of dialectical science. What from the personal, biographical point of view appears desultory has a definite objective continuity: it steadily leads him to an understanding of contradiction as the foundation of all thought and being.

Hegel's preoccupation with Kantian ethics is determined above all by his new view of society. As we have seen, his starting-point was the problems and needs of the individual, the moral problems that confront the individual in his life in society. This brought him in a sense quite close to Kant's ethical doctrines which have their centre, as is well known, in the moral duties of the individual. But even at this stage Hegel's approach was quite different from Kant's and so a critical confrontation was unavoidable, whereas in Berne, where Hegel was almost entirely unconcerned about the fate of the individual, it was possible for him to take up an attitude of benevolent neutrality. The confrontation was aggravated further by the differing attitudes of the two men towards religion. Kant's ethical system culminated with the elevation of God to a 'postulate of practical reason'. (We have already seen—p. 19f.—how Hegel and Schelling reacted to this aspect of Kant's philosophy in Berne.) Hegel's philosophy, too, culminates in a religious position in Frankfurt, but one entirely opposed to that of Kant. However, since this was one of the chief themes of Hegel's thought at this period a confrontation with Kant had to come sooner or later.

It appears further that Kant's view of the relations between religion and the state formed one of the chief matters at issue in this first great confrontation with Kant. I say 'appears', because here *too* we must reflect sadly that this manuscript is among those that have been lost. Even when Rosenkranz was working on his biography of Hegel very little remained of the latter's critique of Kant's doctrine of virtue. But he did at least possess Hegel's commentary on *The Metaphysics of Morals* and on Kant's doctrine of law in toto. Since then all the manuscripts have vanished and all we now have are the notes and quotations to be found in Rosenkranz, who confines himself chiefly to Hegel's views on the relationship between church and state.[1] We can see from our previous examination of Hegel's development in Frankfurt that this problem would have formed an important element in his analysis of Kant, but we must not overlook the possibility that Rosenkranz gave it undue weight because the problem was dear to his own heart and that, placed in its original context, it might have been less significant than would now appear.

Our analysis must begin, therefore, with the fragments that appear in Rosenkranz. But we must proceed with caution, bearing these reservations in mind, all the more so since the very detailed discussions of Kant in *The Spirit of Christianity* relate to very different aspects of ethical philosophy, and the question of church and state plays a much reduced role in the later manuscript. Of course, given the abrupt changes in Hegel's development at this time it is very difficult to surmise to what extent the treatment of Kant in *The Spirit of Christianity* and the present commentary on Kant move along the same lines, to what extent Hegel made use of the commentary for the larger work and whether he

adapted and developed them further. However, despite the risks of biographical inaccuracy we think it is best to violate the precise chronology
and discuss the relevant passages of *The Spirit of Christianity* immediately
after the commentary, partly to avoid repetition and partly to enable us
to reach some sort of coherent conclusions about the disagreements
between the two thinkers at this time.

In his introductory remarks to the Kant commentary Rosenkranz
speaks of Hegel's attempts to resolve the Kantian antithesis between
legality and morality in ethical life, or as Hegel still calls it, 'life'. This is
undoubtedly the groundplan for the Jena *System of Ethics*. The disappearance of these first statements is an irreparable loss for our understanding of Hegel's development. Rosenkranz does not indicate how
Hegel thought of the various gradations in morality at this time; he does
not even say whether they were presented in any dialectical pattern at
all. We have indeed found hints of such a pattern in the Nohl fragments
and in *The Spirit of Christianity* it is already fairly prevalent. We may
assume, therefore, that this may be said also of the Kant commentary, but
we cannot know how clearly it was developed.

There is greater clarity about the nature of Hegel's general critique of
Kantian morality. According to Rosenkranz:

> 'He protested against the suppression of nature in Kant and the frag-
> mentation of man in the casuistry springing from the absolutism of his
> conception of duty.'[2]

This was one of the most common objections to Kant's conception of
morality at the time; quite apart from Hamann and Herder who criticized the whole of classical philosophy, we find it above all in Goethe
and Schiller. Goethe simply rejects the Kantian doctrine in its entirety,
while Schiller attempts to overcome its problematic nature with the aid
of aesthetics and the application of aesthetic principles to life. As we shall
see from *The Spirit of Christianity* Hegel's position is broadly in line with
that of the two poets though his concept of 'life' is more elastic and comprehensive than Schiller's aesthetic ideas. The fragmentation of man resulting from the absoluteness, the metaphysical nature of Kant's
principles is one of the leitmotivs of Hegel's polemics against Kant from
Jena on. In Jena, for instance, he refers to the 'soul-sack of the subject'
stuffed full of 'faculties' arbitrarily separated from each other.[3] and in
Hegel's view the advantage of objective idealism when compared to the
Kantian system consists largely in the fact that it postulates a dialectical
unity in the subject, thus overcoming Kant's fragmentation of man.

The only part of the critique of which enough is preserved to give us
any real insight into Hegel's position is the section dealing with church
and state. Hegel formulates Kant's view of this as follows:

'Both church and state should leave each other in peace, for neither concerns the other.'

Given the crucial importance of religion in his own thought at the time Hegel could not possibly accept this attitude. In particular, he clearly perceived the grounds for conflict: since the state is based on the principle of property, its laws must be utterly opposed to those of the church. According to Hegel the reason for this lies in their differing relations to men. The law of the state affects

'man only very *imperfectly* since it thinks of him only as one who *possesses*, whereas in the church man is a *whole* . . . if a man can live at peace with both, this can only mean that either his relationship with the church or his relationship with the state is not taken seriously.'

Hegel then goes on to discuss the two extremes of the Jesuits and the Quakers, without giving his approval to either. He further rejects as 'inhuman' the domination of the church by the state; such domination must create a fanaticism

'which because it sees individuals and human relationships in the power of the state, sees the state in men and thereby fragments men themselves'.

These arguments culminate in the utopian idea of a union between church and state that will secure the integrity of man.

'The whole church is only fragmented when man within the whole is divided into a man of the *church* and a man of the *state*.'[4]

In our ignorance of the precise context of this critique we must be highly circumspect in drawing any conclusions. But we can certainly see the extremities to which Hegel is driven in his quest for the unity of life and the integrity of a mankind fragmented by capitalism in religion. Even in later life Hegel never worked out a correct view of the relations between church and state, but he never again went so far as to advocate this kind of reactionary theocracy. It is possible that the arguments used here played some sort of a role in the article on *The German Constitution* and may be one of the factors responsible for Hegel's failure to complete it.

Philosophically, what counts is the contrast between the whole man and man fragmented. Even though his search for a religious solution complicated and distorted his arguments, the central point of his ethical studies and his opposition to Kant remains the analysis of bourgeois society based on this insight. Hegel comes more and more to regard the present as a transitory period of crisis, of universal contradiction and disintegration. The task of philosophy (and now of religion) is to overcome these contradictions in life itself. But the contradictions must be genuinely overcome: it is not enough just to weaken or alleviate them, papering over the rifts and divisions in the age. Hegel's thought leads him to emphasize the contradictions, to make them as explicit as possible, even to the point of apparent insolubility. Hence his objections to Kant are based on what Hegel thinks of as Kant's tendency to freeze the various moments of modern bourgeois fragmentation, to turn them into absolutes and thus to perpetuate the contradictions in a primitive, rudimentary state in which they can no longer be superseded or transcended. As we shall see, the objective-idealist critique of Kant developed by Hegel presses increasingly in the direction of a more complete and realistic view of the moral problems of man in society.

At first glance it is something of a paradox to call Hegel 'realistic' at the very moment when he is lost in the murky depths of mysticism to a greater extent than Kant ever was, or even Fichte, Kant's successor in the field of moral philosophy. But when we take a closer look at these two conflicting trends we see not merely that our use of the word is justified, but also that Hegel provides a very decisive critique of the limits and prejudices contained in the radical subjective idealism of Kant and Fichte in the field of ethics, even though he does so from an objective idealism that at this stage is instinctive rather than conscious. The point at issue is the problem of 'the whole man'. In German idealism the capitalist division of labour, particularly in its primitive, pre-revolutionary, ascetic phase, is reflected as the division of man into qualities of the mind and the senses. This division is the heritage of religion, but its implications in the initial stages of classical German philosophy do not stem from religion in general, but from the religious asceticism of those sects that embodied these ideological tendencies at an early stage of capitalism when its ideological and economic development was still rudimentary. We must remind ourselves of the role of the sects in the Peasant War in Germany, the War of Liberation in the Netherlands and even in the English Revolution. And it would be a mistake to overlook the very significant elements of this tradition in Rousseau's ascetic idealism and in a number of his Jacobin disciples, such as Robespierre.

Now the sharp, antagonistic distinction between the mind and the senses with its epistemological and ethical implications makes classical German idealism the heir of this tradition. In addition the reality of the capitalist division of labour itself led to specialization, the separation of the particular human qualities and faculties from each other and the overdevelopment of one at the cost of crippling the others.

In the moral theories of Kant and Fichte this division expresses their own criticism of the morality of their contemporaries while providing a philosophical instrument whereby to affirm the existing social framework. In the purely mental sphere of the 'categorical imperative' first

Kant and then Fichte construct an ideal image of society in which the unconditional devotion to a spiritual and mental 'duty' which no longer belongs to the world of phenomena can function harmoniously and free of conflict. Thus all the antagonisms and contradictions in actual society are now reduced to the single contrast between sensuous and moral man, 'homo phenomenon' and 'homo noumenon'. And according to this doctrine, if men would only conduct their lives in accordance with the dictates of the moral law there would be no more conflict or contradiction in society. This conception of morality can only be validated philosophically by transforming all the moral problems of society into the formal postulates of 'practical reason'. Man appears to be no more than the more or less contingent actor in whom these postulates can be realized. In Fichte this kind of position is maintained even more uncompromisingly than in Kant himself. As he puts it:

'I can and may look after myself simply because, and to the degree that, I am the instrument of the moral law; but this applies to every other human being too.—But this gives us an utterly reliable test to discover whether taking care of oneself is moral, or whether it is merely an instinct.'[5]

These views give expression to two important social trends. First, the morality of the first, ascetic stage of bourgeois development, with the radical spiritualization and the idealist projection of the moral postulates of bourgeois society into heaven. Second, the illusion that bourgeois society, 'in its ideal state', contains no self-contradiction, and that the contradictions that actually appear arise partly from social institutions which have been imperfectly transformed into bourgeois institutions, and partly from the imperfections of man, and especially from an excessive surrender to the claims of the senses, of individual members of society. In this second factor we see the pre-revolutionary narrowness of the idealist constructs of Kant and Fichte (in comparison with the French Revolution). Many revolutionaries have shared these illusions about bourgeois society, though they have not all expressed them in such extravagant, idealist language.

Hegel's opposition to the ethical doctrines of Kant and Fichte is directed at these two points. It was doubtless visible in the Rosenkranz manuscript of which now only the slightest fragments remain. But if we are to consider his views in detail, and the polemic is of the highest importance for Hegel's development and the concretization of his position, we shall have to have recourse to the relevant passages of the later *Spirit of Christianity*.[6]

In the first draft of *The Spirit of Christianity and its Fate*, Hegel's chief objection to the Kantian ethic is that in it man is 'always a slave against a tyrant and at the same time, a tyrant against slaves.'

In the final version he gives a fuller explanation:

'A man who wished to restore man's humanity in its entirety could not possibly have taken a course like this which does nothing for man's divided self but to add to it an obdurate conceit. To act in the spirit of the laws could not have meant for him "to act out of respect for duty and against one's inclinations".[7]

Thus Hegel reproaches Kant with perpetuating that fragmentation of man which Hegel too acknowledges as a fact and hence as the starting-point for philosophy, Kant's solution to his own opposition of duty and inclination (spirit and the senses) is not only not a solution, but even contains elements of inhumanity and its only effect is to add hypocrisy to the other vices of life.

Thus Hegel sees the Kantian ethic as just another form of the philistin-ism that must be combated in the interest of man and of social progress.

We recall here that in the very first Frankfurt notes Hegel associated the Kantian ethic with the religious preservation of positivity (see p. 127–8). And in his further discussion of the ideas already quoted he refers to one of Kant's writings on religion in which Kant sets out to prove the superiority of his ethical theory over the positive religions. (Kant, *Die Religion innerhalb der Grenzen der blossen Vernunft*, Leipzig 1903, p. 206.) Hegel contests Kant's claim here vigorously.

'By this line of argument, however, positivity is only partially removed; and between the Shaman of the Tungus and the European prelate who rules church and state, between the Mongols and the Puritans, on the one hand, and the man who listens to his own com-mand of duty on the other, the difference is not that the former make themselves slaves, while the latter is free, but that the former have their lord outside themselves, while the latter carries his lord in him-self, yet at the same time is his own slave. For the particular instincts, inclinations, pathological love[8], sensuous experience, or whatever else it is called—the universal is necessarily and always something alien and objective. There remains a residuum of indestructible positivity which finally shocks us because the content which the universal com-mand of duty acquires, a specific duty, contains the contradiction of being restricted and universal at the same time, and makes the most stubborn claims for its one-sidedness, i.e. on the strength of possessing universality of form. Woe to the human relations which are not unquestionably found in the concept of duty; for this concept (since it is not merely the empty thought of universality but is to manifest itself in an action) excludes or dominates all other relations.[9]

We see here how Hegel develops a two-pronged attack on the Kantian ethic. He rejects it primarily because it disregards the whole, living man and instead expels man's living existence from ethics, subjugates it by means of laws alien to life and thus transforms morality into a dead 'positive' thing. And secondly he sees clearly that this rigidly mechanical aspect of Kant's thought is intimately connected with the hypostatization of the concept of duty. This insight brings Hegel a significant step forward in the development of the dialectic. He is not primarily interested in the content of Kant's ethics, in whether particular injunctions are morally valid or not. He is concerned to refute the method by which Kant arrives at them. He asserts with increasing confidence that a moral commandment which arises in certain social and historical circumstances, in which alone it is valid, can become false when it is maintained under different circumstances. This not only brings him much closer to the dialectical conception of the relation between true and false, one of the key epistemological themes of Jena, but it leads directly to the heart of Hegel's later approach to ethics.

The different methodological approaches of the two thinkers may be briefly summarized as follows: Kant leaves the social contents of ethics uninvestigated, he takes them as they are given without any historical critique, and attempts to deduce moral laws from the internal coherence of the content of the imperative. For Hegel, on the other hand, every single moral imperative is just a part, a moment, of a living social whole which is in constant flux. For Kant the individual moral laws stand in isolation from each other, each the allegedly inexorable inference from a unified supra-historical and supra-social 'principle of reason'; for Hegel they are all moments of a dialectical process in the course of which they come into collision with each other and, through their own momentum and lively interaction, cancel each other out, wither away in the course of time, or else re-emerge in a different form and with a different content.

The contrast between the two thinkers is not so well defined in sociohistorical terms at this stage as it was to become a few years later in Jena, but at the level of method it is clear enough. And it is also easy to see that Hegel's objections to Kant are based on his different view of civil society. We have already described Hegel's search for a 'reconciliation' with civil society and with the people who live in it, just as they really are. For this reason he rebels against the violation of living human beings by abstract moral injunctions, and the dehumanizing division of man into mental and sensuous halves.

Thus Hegel's critique of Kant is evidently pointing in the same direction as that of Goethe and Schiller. Goethe majestically ignores the methodological problems of idealist ethics and arrives at a humanist position as poet and thinker by a spontaneous materialist route. Schiller for his part rejects the harsh consequences of Kant's doctrine but remains in sympathy with his basic philosophy and refuses to go beyond the limits of Kantian epistemology. Hegel's early method is consciously to elaborate all the contradictions that emerge from Kant's ethical philosophy and with their aid arrive at a definition of what the whole of life, 'religious life', civil society, really demands of man.

We recall our earlier discussion (p. 127) of positivity in which we said that for Hegel at this time everything positive represented a false synthesis. Hegel's conception of positivity naturally implies that the only way to eliminate the positive is through human activity. As long as action was thought of in socially abstract terms, as in Berne, the question was very simple: republican activity in antiquity was free of positivity, the private individuals of the Christian era in their passivity know only the positive. Now, when he has to consider the nature of action on the part of individuals in civil society, another criterion becomes necessary. Action and non-action, activity and passivity are no longer so rigidly opposed to each other as in Berne. One implication of this is that not every action annuls positivity. It does so only if it produces the correct 'union'.

> 'The moral element of action lies in choice and choice is moral when the union achieved is one where that which is excluded is divisive; where the idea that is unified in the action with the thinking subject of the action, is itself already unified—and it is immoral if it is divisive.'[10]

These remarks, too, bear the stamp of the oracular abstraction characteristic of so much of the Frankfurt period. Hegel's starting-point here is Kant's conception of freedom, of the possibility of a free choice between good and evil. The later dialectics of freedom and necessity are scarcely in evidence. In his polemical interpretation he again defines choice as a union: a union of the subject that makes the choice and the object of that choice. Confusing though the word 'union' may be in this context the nature of Hegel's hostility to the Kantian ethical doctrine does emerge very clearly. For Kant the fact of freedom (of the moral outlook expressed in it) suffices to make an action moral. If the motives resulting in an action conform to the dictates of practical reason then, according to Kant, the social content of the action must inevitably be moral too. Hence the social content follows directly, logically from the formal postulates of freedom, from the victory of *homo noumenon* over *homo phenomenon*.

This direct formal and logical necessity is contested by Hegel. In his obscure terminology he seems to be saying: a union can be either real or apparent (i.e. only in the mind, only positive). The choice for its part also achieves a union between the subject that chooses and the object chosen. Whether the action which satisfies these formal requirements is really moral depends according to Hegel on the *content* of the object. If this is a real union then the action is moral; if union is only apparent, positive, then the action is immoral. And this is so whether or not Kant's formal criteria have been satisfied, independently of the state of mind of the subject making his choice.

In blunt contrast to Kant's approach Hegel's criterion is neither formal nor is it a moment of the individual's consciousness (conscience, etc.)—it relates to content, a content bound up with life in civil society. His general use of the word 'life' can no longer disguise this fact. For example,

'Morality is what is fitting, it is union with the law of life—if the law is not the law of life, but something alien, then we have the greatest cleavage, objectivity.'[10]

In the Kantian ethic it is entirely a matter of chance whether there is a union with 'the law of life' and hence it can provide no guarantee that the dead positivity of the world can be overcome by it. Indeed, in Hegel's view, the form of the Kantian injunction to do one's duty with its division of man into two hostile parts, reason and the senses, necessarily precludes the union, the real synthesis of man with the 'law of life', the 'reconciliation' of man with civil society. In Hegel's eyes Kantian 'morality' means dependence on oneself, 'cleavage within oneself'. For this reason positivity simply cannot be annulled in it and through it.

'A moral outlook can annul only the objective (moral) law and not the objective world; man stands isolated and so does the world.'[11]

Hegel's attack on Kant's theory as a doctrine which preserves positivity leads to the other decisive disagreement between their positions: the problem of conflicting duties. It is on this issue that we can see most clearly the development that took place at the time in ideas about the nature of society in an age when the important thinkers and writers were attempting to grapple with the problems of the post-revolutionary world. Given the idealist character of classical German philosophy it was inevitable that the moral problems of life were not deduced from the economic structure of society, but that on the contrary the foundation and starting-point of thought was the reflection of social development in the moral attitudes and the deeds of men. Only after that do they begin to consider society which they conceive as the material and the background for these attitudes and actions. Despite this idealist inversion and distortion of the real state of affairs the methodology of the different moral philosophers clearly reflects their differing views of society.

The problem of conflicting duties is one of the most revealing in this context, the mere assumption that the real demands of morality can come into conflict with each other tacitly acknowledges that civil society contains contradictions. The way in which these contradictions are grasped and philosophically resolved gives us an idea of the way the various idealist philosophers think of the real problems and solutions. Since the idea that there are no contradictions in civil society (apart from the 'eternal' contradiction between phenomenal and noumenal man) is an essential part of the pre-revolutionary illusions about the life history of modern civil society, it is only natural that Kant should resolutely deny the possibility of a conflict of duties. On this point he says:

> '*A conflict of duties* would be a relation of duties in which one of them would annul the other (wholly or in part). But a *conflict of duties and obligations* is inconceivable. For the concepts of duty and obligation as such express the objective practical necessity of certain actions, and two conflicting rules cannot both be necessary at the same time: if it is our duty to act according to one of these rules, then to act according to the opposite one is not our duty and is even contrary to duty.'[12]

Fichte's attitude is precisely similar to this. He is a little more concrete than Kant and speaks not just of conflicts of duties in general, but of conflicts between obligations people have towards themselves and to others. But it is clear that he really provides a restatement of the same position and he naturally arrives at the same conclusion as Kant:

> 'There is no conflict between the freedom of rational beings *in general*: i.e. there is no contradiction in the fact that there are many free beings in the phenomenal world . . . A conflict, not in freedom itself, but between specific free actions on the part of rational beings can only arise if a person makes an *illegitimate and immoral* use of his freedom to suppress the freedom of another . . .'[13]

We have discussed the positions of Kant and Fichte in some detail in order to make clear the extent of Hegel's break with tradition, with the view of morality and society which had obtained hitherto among the classical German philosophers. Of course, Hegel was anticipated here to some extent by Goethe and Schiller. And not merely in their purely literary works whose achievement is, in part, their ability to construct compelling images of conflict in society, which translated into the idiom of moral philosophy yields just those conflicts of duties of which we have spoken, but also in their theoretical writings. Schiller especially in his aesthetic writings and in particular his theory of tragedy placed this issue in the foreground. But since Schiller was never able to liberate himself from his Kantian assumptions there is a constant conflict between the living, authentic, poetically inspired description of particular social and historical antagonism and the strait-jacket of the Kantian principles in which they are confined.[14]

Hegel's critique of Kant increasingly places contradiction in the centre of attention, not so much concrete conflicts between concrete moral imperatives—which was the chief interest of Goethe and Schiller—but the contradictions that necessarily arise from Kant's own definition of duty. We recall that Hegel denied that Kant's ethics could achieve the annulment of positivity. He now characterizes the philosophical quintessence of life in positivity in this way:

'It is true that "positive man", in respect of a specific virtue which in him and for him is service, is neither moral nor immoral, and the service whereby he fulfils certain duties is not of necessity a non-virtuous attitude to these same duties; but from another aspect there is linked with this neutrality of character a measure of immorality, because the agent's specific positive service has a limit which he cannot transcend, and hence beyond it he is immoral. Thus this immorality of positivity does not open on the same aspect of human relations as positive obedience does; within the sphere of the latter the non-moral is not the immoral. Thus the opposite of virtue is not only immorality but also non-morality.'[15]

In a marginal note on this passage Hegel makes the comment, applicable to every moral theory of the Kantian type, that it contains 'neither change, nor gain, nor birth, nor death'. Whereas virtue, as Hegel understands it, is a 'modification of life', it may exist or not exist, it 'can be born and can die'. Hegel goes on to make a contrast between the speculative moralist of the Kantian type who 'can only make war on life' and the pedagogue and reformer 'who addresses himself to human beings' and for whom the problems of birth and death are of decisive importance.

We here see the great importance of the argument that virtue has a two-fold antonym: immorality and positivity. Kant narrowed the field of ethics down to the question of whether duties were fulfilled or neglected. His lack of interest in the possibility of a conflict between the contents of the various duties was matched only by his indifference to the causes or effects in human or social terms of the fulfilment or non-fulfilment of one's moral obligations. This follows inexorably from his fundamental conception of morality and its reduction to a struggle between what is morally reasonable in man and what is merely sensual. Hegel does away with this conflict altogether and searches for the real moral conflicts in the realities of society. We have already seen (p. 209) that his criterion for the rightness of a moral action lies in the content of the 'union' that has been chosen. He now becomes more specific and defines two different kinds of false union: mere positivity, i.e. imprisonment within the immediate, lifeless manifestations of society, and immorality, the direct rebellion against the real, dominant 'unions' in a given society.

Thus Hegel not only regards all those areas utterly neglected by Kant as the very core of ethical thought, but he goes further than this: he is concerned to define the specific, contradictory, human and social meaning of all these very involved and disparate conflicts. At the end of the marginal note referred to above he says:

> 'the destruction of vice lies in the way that it brings about the punishment of the wrong-doer. Punishment is the necessary evil consequence of crime, but not every consequence of crime can be called punishment, e.g. a man's character may deteriorate in the course of crime—it cannot be said that the criminal deserved to become even worse.'[16]

Hegel proceeds from these premises to a ruthless critique of Kant's denial that moral imperatives conflict. He shows that such conflicts must necessarily arise from wealth and the complexity of life. And it is important to note that even in Frankfurt Hegel saw this problem historically. As life becomes increasingly varied and complex (in an emergent bourgeois society) the contradictions lying at the roots of moral conflict increase. By way of illustration we shall cite a lengthy passage dealing with this question, though we must draw the reader's attention to Hegel's annulment of the entire realm of morality by love and religion: in contrast to the contradictions in the sphere of morality, love and religion appear as the principle of a unified life. We must postpone a discussion of the conscious and unconscious contradictions in his view of love and religion until we make a full-scale analysis of the central arguments in *The Spirit of Christianity*. Of the dialectical contradictions inherent in every moral system Hegel writes as follows:

> 'But love reconciles not only the trespasser with his fate but also man with virtue, i.e. if love were not the sole principle of virtue, then every virtue would be at the same time a vice. To complete subjection under the law of an alien Lord, Jesus opposed not a partial subjection under a law of one's own, the self-coercion of Kantian virtue, but virtues without lordship and without submission, i.e. virtues as modifications of love. If the virtues had to be regarded otherwise than as modifications of one living spirit, if every virtue were an absolute virtue, the result would be insoluble conflicts arising from the plurality of absolutes. If there is no such thing as unification in one spirit, every virtue has something defective about it, since each is by its very name a single and so a restricted virtue. The circumstances in which it is possible—the objects, the conditions of an action—are something

accidental; besides, the relation of the virtue to its object is a single one; it precludes other relations to that object as well as relations of the same virtue to other objects. Hence every virtue, alike in its concept and in its activity, has its limit which it cannot overstep. A man of this specific virtue who acts beyond the limit of his virtue can act only viciously, . . A right given up for the one relation can no longer be a right for the other, or, if it is saved up for the other, the first must starve. In proportion as the multiplicity of human relationships grows, the mass of virtues also increases, and so does the mass of inevitable conflicts and the impossibility of fulfilment. If the man of many virtues tries to make a hierarchy of his creditors, all of whom he cannot satisfy, he declares himself as less indebted to those he subordinates than to the others which he calls higher. Virtues therefore may cease to be absolutely obligatory and thus may even become vices.

'In this many-sidedness of human relations and this multiplicity of virtues, nothing remains save despair of virtue and trespass of virtue itself. Only when no virtue claims to subsist firmly and absolutely in its restricted form . . . only when it is simply the one living spirit which acts and restricts *itself* in accordance with the whole of the given situation, in complete absence of external restriction, and without at the same time being divided by the manifold character of the situation; then and then only does the many-sidedness of the situation remain, though the mass of absolute and incompatible virtues vanishes. Here there can be no question of maintaining that underlying all the virtues there is one and the same basic *principle* which, always the same in different circumstances, appears differently modified as a particular virtue. . . . When they subsist together thus absolutely, the virtues simply destroy one another. Their unity on the strength of the rule is only apparent, for the rule is only a thought, and such a unity neither annuls multiplicity nor unifies it; it only lets it subsist in its whole strength.

'A living bond of the virtues, a living unity, is quite different from the unity of the concept; it does not set up a determinate virtue for determinate circumstances, but appears, even in the most variegated mixture of relations, untorn and unitary. Its external shape may be modified in infinite ways; it will never have the same shape twice. Its expression will never be able to afford a rule, since it never has the force of a universal opposed to a particular'.[17]

This passage clearly states the grounds of Hegel's disagreement with the ethical theory of Kant and Fichte. We can see the centrality and the far-reaching implications of his rejection of their approach to the conflict of moral imperatives, and we can also see why their formalism should provoke this frontal attack. However, Hegel is only deceiving himself when, in line with his general tendency in Frankfurt, he explains his position by arguing that the unity of the principle of morality in Kant is only an idea, something merely thought, whereas in his own case that unity exists in being, in life itself. For the most concrete reality that he himself can give this 'life', that of 'objective spirit', is itself only an idea. This self-delusion reveals the insuperable barrier of Hegel's idealism quite plainly, particularly in Frankfurt where it is tinged with religiosity.

But we must beware of exaggerating the importance of this illusion, for even in Frankfurt, to say nothing of later on, his notion of 'objective spirit' is an incomparably richer, more dialectical, more realistic reflection of objective reality than the Kantian position. Its potential is already evident in Frankfurt, in the contrast between Kant's narrow formalism, his crabbed appeal to the conscience and the sense of duty of the isolated individual, and Hegel's appeal to the moral standards inherent in the totality of the effective, living determinations of society, and by implication to the realities of society as the criterion of vice and virtue.

This concentration on the content of morality, these efforts to draw attention to the problematic nature of social content, indicates a very great step forward in the development of Hegel's dialectic. It has a number of important consequences. Above all, society, with all its concrete reality, is made the *direct*, conscious object of morality. It is self-evident that Kantian morality presupposes bourgeois society, no less than Hegel's; both are reflections of the same society. But Kant writes as if from a commanding position far above society. In this sense Kant's standpoint is that of the pre-revolutionary Enlightenment which unconsciously and immediately equated the as yet non-existent bourgeois society with the 'kingdom of reason'. Of course, the situation was different for the French and English Enlightenment, since they found themselves in the midst of the real struggles of the emergent bourgeoisie and so, notwithstanding their equally abstract, idealist and unhistorical beliefs about society, they were able to draw much more concrete conclusions; when it came to action they were able to look at society realistically and not just from the assumptions of their own moral philosophy. Because of the backwardness of German society the idealist method of the Enlightenment culminated there in the particular idealism of Kant and Fichte. Now when this idealism proclaimed its own eternal and absolute validity from the depths of its own subjectivist isolation, it cut itself off from the very social contents that in reality constituted the substratum of its *a priori* constructs. It was essential for it to re-establish contact with these social contents, but from the given position, on its own assumptions, it could only do so by *sleight of hand*. Hegel's critique points unerringly to the weak point in Kant's methodology here; in Jena he will go further and demonstrate Kant's failure with reference to quite specific social problems.

The problem of conflict between moral duties has a further point of interest: the idea that social content supplies the criterion for all moral imperatives. For Hegel this social content amounts to the totality of the social determinations in any given period of history, whereas in Kant's eyes the social concretization and fulfilment of a moral obligation could only mean conferring the support of morality upon a particular institution of bourgeois society. The fact is that Kant dogmatically assumes, firstly, that the particular institutions, moral injunctions, etc. of bourgeois society are in harmony with the postulates of reason and, secondly, that they cannot conflict with each other. Hegel rejects both of these dogmas and this leads him directly to a more dialectical grasp of bourgeois society. In the fragments under discussion we find ourselves at the very beginning of his development. The climax later on comes with the idea that reason, the spirit, can only realize itself in the course of the entire historical development of mankind and that only the whole of this process and its end-result will satisfy the postulates of reason—a conclusion which reveals the bourgeois limitations of Hegel's ideas as clearly as did Kant's dogmatic assumptions. The particular aspects and moments of the process cannot be measured by the requirements of the absolute postulates of reason. They can only be understood and evaluated in the concrete context of the other isolated factors together with which they form a particular historical totality. And every such historical totality (e.g. a nation at a particular stage of its development) can only be thought of as a relatively complete totality, for it is at the same time no more than a moment in the history of the spirit. This gives rise to a complicated dialectic of the relative and the absolute. Hegel was never an historical relativist. He never placed the different periods of history on a level with each other. His dissolution of the dogmatic absolutism of Kant is based on an idea of historical development in which each moment of history is absolute, in the sense that it represents a *necessary* moment in the process, but at the same time, and inseparably from this, it is only relative, since it is *only a moment* in history.

Of course, the idea of historical development was by no means utterly foreign to Kant. His idea of it was the infinite progress of humanity in its advance towards the fulfilment of the dictates of reason. But this view is defective in two respects. On the one hand, it is not able to give a satisfactory account of the different stages of the historical process. On the other hand, it leads to an all-too-simplified view of history based on the battle between reason and unreason, of reason and the senses. Hegel's more dialectical approach overcomes both these limitations. The different stages of history gain a concrete life of their own, the more so as Hegel's thought matures; he constantly labours to analyse the concrete social connections within their real historical context. We have already seen how he broadened his scheme of history by adding the Orient

(Judaism) to his earlier contrast between ancient and modern. This alone suffices to overcome Kant's linear historical scheme.

The more Hegel works at this philosophy of history the more clearly his central belief emerges that history is the journey of the spirit along the road to itself, to complete self-knowledge. But the path to this goal cannot be reduced to such unambiguous moral principles as in the case of Kant. On the one hand, a more advanced stage of history does not necessarily stand higher morally and culturally than the epoch it succeeds. On the contrary, in his fully developed philosophy of history Hegel will show how morally inferior, more selfish passions have provided the stimuli to an objectively higher development. On the other hand, the conquest of a higher stage in historical development always entails irreparable losses for mankind. When we come to analyse his view of history in Jena we shall see the change in his assessment of Greek civilization, a change which, however, only affects the *position* assigned to Greece in his overall scheme: in Berne he had regarded the city-state of antiquity as a model for the present, whereas in Jena he sees that classical civilization is lost beyond recall. But this change is not accompanied by a comparable change in his view of the value of classical culture. Then as now he believed that in certain spheres of human activity—above all in art—classical civilization represented the pinnacle of human achievement. And since this climactic point is necessarily connected with the character of classical civilization, no less necessary than that the higher development of man should advance beyond classical civilization, it becomes apparent that the entire process is a much more complex, contradictory and uneven one in which the higher development of mankind leaves behind it pinnacles which will never again be conquered.

We have argued that the problem of a conflict of duties is one of the starting-points for the development of Hegel's dialectical method. However, it is only in the context of the later, fully-developed philosophy of history that this question really gains in substance. In Frankfurt Hegel only grasped isolated moments of the overall dialectical picture and he worked out the premises and effects of these as well as he could, but the complete picture was still a long way off. For all that, he did not tackle the problem in any narrow spirit; on the contrary, the social breadth and depth of his approach distinguishes him very sharply right from the start from the other contemporary thinkers who objected to the dogmatic narrowness of the categorical imperative. It is a distinction of this kind that forces us to note the senselessness and the lack of scientific rigour which enables the imperialist neo-Hegelians to lump Hegel's Frankfurt period together with vitalist tendencies of the day. E.g. it is true enough that Friedrich Jacobi, one of the genuine vitalists of the time, likewise criticized the inflexibility and narrowness of the categorical imperative. But he opposed to it the richness of the human emotional experience, the emotional world of the individual. He goes on in a highly rhetorical vein to defend certain 'heroic' sins against the categorical imperative but this only leads him straight into the arms of moral relativism. The fact that 'life', Hegel's central category in Frankfurt, has very little in common with views of this sort, but in reality paves the way for the as yet vague idea of the contradictory, living unity of bourgeois society, just helps to illustrate the complexity of the problem of a conflict of moral duties.

Hegel's analysis here moves essentially on a fairly abstract philosophical plane, but two motifs of methodological interest do emerge.

(1) The conflict between moral imperatives springs from the dialectics of the absolute and relative. According to Hegel each moral duty is only a moment in the overall dialectical totality of society, or 'life'. But the entire complex is itself contradictory; contradictions between its particular determinations lie at its very foundations. The situation is not that the particular moral duties are all neatly compartmentalized and govern a neatly segregated area, or that they are arranged in a hierarchy, but that conflict, struggle and contradiction dominate the entire scene. Since every moment, every duty lays claim to absolute validity it must necessarily come into conflict with other moments that make the same claim. And only the living totality of all these determinations can annul this conflict. But the essence of this totality is precisely that it is a totality of such conflicting determinations.

(2) In Hegel's view each moment must necessarily lay claim to absolute validity. This brings us to a point where the profundity of Hegel's analysis of civil society and of the dialectical method become apparent. At the same time we perceive the limits of the idealist approach. The claim of the particular moment to absolute validity forms the focal point of Hegel's later appreciative critique of the so-called philosophy of reflection and of the position of the determinations of reflection (*Reflexionsbestimmungen*) in the dialectical method. Hegel regards the determinations of reflection as an essential part of dialectics, but also as a mere stage in the understanding of reality. This separates him from Kant and Fichte who make the determinations of reflection into absolutes, fail to advance beyond them and hence find themselves unable to progress beyond those insoluble antinomies which follow from the determinations of reflection when these are taken to their logical conclusion. But by the same token a no less firm barrier is erected against vitalism, the philosophy of Romanticism, etc, which also combats the inflexibility and narrowness of the determinations of reflection, while imagining that reality can be understood without them, that they can be dismissed as inferior, merely rational forms of thought; in consequence, such views inevitably end in mystical irrationalism.

However opposed they are to each other both camps believe that the contradictions which they encounter, are merely subjective, things which have their origin in the limitations of the human mind rather than in the nature of reality. They differ from each other only in that Kant draws agnostic conclusions from them, while Romanticism prefers irrational and mystical solutions. Hegel, in contrast to *both* regards the contradictions as something objective, which reveals the nature of reality. Hence for him the determinations of reflection are just a stage on the road to the dialectical understanding of reality. Going beyond the antinomies of reflective understanding annuls their contradictions only to arrive at higher, more developed contradictions of a richer stage, the stage of speculative reason. Hegel's description of the reflective understanding, of the hypostatization of moments with only a relative, partial validation, appears as a necessary moment of the dialectical method itself. It is in this sense that Hegel later presents Kant and Fichte in his history of philosophy as the historically necessary forerunners of his own dialectical method.

Hegel's attitude to the philosophy of reflection is important not only for the development of his own dialectics, but also historically. Romanticism, which according to its modern apologists can lay claim to a much more authentic historicity, is in fact utterly unhistorical on this issue: it regards the metaphysical thought of the seventeenth and eighteenth centuries, whose ultimate consequences and limitations become manifest in the thought of Kant, as a great aberration of the human mind. Hegel, by contrast, sees them from an authentically historical point of view and concludes that dialectics could only be reached via this route. At the same time he senses that the supremacy of metaphysical thought among his predecessors was necessarily connected with the entire cultural development of mankind, that it was an inevitable product of this particular stage of human development. Later on and in the context of a discussion of the development of the natural sciences, Engels provided comprehensive materialist proof that the historical stage of metaphysical thought was indeed indispensable.

Thus from the point of view of the Hegelian system as a whole the necessity of a conflict of moral imperatives is a significant special case of the importance of the determinations of reflection in philosophy, of the necessary emergence of dialectical contradictions from the elevation of the relative determinants into absolute ones so characteristic of the ethical theory of Kant and Fichte. But just from what we have shown it is evident that, however philosophical his formulation may be, we are dealing here with one of those issues that spring directly from his own experience. That is to say, Hegel is not primarily interested in the Kantian ethic because Kant thought it out; he does not see it just as a false picture of reality. Of course, he does criticize what he regards as errors, ideas that have not been followed through to their final conclusion, and Kant's denial that conflicts between moral imperatives can occur is just such a case. Hegel refutes this belief by showing it to be incompatible with the ultimate principles of Kantianism (and Fichteanism) itself. At this point, however, his own position changes. He regards the conflict of duties as a socio-historical reality with which thought has to come to terms and which it must use as a jumping-off point. Thus Hegel looks at and criticizes the antinomic character of Kantianism from a double point of view: firstly, as a prodigious achievement in discovering the necessity of antinomies and treating it as a matter of philosophical importance; and secondly, as a subjectivist limit to Kant's thought (because he wishes to call a halt at the antinomies, regarding them as final).

The insight that antinomies were a necessary part of society was a significant step forward in understanding the nature of bourgeois society. We have already shown why this discovery had to be made firstly and predominantly in the realm of moral thought. His growing awareness of the nature of bourgeois society will increasingly lead Hegel to extend his insights into the realms of economic and social activity.

Of course, even then Hegel does not call a halt once he has discovered contradictions in the conflict of duties. To do so would lead to a so-called 'tragic view of life', to a comprehensive pessimism with regard to bourgeois society. His thought drives him on inexorably in search of a resolution of all the contradictions, and we have already seen that this resolution lies in an understanding of the totality in movement.

We now see how the idealist limits to his thought merge with the bourgeois limits of his mental horizon. Hegel is increasingly concerned to interpret this totality in which the contradictions in the conflict of moral imperatives (i.e. in very general terms: the contradictions of the lives of individuals in bourgeois society) are resolved, as itself something contradictory, as something driven forward by contradictions. Thanks to these efforts he arrives, at the end of the Frankfurt period, at a new and more comprehensive formula for dialectical contradiction than all his predecessors; he will arrive in fact at the most comprehensive statement available to idealist dialectics. But in order to follow this theory through to the end Hegel would have to go beyond bourgeois society, i.e. he would have to have at least a premonition of how bourgeois society might elevate its contradictions to a higher level. But like the English classical economists, Hegel regards bourgeois society as the latest, the most highly developed and final form of historical development. This means that if the contradictions are to be annulled this must be done in a different manner from the earlier stages which led either historically or logically or 'phenomenologically' to this 'highest standpoint'. Hegel finds himself forced, therefore, to annul his own concept of dialectics at the very peak of his own system in order to be able to extinguish all the contradictions and arrive at a harmonious unity. Of course, there is nothing simple about this conclusion, it is the product of a violent internal struggle between two different tendencies in his thought. But an inevitable consequence of the social limitations imposed on him is that he is never able completely to overcome the old type of theory of contradiction. (We shall discuss other limitations of his dialectics in due course.)

Thus the disagreement between Kant and Hegel goes far beyond the confines of a methodology of moral philosophy. It is a significant stage in the growth of dialectical method, even though the transformation that takes place in his thought is relatively slight and abstract for the time being. Over and above that it signals a new stage in the theory of bourgeois society. In the period leading up to the French Revolution German philosophy and literature were worthy contemporaries of pre-revolutionary French ideology and now we find them attempting to perform the same sort of task in post-revolutionary Europe, the age of developing capitalist society. Since this latter enterprise took place on German soil where a bourgeois revolution neither did nor could have taken place, the development of German thought was inevitably provincial and distorted. Marx and Engels have shown this convincingly and comprehensively not only with regard to Hegel's thought but also with reference to Goethe's poetry and above all to that of Schiller. We have shown the common social tendencies underlying the works of Hegel and those of the Weimar classics, insofar as this was possible within the framework of this study. We have also shown that in comparison with his great contemporaries, Hegel displayed a far greater energy both in his analysis of the contradictory character of bourgeois society and in his study of its 'anatomy', viz. political economy. Our further discussions must attempt to show even more clearly that these two features of Hegel's thought are intimately connected with each other.

NOTES

1  Rosenkranz, p. 87f.
2  Ibid., p. 87.
3  *Erste Druckschriften*, p. 211.
4  Rosenkranz, p. 87f.
5  Fichte, *Das System der Sittenlehre* (1798), § 23, Leipzig 1908, Vol. II, p. 675.
6  Hegel takes issue explicitly here only with Kant's ethical doctrine.

We cannot state with any certainty whether he had read Fichte's writings on morality, which had only just appeared. But since Hegel's later detailed writings on ethics and philosophy in Jena almost always discuss Fichte's ethics along with those of Kant, and since he regarded Fichte as the consistent follower of Kant and the heir to his errors, it seems legitimate to assume that the Frankfurt critique of Kantian ethics can be taken to refer also to Fichte.

7   Ibid., p. 266. Knox, pp. 212–13.
8   The phrase 'pathological love' occurs in Kant's discussion of what it means to love God. He calls that love pathological which is a 'love of God, considered as an inclination' and declares that it is impossible 'for He is not an object of the senses'. *Critique of Practical Reason*, Bk 1, chap. 3, trans. T. K. Abbott, London 1967, p. 176.—*Trans.*
9   Nohl, p. 265f. Knox, pp. 211–12.
10  Ibid., p. 387.
11  Ibid., p. 390.
12  Kant, *The Metaphysics of Morals*, trans. M. J. Gregor, New York 1964, p. 23.
13  Fichte, op. cit., p. 694.
14  Cf. my essays on Schiller's aesthetics in my books *Goethe and his Age*, London 1968 and *Beiträge zur Geschichte der Ästhetik*, Berlin.
15  Nohl, p. 276. Knox, p. 224. The last sentence deviates from Knox because G.L. quotes from a divergent text.
16  Ibid., p. 276.
17  Nohl, pp. 293ff. Knox, pp. 244–6.

# CHAPTER FIVE

# The first studies in economics

HERE, at the decisive point in Hegel's intellectual biography, where we might have hoped to clarify the concrete relations between his dialectics and his study of economics we find ourselves baulked by the utter failure of our sources and we are compelled to rely almost entirely on hypotheses. We may think ourselves fortunate that Rosenkranz has at least preserved the bare fact of the date when Hegel first took up economics. All the material that Rosenkranz possessed *in toto* has since been lost.

It is certainly no accident that this section of Hegel's papers has vanished without trace. Of his immediate pupils there was not a single one who had even the slightest comprehension of economic problems, let alone of their importance in the evolution of Hegel's system and methodology. They did not even notice the obvious evidence of such studies in the published works (the *Phenomenology, Philosophy of Right*, etc.).

The backwardness of German society was such that even in the case of Germany's greatest philosophical genius, Hegel himself, the intellectual reflection of social antagonisms appears in an inverted, idealistic form. In the case of his pupils, whose formative years fell, for the most part, in the period of the Restoration, there is an utter failure to comprehend the problems of economics and their significance for an understanding of the problems of society. And this blind spot is as much in evidence on the reactionary right-wing of the Hegelians as in the liberal centre and on the left. The timidity with which the Liberals of the 1830s tackled the great social issues of the time is reflected also in their utter blankness in the face of economic problems. Not until the early 1840s did the intensification of the class struggle awaken a certain interest in economic issues in the ranks of the Hegelians, and even then we find a lack of knowledge and serious study that compares very unfavourably with Hegel. The 'philosophical arrangement' of the economic categories of both the classics and the utopians at the hands of the Hegelians among the 'True Socialists' and also by Lassalle scarcely advanced beyond a superficial formalism.

Not until the early works of the founders of dialectical materialism, of Marx and Engels, do we discover not merely a profound and thorough-going investigation of the problems of political economy, but also the conscious realization that this was the realm in which the great problems of dialectics were to be studied, that here was the great task of taking the material accumulated, but not worked out dialectically, by the classics of bourgeois political economy and by the utopians, of discovering its underlying laws and principles, and advancing from there to an analysis of the dialectical laws of movement in society. As early as Engels' brilliant writings in the *Deutsch–französiche Jahrbücher*, the connection between economics and dialectics stands clearly in the foreground. Shortly after that Marx himself devotes his full attention to the problem in the *Economic and Philosophic Manuscripts*, the last section of which contains his critique of Hegel's *The Phenomenology of Mind*. In this Marx, notwithstanding his incisive and crucial criticism of Hegel's idealism, uncovers the important and positive role of economics in the formation of the Hegelian dialectic, in particular his use of the category of labour in which he follows in the footsteps of the English classics. This work is then succeeded by a series of important polemical writings against Bruno Bauer, Max Stirner, Proudhon, etc, which contain a large number of profound and illuminating observations on these issues.

It is typical of the opportunism of the Second International that a large proportion of these writings gathered dust in the archives, their value recognized by no-one. The development of opportunism coincided with the disappearance of any understanding of dialectics and the rampant growth of metaphysical shallowness then created an atmosphere in which it was easy to twist and distort the clearly formulated propositions of Marxist economics.

Only the Bolsheviks consistently fought against this opportunism on all fronts. Lenin, despite the disadvantage of not having access to a large part of Marx's work on this topic, was the only one to have grasped their full importance.

> 'It is impossible completely to understand Marx's *Capital*, and especially its first chapter, without having thoroughly studied and understood the *whole* of Hegel's *Logic*. Consequently, half a century later none of the Marxists understood Marx!'[1]

Rosenkranz, a moderate liberal and an adherent of the so-called Hegelian centre at the time of the break-up of the school, naturally had no idea of the importance of Hegel's economic studies. To give the reader an idea of the thoroughness with which the documents have been mislaid we propose to quote *everything* that Rosenkranz has to say on the topic in his biography; later biographers have merely copied from Rosenkranz. The discovery of Hegel's manuscripts in recent decades has greatly increased our knowledge of Hegel's study of economics in Jena, but about the years in Frankfurt we are as much in the dark as ever.

Rosenkranz states that Hegel's interest in economic questions began in Frankfurt, and that it was primarily conditions in England that excited his curiosity. He regularly read the newspapers and made detailed notes from them (which have of course been lost). In Rosenkranz's words:

> 'At the same time he moved closer to the immediate arena of politi-
> cal events and found his interest in it greatly increased. Above all he
> was fascinated by the relations of commerce and property especially
> in *England*, partly no doubt in accordance with the general admiration
> which the previous century felt for the English constitution which
> was regarded by many as an ideal, and partly perhaps because no
> other country of Europe could boast such a variety of the forms of
> commerce and property as England, and nowhere else was there such
> a great variety of personal relationships as a result. As his excerpts
> from English newspapers show, Hegel followed with great excite-
> ment the parliamentary debates on the *Poor Law*, the alms by means of
> which the nobility and the aristocracy of wealth attempted to appease
> the rage of indigent masses.'[2]

This passage is followed by a much more detailed account of Hegel's
interest in the Prussian prison system.

Unfortunately Rosenkranz mentions no dates. This is highly regret-
table, especially as the reader of this book can see that he has misinter-
preted Hegel's attitude to England. We do not possess a single remark by
Hegel that would lend support to Rosenkranz's view that Hegel was
ever a great admirer of the English constitution or that he regarded it as a
model. Understandably enough he did not concern himself closely with
England. On the contrary, the annotated translation of Cart which was
written shortly after his arrival in Frankfurt and its sharp criticism of the
reactionary policies of England seems to have arisen as an echo of the
French Revolution (see p. 110). Thus Hegel's interest in England seems
to have grown in connection with his research into the nature and laws
of bourgeois society during his stay in Frankfurt. It would be both
important and interesting to discover the precise moment at which
Hegel took up these studies since, in view of the relatively swift changes
in Hegel's views during the years of crisis in Frankfurt, a knowledge of
the exact dates is very necessary.

But Hegel's interest was not confined to the English economy; he also
took up the study of economic theory. With reference to this Rosenkranz states:

> 'All of Hegel's ideas about the nature of civil society, about need
> and labour, about the division of labour and the wealth of the estates,
> about poverty, the police, taxation, etc, are finally concentrated in a
> *commentary* on the German translation of *Steuart's* book on political
> economy which he wrote between 19 February and 16 May 1799, and
> which has survived intact. It contains a number of magnificent
> insights into politics and history and many subtle observations.

Steuart was a supporter of the mercantilist system. With noble passion and a host of interesting illustrations, Hegel attacked the deadness of this system and sought to preserve man's soul (*das Gemüt*) in the midst of competition, the mechanization of labour and of commerce.[3]

We need not waste words on these jejune, uncomprehending remarks. But even from this meagre summary we can see what an important document we have lost. It is perfectly obvious that Hegel approached the problems of economics from the point of view of his critique of dead positivity and we would have a much clearer picture of his early attitudes to bourgeois society if only we still possessed these first investigations into economic theory.

Another factor here is that Rosenkranz's account poses an insoluble problem. In the last sentence Rosenkranz claims that Hegel sought to save man's soul amidst the mechanism of capitalist society. This would suggest that Hegel's thoughts were running on similar lines to those of the reactionary Romantics. In view of Hegel's later development and the general character of what we have seen of his philosophical and social attitudes, this sounds highly improbable. It is true enough that it was only later on that Hegel made his famous remark that the rational is real and the real is rational, but in a general sense it may be said to constitute the unconscious leitmotiv of all his thought from Frankfurt onwards. In the course of our examination of Hegel's economic notes in Jena we shall have occasion to remark on his closeness to the 'cynical', the ruthlessly truthful views of the English classical economists who were perfectly willing to expose all the horrors and scandals of capitalist society, while asserting that capitalism was essentially progressive. For this reason we believe that Rosenkranz simply misunderstood Hegel. However, since we can offer no irrefutable proof of our assertion, and since it is an abstract possibility that Hegel did for a short time incline towards Romantic economics, we can only regard our rejection of Rosenkranz's interpretation as a hypothesis. Nevertheless, we believe that the reader who has followed the entire development of Hegel's thought will agree that our hypothesis is correct.

It is not really possible to estimate the influence of Steuart's particular economic principles on Hegel. Not only because the commentary has been lost and we cannot know which sections impressed Hegel, which he agreed with and which he rejected, but also because his reading of Steuart did not lead to any immediate attempt to apply the newly-acquired economic principles to bourgeois society. What we have said earlier on about the discontinuities of the Frankfurt period applies with particular force here. Having spent three months on the problems of economics Hegel simply turned to his chief work in Frankfurt, *The Spirit of Christianity*. Of course, as we shall see, this essay does not neglect the

problems of society, but its immediate theme is different and the change
in his socio-economic views only makes itself felt in a few places and
even then in the most general philosophical terms. Not until the period
in Jena do we come across manuscripts which directly concern themselves with social problems and among which economics are given an
explicit and prominent position. Nor can we know with any certainty
just how important economic problems were in Hegel's last work in
Frankfurt, the *Fragment of a System* of 1800, since as we shall see, only two
small fragments of this work have survived. But in the Jena manuscripts
there is evidence that in addition to Steuart Hegel had read the works of
Adam Smith. And given the great abstractness of Hegel's statements
about economics, his exclusive interest in the great, universal problems,
it is hard to show the impact of details.

All the same, it is highly probable that the study of Adam Smith was a
turning-point in Hegel's evolution. The problem which reveals the
striking parallel between Hegel's thought and the classical English economists is the problem of *work* as the central mode of human activity, as
the chief method by which the identity of the subject–object (to use
Hegel's terminology at this time) can be achieved, as the activity which
annuls the deadness of objectivity, as the driving force of the process
which turns mankind into the product of its own activity. And it is
highly probable that this problem emerges for the first time in the course
of reading Adam Smith, since neither a study of the German economy
which was so backward in the context of the development of capitalism,
nor a reading of Steuart could really provide the necessary stimulus.

However, this is another issue which finds us reduced to hypotheses
and guesswork, and we give our view in the full awareness that it is no
more than a hypothesis. The first documentary evidence that Hegel had
read Smith is contained in the manuscripts of some lectures given in Jena
in 1803/4 and which were published not long ago.[4] Hegel refers here to
Adam Smith's statements about developing the forces of production
through the division of labour in the factory and he wrote the name of
Smith in the margin. But as early as 1802, in the *System of Ethics*, a similar,
if, as we shall see, a less well-developed attitude towards work, the division of labour etc., occupies a central position. It is therefore almost certain that Hegel was acquainted with Adam Smith right from the
beginning of his period in Jena and that he had therefore overcome, at
least in part, some of the limitations and defects of Steuart's theories.

Now it is our belief that Hegel's interest in classical English economics
actually dates from an earlier period, namely from the time when he was
already working on the *Fragment of a System*. It is perfectly true that that
work gives us no help at all, at any rate not directly, since the surviving
fragments contain only very meagre references to economic problems
and we have no idea how Hegel had thought of the structure of the

whole essay, nor indeed how far it was from completion. But in the course of some very obscure reflections on the philosophy of religion there is a very remarkable passage which may help to throw light on an extremely dark section of Hegel's intellectual evolution.

In this fragment Hegel deals with the place of religion in man's life, with the annulment of objectivity, of dead positivity in relation to men and things. The social and philosophical problems that this discussion provokes must be postponed for our detailed analysis of the entire fragment. We wish here to emphasize only one moment. Hegel writes:

'But it is necessary that he [man] should also put himself into a permanent relation with objects and thus maintain their objectivity *even to the point of completely destroying them*'.

In the Frankfurt manner already familiar to us, Hegel analyses man's relation to property and hence to the dialectics of positivity and life. In this fragment he finds a solution in a very curious and highly mystical theory of *sacrifice*. He continues:

Man would still be unable to unite himself with the infinite life because he would have kept something for himself; he would still be in a state of mastering things or caught in a dependence upon them. This is the reason why he gives up only part of his property as a sacrifice, for it is his fate to possess property, and this fate is necessary and can never be discarded. . . . Only through this *useless destruction*, through this destruction for the sake of destruction, does he make good the destruction which he causes *for his own particular purposes*. At the same time he has consummated the objectivity of the objects by a destruction unrelated to his own purposes, by that complete negation of relations which is called death. *This aimless destruction* for destruction's sake sometimes happens, even if the necessity of a *purposive destruction of objects* remains, and it proves to be the only religious relation to absolute objects.'[5]

At first sight this passage is certainly obscure enough. Sacrifice is thought of as a religious way out of the necessary 'fate' of the world of property, of bourgeois society. What is of interest to us is the distinction between sacrifice which is viewed as 'useless destruction', 'destruction for destruction's sake', and a concept of 'purposive destruction' which remains utterly unexplained in this context. The fragment from which we are quoting is the last sheet, i.e. the conclusion of Hegel's manuscript. If Hegel fails even to hint at what he means by what is obviously an important concept, this can only be explained by arguing that it must have been elucidated in the earlier parts of the essay, now lost. But enough has been said to indicate that 'purposive destruction' refers to the normal, everyday relation of man to the world of objects. The point of the sacrifice is precisely to raise man beyond that realm.

We must postpone for the time being our discussion of the meaning of sacrifice for Hegel. Our subsequent analyses, especially of his Jena theory of society, will show that the concept is not a religious or mystical one but that it is intimately connected with the illusions Hegel cherished at this time about the possibility of resolving the contradictions of bourgeois society. What interests us here is rather the concept with which it is contrasted, viz. the 'purposive destruction' of the objects. In order to decipher this apparently no less obscure notion we must have recourse to the *System of Ethics* written two years later in Jena. It is evident that the idea is connected with work. Hegel defines work in the *System of Ethics* in language reminiscent of Schelling's, as is much in the first part of his stay in Jena, as the 'destruction of the object', and indeed as its purposive destruction. The first dialectical triad from which his thought proceeds is: need, work, enjoyment. Work is then defined as follows:

> 'The destruction of the object, or of intuition (*Anschuauung*), but as a moment (i.e. not finally and absolutely) so that this destruction is replaced by another intuition or object; or else it establishes the pure identity, activity of the act of destruction; . . . it does not destroy the object as object in general, but in such a way that another is put in its place . . . this destruction, however, is *work*.'[6]

Admittedly, this definition does not contain the word 'purposive', but if we follow Hegel's line of thought carefully here and see how he moves from work to the tools of work and from tools to machines, it is evident that the idea is present and only the word is missing, and the word is only missing because it is supererogatory in this context. The connection between work and purposiveness remains henceforth a basic fact of Hegel's thought. Even in his treatment of theology in the *Logic* work continues to play an extraordinarily important part, as Lenin has expressly pointed out in various notes.

We believe, therefore, that the conception of work which is so essential a category in the Jena *System of Ethics* was already present in the lost parts of the Frankfurt *Fragment of a System*. And this makes it extremely probable that Hegel studied Adam Smith's *Wealth of Nations* as a preliminary to the latter work. (We must add in passing that the works of both Steuart and Smith were available in Germany at this time in various translations.)

In the circumstances it is exceptionally difficult to isolate the influence of particular English economists on particular ideas of Hegel's. However, we may draw attention to a number of elements in Steuart which undoubtedly had a lasting effect. Above all, Steuart was, as Marx shows, the real historian of economics among the classics; he was more interested in the social origins of capitalism than its inner workings which he grasps less well than his successors.[7] And at this stage in Hegel's career, when he was concerned to establish the historical necessity of bourgeois society, the sheer volume of information in Steuart's work and the constant comparisons between ancient and modern economies must have made a deep impression on him.

Beyond that, however, it can be argued that Hegel may have found it much easier to accept certain retrograde elements in Steuart, views which had been superseded by Smith's much clearer and more radical insights. No doubt, Hegel fought dead positivity wherever he found it and this would have led him to sympathize with Smith's efforts to eliminate certain obsolete elements of the old economics, with its wholesale fetishizations. But such outmoded views may have deep roots in the economies of backward nations. The relation between the economy and the state, for example, could only be analysed consistently in England, in the works of Smith and Ricardo. Marx has frequently shown how French economists of the Napoleonic era clung to all sorts of outmoded attitudes on that very question. This was even truer of Germany, and the very much slower growth of economics in Germany meant that misconceptions about the economic role of the state lasted well beyond Hegel's day. (One need think only of Lassalle and Rodbertus.) When in addition we remind ourselves that Hegel in his Jena period entertained many false hopes about the possibilities of resolving the antinomies of bourgeois society along Napoleonic lines, it is only too easy to understand why Hegel should have leant more towards Steuart than Smith on this issue.

But there is one further respect in which Hegel never departs from a view held by Steuart, and never reaches the point of understanding the great advances made by Adam Smith and Ricardo in formulating the laws underlying capitalist economics. We refer to the problem of surplus labour and surplus value. Marx, in his critique of Steuart's economics, makes the point that Steuart remained imprisoned within the old theory of making a 'profit upon alienation'. It is true that Steuart does distinguish between positive and relative profit. The latter is profit upon alienation. Marx says of the former:

> '*Positive* profit arises from "augmentation of labour, industry and ingenuity". *How* it arises from this Steuart makes no attempt to explain. The further statement that the effect of this profit is to augment and swell "*the public good*" seems to indicate that Steuart means by it nothing but the greater mass of use-values produced in consequence of the development of the productive powers of labour, and that he thinks of this positive profit as quite distinct from capitalists' profit—which always presupposes an increase of exchange value.'[8]

When we come to consider Hegel's economic views in Jena we shall see how deeply entangled he is in ideas of this sort which were so retrograde by English standards. The more progressive ideas that he had gained from a study of Adam Smith and a greater awareness of the facts of the English economy do indeed enable him to perceive certain economic contradictions in capitalism, particular antagonisms between capital and labour and he is able to discuss these frankly. But he never succeeds in unveiling the mystery of real capitalist exploitation, indeed he never approaches as close to it as the English bourgeois economists. This is a barrier he will never surmount and the reason is not far to seek: his knowledge of the conflict between capital and labour only comes to him from reading about international economic relations, not from his own experience, from a real insight into capitalism in ordinary life. That is to say, the barrier here is an intellectual mirror of the primitive economy of Germany.

Naturally, the size of the barrier is even further increased by Hegel's own idealism, in particular by his inversion of the relationship between law and the state on the one hand and economics on the other. But, as we have shown, his idealism is itself rooted in the same soil. Thus the economic backwardness of Germany does not have any single direct influence on Hegel, nor does it directly distort many of his most brilliant insights into bourgeois society. Its effects are various, complex and often impinge on his thought in unexpected ways.

We shall discuss Hegel's economic views in detail when we come to analyse his attempts to systematize them in Jena. For the present it is enough if we briefly indicate the immediate effects of Hegel's study of economics and the nature of his approach to the problems of bourgeois society. The decisive moment is contained in the long passage from the *Fragment of a System* already quoted: from this point onwards Hegel regards economics, the economic life of men, their determination by their economic relation to each other and to things as an inexorable 'fate'. (The Hegelian concept of fate will be analysed fully in the next chapter.) We have already seen the seeds of this view (p. 119f.) in the first notes of the Frankfurt period when Hegel made a number of complex observations on the possibility of harmonizing property relations with love.

But the idea was only treated sporadically there; here it becomes a crucial issue. Earlier on it was just one of the problems of subjective love, here we find it defined as fate and opposed to the highest representative of religion, Jesus. Part of Hegel's conception of fate in Frankfurt is the idea that to struggle against a hostile power has the same consequences as to evade it; this is in fact the expression of the inevitability of fate.[9] However mystical many of Hegel's utterances sound on this point, they yet contain a much more realistic core of truth about history and society than is to be found in the other German philosophers of this time: namely his rejection of the very common idea, still prevalent among intellectuals, that a man can stand above his age and his society, that he can take up a theoretical or practical position from a standpoint 'external' to his society.

In this sense property is treated in the *Spirit of Christianity* as an ineluctable fate. Since in that essay Hegel's reflections concentrate on the possibility of realizing the teaching of Jesus in society, it is natural that he should keep returning to the passage in the New Testament about the rich young man whom Jesus advised to dispose of his property to gain salvation. We may remember that Hegel had already referred to this passage in Berne (p. 63), but there he had confined himself to the observation that it illustrated his argument that Christianity is concerned exclusively with 'private individuals'. At that stage he was not interested in the economic implications.

Only now does he focus on the latter, but he does so with a vengeance. In the plan for *The Spirit of Christianity* he is only concerned with Jesus' escape from economics. Since property and possessions cannot constitute 'a beautiful condition of life' Jesus turns away from them. The next step in Hegel's development is that he tacitly dismisses the various subjective compromises with which he had experimented. He says:

> 'The kingdom of God is a condition in which God rules, and all determinations and rights are annulled; hence his words to the young man: go, sell that thou hast—it is hard for a rich man to enter into the kingdom of God;—hence, too, Christ's renunciation of all possessions and all honour—these relations with father, family, property cannot become beautiful, therefore they should not exist at all, so that at least the opposite state of affairs might not exist either. . . .'[10]

No further consequences are deduced in the plan.

But the corresponding passage in the text of the full manuscript speaks a very different language. We shall see that Hegel has a much closer, more approving attitude towards Jesus in this work than he ever had in Berne. Despite this the Berne writings never contained such scathing comments on Jesus' teaching as this one. (In Berne Hegel's satire had been aimed more at Christianity than at the church.) Hegel reverts to the parable of the rich young man and says:

> 'About the command which follows to cast aside care for one's life and to despise riches, as also about Matthew xix, 23: "How hard it is for a rich man to enter the kingdom of Heaven", there is nothing to be said; *it is a litany pardonable only in sermons and rhymes, for such a command is without truth for us. The fate of property has become too powerful for us to tolerate reflections on it, to find* its abolition thinkable. But this at least is to be noticed, that the possession of riches, with all the rights as

well as all the cares connected with it, brings into human life definitive details whose restrictedness prescribes limits to the virtues,
imposes conditions on them, and makes them dependent on circumstances. Within these limitations, there is room for duties and virtues,
but they allow of no whole, of no complete life, because if life is
bound up with objects, it is conditioned by something outside itself,
since in that event something is tacked on to life as its own which yet
cannot be its property. Wealth at once betrays its opposition to love,
to the whole, because it is a right caught in a context of multiple
rights, and this means that both its immediately appropriate virtue,
honesty, and also the other virtues possibly within its sphere, are of
necessity linked with exclusion, and every act of virtue is in itself one
of a pair of opposites. *A syncretism, a service of two masters, is unthinkable*
because the indeterminate and the determinate cannot retain their
form and still be bound together.'[11]

We can see here that Hegel has gone far towards recognizing the
necessity of bourgeois society, even though his insight is still clothed in
the mystical terminology of his view of fate. We see also, harking back
to the last chapter, that his attack on Kantian ethics, his assertion that a
conflict of duties is inevitable is closely bound up with the conception of
society now slowly crystallizing. We shall now see, in the course of our
analysis of the longest manuscript of the Frankfurt period, that on the
basis of this conception the tragic conflict of values now reaches right
into Hegel's view of religion and affects his attitude towards Jesus himself, even though it was Jesus Hegel had looked to, in Frankfurt above
all, to resolve all these conflicts. We shall also see that we are dealing
with a contradiction which runs through Hegel's entire idealist dialectic,
one which he will later attempt to resolve at a much higher level, but
without any greater success.

NOTES
1   Lenin, *Collected Works*, Vol. 38, London and Moscow 1963, p. 180.
2   Rosenkranz, p. 85.
3   Ibid., p. 86.
4   *Realphilosophie*, Vol. I, p. 239.
5   Nohl, p. 349f. Knox, pp. 315–16. All italics by G.L.
6   Lasson, p. 420.
7   Marx, *Theories of Surplus Value*, Vol. I, p. 43.
8   Ibid., p. 41.
9   Nohl, p. 284.
10  Ibid., p. 397.
11  Ibid., p. 273f. Italics by G.L.

CHAPTER SIX

# The Spirit of Christianity and its Fate

WE have already made the acquaintance of a number of important passages from this, the most extensive work of Hegel's Frankfurt period.[1] Our present task is to evaluate the philosophical ideas it contains and estimate their importance in Hegel's evolution. The essay is a great debate with Christianity. We have already shown in detail how Hegel's new view of bourgeois society forced him to reconsider his attitude to Christianity. We have seen how the nature of his development led him to think of Christianity in a more or less approving way. However, his approach in Frankfurt differs qualitatively from that of Jena. As we have seen, and shall see still more clearly, Hegel considers the problems of bourgeois society from the standpoint of an individual living in it. By the time he comes to Jena, the general social perspective prevails over that of the individual. From this time on the individual is no more than a member of society, his individual problems are consistently treated in the light of general social ones. (The role of economics and of a dialectics of the general and the particular, deepened by the assimilation of economic categories, is a matter to be discussed later on in that context.) But since, at present, Hegel's starting-point is the fate of the individual, it is natural that Christianity should have a much more immediate appeal for him than it had done earlier on. Hence the question of how an individual's life should be shaped and conducted was bound to lead to a reconsideration of Christian ethics.

We may say, then, that Hegel never felt so close emotionally to Christianity as at this time. But it would be a great error to infer from this that a feeling of closeness is the same thing as a total doctrinal agreement with the tenets of Christianity, as the reactionary neo-Hegelians never tire of asserting. Lasson and Haering in particular are always at pains to prove that the key to an understanding of Hegel's whole philosophy lies in his complete agreement with Protestantism.

How little these legends have in common with reality can be gauged from the question about which the entire essay revolves and the —admittedly hesitant and contradictory—solution which Hegel advances. Hegel's starting-point is the question: is the solution to the problems of life put forward by Jesus and His church correct and is it still viable in the modern world?

'This idea of a kingdom of God completes and comprises the whole of the Christian religioh as Jesus founded it, and we have still to consider whether it completely satisfies nature or whether his disciples were impelled by any need to something beyond, and, if so, what that need was.'[2]

The answers that Hegel gives in the course of the essay have a fairly negative ring. He proceeds from the mystical dogmas of Christianity and attempts to show that it only achieved its religious objectivity, the supersession of a merely subjective love, through the resurrection of Christ. But this in turn gives rise to a state of mind 'which is more like a hovering between reality and spirit. . . .' And thus an opposition remained

'which, with further development, was bound to become a pairing of living and dead, divine and actual. By conjoining the man Jesus with the glorified and deified Jesus, this vagueness pointed to a satisfaction of the deepest urge for religion, but it did not provide this satisfaction, and the urge was thus turned into an endless, unquenchable, and unappeased longing.'

Thus according to Hegel, Christianity in its maturity does achieve a 'union' (and we have seen what this term means to Hegel in Frankfurt) but one which

'remains eternally in their [i.e. men's] consciousness and never allows religion to become a perfected life. In all the forms of the Christian religion which have been developed in the advancing fate of the ages, there lies this fundamental characteristic of opposition in the divine which is supposed to be present in consciousness only, never in life.'

And Hegel goes on to give a brief account of the various currents in Christianity, showing that none of them is able to achieve the real union with life, the real annulment of positivity. And he concludes the essay with the words:

'And it is its fate that church and state, worship and life, piety and virtue, spiritual and worldly action, can never dissolve into one.'[3]

It is evident that Hegel's final answer is by no means wholly in favour of Christianity. The contradictory character of this essay lies in the fact that he feels impelled to look to religion as the only thing that can provide an answer to positivity in life, and likewise he is driven to regard Christianity as the prototype of religion, and yet, after all the mystical constructions that go a long way towards Christianity, he finds himself forced to come to a negative conclusion about it, viz. that Christianity is incapable of annulling the dead, the positive element of life and that ultimately it is just as subjective a response to the world of dead objects as love and that it likewise allows this world to persist unanulled.

We shall see that Hegel never takes these assertions to their logical conclusion. His attitude will always remain tentative and ambiguous. But of this period less than any other can it be maintained that he was fully in accord with Christianity. Indeed, in Jena we shall encounter a fragment which explicitly speaks of the supersession of Christianity and the birth of a new, third religion. Of course, here too, Hegel's overcoming of Christianity takes place in the name of religion. He can never escape from the trammels of religious ideas which are so profoundly related to his idealism and this has the effect that in his view of society Christianity not only plays the role of a real social force, but it is also invested with a philosophical nimbus precisely because it is a religion.

However, Hegel's attitude to Christianity is riddled with contradictions and we should try and throw some light on them from the outset if we wish to clarify his later writings. He criticizes the Christian community because its love is unable to annul positivity.

> 'But in the lifelessness of the group's love the spirit of its love remained so athirst, felt itself so empty, that it could not fully recognize in itself, living in itself, its corresponding spirit; on the contrary, to this spirit it remained a stranger. To be connected with an alien spirit, felt as alien, is to be conscious of dependence on it.'

Opposition remains and

> 'is something positive, an object which has in it as much foreignness, as much dominion, as there is dependence in the spirit of the group.'[4]

Of course, Hegel is speaking here of the Christian group and not of Jesus himself, and we shall see that this distinction is important for him at this period.

In Hegel's eyes, the discovery that Christianity does not do away with positivity is of decisive importance for the entire subsequent history of the religion. The more complex human relations become, i.e. the more civil society advances, the more blatant this contradiction becomes.

> 'This is the point at which the group is caught in the toils of fate, even though, on the strength of the love which maintained itself in its purity outside every tie with the world, it seemed to have evaded fate altogether. Its fate, however, was centred in the fact that the love which shunned all ties was extended over a group; and this fate was all the more developed the more the group expanded and, owing to this expansion, continually coincided more and more with the world's fate both by unconsciously adopting many of that fate's aspects and also by continually becoming sullied itself in the course of its struggle against that fate.'[5]

Moreover, there is no lack of very explicit statements alleging that even the founder of Christianity was unable to put an end to positivity. Such criticism refers again and again to Jesus' relations with the state, with the organization of society. (We have already discussed his relation to private property in the preceding section.) About society and the state he writes as follows:

> 'The kingdom of God is not of this world, only it makes a great difference for that kingdom whether this world is actually present in opposition to it, or whether its opposition does not exist but is only a possibility. The former was in fact the case, and it was with full knowledge of this that Jesus suffered at the hands of the state. Hence with this [passive] relation one great element in a living union is cut away; for the members of the kingdom of God one important bond of association is snapped; they have lost one part of freedom . . . they have lost a number of active relationships and living ties. The citizens of the kingdom of God become set over against a hostile state, become private persons excluding themselves from it. . . . It is true that from the idea of a kingdom of God all the relationships established in a political order are excluded; these rank infinitely lower than the living bonds within the divine group, and by such a group they can only be despised. But since the state was there and neither Jesus nor his followers could annul it, the fate of Jesus and his following (which remained true to him in this matter) remains a loss of freedom, a restriction of life, passivity under the domination of an alien might which was despised but which ceded to Jesus without conditions the little that he wanted from it—existence among his people.'[6]

The internal contradiction in Hegel's position appears with particular clarity where he makes the attempt to describe the total annulment of all dead objectivity in the kingdom of God. He adduces many illustrations, above all from the sphere of organic life, to show that the relation between the part and the whole (individual and society) need not necessarily conform to the pattern prevailing in bourgeois society of an artificial bond which unites an empty subjectivity with a world of dead objects incapable of being stimulated into life. But when he attempts to describe such a society he is forced to seek analogies in the social relations of primitive peoples:

> 'Even in the expression "a son of Koresh", for example, which the Arabs use to denote the individual, a single member of the clan, there is the implication that this individual is not simply a part of the whole; the whole does not lie outside him; he himself is just the whole which the entire clan is. This is clear too from the sequel to the manner of waging war peculiar to such a natural, undivided people: every single

individual is put to the sword in the most cruel fashion. In modern Europe, on the other hand, where each individual does not carry the whole state in himself, but where the bond is only the conceptual one of the same rights for all, war is waged not against the individual, but against the whole which lies outside him. As with any genuinely free people, so among the Arabs, the individual is a part and at the same time the whole. It is true only of objects, of things lifeless, that the whole is other than the parts; in the living thing, on the other hand, the part of the whole is one and the same as the whole.[7]

The fact that Hegel is forced to appeal to primitive peoples in order to illustrate his belief that the positivity of bourgeois society can be annulled with the aid of religion gives a very clear indication of the impasse in which his thought found itself. Many critics of bourgeois society have sought to escape from its contradictions into less developed, more 'organic' societies. It is this that the Romantics expected from the Middle Ages. Hegel's efforts to do away with positivity necessarily drive him in this direction. It says a lot for his realism that he rejects the Middle Ages and feudalism in favour of peoples still at the tribal level of organization. He sees the relation of man to society in a fundamentally different manner from that obtaining in bourgeois society, and the ideas he works out here prove extremely fruitful later on in his studies of art, history and law. On the other hand, even in Frankfurt Hegel thought of the development of human society from primitive conditions to modern bourgeois society not simply as an actual necessity, but also as an historical advance. After all, he does show, as we have seen, that the Christian community was constantly forced to adapt itself in the course of history to the requirements of a more developed and developing society.

Thus Hegel finds himself confronted by an insoluble contradiction: the 'kingdom of God' which is supposed to resolve the contradictions of modern society turns out to be a long-since-obsolete and superseded condition of man. Hegel is forced to choose between his religious ideal and his belief in the progress of history. It is characteristic of the Frankfurt period that his answer is less incisive than it will be later on. Not that he ever went so far as to proclaim the need to regress to a primitive society or to deny the concept of historical progress. Both ideas, especially the belief in the necessity of progress beyond the primitive, are common in his notes. But on the one hand, he is as yet incapable of giving a comprehensive picture of the general development of world history and hence is unable to place such societies within the process, and on the other hand his discussions of the philosophy of religion frequently show signs of a 'suprahistorical' tendency, a tendency to embrace the 'eternity' of the believer. Then again this tendency is criticized and annulled. It is typical of the Frankfurt manuscripts, however, that criticism and the thing criticized often dwell peaceably side by side. Hegel does indeed expose the tragic contradictions of religion and he regards the founder of Christianity as a tragic figure; but at the same time, a religious solution remains the preferred solution throughout this period, especially, as we shall see, in the *Fragment of a System*.

But all these contradictions have another aspect for Hegel. When we find Hegel recording all these contradictions and uttering negative judgments about Christianity we may well find it hard to understand why he attributed so much importance to the question. We have earlier pointed to the social conditions which necessitated a debate with Christianity and indicated why Hegel found it so hard to break away (cf p. 98ff.). But the question must be raised again here: how did the situation arise which could encourage Hegel to imagine that Jesus might be a serious solution to the contradictions of life and of bourgeois society? The answer is to be sought above all in Hegel's idealism. His entire development, especially in Frankfurt, is an outstanding illustration of Lenin's aphorism that 'Idealism is clerical obscurantism', i.e. philosophical idealism cannot, if it remains true to its premises, evade the claims of religion.[8]

Up to now we have seen Hegel's growing insight into the workings of bourgeois society. This has meant above all an insight into a variety of necessary negative manifestations of that society, of the alienation of man from the world, from his fellow men, from things and the alienated form of the state and society itself. These universal properties of capitalism inevitably appeared in a heightened form in Germany, as Marx was to explain many decades later:

> 'In all the other spheres, we like the rest of Continental Western Europe, suffer not only from the development of capitalist production, but also from the incompleteness of that development. Alongside of modern evils, a whole series of inherited evils oppress us, arising from the passive survival of antiquated modes of production, with their inevitable train of social and political *anachronisms*. We suffer not only from the living, but from the dead.'[9]

Marx's statement here applies doubly to Germany in Hegel's day. What he describes here determined not only what Hegel could see and had to see of society, but also the *way* in which he approached such problems; that is to say, it determined his philosophical idealism. The contradictions he perceived must have seemed all the greater because he was attempting to tackle them from the standpoint and with the equipment of the best bourgeois humanism which was indeed about to cast off the heroic illusions of the pre-revolutionary and revolutionary epochs, but which was very far from acquiescing in the social and cultural monstrosities produced by capitalism. The post-revolutionary character of this humanism inclined it to strive for a solution to the contradictions in society just as it was. All hopes that society might be radically transformed had disappeared, partly because of events in France and partly because of the situation in Germany itself where there was no real social basis for a revolutionary movement or even any sort of radical reorganization. We have repeatedly shown that in this general configuration of events, Hegel followed the same path as Goethe and Schiller, the most outstanding humanists of the period in Germany.

This entire problematic gives Hegel's efforts to overcome positivity the particular shape that is so characteristic of the Frankfurt period. We have already seen, and shall see more clearly still, how in the course of his development an historical dialectic unfolds: the dialectic of the origins of 'dead' forms of life, alienated from society, which retain their positive, dead appearances whilst proving themselves to be the necessary products of the social activity of men themselves.

Because of his basic idealist stance, however, this problem is inseparable from another, more general one, the problem of objectivity. These two issues are linked to each other only because of Hegel's idealism; they have otherwise no necessary connection, but the fact that they are so connected is responsible for the ineradicable religious overtones of his attempts to overcome positivity. For he is not concerned simply to show that all the 'positive' phenomena in society are the products of human activity; his idealism forces him to overstate his case and require the elimination of objectivity as such.

It is evident that this can only be achieved from a religious position. In this respect Hegel is more open and uninhibited in Frankfurt than he is later on. He really does regard religion as the pinnacle of philosophy; it is the annulment of positivity in terms of the religious union of man with God. This goal remains fixed despite the fact that his rapidly growing knowledge of society and history, his own cool self-possession and his integrity as a thinker generate insights in glaring contradiction with such a view. We see here one of the basic and indestructible evils of absolute idealism. And when Hegel in his more down-to-earth phase in Jena does away with the religious key-stone to this system, substituting for it the realm of absolute knowledge and scientific, i.e. dialectical philosophy, the change is more apparent than real. For the identical subject—object of absolute idealism, the return of absolute spirit from its total alienation in nature and its partial alienation in history to the perfected knowledge of itself, is ultimately nothing other than the absorption of all objectivity into the mystified subject which has allegedly created it: viz. the annulment of all objectivity.

But for all this mysticism Hegel's conception of a society and history made by men themselves does provide a firm foundation for a dialectical approach. But it can only do so if it proves possible to dispense with the old Enlightenment view that the real causes of change in society and history are to be sought in the conscious motives of the individual actors, and that the effects can be fully explained in these terms; i.e. a dialectical approach will only work if we go beneath the surface and search for the real and objective causes of historical movement. We know that Hegel was never really able to take this step and that in his view of history the decisive role is played by his idealistically mystified conception of the spirit. Nevertheless, it is sufficiently clear, and Marx and Engels have frequently pointed out, that despite this mystification Hegel's view of history is a decisive advance since he sees both that history is in some sense made by men themselves, and that the conscious actions of men always result in something more than what was intended.

This conception of history only emerged in later years. In order to reach that point it was necessary to abandon his Frankfurt approach from the standpoint of the individual. But even this must not be misconstrued in any rigid or mechanical fashion. Even though the fate of the individual remains a kind of leitmotiv throughout the period and as such is one of the factors responsible for the culmination of his thought in religion, the entire period is marked by an unbroken striving to break out of the subjectivity such an approach must engender. And if his solution is a sort of mystical pseudo-objectivity of the religious life this internal debate does nevertheless prepare the way for his later more objective, dialectical approach to both history and society.

We have seen how this internal debate centres immediately on the dialectics of love, i.e. on the erection of dialectical relations between the dead objectivity of social institutions and the real life of the individual. We have also seen that what Hegel meant by love was the annulment of false objectivity, of positivity.

This set of problems determines Hegel's view of Jesus in Frankfurt. He describes the mission of Jesus in a variety of ways but its content is always the same in essence. In the draft of *The Spirit of Christianity* Hegel writes:

> 'Jesus opposes moral commandments to the moral predisposition, i.e. the inclination to act in a particular way; inclination has its foundation in itself, it contains its own ideal object; and not in anything alien, in the moral law of reason.'[10]

And in the final manuscript he says much the same thing, though perhaps a little more emphatically:

> 'Over against the positivity of the Jews, Jesus set man; over against the laws and their obligatoriness he set the virtues and in these the immorality of "positive" man is overcome.'[11]

These statements about the mission of Jesus are in harmony with what

we have learnt about Hegel's conception of love, of which Jesus is in
Hegel's eyes the greatest incarnation in history. But this does not
exhaust the significance of either Jesus or his teaching. On the contrary,
with increasing clarity Hegel analyses the strengths and weaknesses of
love as a means of overcoming positivity, and we recollect that at this
stage Jesus' mission was precisely to break down all the barriers to love
and to reconcile its contradictions at a higher level. We shall see how
Hegel's efforts led to the reproduction of the contradictions of love on a
higher plane.

The chief defect of love is its tendency to isolate. It is no more than a
passing moment in the flux of life. "Love joins points into moments, but
in love the world, man and domination persist."[12] Of course, love implies
a continual effort to go beyond the momentary, but he states repeatedly
that this effort must fail.

'This is why beautiful souls who are unhappy, either because they are
conscious of their fate or because they are not satisfied in the fullness
of their love, are so full of charity—they have beautiful moments of
enjoyment, but only moments.'[13]

Thus what love lacks according to Hegel is objectivity. It is one manifestation of the divine principle in man, but it is not able to create a living
relationship between subject and object.

'This love is a divine spirit, but it still falls short of religion. To
become religion it must manifest itself in an objective form. As a feeling, something subjective, it must be fused with the universal, with
something represented in idea, and thereby acquire the form of a
being to whom prayer is both possible and due. The need to unite
subject with object, to unite feeling, and feeling's demand for objects,
with the intellect, to unite them in something beautiful, in a god, by
means of fancy, is the supreme need of the human spirit and the urge
to religion.'[14]

This then is the crucial message of the Frankfurt period: religion is the
sphere in which a living objectivity identical with subjectivity is to be
achieved.

Even in the draft we find a dialectical hierarchy of human attitudes.

'Morality annuls positivity, the objectivity of the commandments;
love annuls the barriers of morality; religion annuls the barriers of
love.'[15]

The idea is reproduced a degree more emphatically in the final manuscript.

'Morality annuls domination within the sphere of consciousness; love annuls the barriers in the sphere of morality; but love itself is still incomplete in nature. In the moments of happy love there is no room for objectivity; yet every reflection annuls love, restores objectivity again, and with objectivity we are once more on the territory of restrictions. The religious, then, is the $\pi\lambda\acute{\eta}\rho\omega\mu\alpha$ [fulfilment] of love; it is reflection and love united, bound together in thought.'[16]

This idea is methodologically interesting in two respects. Firstly, we see here a relatively developed form of what was going to become a basic method of approach in *The Phenomenology of Mind*, namely the practice of allowing the various subjective postures towards the world—what Hegel was to call the 'configurations' of consciousness' [*Gestalten des Bewusstseins*]—to develop dialectically from each other. The way this happens is that a given attitude always appears as a resolution of the contradictions to be found on a lower level, while it generates contradictions of its own to be resolved at a higher one. This method is not exclusive to Hegel, but a general characteristic of the whole period. We find it in embryo in Kant, and Schelling's *System of Transcendental Idealism* exemplifies the fully developed method. We shall reserve our analysis of the similarities and differences between Hegel and Schelling for our discussion of the Jena period.

The second point of methodological interest here is the great importance attributed to reflection in his dialectical deduction of religion. We have several times pointed out that the emphasis on reflection as a moment in the dialectical totality is one of the salient characteristics of the Frankfurt period, one which sets Hegel apart from the vitalists and Romantics with whom his imperialist commentators like to associate him. The function of reflection is particularly crucial here, for according to Hegel the absence of reflection is precisely the weak point of love which in consequence can always be destroyed by reflection, since love has merely evaded instead of integrating it. And by contrast with this, the objectivity of religion lies in its union of love and reflection, its reconciliation of these antithetical principles.[17]

But at this stage of Hegel's development these correct insights and anticipations of his future thought simply exacerbate the insoluble problems of the moment. It is clear from what we have said up to now that reflection is a means of getting to grips with reality, a means which is closely bound up with the phenomenon of 'opposition', of which it is indeed the intellectual correlative. Now if the religious unity of life is meant to achieve the total annulment of all objectivity alien to the subject without leaving a trace, then the annulment of reflection is no true dialectical annulment in the Hegelian sense (i.e. with the additional meanings of preservation and elevation to a higher plane). It is rather a total annihilation in the style of Schelling. But if, on the other hand, reflection is annulled in this dialectical sense then how can the objectless 'objectivity' of religious life aspired to by Hegel be realized?

It is obvious that contradictions of this sort in the premises can only lead to contradictions in the conclusions. Later on Hegel will strive to synthesize these contradictions dialectically in 'absolute knowledge' and we shall see that his philosophical idealism prevents any true solution even then. In Frankfurt where he sought the solution in religion rather than knowledge his efforts resulted in two radically opposed solutions. It is characteristic that they should stand side by side in his manuscript. Hegel obviously feels and senses their incompatibility rather than clearly perceiving it. Hence his use of obscure and contradictory categories (such as 'fate' which we shall discuss in a moment); hence too the interpretation of the personality and fate of Jesus in terms of tragedy. It is true that further reflection on these problems does result in the original, specifically Hegelian formulation of the theory of contradiction in *The Fragment of a System*, but even this can only come into its own in Jena when Hegel jettisons the methodological assumptions of the Frankfurt period: above all, the fate of the individual as a starting-point and, following logically from that, the placing of religion above knowledge.

Let us now examine somewhat more closely the contradictory solution at which Hegel had necessarily arrived. Either Hegel must take his objectless objectivity seriously—in that case everything dissolves into a haze of mysticism. Or he must remain true to his premise that reflection does not disappear within religious life but is merely annulled and dialectically preserved in it—and in that case it will become apparent that his concept of religion is utterly unsuited to resolve the contradictions it was designed to deal with because it will turn out to be just another formula for the subjectivity of love and so will possess its defect: its subjectivist inability to annul positivity.

(1) Let us now look at the first side of the contradiction. In the draft Hegel launches an attack on Fichte in these terms:

> 'That which ought to be must of course be an infinite striving if the object simply cannot be overcome, if reason and the senses, or freedom and nature, or subject and object are so opposed to each other that they become *absolutes*. Through the syntheses: no object—no subject, or no Ego—no non-Ego, their absolute character is not annulled. Law is a cogitated relation of objects to each other; in the kingdom of God there can be no cogitated relation, because there are no objects for each other. A cogitated relation is fixed and permanent, without spirit, a yoke, a composite thing, mastery and slavery, activity and suffering, determination and being determined.'[18]

In the manuscript itself Hegel discusses in greater detail the nature of religious elevation above the contradictions. We shall cite a few of the characteristic passages:

> 'The hill and the eye that sees it are object and subject, but between
> man and God, between spirit and spirit, there is no such cleft of objec-
> tivity and subjectivity; one is to the other another in that one recog-
> nizes the other; both are one.'[19]

Here we find the identical subject—object proclaimed in an uncompro-
mising mystical fashion: true knowledge of the world can only be self-
knowledge and absolute idealism must discover a subject which is both
the creator and the knower of the world process. In Frankfurt Hegel declares flatly that this must be God. But this unity of life must at the same
time be a living unity, a relation between human beings within such a
divine harmony. According to Hegel, this harmony is the kingdom of
God. A harmony

> 'in which men's many-sided consciousness chimes in with one spirit
> and their many different lives with one life, but, more than this, by its
> means the partitions against other godlike beings are abolished, and
> the same living spirit animates the different beings, who therefore are
> no longer merely similar but one; they make up not a collection but a
> communion, since they are unified not in a universal, a concept (e.g.
> as believers), but through life and through love. This living harmony
> of men, their communion in God, Jesus calls the kingdom of God.'[20]

It is only logical that Hegel should express the contrast between ordinary knowledge and this, the supreme movement of the spirit, the supreme form of knowledge by using the word 'faith' to describe it. Of
faith he says:

> 'Faith is a knowledge of spirit through spirit, and only like spirits can
> know and understand one another; unlike ones can know only that
> they are not what the other is.'[21]

And Hegel emphasizes that what counts here is not equal intelligence but
the similar intensity of the spirit, of faith. He contrasts this kind of mutual
recognition with the

> 'much-vaunted profound knowledge of men which for divided
> beings, whose nature comprises many and variegated onesidednesses,
> a vast multiplicity without unity, is indeed a science of wide range
> and wide utility; but the spirit, which is what they seek, always eludes
> them . . .'[22]

This contrast is of interest because here too we can see an early mystical
prototype of a later idea of great importance. Hegel's later conception of
the historical process which, as Engels has remarked, seeks to uncover
'non-ostensible causes', is filled with just this sort of contempt for the

merely pragmatic, petty psychologization of history and of the major actors in history. Again and again Hegel refers to the valet's knowledge of human nature. Here, of course, this contempt is different in emphasis since it is the complement of his rhapsodic hymn to the religious unity of mankind in God. It is obvious, however, that we do have the seeds of his later attitude towards psychologizing gossip and scandalmongering in the face of the great events of human history.

The identical subject–object that lies at the roots of every form of objective idealism appears here frankly in the form of religious faith. Through faith Hegel aspires to the union of that divine element inherent in both God and man, a union which will bridge the 'chasm of objectivity'.

> 'How could anything but a spirit know a spirit? The relation of spirit to spirit is a feeling of harmony, is their unification; how could heterogeneity be unified? Faith in the divine is only possible if in the believer himself there is a divine element which rediscovers itself, its own nature; in that on which it believes, even if it be unconscious that what it has found *is* its own nature.'[23]

Here, where Hegel consistently follows his religious mysticism to its logical conclusioh, he finishes by destroying all the dialectical discoveries that he had so laboriously striven for in Frankfurt. Everything is dissipated in the fog of objectless objectivity, the negation of any situation where objects might exist. In all the formulae he uses to describe this stage, his doctrine appears as pure mysticism. At the same time he abandons the very motif that was supposed to enable religion to overcome the limitations of love, viz. the notion that religion is the dialectical unification of love and reflection.

Whenever he begins to take his own idea of an objectless objectivity of religion seriously, he casts reflection ruthlessly to one side and thus demolishes all that he has carefully and artfully constructed. We need quote only a single but highly revealing instance:

> 'The son of God is also son of man; the divine in a particular shape appears as a man. The connection of infinite and finite is of course a "holy mystery", because this connection is life itself. Reflective thinking, which partitions life, can distinguish it into infinite and finite, and then it is only the restriction, the finite regarded by itself, which affords the concept of man as opposed to the divine. But outside reflective thinking, and in truth, there is no such restriction.'[24]

Here then, in contrast to his starting-point, Hegel presents reflection and truth as mutually exclusive concepts. This means that reflection must cease to be a necessary moment in the dialectical road to the truth, as it had been hitherto in Hegel's own view, and as it will be again from Jena onwards—a moment that can only be falsified if it is falsely made into an absolute. Now, as the absolute antithesis of truth, it is banished from the highest sphere of knowledge, from the self-recognition of spirit. It is no accident therefore that Hegel, very much in contrast to his later position, designates the self-cognition of the universal subject as faith and not knowledge. And this comes as no surprise when we see how a cardinal problem of his later dialectic, namely the relation of finite to infinite, a problem that enabled him to do away with so many metaphysical prejudices, has descended here to the level of a 'holy mystery', a religious arcanum.

(2) It is much easier to grasp the other side of the contradiction. Hegel does not consistently dissipate objectivity in a haze of mysticism; he is, especially when he comes to deal with social or historical phenomena, much too down-to-earth and realistic to take the religious postulate of an objectivity without objects seriously. But the alternative is to leave the positivity, the unannulled dead objectivity of the social world in sole possession of the stage, while religion is seen to be a merely subjective phenomenon, not at all superior to love, and burdened with all its limitations and imperfections. A subjectivity that has become purely religious again confronts a world of dead objects and succumbs to its superior power. And this means that even the newly-won concept of God itself becomes something 'positive'. To illustrate this we have selected a passage in which Hegel gives a particularly clear, if unconscious self-criticism of his own mystical extremism.

> 'However sublime the idea of God may be made here, there yet always remains the Jewish principle of opposing thought to reality, reason to sense; this principle involves the rending of life and a lifeless connection between God and the world, though the tie between these must be taken to be a living connection; and where such a connection is in question, ties between the related terms can be expressed only in mystical phraseology.'[25]

Hegel is referring here to John the Baptist and not Jesus himself who in his view represents a higher, more perfect form of the religious. In fact it is Jesus who with the aid of mystical categories such as the 'son of God' and the 'kingdom of God' is assigned the role of bringing into being the state of objectless objectivity. But, as we shall see later in Hegel's treatment of Jesus as a tragic figure, the more concretely and historically he analyses his own concept the less able he is to sustain its mystical implications. This in turn leads him to turn away from the mystical side of the antinomy investigated here and back towards the world of objects.

It is clear, then, that we are not faced with a living dialectical contradiction in reality itself which Hegel has perhaps failed to grasp in its entirety, but by crudely incompatible alternative solutions to the same problem. And the fact that these solutions are incompatible suggests that there are grave defects in Hegel's approach and methodology. Hegel was evidently unaware of the contradiction, otherwise he would not have juxtaposed such contrary solutions in the same manuscript. Undoubtedly he sensed that all was not well and this is perhaps why he fixed on a variety of concepts that might help him out of the difficulty. The most important of these concepts is one of his chief categories in Frankfurt, that of *fate*.

We have already encountered this notion a number of times; we saw Hegel use the term to describe both property and the state and that this was not just picturesque illustration. On the contrary, he wished to point to a specific form of historical necessity, a specific relationship between man and the positivity of the external world. At first glance it might seem as if Hegel were attempting to exorcize the obscurity of his philosophy of religion by means of a no less obscure and mystical philosophy of society and history. And indeed the concept of fate is obscure and contradictory enough. But for all that, it does contain a core of dialectical truth so that it is rewarding to look a little more closely at what Hegel meant by it.

His starting-point here is the comparison of the purely mechanical, inhuman nature of bourgeois society, as expressed in its fetish forms, its penal code and the latter's idealization and internalization in the Kantian ethic, with the vital dialectical movement of human society in general in which man is at the same time both subject and object, active agent and passive sufferer. In the eyes of the law the criminal is only 'a sin existent, a trespass possessed of personality'.[26] And he proceeds from there to search for more broad-minded, more living and above all more human concepts of society where crime is still crime, but where the humanity of a criminal is not abrogated in such a mechanical and inhuman fashion. (We may remind the reader of similar arguments on p. 214f.) In his own words:

'Punishment lies directly in the offended law. The trespasser has forfeited the same right which his trespass has injured in another, i.e. he merits the punishment; the necessity that it should be meted out lies in something external and corresponds to the trespass.'[27]

Hegel goes on to conclude that the rigid necessity of the law, its awful 'majesty' so much admired and glorified by Kant must entail its contingency in life.

'Punishment is inevitably deserved; that is inescapable. But the execution of punishment is not inevitable, because as a characteristic of a living being it may vanish and another characteristic may come on the scene instead. Justice thus becomes something contingent; there may be a contradiction between it as universal, as thought, and it as real, i.e. in a living being.'[28]

It is obvious that these observations are closely parallel to the polemical attitude towards the ethical doctrines of Kant and Fichte which we have already discussed. This will eventually lead Hegel to reject Kant's and especially Fichte's procedure of inferring particular legal precepts from the general concept of law. Instead he will come to emphasize the socio-historical, more or less contingent character of particular moments of positive law.

At this stage, however, we are only concerned with his concept of fate in Frankfurt. These observations about law and crime constitute just one starting-point, just one complementary antithesis to it. Hegel is concerned to show that there is a more extensive, larger, more vital and hence more authentic necessity than the necessity enshrined in the law. The overestimation of the law in Kant and Fichte is part of the heritage of the Enlightenment, it is a widespread illusion stemming from the pre-revolutionary period of bourgeois ideology. Thus Hegel's polemic here is part of a general process to free himself from many traditions of the Enlightenment which he had still accepted unquestioningly in Berne, but which he began to come to grips with in Frankfurt in the process of developing his dialectical method. As we have seen, and shall frequently see again, he often overcomes beliefs of the Enlightenment only to fall into the toils of a mystified form of idealism.

The concept of fate has now become the expression summing up this more broadly conceived, more dialectical and vital form of necessity.

'But fate has a more extended domain than punishment has. It is aroused even by guilt without crime, and hence it is implicitly stricter than punishment. Its strictness often seems to pass over into the most crying injustice when it makes its appearance, more terrible than ever, over against the most exalted form of guilt, the guilt of innocence. I mean that, since laws are purely conceptual unifications of opposites, these concepts are far from exhausting the many-sidedness of life . . . but over the relations of life which have not been dissolved, over the sides of life that are given as vitally united, over the domains of the virtues, it [i.e. punishment] exercises no power. Fate, on the other hand, is incorruptible and unbounded like life itself. . . . Where life is injured, be it ever so rightly, i.e. even if no dissatisfaction is felt, there fate appears, and one may therefore say "never has innocence suffered; every suffering is guilt". But the honour of a pure soul is all the greater the more consciously it has done injury to life in order to maintain the supreme values, while a trespass is all the blacker, the more consciously an impure soul has injured life.'[29]

Anyone acquainted with Hegel's later philosophy of history or his aesthetics will readily see here the contours of his view of historical necessity and his theory of tragedy.

What interests us most about this comparison between fate and the avenging power of punishment is the more vital, more comprehensive nature of fate. It is this that expresses the fundamental, if often unconscious, tendency of Hegel's Frankfurt period to see 'life', the total process of social movement, as opposed to the rigid appearance of its particular moments taken in isolation. The crucial thing here is that Hegel regards the law as emerging 'later than life and on a lower level'. Indeed in this connection he comes very close to his later dialectical view when he says of the law:

> 'It is only the lack of life, defective life appearing as a power. And life can heal its wounds again; the severed hostile life can return into itself again . . . The deficiency is recognized as a part of himself [i.e. the trespasser's self], as what was to have been in him and is not. This lack is not a not-being but is life known and felt as not-being.'[30]

Now since in Hegel's view fate represents the dialectical movement of the totality of life, of society as a whole, since it encompasses the self-destruction and recreation of that life, since it is the uninterrupted dialectical self-reproduction of society, it is not surprising that he should view fate as something essentially human, even though its rigour is even greater than that of punishment by the law.

> 'In fate, however, a man recognizes his own life, and his supplication to it is not supplication to a lord but a reversion and approach to himself.'[31]

Thus in particular instances fate may be unleashed by the deed of another person, but this does not alter the fact that it is still a man's own fate. For Hegel repeatedly emphasizes, as we have seen (p. 115ff.), that for an analysis of the relations between man and fate it is immaterial whether a man meets his fate actively or passively, i.e. whether he flees from it or struggles against it is all one according to Hegel's view at this time.

This is underlined by his radical rejection of the Kantian view in which the individual is mechanically subordinated to society: the individual represents only the particular and society represents only the general and the individual can only attain to the level of the general by unconditionally subordinating himself to its universal principles (the categorical imperative). Hegel repudiates this view and introduces instead a dialectic relation of the particular to the general. Thus the individual and society are seen as conflicting forces: one power opposes the other and the conflict between them gives birth to a revitalized living unity of the whole.

> 'Punishment represented as fate is of a quite different kind. In fate, punishment is a hostile power, an individual thing. . . . In the hostile power of fate universal is not severed from particular in the way in which the law, as the universal, is opposed to man or his inclinations as the particular. Fate is just the enemy, and man stands over against it as a power fighting against it. Law, on the contrary, as universal, is lord of the particular and has subdued this man to obedience.'[32]

The view that individual and society confront each other as forces in conflict is much closer to reality than the Kantian position according to which every deviation from the law can only be regarded as something reprehensible and where, in consequence, social change in the course of history cannot be comprehended as the result of its own movement, its own contradictory self-reproduction. But Hegel's view has another aspect which emerges here: the interconnectedness of all the individual expressions of life in a society. It is the feeling, the experience (for the present no more than feeling and experience) that in everything that happens to the individual, however unique or private it may seem to be, the unity of social life is objectively active. This can be seen precisely in Hegel's treatment of the criminal, of his view of the part played by fate in the criminal's misdeeds and his punishment for them.

It is a general feature of the period that the dialectics of crime became one of the focal points of literary and philosophical debate. This can be explained by the fact that the contradictions of bourgeois society were coming into the open but that their ultimate economic and class nature was not, and could not yet become visible. This process can be seen very clearly in Germany: from Schiller to Kleist's *Michael Kohlhaas* there is a whole series of important contributions to this theme. Moreover, the problem of the criminal is not of merely local German importance as is evident from a glance at European literature from Byron to Balzac.[33]

Thus it is no mere chance or wilfulness on Hegel's part that the contradictions in the concepts of crime and the criminal should emerge so clearly in his work. Hegel emphasizes the vital impact of the whole of society on the criminal, he reveals the self-deception implicit in the notion that nothing but purely individual moments are at work here.

> 'The illusion of crime, its belief that it destroys the other's life and thinks itself enlarged thereby, is dissipated by the fact that the disembodied spirit of the injured life comes on the scene to take sides against the crime, just as Banquo, who came as a friend to Macbeth was not obliterated when he was murdered but immediately thereafter took his seat, not as a guest at the feast, but as an evil spirit. The criminal

intended to engage with another's life, but he has only destroyed his own, for life is not different from life, since life dwells in the one Godhead. In his arrogance he has destroyed indeed, but only the friendliness of life; he has perverted life into an enemy.'[34]

When we come to consider the importance of the concept of fate for Hegel's overall development we must distinguish two moments. There is firstly the more comprehensive dialectical core which is only beginning to emerge in an as yet obscure, confused and illogical form, and secondly there is its particular Frankfurt variant which distorts the dialectical implications and deflects them from their path.

The first moment is clearly present in the passages we have quoted. In them we find a comprehensive and vital principle which divests the lifeless, 'positive' elements of society of their lifeless, 'positive' character, transforming them into moments within the living whole. Hegel's course is here set firmly in the direction of his ultimate mature view of society as a whole which he will later formulate in the *Philosophy of Right* as follows:

'Necessity consists in this that the whole is sundered into the different concepts and that this divided whole yields a fixed and permanent determinacy. However, this is not a fossilized determinacy but one which permanently recreates itself in its dissolution.'[35]

It is obvious that clarity of this sort is nowhere apparent in the passages we have quoted from the Frankfurt manuscripts. We repeat: at this stage Hegel is aware of these interconnections at the level of feeling and experience rather than coherent knowledge. But to say that his perceptions are obscure and amorphous must not blind us to their general *direction*. Especially as we can clearly discern some far from negligible efforts to concretize the dialectics of the universal and the particular. There is, moreover, a strong tendency to overcome the hypostasis of the determinations of reflection by Kant and Fichte and to locate them within the general scheme of his dialectic. And it is vital to see that these efforts to comprehend the 'positive' elements of society as necessary and then to annul them, by viewing them as moments in a dialectical process, stand in glaring contradiction to his religious aspirations, to his obliteration of reflection in the objectless objectivity of religious life. It is just at this point, where we can see in the swirling chaos of their conception, the ideas which will later on become the foundations of Hegelian thought, that the truth of Engels' insight into the contradiction between Hegel's system and his method really comes home to us as something which applies to Hegel's whole career. The seminal importance of his definition of fate in Frankfurt lies precisely in these embryonic formulations of the dialectical method. And all these beginnings which were consciously intended to buttress his religious convictions in fact go in the opposite direction and turn out to be in flat contradiction with their declared objective.

But this is just one side of his conception of fate in Frankfurt, the seminal aspect which provides the foundation for his future thought. The other side, more typical of the Frankfurt period, comes to the surface when we see his attempts to refer his concept of fate, which had sprung after all from an objective base in society, back to the individual himself. Hegel's chief problem in Frankfurt is the fate of the individual in bourgeois society. His treatment of the problems of bourgeois society often drives him beyond this narrow point of view and it is at such moments that he begins to grasp real dialectical interconnections. But he consciously uses all the discoveries made in this way to help him find a solution to his chief problem. And this reference back to the individual results in a series of distortions of his own insights, of lapses to a level he had already overcome.

This is what happens to his concept of fate. When he calls fate 'human' by contrast with the legal system, the system of punishment, the idea is rather confused but its core of truth is his belief that social life is what constitutes the human. But if the idea is then immediately related back to the individual it must relapse into mysticism. And this is what constantly happens to his view of fate, in fact it is the conscious intention underlying the whole notion. For what Hegel deduces from the human character of fate is that it can be 'reconciled'.

Considered in the abstract the idea of reconciliation need not necessarily contradict the social character of his concept of fate. For in his attack on the 'positive' character of punishment and against the Kantian glorification of this positivity it is very clear that he does not feel hostile to the social institutions involved, but only to the form of positivity. That is to say, he stands on the same bourgeois terrain as the civil legal code and as Kantian philosophy. He does not long for another social order, but at most for a definite modification of the present one and above all, philosophically, a different view of the phenomena it contains and their interconnections. The mysticism only arises from the way in which Hegel pictures this reconciliation. And the general drift of his solution is that fate, which is a self-mutilation of life, can be propitiated by love.

'It is in the fact that even the enemy is felt as life that there lies the possibility of reconciling fate . . . This sensing of life, a sensing which finds itself again, is love, and in love fate is reconciled . . . Thus fate is not an alien thing like punishment; it is no firmly fixed thing like an evil action is on the conscience; fate is the consciousness of oneself, but as of an enemy. The whole man can recreate himself in friendship, through love he can return to his pure life; his consciousness again becomes a faith in himself, his perception of himself has become another and fate is thereby reconciled.[36]

It is clear that in this passage, the conscious climax of his view of fate, he effectively retracts the real insights he had gained earlier on: fate which had been seen before as a social necessity, now becomes a feeling, a sensing; it becomes the individual's experience of the necessity that has overtaken him. And this purely subjective experience leads on to the reconciliation with fate through love. This increased subjectivity is already indicative of a complete distortion of reality, for the fate of an individual cannot possibly be inferred with such iron necessity from the objective determinations of society in general. In later years Hegel sees the adventitious elements in the personal fate of an individual perfectly clearly, but here his subjective approach turns them into absolutes and thus creates a false necessity where there is none in reality. But even worse his merely subjective insight into the alleged necessity of this process is then invested with the dignified name of objectivity: the reconciliation of fate through love is the path along which Hegel arrives at the mystical objectivity of his religious life.

It is not surprising, therefore, to see that fate as defined here, i.e. not only the subjective side just discussed, but also those aspects which contain the seeds of his later view of society and history, soon vanishes from Hegel's philosophical vocabulary. The fruitful elements are absorbed into his theory of dialectics, but the word 'fate' is no longer used to describe them. The idea of a reconciliation through love disappears entirely, once Hegel has begun to look at social phenomena exclusively from a socio-historical standpoint, and no longer from the perspective of the individual—a process that takes place already in Jena.[37]

Hegel's use of the concept of fate to give a socio-historical foundation to his philosophy of religion clearly reveals the general conflict between his system and his method. For however much he twists and turns so as to ensure that his view of fate will culminate in a would-be objective realm where fate is reconciled through love, he cannot unmake that objective dialectic of society which he had himself called into being. And viewed from that perspective the supreme religious solution that Hegel seeks looks very much like a *voluntary* abandonment *of the struggle* with the fate embodied in society, in the circumstances of history. But Hegel had clearly shown that to abandon the struggle, to flee from fate, was to invite its attentions no less surely than to take up its challenge. Evasion, then, cannot possibly represent a higher perspective. He had also shown that every evasion of conflict, every withdrawal by the subject into itself necessarily means that the false objectivity, the positivity of the social environment will survive *unannulled* and intact.

Now when Hegel proceeds from these highly contradictory premises to construct a picture of Jesus, the paradigmatic historical incarnation of the religious life, what results—leaving aside the question of Hegel's intentions—is not the realized image of a religious life, the overcoming of positivity through the objectless objectivity of religion, but instead a *tragic figure*, who embodies the intractable nature of these contradictions. And moreover, in even more striking contrast to Hegel's intentions—an *historical* figure.

The introductory words of the draft plan formulate the historical conditions of this tragedy very clearly. Hegel's starting-point is the tense revolutionary situation in which Judaism found itself at the time of Jesus' life. We shall quote Hegel's description here in full, partly because this historical approach reveals the conflict in his intentions very clearly, and partly because we can discern in it a curious variation of that novel, more historical view of positivity that we have already encountered in the two political articles. What we find very clearly expressed here is the idea that an intensification of positivity is one social factor that triggers off a revolution, or more precisely, the growth of the conditions necessary for revolution makes the 'positive' features of society all the more apparent.

> 'At the time when Jesus made his appearance among the Jewish nation it found itself in the situation which sooner or later will give rise to a revolution and which always bears the same general character. When the spirit has departed from a constitution, from the laws, and when it has changed so much that it no longer fits in with them, there comes into being a searching, a striving for something different, so that a large variety of organizations, of modes of life, of claims and needs are created, which if they gradually diverge to the point where they can no longer subsist together, will produce an eruption and a new general form; a new bond uniting mankind will come into being. The looser this bond, the more it leaves ununified, the more it will contain the seeds of new inequalities and future explosions.'[38]

Hegel proceeds from this background to narrate the tragedy of Jesus:

> 'Since Jesus gave battle to the entire genius of his people and had altogether broken with his world, the completion of his fate could be nothing save suppression by the hostile genius of his people. The glorification of the son of man in this downfall is not negative (does not consist in a renunciation of all his relations with the world) but positive (his nature has forgone the unnatural world, has preferred to save it in battle and defeat rather than consciously submit to its corruption or else unconsciously and increasingly succumb to corruption's stealthy advance.) Jesus was conscious that it was necessary for his individual self to perish, and he tried to convince his disciples also of

this necessity.'[39]

Hegel still sees the tragedy of Jesus from a more or less theological point of view: the individual is sacrificed to save, to 'redeem' the corrupted world. But when he concretizes his views of Jesus still further he keeps returning to the question of his flight from the concrete forms of his environment. This leads him to say of Jesus what he used to say, though not so harshly, of subjective love: 'Thus he could discover freedom only in a void'. And now Hegel formulates the tragedy of Jesus in a very different, much more tragic form.

'The fate of Jesus was that he had to suffer from the fate of his people; either he had to make that fate his own, to bear its necessity and share its joy, to unite his spirit with his people's, but to sacrifice his own beauty, his connection with the divine, or else he had to repel his nation's fate from himself, but submit to a life undeveloped and without pleasure in itself. *In neither event would his nature be fulfilled*; in the former case he would sense only fragments of it, and even these would be sullied; in the latter, he would bring it fully into his consciousness, though he would know its shape only as a splendid shadow whose essence is the highest truth; the sensing of that essence he would have to forgo and *the truth would not come alive in act and in reality*.

'Jesus chose the latter fate, the severance of his nature from the world. . . . But the more deeply he felt this severance, the less could he bear it calmly, and his actions issued from his nature's spirited reaction against the world; his fight was pure and sublime because he knew the fate in its entire range and had set himself against it . . . The struggle of the pure against the impure is a sublime sight, but it soon changes into a horrible one when holiness itself is impaired by unholiness, and when an amalgamation of the two, with the pretention of being pure, rages against fate, because in these circumstances holiness is caught in the fate and subject to it. . . .

'What has in part freed itself from fate but in part remains linked therewith, whether there be consciousness or not of this confusion, must destroy both itself and nature all the more frightfully and when nature and unnature are confused, the attack on the latter must also affect the former; the wheat is trodden underfoot with the tares, and the holiest part of nature itself is injured because it is interwoven with the unholy.'[40]

This tragic view of the life of Jesus betokens the collapse of Hegel's conception of the religious life whose greatest historical representative was supposed to be Jesus himself. It turns out that the transcendence of the mere subjectivity of love through religion, the attempt to create an objectivity without objects, simply reproduces at a higher level all the

contradictions of love: the survival of the positivity of social determinations and, as a result of the interaction of this positivity with the subjectivism of love, an escapism which only provokes fate. And at this
higher level of contradiction love becomes manifest as an insoluble tragedy. Thus Hegel's account of Jesus in no sense provides historical evidence for the view that his ideal of the religious life is capable of
realization; it is, on the contrary, much more like a philosophical version
of the tragic figures of his friend Hölderlin, his *Empedocles* in particular.

Of course, there is a very essential difference between them: Hölderlin
remained true to the ideals of the French Revolution right up to his own
tragic end, and not only that, he firmly placed tragedy in the very centre
of his poetic enterprise. Hegel in Frankfurt, on the other hand, wished
precisely to reconcile the contradictions of bourgeois society with the aid
of his view of religion and only arrived at tragedy against his conscious
intentions thanks to the contradictions between his objective and the
method he employed to achieve it, and thanks also to his uncompromis-
ing insistence on the method despite its unpalatable conclusions. In
Hegel's thought, then, the tragic conclusion is far less conscious than for
Hölderlin.

Indeed, when we move on to the *Fragment of a System*, we shall see that
despite the contradictions we have noted Hegel continues to search for a
religious solution. Hence the real gains of the Frankfurt period are
expressed in terms of an internal conflict, in the constant and unconscious
critique of tendencies which form the conscious focus of his thought.
Thus, as we have seen, insoluble antinomies inevitably persist, but since
Hegel simply presses forward exploring both sides of his contradictions,
and constantly acquiring new empirical material in support of them his
dialectical method continues to develop in 'the manure of the contradictions'.

Among these contradictions is the emphasis that Hegel is forced to
place on the societal nature of religious life as a consequence of his search
for its objective mode. We recall that love was subjective in his eyes
partly because it was a necessarily transitory relation between 'two
points', between individuals. Hegel hints (cf. p. 121f.) that its social
maximum is the basis it provides for the family. The religious life,
however, is supposed to provide the foundation for a novel kind of social
relation between men (in the kingdom of God, the community, the
church). The tragic contradiction which we observed in the life and historical fate of Jesus now repeats itself in the impossibility, which is admitted to again and again, of reaching out beyond the foundation of a sect.
Hegel had already observed the sectarian nature of Christianity in Berne.
At that time he had criticized and rejected it from the standpoint of his
preference for the city-states of antiquity. He now approaches the problem from a more sympathetic position, without its being likely that he

could overlook the social limitations of the sect.

This more positive evaluation of the exemplary social function of small communities is a general feature of the age. We may draw attention yet again to Goethe's *Wilhelm Meister* where such a community of intellectually and morally outstanding individuals not only labour to educate each other, to develop each other's various faculties in a general humanist sense, but also seek to further various social goals, in particular, the voluntary harmonious phasing-out of the vestiges of feudalism and the transition from outmoded methods in agriculture to modern capitalist ones. (In the sequel to *Wilhelm Meister's Apprenticeship*, the *Travels*, which was planned at this time though not written until much later, this same society envisages goals which on occasion come close to the ideas of Utopian Socialism.) At the theoretical level Schiller's writings give expression to many of these illusions. In the *Letters on the Aesthetic Education of Man* he confronts the feudal absolutist 'natural state' with a humanist aesthetic state, and concludes his observations with the following remark:

> 'But does such a state of Aesthetic semblance really exist? And if so, where is it to be found? As a need it exists in every finely attuned soul; as a fact we are likely to find it only in a few chosen circles . . .'[41]

When we look a little more closely at Hegel's remarks on the social consequence of the moral reforms of Jesus, of the abolition of the Kantian dualism of reason and sense, duty and inclination, we cannot help being struck by the parallel with Goethe and Schiller. We have already noted their affinity in connection with their responses to Kant's ethical doctrine (p. 154), and we can see it again in this comment on the social implications of that critique. Hegel says of Jesus:

> 'In reconcilability the law loses its form, the concept is displaced by life; but what reconcilability thereby loses in respect of the universality which grips all particulars together in the concept is only a seeming loss and a genuine infinite gain on account of the wealth of living relations with the individuals (*perhaps few*) with whom it comes into connection.'[42]

The similarity to the humanist illusions of Goethe and Schiller is so obvious as to render comment superfluous.

It is more important to discuss the differences within the general similarity, since this will throw light on what is specific to Hegel. Above all, the human and social content of these ideas is much more realistic and clear-headed in Goethe and Schiller than it is in Hegel. Both, especially Goethe, were much more liberated about religion than Hegel was in Frankfurt, and hence were able to criticize Christianity much more freely.

But that is just one side of the story and we must not lose sight of the fact that it is Hegel's search for a religious philosophy that precipitates a theory which for all its obscurity and mysticism goes far beyond anything in Goethe and Schiller in its attempts to get to grips with the real problems of bourgeois society. Hegel is never content with the idea of a small group as the repository of humanistic ideals; he always strives for a moral code, for a theory of human conduct which would be capable of penetrating the whole of society. It is this more comprehensive ambition that leads him to the religious and mystical conclusions which we have already discussed, and in which the pervasive contradiction between method and system could be observed. But Hegel's greatness as a thinker can be seen in the way in which he resolutely faces up to the contradictions that meet him in his search for the ideal, the way he articulates them and strives constantly to discover their nature, their tendency and their underlying laws.

Precisely because of this Hegel was far in advance of Goethe and Schiller both in his understanding of bourgeois society and in his development of the dialectical method. The complex and chequered evolution of the dialectical method in Germany emerges with particular clarity from a comparison of Hegel and Goethe. Goethe is incomparably closer to materialism and much less imprisoned in religious assumptions than Hegel. Nevertheless, Hegel developed the dialectical method to a point that Goethe could not only not achieve, but one that he could not even completely understand in its perfected form (in Hegel's *Logic*), and this despite the fact that by nature he inclined towards dialectics and had strengthened this inclination through study.

We must not forget, therefore, that however far Hegel went astray in Frankfurt, he was throughout the period concerned to understand the problems of bourgeois society in their totality and as a process. His supreme aim was reconciliation with that society, but it was a reconciliation without deceit, without an apologia, a reconciliation which depended on laying bare all the contradictions. And this understanding and exposure of the contradictions contains Hegel's fundamental humanist tendency, his humanist critique of capitalist society. His concepts, such as love, may be confused and over-idealistic, but they always contain an element of protest against the soullessness, ugliness and inhumanity of the capitalist system. If he works towards reconciliation, this means in the first instance the understanding and the recognition of the actual existence and ultimately the progressive nature of capitalism.

Hegel's bourgeois commentators have even vulgarized this aspect of his thought. From his early rejection of Kant's ethical doctrine and the fact that he increasingly treats moral problems as just moments, parts of society as a whole, they infer that he had neither seen nor acknowledged any contradictions between morality and the prevailing customs and attitudes of bourgeois society. The vulgarization lies in their failure to see that Hegel rejects Kantian morality at least in part because its formalism illicitly and mechanically assumes a harmonious congruence between the moral code and the institutions of society. When Hegel then treats individual morality as a moment in the totality and subordinates it to ethical life as a whole, the intention is to express the entire volatile tension between the universal and the particular. Hence his energetic critique of Kantian formalism and of the empty, hair-splitting about morality characteristic of Romantic individualism implies anything but the failure to provide a humanistic analysis of bourgeois morality.

This is particularly clear in the Frankfurt writings since in them Hegel proceeds from the relation of the individual to society. We have already seen how he treats the problem of crime. But he goes much further than this. Behind the categories of love and religion the humanist tendency is quite clear: viz. the tendency not merely to preserve the objective rights of society against the individual, but also to justify the human rights of individuals against society. The tragedy of Jesus springs precisely from this conflict of opposites. But we see it elsewhere also. In another part of the essay he discusses the sins of Mary Magdalene and pours scorn on her philistine judges, ending with these words:

'Would anyone say it had been better for Mary to have yielded to the fate of the Jewish life, to have passed away as an automaton of her time, righteous and ordinary, without sin and without love? Without sin, because the era of her people was one of those in which the beautiful heart could not live without sin, but in this as in any era, could return through love to the most beautiful consciousness.'[43]

It is tempting to argue that the point of view exemplified here was determined by the individualism of the Frankfurt period and that it would disappear entirely with Hegel's later change towards an objectivistic, social point of view. But this would be to over-simplify Hegel's later theory of morality. It is not possible to discuss the matter here fully, and we must content ourselves with one illustration from the *Aesthetics*, making due allowances of course for changes in his method. In this passage Hegel talks about the early works of Schiller and Goethe and this in itself is interesting since it confirms our view that Hegel's affinity is with the German classics and not, as the neo-Hegelians never tire of repeating, with the Romantics. Hegel says:

'The interest in and the need for such a real individual totality and living independence neither can nor will ever leave us, however reasonable and fruitful we acknowledge the character and the conditions of civil and political life to be in their developed form. In this sense we may admire the youthful poetic spirit of Goethe and Schiller in their efforts to recover the lost independence of their characters within the given conditions of the modern world.'[44]

The change in Hegel's attitudes, his greater objectivity *vis-à-vis* history and society, is expressed as an extension of his earlier view, as the synthesizing of the complex moral problems of the individual with the inevitable overall progress of history. This results in a grandiose scheme of history, free of all moralizing and yet able to do justice to the achievement, the greatness and tragedy of man. We shall be able to see how this scheme developed organically from the internal conflicts in Frankfurt we have discussed when we realize that it already existed in a highly advanced form in the beginnings of the period in Jena. In one of the earliest Jena writings, the attempt to complete the essay on the German Constitution, Hegel gives portraits of both Machiavelli and Richelieu in which this genuinely historical approach is perfectly visible. And it is not just that he shows a fine humanist appreciation of particular moments in the historical process; it is one of the sources from which the correct dialectical understanding of history sprang. When Engels claimed that Hegel had a profounder insight into the role of evil in history than Feuerbach himself this raised rather broader issues than the one we have been discussing, but there can be no doubt that it was one of the elements that helped to form the Hegelian view of history as a whole.

## NOTES

1   It is not possible for us to date this essay with absolute precision. Nohl who first published it *in toto* could only deduce from the handwriting that it must have been written either in the winter of 1798–99 or in the summer of 1799. It is our belief that the modification in Hegel's views on the question of the relation of the individual to society and the positivity of property means that in all probability the essay was written after he had read Steuart, i.e. the summer of 1799. Nohl excludes a date later than the summer because Schleiermacher's *Discourses on Religion* appeared at the end of 1799 and Hegel makes no reference to them, even though he constantly attacked them bitterly later on. On all these questions see Nohl, p. 404f.

2   Nohl, p. 321. Knox, p. 270.

3   Nohl, p. 341f. Knox, pp. 300–1.

4   Nohl, p. 33. Knox, pp. 294–5.

5   Nohl, p. 336f. Knox, p. 295.

6   Nohl, p. 327f. Knox, p. 284.

7   Nohl, p. 308. Knox, p. 260. Hegel repeatedly returns to this analogy with primitive peoples, e.g. Nohl, p. 322, where he draws on

reminiscences of English travellers published by Forster.

8  Lenin, op. cit., p. 363.

9  Marx, *Capital*, Preface to the first German edition, London 1967, p. 9.

10  Nohl, p. 388.

11  Nohl, p. 276. Knox, p. 244.

12  Nohl, p. 390.

13  Nohl, p. 389.

14  Nohl, p. 332. Knox, p. 289.

15  Nohl, p. 389.

16  Nohl, p. 302. Knox, p. 253.

17  We would remind the reader that this is not a completely novel problem for Hegel. At the very start of the Frankfurt period he had attempted to reconcile love and reflection (cf. p. 118f.); the problem is now shifted onto the plane of religion.

18  Nohl, p. 395.

19  Nohl, p. 312. Knox, p. 265.

20  Nohl, p. 321. Knox, pp. 277–8.

21  Nohl, p. 389. Knox, p. 239.

22  Nohl, p. 290. Knox, p. 204.

23  Nohl, p. 313. Knox, p. 266.

24  Nohl, p. 309f. Knox, p. 262. The expression 'holy mystery' recurs a number of times in this manuscript in reference to the relation between the infinite and the finite. Cf. Nohl, p. 304.

25  Nohl, p. 308. Knox, p. 259.

26  Nohl, p. 288. Knox, p. 238.

27  Nohl, p. 277. G.L. quotes in part from a deleted text omitted by Knox, p. 225.

28  Nohl, p. 278. Knox, p. 226.

29  Nohl, p. 283f. Knox, pp. 232–3.

30  Nohl, p. 281. Knox, pp. 230–1.

31  Nohl, p. 282. Knox, p. 231.

32  Nohl, p. 280. Knox, pp. 228–9.

33  In Kleist's story *Michael Kohlhaas* the eponymous hero resorts to a series of increasingly spectacular and devastating crimes in order to recover some horses stolen from him by a Junker. His violent quest for justice is eventually rewarded by the recovery of his property, but he is hanged for the crimes he committed in the process—*Trans*.

34  Nohl, p. 280. Knox, p. 229.

35  *The Philosophy of Right*, trans. T. M. Knox, Oxford 1942, p. 283.

36  Nohl, p. 282f. Knox, p. 232. G.L. quotes from a divergent text omitted by Knox.

37  The term 'fate' does of course occur in Hegel's later philosophy,

but not in the meaning under discussion here. As early as the Jena Lectures of 1805/6 fate refers to a kind of necessity about which Hegel says 'we do not know what its law or its content are, or what it wants'. *Realphilosophie*, Vol. II, p. 186. In the same lectures the concept of fate is seen historically and as such is consigned to antiquity; ibid., p. 267. Hegel holds fast to this view in later years. Cf. the *Aesthetics* (ed. Glockner), Vol. II, p. 101f. In the *Logic* fate is always thought of as a mechanical necessity. Cf. *Werke*, Berlin 1841, Vol. V. p. 187f.

38 Nohl, p. 385.

39 Nohl, p. 317. Knox, pp. 271–2. The word 'positive' is used here in its ordinary meaning, and not in the specialized sense that it bears elsewhere in this study.

40 Nohl, p. 328f. Knox, pp. 285–6. Italics by G.L.

41 Twenty-seventh Letter, *On the Aesthetic Education of Man*, trans. E. M. Wilkinson and L. A. Willoughby, Oxford 1967, p. 219.

42 Nohl, p. 269. Knox, p. 215. G.L.'s italics.

43 Nohl, p. 293. Knox, p. 244.

44 *Ästhetik*, ed. Glockner, Vol. I, p. 266.

# CHAPTER SEVEN

# The Frankfurt *Fragment of a System*

IT is not known to us whether or not the contradictions we have been discussing, or whether at least the suspicion that his system was not free of contradiction, were contributory factors in Hegel's decision to break off work on *The Spirit of Christianity* and to refrain from publishing what had been completed. The last part of the Frankfurt period is singularly bare of dates and other information that might be of use in enabling us to establish the further progress of his development. The only thing we possess is the *Fragment of a System* (or perhaps just draft plans for a system) which according to Hegel's own dating was completed on 14 September 1800.[1] We do not know what preparatory studies preceded this fragment and so we are unable to trace in detail the steps that led to it from *The Spirit of Christianity*. We can only survey Hegel's philosophical position about eighteen months after the conclusion of the latter essay, a task which is facilitated by the fact that the *Fragment*, like *The Spirit of Christianity*, portrays religion as the culmination of philosophy; indeed this position only really receives a general philosophical statement in the later work. Our task is made more difficult, however, by the much greater dialectical sophistication of the *Fragment* than the previous Frankfurt writings, and this means that we are unable to follow the route by which Hegel arrived at this, the first clear formulation of the dialectical method. Here once again we are reduced to hypotheses and guess-work.

In view of the very fragmentary nature of the surviving sections of the essay it is obviously not possible to hazard even a guess about the appearance of the general structure of Hegel's philosophical system at this time, the nature of the problems on which his attention was focused, and the way they were organized into a dialectical hierarchy. The only thing to emerge clearly in the first fragment is his view of the relations between religion and philosophy. All we can do, then, is to consider the specific questions raised by Hegel in the context of what we have discovered about his previous development.

In the surviving portions we rediscover the cardinal problems of the Frankfurt period: the antithesis of life and lifeless objectivity and the resolution of this contradiction in the religious life. But although the basic theme of *The Spirit of Christianity* is retained and although the religious climax is even more vigorously asserted in the later work, the entire treatment shows a great advance in dialectical dexterity.

As we have seen, the transition to a dialectical approach involved relativizing rigidly one-sided concepts, shading-off their sharp distinctions from each other, the gradual merging of concepts, the dissolution of their inflexible metaphysical, 'absolute' status. Up to now this has been a general tendency of the Frankfurt writings, but now it seems to become a conscious method. We may remember how rigidly in Berne Hegel had contrasted living and dead, subject and object, etc. In this respect *The Spirit of Christianity* signifies a great step forward, for all its mysticism, and we were able to see how in certain sections, such as the treatment of Kant's ethical doctrine, the tendency to dissolve these rigid opposites gradually became a conscious process. In the *Fragment* Hegel now takes a further conscious step forward in the direction of making his concepts more flexible, in discovering the fluidity of the process of knowledge.

The first fragment of the manuscript starts and ends in the middle of a sentence. Its subject is the problem of life, of the relation of the individual to his environment. Hegel views this relationship as one between two totalities. The picture he gives of the external world is much more clearly that of an organic whole with its own laws than in his earlier writings. It is true that Hegel's ideal of life reborn had always implied the possibility and necessity of such a view, but hitherto the entire problem had been peripheral. In particular, his detailed analysis shows that by the 'external world' of man it was chiefly the problems of man in society that concerned him most deeply. Nature is indeed always on the horizon, but it is always closely bound up with life in society; in fact it always appears in association with the question of whether a particular form of society lives in harmony with nature, or estranged from it and hostile to it.

Up to now Hegel had made no attempt to study the philosophy of nature any more than he had tried to treat epistemological problems independently of concrete social or historical issues. But whereas we have seen how the emergence of contradictions in the study of history and society led Hegel to profound methodological studies and to the development of the dialectical method, the available material does not suggest that he was similarly impelled to study the problems of the philosophy of nature. It is indeed the case that Hegel studied Schelling's writings much more attentively in Frankfurt than he had done in Berne; this is evident from a whole series of terms taken over from Schelling. However, these writings could not possibly have given Hegel any real knowledge of scientific problems. And in Jena we shall see him throw himself into the study of the philosophy of nature and become heavily involved in particular scientific questions. In Jena he became very friendly with a number of scientists. In 1804 he became a member of the Mineralogical Society and in the same year he also joined the Westphalian Society for Scientific Research.[2] From the Frankfurt period we do indeed possess a quantity of notes on geometry but Hegel himself has dated these 23 September 1800, i.e. after he had finished writing the *Fragment*.[3]

The *Fragment* treats the problems of philosophy of nature quite differently from anything that Hegel had done hitherto. How far his ideas go is very difficult to decide from the surviving passages. Nevertheless, the mere fact of such a discussion is of some interest, especially as it occurs repeatedly in these few pages. At the beginning of the second passage we find an admittedly highly obscure and mystical discussion of time and space which is really almost beyond comprehension, particularly since it represents the final conclusions of an argument now lost. We believe, however, that in view of the extreme rapidity with which Hegel immersed himself in scientific problems in Jena, we would not be unduly rash in assuming that the preparatory studies for the *Fragment* must have included a certain amount of work on scientific matters.

In the first of the two fragments life appears as the relation of one totality to another. (One is reminded here of Hegel's later definition of the dialectical structure of any real totality as a circle that consists entirely of other circles.) Both the world and the individual are 'infinite multiplicities' of which one, the individual,

> 'is to be regarded purely as something related, as having its being purely in union,—the second (also an infinite multiplicity) is to be regarded as solely in opposition, as having its being solely through a separation from the first. . . . The first part is called an organization, an individual.'[4]

At first glance this looks like a subjectivization of the relation between the individual and objective reality, and we must not forget that the idealist in Hegel certainly has a tendency towards this, since it is the original assumption or act of 'positing' (*Setzung*) that determines what is to be regarded as a union and what as a separation. We should not overlook the fact, however, that it represents at the same time a relativization of what had been a rigid antithesis of individual and objective reality, and it brings a much more vital, mobile, fluid interaction into being, a process described by Hegel in these words:

> 'The concept of individuality includes opposition to infinite variety and also inner association with it. A human being is an individual life in so far as he is to be distinguished from all the elements and from the infinity of individual beings outside himself. But he is only an individual life in so far as he is at one with all the elements, with the infinity of lives outside himself. He exists only inasmuch as totality of life is divided into parts, he himself being one part and all the rest the other part; and again he exists only inasmuch as he is no part at all and inasmuch as nothing is separated from him.'[5]

Thus the relativization of the antithesis between individual and the world resulting from this assumption does not only imply that each living being can be thought of both as such a centre—relatively speaking —of the union, and merely as a part of a whole, i.e. as the external world of another individual, but also that each individual appears as a unit and the foundation on which it is built is the simultaneous existence of both a unification with and a separation from the world around it.

This relationship can be regarded in two different ways according to Hegel. (1) One may choose the 'undivided life' (i.e. the religious life from *The Spirit of Christianity*) as a starting-point. In that case every individual is only 'an expression of life', and all such expressions are 'crystallized by reflection . . . into stable, subsistent, and fixed points, i.e. into individuals.'[6] Hence reflection is assigned the important, even decisive role of crystallizing the isolated phenomena into individuals. On the other hand, reflection appears as something merely subjective, since life is of itself undivided and reflection imports individuation into it through its own act of positing. Here we see the ambivalent, as yet insoluble paradox of reflection in Hegel's early thought at its most extreme. The other solution open to him of an *objective* reflection is the product of a later, more mature development.

(2) This unresolved duality becomes even more apparent when Hegel comes to speak of the converse assumption. Here 'we presuppose individual lives, namely ourselves, the spectators.' This gives rise to the antithesis of ego and nature,

'as a multiplicity, it is an infinite multiplicity of organizations or individuals, and as a unity it is one unique organized whole, divided and unified in itself.'

This is an admirable and correct definition, which suffers however 'only' from the fundamental idealist defect that it is an assumption, an assumption made moreover from the standpoint of the observer. It is not life itself, but merely

'a positing of life, for reflection has applied to life its concepts of relation and separation, of the self-subsistent particular (something restricted) and the unifying universal (something unrestricted), and by positing these has turned life into nature.'[7]

Here, then, nature is manifestly the product of the positing ego and of the ego as reflection in particular.

This duality now determines Hegel's view of the relation between philosophy and religion. To put it briefly, if what we are considering is the two manifest forms of life, then the first corresponds to religion, the second to spirit and law. According to Hegel the law is 'but a bare unity, something purely conceptual and not a living being. . . . Spirit is an animating law in union with the manifold which is then itself animated.'

For this reason man must advance beyond the positing of the ego and nature in order to arrive at real life in a living relationship. For since

'nature is not life itself, but is only a life crystallized by reflection, even though it be treated by reflection in the worthiest manner, therefore life, in thinking and in contemplating nature still senses . . . this contradiction. . . . And out of the mortal and perishable figure, out of what is self-opposed and self-antagonistic, this thinking life raises that living being, which would be free from transience; raises a relation between the manifold elements which is not dead or killing, a relation which is not a [bare] unity, a conceptual abstraction, but is all-living and all-powerful infinite life; and this life it calls God. In this process it is no longer [merely] thinking or contemplating, because its object does not carry in itself anything reflected, anything dead.'[8]

It is evident that through this philosophical formulation of his chief theme in Frankfurt, the theme of that living life that annuls all that is dead, positive, objective and reflected, Hegel has arrived at an authentic mystical position. Hence his view of the relation between philosophy and religion is, logically enough, that philosophy is superseded by religion. Philosophy as philosophy can only lead to a Kantian 'infinite progress'[9] (Hegel was later to term it a 'bad infinity'). According to Hegel's views at this stage, an infinite progress cannot be brought to any conclusion within philosophy. Such a conclusion would imply going beyond the infinite progress, the 'bad infinity' which must continually posit the lifeless and positive as lifeless and positive, and this is only possible by reaching a form of reality beyond reflection. Hegel describes what this involves in the following way:

'Every expression whatsoever is a product of reflection, and therefore it is possible to demonstrate in the case of every expression that, when reflection propounds it, another expression, not propounded, is excluded. Reflection is thus driven on and on without rest; but this process must be checked once and for all by keeping in mind that, for example, what was earlier called a union of synthesis and antithesis [the argument referred to here has not survived in the extant fragment, G.L.] is not something propounded by the understanding or by reflection but has a character *of its own*, namely, that of being a *reality beyond all reflection*. . . . Philosophy therefore has to stop short of religion because it is a process of thinking and, as such a process, implies an opposition with non-thinking [processes] as well as the opposition between the thinking mind and the object of thought. Philosophy has to disclose the finiteness in all finite things and require their integration by means of reason. In particular, it has to recognize the illusions generated by its own infinite and thus to place the *true* infinite *outside* its confines.'[10]

The task of philosophy then, is its own self-annulment in favour of religion.

This 'reality beyond all reflection' is the realm of religion. In Hegel's view it cannot be a thought-out, reasoned relation of man to the world, but something lived. In the course of a polemic against contemporary philosophy Hegel emphasizes that the elevation of man in religion does not proceed

'from the finite to the infinite (for these terms are only products of mere reflection, and as such their separation is absolute), but from finite life to infinite life.'[11]

In this infinite life the separate partial existence of the parts, i.e. including human beings, ceases to be.

'Finite life raises itself to infinite life. It is only because the finite is itself life that it carries in itself the possibility of raising itself to infinite life.'[12]

Hegel goes on to explain how the process of the self-elevation from finite life to infinite life should proceed.

'When man . . . takes the infinite life as the spirit of the whole, and at the same time as a living being outside himself (since he himself is restricted), and when he puts himself at the same time outside his restricted self in rising toward the living being and intimately uniting himself with him, then he worships God.'[13]

In our discussion of the manuscript of *The Spirit of Christianity* we dealt very fully with the question of the social issues that impelled Hegel in the direction of the religious life. Now, when faced with the extreme mystical formulations of his concluding piece of work in Frankfurt we must briefly turn to the philosophical problems that determine their particular shape. These statements, like Schelling's almost exactly contemporary *System of Transcendental Idealism*, mark the point at which classical German philosophy takes the road towards objective, absolute idealism.

The transition from subjective to objective idealism raises the question of philosophical attitudes towards reality, towards existence independently of consciousness. For this reason it also involves an attitude (whether open or covert) to philosophical materialism. Kant's subjective idealism had really hesitated, as Lenin observes, between idealism and materialism; it compromised between the two.

'When Kant assumes that something outside us, a thing-in-itself corresponds to our ideas, he is a materialist. When he declares this thing-in-itself to be unknowable, transcendental, beyond this world, he is an idealist.'[14]

As is well known, Fichte rejected this compromise in the *Theory of Science* in favour of a radical and logically coherent subjective idealism. Both Hegel and Schelling then strove to advance beyond both Kant and Fichte in a quest for a solution to the problems of philosophy that tended towards objective idealism. And since it is a widely-held belief among historians of philosophy that Hegel was in a certain sense the disciple, and that he extended lines of thought developed by Schelling, we must at once devote a little space to their relations with each other (though we must postpone our detailed comparison of Schelling and Hegel for later chapters when we shall be able to examine their collaboration in Jena and Hegel's critique of the Schellingian version of dialectics).

In brief we may say at this point that Hegel's first attempt to formulate an objective idealism owes nothing to the influence of Schelling, but grows organically from the contradictions arising from his own reflections on socio-historical problems. Of course, there can be even less truth in the suggestion that Hegel might have exerted an influence on Schelling. The latter's objective idealism grew from his own desire to supplement Fichte's philosophy with a philosophy of nature. It took Schelling a relatively long time before he became fully aware of the gulf between Fichte's dialectics and his own, and in all probability Hegel did have something to do with hastening his realization of this fact. But in general it may be said that at first sight the paths of the two leading representatives of objective idealism in Germany ran parallel with each other.

But even this parallelism is more apparent than real and we should not be led astray by the two thinkers themselves who believed for a number of years that their philosophical ideas were intimately related. In reality they were proceeding in opposite directions and their collaboration in Jena was the meeting-place of paths that diverged both and after. That they coincided at this point was due to the need felt by both to join forces in a common battle against subjective idealism and this need was able to override differences which in any case had not yet become fully apparent.

To explain the problem schematically, objective idealism has two general methods for coming to grips with objective reality (both of which are in fact pseudo-solutions, even though the differences between the two types are of importance). The first approach can be seen in Hegel's Frankfurt writings. As with Kant and Fichte, empirical reality is thought

of as something 'posited' by the philosophical subject. Beyond that there
is a further 'non-posited' reality which is the authentic reality independent of human consciousness. This latter is in fact a religious reality
whose extreme idealistic nature is expressed in the notion that it is supposed to be the lived union of the subjective and objective principles, the
dissolution of the opposition between man and the world in the union of
man and God. We thus find ourselves in a pseudo-mystical realm which
is either entirely empty—a night in which all cows are black, as Hegel
was later to observe in the *Phenomenology*—or an irrationalist receptacle
in which all sorts of reactionary contents may be deposited at will. The
most important manifestation of this type of idealism is Schelling's later,
so-called 'positive' philosophy (designed to complement the 'negative'
philosophy of his youth). Here Schelling was the predecessor of a whole
series of later reactionary philosophies from Kierkegaard to Heidegger.
(On Schelling's later thought cf. Chapter II of my book *The Destruction
of Reason*, Berlin 1950, *Werke*, Vol. 9, 1962.)

    The second type of objective idealism to be found in Hegel's mature
philosophy and its programme, proclaimed in *The Phenomenology of
Mind*, states that the task of philosophy is to transform all substance into
subject, i.e. that the whole world is to be depicted as the self-production
and self-recognition of spirit and every objective reality is just one of the
various possible forms of spirit in a state of 'externalization'. This means,
of course, that all the relations between subjectivity and objectivity are
turned upside down and are distorted in detail, as we shall see clearly
when we come to discuss Marx's critique of the *Phenomenology*. All we
need say at this point, however, is that for all its idealist distortion, this
was the only form of objective idealism capable of yielding a dialectic of
human progress, a progressive view of the laws underlying nature and
society; the only form of objective idealism capable of being turned right
way up again and converted into a materialism. The other version of
objective idealism is necessarily reactionary.

    To put the matter schematically, and anticipating our own detailed
analysis, we may say that Hegel's development begins with the reactionary form of objective idealism and advances to its progressive form,
whereas Schelling proceeds in the reverse direction. We shall see how
Schelling begins quite naively with an attempt to build a philosophy of
nature into Fichte's theory of knowledge and that these first essays in
natural philosophy reveal far-reaching materialist leanings such as Hegel
never experienced. But because he was unable ever to reach the same
level of dialectical thought as Hegel and because too of his much more
superficial knowledge of the problems of society and history, he was
gradually driven to adopt the sort of solution that Hegel arrived at
during the crisis of his thought in Frankfurt.

    The contradictions arising from this crisis leave their marks also on the few fragments remaining from his plan for a system. In the first place it is interesting to note that even when Hegel follows his extremist, irrationalist and mystical tendencies right through to their conclusions he never entirely loses his ordinary sense of reality and would prefer his mysticism to be disfigured by the most blatant contradictions rather than fall victim to an out-and-out irrationalism. Thus we have seen how the whole point of this *Fragment* is to show how religion annuls and transcends philosophy. We have also seen that this act of supersession involves abandoning the realm of thought, of reflection. But at the same time it is interesting to observe that just at the point where he seeks to define the worship of God beyond all thought (see the quotation on p. 214) he unconsciously re-introduces his philosophical categories into the worship of God, thus destroying the entire edifice of religious irrationalism. For at this point he remarks that man 'takes', 'posits' both the infinite life and himself within religion as something 'outside himself', i.e. he implies that the religious life is likewise the product of the philosophical activity of the subject and—to use the terminology of the *Phenomenology*—is in a certain sense no more than one of the 'configurations of consciousness'.

The second contradiction between system and method is even more important and influential. We have seen that Hegel only allows philosophy a negative, preparatory role as the hand-maiden of religion, a role in which philosophy as it were prepares the way for its own critical self-abolition. In explaining the necessity for this he argues that the most philosophy can achieve is the 'infinite progress' of Kant and Fichte, or what he will later call a 'bad infinity'. In harmony with this is the fact that Hegel here simply equates philosophy with what in Jena he will call 'the philosophy of reflection'. (It is very revealing that this equation should be found again in Schelling's later 'positive' philosophy, but there it is used as a weapon with which to attack Hegel.)

But without noticing it or drawing any conclusions from it Hegel has nevertheless gone beyond this point of view here. A number of isolated remarks show that he has already anticipated his later definition of dialectics, even if only in an obscure and confused manner. But in the course of his argument showing that philosophy is incapable of really annulling opposition and is therefore compelled to annul itself and to allow itself to be absorbed into religion he arrives at a relatively clear statement of his later dialectical method.

'Although the manifold is here no longer regarded as isolated but is rather explicitly conceived as related to the living spirit, as animated, as organ, still something remains excluded, namely, the dead, so that a certain imperfection and opposition persists. In other words, when the manifold is conceived as an organ only, opposition itself is excluded; but life cannot be regarded as union or relation alone but must be

regarded as opposition as well. If I say that life is the union of opposition and relation, this union may be isolated again, and it may be
argued that union is opposed to non-union. Consequently, I would
have to say: *Life is the union of union and non-union.*'[15]

It is evident that this statement incorporates the mature form of
Hegel's dialectic; it embodies the view of contradiction which raises
Hegel above all his predecessors because of its realization that contradiction is the profoundest principle of all things and their movements,
whereas they are all content with the simple resolution of antithetical determinations and so inevitably drift towards a realm (always more or less
religious) where all contradictions are extinguished. (And of this Schelling is a cardinal instance.) With Hegel's formulation, however, contradictoriness appears as the living and moving principle. It simply cannot
be abolished for good and all but continually reproduces itself at a higher
level. (When we come to examine Hegel's development in Jena we shall
see that this implies a radical change in the status of reflection since
reflection now becomes a necessary moment in the overall dialectical
movement. But at the moment it is necessary to point out only that sporadic elements of this view were always present in Hegel's thought in
Frankfurt, even though they were never fully thought out at this stage.)
It is no less clear that this view of dialectics, if thought through, would
inevitably explode the idea that the religious life could be the culminating moment of philosophy. Hence when Hegel does follow up his
conception of dialectics his analysis leads him directly to the form of
speculation', characteristic of his mature philosophy.

This doctrine of contradiction can only be worked out adequately and
consistently within a *materialist* dialectic in which it can be regarded as
the intellectual mirroring of the dynamic contradictions of objective reality. But this insight into the necessary limitation of Hegel's philosophical idealism does not in the least diminish his great achievement in
perceiving the real character of contradiction in both life and thought. In
this context Lenin has emphasized the importance of the much clearer
and more accurate statements in the *Logic* and has shown how the path
leads from them to the materialist 'inversion' of the Hegelian dialectics.
He cites a number of passages from the *Logic*, among them the place
where Hegel discusses the relation between identity and contradiction:

'But indeed, if there were any question of rank, and the two determinations had to be fixed as separate, contradiction would have to be
taken as the more profound and the more fully essential.'

Lenin side-lined this passage approvingly and remarked at the end of the
whole excerpt:

Movement and "*self-movement*" (this NB! arbitrary [independent], spontaneous, *internally-necessary* movement), "change", "movement and vitality", "the principal of all self-movement", "impulse", [*Trieb*] to "movement" and to "activity"—the opposite to "*dead Being*"—who would believe that this is the core of "Hegelianism", of abstract and abstruse (ponderous, absurd?) Hegelianism?? This core had to be discovered, understood, "*hinübergerettet*" [rescued], laid bare, refined, which is precisely what Marx and Engels did.'[16]

This formulation of dialectical contradiction is the greatest achievement of Hegel's period in Frankfurt. We might say that it brings his phase of philosophical 'Sturm und Drang', the period of intellectual crisis, to a conclusion. But we have also established that this same formulation stands in the most glaring contradiction to the positions finally adopted in Frankfurt, to the structure of the *Fragment of a System* as a whole. We can do no more than point to this contradiction, without being able to show in detail how Hegel arrived at it. For that we would need the preparatory studies in Frankfurt, the missing sections of the *Fragment* itself, together with the other studies carried out by Hegel just before he left for Jena. The importance of this lost material can be gauged from the remark he let fall to the effect that he had already talked about the 'union of synthesis and antithesis'. Since neither Fichte nor Schelling had gone further than the idea of synthesis as the union of thesis and antithesis we may assume that we have lost an important statement about Hegel's view of his innovations in dialectics.

In our analysis of the general tendencies found in Hegel during the Frankfurt period, we have attempted to show the factors in his thought that led to an intensified antagonism between his system and his method. In the context of our earlier discussions we now believe that we are justified in airing the hypothesis that one of the decisive moments that helped to determine his view of contradictoriness was the dynamic contradiction to be found most strikingly in human activity, in work. In an earlier chapter (p. 174–5ff.) we suggested that a plausible case might be made to show that Hegel was already familiar with Adam Smith's writings on economics and had taken over his concept of work at the time when he was writing the *Fragment of a System*. If we now look at what Hegel wrote a few years later about the economic problems connected with work we can see that what is essential to them is that concepts such as the particular and general, which are mutually exclusive in metaphysical thought, not only merge into each other, but that they always appear simultaneously and inseparable from each other, united in contradiction —and that in Hegel's eyes this is their salient characteristic. We may look, for example, at what he says in the *System of Ethics* (Jena 1802) about tools and their relation to man and his work:

'On the one hand, they are subjective, in the power of the subject who works, and quite definitely prepared and operated by him; and on the other hand, they are objectively directed towards the object of work. Tools are thus a means through which the subject annuls the immediacy of annihilation; for work as an annihilation of intuition is equally an annihilation of the subject, a negation, positing him as a mere quantity; both hands and mind are blunted by it, i.e. they themselves assume the nature of the negative and formless, just as on the other side (for the negative, the difference is doubled) work is simply single and subjective. Through tools the subject creates a middle thing between itself and the object and this medium is the real rationality of work. . . . Through tools the subject divests himself of his objectivity and ceases to be blunted . . . at the same time his work ceases to be something single; through tools the subjectivity of work is raised to the level of the universal; anyone can imitate it and work in the same fashion; to that extent it is the constant rule of work.'[17]

We are not concerned here to offer a critique of Hegel's economic views, but only with his methodology. And here the reader can see that Hegel's novel interpretation of dialectics is particularly well-developed when the subject under discussion is work, activity. Not only do we find the merging of the general in the particular and vice versa, but also we see that Hegel views the activity of work, man's active relation to the world of objects mediated by tools, simultaneously as something general and particular. Obviously, the evidence of such passages even though they were written only a few years later cannot provide any conclusive proof that his reflections on the contradictions in the notion of work provided one of the chief sources for the specifically Hegelian form of dialectics. But since the mainstream of his development does flow towards the *Phenomenology* whose central idea is the self-production of man through his own activity and since we have already observed such views in embryonic form at an earlier stage of his thought, we think it legitimate to use this passage as the basis for an hypothesis by which to explain a stage in his development for which no incontestable evidence is available.

The second surviving passage from *The Fragment of a System* forms the conclusion of the essay and focuses on those discussions of property, work and sacrifice which we have already examined in some detail in connection with the growth of Hegel's views on economics. They form a part of that complex of ideas familiar to us from our analysis of *The Spirit of Christianity* and centring on the question of whether religion is adequate to the task to which it has been appointed, according to Hegel, of overcoming the false, lifeless, 'positive' objectivity of the world. The answer we discover here sounds rather more sceptical than one was entitled to expect after the enthusiastic mystical outpourings of the fragment already discussed. Hegel refers here to discussions—now lost —according to which the religious life was defined as something which kept objects alive or breathed new life into them, views known to us from earlier chapters. Nor is there anything fundamentally new in his reference to the fate of the religious life

'which demands of him that he admit the existence of the objective as objective or even that he make the living being itself into an object.'

The later formula is even more incisive than those in *The Spirit of Christianity*, for there, although Hegel went no further than to acknowledge that religion could not annul objectivity, it was only Judaism which was accused of causing living relations with objectivity to ossify. This process of objectification may well be momentary and revocable.

'But it is necessary that life should also put itself into a permant relation with objects and thus maintain their objectivity even to the point of completely destroying them.'

Here once again the Hegelian definition of work as a permanent relation, not capable of being annulled by religion, comes to the surface. The process of realizing religion in the modern world is seen by Hegel to be one in which the religious life must continually come to terms with the conditions of life which have become objective and constantly reproduce objectivity. This goes so far that Hegel even admits that for modern priests the social division of labour is unavoidable.[18]

We can see, then, that Hegel's extravagant hopes about the redemptive power of religion fade in proportion as he approaches the concrete history and social reality of the modern world. In line with this the concluding sentences of the *Fragment* have a certain air of resignation. Hegel believes that

'an elevation of finite life to infinite life such that as little as possible of the finite and restricted . . . remains . . . is not absolutely necessary. Religion is *any* elevation of the finite to the infinite . . . and some such elevation is necessary. . . . But the stage of opposition and unification on which the determinate nature of one generation of men persists is accidental. The most perfect integration is possible in the case of peoples whose life is separated and disintegrated as little as possible, i.e. in the case of happy peoples. Unhappy peoples cannot reach that stage, but they, living in a state of separation, *must* take anxious care for the preservation of one member [of the whole], i.e. for their own independence.'[19]

We can see that the intoxicating wine of religious mysticism has been watered down considerably by this point.

Of philosophical importance in these and the sentences directly following them is Hegel's attempt to take up a critical stance towards the philosophies of his age (which he has now seen to be necessary) and to judge them from a loftier perspective. It comes as no surprise to see him equating pure objectivity and pure subjectivity in the course of his strictures on the limitations of the finite life and on fragmentation. For this is no more than a general philosophical re-statement of the idea already familiar to us according to which activity and passivity, struggle against fate or flight from it, amount to the same thing.

But his arguments, which are evidently aimed at Kant and Fichte, go beyond this. It occurs to him for the first time that the subjectivity of Kant and Fichte is part of the same complex as the unknowable thing-in-itself. He writes:

> 'One may consider this situation from the side of subjectivity as independence, or from the other side as an alien, remote, inaccessible object. Both seem to be compatible with one another, although it is necessary that, the stronger the separation is, the purer must the Ego be and the further must the object be removed from and above man. The greater and more isolated the inner sphere, the greater and more isolated is the outer sphere also . . . it does not matter what mode of consciousness a man prefers. . . . When the separation is infinite, it does not matter which remains fixed, the subject or the object, but in either case the opposition persists, the opposition of the absolutely finite to the absolutely infinite.'[20]

Thus Hegel is no longer content to criticize the philosophy of Kant and Fichte purely from a moral point of view: this critique is directed at their system in its entirety and hints that its epistemological foundations, viz. the unknowable thing-in-itself, are the philosophical correlative of their subjectivity. On the other hand, he regards their philosophy as the most important world-view of the age since it expresses its intractable contradictoriness, a condition that he will term 'disintegration' [*Zerrissenheit*] in Jena. Thus Hegel sees Kant and Fichte as the representatives of the crisis which he perceives in the social situation of the age. To discover a philosophical cure for this crisis is the task he has proposed to himself.

We know already what this cure appeared to him to be in Frankfurt. We have also seen the internal contradictions it contained. The historical and epistemological evaluation of Kant and Fichte remains a constant in his later philosophy. The process of overcoming the religious mysticism of his Frankfurt period will enable him to place this critique of them in a more comprehensive, more scientific framework. That is to say, the elements of his later historical method are already present. In this he does not criticize particular aspects or doctrines of these philosophers, but instead sees them as philosophical totalities which are at the same time the necessary product of their age. 'Sublime and awful, but not beautiful and humane'—this is Hegel's judgment on their *Weltanschauung* and it points at the same time to the general humanist philosophy by which he hoped to overcome it.

## NOTES

1 What remains of this manuscript are two written sheets each filling three printed sides in the Nohl edition. According to Hegel's own pagination the manuscript seems to have contained 47 such sheets. What has survived are pp. 8 and 47 (Nohl, p. 345). It is doubtful whether Hegel regarded the work as finished. In a later letter to Schelling dated 2 November 1800 he speaks of his work on the system as if it were still going on. But we cannot say whether this remark refers to the present fragment or to the initial stages of some other work (cf. Rosenkranz, p. 143). No preparatory studies for this or any other works from the same period have come to light. We shall have something to say about the new introduction to *The Positivity of Christianity* in the next chapter. Hoffmeister maintains that an examination of the manuscripts shows that the brief essay on Schiller's *Wallenstein* also falls within this period, although it has always been included in Hegel's later Berlin writings (Vol. XX of the Glockner edition, pp. 456ff.) cf. Hoffmeister, p. 456f. Since this essay merely presents a number of variations on the view of fate already familiar to us we do not intend to comment on it further.

2 Cf. Rosenkranz, p. 220 for an account of these activities and relations in Jena.

3 Hoffmeister, pp. 288ff. and 470ff.

4 Nohl, p. 346. Knox, p. 309.

5 Nohl, p. 346. Knox, p. 310.

6 Ibid.

7 Nohl, p. 346f. Knox, p. 310.

8 Nohl, p. 347. Knox, pp. 310–11.

9 Hegel's mature discussion of Kant's 'infinite progress' can be found in the *Science of Logic* (trans. Miller, London 1969, pp. 150–54 and 227–34). He remarks there: 'The spurious infinite, especially in the form of the quantitative progress to infinity which continually surmounts the limit it is powerless to remove, and perpetually falls back into it, is commonly held to be something sublime and a kind of divine worship, while in philosophy it has been regarded as ultimate. This progression has often been the theme of tirades which have been admired as sublime productions. As a matter of fact, however, this *modern* sublimity does not magnify the *object*—rather does this take flight—but only the *subject* which assimilates such vast quantities.' He goes on to criticize the 'hollowness of this exaltation' as he finds it in the 'tirade' at the end of the *Critique of Practical Reason* where Kant finds it sublime 'when the subject raises himself in

thought above the place he occupies in the world of sense, reaching out to infinity, to stars beyond stars, worlds beyond worlds, systems beyond systems' etc. Hegel goes on to castigate the love of infinity as displayed by modern astronomers and finally attacks its role in Kant's moral dualism: 'To the infinity of outer, sensuous intuition, Kant opposes the other infinite, when "the individual withdraws into his invisible ego and opposes the absolute freedom of his will as a pure ego to all the terrors of fate and tyranny, and starting with his immediate surroundings, lets them vanish before him, and even what seems enduring, worlds upon worlds, collapse into ruins, and, alone knows himself as equal to himself."' Hegel comments: 'The ego in being thus alone with itself is, it is true, the reached beyond; it has come to itself, is with itself, here and now; the absolute negativity which in the progress beyond the quantum of sense was only a flight, in pure self-consciousness becomes affirmative and present. But this pure ego, because it has fixed itself in its abstraction and emptiness, has determinate reality, the fulness of the universe of nature and mind, confronting it as a beyond. We are faced with the same contradiction which lies at the base of the infinite progress, namely a returnedness-into-self, which is at the same time immediately an out-of-selfness, a relation to its other as to its non-being; and this relation remains a longing, because on the one side is the insubstantial, untenable void of the ego fixed as such by the ego itself, and on the other, the fullness which though negated remains present, but is fixed by the ego as its beyond.' Thus Hegel's critique of 'infinite progress' is crucial to his rebuttal of the philosophy of Kant and Fichte, just as his concept of 'bad or spurious infinity' is pivotal to his attack on Romantic Irony. Cf. his remarks on the Ought where similar arguments are employed (*Science of Logic*, op. cit., pp. 131–6)—*Trans.*

10  Nohl, p. 348. Knox, pp. 312–13. G.L.'s italics.

11  Nohl, p. 347. Knox, p. 311.

12  Nohl, p. 348. Knox, p. 313.

13  Nohl, p. 347. Knox, p. 312.

14  Lenin, *Materialism and Empirio-Criticism*, Collected Works, Vol. 14, London 1962, p. 198.

15  Nohl, p. 347f. Knox, p. 312. G.L.'s italics.

16  Lenin, Collected Works, vol. 38, pp. 139 and 141.

17  Lasson, p. 428.

18  Nohl, p. 349f. Knox, p. 316f.

19  Nohl, p. 350. Knox, p. 317.

20  Nohl, p. 351. Knox, pp. 317–18.

# CHAPTER EIGHT

# Reformulation of the problem of 'positivity'

THE last piece of work undertaken by Hegel in Frankfurt was a new introduction to the great Berne manuscript *The Positivity of the Christian Religion*. Hegel himself gives 24 September 1800 as the date when he started work on it, i.e. shortly after finishing *The Fragment of a System*, and since the essay is brief no further chronological problems are involved. Hegel's general approach to the problem here is radically opposed to that of the original study; it is not known, however, whether he seriously intended to rewrite it or not; nor do we know when he stopped working on it.

The analysis of the new introduction presents no special problems in view of our familiarity with Hegel's other Frankfurt writings since in the main it summarizes ideas which we have frequently encountered. We shall concentrate, therefore, on those features which come closer to his later views as well as those which point up the change from earlier positions and in particular his rejection of ideas he had entertained in Berne.

A point of particular methodological interest is his definition of an 'ideal' since it represents the as yet unclear formulation of what he was later to call the 'concrete concept'. Both in Berne and Frankfurt the word 'ideal' recurs often enough but it is used either in its ordinary meaning or in its Kantian sense. The term is not particularly well adapted to what Hegel wants it to mean and he soon dropped it, but the substance is of the first importance. After the new conception of dialectical contradiction in the *Fragment of a System* it comes as no surprise to see Hegel moving in the direction of the concrete concept. However, our thesis that his method and system were in conflict during the Frankfurt period and that his development of the dialectic worked *against* his systematic aims, is confirmed by the fact that he now looks for and finds the concrete totality within the categories of philosophy, even though in the *Fragment* the concrete had been placed in the realm of the religious and philosophy had been assigned the lesser role of preparing the way for religion through its negative criticism; which task accomplished, it would find itself superseded by it.

Here Hegel contrasts the ideal which is concrete and historical, with universal concepts which are abstract and anti-historical. He writes:

'An ideal of human nature, however, is quite different from general

concepts of man's vocation or of man's relation to God. The ideal
does permit of particularization, of determination in detail, and therefore it demands appropriate religious actions, feelings, usages,
demands an excess of these, a mass of excessiveness which in the
lamplight of general concepts seems only ice and stone.'[1]

This statement certainly lacks methodological rigour and precision, but
it represents the first appearance of Hegel's discovery that generalization
does not necessarily entail the impoverishment of content (as formal
logic assumes), but that, on the contrary, because true philosophical
generalizations contain rich deposits of material that has been superseded
they become richer and more concrete the higher the level of generalization becomes.

Hegel's reliance in Frankfurt on experience as a basis for the formation
of conceptual schemes is demonstrated here by the way in which necessary generalizations have not yet been fully emancipated from the actual
historical occasion that engendered them. Instead they simply carry the
signs of their origin along with them in an undigested or only partly
digested form. In the present instance, the 'ideal', the general concept by
means of which Hegel is moving towards the concrete concept, has still
not freed itself from the realm of religious positivity to which it is being
applied. Of course, the later Hegel, too, always enlivens and illuminates
the most abstract ideas with a mass of concrete material, but there is a
great difference between that and the confused, unmediated union,
which we see here, between the problem itself and the factors that
brought it into existence.

Like all of Hegel's developmental processes this one too has a dual
character. On the one hand, as we have shown, it contains the seeds of a
new logic which make it possible to accommodate the particularity of
objects and of historical phenomena within dialectics and so to construct
a methodology which—even though unconscious at this stage and full of
idealist distortions—is capable of reflecting the richness and mobility of
objective reality. On the other hand, Hegel employs this more concrete
logical structure in order to defend religion against the encroachments of
reason and the understanding.

In line with this the opening remarks of the new introduction contain
a full-scale attack on the philosophy of the Enlightenment and its view of
history and religion in particular. From the outset Hegel protests energetically against the distinction drawn by the Enlightenment between
positive and natural religion. He rejects the premise

'that there is only one natural religion, since human nature is one and
single, while there may be many positive religions.'[2]

Hegel rejects the idea that religion and its historical role can be deduced from such generalized concepts of human nature.

'The general concept of human nature is no longer adequate. The [concept of the] freedom of the will is a one-sided standard, because human manners and characteristics together with the accompanying religion cannot be determined by concepts at all. . . . The universal concepts of human nature are too empty to afford a criterion for the special and necessarily manifold needs of religious feelings.'[3]

Hegel's aim here—and this is the progressive side of his method—is to refrain from passing moral and philosophical judgment on the past, and to limit himself to attempting to comprehend its dynamics and complexity. After listing a series of arguments against religion advanced by the Enlightenment, he adds:

'But this method of explaining the matter presupposes a deep contempt for man and the presence of glaring superstition in his intellect. . . . The sole question raised . . . is the question about the truth of religion in abstraction from the manners and characteristics of the nations and epochs which believed it, and the answer to this question is that religion is empty superstition, deception and stupidity.'[4]

Hegel raises a passionate protest against the notion that

'the convictions of many centuries, regarded as sacrosanct, true and obligatory by the millions who lived and died by them in those centuries, were . . . at least on their subjective side, downright folly or plain immorality.'[5]

These quotations show clearly enough that the strengthening of Hegel's historical consciousness was accompanied by the need to provide an historical and philosophical apologia for religion, and not just in the sense that he was able to recognize the religions of the past as real factors in history the social causes of whose rise and fall were worthy of study, but in the sense of wishing to justify the permanent and hence contemporary relevance of religion. Knowing as we do the course of Hegel's development in Frankfurt this does not come as any surprise to us. We must, Hegel says,

'at least presume that man has a natural sense or consciousness of a supersensible world and an obligation to the divine . . . that everything high, noble and good in man is divine, that it comes from God and is His spirit, issuing from Himself.'[6]

This is essentially the application to history of the philosophy of religion contained in the *Fragment of a System*. But it would be one-sided to regard this as the sole aim of Hegel's thought at this time. We do indeed witness that tendency to idealize religion which never disappears, even after he has long since overcome the mystical excesses of the Frankfurt period. But it would be an error to see only this and to overlook his serious attempts to understand Christianity historically, to see it as that spiritual force that for two thousand years has determined European culture for good and evil, in a progressive or reactionary sense. Hegel opens the essay with a broad survey of the political, social and cultural influence of Christianity in which, characteristically, many of the strictures dating from the Berne period were taken over almost word for word. Since this is Hegel's first historical survey of this kind we think it is important to reprint the passage in its entirety despite its length.

'The Christian religion has sometimes been reproved, sometimes praised, for its consistency with the most varied manners, characters and institutions. It was cradled in the corruption of the Roman state; it became dominant when that empire was in the throes of its decline, and we cannot see how Christianity could have stayed its downfall. On the contrary, Rome's fall extended the scope of Christianity's domain, and it appears in the same epoch as the religion of the barbarians, who were totally ignorant and savage but completely free, and also of the Greeks and Romans, who by this time were overcivilized, servile, and plunged in a cesspool of vice. It was the religion of the Italian states in the finest period of their licentious freedom in the Middle Ages; of the grave and free Swiss republics; of the more or less moderate monarchies of modern Europe; alike of the most heavily oppressed serfs and their overlords: both attended one church. Headed by the Cross, the Spaniards murdered whole generations in America; over the conquest of India the English sang Christian thanksgivings. Christianity was the mother of the finest blossoms of the plastic arts; it gave rise to the tall edifice of the sciences. Yet in its honour too all fine art was banned, and the development of the sciences was reckoned an impiety. In all climates the tree of the Cross has grown, taken root, and fructified. Every joy in life has been linked with this faith, while the most miserable gloom has found in it its nourishment and its justification.'[7]

This general account is indeed rather more of a question than an answer and at this point Hegel is far from being able to provide a solution to a problem of such complexity. But the very breadth of his approach here shows a noteworthy advance in historical concreteness since his first efforts in Berne. At the same time, we can see how his improved understanding of the tortuous course of historical development is a function of his rejection of Enlightenment methodology with its starting-point in a general concept of 'man'. It is precisely this sort of historical insight that favours the formation of concrete concepts. In the passage directly following this one Hegel supplements his definition of 'ideal' with this remark:

> 'But the living nature of man is always other than the concept of the same, and hence what for the concept is a bare modification, a pure accident, a superfluity, becomes a necessity, something living, perhaps the only thing which is natural and beautiful.'[8]

It is evident that such an approach must lead to a much more historical view of the concept of positivity. Hegel no longer inquires: what *is* positivity? What excites his interest now is the question: how does a religion *become* 'positive'? Despite this historicism, however, which we were able to see in embryonic form in all his writings from the political pamphlets onward, it would be a mistake to follow the bourgeois historians here and make a sharp distinction between Hegel the 'historicist' and the 'unhistorical' Hegel influenced by the Enlightenment. Even though the majority of Hegel's concepts in Berne may have been metaphysical and unhistorical, his aim was to acquire an overall picture of the course of history. And even though the assumptions he shared with the Enlightenment undoubtedly were an obstacle to the development of a conceptual system capable of doing justice to the complexity of history, the broad sweep of his first exercises in historiography owed much to the beneficial influence of Enlightenment historians. The apologists of reaction can only reach their conclusions by denying that the entire period of the Enlightenment from Gibbon to Condorcet was an age which gave birth to great historical works of lasting importance.

On the other hand, we should not lose sight of the idealist limitations of Hegel's present view of history. The reactionary historians overemphasize and overvalue certain carefully selected aspects of the Hegelian view of history, with which they sympathize because their own view of the development of the historical consciousness is that it stems from the reaction against the French Revolution (i.e. from Burke) and then proceeds via Hegel to Ranke and later apologists. If we wish to understand both the strengths and weaknesses of Hegel's developing system we must see through this sham tradition. The real line of the tradition begins indeed with the ideological debates surrounding the French Revolution but their main tendency is just as powerful a defence of human progress as was found in the Enlightenment but from a much more profound awareness of the facts, the tendencies and the underlying laws of history. It is only if this is understood that it becomes possible to site Hegel within the historical tradition.

It then becomes apparent that Hegel's 'recognition' of the facts, in this case the facts of religion, represents a definite ideological weakness in his view of history, one arising from his philosophical idealism. The assumption that religion is 'eternal', that it corresponds to an 'ideal of mankind' is not a whit less metaphysical than the concept of a general human nature which he criticizes so incisively. If an authentic historicism is emerging in Hegel's mind, then it must spring from quite different sources than the ones singled out for praise by his reactionary apologists. He constructed an important approach to history *despite* and not *because* of what they have found to praise.

Let us now turn to the effect of his new attitude on his definition of positivity. We have already seen the various stages that preceded his present position. Cf. the pamphlet on Württemberg (p. 132f.), the article on *The German Constitution* (p. 139ff.), and his treatment of certain passages in *The Spirit of Christianity* (p. 200f.). Now he has a much more forthright and decisive formula for the same phenomenon:

> 'To shudder before an unknown Being; to renounce one's will in one's conduct; to subject one's self throughout like a machine to given rules; to abandon intellect altogether in action or renunciation, in speech or silence; and to lull one's self into a brief or lifelong insensibility—all this may be "natural", and a religion which breathes this spirit would not on that account be positive, because it would accord with the nature of its time. A nature demanded by such a religion would doubtless be a deplorable one; but the religion would have fulfilled its purpose by giving this nature the only higher Being in which it found satisfaction and with which it was compatible.'

And consistently with the observations already discussed Hegel now supplies an answer to the new question:

> 'Of course religion has become positive at this stage, but it has only become so; it was not so originally.'

When does a religion become positive? We have seen that a religion suited to 'a deplorable nature' was not positive.

> 'Only when another more courageous mood awakens, when this nature begins to have a sense of itself and thereby to demand freedom in and for itself . . . then and only then can its former religion begin to appear a positive one.'[9]

Thus the fact that a religion appears positive is the sign of an approaching revolution. Hegel has strongly historicized the concept of positivity here and thus finds himself at the opposite end of the spectrum to the Romantics, who regarded the mere existence of an institution, its very positivity, as an excuse to defend and canonize it (like the later historical school of law).[10] Hegel, by contrast, regards positivity as a sign that history has superseded a religion, that it deserves to be destroyed by history and that it must be so destroyed.

The comparison with Romanticism throws light on another issue of methodological importance. Hegel refuses to decide whether particular

Christian dogmas or institutions are positive or not. He demands that analysis should concern the *whole*:

> 'but the content of this inquiry will nevertheless always concern the whole rather than the parts.'[11]

On this question Hegel makes only a few general remarks here, but they are enough to give us pause. Firstly, because we see here the first announcement of what will become a conscious method of philosophical totalization in the *Phenomenology* with the statement: 'The true is the whole'. Secondly, because the reactionary philosophy of our own day claims a monopoly of philosophical totalization. It does so by converting the whole into a metaphysical concept which is emptied of every real observation of history, i.e. of every development which creates a succession of totalities, while at the same time it is consciously opposed to any kind of causal analysis. (Othmar Spann is a characteristic exponent of this view.)

Since there has been no lack of attempts to assimilate Hegel to reactionary postures of this sort it may not be out of place to cite a passage written a few years later in which Hegel applies his view of totality to a concrete example which helps to clarify the concept of positivity. In the *Scientific Modes of Treatment of Natural Law* written in Jena 1803,[12] Hegel has occasion to discuss the problem of feudalism and its survival in Germany and in this context he raises the question of its positivity.

> 'The feudal constitution, for example, can indeed appear utterly positive . . . but whether it does in fact confront life in a positive manner depends on whether the people has organized itself into a true individuality, whether it entirely fills the system and penetrates it with life. . . . Whereas if, for instance, the genius of a nation is generally on a lower plane and of a feebler kind—and the feebleness of ethical life is at its most extreme in a barbaric or a formal society if it allows itself to be conquered by another and is forced to surrender its autonomy, i.e. if it has preferred the misfortune and degradation of losing its independence to struggle and death, . . . then it may very well be the case that feudalism and servitude are absolute truth and that this system is the only possible form of ethical life and for that reason it is necessary, just and ethical.'[13]

It is evident that the bitterness Hegel feels about the primitive social and national conditions of Germany leads him here to regard the remnants of feudalism as suited to the 'deplorable nature' of the Germans and as *nonpositive* for that reason. Had there been any real movement in Germany to change the situation feudalism in Hegel's present view would surely have to be thought 'positive'.

The shift towards greater historical concreteness has a further by no

means unimportant implication. We recall that in Berne certain attitudes, religions and institutions were marked from the outset with the
stain of positivity, whereas others were metaphysically and absolutely
free of such stains. Hegel now throws this assumption overboard.

> 'Any doctrine, any precept, is capable of becoming positive . . . and
> there is no doctrine which might not be true in certain circumstances,
> no precept which might not impose a duty in certain circumstances,
> since what may hold good universally as truth unalloyed requires
> some qualification, because of its universality, in the particular cir-
> cumstances of its application; i.e. it is not unconditionally true in all
> circumstances.'[14]

This brings Hegel very close indeed to the conception of the historical
dialectics of the true and the false, contained in the *Phenomenology* and in
his later system.

Needless to say, this insight has two sides, like all of Hegel's discoveries about the dialectical method. And the idealist, non-progressive
side of the present argument is that it once again involves the unconditional acceptance of the Christian religion and the adulteration of the
historical polemic against it. The remark with which Hegel opens the
passage just quoted may seem innocent enough at first sight:

> 'The question of whether a religion is positive affects the content of its
> doctrines and precepts far less than the form in which it authenticates
> the truth of its doctrines and requires the fulfilment of its precepts.'[15]

This sentence does indeed contain a core of truth since Hegel distinguishes between a doctrine which freely and through its own force
takes possession of the minds and hearts of men, and one which can
only perpetuate itself with the aid of violence and reprisals, etc. But if
we read this sentence together with one quoted earlier (cf. p. 227)
which maintained that the religious relation to God was something
eternal and that all that is good and noble in man stems from God,
then we may fairly see it as an instance of the reactionary idealist
attempt to distinguish between the particular historical manifestations
of religion, which may lapse into positivity and be subjected to criticism, and the 'essence of religion' which is to be enshrined in a realm
beyond history.

This duality, even ambivalence, in Hegel's attitude to Christianity
appears again and again in varying guises. The quotations just referred
to may well give the impression that Hegel's essay will end up in a
glorification of Christianity. But they are at once followed by a vigorous attack on the fundamental dogma of Christianity, on Christ's mission as redeemer, on his role of mediator between God and man.

'But this view becomes glaringly positive if human nature is absolutely severed from the divine, if no mediation between the two is conceded except in one isolated individual, if all man's consciousness of the good and the divine is degraded to the dull and killing belief in a superior Being altogether alien to man.'[16]

Nor is there any possibility of ironing out apparent ambivalences by claiming that Hegel's views accord with one or other Christian sect, as is sometimes maintained. For we have seen that it is precisely the element of sectarianism that Hegel finds so reprehensible in Christianity and he is generally much more hostile to the various sects than he is towards the church itself.

Hegel's idealism in short is irreducibly ambivalent. His understanding of history and society often forces him to go beyond Christian points of view. His insight into dialectical interconnections increasingly brings him closer to a position from which the God of Christianity is entirely superfluous. It is very revealing that almost immediately after the last passage quoted he goes on to say that the problem of the positivity of Christianity, of mediation between man and God, could only be resolved by first solving the problem of the relation between the finite and the infinite. Obviously it was not possible for Hegel to undertake a task of that sort in the framework of an introductory essay and we cannot know with any certainty what views he had put forward on this matter in *The Fragment of a System*. But we do know that as early as Jena he does set out in search of a dialectical solution to the problem, in the course of which he divests the infinite of every trace of transcendence and other-worldliness. This dialectical approach to the infinite—very like parallel ideas in Goethe—has a pronounced tendency to dismantle the philosophical bases for every religious belief in God. But at the same time, we see that because of its own idealism, religious ideas that have apparently been superseded always make their re-appearance in philosophy in a different shape. As we have indicated, the irrepressible duality and ambivalence of Hegelian philosophy is a necessary consequence of his idealism, and this in turn arises from the particular circumstances of the development of bourgeois society in Germany. Even Goethe who, as we know, was much closer to materialism and much more hostile to Christianity than Hegel, could not free himself entirely from such religious ideas.

Of course, Hegel's own attitudes towards religion were subject to major changes in the course of his development. In Frankfurt the period of mental crisis represents a high point in his religious beliefs. But the roots of his ambivalent attitude towards Christianity are deep and their influence extends into Jena where his beliefs are even more clearly defined than here. In particular his illusions about the possibility of overcoming the contradictions of bourgeois society within the framework of

that society both strengthen his general idealism and lend a special force
to his religious views. They enable him to accept the contradictions in
Christianity, to combine what is in places very incisive criticism with a
generally religious orientation, because he is able to imagine the new,
contradiction-free society in the form of a new post-Christian religion.
(We shall have more to say about the latter when we come to the Jena
period itself.)

Only after the collapse of the Napoleonic empire and with that, the
disappearance of his illusions about Napoleon, will Hegel find himself
compelled to come to terms with the capitalist world, or as he terms it
the 'world of prose'. When that happens Christianity finally becomes a
specifically historical form of religion and the ambivalence in Hegel's
position reaches its peak. At the same time, his very late writings contain
the most complete and most dialectic view of bourgeois society of which
he was capable. If we may anticipate our later discussion by calling attention to one very significant point, it is characteristic of Hegel that his
philosophical justification of the 'Estates' (i.e. of the class structure of
civil society) becomes progressively less ideological, and much closer to
a grasp of society's material foundations.

We may therefore venture the paradoxical statement, which,
however, really does sum up the contradictory course of Hegel's development, that the more he is driven to abandon the revolutionary ideals of
his youth, the more resolutely he 'reconciles' himself to the rule of bourgeois society and the less his thought reaches out to new possibilities—then the more powerfully and consciously the dialectician in
him awakens. Given the existing historical conditions, the dialectical
view of human progress which is given its first comprehensive and philosophically significant shape in *The Phenomenology of Mind* could only
have been constructed from such a contradictory position. We have seen
the birth and growth of these contradictions in Frankfurt. In Jena we
shall encounter them again in a more distinct and more highly developed
form. That will be the moment to examine them fully.

It cannot be doubted, however, that the foundations for the later ideas
were laid during the crisis in his mental life in Frankfurt. From a literary
point of view Frankfurt, like Berne, produced a heap of fragments and
sketches. But whereas a reconstruction of the Berne writings yields an
ambitious and coherent design, the result of the Frankfurt years is a chaos
of conflicting tendencies. But—and this has been our task in Part II—it is
from amidst this chaos of unresolved contradictions that the Hegelian
dialectic was born. The creative product of the Frankfurt years is the intellectual framework necessary for gaining a philosophical purchase on
reality.

In later years Hegel apparently attached as little importance to the
Frankfurt writings as to those from Berne. At any rate his stay in Jena is

notable for his extraordinarily prolific productivity which is entirely unconnected with any of the projects he was concerned with in Frankfurt—with the single exception of an attempt to complete the essay on *The German Constitution*. Hegel went to Jena at the age of thirty, without a public reputation of any kind, and without a single manuscript which he could or would have seriously intended to publish. Despite this it is apparent that he went to Jena justifiably confident that he was the equal of his school friend Schelling, the most important philosopher of the age.

In the year 1800 Hegel's father died. The very modest estate bequeathed to Hegel enabled him to give up his post as a private tutor and devote himself for a few years entirely to his studies without material cares or other obligations. He fixed upon Jena as a suitable place for this and wrote to Schelling announcing his decision in a letter which broke the silence into which their correspondence had apparently lapsed. The most important parts of this letter show how Hegel, although he was completely unknown, could approach a friend who had become a celebrity, with the utmost self-assurance. On 2 November 1800 he wrote as follows:

'I have watched your great public progress with admiration and joy. You will overlook it if I do not speak about it or do not present myself to you with any false humility. I prefer a middle course and hope that we shall meet again as friends. —In my education which began with the inferior needs of man I was driven towards science, and my youthful ideals had to be transformed into reflection and at the same time into a *system*. While still engaged on this I find myself wondering *how to find my way back to the point where I might involve myself once more in the lives of men.* —Of all the people I see around me you are the only one whom I should like to have for a friend, even in respect of appearing before the public and producing an effect on the world. For I can see that you have striven purely, i.e. wholeheartedly and without vanity to understand man. It is for this reason that I approach you with such confidence on my own behalf, for I am sure that you will recognize my disinterested efforts and discover some value in them, even if they have taken place in a lesser sphere. In the desire and the hope to meet you I must yet respect fate and hope that it will preside with favour over our reunion.'[17]

It is the mood of the epigram that we mentioned in our introductory pages as providing a fitting conclusion to his stay in Frankfurt:
'Then you will be not better than the age,
but the age at its best.'

## NOTES

1   Nohl, p. 142. Knox, p. 170.
2   Nohl, p. 139. Knox, p. 167.
3   Nohl, p. 141. Knox, pp. 169–70.
4   Nohl, p. 144. Knox, p. 173,
5   Nohl, p. 143. Knox, p. 172.
6   Nohl, p. 146. Knox, pp. 175–6.
7   Nohl, p. 140. Knox, pp. 168–9.
8   Nohl, p. 141. Knox, p. 169.
9   Nohl, p. 141. Knox, pp. 169–70.
10  The historical school of law opposed natural law, arguing that law
    was a product of the historical process and hence varied in accor-
    dance with the culture of different peoples. Its founder was
    Friedrich Karl von Savigny (1779–1861).—Trans.
11  Nohl, p. 144. Knox, p. 173.
12  Referred to later in this text as the essay on Natural Law—Trans.
13  Lasson, p. 405f.
14  Nohl, p. 143. Knox, pp. 171–2.
15  Nohl, p. 143. Knox, p. 171.
16  Nohl, p. 146. Knox, p. 176.
17  Rosenkranz, p. 143f.

## Chronological Table of the Nohl Fragments

For the convenience of the student of Hegel's early development we present the following chronological table of all the early writings as contained in Nohl.

Pagination in

| Nohl | Knox | Title | Authenticated Dates |
|---|---|---|---|
| Tübingen | | | |
| 3–30 | | *Popular Religion and Christianity*[1] | Before 1793 |
| 355–59 | | Drafts | |
| Berne | | | |
| 30–35 | | *Popular Religion and Christianity* | |
| 359–60 | | Drafts | |
| 36–47 | | *Popular Religion and Christianity* | |
| 48–60 | | *Popular Religion and Christianity*[2] | |
| 70 71 | | *Popular Religion and Christianity* | |
| 60 69 | | *Popular Religion and Christianity* | |
| 75 136 | | *The Life of Jesus* | From 9·5 to |
| | | | 24·7., 1795 |
| 361–2 | | Drafts | |
| 362–66 | | Drafts | |
| 152–213 | 67–145 | *The Positivity of the Christian Religion* | 2.11.1795 to |
| | | | 29.4.1796 |
| 213–239 | 145–166 | *The Positivity of the Christian Religion* | |
| 366–367 | | Drafts | |
| Frankfurt | | | |
| 368–374 | | Drafts for *The Spirit of Judaism* | |
| 374–377 | | *Morality, Love, Religion* | |
| 377–378 | | *Love and Religion* | |
| 378–382 | 302–308 | *Love* | |
| 382–385 | | *Faith and Being*[3] | |
| 385–395 | | First draft of *The Spirit of Christianity and its Fate* | |
| 243–342 | 182–301 | *The Spirit of Christianity and its Fate* | |
| 398–402 | | Additions to *The Spirit of Christianity and its Fate* | |
| 345–351 | 309–319 | *Fragment of a System* | completed 14.9.1800 |
| 139–151 | 167–177 | New introduction to *The Positivity of the Christian Religion* | Begun on 24.9.1800 |

1 Trans. H. S. Harris, *Hegel's Development towards the Sunlight*, Oxford 1972, pp. 481–507.
2 Pages 48–50 in Nohl. Trans. H. S. Harris, *Hegel's Development towards the Sunlight*, Oxford 1972, pp. 508–510.
3 Trans. H. S. Harris, *Hegel's Development towards the Sunlight*, Oxford 1972, pp. 512–515.

# PART III

# Rationale and Defence of Objective Idealism (Jena 1801–1803)

In the letter to Schelling in which Hegel announced his intention of coming to Jena, he admitted that he felt apprehensive at the prospect of the 'riotous literary life' of the town. His anxiety, which was evidently aroused by the fact that Jena was the focal point of the Romantic Movement, was no longer as well-founded as it might have been a little earlier. The group of Romantic poets and thinkers with whom Schelling had been closely associated had gradually broken up. The *Athenäum*, the movement's journal published by the Schlegel brothers, had ceased to appear. Relations had become increasingly tense between Schelling and Friedrich Schlegel, the chief theoretician of the Romantic school. The divorce of August Wilhelm Schlegel from his wife Caroline and her subsequent marriage to Schelling had introduced personal sources of conflict to aggravate the intellectual disagreements. By the time Hegel arrived, Jena had ceased to be the centre of the Romantic Movement.

Yet another figure of great philosophical importance was lost to Jena at this time, namely Fichte. In 1798–9 Fichte had been the centre of a storm which had been triggered off by accusations that he was an atheist, and this had led eventually to his resignation from his Chair in Jena and his move to Berlin. This conflict united Fichte, Schelling and the Romantics for the last time in an onslaught on their common enemies. Fichte's departure, the impossibility of reconciling diverging views in the course of conversation undoubtedly accelerated the process of disintegration and prepared the way for the philosophical disputes of the future, although the ultimate causes of those disputes were much too profound to be more than postponed by personal friendships.

# CHAPTER ONE

# Hegel's role in Schelling's breakaway from Fichte

Despite these events Hegel's arrival in Jena coincided with an important development in German classical philosophy: the split between Schelling and Fichte and the founding of objective idealism. In this event Hegel played an important, indeed one may say the decisive part, making at the same time his own first public appearance (since the anonymous translation and annotation of the Cart pamphlet does not merit the title of public appearance). It was the young Engels who first perceived and drew attention to the significance of Hegel's role.

'Only this is certain, that it was Hegel who made Schelling aware of how far he had, without realizing it, gone beyond Fichte.[1]

Hegel himself puts the same view in the Preface to his first published work: *The Difference between the Fichtean and Schellingian Systems of Philosophy*.

'Neither the immediate appearance of the two systems as they present themselves to the public, nor, for example, Schelling's reply to Eschenmayer's idealist objections to the Philosophy of Nature, gave expression to this difference.'[2]

At around this time German Idealism underwent a series of extraordinarily rapid changes. Scarcely two years earlier Kant had published his well-known declaration against Fichte's *Theory of Science (Wissenschaftslehre)*. Up to that point Fichte could and undoubtedly did believe that he was simply providing a logical interpretation of Kantianism, that he was merely defending what he called the 'spirit' of Kant against the 'letter', i.e. the vulgarizations of other Kantians. Kant's declaration put an end to this confused state of affairs.

A detailed analysis of the differences between Kant and Fichte is clearly beyond the scope of this work and we must content ourselves with two observations. Firstly, Kant protested vigorously against the separation of spirit from letter. Although his statement is not notable for its sympathetic understanding, he obviously realized that Fichte's philosophy was an independent system and not just an interpretation of his own. This is not unimportant because it repeats itself *mutatis mutandis* in the breach between Fichte and Schelling. At the same time it says something about Hegel's position in classical German philosophy that when he comes into conflict with Schelling he simply opposes his own new philosophy to Schelling's old (and obsolete) one: the problem of whether his new position represents a re-interpretation just does not arise for him.

Secondly, it is of importance for the later development of German Idealism that Kant objected to Fichte's introduction of problems of content into his form of 'transcendental philosophy', i.e. into the *Theory of Science*. In line with his general views (although in unconscious contradiction to the dialectical implications of his own 'transcendental philosophy'), he maintains that pure logic must abstract from content of every kind. We shall see that the inclusion of problems of content in logic is a very essential part of Hegel's dialectical logic. But he is the first person to take this step consciously and make it part of his programme. Kant, Fichte and Schelling allow the old formal logic to go its own way *alongside* the newly emerging dialectical logic. This produces all sorts of contradictions which are intensified as the unconsciously incorporated elements of content, the general growth of the dialectic and its application to ever new areas, become more and more prominent.

Schelling and Fichte met Kant's declaration with a united front. They both believed that open dissociation from Kant had become inevitable and was essential for the further development of philosophy. At the same time, it is noteworthy that neither Fichte nor Schelling regarded the new philosophy as complete in itself; on the contrary, both of them knew it to be in a state of flux and that the philosophical revolution still had far to go. This mood is very obvious in a letter written by Fichte to Schelling in 1799, after Kant had issued his statement. Fichte refers to what he regards as Kant's inability even to understand the latest developments in philosophy and in the course of the letter he makes an interesting remark which points almost prophetically to Hegel:

> 'Who knows whether or not some young fire-eater isn't already at work, who will be able to go beyond the *Theory of Science* and attempt to expose its failings and inadequacies. May Heaven spare us then from contenting ourselves with the confident assurance that such criticism consists of sterile quibbling—something we should certainly not permit ourselves—[a reference to some slighting remarks in Kant's declaration—G.L.] Let us rather hope that one of us would stand his ground like a man either able to *prove* the nullity of these new discoveries, or else, if we cannot do this, willing to accept them gratefully in both our names.'[3]

The next few years were to show that Fichte found it impossible to live up to these good intentions.

At around this time differences of opinion between Fichte and Schelling began to emerge, initially in personal and technical disagreements to do with various common projects for journals and internal realignments with the Romantic movement. But they only came out into the open with the appearance of Schelling's first comprehensive, systematic work, the *System of Transcendental Idealism* of 1800. It is true that this work was conceived as an elaboration and complement of Fichte's *Theory of Science*, and not as a criticism or refutation of it. But in substance and notwithstanding Schelling's intention, it was already an attempt to systematize a philosophy of *objective* idealism. It is easy to understand, then, that Fichte felt unable to approve of the work, even though he did not in the least distrust Schelling or suspect, for a long time to come, that they were not in complete agreement about the *fundamental principles* of philosophy. The book gave rise to a protracted and detailed exchange of letters to clear up any 'misunderstandings' and to reestablish their former harmony.

Fichte purified Kantian philosophy of its 'materialist deviations'. He created a pure subjective idealism which, however, has a quite definite character of its own. Obviously, since he is perfectly consistent he must end up objectively in a completely agnostic position. But this is not his intention as a philosopher. On the contrary, his plan is to eliminate Kant's own agnosticism, his belief that we can know nothing about things-in-themselves. His method of doing this is the radically subjective one of disputing, not that things are *knowable*, but that they *exist*. He regards the universe as something 'posited' by the Ego (a concept which for him is not identical with the empirical consciousness of particular human beings) and consequently it is something that can be known perfectly by this imagined, mystificatory subject. According to Fichte, the Ego created the universe and for that reason can have knowledge of it, since—according to Fichte—apart from the universe as 'posited' by the Ego, nothing either can or does exist at all.

With this iridescent, contradictory conception of the Ego which replaces Kant's 'consciousness' but which is not counterpoised to any alien, independent, unknowable world of things-in-themselves, Fichte paves the way for the birth of objective idealism, even though his own project is the most extreme formulation of subjective idealism imaginable. All that is required for the change is that the concept of the Ego should be clarified and concretized (admittedly in an even more idealistic, mystificatory sense) and that Fichte's merely epistemological 'positing' of the world should be transformed into real creation—and objective idealism will be complete. This is what happens in Schelling's *System of Transcendental Idealism*, and later also in Hegel.

Fichte's philosophy, however, paves the way for Schelling and

Hegel in yet another important sense: in connection with the systematic deduction of the categories. In Kant as in Fichte, the categories are subjective-idealist in character. But in Kant's case they have been assembled empirically, rather than deduced. Kant took the categories over from the traditional school-logic and then gave them fresh interpretations, but without raising the question of their deduction from each other. The typical Kantian approach is: There are synthetic judgments *a priori*—how are they possible? This shows the extent to which Kant simply accepted the categories and their interrelations as something pre-existing. (And here too we see Kant wavering between materialism and idealism.) For Fichte, however, the categories spring from the positing activity of the Ego: they result from the interaction of Ego and Non-Ego—which means that the dialectical triad of thesis, antithesis and synthesis can be found already in Fichte.[4]

This leads in Fichte to that strengthening of the 'active side' of classical German philosophy to which Marx refers in his First Thesis on Feuerbach, although even this remains within the framework of pure idealism. In Kant it is only through his moral activity that man can break through the realm of appearances and take part in the world of reality, the world of essence. Thus the structure of Kantian ethics has implications for Fichte's theory of knowledge: the Ego's positing of the world is, according to Fichte, an 'action' [*Tathandlung*].

Even this crude outline makes it perfectly clear that disagreement between Kant and Fichte was inevitable. At the start Fichte could imagine that he was just spelling out Kant's philosophy more consistently even than Kant himself, defending the spirit against the letter. But in fact he had created a different philosophy which Kant could not possibly have accepted as his own.

The relation between Fichte and Schelling has a certain similarity with this, but it should not be exaggerated. Schelling's point of departure is in fact very different. Fichte's philosophy is the revolutionary activism of the age translated into philosophy. It is no accident that his first works were written in defence of the French Revolution and of the right to embark on revolutionary activity. Moreover, Fichte remained true to these sentiments for a relatively long period. We shall have occasion to look at his views when we come to consider Hegel's polemics against his moral theory and philosophy of law. In 1800 Fichte published his *Geschlossener Handelsstaat [The Closed Commercial State]* which Benjamin Constant, for example, considered to be a belated echo of Robespierre's economic policy. Fichte's subjectivism gives expression to a revolutionary faith in man's ability to transform and revitalize everything, but in a typically German, excessively idealist form. Beyond man—who is equated by Fichte with moral man, Kant's phantom '*homo noumenon*'—Fichte sees no reality at all. The world, and above all nature, is merely a passive arena for man's activity.

Schelling's philosophy, by contrast, grows out of the contemporary crisis in scientific knowledge. He belongs in the ranks of those 'nature enthusiasts' whom Marx talks about (with reference to Feuerbach) in a letter to Ruge.[5]

At first Schelling was just as unconscious of the divergence between his views and Fichte's as the latter had been of the growing differences between himself and Kant. He too imagined that his thought had grasped the 'spirit' of the *Theory of Science*—and he even believed this more whole-heartedly than Fichte had in his own dealings with Kantianism. In consequence, it was a long time before either of them began to free himself from the Kantian matrix. Indeed, we shall see later that on many important points Schelling never overcame certain limitations of Kantian philosophy. However, in accordance with their different inner development, each thinker attached himself to a different aspect of Kant. The *Critique of Practical Reason* supplied Fichte with the model for his *entire* philosophical system, whereas Schelling began by re-interpreting the *Critique of Judgement* in the spirit of objective idealism. Thus both thinkers resemble each other in the way in which they go about cleansing the Kantian system of its logical impurities, but as far as the content of their own thought is concerned they are diametrically opposed. The similarity between them is based on their adoption of Kant's own problematic. But Schelling moves in the direction of objective idealism from what in Kant had been a subjective agnosticism. The real point of departure for Schelling's philosophy is Kant's new approach to questions about teleology (which we shall discuss in detail later on) and what he does is to apply these in a novel and highly characteristic fashion to organic life, nature and art.

Schelling's use of Kant made it even more imperative than it had been for Fichte to establish the categories on a deductive basis. Kant's thought about contradiction had not progressed beyond the discovery of necessary *antinomies*. Contradiction signified only the dialectical self-dissolution of the phenomenal world. Beyond that there could be no synthesis, no knowledge based on the contradictory nature of the world. The only point at which man comes into contact with reality, namely the world of ethics, lay beyond all contradiction. We have already seen how Fichte made use of contradiction as a sort of methodological springboard with the help of which he strove to construct the system of categories. Schelling now took over the Fichtean triad and transformed it into an *objective* element in the structure of the universe.

One question that arises from this approach is: *how*, with the aid of *what* organ, can this knowledge of the universe be obtained? For Kant and Fichte such knowledge had been founded on the experiences of pure morality (conscience, etc.). Extending this principle Fichte arrived at his concept of 'action', the master-concept of his theory of knowledge. In line with the moral basis of his system Fichte denied the existence of any object independent of human consciousness. That it is possible to have knowledge of a self-created world (posited by the Ego) was self-evident to Fichte: it is the self-knowledge of the positing Ego.

Schelling's approach is the very opposite of this: he directly confronts the problem of how we can have objective knowledge of the external world and especially of nature. In the process he wholeheartedly embraces all those agnostic arguments which Kant puts forward in *The Critique of Pure Reason* with regard to our knowledge of what he calls the phenomenal world. Thus Schelling sets out to appropriate an epistemological theory which leads to a series of antinomies about our knowledge of the world of phenomena but his goal is to use it in order to reach a higher mode of cognition, one which will ground and guarantee an adequate knowledge of objective reality. In a celebrated section of *The Critique of Judgement* (§ 76) Kant himself postulates such knowledge, though in a purely hypothetical manner. He says there that in ordinary knowledge which subsumes the particular beneath the general the particular always remains random. Such knowledge can never give us an adequate grasp either of life as a whole or of organic life. He therefore postulates another kind of intelligence (*intellectus archetypus*) which would eliminate the disharmony between general and particular.

This hypothesis had an incalculable effect on the entire course of German philosophy. In particular it became of crucial importance for Goethe, who of course interpreted it quite differently from Schelling. Schelling adapts Kant's philosophy here in a very simple way which asserts rather than argues. He simply converts Kant's hypothetical postulate into an existing reality which he calls *intellectual intuition*. This intuition is the faculty by means of which man arrives at a true understanding of objective reality; it reveals that objective reality (nature) and human knowledge are but two arms of the same river and man becomes conscious of their identity through the act of intuition. In *The System of Transcendental Idealism* Schelling defines intellectual intuition in this way:

> 'This knowledge must (a) be absolutely free simply because all other knowledge is *not free*; hence it must be knowledge not attainable by way of proof, deduction or the mediation of concepts of whatever sort, i.e. it must be a pure intuition. And (b) it must be knowledge whose object is *not something independent* of the process of knowing, i.e. knowledge which both knows and *produces its own object*—an intuition which produces freely and in which the producer is one and the same thing as the product. We call such intuitions *intellectual* to distinguish them from sensuous intuitions which do not become

manifest as the producers of their own objects, i.e. the intuition is distinct from what is intuited.[6]

In this statement the identical subject–object, the foundation of objective idealism is already fully developed.

We shall discuss the internal contradictions in Schelling's position in full detail when we come to consider the disagreements between him and Hegel. All we need say here is that as far as Schelling is concerned the objectivity of nature is adequately demonstrated and guaranteed. Contradictions within human knowledge and between human knowledge and the external world (such as we find in Kant) do not exist for Schelling but are viewed instead as contradictions within objective reality itself. Thus Schelling, like Fichte, does away with contradictions within human knowledge and so in this respect his thought is in sharp disagreement with Kant. But since these contradictions are objective in nature they also entail a rejection of Fichte's position. It is this fact that securely establishes contradictions and their dialectical supersession in the centre of philosophy as a whole.

We should perhaps round off our account by mentioning that Schelling looks to aesthetic contemplation to provide a 'proof' that intellectual intuition is both possible and actual. This too is already anticipated in *The Critique of Judgement* where Kant's formulation of the problem of teleology is closely connected to aesthetics. This had already had the effect of leading Schiller in the direction of objective idealism within aesthetics itself. Schelling now continues this process with the result that for a time aesthetics is assigned a central position in his philosophical system. (I have discussed these problems at length in my studies of Schiller's aesthetics.)

Schelling's concern in the sphere of dialectics is to appropriate for philosophy the great scientific discoveries of the day. He wished to systematize them and integrate them in his complete system of natural philosophy. It is not possible to examine these problems in the present study.[7] Engels has described the great effect of these discoveries on a number of occasions: the transformation of chemistry as a result of Lavoisier's work, the new discoveries in electricity (thanks to the work of Volta and Galvani) and the beginnings of scientific biology and the theory of evolution. The effect of these new ideas can already be seen in the kind of problems Kant poses in *The Critique of Judgement*. Goethe's life-long preoccupation with science played an important role here too and exerted an influence on Schelling's philosophy. Throughout this entire scientific revolution the limits, the failings of metaphysical thought became increasingly clear. Nor was the old form of materialism immune. The German nature philosophy of the day then makes the attempt to save the situation by regarding the emerging contradictions as the objective contradictions of reality itself and by making these into the foundation on which to construct its own system of philosophy. We referred above to Marx's epithet 'nature enthusiast' which he applied to Feuerbach and we in our turn used it to describe the young Schelling. Our justification for this is to be found in a letter from Marx in which he asked Feuerbach to contribute a critical essay on Schelling to the *Deutsch–Französische Jahrbücher*. Marx referred to Feuerbach as a 'Schelling *in reverse*' and went on to say:

> 'Schelling's *genuine youthful insight*—to be charitable to our enemy —was one for the realization of which he had no tools but the imagination, no energy other than vanity, no stimulus other than opium, no mental faculty but the irritability of a feminine receptivity—this genuine youthful insight became nothing more than a youthful fantasy for him. But in you it has become truth, reality, with a really masculine seriousness. Hence we may say that Schelling is a *distorted prefiguration* of yourself. . . .'[8]

During the period with which we are concerned Schelling's 'genuine youthful insight' was very much to the fore. Needless to say, the seeds of his later reactionary views were also in evidence but for a brief period they were largely overshadowed by his enthusiastic efforts to found a new philosophy of nature, a unified dialectical system of all the phenomena of nature. His excitement was such that for a time his ideas even verged on materialism and on a number of occasions he passionately attacked the rarefied spiritualism of the same Romantics with whom he had had such close affinities in other respects. Since we have no room here for a full discussion of this issue we must content ourselves with a single illustration. In 1799 in opposition to Novalis' spiritualism Schelling experienced what Friedrich Schlegel has called 'a new access of his old passion for irreligiosity' and wrote his tract *Heinz Widerporst's Epicurean Confession of Faith*, from which we quote the following very characteristic lines:

> Seit ich gekommen bin ins Klare,
> Die Materie sei das einzig Wahre,
> Unser aller Schutz und Rater,
> Aller Dinge rechter Vater,
> Alles Wissens Anfang und End'.
> Halte nichts vom Unsichtbaren,
> Halte mich allein am Offenbaren,
> Was ich kann riechen, schmecken, fühlen,
> Mit allen Sinnen drinnen wühlen,

Glaub', die Welt ist seit jeher gewesen,
Wird auch nimmer in sich verwesen.[9]

Schelling's commitment to materialism here is passionate and perfectly explicit, but it is by no means clearly thought out. For almost with the same breath in which he asserts his atheism Heinz Widerporst declares that he is in fact irreligious, but if he had to choose a religion—he would choose catholicism. And in the course of the poem there is a plethora of mystical motifs derived from Böhme's philosophy of nature.

Even from these bare hints the reader will have been able to gauge the profound differences that distinguish Fichte and Schelling from each other right from the beginning. However, these differences were hidden from them above all by their common struggle against the followers of Kant who wished to freeze philosophy at the point it had reached in Kant himself. In his *Difference* Hegel pours scorn on Kantians of this type. Thus he makes this comment about Reinhold and the image he uses is very revealing:

> 'Just as *la révolution est finie* has been frequently decreed in France, so too Reinhold has frequently proclaimed the completion of the philosophical revolution. Now he announces the final completion of all the completions. . . .'[10]

If we juxtapose this statement with the letter we quoted above from Fichte after Kant had published his declaration we catch a glimpse of the prevailing warlike mood in which the need to make common cause made it all too easy to gloss over existing differences of opinion. Moreover, Schelling's vagueness about his own real tendencies, his shifting between fits of materialism and mystical extravaganzas, both of which were bound up with Fichte's theory of knowledge, helped to conceal these differences for a relatively long time. Schelling's vagueness extends to the manner in which he presents his own philosophy, a manner which Hegel summed up accurately and perceptively in his *History of Philosophy*.

> 'Schelling completed his philosophical education in public. The list of his philosophical *writings* is simultaneously the history of his philosophical education. It represents his gradual emancipation from the Fichtean principles and Kantian contents with which he began. It does not contain an analysis of the different parts of philosophy in logical sequence, but the stages in his education.'[11]

Schelling never systematically worked through the problems of philosophy as a whole. He left large and important areas completely untouched in order to go in search of ever new discoveries. Imperceptibly the Fichtean Ego became transformed into the identical subject

—object of objective idealism. He began by writing his philosophy of nature as a mere *appendix* to the *Theory of Science* and since Fichte was himself engaged at this time on the application of the theory to morality, law, the state, etc., the illusion could be sustained that they were in basic agreement on fundamental principles but that each had selected specific areas to follow up.

These illusions began to fade soon after the appearance of Schelling's first systematic work. The publication of his *System of Transcendental Idealism* was followed by a long correspondence ending with a complete breach. It is true that in his next work, the *Presentation of My System of Philosophy* (1801), Schelling still thought of transcendental philosophy and the philosophy of nature as two aspects of the same system. And a letter of 19 November 1800 reveals that he still regarded the *Theory of Science* as complete in itself, to which the philosophy of nature was no more than an adjunct, a supplement. He observed:

> 'Firstly, as far as the *Theory of Science* is concerned, I would separate it off entirely; it is complete in itself, it should not be changed or tampered with; it is perfect and must be by its very nature. But theory of science . . . is not itself philosophy. . . . It involves only logic and has nothing to do with reality.'[12]

Thus a fundamental disagreement was very far from Schelling's mind. He considered the *Theory of Science* to be the immutable foundation of all philosophy, his own included.

For his part Fichte began by conducting the discussion with extreme caution. He too had no desire to break with his greatest and most gifted ally. But right from the start he demurred at the autonomy conferred on nature by Schelling's system. In a letter dated 15 November 1800 which provoked the answer we quoted above, he described Schelling's 'self-construction of nature' (i.e. his objective-idealist view of the objectivity of the categories of nature) as self-deception. He wrote:

> 'The *reality of nature* is quite another matter. In the transcendental philosophy nature appears as something *given* and as such it is perfect and complete in itself. Moreover, it is "given" not in terms of its *own* laws but according to the *immanent laws of intelligence*. . . . If, by means of a subtle process of abstraction, science concentrates on nature in isolation, it must of course (precisely because it abstracts from intelligence) do so on the premise that nature is something *absolute* in order to make room for the *fiction* that it *constructs itself*.'[13]

Later, when the split had become irrevocable Fichte gave vent to the same idea in a much blunter and more forceful manner. In his letter of 31 May 1801 he remarks that all that can be known is contained in consciousness and that 'only there in a small area of the mind do we find a world of the senses: nature.'[14]

The distinction between subjective and objective idealism is clearly stated here. Fichte denies Schelling's nature philosophy the right even to the relative *autonomy* of an addendum to the *Theory of Science*. He re-affirms that every external reality is no more than a moment posited by the sovereign action of the Ego and that accordingly the *Theory of Science* embraces the whole realm of knowledge.

As we have seen, Schelling's conduct of the debate was a good deal less incisive than Fichte's. His uncertainty would emerge much more clearly if we had space to analyse the correspondence in its entirety. However, we are concerned with one point only: Hegel's role. We may remind the reader of Hegel's letter to Schelling of 2 November 1800 in which he an-nounced his forthcoming arrival in Jena though indicating his intention to spend a certain amount of time in Bamberg first. On 15 November Fichte wrote the letter we have quoted containing his criticisms of the *System of Transcendental Idealism*. Schelling's reply to Hegel has been lost but since Hegel came to Jena in January 1801, much sooner than he had originally intended, Haym is probably right in surmising that Schelling's letter was instrumental in bringing about his earlier arrival.[15] And the reason for coming sooner could only be connected with the present debate. What follows entirely confirms these suppositions. Hegel who up to then had just produced one fragment after another suddenly became extraordinarily productive and completed one polemical essay after another. By July 1801 the *Difference* was finished. In August of the same year he defended his doctoral thesis and by the autumn he was giving lectures as a *Privatdozent* at Jena University. Before the year was out he and Schelling had founded the *Kritisches Journal der Philosophie* in order to propagate the philosophy of objective idealism. In this period-ical Hegel displayed the same energy in elaborating what was a new parting of the ways in philosophy, the birth of a new stage in the devel-opment of thought. Although objective idealism had already made its appearance in Schiller's aesthetic writings and above all in Schelling's own systematic works, it was only now openly proclaimed as a new philosophy. And it was Hegel who so proclaimed it. Both the *Difference* and the great essays produced for the periodical (*Faith and Knowledge* and on the *Scientific Modes of Treatment of Natural Law*) contain a compre-hensive and systematic critique of subjective idealism. That is to say, they deal not just with Fichte but also with Kant, the Kantians and with the chief advocate of a subjectivist 'philosophy of life' namely Friedrich Heinrich Jacobi. In a series of reviews of varying length both in the *Kri-tisches Journal* and in the *Erlanger Zeitung* Hegel settles accounts with the large crowd of lesser figures—Schulze, Krug, Bouterwek etc.

At every point Hegel emerges as the chief protagonist of the new direction in philosophy. Up to that time, however, this philosophy had made its *public* appearance only in the writings of Schelling. This explains why Hegel constantly emphasizes the distinction between the objective idealism of Schelling and the subjective idealism of Kant, Jacobi, Fichte. This is why he sharply contrasts the two tendencies highlighting the failure of subjective idealism, its inability to resolve its own contradictions showing at the same time that only objective idealism is capable of providing a satisfactory solution to all the problems involved. Hegel makes no attempt to subject Schelling's philosophy to scrutiny and there is not even a hint of criticism. The most that can be claimed is that the modern reader who is already familiar with the differences between Hegel and Schelling can see that in a number of places Hegel imputes to Schelling a view or a tendency which seems to fit in better with his own thought than with that of Schelling.

All this can be readily explained by reference to the exigencies of a philosophical polemic. But setting that aside how are we to define Hegel's position *vis-à-vis* Schelling in those first Jena years? The available material does not permit us to provide a fully-documented answer. From the period before Schelling's departure for Würzburg in 1803 not a single negative or even critical utterance about Schelling by Hegel is known to us. Not until the period 1803–6 does Hegel begin to criticize Schelling's supporters and disciples and finally Schelling himself. This criticism is formulated systematically in *The Phenomenology of Mind*: Hegel's first public disagreement with Schelling's philosophy is also decisive and conclusive.

Is it then fair to say that in his early years in Jena Hegel supported Schelling without any reservations whatever? Or was his collaboration with Schelling no more than 'diplomacy', 'tactics'? The first view is propagated in the usual histories of philosophy; the second is purveyed e.g. by Stirling who discovers a certain 'cunning', an element of 'calculation' in Hegel's rapprochement with Schelling at this time.[16] That the first view is false will be evident to the reader of our discussion of Hegel's Frankfurt period. As we saw there, even before coming to Jena Hegel had already arrived at an objective dialectics which was in advance of Schelling's on the crucial point (the theory of contradiction). We saw too that in his fragmentary notes Hegel had made more progress than Schelling on a whole series of other problems concerning dialectics. And the most important tendency of Hegel's philosophy, his creation of a novel dialectical logic, always lay well beyond Schelling's horizon. Hence when Hegel objected in the *Kritisches Journal* to being described as a supporter of Schelling, he was undoubtedly justified in doing so.[17]

But this is not to imply that Stirling and his like have correctly interpreted the relations between the two thinkers at this time. Stirling's attitude to Hegel is much like the attitude revealed by Erich Schmidt in his analysis of the relations between Lessing and Voltaire, an attitude which Franz Mehring has exposed with such irony. Mehring's scorn was aroused particularly by the way in which 'scholars' like Schmidt insinuate that the great poets and thinkers of the past possess the obsequious mentality shown by ambitious lecturers towards powerful professors, a mentality to which they themselves owe their university careers. But a Lessing and a Hegel are humanly as well as intellectually superior to a Professor Schmidt or a Professor Stirling.

The Frankfurt *Fragment of a System* makes it quite clear that Hegel had succeeded in clarifying his own specific method on a number of the fundamental problems of dialectics before he joined forces with Schelling. But this is far from implying that his own approach to dialectics was fully thought out by the time he arrived in Jena, let alone elaborated in a systematic and concrete manner. I am not thinking here of such important systematic problems as the relation of philosophy to religion. We have seen (p. 212ff.) how in Frankfurt Hegel thought that philosophy should terminate in religion, i.e. that man's religious position constituted the apex of philosophy. And we shall soon see how he took up another stance on this issue in his very first work in Jena, one which was continually modified and developed right up to the *Phenomenology*. But if we set aside such major issues and just glance at the first version of his views on logic, the so-called *Jena Logic* of 1801/2, we cannot help seeing how side by side with the lucid exposition of problems of pivotal importance for his later logic (e.g. the transition from quantity to quality) there remains much that Hegel silently rejected as early as the *Phenomenology* itself. And above all on the crucial problem of the dialectical deduction of the categories from the movement of their internal contradictions, the *Jena Logic* is still riddled with confusions, even by comparison with the later Jena period. The precise division into formal and dialectical logic, and the definition of the relationship between them—this is all there *in nuce* and is clarified to a degree never attained by Schelling—but by the standard of Hegel's later development it is still rudimentary.

Hence it is no mere accident that in the first part of his stay in Jena Hegel published only polemical tracts—if we ignore his dissertation *De orbitis planetarum* which is of negligible importance for his life's work. In these polemical writings he combats the contradictions and inadequacies of subjective idealism and in the process he develops his own views above all in the sphere of social philosophy. At the same time he either refrains entirely from presenting a detailed concrete discussion of the methods and content of objective idealism or else, where there is such a discussion, it remains very general.

Simultaneously with these polemical activities Hegel energetically set about constructing an independent system both in his lectures and in manuscript form. However, he did not get beyond the stage of plans and

sketches. Neither at this stage nor later on did he contemplate publishing
them. He did indeed draw on them for his later published work but they
remained raw material and the systematic framework in which they
were cast was constantly subjected to criticism and revision. This continuous process of modification in fundamentals gives some indication of
the extent tö which his basic thought was still in a state of flux. We have
already referred to his description of Schelling as that of a thinker whose
development took place in public. It may be that at times this method
held some attractions for the young Hegel as he toiled away laboriously
at the construction of a system. But we can be quite sure that it was ana-
thema to his deepest philosophical convictions.

The first phase of Hegel's stay in Jena, then, was a time of philosophical *experimentation*, though on a far higher plane than in Frankfurt,
as a comparison between the products of the two periods makes quite
clear. In Frankfurt we find Hegel writing a series of essays in which he
struggles with problems of the greatest importance for him, essays which
show a definite coherence, but which do not consciously put the problem of a system in the foreground. In Jena, however, the sketches are all
sketches for a *system* so that the progress is quite apparent, even if the
methodological foundations of a system are still insecure.

A glance at Hegel's intimate diary from the later part of Hegel's stay in
Jena furnishes us with interesting insights into his intellectual workshop.
This diary was published by Rosenkranz as 'Hegel's notebook'. Typically more recent Hegel scholars have ignored both Rosenkranz's publication and his correct dating of the diary (1803–6). Dilthey discussed its
contents but clearly regarded them as general statements valid for the
entire Jena period and he neglected even to hint that they had been published by Rosenkranz. Haering went even further: he praised Dilthey for
his 'great achievement' in having 'published' them and he placed them
right at the start of the Jena period.[18]

An attentive study of these diaries will show anyone who has even the
slightest understanding of Hegel's development that the statements they
contain about his method of work are *retrospective* in character; Hegel has
become clear about his own methods and now looks back self-critically
at his earlier efforts. That is to say, if we stick to Rosenkranz's dating we
gain a very useful account of Hegel's mood and his method of work
during his earlier period in Jena. We give a number of typical passages:

> '*The most pernicious vice is to seek to preserve oneself from errors.* The fear
> of actively bringing error upon oneself is complacency and renders
> absolute passive error inevitable. Thus a stone has no active error,
> except e.g. for limestone when nitric acid is poured on it. It then gets
> quite out of hand. It really goes wildly astray, it flares up and enters
> another world—knowing nothing of this other world it is destroyed.

Contrast man. He is substance, maintains himself. . . . This stoniness or stoneness . . . this rigidity must be abandoned. Flexibility *educability* . . . is truth. Not until one understands the thing, something which comes after learning about it, does one stand above it.'

This passage is finely elucidated by the entry immediately preceding it. There Hegel says:

'An essential part of studying a science is that one should not be led astray by its principles. They are general and do not mean much. It appears that you only grasp their meaning if you grasp the particular. Often they are simply bad. They are consciousness of a thing, and the thing is often better than the consciousness. One goes on studying. At first consciousness is unclear. *Anything rather than understand and prove everything step by step.* Instead one puts the book aside, reads on half asleep, resigned to one's own consciousness, i.e. one's singularity, which is painful.'[19]

A careful reading of this passage reveals that Hegel is describing his own method of work in this period of transition. The central problem has become clear to him, though not entirely so, but he presses on, undeterred by errors to test the correctness of his views against all the particularities of the real world. And he stubbornly holds fast to the principle of accepting only ideas that withstand this confrontation with the particular. 'The thing is often better than the consciousness.' This is the key to his whole mode of philosophy during his youth. He takes over Schelling's idea of the world as a unified process which embraces nature and history and treats it with total seriousness, much more seriously than Schelling who put the same idea forward in a different system, a different abstract form every year. Hegel wants to grasp the essence of this process, to see just how it comprehends all particulars, and as long as he does not possess a method which will guarantee this comprehensive knowledge he will accept the general principle only with reservations, i.e. he tests it against the facts, the particulars and rejects it at once if he finds it abstract, i.e. if it fails to explain the particulars. This 'empiricism' which has gravely embarrassed Hegel's bourgeois exegetes is a feature of his *specific form* of the dialectic. We shall see later just where its limits lie for him. Here it was necessary only to point to this feature of his thought, partly to make the difference between him and Schelling absolutely clear, and partly to explain why Hegel did not *at once* take up a negative stance on a number of the fundamental tenets of objective idealism, but spent some time experimenting with them, testing them, to convince himself of their validity or nullity.

Another passage in the diaries reveals Hegel's attitude to Schelling even more clearly, though Schelling is not referred to by name.

'I remember very well how for a long time I drifted around among the sciences, honestly believing that what had become apparent on the surface was not the whole of it. From the way it was all discussed I concluded that the heart of the matter still lay behind the scenes and that everyone knew far more than they admitted, that in fact they knew the spirit and reasons justifying what they were proposing. After I had long sought in vain for the right way and its justification, things they were all talking about and acting as if they were generally known and the normal way of proceeding, I came to the conclusion that there was nothing beyond what I had understood except for the confident tone, wilful argument and arrogance.'[20]

This remark comes at the very end of the notebook. His own tone reveals that he had himself seen through the abstraction, the formalism and the philosophical defects of Schelling's philosophy. In the form of self-criticism he gives us an idea of the way he had been influenced by Schelling's philosophical dexterity, and his self-confident and impressive manner. When we come to analyse the differences of substance between Hegel and Schelling the reader will be better able to understand Hegel's attitude than here where we are concerned merely with sketching in the 'intellectual physiognomy' of the two men.

However, we must beware of exaggerating the contrast between them. If we wish to understand the period 1801–3 rightly we must not be prejudiced by what we know *today* about Schelling's *later* career. It is true that the seeds of Schelling's reactionary tendencies were already to be seen, but they were no more than seeds. And in 1801 no-one could have foreseen that the originator of the philosophical revolution in Germany would end as the philosopher of theological reaction. Even the vapidity of his philosophical constructs looked different then from how they would appear when examined in the light of his later thought. At that time a revolution in philosophy was imminent—we recall Hegel's biting remarks about people who wanted to bring it to a conclusion—and Schelling's abstractions had necessarily the appearance of the sort of abstraction that inevitably accompanies the birth of a new philosophy in a new age. (When we come to discuss *The Phenomenology of Mind* we shall see that this feature was very much in Hegel's own mind too.)

Marx as a dialectical historian criticized Schelling unsparingly, but he nevertheless singled out his 'genuine youthful insight' for special praise and compared him with a thinker of the stature of Feuerbach. It is evident that for the young Hegel, struggling to discover the principles of objective dialectics, this 'genuine youthful insight' must have been what attracted him most in Schelling, especially since despite all his later criticism he was never able to see through him as clearly as Marx could from the vantage-point of materialism. For the truth is that the idealist dialectics of objective idealism *always* remained common ground. There are then definite limits to Schelling's philosophy which turned out to be limits of the Hegelian dialectic too, while Marx could go further and criticize them with annihilating effect.

We have already stated that Schelling's 'genuine youthful insight' was his attempt to view nature and history as a single unified dialectical process. This answered to the deepest intellectual aspirations of the young Hegel. Furthermore, if it is true that Hegel's ideas at this time were much more profound than those of Schelling, particularly in the sphere of social philosophy and the lógical problems of dialectics, it remains the case that Hegel was not yet capable of gathering his ideas together into a comprehensive unified system. Yet this is precisely what Schelling achieved and moreover he was able to present his system in an exceptionally brilliant and dazzling literary form. We have already seen that Hegel thought it essential to test Schelling's views against his own independent work before venturing any criticism and we see from his diary entries that his procedure might be called *experimental*. Only if we see their relations in this way will we be in a position to interpret correctly the appearance in some of his writings especially the *System of Ethics*, of Schellingian terminology, i.e. only then will we be able to do justice to the influence of Schelling on Hegel without feeling the need to describe him either as a simple supporter of Schelling or as an ambitious climber and a hypocrite who failed to disclose differences of opinion for 'tactical reasons'.

A further factor of importance here is that for all the literary accomplishment of each publication, Schelling's thought too was in flux. Of course, we know nothing of the personal relations between the two men. They lived in the same place, taught at the same university and published a periodical together. They obviously must have had very detailed discussions about the principles of philosophy. And if it cannot be denied that Hegel's early Jena writings show the impact of Schellingian language, it is also true that we can sometimes hear the voice of Hegel in certain of Schelling's writings at this time. Thus for a long time there was a debate about the authorship of the introductory article in the periodical on the *Relationship of the Philosophy of Nature to Philosophy in general*. It was not possible to say whether it had been written by Schelling or by Hegel. Not until an autobiographical note by Hegel from the year 1804 was discovered could it be shown that Schelling was in fact the author.[21] In circumstances such as these we may easily imagine that on certain contentious points Hegel must have striven to convince Schelling of his errors in the course of conversation over long periods of time and attempted to bring him back to the right path before he finally entered the lists in public.

We must also bear in mind that although in many respects Hegel held profounder and more progressive views than Schelling, he must have been a disciple in the sphere of the philosophy of nature—at least in the early stages. We know that he had made an intensive study of scientific problems while he was still in Frankfurt, but this must be set against the major achievements of Schelling, his disciples and above all, and quite independently of them, Goethe, with whom Hegel became acquainted at around this time. And Hegel had to familiarize himself with these discoveries and assess them critically before constructing an independent system of his own.

This examination of the relations between Schelling and Hegel bears out the contention made earlier on (p. 215ff.): their collaboration in Jena was the point at which the paths of two important minds *crossed*. Hegel was in the process of working out his specific form of dialectics. From the available documents we can see that he did not discard Schelling's terminology entirely before the lecture manuscripts of 1805–6 —and of course this is by no means just a matter of terminology. When we come to look at the various drafts of Hegel's social philosophy we shall have cause to remark the close connection between the clear and concrete evolution of ideas and his emancipation from the language of Schelling.

In 1803 Schelling left Jena and went to Würzburg, thus bringing the period of close personal contact to an end. The *Kritisches Journal* did not survive the separation; it had fulfilled its historic mission of drawing a dividing line between subjective and objective idealism. The process of distinguishing various strands within objective idealism itself could now begin. It would be an error, however, to see this process entirely in terms of a clarification of Hegel's ideas. We repeat: Schelling's thought too was in flux. And the increasingly definite emergence of the reactionary elements in Schelling's philosophy stands in continuous interaction with the evolution of Hegel's thought, with his ever more pronounced emancipation from the Schellingian concepts with which he had 'experimented' for a time. In Würzburg, as early as 1804, Schelling's *Philosophy and Religion* already contained a number of fairly definite reactionary features. His abandonment of his 'genuine youthful insight' had already begun to assume philosophical dress: the world was now seen as a 'defection' from the Absolute (i.e. from God). The basic tendency of his later openly reactionary position, of his so-called 'positive' philosophy appeared here for the first time in a fairly explicit manner. (The later Schelling came to regard his own philosophy of nature and dialectics as 'negative' philosophy complementing and preparing the way for his final synthesis.)

It would be absurd to ignore the effect upon Hegel of these changes in Schelling. Hegel's later view of the matter finds expression in the *History of Philosophy*. There he makes it plain that Schelling has earned his place in the world history of philosophy exclusively by virtue of his first period in Jena. He does not even bother to attack his later works (there is a parallel here to his attitude towards Fichte's later works). On the other hand, we must not forget that Hegel who had such intimate knowledge of Schelling's character as well as his work, did not regard the latter's new phase as definitive. For a long time he continued to hope that criticism would bring Schelling back to the true path of dialectical philosophy. The correspondence between them, even at the time of *The Phenomenology of Mind* shows that Hegel still reckoned with the possibility of a philosophical rapprochement. Only after the *Phenomenology* was published in 1807 did the split become definitive when Schelling broke off relations.

## NOTES

1  Engels, *Schelling und die Offenbarung*, MEGA 1, Vol. 2, p. 186.
2  *Erste Druckschriften*, p. 3. For the sake of brevity we shall refer to Hegel's essay as the *Difference*.
3  Fichte, *Briefwechsel*, Berlin 1925, Vol. II, p. 165.
4  The Kantian 'categories' are the pure or *a priori* concepts of the understanding (*Verstand*) and they constitute the indispensable prerequisites of our knowledge of things in the world. For without them objects cannot be thought and without being thought they cannot really be said to be known. The categories enumerated by Kant were: quantity, quality, relation and modality and each possessed three sub-divisions. See *The Critique of Pure Reason*, 'The Analytic of Concepts'.
5  Marx to Ruge, 13 March 1843. MEGA 1, Vol. 1(2), p. 308.
6  Schelling, *Werke*, Stuttgart and Augsburg 1858, Division I, Vol. 3, p. 369.
7  More about Schelling can be found in my book *The Destruction of Reason*, Berlin 1954, Chap. 2; *Werke*, Vol. 7, pp. 114–72.
8  Marx to Ludwig Feuerbach, 20 October 1843. MEGA 1, Vol. 1(2), p. 316.
9       Since the day I understood
        That the only truth is matter,
        It alone our friend and shelter,
        All things' father true and good,
        Start and end of every science—
        I can no longer be impressed
        By the Unseen; the Manifest
        Is what I hold to,—what I taste
        And touch and smell, and hold embraced
        with every sense . . .
        The world I trust

> was always there and always must
> Be there, not moulder into dust.

(Plitt, op. cit., Vol. I, pp. 283f. and 286.)

10  *Erste Druckschriften*, p. 98f.

11  *History of Philosophy*, Glockner, Vol. III, p. 647. It is interesting that the chapter on Schelling shows many parallels with Hegel's Jena lectures of 1806, which suggests that his later description of Schelling contains the views he held at the time of the breach.

12  Fichte's *Briefwechsel*, op. cit., Vol. II, p. 295.

13  Ibid., p. 292f.

14  Ibid., p. 326.

15  Haym, p. 123.

16  J. H. Stirling, *The Secret of Hegel*, Edinburgh 1908, p. 662. Stirling was one of the first to attempt to reduce Hegel entirely to Kant. Of the opinions of Marx and Engels, *Correspondence,* Berlin 1950, Vol. IV, pp. 70 and 304. Marx to Engels, 23 May 1868 and 4 April 1870.

17  Rosenkranz, p. 162f.

18  Rosenkranz, pp. 198ff.; Dilthey, Vol. IV, p. 195f. Haering, p. 603.

19  Rosenkranz, p. 545.

20  Ibid., p. 554.

21  Nohl, p. VIIIf.

# CHAPTER TWO

# The critique of subjective idealism

HEGEL's first published works in Jena are essentially polemical in nature. The passion with which they are imbued springs from his conviction that the philosophical revolution he is proclaiming is but the intellectual expression of a great general revolution. The defeat of subjective idealism at the hands of objective idealism is not merely the narrow parochial concern of a few philosophers but the intellectual apex of a great socio-historical transformation. This explains the recurrence in these writings of images which establish precisely this connection between the changes in philosophy and the emergence of a new world. We have already given one example. (p. 249.) The following quotation is perhaps even more characteristic of his mood in this first period in Jena.

> 'The lawgivers of Athens prescribed the death-sentence for political abstention at times of political unrest. Philosophical abstention, the decision not to defend one's own position but to resolve in advance to submit to whomever fate crowns with victory and general acclaim, is the decision to condemn oneself to the death of one's speculative reason.'[1]

The weapons he employs are already specifically Hegelian. His refutation of subjective idealism does not confine itself simply to demonstrating its limitations and defects. His method is less direct, but far more radical than that. He regards subjective idealism not simply as a false direction in philosophy, but as a trend which *necessarily* came into being and whose errors also bear the stamp of necessity. His demonstration that subjective idealism is false shows the logic both of this necessity and of the limitations it entailed. Now as later he uses both historical and systematic arguments, and ultimately the two are inseparable. Historically, he shows that subjective idealism necessarily arose out of the deepest problems of the present and that this was its historical justification and its permanent achievement. Yet at the same time he shows that subjective idealism cannot possibly do more than present the problems posed by the age and translate them into the language of speculative philosophy. Subjective idealism, however, has no answer to these problems: this is its failure.

Thus by confronting subjective idealism with objective idealism he fixes the *historical position* of both in the history of philosophy and indeed of mankind. He thereby elevates the discussion to a level not dreamed of by Fichte and Schelling in their correspondence on the subject. Moreover Hegel's historical grasp of the problem represents an enormous advance in his own development, one which clearly points to the mature Hegel of the future. Of course, having studied his Berne and Frankfurt fragments in detail we can see the long preparation that preceded this. For Hegel philosophy was always connected intimately with the general, socio-political and cultural problems of the present; it would provide the final intellectual solution for all the problems of the past pressing upon the present.

Thus the 'sudden' emergence of an historical approach in such a perfected form is not hard to explain. In Berne and Frankfurt Hegel had attempted to tackle the great problems of society head on and even though he advanced to the point where he had to deal with some of the central problems of dialectics he was not able to bring his views together in an overall system. Moreover although he was in continuous contact with developments in philosophy throughout this period (above all in Frankfurt), he only took issue with them when it became unavoidable and then only on particular problems. Only when he came to Jena did he feel the necessity of coming to terms with contemporary philosophy as such. It was his profound and comprehensive grasp of the problems of the present, his ability to relate them to a single problem: the turning-point from subjective to objective idealism, that 'suddenly' produced the fully-fledged historical approach.

In his polemical writings the historical method is inseparable from the systematic one. We repeat: Hegel is not concerned to refute subjective idealism from 'outside', but by unravelling internal contradictions which remained hidden from Fichte. The internal dialectic of these contradictions, the solution which the movement of the contradictions brings about, is what will demonstrate the necessity for objective idealism. Since Hegel regards these contradictions as the products of events and processes in society we witness the emergence here in these early polemics of that inner organic unity of philosophy and history so typical of his maturity.

Thus Hegel's approach is historical and systematic at the same time. He raises the question of the need for philosophy in the present. From our knowledge of the Frankfurt *Fragment of a System* it cannot surprise us to learn that Hegel sought the source of this need for philosophy in fragmentation and disunity. This enabled him to deduce what he regarded as the crucial weakness of non-dialectical thought, viz. that it simply reflected this fragmentation through its separation of the categories of reason from the living and moving totality of the world, the absolute. He says:

'If we look more closely at the particular form of a philosophy we can see how it springs on the one hand from the living originality of a mind which has created and actively shaped a fragmented harmony; and on the other hand, it springs from the particular form of disunity from which the system arises. Disunity is the source of the *need for* philosophy and as the culture (*Bildung*) of the age it is its unfree, pre-determined aspect. In culture manifestations of the absolute have become isolated from the absolute and have become fixed as autonomous things.'[2]

This description of the present as an age of culture once more reminds us of the close links between Hegel's philosophy and the classical period of Goethe and Schiller. Indeed, at first glance it almost looks like a philosophical statement of the aspirations formulated in Schiller's aesthetic essays and especially in Goethe's *Wilhelm Meister's Apprenticeship*. But the term 'culture' has a different emphasis in Hegel. He stresses the disharmonies and contradictions which make such a dramatic appearance at this stage of human history. When we come to discuss *The Phenomenology of Mind* we shall see that the age of culture is in Hegel's eyes the age when dialectics is reborn in its final and most perfect form, i.e. that the convulsions and struggles of this fragmented and disharmonious age are the birthpangs of the final harmony of Hegel's absolute spirit.

The distinction is important but is nevertheless just a matter of emphasis, involving a different evaluation of the preceding periods of transition and especially of the Enlightenment. Goethe and Hegel always agree in seeing themselves as the successors of the Enlightenment, as its consummation; their critique of Enlightenment never reaches the point of rejecting its heritage outright as do the Romantics. (The modern swindle in Goethe and Hegel studies depends on obscuring precisely this circumstance and it thrives on isolated quotations wrenched from their contexts.) In this area a typical example of the way in which Goethe and Hegel see eye to eye is to be found in Goethe's discovery of the manuscript of Diderot's *Le Neveu de Rameau* early in the nineteenth century. He immediately translated it and published it with a commentary while Hegel no less eagerly made use of it to define the particular form of dialectics operative in the Enlightenment. The characters depicted by Diderot are assigned a crucial role in the most important chapter in *The Phenomenology of Mind*.

Now Hegel thinks of his age as the point in time when the disintegration of culture has reached its peak and the possibility of a reversal of the trend and the emergence of a new harmony is very real.

'The more progress there is in culture and the more various the manifestations of life exposed to fragmentation, the greater the power of fragmentation becomes . . .'

But this fragmentation holds out the possibility of new harmony and its appointed agent is philosophy itself:

'When the power of unification vanishes from the lives of men and opposing tendencies lose their ability to interact with each other and become autonomous, the need for philosophy is born.'[3]

These statements are enough to persuade us that Hegel is pursuing ideas he had conceived in Frankfurt in a more explicit and conscious fashion, above all, the notion that all the contradictions and conflicts that arise in philosophy can be reduced to conflicts and contradictions in life, that they are rooted in society itself. This idea is not only the source of Hegel's historicism but it also defines his particular approach to contradictions and their elimination. It is made quite explicit in the programmatic introduction to the first of the polemical essays written at this period.

'To do away with such rigid antagonisms is the exclusive task of philosophy. This does not mean that it is opposed to opposition and limitation as such; for a necessary disunity is a factor of life itself which develops through an eternal process of oppositions and the totality can only be reconstructed in all its vitality from a state of the greatest possible division. However, reason is opposed to the absolute fixation of disunity by the understanding, all the more when absolute opposites have sprung from reason itself.'[4]

Thus in Hegel's view disunity is a feature of life itself, the philosophy of culture is not in the wrong because it gives it philosophical expression; on the contrary, that is its achievement. Its defect lies in its inability to discover the unifying principle which lies objectively at the base of all disunity and its consequent failure to find the path back to harmony.

Such considerations elevate the conflict between Fichte and Schelling, between subjective and objective idealism, to the plane of a decisive polarity in history itself. Fichte's philosophy appears in it as the highest intellectual expression of disunity, as its systematic philosophical statement. However, it is unaware of its own origins, its analysis of the problem is in fact spurious and its claims to offer a solution are specious. Criticism must demonstrate the philosophical and historical justification and necessity for the problems while showing that Fichte's solutions only appear as such to the superficial glance while in reality they merely formulate unsolved and on this plane insoluble problems in terms of rigid polarities. Objective idealism will provide the solution to these problems, it is the philosophy which arises from the living contradictions of the age and its thought: in the language of Hegel's later philosophy, objective idealism is 'the truth of subjective idealism'.

The view expressed in these early writings already stamps Hegel as the founder of a new scientific method in the history of philosophy. He is the first thinker to have refused to content himself with the mere collation of facts or abstract criticisms. His new approach is attempted quite consciously in the *Difference*. He launches an attack there against the view that philosophy and its history

'is a sort of craft which can be improved by the constant development of "tricks of the trade".'

At the same time he turns against thinkers who would deal with the subject from a 'particular point of view'. In this he can see nothing but a bad subjectivity.

'Anyone who is trapped in a particular point of view can only see peculiarities in others.'

His position is that philosophy is a great, unified historical process whose content is the dialectical unfolding of reason in its unity.

Needless to say Hegel was not the first to attempt to give the study of the history of philosophy a scientific foundation. Kant had made a plea for such a study and so had all the important figures in classical philosophy. But his predecessors here had never gone beyond the stage of programmatic declarations. Hegel was the first person to tackle the problem in all seriousness and to try to produce a comprehensive history of philosophy and to provide it with a methodological basis which would show how it unfolds logically by virtue of the inner dialectic of thought, of human progress. We could only know how far Hegel had advanced with this programme if we still had the text of his lectures on the history of philosophy from the year 1806. His editors did possess them but the printed version only indicates in a few isolated places which passages date from the 1806 lectures. A really conclusive statement on this issue is therefore no longer possible.

Nevertheless, we can attempt an approximate reconstruction of Hegel's view of the history of philosophy in his Jena period, because even though his polemics against subjective idealism concentrate on the historical necessity both of its emergence and its demise, they do not limit themselves to this theme in any narrow or one-sided way. On the contrary, in order to present the problem from as many points of view as possible and to document it as fully as he can, he takes the opportunity to discuss a wide variety of problems. Since it lies to one side of our main arguments we must confine ourselves to a list of some of the more important of the *excursi* he makes in the course of his polemics. In his essay on Schulze he makes a detailed comparison between scepticism in antiquity and the modern world. In the essay on natural law he contrasts the social philosophies of Plato and Aristotle with the moderns and compares the views of important representatives of the Enlightenment such as Hobbes and Montesquieu on the subject of law, the state and society, with the views of Kant and Fichte. In his attack on Jacobi he sets Spinoza's authentic dialectic against Jacobi's vulgarized version of it and in his discussion of teleology he opposes Voltaire's ideas to those of Kant and Fichte.

However, we must consider one problem—Hegel's position *vis-à-vis* the Enlightenment—a little more fully, since it is closely bound up with Hegel's approach to dialectics and is a crucial factor in the disagreements which led to the breach with Schelling. The main thrust of classical German philosophy was a struggle against philosophical materialism. The struggle became sharper as German philosophy gained in strength and assurance. Schelling's occasional lapses into a sort of materialism were merely episodes that did not affect the main trend any more than Kant's well-known hesitations. As far as Hegel is concerned, we know that he never had any hesitations at all; he was always consciously an idealist and a declared opponent of materialism.

But this hostility should not be allowed to obscure the fact that the philosophy of the Enlightenment left an *indelible* imprint on Hegel's development and throughout the Jena period he considered himself as its heir. That the Enlightenment was the point of departure for his own philosophy and that he was profoundly influenced by it in his youth is nothing out of the ordinary; the same could be said of almost all his contemporaries. What is important is that unlike the majority of them —with Goethe almost the only exception,—he did not renounce the Enlightenment. Schelling and the Romantics became more and more opposed to the Enlightenment and expressed their hostility in increasingly sharp terms. It is not without significance that they tended to identify the Enlightenment with the second-rate mediocrities prominent at the end of the eighteenth century in Germany. In the eyes of many Germans the real greatness of the Enlightenment was obscured by such caricatures as Nicolai. Hegel's attitude was quite distinct from this. The broad cosmopolitan outlook which we have already observed in his attitude to the French Revolution and English economics proved its worth here too. In his Jena diaries we find the following very revealing comments on the issue.

'In Germany people are always rushing to defend *healthy common sense* from what are thought of as the *arrogant attacks of philosophy*. It's all wasted effort since even if philosophy were to concede everything it would be of no service to them—since they have no common sense. Genuine common sense is not peasant coarseness, but something in the educated world which freely and forcefully confronts the fetishes of culture with the truth; or it may appear in the form of a Rousseauesque paradox which formulates principles to express its objections both to culture and its fetishes; or else in the form of experience, reasoning, wit, as in Voltaire or Helvétius.'[5]

Hegel regards objective idealism as the highest and indeed the final form of philosophy. In his polemics against Kant and Fichte he elaborates its claims. But he sees the direct antecedents of his own philosophy not just in subjective idealism but also in the philosophy of the Enlightenment. In the process of settling accounts with the past we frequently come across situations where he puts the views of the Enlightenment or of particular Enlightenment thinkers on the same plane as those of Kant or Fichte or even praises the former at the expense of the latter. This is a matter we shall return to in our treatment of the particular issues where we shall see how these comparisons and contrasts constantly recur. We shall also have occasion to observe that his view of the Enlightenment is intimately bound up with his entire view of history and as such it has a decisive impact on *The Phenomenology of mind*.

All that need be said here is that Hegel's general repudiation of philosophical materialism does not restrain him from assigning a prominent place in the history of philosophy to its most important representatives Holbach and Helvétius. In the *Difference* Hegel takes issue with the Kantian thinker Reinhold and his superficial and purely negative view of materialism as a mere 'aberration' 'alien to Germany'. Reinhold sees nothing of its authentic philosophical desire to abolish the dualism of mind and matter.

'If the Western locality of the culture which produced this system prevents the system from migrating to another country we may inquire whether this enforced separation does not stem from the opposite cultural one-sidedness. Even if its scientific value were negligible we cannot but see that e.g. in [Holbach's] *Système de la nature* a mind estranged from its age reproduces itself in scientific form. We cannot but see how the sorrow at the universal deceit of the age, the thorough-going destruction of nature, the endless lies that go by the name of truth and law—how this sorrow which permeates the entire work still has the energy, the philosophical need and the passion for speculation to construct into a science the absolute that has vanished from life. And the form that science takes is that of objectivity, just as German culture often without any speculative power at all makes its home in subjectivity (to which faith and love also belong.)'[6]

The defects of Hegel's arguments here are plain to see. He believes that objective idealism will provide the principle that will overcome both one-sided attitudes: those of subjective idealism and philosophical materialism. What is more interesting is that he places Holbach's materialism *on the same plane* as the philosophy of Kant and Fichte. No doubt, he greatly exaggerates the 'desperation' contained in the social criticism and the general philosophy of the eighteenth-century materialists. He overlooks the optimistic, self-confident mood in which they anticipate the coming transformation of society, the approaching rule of the bourgeoisie. This misconception has its roots in his general view of history. He views the French Revolution as the climactic point of a crisis which will lead to a new age of the spirit. Hence the French materialists are regarded exclusively as the intellectual spokesmen of this crisis. Hence he is as right about the materialists as he is about the Revolution, and where he goes wrong about the Revolution we can also perceive the limitations of his view of Holbach and Helvétius. What is important, however, is that he sees Kant and Fichte as products of the same crisis. That is to say, he places Holbach on the same philosophical plane as Kant and Fichte and high above the subjective idealists whose philosophy ends in mere feeling and declamatory statement. The last sentence of the passage just quoted is an energetic dig at the whole school of sentimental philosophy and of Romanticism, and not just at Kantians like Reinhold.

This parallel between subjective idealism and materialism is not an isolated incident in Hegel's polemical essays. He keeps returning to it and always with the intention of showing how their complementary limitation can be overcome by objective idealism. For example, in the course of an argument against superficial conceptions of 'common sense'.

> 'The matter of the materialists or the Ego of the idealists—the former is no longer the dead matter which turns out to have life of its own in opposing and shaping; the latter is no longer the empirical consciousness, that as a limited thing finds itself forced to posit infinities outside itself.'[7]

Hegel's early critique of subjective idealism differs from his later views. The celebrated criticism of the thing-in-itself which both Engels and Lenin praised so highly is not yet present in Hegel's objections to Kant. Such criticism was only possible after the full development of the system of objective idealism. Of course, when we come to examine Hegel's discussions of 'externalization' in the *Phenomenology* the attentive reader will readily see that his view of this concept implicitly contains his critique of subjective idealism. Hegel's later criticism is retrospective and conclusive. It takes the line that subjective idealism has been completely superseded. But at the time under consideration we are still witnessing the birth of absolute idealism. Hence the connections between the two philosophies are sometimes more apparent than their opposition, since the new philosophy emerges as the necessary solution to the unresolved contradictions in the old. In consequence the young Hegel tends to focus attention on Fichte. Not simply because the disagreement between Fichte and Schelling provided a suitable point of departure, but because it was Fichte who had successfully completed the Kantian system and who thereby became Hegel's chief target. Hegel's attitude to Fichte never changed throughout his life. But in the great debates in the *Logic* and the *Encyclopaedia* there was a shift in emphasis and Kant as the founder and the greatest exponent of subjective idealism became the chief object of Hegel's attack. This change in emphasis reflected Hegel's greater maturity and a surer grasp of the history of philosophy than he could have had in the heat of the debate during his youth.

At the centre of his analysis is his demonstration that Fichte was unable to carry out his intention of proving that the Ego is an identical subject –object and so resolving the Kantian dualism of consciousness and things-in-themselves. We observe that the Schelling–Hegel critique of Fichte is the reverse of Kant's. Both, however, throw light on the half-hearted way in which Fichte attempts to supersede Kant. Fichte's inadequacy lies in the fact that he aims to overcome Kantian dualism with the aid of a concept which in reality takes the agnostic and subjectivist tendencies in Kant to an extreme by transforming the entire world into consciousness whilst at the same time requiring that the Ego should possess an objectivity which goes well beyond the limits assigned to consciousness by Kant. Kant in his criticism of Fichte emphasized that from the standpoint of consciousness it is not possible to overcome the dualism of consciousness and external world, Hegel starts at the other end: he acknowledges Fichte's purpose of providing an idealist solution to the problem of the objectivity of the world by discovering an identical subject-object, but maintains that Fichte does not get beyond *postulating* this solution. In Hegel's own words:

'Thus the Ego does not itself become the subject–object within the system. The subjective does indeed become the subject–object, but not the objective; and so the subject is not equal to the object.'[8]

It is easy to see the historical necessity underlying these formulations. Kant provided the agnosticism of subjective idealism with its most advanced theoretical statement. At the same time it became apparent that the materialism of the seventeenth and eighteenth centuries was utterly unable even to formulate let alone resolve the problems of dialectics thrown up by the advances in the natural sciences and the progress of society. In view of the prevailing conditions of society and hence of scientific thought the road from metaphysics to dialectics had to go through idealism. Now from an idealist point of view a dialectics of objective reality can only be achieved on the basis of the identical subject–object.

There can only be an objective-idealist dialectics (a) if we may assume
the existence of something that goes beyond the consciousness of individuals but is still subject-like, a kind of consciousness, (b) if amidst the dialectical movement of the objects idealism can discern a development
which moves towards a consciousness of itself in this subject, and so (c) if
the movement of the world of objects achieves an objective and subjective, real and conscious union with knowledge. Thus the identical subject–object is the central pillar of objective idealism just as the reflection
in human consciousness of an objective reality subsisting independently
of consciousness is the crux of materialist epistemology.

The great economic and social upheavals at the turn of the century and
the upsurge of the natural sciences laid bare the limitations of the old
materialism which Lenin defines in the following terms:

> 'the fundamental *misfortune* of ["metaphysical" materialism] is its in-
> ability to apply dialectics to the theory of reflection [*Bildertheorie*], to
> the process and development of knowledge'.[9]

The development of society had thrust the problem of dialectics to the
centre of the stage so vigorously that Kant's agnosticism had made its appearance in dialectical form (in sharp contrast to that of Berkeley and
Hume), but at the same time dialectical materialism was neither socially
nor theoretically possible. In this situation only two roads were open to
further philosophical development. Either one could hold fast to Kantian positions or one could go on to invent the identical subject–object
and arrive at a dialectics of objective reality by means of a detour
through philosophical mystification. It is with this in mind that Lenin
goes on to say after the passage just quoted:

> 'Philosophical idealism is *only* nonsense from the standpoint of crude,
> simple, metaphysical materialism. From the standpoint of a *dialectical*
> materialism, on the other hand, philosophical idealism is a *one-sided*,
> exaggerated, *überschwenglich* (Dietzgen) development (inflation, dis-
> tention) of one of the features, aspects, facets of knowledge into an
> absolute, *divorced* from matter, from nature, apotheosised. Idealism is
> clerical obscurantism.'[10]

With his usual precision Lenin points to both sides of the problem. He
makes it quite clear that the idealist approach necessarily entails religious,
clerical overtones. We shall see later on the profound social reasons
which prevented Hegel from emancipating himself from religion.
Naturally enough, the identical subject–object which was itself born on
religious soil nourished his religious beliefs and strengthened them still
further. A proper study of the history of classical idealism in Germany
will have to come to terms with both the aspects stressed by Lenin and to
explore their dialectical interrelations.

Looked at from this point of view Fichte's philosophy is an odd mixture of logic and inconsistency. When he insists on the purely subjective and conscious character of the Ego he is more logical than his successors. And when he attacks Schelling's illusions and inconsistencies from this vantage-point he has a certain amount of right on his side. (Of course, using that logic, Kant is no less justified in the strictures he makes about Fichte from *his* point of view.) If Fichte were to be truly consistent he would *necessarily* end up in a Berkeleyan position. By conferring the quality of an identical subject–object on his Ego he involves himself in inconsistency—even from the standpoint on an immanent idealism. Nevertheless, by stopping half-way he arrives at a position pregnant with consequences of the most fruitful kind for the development of idealist dialectics in Germany.

Hegel's critique is directed exclusively at this latter failing. His and Schelling's search for an objective–idealist dialectic forces them to take the mystification of an identical subject–object really seriously. He therefore subjects Fichte's thought to a quite ruthless scrutiny. As we have seen, he proceeds from the premise that the Fichtean Ego really ought to be an identical subject–object, but that it cannot fulfil this function because of Fichte's own illogicality.

'Absolute identity is indeed the principle of speculation, but like his phrase I=I it remains no more than the rule whose infinite fulfilment is postulated but never carried out in the system.'[11]

Hegel goes on to show us the systematic aspect of the view already familiar to us that metaphysical materialism belongs on the same plane as subjective idealism. He pursues the comparison as follows:

'The existence of pure consciousness in the empirical world cannot be proved or disproved anymore than can the thing-in-itself of the dogmatist (i.e. the materialist—G.L.) Neither the subjective nor the objective alone constitutes consciousness; the purely subjective is just as abstract as the purely objective; dogmatic idealism posits the subjective as the real ground of the objective, dogmatic realism posits the objective as the real ground of the subjective. . . . But just as idealism asserts the unity of consciousness, realism can with no less validity insist on its duality. The unity of consciousness presupposes a duality, a relation of opposition. The proposition I=I is confronted by an equally absolute proposition: The subject is not identical with the object. Both statements have the same status.'[12]

Thus Fichte's Ego is no identical subject–object of the sort that could produce and guarantee the dialectics of objective reality.

'Amid the infinite progress of existence it endlessly produces parts of itself, but it will not produce itself as subject–object in an eternity of self-contemplation.'

In Hegel's view this defect in Fichte's concept is revealed most strikingly in the relationship of the Ego to nature. Here too Hegel underlines Fichte's failure to overcome materialist metaphysics.

'The dogmatic postulate of an absolute object becomes transformed in this idealism into a self-limitation utterly opposed to free activity.'[13]

Fichte's negative attitude here converts nature into a lifeless thing incapable of possessing any dialectical movement of its own. Hegel pursues the implications of this for the rest of Fichte's philosophy. He shows that Fichte fails to provide firm foundations for the unity of subject and object, Ego and nature, in nature, so that they are in fact torn apart and frozen in a rigid duality.

However, it is above all in the relation between man and society that Fichte fails most signally, in Hegel's view, to overcome the Kantian dualism which he in fact merely reproduces on a higher plane. We shall shortly consider the moral and social views of subjective idealism in greater detail. All we need do here is outline the chief area of disagreement between Fichte and Hegel. Hegel points out that in Fichte's philosophy society constitutes just such a *limitation* of man's freedom as nature had done. The main lines of this argument are already familiar to us from the Frankfurt critiques of Kantian philosophy (cf. p. 128). Hegel's present objections are quite in harmony with his earlier arguments:

'If the community of rational beings really constituted a limitation of true freedom, it would in fact amount to the highest form of tyranny.'[14]

Thus Hegel demonstrates that Fichte is still a long way from removing the dualism of Kantianism. He levels at him the criticism with which he would always attack subjective idealism, viz. that it is unable to go beyond the abstract 'ought'.

'This impossibility, namely that the Ego should reconstruct itself from the opposition of subjectivity and the X that arises in the process of unconscious production and that it should become one with its manifestation, is expressed in such a manner that the highest synthesis of which the system is capable is an *"ought"*. I=I is transformed into: I *ought* to equal I: the end of the system does not return to its beginning.'[15]

And this brings us back to Kant's (essentially agnostic) infinite progress which according to Hegel simply reiterates the problem in philosophical terms.

'The bad infinity', Hegel remarks in the *Jena Logic*

'is the last resort of that failed attempt to synthesize and transcend the contradiction in a conclusive manner since it merely stipulates the need for this synthesis, and contents itself with the description of this need, instead of putting it into practice . . .'[16]

The account given of objective idealism in the *Difference* is essentially that of Schelling; in fact Hegel simply adopts Schelling's first, primitive formulation of objective idealism in which the parallel existence and equal status of the philosophy of nature and transcendental philosophy are put forward as a solution to the difficulties of subjective idealism. Like Schelling, Hegel's starting-point is the proposition in Spinoza:

'The order and connection of ideas is the same as the order and connection of things'.[17]

Of course, the statement has a somewhat different meaning for Hegel and Schelling. In Spinoza it had been an expression of his materialist tendencies. Schelling and Hegel aim to transform it into a constituent of objective idealism. From the materialist standpoint the strength of the statement had been its anticipation of the materialist theory of reflection, but this becomes a defect in the context of idealism. Schelling never goes beyond the idea of a parallel between inner and outer, subjective and objective. Hegel alone attempts to overcome this vestige of dualism, and then not for a number of years. In the *Difference* he still accepts Schelling's view of two mutually complementary aspects that ultimately form a synthesis. This synthesis is supposed to occur through a sort of merging, but this is merely proclaimed and never demonstrated systematically. Such a merging process would according to Hegel's later views (of which the seeds are already present) provide a real guarantee that the two sciences of nature and consciousness really can subsist side by side, in a mutually complementary fashion without either of them gaining primacy over the other, a primacy that would destroy the synthesis to the advantage of either materialism or subjective idealism. Schelling's views are reflected further in Hegel's employment, without even a hint of criticism, of his most important concepts like 'unconscious production' and 'intellectual intuition'.

Thus far Hegel seems content merely to advance Schelling's views, though he goes much further than Schelling himself in their defence. But even in the early Jena period independent elements of the Hegelian dialectic are already active, elements that will later lead to a parting of the ways. Thus Hegel defends Schelling's attempt to co-ordinate transcendental and nature philosophy. But even as early as 1803 in the essay on *Natural Law* which appeared in the *Kritisches Journal* Hegel also defends a very characteristic later doctrine, though without polemicizing against Schelling. This is the idea that spirit stands higher than nature.

> 'If the absolute is what contemplates itself and sees itself for what it is, and if that absolute contemplation and self-recognition, that infinite expansion and no less infinite retraction within the self, are but one and the same, then if both aspects are real, spirit stands higher than nature.'[18]

Here then, on a crucial point, Hegel has completely freed himself from Schelling's position. It is typical of both men at the time, however, that although differences of opinion emerge at various points they are not treated as such by either. Outwardly all is harmony, a harmony which then 'suddenly' breaks down when the differences have crystallized out into conscious principles.

We may mention just one of these important differences of opinion here. For Schelling philosophy in the Jena period culminates in art. Following the *Critique of Judgement* Schelling discovers the immediate unity of subject and object, of conscious and unconscious production in art alone. Hence art provides the philosopher with a guarantee that there really is such a thing as intellectual intuition and that conscious and unconscious production really do merge in reality, in nature and history. Not until he was in Würzburg did religion begin to usurp the place that art had held in his system.[19] Hegel's development is diametrically opposed to this. In the Frankfurt *Fragment of a System* (p. 213ff.) philosophy culminates in religion, religion is the highest level of thought. In Jena this view quickly yields to others. We cannot pursue all the changes that take place here, all the less since in our discussion of *The Phenomenology of Mind* we shall have to consider Hegel's views on religion in detail. All we need say here is that in the *Difference* there are both vestiges of the Frankfurt standpoint (admittedly mainly in terms of emphasis and tone) and also radically new attitudes. Thus at one point Hegel refers to art, philosophy and religion as 'divine worship' (*Gottesdienst*) and on the other hand in his important programmatic introduction he remarks that religion stands to one side of the great march of culture.

> 'As culture has advanced it has quarrelled with religion and placed religion *beside* itself, or itself *beside* religion. . . .'[20]

In all essentials this is the view of *The Phenomenology of Mind*, or at least, since this too is contradictory, its most important component.

We must however discuss in greater detail one matter on which Hegel diverges significantly from Schelling. For a number of years Hegel accepted Schelling's terminology on the subject of contradiction. He speaks constantly of 'the point of indifference', 'intellectual intuition' etc. But at the same time, without any attempt at mediation we also find him taking up the view of contradiction contained in the *Fragment of a System* (p. 217f.). Moreover this is not confined to isolated remarks, but it occurs so frequently and in such important passages that it becomes clear that Hegel never really abandoned his own standpoint on this issue, even though he was prepared to experiment quite seriously with Schelling's ideas. Thus in the *Jena Logic* Hegel says quite explicitly that opposites are not completely annulled or extinguished in the absolute (which was the crux of Schelling's position).

> 'Opposition is the decisive element here and since there is nothing outside the absolute, it is itself absolute and only because it is absolute does it annul itself, and the absolute resting in the peaceful *state* of annulment is just as absolutely the movement of being or annulment of absolute opposition. The absolute state of opposition, or if one prefers, the state of *opposition in the absolute itself*. . . .'[21]

this is what constitutes the absolute in Hegel's eyes. He reiterates the point in another passage:

> 'The very concept of infinity shows that it is not the simple annulment of opposition, it is not the state of annulment; the latter is the emptiness to which opposition is itself opposed.'[22]

The distinction is particularly striking in the *Difference* where Hegel formulates the matter as follows:

> 'Just as identity must be made to prevail, so too must division. To the extent to which identity and division are opposed to each other, each is absolute; and if identity is to be maintained by annihilating duality, then they remain opposed to each other. Philosophy must allow division in subject and object its due; however, by postulating it to be as absolute as the identity opposed to division, it postulates it as relative: just as such an identity can only be relative—since it is premised on the destruction of opposition. *For that reason, however, the absolute is the identity of identity and non-identity;* both opposition and unity dwell in it at one and the same time.'[23]

This is a clear continuation of the view contained in the *Fragment of a System* and so it is important to stress that Hegel would never again depart from the view of contradiction given here. I need refer only to the well-known passage in the *Logic* where Hegel affirms the equality of identity and contradiction, adding that if either of the two is to receive preference then contradiction is the more profound and the more important. Lenin particularly drew attention to this passage in his study of Hegel.[24]

It is of the greatest importance that we should understand what is involved for Hegel in his view of contradiction and annulment. We have just seen how in the *Jena Logic* Hegel even opposes annulment to the state of annulment and his aim there is to ensure that the preservation of division, duality, difference, non-identity in the ultimate philosophical unity is seen as a *movement*, a movement which is continuously renewed since its moments are constantly postulated and annulled. This view of annulment is stated most clearly in *The Phenomenology of Mind*. Here too Hegel returns to the discussion of identity and non-identity and he says that whichever side one stands on, whichever of the two concepts is held to be fixed and true, one is nevertheless both in the right and in the wrong.

'Neither the one or the other has the truth, their truth is their *movement*.'[25]

This formulation of dialectical contradiction and its annulment makes Hegel's view of it perfectly clear. From it we can understand why materialist dialectics could make use of Hegel's version but not of any other existing models. The union of opposites dates back to classical times. From Nicholas of Cusa to Schelling the '*coincidentia oppositorum*' recurs repeatedly. But nowhere is a theoretical solution to the problem of the relations between the act of annulment and the state of having been annulled to be found. Among idealist dialecticians the state of annulment always triumphs over the movement. The religious impulses present either explicitly or just beneath the surface in almost all of them strengthen this tendency still further. For if God is to be the point at which all the contradictions are resolved, the victory of stasis over movement is almost a forgone conclusion. As we shall see the urge to make the state of annulment into an absolute is also present in Hegel and where it makes itself felt it drags him down to the level of his predecessors.

Despite such frequent and unavoidable lapses which have a lot to do with the general limitations of idealist dialectics, this view of dialectics represents an enormous step forward. For it alone can adequately reproduce and reflect the unbroken movement of contradictions with its regular rhythm of creation and annulment. Of course, Hegel's brilliant idea has to be turned the right way up, materialistically, if it is really to do justice to reality, i.e. what is necessary is the clear recognition that the dialectical movement is an objective law governing things in the world, independently of consciousness. Only then will this constantly self-renewing movement remain a movement, rather than a pseudo-movement which ultimately comes to rest in God or a 'spirit'. We may cite a single (albeit very important) discussion of dialectical annulment by Marx so that the reader may see both how materialist dialectics are linked to Hegel's and how at the same time a materialist view works in quite a different way from Hegel's prefiguration of it, however brilliant that may have been. In *Capital* Marx has occasion to discuss the contradictions that emerge in the course of commodity exchange. He goes on to say:

'The differenciation of commodities into commodities and money does not sweep away these inconsistencies, but develops a *modus vivendi*, a form in which they can exist side by side. This is generally the way in which real contradictions are reconciled. For instance, it is a contradiction to depict one body as constantly falling towards another, and as, at the same time, constantly flying away from it. The ellipse is a form of motion which, while allowing this contradiction to go on, at the same time reconciles it.'[26]

Thus despite the limitations of idealism Hegel's dialectic never ceases to insist that the independence of the partial moments is preserved even when they are annulled. The elevation of particular objects and relations into the absolute entails not the extinction but the preservation of their concrete nature right down to and including the empirical features of objects and their interrelations. Hegel affirms this shortly after the passage cited earlier from the first polemic against Fichte:

'When philosophy separates things it cannot posit the things separated without positing them in the absolute . . . This relation to the absolute does not entail annulling both . . . but they are to subsist as separate things and retain this quality as long as they are posited in the absolute or the absolute in them.'[27]

This view has two important closely linked consequences for Hegelian philosophy. (1) In the first place this definition creates great scope for empirical research within an objective dialectics, i.e. for the unconstrained discovery of all that is to be found in the external world, in nature and society. Because Schelling's view of annulment ends in the immediacy of 'intellectual intuition' it extinguishes the empirical world and one consequence of this is that Schelling's philosophical constructs become increasingly formalistic and arbitrary. The methods of philosophy are directly and bluntly opposed to those of empirical research. The philosopher constructing his system from the lofty heights of 'intellectual intuition' feels increasingly disdainful of the need to respect the facts of empirical reality. Of course, there are counter-pressures here, especially in the case of Schelling himself, and far weaker ones in his disciples. These are related to his fitful moods of materialism, his efforts to see nature as it really is (and the connection with Goethe is important in this context). But his philosophical method does nothing to buttress these healthy instincts. On the contrary, the supremacy of speculative constructs that operate in terms of analogies which become increasingly formalistic and superficial as time passes, leads him further and further away from real empirical research. When later on he does make 'experiments' his philosophical method is no defence against mystical and reactionary swindles. Very typical in this respect are the letters that Schelling wrote to Hegel in the years 1806/7, the period just before he received a copy of *The Phenomenology of the Mind*. He describes in great detail the 'experiments' he is making with a divining rod and he also refers to highly important and allegedly empirical discoveries in the realm of magic.

Hegel's dialectic, by contrast, is a method by means of which the thinker can educate himself to acquire the true stuff of knowledge. We shall see later that sometimes Hegel even goes too far in this direction and loses himself in a plethora of empirical facts. This is connected with inadequacies in his concept of dialectics which as Marx observed has the double defect of an 'uncritical positivism' and an 'equally uncritical idealism'.[28]

But even this Marxian criticism suggests that Hegel had far more scope for really objective research than Schelling. Marx and Engels frequently drew attention to Hegel's encyclopaedic knowledge in contrast to the formalistic and arrogantly inflated ignorance of the Young Hegelians. This knowledge should not be thought of as an incidental personal virtue of Hegel's but as something intimately bound up with his specific conception of dialectics.

(2) The second important motif we must mention relates to the real dialectical interaction of the various categories and in particular the need to respect the autonomy and the particular nature of the so-called 'lower' categories that are closer to the empirical world. The more Schelling severs the links between absolute and relative knowledge the more he tends to treat the lower spheres in an arbitrary, undialectical and negligent manner. There is a great amount of documentary material which enables us to chart Schelling's course from a dialectic based on instinct to an entirely decadent, formalistic system in which grandiose intellectual structures are based on the most tenuous analogies. At the same time we see the opposite tendency emerging more and more clearly in Hegel. Fichte's point of departure had been the absolute (the Ego) from which he had gradually descended proceeding deductively to the empirical world. Schelling too had often lapsed into this mode of thought. Hegel employed a different method: beginning with the empirical categories he develops their internal dialectic and advances gradually to higher, more complex determinations. *The Phenomenology of Mind* provides the key instance of this method, as we shall show in due course, together with the limitations of Hegel's approach.

But even apart from the question of the structure of his philosophical system, the distinction between his approach and Schelling's has one other extremely important consequence. Hegel is compelled to relativize the dialectical transitions between absolute and non-absolute, infinite and finite, reason and understanding thus constructing an ever richer and more complex system of mediations. In contrast to this, as Schelling advances along the road of 'intellectual intuition' postulating first an aesthetic and later a religious genius as the prerequisite of philosophical insight, he increasingly opens up an abyss between the 'common understanding' and his philosophy. Thus he finds it harder and harder to discover any real mediations, and real dialectical bonds linking the categories of the understanding and of reason, finite and infinite, absolute and relative.

Here we see the systematic, methodological implications of the different approaches of the two thinkers to the history of philosophy. Schelling's contempt for the philosophy of the Enlightenment is grounded in his contempt for the categories of 'common' thought which are not allowed to have any truck with the absolute. Hegel's quest for transitions and mediations, however, leads him to regard the philosophers of the Enlightenment as among the forerunners of his own dialectics. Thus while Schelling's formalism drives him further and further into an historical and even anti-historical position, the development of Hegel's system runs parallel in his growing appreciation of the problems of history.

The most important issue here as far as we are concerned is Hegel's treatment of the categories of the understanding, the so-called determinations of reflection.[29] Together with Schelling Hegel combats the tendency present in both Kant and Fichte to stick fast at the determinations of reflection with their rigid antinomies. The latter remain openly unresolved in Kant, and Fichte can only resolve them with the aid of a specious logic. Schelling for his part soon falls into the opposite extreme: he takes refuge entirely in the categories of reason (*Vernunft*) where the contradictions are all eliminated, a procedure accomplished, as we have seen, with the aid of 'intellectual intuition'. Hegel, however, sets out to combat Kant and Fichte on their own territory. That is to say, he acknowledges the relative validity and indeed the indispensability and necessity of the determinations of reflection. What he objects to is that Kant and Fichte artificially isolate them and thus lapse into the rigidities of metaphysics, whereas an attentive investigation of the internal dialectical movement of the determinations of reflection would necessarily lead beyond metaphysics to a knowledge of the absolute.

Thus while Schelling's whole bent leads him gradually to the point where he utterly rejects the determinations of reflection (despite certain counter-tendencies and reversions to earlier positions which we must leave to one side in our search for the mainstream of his thought), Hegel comes to accept the necessity for a *philosophical reflectivity* as early as the *Difference*. In view of the importance of the whole issue for his entire system we must cite the relevant sections at greater length.

> 'The absolute must be constructed for consciousness—that is the task of philosophy. But since both the production and the products of reflection are just limitations, a contradiction arises. The absolute must be reflected, postulated; but in this manner it is not postulated but annulled; for the very act of positing it, limits it.

Hegel then rebukes Kant and Fichte for remaining in this impasse.

> 'Isolated reflection, viz. the postulating of opposites, annuls the absolute; it is the characteristic of being and limitation.'

But Kant and Fichte, no less than metaphysics as a whole, fail to observe that there is here an *objective* bond with the absolute, based on the general and comprehensive dialectical interactions between all objects both in thought and reality.

> 'But as reason reflection is related to the absolute and reflection is reason through this relation alone. To that extent reflection annihilates itself and all being and limitation, by relating all to the absolute. But at the same time just through this relation to the absolute all that is limited has its being.'

Thus the task of philosophy is to make *conscious* the objective contradictory relations underlying reflectivity. This philosophical consciousness of the dialectical path traversed by the determinations of reflection, the perception of the barriers, apparently so insurmountable, of their immediate manifestation as the categories of the understanding, leads Hegel to the idea of philosophical reflectivity. Philosophical reflectivity is the most important driving force of the dialectic, of his system, it is the methodological foundation both of the dialectic and of his view of history as a moment of the dialectic.

> 'When reflection turns its gaze upon itself its highest law, given to it by reason and making it a part of reason, is its annihilation. Like all else it subsists only in the absolute, but as reflectivity it is opposed to the absolute. So in order to exist it must make self-destruction its law. The immanent law enabling it to make itself absolute through its own efforts is the law of contradiction; viz. that it be postulated and once postulated, that it subsist. In so doing it defines its products as absolutely opposed to the absolute and dooms itself to remain understanding for all time, and not to become reason, and to hold fast to its own works which, as opposed to the absolute, are nothing and so as something limited it remains opposed to the absolute.'[30]

These arguments are evidently related to the Frankfurt writings about the dialectics of the absolute and the relative, but they provide a much clearer and more systematic foundation for the later Hegelian Logic.

That Hegel should still be experimenting with Schellingian concepts (such as 'potency') throughout this period will not come as any surprise after what we have already said. But it is no less evident that for all the undoubted influence of Schelling it would be as wrong to speak of a Schellingian period in Hegel's thought now as it was to speak of a theological and mystical period earlier on. Hegel's independence on a number of quite crucial dialectical problems is well established by now.

This independence is borne out still further when we compare his discussion of subjective idealism with the correspondence between Fichte and Schelling. Not only does he raise completely novel questions about the differences between subjective and objective idealism, questions that did not occur to either Fichte or Schelling, he also enters areas of philosophy where these differences become vital. In particular, we shall have to say a few words about the sphere of 'practical reason': ethics and the philosophy of law and the state.

On questions such as these Schelling was always a derivative thinker. His early and immature essay the *New Deduction of Natural Law* remained an insignificant episode which he failed to follow up. Of course, once he had embarked on a whole series of great systematic projects in Jena, he could not utterly ignore ethical and political problems. But his treatment of them always forms the weakest part of his philosophy, both in terms of originality and the factual material at his disposal. And not unexpectedly the reactionary elements in his thought emerged here much sooner and more explicitly than in his treatment of general problems of dialectics or the philosophy of nature. We have already drawn attention to the circumstance that Hegel never takes the trouble to criticize Schelling's views on these subjects even though he regards the critique of Kant's and Fichte's 'practical philosophy' as crucial. He simply ignores Schelling's ideas here altogether. For this reason we shall ourselves only discuss them to the extent to which it is necessary in order to lay bare some of the social pressures underlying the breach.

Before proceeding to Hegel's critique of the 'practical philosophy' of subjective idealism we should perhaps just glance at the rich variety of Hegel's discussions and the wealth of problems that he treats. When we do so we shall see that Fichte's objections to Schelling's philosophy of nature, to the existence of objective categories in our knowledge of nature, pale into insignificance.

Nevertheless, like all the facts in the highly complex history of idealism in Germany, even this question has two sides to it and they should not be utterly ignored. Up to now we have emphasized the positive aspects of Hegel's distinctions between subjective and objective idealism, and our concluding discussion will emphasize this still further. But we should briefly note the negative side too.

Fichte passionately accuses Schelling of self-delusion, his 'self-construction' of the categories of nature is an illusion. When he insists on confining nature to 'a small area of the mind' he criticizes Schelling not just from the standpoint of subjective idealism, but from that of any possible idealism. For *all* idealism nature is in fact a region of consciousness, whether large or small makes no difference. If nature is not to be regarded thus the philosopher must demonstrate its existence *outside* consciousness. In the absence of this demonstration—and nothing could be further from the minds of either Schelling or Hegel—Fichte's criticism remains valid in a certain sense. Hegel is unable to refute Fichte on this point; he can only ignore him. Even the most highly developed form of the Hegelian dialectic in *The Phenomenology of Mind* or the *Encyclopaedia* is vulnerable to this criticism. Hegel and Schelling can only assert the objectivitify of spirit; they cannot prove it, since spirit's independence of consciousness is in fact the basic fallacy of objective idealism.

Coming from the other side, from materialism, Feuerbach is able to carry through Fichte's argument with greater consistency than Fichte. Moreover, he directs his fire not at the early works but at *The Phenomenology of Mind* itself. As we shall see, Hegel's strategy there is to chart the dialectical journey from sensuous perception to spirit itself, justifying the necessity of his own position by demonstrating the necessity of this journey. Feuerbach shows that even here Hegel remains within the bounds of thought, of consciousness, and that his appeal to the sensuous reality of the external world is based on a fallacy.

> 'The "Here" is, for instance, a tree. I turn around and this truth disappears. True enough in the *Phenomenology* where turning-round costs no more than a word. But in reality, where I must also turn my ponderous body the Here retains a very real existence even behind my back. The tree sets limits to my back; it prevents me from occupying the place it occupies. Hegel does not refute the Here as an object of sensuous consciousness and as an object for us as opposed to pure thought, but the logical Here. . . . It [i.e. Hegelian philosophy] begins not with the otherness of thought but with the *thought of the otherness* of thought.'[31]

This clearly exposes the fallacy in Hegel's process of reasoning about objective reality.

It was necessary to refer to this aspect of Hegel's disagreement with Fichte since it is closely related to the ultimate limitations of his dialectics. Looked at historically, Schelling and Hegel simply had to ignore Fichte's not entirely otiose objections in the interest of the fruitful further development of the dialectic, just as Fichte had in his day overridden no less defensible arguments from Kant. In the absence of this philosophical self-deception, which is closely bound up with a whole series of societal self-deceptions—both heroic and petty—Hegel's dialectics would never have come into being. We have seen that Feuerbach was right to criticize this particular delusion. But we know also that this correct insight in no way helped Feuerbach to extend Hegel's dialectic on a materialist basis. Only Marx was able to do that and he could do it only on the basis of a critique of Hegel *and* Feuerbach. And we have no need to demonstrate that if Marx was in a position to overcome both objective idealism and metaphysical materialism, this was because he could and did criticize bourgeois philosophy as a whole from the standpoint of the proletariat. It is this that highlights the impotence of Fichte's strictures on Schelling and above all Hegel. For even if the economic situation and the class structure in Germany at the beginning of the nineteenth century had been such as to permit the emergence of a materialist philosophy of the stature of Feuerbach's, the objections raised by such a philosophy to Hegel's idealism would have been sterile, however correct in themselves. Feuerbach's critique could only bear fruit after the development and triumph of his philosophy in a Germany where class tensions were reaching breaking-point and where the pressures leading to a bourgeois democratic revolution were at a peak. And even then it could only do so in the sense that it provided the impetus for the emergence of dialectical materialism. The bourgeois successors of Feuerbach degenerated to a level well below that of the Hegelian dialectic.

## NOTES

1  *Erste Druckschriften*, p. 163.
2  Ibid., p. 12.
3  Ibid., p. 14.
4  Ibid., p. 13f.
5  Rosenkranz, p. 540.
6  *Erste Druckschriften*, p. 96f.
7  Ibid., p. 24. Cf. also pp. 82 and 84.
8  Ibid., p. 48.
9  Lenin, *Philosophical Notebooks*, Collected Works, Moscow and London 1961, Vol. 38, p. 362.
10  Ibid., p. 363.
11  *Erste Druckschriften*, p. 46.
12  Ibid., p. 47.
13  Ibid., p. 56.
14  Ibid., p. 65.
15  Ibid., p. 52f.
16  *Jena Logic*, p. 29.

17    Spinoza, *Ethic*, Part II, Proposition 7.

18    *Schriften zur Politik und Rechtsphilosophie*, ed. Lasson, p. 387f.

19    Cf. my book *The Destruction of Reason*, Berlin 1954, Chap. 2; *Werke*, Vol. 9, pp. 84–269.

20    *Erste Druckschriften*, p. 91.

21    *Jena Logic*, p. 13. G.L.'s italics.

22    Ibid., p. 33.

23    *Erste Druckschriften*, p. 76f. G.L.'s italic.

24    Op. cit., p. 139.

25    *The Phenomenology of Mind*, trans. J. P. Baillie, London 1964, p. 777. G.L.'s italics.

26    *Capital*, Vol. I, London 1967, pp. 103–4.

27    *Erste Druckschriften*, p. 77.

28    Marx, *Economic and Philosophic Manuscripts of 1844*, trans. M. Milligan, London 1970, p. 176.

29    The determinations of reflection (identity, difference and contradiction) are dealt with in the *Logic*, Bk. 2, *Essence*, Chap. 2, pp. 408–44.—*Trans.*

30    *Erste Druckschriften*, p. 17.

31    Feuerbach, *Zur Kritik der Hegelschen Philosophie, Werke*, Leipzig 1846, Vol. II, p. 214f.

# CHAPTER THREE

# Against abstract idealism in ethics

IF we now turn to Hegel's criticisms of the 'practical philosophy' of subjective idealism we find a much larger body of material available from
his earlier period to provide a comparison. We have already discussed in
detail Hegel's arguments against Kant's ethics in Frankfurt (p.146ff.). We
shall see that the basic direction of his criticism remains the same but that
it has now become much more concrete, detailed and above all more systematic. He no longer concerns himself just with the specific problems of
Kantian ethics as they arise in the course of his own analyses. Instead, he
now subjects the whole 'practical philosophy' of subjective idealism to a
searching scrutiny. Moreover, his discussions relate these issues to the
general philosophical positions of Kant, Fichte and Jacobi. Hegel considers the inadequacies of their moral philosophy to be the direct consequence of the fallacies and the one-sidedness of their world-view. He
regards their treatment of moral problems as a test of the way in which
subjective idealism must fail to deal with the salient problems of real life
in society.

In the *Difference* Hegel only touches on isolated aspects of their ethical
thought. In *Faith and Knowledge* he carries out a thorough analysis of subjective idealism in all its aspects, culminating in a criticism of ethical
ideas. The last great polemical essay from the *Kritisches Journal*, the essay
on *Natural Law,* is almost exclusively devoted to this question. In *Faith
and Knowledge* Hegel locates the defect of a merely reflective philosophy
in its inability to bridge the gulf between the universal and the empirical.

> 'The one and the many confront each other as abstractions so that the
> polar opposites are opposed to each other, both positively and nega-
> tively, so that to the universal concept empirical reality is both an ab-
> solute something and an absolute nothing. By virtue of the former
> they are old-fashioned empiricism, by virtue of the latter they are
> both idealism and scepticism.'[1]

And Hegel adds with particular reference to Fichte:

> 'The immediate product of this formal idealism . . . manifests itself in
> the following form: an amorphous empirical realm composed of a
> purely arbitrary variety of things stands opposed to an empty world
> of thought.'[2]

This view of reality has particularly disastrous implications in the field of ethics. The ethical philosophy of subjective idealism is not able to attain to a true understanding of the general nature of moral imperatives and of the social content of ethics.

> 'Because the emptiness of pure will and of the universal is the true *a priori* requirement, the particular is simply an empirical datum. It would be inconsistent to give a definition of what right and duty are in and for themselves; for the content at once annuls the pure will, duty for duty's sake, and turns duty into something material. The vacuity of the pure feeling of duty constantly runs athwart the content.'[3]

Following this general criticism Hegel raises the same objections to Kant and Fichte that we saw in the Frankfurt fragments: that their morality brings tyranny not freedom, that to live according to such a morality must lead to hypocrisy etc.

In his general discussion of Kant and Fichte Hegel had already shown that their method leads only to an empty and abstract 'ought', to the vacuous notion of 'infinite progress'. In the realm of ethics these concepts are given a more concrete form which reveals the nullity of subjective idealism even better than in the realm of pure theory. By postulating the 'ought' of morality Kant and Fichte had hoped to raise themselves above the ordinary empirical consciousness of the individual and to achieve a true ethical universality. Hegel lays bare the fallacy involved in this and shows that the 'ought' leads straight back to the vulgar empirical individualist posture *vis-à-vis* society and the world.

> '. . . for from the very outset the "ought" admits of no totality; but instead the manifold variety of the world appears as an incomprehensible, basic determinacy and empirical necessity. Particularity and difference as such are absolute. The standpoint for this reality is the empirical standpoint of each individual; and for each individual, the actual is the incomprehensible sphere of a vulgar reality by which he happens to be enclosed.'[4]

Thus in this system of morality the general sterility of subjective idealism, its failure to comprehend concrete reality, is clearly exposed.

We may recollect Hegel's argument that the concept of infinite progress is not able to solve any significant problem and that it merely repeats and reproduces in philosophical language the unsolved problems of subjective idealism. In 'practical philosophy' the connection between the 'ought' and the infinite progress is even clearer. Hegel shows that the concept of infinite progress itself points to the unrealizability of the programme of subjective idealism, that it is an admission that even if the programme of subjective idealism were to be realized this would only invalidate its own premises, and that therefore these premises are in contradiction with reality. In the course of an argument where Hegel shows that Jacobi really shares the assumptions of Kant and Fichte even though he is vigorously attacking them Hegel goes on to say:

'The moral world-order that resides in faith ['faith' is the central concept in Jacobi's philosophical system—G.L.] is utterly *external* to the Ego; the Ego can enter it, or it can enter the Ego, acquire reality for the Ego—solely in an infinite progress. For the Ego things simply cannot become what they ought to be, for then the Non-Ego would cease to exist and would become Ego, because Ego=Ego would stand as an absolute identity without any other axiom, and because the Ego would be annulled by something it had itself posited, thereby ceasing to be Ego. Thus this method of escaping from dualism is as futile as Jacobi could hope for.'[5]

(Jacobi consistently opposed every type of monism, not merely the authentic monism of Spinoza but the ostensible monism of Kant and Fichte. Hegel's remarks here have a double edge. On the one hand, he shows that what is apparently monism in Kant and Fichte is really dualistic, while on the other hand he shows that Jacobi, who thought that his unmediated concept of faith placed him above Kant and Fichte, really shares the same subjective–idealist assumptions.)

Hegel pulls no punches in the language he employs to describe the philosophy of Kant and Fichte. At one point he speaks of their 'sublime hollowness and uniquely consistent vacuity', and elsewhere he refers to the 'distasteful pure heights' of abstraction.[6] The appeal of subjective idealism to the most noble and sublime sentiments of man, to the function of pure ethics in binding man to a supernatural world, makes absolutely no impression on Hegel. On the contrary, he just observes that 'the supernatural world represents merely a flight from the natural one'. The longing for freedom expressed in both Kant and Fichte is in Hegel's eyes only a failure to grasp the real movement of society in its concrete totality. He regards this longing for freedom as 'overweening pride'. Fichte's philosophy consists in

'Sorrow that he is at one with the universe, that eternal nature acts through him; he feels loathing and horror at the idea of subjecting himself to the eternal laws of nature with their sacred and immutable necessity, and he feels sorrow and even despair if he is unable to free himself from the eternal laws of nature with their stern necessity. . . . Just as if these laws were not rational, as if they were laws which would put the Ego to shame if it were to accept their authority, as if it would make him indescribably wretched to have to obey them, as if it would make him despair if he were to be subjected to them.[7]

There can be no doubt that Hegel's position here is both more true and more progressive than Fichte's and that the construction of an effective ethical system, one that will be able to encompass all the problems of man in society, can be accomplished only with his methods rather than those of Kant and Fichte. Nevertheless, this disagreement between them reflects the great general contradictions of the age which none of them were able fully to resolve. Engels' pronouncement about the dialectics of organic development 'that every step forward is . . . at the same time a step backward, since it hardens out a one-sided development' is particularly relevant to this debate.[8]

Hegel's criticism makes the defects of Fichte's position stand out very clearly. But when we pass judgment on Fichte's concept of freedom we must not forget that it came into being in the context of the French Revolution of which it is an ideological reflection. Fichte may indeed overestimate the gulf dividing freedom from reality in a manner characteristic of abstract idealism, but this exaggeration should not blind us to his realistic assessment of the political situation. And this is not just true of Germany where the French Revolution had as yet done nothing to remove the vestiges of feudalism—not until Napoleon was the French occupation effective in liquidating certain feudal remains in some parts of Germany and in provoking a reform movement in Prussia. The demands for freedom put forward in the Revolution do indeed clash head-on with the realities of Germany, much as Fichte claims that the need for freedom will clash with reality in any society at any time. But the failure of the French Revolution to satisfy demands for freedom, both in general and those of Fichte in particular, was not just confined to Germany. We have already indicated that Fichte was a radical democratic supporter of the Revolution and shared the view that the concepts of freedom and equality should be extended to the realm of private property. The fact that the proposals he advanced were more than a little naïve (and even more naïve than the ideas of Babeuf in France) is an inevitable consequence of the entire historical situation. Thus the disagreement between Hegel and Fichte is a reflection of a great world-historical conflict of the age. On the one hand, bourgeois society actually came into being in consequence of the French Revolution and the Industrial Revolution in England. Hegel's philosophy was an attempt to provide this bourgeois actuality with a philosophy. On the other hand, neither the English nor the French Revolution was able to achieve such a perfect state of democracy or to have such complete success in eliminating the remnants of feudalism as the real democratic revolutionaries had longed and fought for. In this sense even in Western Europe the bourgeois democratic revolution could not be said to have been completed. It is this aspect of the historical situation that Fichte reflected in his philosophy, albeit in a subjectivist, exaggerated manner. The entire dispute was exacerbated still further because it took place in Germany where, as we know, a bourgeois democratic revolution could not be considered except as a possibility in the distant future.

Hence both Fichte and Hegel may be said to stand rather one-sidedly for one aspect of this world-historical conflict. And if we contemplate the later course of democratic revolutions in Western Europe we can see that neither of them had the whole truth about the Revolution itself and the bourgeois society to which it gave birth. By the middle of the nineteenth century the role of the proletariat had become extraordinarily important—notwithstanding the bourgeois-democratic content of the revolutions themselves—and with the passage of time even bourgeois-democratic revolutions could only be understood properly from the standpoint of the proletariat. In this context too we can see the relevance of Marx's comment that

> 'rudiments of more advanced forms in the lower species of animals can only be understood when the more advanced forms are already known. Bourgeois economy thus provides a key to the economy of antiquity, etc.'[9]

A truly dialectical theory of bourgeois revolution and bourgeois society is to be found only in dialectical materialism.

It is this situation that gave rise to Fichte's abstract utopianism. He was a revolutionary thinker in a country that lacked a revolutionary movement. And when later, at the time of the war of liberation against Napoleon, he did come into contact with a popular movement, its reactionary features had a disastrous impact on his philosophy. The objectivism of Hegel's philosophy was rendered possible by the fact that right from the start he unreservedly accepted the bourgeois society that emerged from the French Revolution as an incontrovertible reality. In his thought he was concerned above all to understand it as it was, to recognize its underlying principles and explain them philosophically. The fact that a former supporter of the French Revolution could advance logically to such a position is explained by the circumstance that Hegel, as we know, was never in sympathy with the radical democratic wing of the Jacobins. There was accordingly no contradiction in his development from supporter of the French Revolution to supporter of Napoleon.

This leads us to the paradoxical conclusion that Hegel's superiority over Fichte as a philosopher, his superiority as a social philosopher, is connected with the more undemocratic basis of his social and political thought. Such paradoxes are not infrequent in history. In this case we may explain it by the unreality of political commitments for or against democracy or revolution in Germany in practice: such commitments

were purely ideological in nature. No sooner did they come into contact
with concrete political movements in Germany than the reactionary features of German society began to exercise an undue influence on their
thought. In Fichte's case this happened, as we have seen, at the time of the
Wars of Liberations in 1813; in the case of Hegel, not until his Berlin
period (from 1818 to his death). Wherever the democratic aspirations of
ideologists have some foundation in a real popular movement, however
feeble, contradictions of this sort are not possible. We need think only of
the ideological superiority of the revolutionary democrats in Russia over
all their ideological opponents.

The contrast between Hegel and Fichte is nowhere more clearly
expressed than where Hegel takes issue with Fichte's ideas about insurrection and 'right to rebel'. In his *Foundation of Natural Law* (1796) Fichte
puts forward radical revolutionary views. He says:

> 'However—and this is something we must not lose sight of—the
> people is never rebellious and to use the expression *rebellion* with ref-
> erence to it is the greatest nonsense imaginable. For the people is in
> fact and in law the highest power beyond which there is no other: it is
> the source of all power and is responsible to God alone. When it
> assembles the executive power loses its authority both in fact and ac-
> cording to law. Rebellion must be directed against a higher authority.
> But what is there on earth that is higher than the people! It could rebel
> only against itself, which is nonsense. Only God stands above the
> people. So if it is said that a people has rebelled against its ruler then
> we must assume that the ruler is a god, an assumption that might be
> difficult to prove.'[10]

Fichte conceives of the sovereignty of the people as taking the following form in actual practice: in normal times the executive power will
have all the power in its hands. Alongside the executive, however, there
is another body, the so-called ephors or governors. They have no real
power unless the executive oversteps the limits of the constitution,
whereupon they are entitled to proclaim an interdict, suspend the power
of the executive, and summon the people together as the final arbiters in
the particular dispute.[11] Similarly the debate about the right of the people
to rebel is not confined to academic circles. It played a very important
role in the struggles surrounding the French constitution during the
Revolution. Robespierre and the Jacobins consistently defended the
people's right to revolution; Condorcet as the ideologist of the Girondins was opposed to it and wished to devise institutions which would
resolve constitutional conflicts in a legal manner. The argument between
Robespierre and Condorcet was taken up with great energy by German
theorists, including Hegel who refers to the problem in his pamphlet on
the German constitution.[12]

In his essay on *Natural Law* Hegel savagely attacks this Fichtean theory. His arguments are as close to Condorcet as Fichte's are to those of Robespierre. That is to say: in both men we find that a French reality has evaporated into a German philosophical abstraction. The decisive point in Hegel's argument is his total rejection of the right to rebel:

'since this pure power consists merely of a host of private wills which for that reason cannot constitute themselves as the common will.'

Thus Hegel defends the undemocratic position that the immediate expression of the will of the people cannot create a real, ordered state of law. The weakness of his position is thus clearly exposed.

But Hegel's strength and his sober assessment of actual conditions is very apparent in his refutation of Fichte's proposed constitution. His analysis of the relations between the executive and the ephorate does not just content itself with the formal legal problem (as does Fichte) but instead he examines their actual power-relations. And this leads him to the irrefutable conclusion that if both executive and ephorate had the same powers then the state would become a kind of 'perpetuum mobile' which 'instead of moving would find itself in perfect balance and so in a perpetuum quietum'. Hegel realizes that in a normally functioning state —and every constitution is designed to function normally over a long period of time—a dual authority is untenable in the long run. And if either the executive or the ephorate gains the upper hand, i.e. if there is in effect a unified authority, then the entire Fichtean edifice falls to the ground.

Thus we can see the historical limitations of both parties to the dispute who for all their differences nevertheless share common ground. It is evident that the core of the dispute is the question of a dual authority. This issue was a practical one in the French Revolution—in the Paris commune, the Jacobin Club etc., *vis-à-vis* the Convention. But even those who were involved in events or who, like Robespierre, helped to organize and lead and even exploit this dual authority did not and could not understand its social nature. This is why Robespierre wished to build the right to rebel into the constitution of 1793. Fichte's philosophy is a simple if idealistically magnified reflection of this misunderstanding, of these legalistic prejudices about the nature of revolution. (The tenacity of such prejudices can be seen from the role they play in Lassalle's *System of Acquired Rights*.) Hegel reached the point where he could see through the formalistic and impotent definitions of constitutional law and grasp the underlying issues of political power. But this vision was blurred by his inability to perceive the creative force inherent in a revolutionary movement of the people.

Very interesting, and very typical of Hegel, is the fact that he ends his polemic against Fichte with a reference to Bonaparte's *coup d'état* of the

18th Brumaire. His aim is not simply to point up the impotence of Fichte's ephorate (since all French governments at this period had similar if less far-fetched supervisory bodies) but also to show how in his view changes in a constitution are in fact brought about. He does not mention Napoleon by name. But since the *coup d'état* took place in 1799 and the essay was written in the winter of 1802–3 there can be no doubt that he is referring to it:

> 'It is well known that on a recent occasion when a government succeeded in dissolving a legislative body in competition with it and paralysing it, it was suggested that a supervisory body along the lines of Fichte's ephorate would have prevented such a *coup de main*. A man who was closely involved in the affair gave it as his view that had such a council attempted to offer any resistance it would have been treated in like fashion.'[13]

We shall see that Hegel later thought of Napoleon as the 'great teacher of constitutional law in Paris'. It is very characteristic that he used him as an argument against Fichte even at this early stage.

This disagreement between Hegel and Fichte goes back ultimately to Fichte's belief that all social and juridical institutions are merely restrictions on human freedom, whereas Hegel maintains that

> 'the highest community is the greatest freedom both in terms of power and of the exercise of one's rights.'[14]

It is obvious that this dispute was based on the disagreement discussed above about the nature of the bourgeois society that succeeded the French Revolution. Its effect on Hegel was that he could detect nothing in Fichte's ethics and political theory but servitude and the suppression of man and nature.

We have already had occasion to discuss the purely moral problems that arise here in our analysis of Hegel's Frankfurt critique of Kant and we showed then that Hegel's remarks held good for Fichte too. The explicit polemic against Fichte fully bears this out so that we need not concern ourselves further with it here. On the issue of the theory of law and the state Hegel consistently satirized Fichte's efforts to regiment everything and to deduce all his regulations *a priori* from the nature of philosophy. Thus Fichte attempted to prove that regulations can be drawn up which will prevent the forgery of money and bills of exchange, or determine which passport a person should have and how it is to be issued etc.[15] Elsewhere he refers to a statute-book drawn up according to Fichtean precepts as a 'price-list'.[16]

There is much more at issue here than satire at the expense of the more eccentric forms of Fichte's idealism. Behind his ironical remarks lie two fundamental theoretical positions. First, there is his view that the real motor force powering society is society's own uninterrupted organic self-reproduction, that therefore society in the course of its development will produce the institutions it requires, and that these cannot be imposed on it by any external authority, not even that of a deductive philosophy. (We shall see later on at what point and for what reason Hegel fails to carry out his own perfectly correct prescriptions.) Second, he holds to the principle that the general content of law is systematically and historically necessary, but that, just because of this, the particular determinations of the law and above all their application to isolated instances must always contain a chance element. According to Hegel it will always be a contingent matter to decide whether a given crime should be punished by three or four years in prison; problems of this sort cannot be resolved by an appeal to philosophy. We see here the great fundamental frontier between the concrete objective idealism of Hegel and the abstract subjective idealism of Fichte.

This abstractness stems in Hegel's view from the formalist nature of subjective idealism. It avoids all problems of content on principle. The content of moral of legal imperatives is always established by a sort of swindle, never by a true deduction from its own premises. Hegel had already come to this conclusion in Frankfurt. Now he reiterates the same idea, but in a more resolute and theoretically better-grounded way. As he puts it:

'But the will is pure identity without any content, and it is pure only insofar as it is entirely formal and without content. It is not possible for its object to generate a content of its own. . . .'[17]

The concrete implications of this disagreement can be seen from a passage where Hegel criticizes a crucial argument from Kant's *Critique of Practical Reason*. Kant is in the process of concretizing the supreme law of morality, the categorical imperative, by arguing that a criterion for moral rightness or wrongness is to be found in the absence or presence of contradiction in the actions of men. He believes that if a man can convert a particular moral maxim into a universal law without involving himself in contradiction, he will thereby establish the rightness of the maxim in question. As an example Kant argues that it can never be right to embezzle a deposit.[18] He says:

'I at once became aware that such a principle, viewed as a law, would annihilate itself, because the result would be that there would be no more deposits.'[19]

Kant believes then that the principle of contradiction will suffice to enable the social content of the categorical imperative to be deduced in any given case.

Hegel's reply to this argument is clear and incisive:

'What if there were no deposits, where is the contradiction in that? For there to be no deposit would contradict other necessarily determined facts: just as the possibility of deposits is connected with yet other necessary facts and so itself becomes necessary. But it is not permissible to invoke other purposes and other material grounds; only the immediate form of the concept may decide which of the two assumptions is correct, but each of the opposed facts is as immaterial to the form as the other.'[20]

In the first place, Hegel refuses to accept that any social content can be derived from a formal moral maxim. The various institutions of society are a coherent and constantly changing concrete totality. Their necessity is something that can be deduced only from their position within that totality. Since Kant does not even consider this question (because he is concerned only to derive them from a formal moral law) his proof is *ipso facto* illicit. In the second place, Hegel is concerned here to combat the antithesis between internal and external in ethics, the antithesis between morality and legality. According to Hegel morality is an important part, but no more than a part of the social activity of man. Hence it cannot be separated from the concrete totality of society with its external laws and institutions. Hegel argues that in Kant and Fichte there is a division between the rigid and lifeless set of institutions on the one hand, and the empty abstract inwardness of moral man on the other. Hegel defends an opposing view in which there is a continuous interaction between all the moments of the dialectical movement according to which men make their society with all its institutions, a society in which they then work and live as independent beings.

This abstract and undialectical division of internal and external is in Hegel's view the real reason why Jacobi shares the same ground as Kant and Fichte and is implicated in all their errors, even though he relentlessly attacks them in all his writings, frequently with extremely pertinent arguments.

Superficially Jacobi's philosophy does indeed represent the exact opposite of Kant and Fichte. The latter proclaim the majesty of the abstract and universal moral law and allow the aspirations of individual men, actual living men, only as much scope as is compatible with the moral law. Jacobi, on the other hand, appeals to actual man as a unique being. From history, literature and legend he draws on a vast number of anecdotes and exempla which prove that actions which appear criminal according to the commandments of formal ethical codes or customary moral beliefs are in reality the expression of a lofty human morality. He actually demands the right to such 'crimes' because 'the law was made for the sake of man, not man for the sake of the law.'[21]

Now Hegel does not dispute that the objections to Kant and Fichte raised here have a certain force. He himself had opposed the Kantian ethic in Frankfurt on the grounds that it fragmented, violated and tyrannized over actual, living men. But he shows that from a quite different angle Jacobi too, no less than Kant and Fichte, opposes the isolated individual to a wholly alien society. According to Hegel living human beings are human beings living in a concrete society, and their human totality and vitality can only be expressed in the context of that society. Isolated from this man becomes just as abstract and schematic as the human beings posited by the abstract moral law of Kant and Fichte.

In support of his own view Jacobi mentions the story of the two Spartans who, when asked by the King of the Persians whether they would not remain and live in his country, replied:

'How could we live here and abandon *our land*, *our laws* and *our people*, for whom we have freely undertaken this great journey so that we might lay down our lives for them?'

Jacobi interprets this incident in the following manner:

'They did not attempt to convince him of *their* truth. . . . They did not appeal to their understanding, their fine judgement; they appealed only to *things* and their preference for these things. They did not lay claim to any virtue, nor to any philosophy. They simply declared what lay in their hearts, *their feelings*, *their experience*. . . .'

It is at this point that Hegel detects a subjectivism similar to that in Kant and Fichte. He says of Jacobi's interpretation:

'But Jacobi refers to the most vital matters: country, people and laws, as *things* to which they are accustomed as one is accustomed to things. He thinks of them not as sacred things but as common ones. . . . He regards as chance and contingency things which contain the highest necessity and the highest energy of ethical freedom, viz. to live in accordance with the laws of a people, of the Spartan nation moreover. He thinks of that which is most rational as if it were something ordinary and empirical.'[22]

Hence Hegel thinks of Kant/Fichte and Jacobi as possessing mutually complementary, one-sided philosophies which have at least one common feature: they all neglect the actual concrete realm of human activity. They are blind to it and treat it as contingent, external and secondary. The critique of Jacobi supplements the criticism of the Kantian categorical imperative, so that Hegel can say by way of summing up:

'Ethical beauty may not dispense with either aspect: either with living individuality, without which it becomes subservient to lifeless concepts, or with the form of the concept and the law, universality and objectivity.'[23]

This attack on Jacobi was highly topical at the time it was written. It was the heyday of Romanticism and although Jacobi himself was not personally a member or supporter of the Romantic school in the narrower sense, he was the representative of an ideological current that helped to prepare the way for certain reactionary elements of Romanticism. In brief, the issue turns on the situation that arose when the Enlightened democratic rebellion of the most progressive elements of the German intelligentsia against feudal absolutism in Germany began to disintegrate rapidly. The most striking achievements of this phase had been Goethe's *Werther* and Schiller's *Robbers* and *Love and Intrigue*. The degeneration set in partly because of the disaffection of important sectors of the bourgeoisie from the actuality of the French Revolution.

The passionate individualism of Goethe and Schiller in their youth had an explicitly anti-feudal bias and their demand for freedom was no less explicitly critical of the existing social order. Their successors simply took over their call for individual fulfilment without any attempt to fight against the concrete social obstacles impeding the development of the individual in Germany. Some of them simply lost all interest in social criticism, others criticized society in general as an obstacle to individual fulfilment. In the process they intellectually and artistically detached the individual from all social bonds and set him abstractly and exclusively over against society.

This development corresponds to the general ideological situation. The literary and intellectual activity of Goethe and Schiller in their youth was a final climactic moment of the pre-revolutionary Enlightenment. In the Prometheus fragment and other poems of his youth we find Goethe proclaiming a Spinozistic philosophy. The degeneration of the socially critical revolt of the individual into an abstract cult of individuality leads also to a defection from the general principles of the Enlightenment, which as we have seen was never really materialist in Germany and which culminated in the Spinozism of the later Lessing, Goethe and Herder. With Jacobi the attack on Spinoza's atheism began in Germany.

The Romantic School, in its later increasingly reactionary view of individuality, could take their cue from Jacobi and his like. From this vantage-point they could resume the attack on the Enlightenment. Of course, the later Romantics had the additional refinement of claiming that the Middle Ages had permitted a freer development of the individual than the 'atomism' of the present. The Romantic School in Jena had not yet fully explored these possibilities. Nevertheless, the idea of a limitless, empty individualism already played a crucial role in Jena. In his early republican phase Friedrich Schlegel the chief ideologist of the group had mocked Jacobi claiming that he had no concept of humanity, but only of 'Friedrich Heinrich Jacobity.'[24] But only a few years later, in

1799, he published his notorious novel *Lucinde* in which abstract individualistic and irrationalist tendencies were already taken to extremes. Schleiermacher, the other leading ideologist of the Romantic School, followed this up with an anonymous defence of the novel in which he provided this individualism and irrationalism with a theoretical basis. Independently of the Romantic School and indeed partly in opposition to it the novels of Jean Paul were widely read and highly esteemed at around this time, and Jean Paul always claimed to be a disciple and follower of Jacobi.

This sketchy outline may perhaps convey some idea of the topicality of Hegel's sharp criticism of Jacobi's views on morality. This must be emphasized because the neo-Hegelians are constantly at pains to turn Hegel into a 'philosopher of life' and an irrationalist. In this context it is of great importance to bear in mind that Hegel puts the abstract and empty individualism of Kant and Fichte on the same plane as Jacobi's irrationalist 'philosophy of life'. For we have seen how the neo-Kantianism of the Imperialist period (Simmel) contrived to create a synthesis of Kantianism and the 'philosophy of life', thus converting Hegel's critical view of this affinity into one of positive affirmation. As we have seen, neo-Hegelianism also attempted to obscure the distinction between Kant and Hegel and to assimilate Hegel to the Romantic 'philosophy of life'. Ignoring overtly Fascist interpretations (Hugo Fischer) we can still find the following description of Hegel in the 'standard work' of the neo-Hegelian Richard Kroner:

> 'Hegel is undoubtedly the greatest irrationalist known to the history of philosophy.'[25]

The blatant falsifications committed during the Fascist and pre-Fascist era must be countered by a presentation of the true facts of the intellectual situation at the time and a concrete analysis of Hegel's attitude towards them.[26]

The true fact of the matter is that Hegel together with Goethe (whom the modern irrationalistic revisors of German history also claim for their cause) always stood out against Romantic individualism and the irrationalist 'philosophy of life'. Hegel's final judgment of Jacobi's philosophy is that his narrow emphasis on the individual,

> 'his eternal meditation on the subject, which replaces ethical freedom with excessive scrupulosity, nostalgic egoism and ethical debility'

can lead only to an 'inward idolatry'. Revealingly, Hegel refers to the life of a man trapped in his own individuality as a 'Hell', and no less revealingly he appeals to the authority of Goethe who in his *Iphigenie* dramatizes this hell as the fate of Orestes but is evidently fully aware both of its disintegrating, problematic nature and of the fact that the task of progressive humanism is to discover a way out of this impasse of individualism in the modern world. Goethe's awareness of his humanist mission is what makes him the great poet of his age. Hegel goes on to measure Jacobi's poetic works against the artistic, moral and intellectual standard set by Goethe:

> 'Thus in his heroes Allwil and Woldemar we witness the torment that springs from an eternal contemplation of the self not even in the course of acting, but in the still greater boredom and lassitude of an empty existence; this self-prostitution is portrayed as the explanation for the catastrophe that befalls them in their non-novelistic adventures but it is not annulled at the moment of disaster and the uncatastrophic virtue of their whole environment is also more or less tainted by the same hell.'[27]

It is very revealing that the section of *Faith and Knowledge* which treats of Jacobi concludes with a discussion of Schleiermacher's *Discourses on Religion* one of the programmatic works of the Jena Romantic School. Hegel reproaches Schleiermacher with cultivating the same empty subjectivity as Jacobi:

> 'Thus even the contemplation of the universe is turned into subjectivity since . . . it is a piece of virtuosity and not even nostalgia, but a search for nostalgia . . . the expression of something utterly inward, the unmediated explosion or succession of isolated and particular enthusiasms and not the truthful statement that a work of art should be.'

Thus Hegel castigates in Schleiermacher what he criticized in Jacobi. Scheiermacher wishes 'to cultivate art without works of art'[28], and the 'philosophy of life' is to achieve its 'practical' fulfilment as '*Lebenskunst*', the art of living. Hence Schleiermacher remains at the same level of individualistic immediacy as Jacobi.

To bring out the profound affinity of such views with the philosophy of Kant we would just like to cite one comment in Hegel's Jena Notebook:

> 'Of Kant it is admiringly claimed that he teaches *philosophizing*, not *philosophy*, just as if a man were to teach carpentry without ever making a single table or chair, door or cupboard.'[29]

Thus Hegel views Kant, Jacobi and Fichte as part of the same philosophical trend in which with historical necessity the hollowness and problematic nature of modern individualism is reproduced in its various stages. The morality of objective idealism with which he now confronts the advocates of subjective idealism culminates in the proposition that 'absolute ethical totality is nothing other than *a people*'.[30] And he goes on to summarize his own position by citing the answer given by a Pythagorean in Diogenes Laertius to a question about the nature of the best education: 'Make him the citizen of a well-ordered nation'.[31]

Engels clearly perceived this fundamental tenet of Hegelian morality and he counterpoised it to Feuerbach's abstract ethical views.

'Hegel's ethics or doctrine of moral conduct is the philosophy of right and embraces: (1) abstract right: (2) morality: (3) social ethics, under which again are comprised: the family, civil society and the state. Here the content is as realistic as the form is idealistic. Besides morality the whole sphere of law, economy, politics is here included.'[32]

Both in content and structure Hegel's ethics in his Jena period differs from its later formulation. But as a general account of the tendencies operative in his views on ethics Engels' description may be taken to apply to this period also. Now that we have to some extent extracted Hegel's positive ideas from his polemic with subjective idealism we must confront the problem of presenting the issues discussed by Hegel in their proper context. The first prerequisite for this is an understanding of how, according to Hegel, modern civil society came into being, for it is the substantive nature and the institutions of that society that form the context for his ideas on morality.

## NOTES

1  *Erste Druckschriften*, p. 230.
2  Ibid., p. 323.
3  Ibid., p. 340.
4  Ibid., p. 315.
5  Ibid., p. 328.
6  Ibid., pp. 323 and II.
7  Ibid., p. 333f.
8  *Dialektik der Natur*, Berlin 1952, p. 327.
9  *A contribution to the Critique of Political Economy. Introduction*, London 1971, p. 211.
10  *Werke*, Vol. II, p. 186.
11  Ibid., pp. 176ff. This artificial procedure is not simply Fichte's own invention. The ephorate has always formed part of the tradition of revolutionary natural law; it is to be found in Calvin and later in the so-called monarchomachic writers. (i.e. 'The Bearers of the sword against monarchy'. The reference is to an anonymous French pamphlet *Vindiciae Contra Tyrannos* of 1579 and the monarchomachic tradition includes writers like Althusius and Grotius, better known for their contributions to the debate on natural law.—*Trans.*) Cf. K. Woltzendorff, *Staatsrecht und Naturrecht in der Lehre vom Widerstandsrecht des Volkes*, Berlin 1916, p. 123ff.

12   Lasson, p. 79.
13   Ibid., pp. 360ff.
14   *Erste Druckschriften*, p. 65.
15   Ibid., p. 67.
16   Lasson, p. 367.
17   *Erste Druckschriften*, p. 331f.
18   Kant has in mind here the situation arising when the original owner of the deposit has died and no-one except the man with whom he has left it for safe-keeping knows of its existence. The question is: can it be moral for its present possessor to keep it for good?—*Trans.*
19   *Critique of Practical Reason*, Chap. I, § IV, Theorem III, Abbott's translation, London 1967, p. 115.
20   Lasson, p. 352.
21   Quoted by Hegel, *Erste Druckschriften*, p. 305.
22   Ibid., p. 306f.
23   Ibid., p. 306. In this context it is not without interest to observe that the highly influential modern 'philosopher of life', Georg Simmel, also criticized the Kantian argument about deposits, but from a Jacobian rather than a Hegelian position. He believed that Kant overlooked the uniqueness of every moral action, that the circumstances surrounding every moral action, both the external and internal factors, are different. He concluded from this that there are such things as moral laws, but they are what he calls 'individual laws', i.e. there is an individual law for each individual case. Since Hegel has often been linked with irrationalism and the 'philosophy of life' in recent years (e.g. by Kroner) this 'parallel' between Hegel, Simmel and Jacobi is highly instructive. Cf. Simmel, *Kant*, 6th edition, Munich and Leipzig 1927, pp. 145ff.
24   F. Schlegel, *Prosaische Jugendschriften*, Vienna 1906, Vol. II, p. 86.
25   Kroner, *Von Kant bis Hegel*, Tübingen 1921, Vol. II, p. 271.
26   On this point cf. the chapter on neo-Hegelianism is my book *The Destruction of Reason*, Berlin 1954; *Werke*, Vol. 9, pp. 474–505.
27   *Erste Druckschriften*, p. 307f.
28   Ibid., p. 312f.
29   Rosenkranz, p. 552. This type of enthusiasm for Kant became very fashionable in the Age of Imperialism, especially in Simmel's conflation of Kantianism and '*Lebensphilosophie.*'
30   Lasson, p. 368.
31   Ibid., p. 392.
32   Engels, *Feuerbach*, Selected Works, Vol. II, p. 345.

# CHAPTER FOUR

# Hegel's view of history in his first years in Jena

THE main thrust of Hegel's thought was historical right from the start. In his Berne period, as we have seen, his historical approach even antedated his philosophical consciousness of the problems of history. The latter was only activated after he had abandoned his Jacobin illusions about the possibility of a classical revival and was able to face up the problems of the dialectics of modern civil society. From that point on Hegel's thought focused on the dialectical interaction of historical development and philosophical system. We may remind the reader that both the *Philosophy of Right* and the portrayal of objective mind in the *Encyclopaedia* culminate in world history as the highest expression of human reason. Moreover, one of Hegel's chief objections to Fichte was that Fichte's notion of freedom was isolated from the objective laws of nature and history.

Hence respect and even reverence for the realities of history form the foundation of Hegelian philosophy. In the introductory remarks to the Jena continuation of the Frankfurt essay *The German Constitution* Hegel saw it as his task 'to understand what is'. And elsewhere in the same introduction he elucidated that remark in a manner which high-lights both the idealistic and the forward-moving dialectical elements on his thought: 'Whatever can no longer be understood, has ceased to exist.'[1]

Hegel's historicism, then, by no means implies the glorification of the past or even the vindication of certain aspects of the present, by suggesting that they have a long, honourable past behind them. That is the standpoint of the Romantic historians or of those influenced by Romanticism in one form or another. Hegel always repudiated such attitudes. Earlier on (p. 231f.), we quoted a passage from Hegel's essay on *Natural Law* in connection with the problem of positivity. He spoke there of the way in which the institutions of feudalism which had once corresponded to the historical conditions of the people had, in the course of time, developed the symptoms of a lifeless 'positivity'. Hegel calls for a real historical understanding of the question.

> But 'it would exceed its competence and its truth if this meant that it was necessary to justify for the present a law that had truth only in the past. On the contrary, the historical understanding of a law which had its ground in past customs and a now defunct life alone shows precisely that it lacks all meaning and sense in the living present. . . .'

And in this context he makes a distinction between the 'history of a past life' and the 'definite idea of a present death.'[2] It is therefore a straightforward falsification to try and assimilate Hegel to the pseudo-historicism of the Romantic movement.

Nor did he share the historical methodology of Romanticism which came into existence at around this time. Under the influence of counter-revolutionary journalism we witness the spread of a view according to which the 'organic nature' of historical structures and processes precluded the intervention of the conscious will of men to change their own fate in society. Furthermore, the 'continuity' of history is placed in sharp contrast to attempts to interrupt the process once it has *begun to take place*. Both these views imply that revolution is essentially an 'unhistorical aberration', an 'unhistorical piece of bungling' which simply disrupts the 'true course' of history. It is highly characteristic of the growing reactionary and romantic elements in Schelling's thought that he began to make significant concessions to this theory in his *Lectures on the methodology of academic study* of 1803—the very time when he was collaborating with Hegel.

The practical methodological significance of what we have come to recognize as Hegel's specific form of dialectics can now be seen in his approach to history. All of his comments on history at this period show that he has remained true to his conception of dialectics, to the idea that historical continuity is a union of continuity and discontinuity. We shall see later on how the French Revolution occupied a central place in Hegel's view of history in Jena. And we may easily appreciate that this should be reflected in his methodology too. We have already shown that the *Jena Logic* contains a version of the theory of the transition from quantity to quality. The 'nodal line of measure relations' (which was not finally formulated until much later)[3] enshrines the doctrine which enables Hegel to view qualitative leaps, violent disruptions of continuity as necessary, organic constituents of a process.

In the concluding paragraphs of the essay on *Natural Law* Hegel does in fact raise the matter of qualitative leaps in history—and even though he does not explicitly name the Romantics, the polemic is clear enough. Although the passage is rather long we must quote it in full because of the sharp contrast it presents between Hegel and Romanticism. It should be noted incidentally that by 'individuality' he means the individuality of a people.

'And although nature advances regularly within a particular configuration, its advance is not mechanical, but accelerates progressively and enjoys the new configuration it has reached. Having leapt into it, it reposes there a while. Just like a shell that gives a final burst as it reaches its goal and there rests a moment, or the heated metal which melts not like wax, but suddenly, and then remains in that condition. For a phenomenon is a transition to its absolute opposite, i.e. it is infinite, and this emergence from infinity, or from nothing is a leap, and a configuration in all its newly born strength is something that at first exists for itself, before it becomes aware of its relation to another. And in the same way a growing individuality has both the joy of the leap and also the duration of enjoyment in its novel form. Until it gradually becomes exposed to the negative and then suddenly is shattered.'[4]

This clearly demonstrates the worthlessness of the modern theories of Meinecke, Rosenzweig and Heller which attempt to turn Hegel into a forerunner of Ranke.

Turning now to an analysis of Hegel's detailed historical views, we must begin by observing that we do not possess any comprehensive historical survey from his own hand at this period. All we have are scattered remarks in a number of writings, especially in the essay on *The German Constitution* which he worked over again in 1801–2 only to leave it finally as a fragment. In addition a number of ideas can be gleaned from the polemical essays, projected systematic works, etc. Although we shall concentrate on the first few years in Jena we shall also refer to the recently published manuscripts of his lectures for the years 1803–4 and 1805–6, both for his views on history and for our next chapter on economics. These lectures often contain superior formulations of the problems which emerged in the period following his arrival in Jena. It is true that *The Phenomenology of Mind* already contains a systematic survey of the history of mankind, but as we shall see later on, Hegel's objectives in that work are quite specific and so even the *Phenomenology* does not present us with a comprehensive account of world history in the sense that this may be said of the later lectures on the philosophy of history.

*The German Constitution* though begun in Frankfurt was not given any more detailed historical backing until Hegel took it up again in Jena. When he did so he focused on one problem: that of the origins of the national and political disunity of Germany, much more clearly than he had earlier on. The other side of Hegel's interest, however, the question of a solution to this problem is as intractable for Hegel now as it had been before. Indeed, his more penetrating historical analysis forces Hegel to give this lack of clarity concrete shape.

In the course of a discussion of the national disunity of Italy and the attempts made to remedy it—a situation which offered many parallels with Germany—Hegel has occasion to mention Macchiavelli. He too had made an acute analysis of his country's disunity, and he too had failed to discover a definite path to national unification. This was why the figure of Theseus was to be found in his writings, for according to legend Theseus had succeeded in putting an end to the discord and anarchy of the Athenian people and had laid the foundations for the political and national unity of Athens. Macchiavelli longed for an Italian Theseus and the young Hegel, no less muddled than he, followed suit.[5]

The legendary figure of Theseus is to be found not only in *The German Constitution* but in a number of other early writings and the Hegel-literature is full of the most ingenious conjectures about his possible identity. (Macchiavelli had had Cesare Borgia in mind, at least for a time.) According to Dilthey, Hegel's Theseus was Napoleon. Rosenzweig has a very tortuous argument that identifies Theseus with the Austrian Archduke Charles.[6]

Since the latter hypothesis is an important stone in the edifice designed to show that Hegel is a forerunner of Ranke and Bismarck, we must comment on it a little more fully. This will have the useful advantage of enabling us at the same time to isolate Hegel's views of Austria and Prussia, the two great German powers of his day. His attitude towards Prussia is one of radical rejection. He considers it to be an alien power threatening Germany from without.

> 'Just as the old Roman Empire was destroyed by barbarians from the North, so too the principle of destruction entered the Romano-German Empire from the North. Denmark, Sweden, England and above all Prussia are the foreign powers whose standing as estates of the Empire has given them at one and the same time a centre separate from the German Empire and a constitutionally proper influence on its affairs.'[7]

The young Hegel does not allow himself to be dazzled by legends about Frederick the Great of Prussia. He discerns no national interest in the wars fought by Prussia, but merely 'the private interest of the warring powers'. They are comparable to the cabinet wars of the *ancien régime*. Nor does Hegel see any merit in the aggrandizement of Prussia in the course of the eighteenth century as far as Germany as a whole is concerned. It just means the enlargment of that power 'whose size is the greatest impediment to the unity of the German state'. And elsewhere he speaks with the greatest contempt of the soulless bureaucracy of the Prussian state.[8] This view of Prussia remains dominant up to the fall of Napoleon. We find it expressed in letters from the Bamberg and Nuremberg periods, as well as Hegel's Nuremberg writings. At the time of the transformation which caused Hegel to come to terms with the fall of Napoleon and the Restoration, a transformation which was precipitated by an inner crisis and which ushered in the resigned mood of his entire later life, there was also a change in Hegel's view of Prussia. A discussion of the development in Hegel's views in this later period is quite beyond the scope of the present work. His attitude towards Austria as expressed in *The German Constitution* is a shade friendlier than his view of Prussia and there is even a certain sympathy, especially for Joseph II's attempted reforms. But with reference to the overall fate of Germany, Austria and Prussia stand on much the same footing.[9] This gives us some idea of the value of Rosenzweig's hypothesis.

As to the identification of Theseus with Napoleon, this is altogether more plausible. Some years later, at the time when he was engaged in writing *The Phenomenology of Mind*, Hegel was unquestionably a supporter of Napoleon's. From his letters it is quite clear that he was in favour of the policy of the Confederation of the Rhine and remained so until the fall of Napoleon. We have also seen how in 1803 in the course of his criticism of Fichte's ephorate he implied approval of Napoleon's *coup d'état*. It looks as if we can trace the origins of this view back to 1801, but we cannot do this with absolute certainty. For in the fragments dealing with religion and the philosophy of history from the earliest period in Jena, published by Rosenkranz and dating in all probability from the time of the essay on the German constitution, Hegel talks of the birth of a new religion in the following terms:

> It will come into being 'when there is a *free people* and when reason has once again given birth to reality as an ethical spirit which will be bold enough *to take shape on its own soil and from a sense of its own majesty.*'[10]

This seems to suggest that at this time Hegel still cherished the hope of a complete national liberation of Germany, even though the basis for such hopes is of course completely obscure. However, the impossibility of resolving this problem is of no great moment for our understanding of Hegel's development since we have a completely clear picture of the road he took from disillusion with the revolution to enthusiastic support for Napoleon. The question of *when* he began to feel this enthusiasm and what hesitations he experienced is of secondary importance.

The importance of the pamphlet on the German Constitution for Hegel himself was that for the first time he established the developmental pattern of social formations and states. Later on he would fill in various gaps in the pattern, but he never modified the main points. He regarded the Migration of Nations and the feudal system arising out of it as the social and political starting-point of the nations of modern Europe.

> 'The system of representation is the system of all modern European states. It did not exist in the forests of Germany, but it did arise from them; it marks an epoch in world-history. The continuity of world-culture has led the human race beyond oriental despotisms, through a republic's world-dominion, and then out of the fall of Rome into a middle term between these extremes. And the Germans are the people from whom this third universal form of the world-spirit was born. This system did not exist in the forests of Germany, because each

nation must on its own account have run through its own proper
course of development before it encroaches on the universal course of
world-history. The principle which elevates it to universal dominion
first arises when its own peculiar principle is applied to the rest of the
unstable cosmos. Thus the freedom of the German peoples necessarily
became a *feudal system* when in their conquests they deluged the rest of
the world.'[11]

Starting from this general position Hegel proceeds to give a sketch of
the development of feudalism and its collapse in the most important European states. These he divides into two major groups. The first, includes
England, France and Spain where the central monarchical power was
able to subdue feudalism. The second comprises Germany and Italy
where the dissolution of feudalism disrupted national life and prevented
the emergence of unified nations.

Of the nations belonging to the first group it is only France that Hegel
analyses in any detail. He shows how France and Germany arrive at
opposed national formations from a common source in feudalism.

'France as a state and Germany as a state had both of them the same
two inherent principles of dissolution. In the one Richelieu completely annulled these principles and thus raised it to be one of the
most powerful states; in the other he gave these principles full play
and thus cancelled its existence as a state.'[12]

Hegel relates how in France the absolute monarchy was able to subjugate
both the nobility which had hitherto asserted its independence and the
Huguenots who had for a time maintained a state within the state. He
shows how the power of both had to be destroyed if the unity of the
French monarchy were to be maintained. He emphasizes the part played
by Richelieu and does so in such a way that we can clearly discern his
later concept of the 'world-historical individual'.

Here too the neo-Hegelians have attempted to distort a Hegelian
theory, this time by connecting it with the cult of the hero stemming
from Treitschke and Nietzsche. However, Hegel is never concerned
with the person but with the world-historical principle which takes possession of a person at a particular moment in time, using him as an instrument for its own ends. This is undoubtedly his later position and we find
it quite explicit here too. Writing of the French feudal lords he says:

'They gave way not to Richelieu as a man but to his genius, which
linked his person with the necessary principle of the unity of the
state . . . . And herein lies political genius, in the identification of an
individual with a principle. Given this linkage, the individual must
carry off the victory.'[13]

Hegel's remarks about England, Spain and the other nations in this group are brief and even cursory. The only point to notice is that he is completely indifferent to the relative merits of political forms (monarchy or republic). What is important in his eyes is that these countries

'have succeeded in attaining a centre in which all power is concentrated . . . it does not matter in this connection whether this centre has a strictly monarchical or republican form.'[14]

(On this point as on a number of others Hegel follows the example of Hobbes.)

In his remarks on Italy pride of place goes to a frank and objective analysis of Macchiavelli's theories. It should be noted that Hegel does not regard Macchiavelli as the general theoretician of mindless power-politics, a view favoured by the Meinecke school. Hegel sees Macchiavelli as a despairing protagonist of the Italian national unity that had been lost but which he wished to restore; he views him as a national revolutionary who is eager to attain this great goal with whatever means present themselves. In this context Hegel briefly turns aside to discuss Frederick the Great's pamphlet attacking Macchiavelli, dismissing it as a 'school-exercise' whose empty sanctimoniousness was revealed by Frederick's own actions. Nor does Hegel omit to point out the contrasting historical actions of the two men: Macchiavelli fought for the unity of Italy, his critic, the Crown Prince Frederick, was

'a modern monarch whose whole life and actions have expressed most clearly the dissolution of the German state into independent states.'[15]

Hegel's views about the dissolution of German feudalism and the origins of the fragmentation of Germany into a host of petty states are already known to us from the Frankfurt version of this essay (see p. 138ff.). According to Hegel the decisive turning point here was the Peace of Westphalia (1648) which brought the Thirty Years' War to an end:

'In the Peace of Westphalia this statelessness of Germany was organised. . . . Germany renounced establishing itself as a secure state-power and surrendered to the good will of its members.'[16]

On the basis of this historical outline Hegel goes on to speak of the necessity of the modern state. In his eyes it came into being with the *over-coming* of the French Revolution. To understand Hegel rightly on this point we should recollect that Hegel thinks of the French Revolution as having been overcome in the double sense of *aufgehoben*: annulled but also preserved. In his remarks about the Revolution in *The German Constitution* his dislike of its radical democratic elements is again quite explicit: he talks of them as if they were to be simply equated with anarchy. But his conclusions, which we quote at length, make it obvious that he was very far from agreeing to Restoration of any type and that, once the threat of 'anarchy' was removed, he saw the French Revolution as the opening of a new epoch in world history.

'Anarchy has become distinguished from freedom; the notion that a firm government is indispensable for freedom has become deeply engraved on men's minds; but no less deeply engraved is the notion that the people must share in the making of laws and the management of the most important affairs of state. The guarantee that the government will proceed in accordance with law, and the co-operation of the general will in the most important affairs of state which affect everyone, the people finds in the organisation of a body representative of the people. This body has to sanction payment to the monarch of a part of the national taxes, but especially the payment of extraordinary taxes. Just as in former days the most important matter, i.e. personal services, depended on free agreement, so nowadays money, which comprises influence of every other kind, is equally so dependent. Without such a representative body, freedom is no longer thinkable. . . .'[17]

It is quite clear from this that Hegel's standpoint is that of a constitutional monarchy (with the reservation we have mentioned of his indifference, not always explicit, to the relative merits of republics and monarchies). And on closer examination we can see that the model to which his ideal increasingly approximates is that of the Napoleonic states. On the other hand, we can also perceive his later conception of the organic growth of the modern state out of feudalism and the collapse of feudalism.

But in this process the French Revolution makes a definite caesura. We must emphasize this, since the more recent critics have made repeated efforts to obscure his anti-feudalism and his contempt for the Restoration, so as to buttress their view of a development from Hegel through Ranke to Bismarck. This interpretation occasionally resorts to quite crude methods of falsification. Thus Rosenzweig, who knows Hegel's writings much too well to be unable to detect his affinities with Napoleonic conceptions of the state, simply falsifies the whole character of the Napoleonic age: he regards it as a restoration of the *ancien régime* in the style of Louis XIV.[18] On this premise it is not hard to convert Hegel firstly into an adherent of the *ancien régime* and secondly into a forerunner of Bismarck. In reality the conception of constitutional monarchy we have outlined goes back to Montesquieu and is a construct based partly on the model of England, partly on that of the Napoleonic states, i.e. it is grounded above all in the idea of a state that has undergone a bourgeois revolution. We can see this theme running through all of Hegel's reflections on the constitution. We shall come back to his discussion of the character of the Estates in another context. All we need say here is that his proposals for a system of taxation are derived largely from English models (especially that of Adam Smith) and that he is implacably opposed to all vestiges of feudalism in financial affairs (in particular to incomes derived from royal domains.)[19]

We can see Hegel's view of the modern state most clearly if we return to his mystical redeemer, Theseus. Theseus makes his appearance not just in the section of *The German Constitution* dealing with Macchiavelli, but also in a later, rather obscure passage, whose meaning, however, we hope to be able to elucidate by means of reference to his later lectures (1805–6). Hegel says:

> 'This Theseus would have to have the magnanimity to grant to the people he would have had to fashion out of dispersed units a share in matters that affected everyone. Since a democratic constitution, like the one Theseus gave to his own people, is self-contradictory in modern times and in large states, this share would have to be some form of organization. Moreover, even if the direction of the state's power which he had in his hands could insure him against being repaid, as Theseus was, with ingratitude, still he would have to have character enough to be ready to endure the hatred with which Riche-lieu and other great men who wrecked men's private and particular interests were saddled.'[20]

Hegel's repudiation of democracy is no longer a novelty for us. Nor is there anything original, either for Hegel or in itself, in the idea that democracy was a form of government adapted to the city-states of anti-quity, but not for the great states of the modern world. It is in fact a com-monplace of the French Enlightenment. Hegel's bluntness about it is of interest mainly because it is linked to the idea that had begun to emerge in Frankfurt and would appear in its mature form in Jena to the effect that classical civilization now *belonged entirely to the past* and that by that token it had ceased to act as an ideal for us. We shall return to this issue later and deal with it in detail.

As to Theseus himself, we must not allow ourselves to be misled by Hegel's very general and in parts obscure language. Of course, for Hegel the 'world-historical individual' is always the executive organ of the world-spirit. But, as we shall see at once, what always matters to him is the hegemony of the historically necessary principle and Theseus is no more than an organ, an instrument of world history, who is needed to carry out the latest part of the process. The antithesis that Hegel estab-lishes here between Theseus and the masses is the antithesis between the 'world-historical individual' who has grasped the necessity for a general change after the French Revolution, and the inert, retrograde German nation that has fallen asleep in the midst of its wretched semi-feudal and petty-bourgeois existence and that defends this existence against all attacks by appealing to its 'private interests and particular nature'. When Hegel speaks of the ingratitude that has been the lot of great men like Richelieu, his expression is unfortunate although its meaning is clear enough: Richelieu earned the deadly hatred of the feudal nobility of France whose independent power he destroyed. Hegel recognizes this fact and applies it to Germany. The observation is correct, but the expression is misleading because the nobles had no grounds for gratitude towards Richelieu and so their hatred cannot be construed as ingratitude.

In the Lectures of 1805–6 Hegel again reverts to the idea of Theseus as the founder of states. He remarks that all states were founded through force and that the agents of this force were often great men.

> 'This is the merit of the great man: that he knows and can express the absolute will. All assemble around his banner; he is their god. It was thus when Theseus founded the state of Athens; so it was too when a terrible force took hold of the state, and indeed everything, in the French Revolution. This force is not despotism, but *tyranny*, pure, terrifying dominance. But it is *necessary* and *just* to the extent to which it *constitutes and maintains the state as a real individual entity*. This state is the simple absolute spirit which is certain of itself and which acknowledges nothing but itself, neither concepts of good and evil, scandalous and base, nor cunning and deceit. It is above all these since in it evil is reconciled with itself.'[21]

Hegel goes on to say almost at once that this tyranny is necessary to educate the people to 'obey' the new institutions. Here too it would be an error to put too much weight on the word 'obey'. Undoubtedly, these remarks do convey Hegel's anti-democratic sentiments. But their main thrust is generated by the realization that outmoded institutions such as feudalism must not only be destroyed by force, but that tyranny is essential if attempts to restore them are to be frustrated. Hegel regards tyranny as an essential *transitional* phase between two social and political systems.

> 'Tyranny is overthrown by the people because it is abhorrent and base, etc.: but in reality only because it is superfluous. *The memory of the tyrant is execrated*; but in this respect too he is only spirit certain of itself. As such he has acted as a god only in and for himself and expects the ingratitude of his people. If he were wise he would divest himself of his powers as they became superfluous; but as things are his divinity is only the divinity of an animal: blind necessity which deserves to be abominated as sheer evil. This was the case with *Robespierre*. His power abandoned him, because *necessity had abandoned him* and so he

was violently overthrown. That which is necessary comes to pass, but each portion of necessity is normally assigned to individuals. One is counsel for the prosecution and one for the defence, another is judge, a fourth executioner; but all are necessary.'[22]

Here too it is easy enough to criticize the obscurities in Hegel's mythological view of history. It is obvious that he understood very little of the actual class struggles in France and the processes which led to the establishment and the fall of the Jacobin dictatorship. But his great understanding of history enabled him to see that this dictatorship, which he abhorred so profoundly, was a necessary and inevitable turning-point in world history: the establishment of the modern state. But even if it is true that Hegel did not understand the actuality of the class struggles in France, he was by no means blind to their social import. On the contrary, in a marginal note to the same course of lectures he wrote:

'Thus the French Revolution, abolition of formally *privileged estates*, once this achieved, abolition of inequality between estates, *idle talk*.'[23]

This makes it quite clear that Hegel unreservedly accepted the bourgeois content of the French Revolution, its achievement in establishing modern bourgeois society and the liquidation of feudal privileges and could even accept the historical necessity of the Jacobin Terror as an instrument for effecting this world-historical transformation (in which it is Robespierre who is equated with Theseus.) But he at once expresses his disapproval ('idle talk') when the radical democracy of the day overshoots the limits of bourgeois society. We believe that these observations should help to clarify the social and historical significance of Hegel's obscure and even mystical references to Theseus.

We shall return later to the question of how Hegel envisaged the internal social structure of the modern state. For the moment we need only point out that the figure of the monarch is not thought of as a ruler after the style of the *ancien régime*.

'He is the fixed, *immediate* knot binding the whole. The spiritual bond is *public* opinion.'

Clearly, what Hegel has in mind here is a society whose free, self-activating movement holds the whole in balance.

'The whole, however, is the mean, it is the free spirit which comports itself independently of these wholly fixed extremes [i.e. the particular spheres of society—G.L.]; the whole is independent of the knowledge of individuals or of the nature of the ruler; he is a knot that binds nothing.'[24]

And just as it is not possible to identify the hereditary monarch with the ruler of the *ancien régime*, so too it is quite illicit to equate the first or the universal class of the Jena philosophy of society with the old hereditary nobility, as Rosenzweig does. At this period Hegel still had not lost his old antipathy for the aristocracy that he had felt in Berne. When he wrote about democracy, aristocracy and monarchy in the *System of Ethics* he described aristocracy in these terms:

'It is distinguished from the absolute constitution by heredity and even more by its possessions, and because it has the form of the absolute but not its essence, it is the worst of all.'[25]

As we shall see, Hegel accepts the principle of heredity only for the monarchy; he rejects it for the nobility. In another passage where he makes a comparison between the monarch and the rest of the population he observes:

'*Other individuals have value only to the extent to which they are "externalized" cultivated beings, as what they have made of themselves.*'[26]

Thus Hegel holds fast to the view of a society divided into classes, the individual membership of those classes, however, is to be determined by individual talents and achievements, and not by heredity. Hegel's conception of the 'universal class' at this time corresponds much more closely to the military and bureaucratic nobility of Napoleon than to the hereditary nobility of the semi-feudal states.

Hegel gives a comprehensive historical survey of medieval and modern Europe. He regards the entire development from the Migration of Nations to the present as a single unified process. The French Revolution is not a discordant note, disrupting the 'organic' process, as the thinkers of counter-revolutionary Romanticism believed, but on the contrary: it is a great purifying world-crisis which releases vital new elements and activates existing tendencies which will promote the healthy development of the different nations. Of course, 'anarchy' has to be conquered. But we have also seen how this anarchy is an essential constituent of the dialectical course of history and that Robespierre plays as vital a role in French history and indirectly in world history too, as Richelieu had done before him. The function of both was to create an opening for a new constellation of the spirit.

With this far-sighted and uninhibited view of history Hegel stands more or less alone in his age, and not merely in Germany. With its freedom from moralizing, from all antipathy and sympathy his attitude to the great events of the day and their interconnections is reminiscent of Balzac, who had also understood the history of France from the collapse of feudalism to the February Revolution in terms of a unified, if crisis-ridden, process. This becomes quite explicit in an ingenious and witty conversation between Catherine de Medici and the young lawyer

Robespierre who are brought together to make the point that both had striven for the same thing, namely the unity of the French nation, and although she had failed, he would succeed. And the disciple of Hegel, Heinrich Heine, put forward the same idea—admittedly from a more highly developed stage of society when he linked Richelieu, Robespierre and Rothschild as 'the three most terrible levellers in Europe, the greatest scourge of the nobility'.[27]

This perspective on history spells the conscious and final demise of Hegel's youthful dream of the revolutionary return of classical civilization. Its central problem is not just to discover and isolate the specific features of the modern world, which ever since Frankfurt had ceased to be thought of entirely as symptoms of decadence. Quite on the contrary, his present view is based on an overall conception of history as a whole, so that the dissolution of the classical city-states is not merely historically necessary—it had been necessary even in Berne—but a *higher* social principle has emerged from the ruins.

Thus Antiquity has definitively lost its privileged place in the philosophy of history. As early as the fragment from the first part of his stay in Jena published by Rosenkranz Hegel had referred to the beautiful world of antiquity as 'only a memory'.[28] In his later Jena writings Hegel describes this higher principle of the modern world in detail. In his Lectures of 1805–6 Hegel draws the following parallel between a Greek community and a modern society:

'*This is the higher principle of the modern age that the Ancients and Plato did not know*. In days of old a *beautiful* public life was the custom of all, beauty as the immediate union of the universal and the particular, a work of art in which no part was separated from the whole, but a wonderful union of the self-knowing self and its representation. But the absolute self-knowledge of the individual did not yet exist, this absolute being-in-oneself was not present. The Platonic republic, like the state of Sparta, is the disappearance of the self-knowing individual.'

And in a marginal note Hegel adds, by way of explanation:

'Plato did not set up an ideal, he interiorized the state of his age within himself. But this state has perished—the Platonic republic is not realizable—because it lacked the principle of absolute individuality.'[29]

Thus individuality or, more precisely, the absolute value of personality in its singularity, is the novel principle that divides the ancient and the modern worlds. This idea too is familiar to us from Frankfurt and its roots, i.e. the individual as crucial in distinguishing between ancient and modern society, go back even into the Berne period. Even in Berne Hegel had observed that the 'privatization' of human life which entered the ancient city-states at the time of their decay had led to individuality and individualism in the modern sense. At that time, however, he had steadfastly opposed the inroads of the private on the public. It represented for him merely the subjective side of lifeless 'positivity', of societal existence. The Frankfurt crisis was precipitated by the fact that Hegel gradually began to modify this blunt rejection of 'positivity'. We have already seen how the concept of 'positivity' gradually became historicized and how it became saturated with an increasingly complex dialectic of progressive and reactionary elements. This dialectic was set in motion as Hegel came to believe that the 'positive' spheres of modern society were also the products of human activity, and that they came into being and perish, flourish or petrify, in constant interaction with the actions of men. Hence they cease to appear as something ready-made, as an inexorably objective 'Fate'.

The change in his views had begun in Frankfurt. For the time being it was confined to an objective dialectic of 'positivity' itself. Then the increasing interaction between subject and object, between the subjectivity of the action of individuals in society and the objectivity of the social formations 'rigidly' confronting them, came to influence and even to determine the dialectic, without ever reaching the point of being identified as its central principle. This was reserved for the Jena period and became fully conscious in its culminating phase in The *Phenomenology of Mind*. There, as we shall see, the old concept 'positivity' is replaced by the new terms 'externalization' or 'alienation'.

As with all genuine thinkers, the change is not merely one of terminology. The distinction between 'positivity' and 'externalization' conceals a profound extension of Hegel's earlier ideas; 'Positivity' refers to a *quality* of social formations, objects, *things*. 'Externalization' is a specific mode of human *activity* as a result of which specific social institutions *come into being* and acquire the objective nature peculiar to them. The change in terminology is very gradual indeed. The term 'externalization' recurs with increasing frequency, 'positivity' becomes more and more rare, but for years the two terms are used alongside each other. Not until the Lectures of 1805–6 are the two concepts properly distinguished.

What the change involves is a growing understanding of the real nature of modern civil society and above all of its progressive nature. We have already seen how Hegel had begun in Frankfurt to think of antiquity as irrevocably belonging to the past. In Jena he becomes more firmly convinced of this. But his conviction is accompanied by a profound feeling of sorrow that this world of really living and really human beings should have vanished forever. We have quoted the remark in Rosenkranz where Hegel refers to antiquity as 'only a memory'. The continuation of the same passage is very revealing of his mood at that time:

'The union of mind and its reality must be sundered. The ideal principle must constitute itself as a universal, the real must become fixed as a particular, and nature must lie between them, a *desecrated corpse*.'[30]

The sorrow expressed here forms the basic mood of Hölderlin's poetry and it also confers undying beauty on the great philosophical poems of Schiller. Schiller did not stop short at that point, but advanced in the realm of aesthetics—and of course on the basis of a broad philosophical culture—to an understanding of the specific characteristics of the modern world and its poetry. Hegel travelled the same path, but in a much more resolute and systematic fashion. It is worth remarking, however, that the greatness of both Schiller and Hegel in their reflections on the philosophy of history rests in great measure on the fact that they never really overcame this sorrow. In the absence of a proletariat, the humanist critique of capitalism could only discover a concrete standard of what man had lost and had to lose in the course of the undeniable progress made by capitalism by recalling that authentic humanity which had flourished in the city-states of Greece. The recognition of the progressive nature of capitalism never degenerated in the writings of the German classics into a superficial glorification of modern bourgeois society after the manner of Bentham. The notion, developed by idealist dialectics, of a contradictory progress is very intimately bound up with this relationship to antiquity.

The opposition between ancient and modern society develops increasingly into a distinction between the immediate and the mediate socialization of man. And the more Hegel comes to appreciate the necessary and progressive nature of mediation, the more he perceives that the increasingly complex system of mediations that results is the product of man's own activity. This in turn leads him to the discovery that the involvement of human personality in these social mediations and the sharp decline of unmediated relationships between men does not entail the diminution of human individuality. On the contrary, real human individuality only begins to unfold in the course of this process, through the creation of a mediating system of institutions which progressively become more 'thing-like' and which increasingly 'externalize' human personality. We have just cited Hegel's remark (p. 312) to the effect that in modern civil society individuals exist only as externalized beings, 'as what they have made of themselves'. What this means is that Hegel was beginning to see that if mankind is to develop all its capacities and awaken into deed all the talents that sleep within it, then it must overcome its merely natural immediacy. His regret at the passing away of that beauty that was to be found in the natural immediacy of life in antiquity expresses his dialectical conviction that human progress has been dearly bought.

Since for Hegel modern civil society was the highest stage of mankind, beyond which he neither did nor could see anything higher, his recognition of the passing of antiquity had the sense of an irrevocable loss. His greatness as a thinker is that he was able to hold fast to both aspects of this contradiction without concerning himself overmuch with the further contradictions that it provoked in him. (These contradictions are connected partly with certain illusions about a classical revival prevalent in the Napoleonic era.) When Hegel's first liberal critics, such as Haym, reproach him with a nostalgia for antiquity, a failure to recognize the merits of modern bourgeois society, what they really lament is Hegel's failure to become the German Bentham.

The insoluble contradiction that appears here in Hegel, one with which we shall concern ourselves in a later chapter, is a contradiction in history itself. The contradictions in the nature of progress could only be fully grasped in a concrete, materialist and dialectical manner once the class struggle had developed to the point where a proletarian humanism could envisage the recovery of immediate personal and social relations as the result of the emancipation of humanity through socialism. The proper understanding of human development in historical materialism provides an essential corrective to Hegel, but in a manner diametrically opposed to those who have criticized him from the point of view of a vulgar and superficial liberal belief in progress. Marx's view of antiquity as the normal childhood of mankind, the theory of primitive communism, of tribal society and its dissolution as the foundation of classical civilization is infinitely superior to Hegel's conception, but does not conflict with its basic historical premises or his brilliant insights into the development of mankind.

In the Lectures of 1805–6 Hegel formulates the difference between ancient and modern civilization as follows:

'This is the beautiful, happy freedom of the Greeks which has been and still is the subject of such envy. The nation is divided into citizens and is at the same time *one individual*, the government. It interacts only with itself. The same will informs *the individual* and the universal. The renunciation of the particular will is the immediate preservation of that same will. But a higher abstraction is necessary, a greater opposition and culture, a *deeper* spirit. It is the realm of ethical life: each man is himself *ethical*, immediately at one with the universal. There are no protests here; each man knows himself to be *immediately* universal, i.e. he renounces his particularity, without knowing it as such, as *this* self, as essence. The higher division [of the modern world—Trans.] is that each person *retires completely into himself*, knows his self *as such* to be the essence; he comes to the wilful idea that although separated from the universal, he is yet absolute and in his knowledge he possesses his *absoluteness immediately*. As a particular being he leaves the universal quite free; he has complete autonomy, he relinquishes his *reality* and has value only in *his knowledge*.'[31]

We shall have to analyse at length the problems that emerge from this comparison. In the process we shall encounter the philosophical sources of a number of the social and political limitations of Hegel's thought, such as, for example, Hegel's belief that his use of 'externalization' as the foundation of modern individuality provides him with a philosophical reason for rejecting democracy in modern society. For the present it is sufficient to focus on the contrast which lies at the roots of his conception of history. On the one hand, he sees the development of human personality as a product of the process of 'externalization' or alienation, and, on the other hand, he recognizes that the man-made system of 'externalized' mediations injects into society an objective means of propulsion and that one of the chief tasks facing the philosophy of history is to investigate the laws of that process. After some observations concerning the monarch as a 'natural' person and the rest of the citizenry as 'externalized' persons Hegel adds:

'The entire community is tied as little to the one as to the other; it is the self-supporting indestructible substance. Of whatever sort the ruler or the citizens may be, the community is complete in itself and preserves itself.'[32]

The increasing tension apparent here between the growing subjectivity and autonomy of human individuality on the one hand, and the simultaneous emergence of a no less autonomous system of man-made social mediations—this is in Hegel's eyes the fundamental problem of modern civil society, and of his own philosophy of history.

Although the term has not yet been employed, it is very clear that *political economy* provides this problem with its scientific underpinning. It is necessary, therefore to consider Hegel's views on economics and to estimate their importance for his dialectics. This will involve us in two sets of problems. On the one hand, there is the question of the extent to which Hegel's understanding of the contradictions of capitalism advanced his dialectical method. On the other hand, we must consider the problem arising from Hegel's inadequate grasp of the contradictions of capitalism and the difficulties that this involved him in, i.e. the way in which his defective understanding of economics and the limitations of his idealist dialectics mutually determined each other.

NOTES

1   Lasson, pp. 5 and 3.
2   Ibid., p. 408f.

3   Hegel's decisive discussion of the extremely important concept of 'the nodal line of measure relations' *(die Knotenlinie der Massverhält-nisse* can be found in the *Logic*, Section 3, Chapter 2 (pp 366–371 in Miller's translation, London 1969). It is here that he defines what he means by the transition from quantitative to qualitative change. He is primarily concerned to attack the maxim that 'nature does not make leaps', repudiating the notion that the concept of 'gradualness' can help to elucidate the phenomenon of change. From his illustrations it is evident that that his view of transition can be applied widely to areas ranging from musical scales and chemical combinations to moral and political history.—*Trans.*

4   Lasson, p. 410.
5   Ibid., pp. 111ff.
6   Dilthey, Vol. IV, p. 136. Rosenzweig, Vol. I, p. 125f.
7   Knox and Pelczynski, p. 198.
8   Rosenzweig, pp. 93, 91 and 31.
9   Ibid., p. 127.
10   Rosenkranz, p. 141.
11   Knox and Pelczynski, p 203. The reference to 'the forests of Germany' is a polemical corrective to Montesquieu, *L'Esprit des Lois*, Bk IX, chap. 4 Hegel historicizes Montesquieu's account but does not explicitly take issue with his overall view.
12   Knox and Pelczynski, p. 216.
13   Ibid., p. 216.
14   Ibid., p. 217.
15   Ibid., p. 223.
16   Ibid., p. 214.
17   Ibid., p. 234.
18   Rosenzweig, Vol. II, p. 3f.
19   Ibid., p. 493f. *Realphilosophie*, Vol. II, p. 253f.
20   Knox and Pelczynski, p. 241.
21   *Realphilosophie*, Vol. II, p. 246.
22   Ibid., p. 247f.
23   Ibid., p. 260.
24   Ibid., p. 250f.
25   Lasson, p. 498.
26   *Realphilosophie*, Vol. II, p. 252.
27   Heine, *Ludwig Börne, Werke*, ed. Elster, Vol. VII.
28   Rosenkranz, p. 136.
29   *Realphilosophie*, Vol. II, p. 251.
30   Rosenkranz, p. 136.
31   *Realphilosophie*, Vol. II, p. 249f.
32   Ibid., p. 252.

# CHAPTER FIVE

# Hegel's economics during the Jena period

THE *Economic and Philosophic Manuscripts* contain a crucial criticism of *The Phenomenology of Mind* in the course of which Marx gives a precise account of the achievement and the failing of Hegel's views on economics.

> 'Hegel's standpoint is that of modern political economy. He grasps *labour* as the *essence* of man—as man's essence in the act of proving itself: he sees only the positive, not the negative side of labour. Labour is man's *coming to be for himself* within *alienation*, or as *alienated man*'.[1]

The present analysis of Hegel's economic views will confirm the accuracy of Marx's observations, both in their positive and in their negative aspects. Hegel did not produce a system of economics within his general philosophy, his ideas were always an integral part of his general social philosophy. This is in fact their merit. He was not concerned to produce original research within economics itself (for this was not possible in Germany at the time), but instead he concentrated on how to integrate the discoveries of the most advanced system of economics into a science of social problems in general. Moreover—and this is where we find the specifically Hegelian approach—he was concerned to discover the general dialectical categories concealed in those social problems.

Needless to say, Hegel was not the first to attempt a synthesis of economics, sociology, history and philosophy. The isolation of economics from other areas of the social sciences is a feature of the bourgeoisie in its decline. The leading thinkers of the seventeenth and eighteenth centuries ranged through the whole territory of the social sciences and even the works of the outstanding economists such as Petty, Steuart and Smith constantly ventured forth beyond the frontiers of economics in the narrower sense. The real originality of Hegel's exploitation of economic discoveries would only be determinable in the context of a history which sets out to explore the interplay between philosophy and economics in modern times (and even in Plato and Aristotle). Unfortunately Marxist historiography has entirely failed to make such a study, so that almost all the necessary groundwork still remains to be done. The pointers to such work in the writings of the classics of Marxism–Leninism have been largely ignored.

Nevertheless, something can be said about Hegel's originality here with relative accuracy. For the philosophy of the Renaissance and the Enlightenment, mathematics, geometry and the burgeoning natural sciences and especially physics were the decisive models. The outstanding thinkers of the day consciously based their method on that of the natural sciences, even when their own subject-matter was drawn from the social sciences. (Of course for that very reason, it would be interesting and important to discover whether and to what extent the study of economics had had any influence on their general methodology.) Not until the advent of classical German idealism can any other methodological model be found. Naturally, this model also had its antecedents, I need refer only to Vico whose great achievement in this area has likewise been consigned to oblivion by the scholars of subsequent ages.

The shift in methodology is a product of the new emphasis on the 'active side' in philosophy, an emphasis to be found more clearly in Fichte than in Kant. But subjective idealism necessarily held a far too constricted and abstract view of human praxis. In subjective idealism all interest is concentrated on that aspect of human praxis that can be included under the heading of 'morality'. For this reason the economic views of Kant and Fichte had little bearing on their general method. Since Fichte viewed society, as well as nature, as a merely abstract backdrop for the activities of moral man, for '*homo noumenon*', and since that backdrop confronted morality as an abstract negative, rigidly indifferent to the moral activity of man, it naturally did not occur to him to investigate the particular laws governing it. His *Closed Commercial State* shows that he had made a study of the Physiocrats. However, the main ideas of the work are not influenced by the knowledge he had acquired. It is a dogmatic attempt to apply the moral principles of his philosophy to the various spheres of society and represents a Jacobin dictatorship of morality over the whole of human society.

Kant's thought is in some respects more flexible and less narrow than Fichte's but he too does not get beyond the point of applying general abstract principles to society. Kant had indeed read the works of Adam Smith and gleaned from them an insight into the nature of modern bourgeois society. But when he attempts to put this knowledge in the service of a philosophy of history he arrives at quite abstract formulae. This is what happens in his interesting little essay *Idea for a Universal History with a Cosmopolitan Purpose*, where he attempts to make a philosophical study of the principles of progress in the development of society. He comes to the conclusion that Nature has furnished man with an 'unsocial sociability' as a result of which man is propelled through the various passions towards progress.

'Man desires harmony; but Nature understands better what will profit his species; it desires conflict.'[2]

The influence of English thinkers is clear enough. All that has happened is that the discussions have become more abstract without gaining any philosophical substance. For the end-product is nothing but the bad infinity of the concept of infinite progress.

When considering Hegel's critique of the ethics of subjective idealism, we saw how unremittingly hostile he was to this moralistic narrow-mindedness, this unyielding contrast between the subjective and objective sides of social activity. We may infer from this that his view of economics differed fundamentally from that of Kant and Fichte. It was for him the most immediate, primitive and palpable manifestation of man's social activity. The study of economics should be the easiest and most direct way to distil the fundamental categories of that activity. In our discussion of the Frankfurt period we pointed out in a rather different context that Hegel was decisively influenced by Adam Smith's conception of labour as the central category of political economy. Hegel's extension of the idea and systematic exposition of the principles underlying it in *The Phenomenology of Mind* have been fully defined by Marx in the work previously referred to:

> 'The outstanding achievement of Hegel's *Phenomenology* . . . is thus first that Hegel conceives the self-creation of man as a process, conceives objectification as loss of the object, as alienation and as transcendence of this alienation; that he thus grasps the essence of *labour* and comprehends objective man—true, because real man—as the outcome of man's *own labour*. The *real*, active orientation of man to himself as a species being, or his manifestation as a real species being (i.e. as a human being), is only possible by the utilization of all the *powers* he has in himself and which are his as belonging to the *species*—something which in turn is only possible through the cooperative action of all mankind, as the result of history—is only possible by man's treating these generic powers as objects: and this, to begin with, is again only possible in the form of estrangement.'[3]

Our examination of Hegel's historical attitudes has shown us that he was guided in his ideas by an image of modern bourgeois society, but that this image was not simply a reproduction of the retrograde conditions of Germany in his age (even though this did sometimes colour his view of the world much against his will). What he had in mind was rather a picture of bourgeois society in its most developed form as the product of the French Revolution and the Industrial Revolution in England. With this image in his mind and with his insight into the role of human activity in society Hegel attempted to overcome the Kantian and Fichtean dualism of subjectivity and objectivity, inner and outer, morality and legality. His aim was to comprehend socialized man whole and undivided as he really is within the concrete totality of his activity in society.

His efforts were directed at the ultimate questions of philosophy. Kant had greatly advanced the 'active side' of philosophy, but the price he had paid was to tear philosophy into two parts, a theoretical and a practical philosophy which were only tenuously connected. In particular, Kant's idealist sublimation of morality barred the way to an explanation of the concrete interplay between man's knowledge and his praxis. Fichte's radicalism only deepened the gulf still further. Schelling's objectivity did indeed take a step towards reconciling the two extremes but he was not sufficiently interested in the social sciences and his knowledge of them was too slight to make any real difference here. Moreover, he was far too uncritical of the premises of Kant and Fichte.

It was left to Hegel to introduce the decisive change here and what enabled him to do so was the possibility of exploiting the conception of labour derived from Adam Smith. We shall show later on that, given his own philosophical premises, it was not possible for Hegel to explore the economic, social and philosophical implications of this idea to their fullest extent. But for the present the important thing is to emphasize that his approach to the problem was determined by his complete awareness of its crucial significance for the whole system.

To clarify the interrelations between knowledge and praxis it is essential to make the concept of praxis as broad in thought as it is in reality, i.e. it is vital to go beyond the narrow confines of the subjective and moralistic approach of Kant and Fichte. We have looked at the polemical aspect of this problem in some detail. If we now move on to Hegel's own views on economics in Jena we notice at once that he thinks of human labour, economic activity as the starting-point of practical philosophy. In the *System of Ethics* Hegel introduces his discussion of economics with these words:

'In the potency of this sphere . . . we find the very beginning of a thorough-going ideality, and the true powers of practical intelligence.'[4]

In the Lectures of 1805–6 this idea has gained in profundity. In a discussion of tools Hegel remarks:

'Man makes tools because he is rational and this is the first expression of his *will*. This will is still abstract will—the pride people take in their tools.'[5]

As is well known the 'pure will' is the central category of the ethics of Kant and Fichte. If Hegel now sees tools as the first expression of the human will it is evident that he is employing the term in a way directly opposed to theirs: for him it implies a conception of the concrete totality of man's activity in the actual world. And if he describes this will as abstract this just means that he intends to proceed from there to the more complex and comprehensive problems of society, to the division of labour etc., i.e. that one can only talk concretely of these human activities by talking of them as a whole.

In economics Hegel was an adherent of Adam Smith. This is not to say that his understanding of all the important problems of economics was as profound as that of Smith. It is quite clear that he did not have the sort of insight into the complex dialectic of the 'esoteric' economic issues that Marx reveals in the *Theories of Surplus Value*. The contradictions in the basic categories of capitalist economics that Marx unveils there never became apparent to Hegel. But what Hegel does succeed in doing is to clarify a number of categories objectively implied by Smith's economics to a degree that goes far beyond Smith himself.

Hegel's views on economics are put forward first in the *System of Ethics*. This work represents the high point of his experiments with Schelling's conceptual system. In consequence the whole argument in this work is tortuous, over-complicated and over-elaborate. Moreover, the static mode of presentation often impedes the dialectical movement implicit in the ideas themselves. Much more mature and characteristic of Hegel himself are the essays on *Natural Law* and the economic arguments contained in the Lectures of 1803–4 and especially those of 1805–6. The latter contain the most developed statement of his economic views in Jena before the *Phenomenology* and embody an attempt to trace a systematic dialectical progression from the simplest categories of labour right up to the problems of religion and philosophy. Wherever possible we shall refer to this latest stage of his development. It goes without saying that the *Phenomenology* is a much more advanced stage even than this. But the particular method used in that work has such profound implications for his general approach that it is very hard to select extracts from it for discussion for our present purposes, although we shall of course return to it later on.

Since the literature on Hegel has with very few exceptions simply ignored his preoccupation with economics, and since even those bourgeois writers who were not unaware that it did form an important part of his work were nevertheless quite unable to assess its significance, it is absolutely essential in our view to begin by stating just what his views were. Marx has shown both the importance and the limitations of Hegel's ideas in the passages we have quoted. But he presupposes a knowledge of those ideas; it is obvious, then, that we must begin with exposition if we wish to be able to appreciate the rightness of Marx's assessment. We can reserve our own criticisms for a later stage.

It is very striking that even in his earliest attempts to systematize economic categories Hegel not only uses the triadic form but also that the various categories are grouped together by means of Hegel's very characteristic mode of deduction. Thus in the *System of Ethics* he begins his discussion with the triad: need, labour and enjoyment and he advances from there to the other, higher triad: appropriation, the activity of labour itself and possession of the product.[6] We have already spoken of Hegel's definition of labour as a purposive annihilation of the object as man originally finds it and we have quoted Hegel's own statements about this (p. 172ff.). In the Lectures of 1805–6 we find the whole matter treated much more clearly, both the content (the relations of man to the object in the work-process) and the form (the dialectics of deduction as the dialects of reality itself). Hegel writes:

'Determination [dialectic] of the object. It is, therefore, content, distinction—distinction of the deductive process, of the syllogism, moreover: singularity, universality and their mediations. But (a) it is *existent*, immediate; its mean is thinghood, dead universality, *otherness*, and (b) its *extremes* are *particularity*, *determinacy* and individuality. In so far as it is other, its activity is the self's—since it has none of its own; that extreme is beyond it. As thinghood it is passivity, communication of [the self's] activity, but as something fluid, it contains that activity within itself as an alien thing. Its other extreme is the antithesis (the particularity) of this its existence and of activity. It is *passive*; it is for another, it [merely] touches that other—it exists only to be dissolved (like an acid). This is its being, but at the same time, active shape *against* it, communication *of the other*.

'Conversely, [dialectic of the subject]: in one sense, activity is only something communicated and it [the object] is in fact the communication; activity is then pure recipient. In another sense, activity is activity *vis-à-vis* an other.

'(The gratified impulse is the *annulled labour* of the self; this is the object that labours in its stead. Labour means to make oneself immanently [*diesseitig*] into a *thing*. The division of the impulsive self is this very process of making oneself into an object. ((Desire [by contrast] must always start again from the beginning, it does not reach the point of separating labour from itself.)) The impulse, however, is the unity of the self as made into a thing.)

'Mere activity is *pure* mediation, movement; the mere gratification of desire is the pure annihilation of the object.'[7]

The dialectical movement that Hegel attempts to demonstrate here has two aspects. On the one hand, the object of labour, which only becomes a real object for man in and through labour, retains the character which it possesses in itself. In the Hegelian view of labour one of the crucial dialectical moments is that the active principle (in German idealism; the idea, concept) must learn to respect reality just as it is. In the object of labour immutable laws are at work, labour can only be fruitful if these are known and recognized. On the other hand, the object becomes another through labour. In Hegel's terminology the form of its thinghood is annihilated and labour furnishes it with a new one. This formal transformation is the result of labour acting on material alien to it yet existing by its own laws. At the same time this transformation can only take place if it corresponds to the laws immanent in the object.

A dialectic of the subject corresponds to this dialectic in the object. In labour man alienates himself. As Hegel says, 'he makes himself into a thing.' This gives expression to the objective laws of labour which is independent of the wishes and inclination of the individual. Through labour something universal arises in man. At the same time, labour signifies the departure from immediacy, a break with the merely natural, instinctual life of man. The *immediate* gratification of one's needs signifies, on the one hand, the simple annihilation of the object and not its transformation. On the other hand, thanks to its immediacy it always starts up again in the same place: it does not develop. Only if man places labour between his desire and its fulfilment, only if he breaks with the instinctual immediacy of natural man will he *become* fully human.

The humanization of man is a theme treated at length in the Lectures of 1805–6. Hegel's idealist prejudices make themselves felt in his belief that man's spiritual awakening, his transition from the world of dream, from the 'night' of nature to the first act of conceptualization of naming, his first use of language, can take place independently of labour. In tune with this he puts labour on a higher plane altogether, one where man's powers are already developed. However, isolated remarks indicate that he did have some glimpses of the dialectic at work here. Thus in his discussion of the origins of language he shows how in the process both object and the self come into being. In a marginal note, however, he observes:

'How does this necessity or stability *come about* so that the self becomes its *existence*, or rather, that the self, that is its *essence*, becomes its existence? For existence is *stable*, thing-like; the self is the form of pure unrest, movement or the night in which all is devoured. Or: the self is *present, (universally)* immediate in the name; now through mediation it must become itself through itself. Its unrest must become stabilization: the movement which annuls it as unrest, as pure movement. This [movement] is *labour*. Its *unrest* becomes *object*, stabilized plurality, order. Unrest becomes *order* by becoming object.'[8]

The decisive importance of labour in the process of humanization is shown most vividly when Hegel writes his 'Robinsonade': his story of the transition to civilization proper. His attitude to the so-called state of nature is quite free of the value judgement, whether positive or negative,

which the state of nature so frequently invited in the literature of the Enlightenment. His view is closest to that of Hobbes and is expressed most
trenchantly in a paradoxical thesis which he defended at his doctoral
examination:

> 'The state of nature is not unjust, and for that very reason we must
> leave it behind us.'[9]

The development of this idea leads Hegel as early as *The System of
Ethics* to formulate his 'Robinsonade' of 'master and servant'. This theme
is taken up again in *The Phenomenology of Mind* and remains an integral
part of his philosophy ever after.[10]

Let us now consider this, Hegel's most mature statement of the transition from a state of nature of civilization, as we find it set out in *The
Phenomenology of Mind*. The starting-point is Hobbes' *bellum omnium contra
omnes*, the internecine wars of man in his natural condition which Hegel
describes as annihilation without preservation. The subjugation of some
people by others gives rise to the condition of mastery and servitude.
There is nothing novel or interesting in this. What is important is
Hegel's analysis of the relations between master and servant and between
them and the world of things.

> 'The master, however, is the power controlling this state of existence,
> for he has shown in the struggle that he holds it to be merely some-
> thing negative. Since he is the power dominating existence, while this
> existence again is the power controlling the other (the servant), the
> master holds, *par conséquence*, this other in subordination. In the same
> way the master relates himself to the thing mediately through the ser-
> vant. The servant being a self-consciousness in the broad sense, also
> takes up a negative attitude to things and annuls them; but the thing is,
> at the same time, independent for him, and, in consequence, he
> cannot, with all his negating get so far as to annihilate it outright and
> be done with it; that is to say, he merely works on it. To the master,
> on the other hand, by means of this mediating process, belongs the
> immediate relation, in the sense of the pure negation of it, in other
> words he gets the enjoyment. What mere desire did not attain, he
> now succeeds in attaining, viz. to have done with the thing, and find
> satisfaction in enjoyment. Desire alone did not get the length of this
> because of the independence of the thing. The master, however, who
> has interposed the servant between it and himself, thereby relates
> himself merely to the dependence of the thing, and enjoys it without
> reserve. The aspect of its independence he leaves to the servant, who
> labours upon it.'[11]

It is just this unconfined dominion, this wholly one-sided and unequal
relationship that precipitates its own reversal and makes of the master a

purely ephemeral episode in the history of the spirit while the seminal moments in the development of man spring from the consciousness of the servant.

'The *truth* of the independent consciousness is accordingly the *consciousness of the servant*. . . . Through work this consciousness comes to itself. In the moment which corresponds to desire in the case of the master's consciousness, the aspect of the non-essential relation to the thing seemed to fall to the lot of the servant, since the thing there retained its independence. Desire has reserved to itself the pure negating of the object and thereby unalloyed feeling of self. This satisfaction, however, is purely ephemeral, for it lacks *objectivity* or *subsistence*. Labour, on the other hand, is desire restrained and checked, it is the ephemeral postponed; in other words labour shapes and fashions the thing. The negative relation to the object passes into the *form* of the object, into something that is permanent and remains; because it is just for the labourer that the object has independence. This negative mediating agency, this activity giving shape and form, is at the same time the individual existence, the pure self-existence of that consciousness, which now in the work it does is externalized and passes into the condition of permanence. The consciousness that toils and serves accordingly attains by this means the direct apprehension of that independent being as its self.'[12]

We know from Hegel's philosophy of history that individuality is the principle that elevates the modern world to a higher plane than that reached by antiquity. In his youth Hegel had completely overlooked the presence of slavery in Greek civilization and directed his attention exclusively towards the non-labouring freeman of the city-states. Here, however, the dialectics of work leads him to the realization that the high-road of human development, the humanization of man, the socialization of nature can only be traversed through work. Man becomes human only through work, only through the activity in which the independent laws governing objects become manifest, forcing men to acknowledge them i.e. to extend the organs of their own knowledge, if they would ward off destruction. Unalloyed enjoyment condemns to sterility the master who interposes the labour of the servant between himself and the objects and it raises the consciousness of the servant above that of his master in the dialectics of world-history. In the *Phenomenology* Hegel sees quite clearly that the labour of man is sheer drudgery with all the drawbacks that slavery entails for the development of consciousness. But despite all that the advance of consciousness goes through the mind of the servant and not that of his master. In the dialectics of labour real self-consciousness is brought into being, the phenomenological agent that dissolves antiquity. The 'configurations of consciousness' which arise in the course of this dissolution: scepticism, stoicism and the unhappy consciousness (primitive Christianity) are without exception the products of the dialectics of servile consciousness.

Hegel's discussion of work has already shown that the mere fact of work indicates that man has exchanged the immediacy of nature for a universal mode of existence. As he investigates the determinations of work he uncovers a dialectic in which technology and society interact to the benefit of both. On the one hand, Hegel shows how tools arise out of the dialectics of labour. Starting with the man, who by using tools, exploits the laws of nature operative in work, he passes through various transitions until he reaches the nodal point where the concept of the machine emerges. On the other hand, though inseparably from the first process, Hegel shows how the universal, i.e. the socially determined aspects of work lead to the increasing specialization of particular types of labour, to a widening gulf between the labour of the individual and the satisfaction of the needs of the individual. As we have emphasized, these two processes are intimately connected. As a disciple of Adam Smith Hegel knows perfectly well that a high degree of technical competence presupposes a highly advanced division of labour. By the same token he is no less aware that the perfection of tools and the development of machinery itself contributes to the extension of the division of labour.

Descriptions of this process can be found in all of Hegel's writings on economics. We shall quote his most mature statement of the theme in the Lectures of 1805–6:

'The existence and scope of natural wants is, in the context of existence as a whole, vast in number; the things that serve to satisfy them are processed, their *universal inner* possibility is posited as something external, as *form*. This processing is itself manifold; it is *consciousness transforming itself into things*. But since it is universal it becomes abstract labour. The wants are many; to absorb this quantity into the self, to work, involves the *abstraction* of the *universal* images, but it is also a self-propelling formative process. The self that *exists for self is abstract*; it does indeed labour, but its labour too is abstract. Needs are broken down into their various aspects; what is abstract in them is their self-existence, activity, labour. *Because work is only performed for an abstract self-existing need the work performed is also abstract.* This is the concept, the truth of the desire we have here. And the work matches the concept. There is no satisfaction of all the desires of the individual as he becomes an object for himself in the life he has brought forth. *Universal* labour, then, is *division* of labour, saving of labour. Ten men can make as many pins as a hundred. Each individual, because he is an individual labours for *one* need. The content of his labour goes beyond *his own* need; he labours for the needs of many, and so does everyone. Each person, then satisfies the needs of many and the satisfaction of his many particular needs is the labour of many others.'[13]

Hegel also deduced technical progress from this dialectic of the increasing universality of labour. Naturally, his arguments relating to tools and machines were determined down to the very last detail by Adam Smith. Germany as it then was, and especially those parts known personally to Hegel, could not provide him with the direct experience of the sort of economic realities that might yield such knowledge. On such matters he had to rely almost exclusively on what he had read about England and the English economy. His own contribution was to raise the dialectic immanent in economic processes to a conscious philosophical level.

The double movement which takes place in man and in the objects and instruments of work is on the one hand the increasing division of labour with its consequent abstraction. On the other hand, there is a growing understanding of the laws of nature, of how to induce nature to work for man. Hegel always emphasizes the connection between the division of labour (together with the human labour transformed by it) and technical progress. For example he demonstrates the necessity for machines in the following passage:

'His [i.e. man's] labour itself becomes quite mechanical or belongs to a quite simple order of things. But the more abstract it is, the more he becomes pure abstract activity, and this enables him to withdraw from the work-process altogether and to replace his own labour with the activity of external nature. He requires only movement and this he finds in external nature, or in other words, pure movement is just a relationship of the abstract forms of space and time—abstract external activity, *machines*.'[14]

But Hegel is the disciple of Adam Smith (and *his* teacher Ferguson) not only as an economist, but also as a critical humanist. That is to say, he is concerned to describe a process, to explain its subjective and objective dialectic as fully as possible and to show that it is not just an abstract necessity but also the necessary mode of human progress. But he does not close his eyes to the destructive effects of the capitalist division of labour and of the introduction of machinery into human labour. And unlike the Romantic economists he does not present these features as the unfortunate side of capitalism which has to be improved or eliminated so as to achieve a capitalism without blemish. On the contrary, he can clearly discern the necessary dialectical connections between these aspects of capitalism and its progressive implications for both economics and society.

In the Lectures of 1803–4, too, Hegel speaks of the movement towards universality as a result of the division of labour and the use of tools and machinery. He begins by illustrating the dialectical process, by showing how the inventiveness of an individual may lead to a general improvement, a higher level of universality:

'Faced with the general level of skill the *individual sets himself up as a particular,* sets himself off from the generality and makes himself even more skilful than others, invents more efficient tools. But the really universal element in his particular skill is his *invention* of something universal; and the *others acquire it from him* thereby annulling his particularity and it becomes the common immediate possession of all.'

Thus through the use of tools the activity of man becomes formal and universal, but it remains 'his activity'. Not until the arrival of the machine is there any qualitative change. He goes on to describe the impact of machinery on human labour.

'With the advent of *machines* man himself annuls his own formal activity and makes the machine perform all his work for him. But this deception which he practises against nature and with the aid of which he remains fixed within the particularity of nature, does not go unavenged. For the more he profits from the machine, the more he subjugates nature, then the more degraded he himself becomes. He does not eliminate the need to work himself by causing nature to be worked on by machines, he only postpones that necessity and detaches his labour from nature. His labour is no longer that of a living being directed at living things, but evades this negative living activity. Whatever remains becomes more *mechanical.* Man only *reduces* labour for society as a whole, not for the individual; on the contrary, he increases it since the more mechanical the work is the less valuable it is and so the more labour he must perform to make good the deficiency.'[15]

When one considers the time when these remarks were written, and especially the fact that they were written in Germany they clearly represent a quite remarkable insight into the nature of capitalism. He cannot be reproached for thinking of capitalism as the only possible form of society and for regarding the function of machines in capitalism as their only possible function. On the contrary, it must be emphasized that Hegel displays the same refreshing lack of prejudice and narrowmindedness that we find in the classical economists Smith and Ricardo: he can see the general progress in the development of the forces of production thanks to capitalism and the capitalist division of labour while at the same time he is anything but blind to the dehumanization of the workers that this progress entails. He regards this as inevitable and wastes no time in Romantic lamentations about it. At the same time he is much too serious and honest a thinker to suppress or gloss over unpalatable truths.

This can be seen particularly clearly when he proceeds to argue that the division of labour in capitalism and the increase in the forces of production leads necessarily to the pauperization of great masses of people. The economic causes of this have already been indicated in the remarks just quoted. In the Lectures of 1805–6 he describes the process even more vividly:

'But by the same token the abstraction of labour makes man more mechanical and dulls his mind and his senses. Mental vitality, a fully aware, fulfilled life degenerates into empty activity. The strength of the self manifests itself in a rich, comprehensive grasp of life; this is now lost. He can hand over some work to the machine; but his own actions become correspondingly more formal. His dull labour limits him to a single point and the work becomes more and more perfect as it becomes more and more one-sided. . . . No less incessant is the frenetic search for new methods of simplifying work, new machines etc. The individual's skill is his method of preserving his own existence. The latter is subject to the web of chance which enmeshes the whole. Thus a vast number of people are condemned to utterly brutalizing, unhealthy and unreliable labour in workshops, factories and mines, labour which narrows and reduces their skill. Whole branches of industry which maintain a large class of people can suddenly wither away at the dictates of fashion, or a fall in prices following new inventions in other countries, etc. And this entire class is thrown into the depths of poverty where it can no longer help itself. We see the emergence of great wealth and great poverty, poverty which finds it impossible to produce anything for itself.'[16]

Hegel elsewhere presents this insight in summary, almost epigrammatic, form:

'Manufacturers and workshops found their existence on the misery of a class.'[17]

Hegel here describes social realities with the same ruthless integrity and the same habit of plain speaking that we find in the great classical economists. The insight is almost incredible by German standards of the time and it is not in the least diminished by certain misconceptions that make their appearance from time to time, such as the illusion that the ills he describes could be remedied by the intervention of the state or the government. For such idealistic illusions are always accompanied by a sober assessment of the limits imposed on state intervention. Moreover, as we know, he consistently opposes all theories that advocate what he regards as excessive government control of economics and society. He does indeed cherish the belief that the state and the government have it in their power to reduce the glaring contrast of wealth and poverty, and above all the notion that bourgeois society as a whole can be kept in a state of 'health' despite the gulf between rich and poor. We can obtain a clear picture of Hegel's illusions in this respect if we quote one of his remarks from the *System of Ethics*:

> 'The government should do all in its power to combat this inequality and the destruction it brings in its wake. It may achieve this immediately by making it harder to make great profits. If it does indeed sacrifice a part of a class to mechanical and factory labour, abandoning it to a condition of brutalization, it must nevertheless preserve the whole in as healthy a state as is possible. The necessary or rather immediate way to achieve this is through a proper constitution of the class concerned.'[18]

This amalgam of profound insight into the contradictions of capitalism and naive illusions about the possible panaceas to be applied by the state marks the whole of Hegel's thought from this time on. In *The Philosophy of Right* Hegel formulates his view in essentially the same terms but on a higher level of abstraction. And we see that his illusions are largely unchanged except that he now regards emigration and colonization as possible methods of ensuring the continued health of capitalist society. He says there:

> 'It hence becomes apparent that despite an excess of wealth civil society is not rich enough, i.e. its own resources are insufficient to check excessive poverty and the creation of a penurious rabble.'[19]

Thus in Hegel's eyes capitalism becomes an objective totality moving in accordance with its own immanent laws. In the *System of Ethics* he gives the following description of the nature of its economic system (or as he calls it: the system of needs):

> 'In this system the ruling factor appears to be the unconscious, blind totality of needs and the methods of satisfying them. . . . It is not the case that this totality lies beyond the frontiers of knowledge in great mass complexes. . . . Nature itself ensures that a correct balance is maintained, partly by insignificant regulating movements, partly by greater movements when external factors threaten to disrupt the whole.'[20]

Thus, like Adam Smith, Hegel sees the capitalist economy as an autonomous self-regulating system. It is self-evident that in 1801 he could only think of disruptions as caused by external factors and not as crises brought about by contradictions within the system itself.

In the context of this self-propelling system of human activities, of objects which generate this activity and are activated by it, Hegel's concept of alienation receives a new, more concrete definition. In the Lectures of 1803–4 Hegel describes this system as follows:

> '*These manifold* exertions of needs as things must realize their concept, their abstraction. Their general concept must be a thing like them, but one which as an abstraction can represent them all. *Money* is that materially existing concept, the unitary form or the possibility of all objects of need. By elevating need and work to this level of generality a vast system of common interest and mutual dependence is formed among a great people, a self-propelling life of the dead, which moves hither and thither, blind and elemental and, like a wild animal, it stands in constant need of being tamed and kept under control.'[21]

This 'self-propelling life of the dead' is the new form that 'positivity' assumes in Hegel's thought: 'externalization'. Work not only makes men human according to Hegel, it not only causes the vast and complex array of social processes to come into being, it also makes the world of man into an 'alienated', 'externalized' world. Here, where we can see the concept embedded in its original, economic context, its dual character becomes particularly obvious. The old concept of 'positivity' had placed a one-sided emphasis on the dead, alien aspect of social institutions. In the concept of 'externalization', however, we find enshrined Hegel's conviction that the world of economics which dominates man and which utterly controls the life of the individual, is nevertheless the product of man himself. It is in this duality that the truly seminal nature of 'externalization' is to be found. Thanks to it the concept could become the foundation and the central pillar of the highest form of dialectics developed by bourgeois thought.

At the same time this duality points to the limitations of Hegel's thought, the dangers implicit in his idealism. His great sense of reality leads him to emphasize this duality in his analysis of bourgeois society and its development, erecting its contradictions into a conscious dialectic. Despite the sporadic appearance of illusions he is much too realistic even to play with the idea that 'externalization' could be overcome within capitalist society itself. But, for that very reason, as our discussion of *The Phenomenology of Mind* will show, he extends the concept of 'externalization' to the point where it can be annulled and reintegrated in the subject. Socially, Hegel cannot see beyond the horizon of capitalism. Accordingly, his theory of society is not utopian. But the idealist dialectic transforms the entire history of man into a great philosophical utopia: into the philosophical dream that 'externalization' can be overcome in the subject, that substance can be transformed into subject.

In the Lectures of 1805–6 Hegel gives a very simple and succinct definition of the process of 'externalization' '(a) In the course of work I make myself into a thing, to a form which *exists*. (b) I thus externalize this my existence, make it into *something alien* and *maintain* myself in it.'[22]

These latter remarks refer to exchange. The previous quotation alluded to money. Thus in the course of our discussion of Hegel's view of capitalist society we have advanced to the higher categories of political economy: exchange, commodity, value, price and money.

Here too, in all essentials, Hegel's remarks do not diverge from their basis in Adam Smith. But we know from Marx's criticism that this is where the contradictions in Smith's work appear, rather than in what he has to say about work and the division of labour. And naturally enough Hegel's dependence on Smith shows to much greater disadvantage here than in his discussion of work. There was no economic reality in Germany at the time which might have given Hegel the opportunity to test these categories himself and perhaps arrive at his own critique of Smith. Hegel's achievement is that he was not confined to the contemporary economic state of Germany, his philosophical examination of economic ideas does not reflect the backwardness of Germany, but is an attempt to analyse what his reading had taught him about the English economy. Given the greater complexity of economic categories and the fact that they inevitably contained contradictions, the effect on Hegel was that partly he just accepted those contradictions without comment and without recognizing them for what they were and partly he was forced to seek analogies in German conditions and to explain advanced theories in terms of the backward German economy.

This situation is apparent at many points in Hegel's discussions of economics, most of all in the fact that despite his fine dialectical appraisal of the philosophical implications of the Industrial Revolution in England he comes to the conclusion that the central figure in the whole development of capitalism was that of the merchant. Even where Hegel speaks with perfect justice about the concentration of capital and where he shows his understanding that this concentration is absolutely indispensable in capitalism he thinks of it in terms of merchants' capital.

'Like every mass wealth becomes a force. The increase of wealth takes place partly by chance, partly through its universality, through distribution. It is a focus of attraction which casts its net widely and collects everything in its vicinity, just as a great mass attracts a lesser. To him that hath, more is given. Commerce becomes a *complex* system which brings in money from all sides, a system which *a small business could not make use of*.'[23]

Hegel talks here in very general terms. But we shall later on consider other statements, especially those concerned with the class structure of society from which it is apparent what when Hegel thinks of concentration of capital on a large scale, he always has merchants' capital in mind. For example, in the *System of Ethics* he refers to commerce as the 'highest point of universality' in economic life. This cannot be a matter for astonishment if we reflect that the most developed form of manufacturing in Germany at that time was linen weaving which was still organized as a cottage industry.

For these reasons we can see all sorts of uncertainties and confusions in Hegel's definition of economic categories, especially in his notion of value. Hegel never understood the crucial development in the classical theory of value, viz. the exploitation of the worker in industrial production. It is in this light above all that we may interpret Marx's criticism of Hegel, quoted above, that Hegel only took the positive ideas about labour from classical economics, and not the negative sides. We have seen that he clearly sees and frankly describes the facts about the division of society into rich and poor. However, many progressive French and English writers saw and proclaimed this before him without coming any closer than he to a labour theory of value.

Hegel's confusion here is reflected also in his definition of value. He constantly hesitated between subjective and objective definitions, without ever coming down on one side or the other. Thus in the later Lectures we find such subjective definitions as: 'Value is *my opinion* of the matter.'[24] And this despite earlier statements, both in the same lectures and elsewhere, from which it is quite clear that he wishes to think of value as an objective economic reality. Thus in the *System of Ethics* he says that the essence of value lies in the equality of one thing with another:

> 'The abstraction of this equality of one thing with another, its concrete unity and legal status is *value*; or rather value is itself equality as an abstraction, the ideal measure; whereas the real, empirical measure is the price.'[25]

However, all these unclarities and hesitations, and the confusion of economic and legal categories such as we find in this quotation and which we shall consider in detail later on, do not prevent Hegel from pursuing the dialectics of objective and subjective, universal and particular right into the heart of the categories of economics. In the process he brings a mobility into economic thought which was only objectively present in the works of the classical economists, or to put it in Hegelian terms; a mobility which was only present in itself, implicitly, and not explicitly, for us. Not until forty years later in the brilliant essay of the young Engels in the *Deutsch–Französische Jahrbücher* do the dialectical structure and the interplay of the various categories of economics come to the surface once again, and this time, of course, at quite a different theoretical level, both economically and philosophically.

For example, in his analysis of exchange Hegel writes as follows:

'The concept [of exchange] is mobile, it is destroyed in its antithesis, it absorbs the other thing opposed to it, replacing that which it previously possessed; and it does so in such a way that that which existed before as an idea, now enters as a reality . . . an ideal which by its nature was at first a practical ideal, existing prior to enjoyment. Externally, exchange is two-fold, or rather a repetition of itself; for the universal object, superfluity, and then the particular, viz. need, is in substance a single object, but its two forms are necessarily repetitions of the same thing. But the concept, the essence of the matter is transformation . . . and its absolute nature is the identity of opposites. . . .'[26]

The dialectic of the categories of economics is much more striking in Hegel's discussion of money where the reader can see even more clearly how in his view the structure of capitalism culminates in trade. Writing about the role of money he says:

'All needs are comprehended in this single need. Need which had been a need for a thing, now becomes merely an *idea*, unenjoyable in itself. The object here is valid only because it *means* something, and no longer *in itself*, i.e. to satisfy a need. It is something utterly *inward*. The ruling principle of the merchant class then is the realization of the identity of the *essence* and the *thing*: a man is as real as the money he owns. Imagination vanishes, the meaning has immediate existence; the essence of the matter is the matter itself; value is hard cash. The formal principle of reason is present here. (But this money which bears the *meaning* of all needs is itself only an *immediate thing*)—it is the abstraction from all particularity, character, etc., individual skill. The outlook of the merchant is this hard-headedness in which the particular is wholly estranged and no longer counts; only the strict letter of the *law* has value. The bill must be honoured whatever happens —even if family, wealth, position, life are sacrificed. No quarter is given. . . . Thus in this abstraction spirit has become object as *selfless* inwardness. But that which is within is the Ego itself, and this Ego is its existence. The internal constellation is not the lifeless thing —*money*, but likewise the Ego.'[27]

For all the obscurity of parts of this argument two highly progressive and extremely profound ideas emerge from these passages. First, Hegel has a much greater understanding of the nature of money than many eighteenth century English writers on economics (such as Hume) who failed to recognize the objectivity of money, its reality as a 'thing', in

Hegel's term, and who saw money as no more than a relation. Second, here and in a number of other places it is evident that Hegel had at least a glimmering of the problem that Marx was later to describe as 'fetishism'. He stresses the objectivity of money, its thinghood, but sees no less clearly that in the last resort it is a social relation between men. This social relation appears here in the form of an idealist mystification (The Ego), but this does not detract in the least from the brilliance of Hegel's insight; it merely shows us once again the intimate connections between his achievements and his failings.

## NOTES

1   Marx, *Economic and Philosophic Manuscripts of 1844*, p. 177.
2   Kant, *Kleinere Schriften zur Ethik und Religionsphilosophie*, Leipzig 1870, pp. 7 and 8.
3   Marx, op. cit., p. 177.
4   Lasson, p. 436.
5   *Realphilosophie,* Vol. II, p. 197.
6   Lasson, pp. 418f. and 421.
7   *Realphilosophie*, Vol. II, p. 197.
8   Ibid., p. 185.
9   *Erste Druckschriften*, p. 405.
10  Lasson, pp. 442ff. Works, Vol. II, pp. 140ff. Encyclopaedia, § 433f.
11  *The Phenomenology of Mind*, pp. 235–6.
12  Ibid., pp. 237–8.
13  *Realphilosophie*, Vol. II, p. 214f. Cf. also Lasson, p. 433f. and *Realphilosophie*, Vol. I, pp. 236ff.
14  Ibid., p. 215.
15  Ibid., p. 237.
16  *Realphilosophie,* Vol. II, p. 232. Cf. also Lasson, p. 491f.
17  *Realphilosophie*, Vol. II, p. 257.
18  Lasson, p. 492.
19  *Philosophy of Right*, trans. Knox, Oxford 1942, § 245, p. 150.
20  Lasson, p. 489.
21  *Realphilosophie,* Vol. I, p. 239f.
22  *Realphilosophie*, Vol. II, p. 217.
23  Ibid., p. 232f.
24  Ibid., p. 217.
25  Lasson, p. 437.
26  Ibid., p. 437f.
27  *Realphilosophie*, Vol. II, p. 256f.

# CHAPTER SIX

# Labour and the problem of teleology

BEFORE we can proceed to a critical analysis of Hegel's views on economics we must turn our attention to a specific problem which has not only played a crucial role in the history of classical German philosophy, but is also one of the issues which, as Lenin has pointed out, show Hegel to have been one of the precursors of historical materialism. And it is certainly no mere accident that Hegel's novel and seminal approach grew out of his reflections on the problems of modern economics.

The problem we refer to is the problem of teleology, the right definition of the concept of purpose, above all as a concept of praxis, of human activity. Here too it was Marx who ultimately provided the solution. He defined human labour in the following manner:

'We presuppose labour in a form that stamps it as exclusively *human*. A spider conducts operations that resemble those of a weaver, and a bee puts to shame many an architect in the construction of her cells. But what distinguishes the worst architect from the best of bees is this, that the architect raises his structure in imagination before he erects it in reality. At the end of every labour-process, we get a result that already existed in the *imagination of the labourer* at its commencement. He not only *effects* a change of form in the material on which he works but he also *realizes a purpose* of his own that gives the law to his *modus operandi*, and to which he must subordinate his will.'[1]

Marx does not simply leave the idea there in the labour-process, the basic chemical interchange between man and nature. He applies it also to a variety of the spheres of human action above all that of economics. We shall confine ourselves, however, to one further quotation from Marx's discussion of the relation of production to consumption:

'Consumption furnishes the impulse to produce, and also provides the object which acts as the determining purpose of production. If it is evident that, externally, production supplies the object of consumption, it is equally evident that consumption *posits* the object of production as a *concept*, an internal image, a need, a motive, a purpose.'[2]

The philosophy of the modern world had failed utterly to clarify the problem of purpose. Philosophical idealism, quite unaware of the human character of purposefulness, had projected purpose into nature where it sought—and found—an 'authority' [*Träger*] to vouch for it, namely God. God was alleged to have created the world with a purpose in view and to have taken care both directly and indirectly that the purposes intended by Him should be faithfully realized. Engels rightly pours scorn on all schemes of this sort:

> 'The highest general idea to which this natural science attained (i.e. up to the eighteenth century) was that of the purposiveness of the arrangements of nature, the shallow teleology of Wolff, according to which cats were created to eat mice, mice to be eaten by cats, and the whole of nature to testify to the wisdom of the creator. It is to the highest credit of the philosophy of the time that it did not let itself be led astray by the restricted state of natural knowledge, and that —from Spinoza down to the great French materialists—it insisted on explaining the world from the world itself and left the justification in detail to the natural science of the future.[3]

In fact the important thinkers of modern times vigorously assailed this notion of teleology. However, their arguments led them logically enough to the complete repudiation of the concept of purpose however defined. They perceived quite correctly that the postulate of purpose must be something subjective and human and inferred that it must be subjective in the bad sense. In their eagerness to dismiss the theological arguments in favour of an objective purpose, what appeared to be an unbridgeable gulf opened up between causality and teleology and this led metaphysicians—and even the earliest, still somewhat tentative dialecticians—to repudiate teleology in all its forms. For example, Hobbes argued that:

> 'A *final cause* has no place but in such things as have sense and will; and this also I shall prove hereafter to be an efficient cause.'[4]

Hobbes was perfectly justified in reducing all events, even the fact that the realm of purposes occupies a specific place *within* the network of causal relations.

Spinoza's view is very similar to this:

> 'There will now be no need of many words to show that nature has set no end before herself, and that all final causes are nothing but human fictions. . . . Thus much, nevertheless, I will add, that this doctrine concerning an end altogether overturns nature. For that which is true in the cause it considers as the effect, and *vice versa*. Again, that which is first in nature it puts last.'[5]

Spinoza was of course not unaware that final causes play an important role in the affairs of men. But, like Hobbes, he regarded them as merely

subjective appearances and his correct insistence on the primacy of causality extinguished that particular dialectic in human actions which
Marx discovered and formulated so definitively. Spinoza returns to the
theme elsewhere:

> 'and since He has no principle or end of existence, He has no principle
> or end of action. A final cause, as it is called, is nothing, therefore, but
> human desire, in so far as this is considered as the principle or primary
> cause of anything. For example, when we say that the having a house
> to live in was the final cause of this or that house, we merely mean that
> a man, because he imagined the advantages of a domestic life, desired
> to build a house. Therefore, having a house to live in, in so far as it is
> considered as a final cause, is merely this particular desire, which is
> really an efficient cause, and is considered as primary, because men are
> usually ignorant of the causes of their desires.'[6]

The defect of this persuasive argument is that Spinoza, too, in his
eagerness to establish the causal necessity of human desires, overlooks the
specific dialectic of purpose and causality in labour—where of course
the realization of a purpose through labour is likewise subject to the laws
of causality.

In classical German philosophy the problem of teleology was posed
afresh, together with a large number of other fundamental problems in
philosophy, and the tendency towards the development of a dialectics
initiated discussion at a relatively high level. This movement began with
Kant. Kant asked a number of new questions about teleology, but as we
shall see, they had no immediate connection with Hegel's approach to
the problem. Nevertheless, it is useful to begin with Kant's arguments, if
only briefly, since on the one hand, they provide us with ammunition
against the more recent theories of the history of philosophy which
attempt to show that Hegel merely continued what Kant had begun, and
on the other hand, Hegel's own method of solving the problems of teleology was undoubtedly influenced indirectly or at least made easier by the
fact that the entire complex of questions had been raised and was very
much in the air. For if we must reject as unscientific and confusing any
assumption that classical German philosophy is to be treated as a single
undifferentiated unity, we must also be on our guard against the opposite
fallacy which assumes that Hegel lived in a philosophical vacuum in
which he simply proposed problems as they occurred to him and solved
them as best he might.

In Kant we find three different attempts to analyse the problems of
teleology. Before we discuss them it is as well to begin by stating that
Kant rejected the tenets of the old teleology just as firmly as all the
important philosophers of his day. Even though in his philosophy objective reality is degraded to the status of mere appearance, this phenomenal

world is wholly subject to the laws of cause and effect, leaving no room for teleology.

The first point at which Kant re-introduces the concept of purpose into philosophy is in his discussion of human action, of morality. His application of the notion here suffers from all the defects of subjectivism and abstractness which Hegel criticized and which were noted earlier on. The central idea put forward by Kant in this context was the proposition that man is an end in himself and may not under any circumstances be used as a means to any other end whatsoever. This theory which Fichte then extended even more radically obviously represents an ideological revolt against the treatment meted out to human beings in the system of feudal absolutism. It contains an ethic which reflects the moods of the period of the French Revolution after the fashion of German idealism.

Objectively this theory again opens up an unbridgeable gulf between man and nature, between purpose and causation. Since Kant and Fichte are under the necessity of establishing some contact between the world of pure morality and that of objective reality, they end up by reproducing the old view of teleology, as Hegel shows in *Faith and Knowledge*, despite an intention which runs contrary to it.

'In the older teleology particular aspects of nature were related to particular final causes which themselves lay outside those aspects of nature, so that everything existed only for the sake of something else.—Fichte's teleology likewise represents everything which manifests itself naturally as existing for the sake of something else, namely to create a realm for free beings and to allow itself to be shattered so that those free beings may rise above the ruins and fulfil their destiny. Fichte's philosophy thus shares the assumption common to all teleology that nature is nothing in itself but only in relation to something else, to something absolutely profane and lifeless.'[6]

It is perhaps not uninteresting to note that Hegel remarks on the achievements of Voltaire in satirizing the old teleology and acknowledges the value of criticism from an empirical point of view. He sees his work as a critique *ad hominem* which ridicules the unphilosophical amalgam of idea and manifestation by confronting it with a matching satirical hybrid.

Of much greater importance for philosophy was Kant's second attempt to find an adequate concept of purpose in the activities of man. His theory of aesthetics, his definition of a work of art as 'purposiveness without a purpose' became fundamental to all discussions of aesthetics throughout the entire period. Schiller extended the idea in the direction of objective idealism; Schelling put it in the very centre of his aesthetics and it exerted a powerful influence on Hegel's aesthetics too, an influence always acknowledged by Hegel. A more detailed analysis of this subject lies beyond the scope of this study (although more can be found in my books *Goethe and his Age* and *Contributions to the History of Aesthetics* where I discuss Schiller's aesthetic theory in greater detail).

Finally, in the *Critique of Judgement* after his discussion of aesthetics Kant took up the problem of teleology itself and devoted an extended philosophical discussion to it. The main thrust of his arguments is concerned with an attempted difinition of organic life. Kant was faced by the following antinomy. On the one hand, he holds fast to the idea that nature (or, in his philosophy, the phenomenal world) is subject to causality. And since causality and teleology were mutually exclusive the latter must be eliminated from the scheme of natural phenomena. On the other hand, the newly arising science of the organic brought with it problems that were not capable of solution on the old mechanistic model. It goes without saying that Kant was unable to find a solution to this crisis in the organic sciences. Indeed, he even declared that the impossibility of discovering a way out of the impasse showed that an absolute frontier of human knowledge had been reached. As he put it:

'And we can say boldly it is absurd for men . . . to hope that another Newton will arise in the future, who shall make comprehensible by us the production of a blade of grass according to natural laws which no design has ordered.'[8]

Kant could have had no idea that half a century later this 'Newton of the organic realm' would appear in the person of Darwin. It is in keeping with his acknowledgment that the problems of organic nature were insoluble that Kant never went further than to recommend the 'regulative' use of judgment. The title of 'constitutive', (i.e. something which defines the object), of what he regards as objective reality was reserved for the categories of mechanical causality.

Despite this agnostic solution, despite this conversion of the existing limits of scientific knowledge into the absolute frontiers of cognition, we can clearly see how the transition to dialectics was being prepared in the *Critique of Judgement*, how the central problems of dialectics were presented, albeit as yet in an unsatisfactory form. When, for example, Kant states that these problems are inaccessible to the human understanding he vividly illustrates the limitations of metaphysical thought and, in part, those of idealist dialectics also. He explains the 'regulative' use of the category of purposiveness in this way:

'Between natural mechanism and the Technic of nature, i.e. its purposive connection, we should find no distinction, were it not that our understanding is of the kind that must proceed from the universal to the particular. The judgement then in respect of the particular can cognize no purposiveness and, consequently, can form no determinant judgements, without having a universal law under which to subsume that particular. Now the particular, as such, contains something contingent in respect of the universal, while yet reason requires unity and conformity to law in the combination of particular laws of nature. This conformity of the contingent to law is called purposiveness; and the derivation of particular laws from the universal, as regards their contingent element, is impossible *a priori* through a determination of the concept of the object. Hence, the concept of the purposiveness of nature in its products is necessary for human judgement in respect of nature, but has not to do with the determination of objects. It is, therefore, a subjective principle of reason for the judgement, which as regulative (not constitutive) is just as necessarily valid for our *human judgement* as if it were an objective principle.'[9]

Kant then proceeds to contrast this human faculty, this discursive understanding which always retains an element of contingency when it subsumes a particular under a universal, to an understanding of a different kind. This understanding has

'a complete spontaneity of intuition'; it is 'an intuitive understanding . . . which does not proceed from the universal to the particular, and so to the singular (through concepts). In this mode of cognition we do not find that the *particular* laws governing nature in its products *are* afflicted with the same contingency that had been present in the understanding.'[10]

In this way Kant postulates the idea of a particular form of intelligence, of an *intellectus archetypus* but with the explicit reservation that it is only an 'idea' and that this mode of cognition is inaccessible to human understanding.

It is evident that we have here a programme for advancing beyond the limits set to metaphysical thought. And the outstanding minds of Germany, Goethe and Schiller above all, embraced it with enthusiasm, without concerning themselves overmuch with Kant's protestations that this mode of cognition was inaccessible, that it exceeded the powers of man. Once again it would go beyond the bounds of our present subject if we were to chart the further course of this idea through the philosophy of nature of Goethe and Schelling. No doubt the question is very closely connected with the philosophical movement which developed from Goethe and Schelling and was strongly influenced by the *Critique of Judgement*. A discussion of Hegel's originality in this area would require much specialized research. What is certain, however, is that on this issue of an inner purpose Engels, who usually establishes the fundamental distinctions between Kant and Hegel, here brackets them together. In the course of a polemic against Haeckel, who had argued that mechanism and teleology were rigidly opposed principles, Engels says:

> 'Already in Kant and Hegel *inner* purpose is a protest against dualism. Mechanism applied to life is a helpless category, at the most we could speak of chemism, if we do not want to renounce all understanding of names. . . . The *inner purpose* in the organism, according to Hegel (V. p 244), operates through *impulse*. *Pas trop fort*. Impulse is supposed to bring the single living being more or less into harmony with the idea of it. From this it is seen how much the whole *inner purpose* is itself an ideological determination. And yet Lamarck is contained in this.'[11]

This brief survey will perhaps suffice to show the reader that the old dogmas about causality and teleology had begun to totter in the period of German idealism even before Hegel. It was important to register the general atmosphere of change before proceeding to Hegel's own particular contribution to this discussion. Hegel's new view of teleology appears first in connection with his analysis of labour, and, specifically, where he talks about man's use of tools. We shall quote from the Lectures of 1805–6 his most mature statement of his position:

> 'It is also the content in so far as it is the object of will, the means of desire and their *definite possibility*. In tools or in the cultivated, fertilized field I possess a *possibility, content,* as *something general*. For this reason tools, the means, are to be preferred to the end or purpose of desire, which is more individual; the tools comprehend all the individualities.
>
> But a tool does not yet have activity in itself. It is inert matter, it does not turn back in itself. I must still work with it. I have interposed *cunning* between myself and external objects, so as to spare myself and to shield my determinacy and let it wear itself out. The Ego remains the soul of this syllogism, in reference to it, to activity. However, I only spare myself in terms of quantity, since I still get blisters. Making myself into a thing is still unavoidable; the activity of the impulse is not yet in the thing. It is important also to make the tool generate its own activity, to make it self-activating. This should be achieved (a) by contriving it so that its line, its thread, its double edge or whatever, is used to reverse its direction, to turn it in upon itself. Its passivity must be transformed into activity, into a cohesive movement. (b) In general nature's own activity, the elasticity of a watch-spring, water, wind, etc. are employed to do things that they would not have done if left to themselves, so that their blind action is made purposive, the opposite of itself: the rational behaviour of nature, *laws*, in its external existence. Nothing happens to *nature* itself; the *individual purposes of natural existence* become universal. Here impulse departs entirely from

labour. It allows nature to act on itself, simply looks on and controls it with a light touch: *cunning*. The broadside of force is assailed by the fine point of cunning. The *point d'honneur* of cunning in its struggle with force is to seize it on its blind side so that it is directed against itself, to take a firm grip on it, to be active against it or to turn it as movement back on itself, so that it annuls itself. . . .'

And in a note in the margin he adds:

'Wind, mighty river, mighty ocean, subjugated, cultivated. No point in exchanging compliments with it—puerile sentimentality which clings to individualities.'[12]

The exceptional philosophical importance of these arguments is easily grasped. Hegel's concrete analysis of the dialectics of human labour annuls the unyielding antithesis of causality and teleology, i.e. it locates conscious human purposes concretely *within* the overall causal network, without destroying it, going beyond it or appealing to any transcendental principle. Nor does it fall into the opposite error which we have noted in earlier philosophers: of losing sight of the specific determinants of final causes in the sphere of labour.

Like almost every major turning-point in philosophy Hegel's discovery here is extraordinarily simple: every working man knows instinctively that he can only perform those operations with the means or objects of labour that the laws or combinations of laws governing those objects will permit. That is to say, the labour-process can never go beyond the limits of causality. And every human invention must therefore consist in discovering concealed causal relationships which are then introduced into the labour-process. The specific nature of final causes as both Hegel and Marx correctly saw is just that the idea of the objective to be attained comes into being before the work process is set in motion and that the work process exists for the purpose of achieving this objective by means of an ever greater penetration of the causal relationships existing in reality. It is true and indeed self-evident that the final cause is itself causally conditioned—as Spinoza insists. This insight did escape Hegel since he derives the labour-process from immediate need and then constantly reduces all perfected labour processes to their social origins and ultimately to man's impulse to satisfy his essential wants. But far from annulling the specific teleological nexus in labour—as Spinoza believed—it only makes the dialectical unity of cause and purpose more transparent. For it becomes perfectly obvious that the breadth and depth of man's knowledge of cause and effect in nature is a function of the purposes man sets himself in the work process. Man comes to recognize the chain of cause and effect more and more precisely in order to make nature work for him. Thanks to this purposiveness he gives objects a different form and function, he gives different directions and effects to the forces of nature than they would have had without his intervention. In Hegel's view this novel function of objects and of the forces of nature is both new and not new. Man can only make use of 'nature's own activity' for his own purposes; he can add nothing new to the essence, the laws of nature. Nevertheless, through the intervention of his causally determined purpose these laws may give birth to new effects which were either unknown before or whose appearance had been a matter of chance. Thus Hegel's concrete analysis of the human labour-process shows that the antinomy of causality and teleology is in reality a dialectical contradiction in which the laws governing a complex pattern of objective reality become manifest in motion, in the process of its own constant reproduction.

It is quite evident from the foregoing that Hegel has made a great advance on his predecessors. He has taken the first step towards a correct philosophical understanding of the real relations and interactions between man and nature. In Kant and Fichte an abstract dualism had prevailed: nature was thought of either as the passive arena for man's activity or else as a mere frontier delimiting human action. In consequence, this activity became elevated, as Hegel said about Fichte, onto the 'pure and vertiginous heights' of abstract morality. And this would always end up in the 'bad infinity' of the concept of infinite progress.

Schelling did indeed make a serious effort to translate the subjective principles of the *Critique of Judgement* into objective ones, but the method he chose was so unmediated, abstract and assertive that he never really advanced beyond the confines of Kantianism, and where he did it was to lapse into mysticism. His aim was to bring about the unity of man and nature by means of an idea which in itself was not without profundity: he saw the whole universe as consisting of a unified process of activity. Within this process the only distinction between man and nature was that man's activity was conscious while that of nature was unconscious. But the real profundity (and the real limitation) of this idea could only have been demonstrated in the course of a real, concrete analysis. Schelling did not possess the knowledge that might have enabled him to analyse the 'unconscious production' of nature. Where his knowledge failed him he filled the gap with more or less ingenious inventions. And as for the conscious activity of man Schelling never made any serious attempt to concretize that with the sole exception of man's aesthetic activity. And even here his efforts served in the last analysis only to furnish a real, palpable analogy for the mystical doctrine of intellectual intuition. For this reason he never escaped the confines of the concept of infinite progress postulated by Kant and Fichte:

'The antithesis between conscious and unconscious activity is infinite, since, if it were to be annulled, this would entail the annulment of freedom as a manifestation, because freedom depends simply and solely on this antithesis for its survival.'[13]

In Hegel, on the other hand, the precise analysis of the labour process led to the real concretization both of human praxis and of man's relationship with nature. Whereas the Romantics expended their lyrical energy declaiming about the unity of man and nature, Hegel, while brusquely rejecting 'wretched sentimentality', in any form took the trouble really to think the matter out. In *The German Ideology* Marx makes this comment on the problem:

'. . . the celebrated "unity of man with nature" has always existed in varying forms in every epoch according to the greater or lesser development of industry.'[14]

There can be no doubt that Hegel made a significant advance in the direction of this real understanding of the relationship between man and nature.

The dialectical concretization of human activity which we find in Hegel's teleology of labour also dramatizes the mediating processes that link human praxis with the idea of social progress. In the old teleology the relative values placed on means and ends were necessarily false. The metaphysical analysis tended towards a rigid polarization of the two concepts; since the ends were inevitably idealized and since they were the product of a consciousness, idealist philosophies always placed a higher value on them than on the means. In the earlier teleologies theological motives were clearly at work, since the authority which guaranteed the ends was always God. But even the subjective idealism of Kant and Fichte foundered upon this rock: even though their notion of ends was inspired by an utterly sincere and revolutionary sense of the dignity of man, the relationship between ends and means remained metaphysical and idealistic.

As far as immediate needs are concerned Hegel too does not dispute that in the first instance the ends stand higher than the means. Man naturally wishes to satisfy his needs immediately and all work, every tool, etc., only appears to his immediate consciousness as a means to this end. But Hegel also shows the concrete objective dialectics of the labour-process which necessarily lead beyond the standpoint of immediate consciousness. And it is here that progress lies. We earlier quoted Hegel's statement that 'desire must always start again from the beginning', and his philosophy of history shows that the course of human development (or, in Hegel's language, the historical origins and growth of mind) passes through the labour of the 'servant', whereas the 'master' sticks fast in immediate enjoyment, the immediate satisfaction of his needs, all of which remains barren as far as the progress of mankind is concerned.

Hegel's dialectic of labour also shows why this is necessarily so: what is expressed in labour, in tools, etc., is a higher more universal, more social principle. A new terrain is conquered which leads to a broader and deeper understanding of nature; and this conquest redounds to the advantage of not just of one single man, but of mankind as a whole. And when this process continuously reproduces itself it does not lead to the monotony of 'infinite progress', but to the constant self-reproduction of human society at an ever-higher level—even though this progress is sometimes uneven and may be punctuated by setbacks. For this reason Hegel can rightly say that tools, the means, are more valuable than the ends for which they are employed, i.e. than desire, the impulse to satisfy one's needs.

Hegel did not draw out all the philosophical consequences of this new view of teleology until some years later, in the *Logic*. (We do not know exactly whether Hegel made use of the Jena lecture notes for these sections of the *Logic*, but we shall see that its fundamental ideas do in fact go back to the passages we have quoted from the Jena period.) We shall now turn to some of Hegel's most important systematic statements in the *Logic* on the subject of teleology. We do this partly because it is *important* to show that the dialectical analysis of the labour-process provided the foundations for the later systematic discussion in the *Logic* of the relations between causality and teleology, theory and praxis, and partly because Lenin, in his *Conspectus of Hegel's Logic*, made a series of extremely important comments on precisely these passages, comments which throw a completely new light on the relations between Hegel's dialectics and historical materialism. Moreover, it is not without interest to see that those of Hegel's views which in Lenin's opinion brought him closest to historical materialism were the very ones which sprang from his comprehensive and accurate analysis of economic problems. That is to say, the proximity of Hegel's ideas to historical materialism was not a coincidence, not the expression of the mysterious intuitions of a genius, but the results of his study of the same objective problems which were solved so brilliantly by the founders of historical materialism.

Lenin quotes the following passage from Hegel's *Logic*:

'Further, since the end is finite it has a finite content; accordingly it is not absolute or utterly in and for itself *reasonable*. The means, however, is the external middle of the syllogism which is the realization of the end; in it, therefore, reasonableness manifests itself as such —as preserving itself *in this external other* and precisely *through* this externality. To that extent the *means* is *higher* than the *finite* ends of *external* usefulness: the *plough* is more honourable than those immediate enjoyments which are procured by it, and serve as ends. The *instrument* is preserved while the immediate enjoyments pass away and are forgotten. In his tools man possesses power over external nature, even though, as regards his ends, nature dominates him.'[15]

Lenin made the following notes in the margin to this passage: 'the germs of historical materialism in Hegel' and 'Hegel and historical materialism.' And immediately after the quotation he adds:

'Historical materialism as one of the applications and developments of the ideas of genius—seeds existing in embryo in Hegel.'[16]

The reader of our earlier remarks will require no commentary to convince him that these excerpts from Hegel's *Logic* merely present in a more systematic form ideas which we have already found in the Jena Lectures, but that they do not go beyond them. Even the idea that the labour man performs with the aid of tools is a syllogism is already present in various places in Hegel's economic writings in Jena. What Lenin says about the *Logic* may be applied also then to Hegel's Jena arguments.

However, in the *Logic* Hegel does take the idea further when he says that teleology, human labour, and human praxis are the truth of mechanism and chemism. This idea represents an advance on his Jena ideas, even though at the same time its underlying assumptions are contained there. In particular, his interest in the relationship of teleology to mechanism and chemism focuses on the way in which mechanical and chemical technology bear on the objective reality of nature. That is to say, the economic process of production is the moment thanks to which teleology becomes the truth of mechanism and chemism. Lenin has given a running commentary on all these sections, modulating them into the language of dialectical materialism. To give the reader a clear idea of this process we shall quote the central passage from Hegel in full together with Lenin's materialist critique:

| *Hegel* | *Materialist Dialectics* |
|---|---|
| '. . . From this results the nature of the subordination of the two previous forms of the objective process: the other, which in them lies in the "infinite Progress", is the concept which at first is posited as external to them, which is end; not only is the concept their substance, but also externality is the moment which is essential to them and constitutes their determinateness. | 'Two forms of the objective process: nature (mechanical and chemical) and the *purposive* activity of man the mutual relation of these forms. At the beginning, man's ends appear foreign ("other") in relation to nature. Human consciousness, science "*der Begriff*"), reflects the essence, the substance of nature, but at the same time this consciousness is |

*Hegel*

Thus mechanical or chemical tech-
nique spontaneously offers itself to
the end-relation by reason of its
character of being determined
externally; and this relation must
now be further considered.'

*Materialist Dialectics*

something external in relation to
nature (not immediately, not
simply, coinciding with it).
Mechanical and chemical tech-
nique serves human ends just because its character (essence)
consists in its being determined by
external conditions (the laws of
nature).'

Lenin concludes his comments on this section of Hegel's *Logic* with the
following remarks:

> 'In actual fact, men's ends are engendered by the objective world and
> presuppose it—they find it as something given, present. But it *seems*
> to man as if his ends are taken from outside the world, and are inde-
> pendent of the world ("freedom"). NB. All this in the paragraph on
> the *Subjective End*.)'[17]

Thus Hegel proposes here a quite new approach to the place of human
praxis in the system of philosophy. And we do not have to waste any
more words in showing that the prototype of human praxis for Hegel is
to be found in labour, in economic activity. As Marx noted in his *Theses
on Feuerbach*, the great achievement of German classical idealism was to
develop the 'active side' of reality which had been neglected by the older
forms of materialism. This development began with Kant and Fichte, but
their concept of praxis was so moralistic and exaggerated that it led to the
rigid confrontation of theory and praxis, and to the abstract isolation of
practical philosophy which Hegel criticized so trenchantly. But we have
now seen not only his criticism but also his positive concrete proposals
for a theory of human praxis. We may refer the reader back to his
remarks about labour and tools etc. and to his analysis of master and servant in *The Phenomenology of Mind*. These ideas are synthesized in the
*Logic* which Lenin then subjected to a thorough-going critique in his
commentaries on Hegel.

In the *Logic* Hegel compares the 'idea' of praxis with merely theoretical knowledge and arrives at the following conclusion:

> 'But in the practical idea it [the notion, concept] stands opposed as
> actual to the actual. . . . This idea is higher than the idea of theoretical
> cognition, for it has not only the dignity of the universal but also of
> the simply actual.'[18]

In what follows Hegel provides a more detailed explanation of the concrete superiority of the practical over the theoretical idea, a superiority

which, the reader will need no further telling, has nothing in common with and is indeed diametrically opposed to the 'primacy of the practical reason' of Kant and Fichte. Hegel says:

'Another way of regarding this defect is that the *practical* idea still lacks the moment of the *theoretical* idea. That is to say, in the latter there stands on the side of the subjective concept—the concept that is in process of being intuited within itself by the concept—only the determination of universality. Cognition knows itself only as apprehension, as the self-identity of the concept, which for itself is indeterminate; fulfilment, that is, objectivity determined in and for itself, is *given* to it, and that which *truly is* is the actuality that is present independently of subjective positing. The practical idea on the other hand counts this actuality (which at the same time opposes it as an insuperable barrier) as that which in and for itself is null, which is to receive its true determination and sole value through the ends of the good. Will itself consequently bars the way to its own good insofar as it separates itself from cognition and external actuality does not, for it, retain the form of that which truly is; consequently the idea of the good can find its complement only in the idea of the true.'[19]

Lenin excerpted the entire passage and added this commentary:

'Cognition . . . finds itself faced by that which truly is as actuality present independently of subjective opinions, (positings). (This is pure materialism!) Man's will, his practice, itself blocks the attainment of its end . . . in that it separates itself from cognition and does not recognize external actuality for that which truly is (for objective truth). What is necessary is the *union of cognition and practice*.'[20]

A number of other comments by Lenin arising more or less directly from these quotations from the *Logic* are highly illuminating on the subject of our present discussion: Hegel's efforts to acquire an understanding of the subject-matter and methodology of economics and the way in which these made him the forerunner of historical materialism. Immediately following the passage just quoted Lenin points out with a substantial measure of agreement, but also with critical reservations of a materialist nature, that Hegel uses the syllogism as a practical principle for getting to grips with objective reality:

'The "syllogism of action" . . . For Hegel *action*, practice, is a *logical* "syllogism", a figure of logic. And that is true! Not, of course, in the sense that the figure of logic has its other being in the practice of man (= absolute idealism), but *vice versa*: man's practice, repeating itself a thousand-million times, becomes consolidated in man's consciousness by figures of logic. Precisely (and only) on account of this thousand-million-fold repetition, these figures have the stability of a prejudice, an axiomatic character.'[21]

And a few pages earlier on, but still in the same critical commentary of Hegel's discussion of cognition and praxis, Lenin gives a summary of the links between Hegel and Marx:

> 'All this in the chapter "The Idea of Cognition" (Chapter II)—in the transition to the "Absolute Idea" (Chapter III)—i.e., undoubtedly, in Hegel practice serves as a link in the analysis of the process of cognition, and indeed as the transition to objective ("absolute" according to Hegel) truth. *Marx, in consequence, clearly followed Hegel's* lead in introducing the criterion of practice into the theory of knowledge: see the *Theses on Feuerbach.'[22]*

We see, then, that Hegel's new approach to the problem of teleology, of the connections between final causes and man's economic activities in particular and—branching out from there—human praxis in general, is of cardinal importance for his entire philosophical system. It leads to the abolition of the mechanical separation between theory and praxis established by the subjective idealism of Kant and Fichte. Consequently it reaffirms the objective link between human praxis and reality. This return to objectivity indicates a partial return to major philosophers of the past such as Spinoza or Hobbes, but with the reservation that Hegel's objectivity stands on a higher plane than theirs, since it incorporates the dialectics of man's 'active side' in its conception of reality. Indeed as far as the theory of knowledge of Hegel's own dialectical method is concerned this 'active side' may be considered to be the decisive factor. The relationship of theory to practice was thereby clarified in a manner unknown in philosophy up to that time, so much so that Marx could take up the matter where Hegel left off and was in a position to introduce his final and decisive clarifications.

This deepened understanding of the relationship of theory to practice had the most far-reaching consequences for the dialectics of the essential concepts of philosophy. We shall now attempt to demonstrate this with reference to a number of the relevant issues, such as freedom and necessity, contingency and necessity. We shall see how Hegel's enlarged understanding of these issues springs from the same source as the philosophical insights we have been discussing. At the same time we shall also see that the limitations of his dialectics, the point at which his profound dialectics of reality lapse into an idealistic mystification, is located at the very point at which, for various reasons, his knowledge of economics lets him down and his understanding of society loses itself in the miasmas of mysticism.

Hegel is surprisingly conscious of economic problems and their philosophical implications. We have already seen how consciously he established a connection between praxis and labour, economic activity. But his clear understanding is by no means confined to isolated issues. He is fully aware that the categories of action emerge most clearly in the sphere of economics and he comments on the methodological issue involved in the introductory remarks to his essay on *Natural Law*. It is true that he is dealing expressly with natural law and not with economics, but since we have come to understand the crucial role of economic categories in the overall structure of society and its scientific analysis we may not take it as read. In a discussion of the way in which the world is reflected in the mirror of science he observes:

'that the state of natural law is the closest [to reality] since it pertains directly to the ethical, the mover of all things human, and insofar as there is a science of such things to which necessity may be ascribed, it must be at one with the empirical form of the ethical, which is equally necessary, and as a science it must express the latter in universal form.'[23]

The problem of freedom and necessity is concretized above all by being placed in a specific socio-historical framework. Hegel is concerned as we have seen to combat the ethical views of subjective idealism, with its isolation of the concept of freedom from the real world of history and society. Since Hegel's study of the modern world represents an effort to comprehend the isolation of the individual with the aid of classical economics, the overall self-movement of society must appear as the product of the isolated and hence contingent activities of individuals. We have already quoted various statements in which the identity of Hegel's position with that of Adam Smith is established beyond doubt. But in order to gain a clear picture of what it entails we must consider his later description of economics as a science, for it is there that he synthesizes his view that the problem of necessity and contingency is the fundamental problem of the discipline. This view is in complete accord with his position in Jena except for the fact that the stage he had reached in Jena did not make it necessary for him to make a formal statement on the subject. In the *Philosophy of Right* he writes:

'But this medley of arbitrariness generates universal characteristics by its own working; and this apparently scattered and thoughtless sphere is upheld by a necessity which automatically enters it. To discover this necessary element here is the object of political economy, a science which is a credit to thought because it finds laws for a mass of accidents. It is an interesting spectacle here to see all chains of activity leading back to the same point; particular spheres of action fall into groups, influence others, and are helped or hindered by others. The most remarkable thing here is this mutual interlocking of particulars, which is what one would least expect because at first sight everything seems to be given over to the arbitrariness of the individual, and it has a parallel in the solar system which displays to the eye only irregular movements, though its laws may none the less be ascertained.'[24]

On this basis Hegel proceeds both to pose and for the first time correctly and concretely to solve the question of the relationship between freedom and necessity within the framework of the concrete and dynamic totality of man's life in history and society. Engels discussed Hegel's solution in these terms:

'Hegel was the first to state correctly the relation between freedom and necessity. To him, freedom is the appreciation of necessity. "Necessity is *blind only in so far as it is not understood.*" Freedom does not consist in the dream of independence from natural laws, but in the knowledge of these laws, and in the possibility this gives of systematically making them work towards definite ends.'[25]

As we have seen, this view of freedom and necessity stands in the very centre of Hegel's study of teleology and hence of his discussion of human activity in general. We are already familiar with the purely economic side of the problems and also with its basis in the dialectical progress of human knowledge about the laws of nature. Furthermore, we will recollect Hegel's passionate attack on the abstract concept of freedom held by Kant and Fichte, with all its pretensions to the sublime. What remains, then, is briefly to consider what Hegel's definition actually implies for our understanding of society and history as a concrete totality. For given Hegel's position it goes without saying that history is the real framework of freedom, the actual arena in which the dialectical conflict between freedom and necessity is to be fought out.

It is well known that the 'cunning of reason' is the central concept in Hegel's later philosophy of history. Translated into more prosaic terms the expression referss to the idea that men make their own history themselves and the actual driving-force behind the events of history is to be found in the passions of men and in their individual, egoistic aspirations; but the totality of these individual passions nevertheless ends by producing *something other* than what the men involved had wanted and striven to attain. Nevertheless, this other result is no fortuitous product, on the contrary, it is here that the laws of history, the 'reason in history', the 'spirit' (to use Hegel's terms) actually makes itself manifest.

The term 'ruse', 'cunning' (*List*) has a long history in Hegel's thought, reaching back to Jena. We may recollect his use of it in the methodologically important analysis of tools (p. 344f.) as a concept with which to relate man to nature through labour. Closely associated with that is his use of the same concept to establish the relation of the state and the government to the individual, and especially to the total network of man's economic activities. In the next section we shall show in detail how the frontiers of Hegel's ideas on economics and above all his idealist illusions about the state make their appearance at this point, illusions which are intimately bound up with his general attitude towards Napoleon.

But this is not the sole source of Hegel's views. Of course, the influence of contemporary events on his mind is very apparent; but their remoter origins are to be found in the ideas of Hobbes and Mandeville according to which the interaction of the egoistical and even evil and vicious passions of men gives rise to the balance of forces prevailing in capitalist society and even guarantees its future progress. This conception was extended and generalized by the leading thinkers of the French Enlightenment into a utilitarian philosophy (which admittedly, as Marx points out, also perpetuates the accompanying illusions of idealism). The economics of Adam Smith provides all these theories with a firm foundation and its sober emphasis on the actual facts of the given situation shows how far these views can lead.

Hegel is heir to this tradition. How close he is to it can be seen from this passage from the Lectures of 1805–6:

'From the outside the actual does not indeed look like the ideal, because the observer holds fast to what is immediate, namely necessity. The eccentricity, ruin, licentiousness and vice of others must be borne; the state is *cunning*.'[26]

And elsewhere Hegel sums up his view as follows:

'The cunning of the government is to allow free rein to the self-interest of others—the right, the understanding of the merchant tells him what counts in the world: utility—the government must turn its *utility* to account and ensure that it returns back into the world.'[27]

What is remarkable about Hegel's general theory of the relations between civil society and the state at this point is the way in which he compares it to that of the merchant in society and attempts to assimilate his idea of the 'cunning' of the government to his general economic use of the notion of cunning. This appears even more clearly in another marginal comment in the same work:

'Not the *artificial* [actions] of the *legislative*, etc. organs—the *self* is the highest authority.—*Free rein for the powers of necessity*—the cunning to leave individuals a free hand, each *looks after himself*—this flows into the universal—a higher reflection of spirit in itself.—Guarantee against arbitrariness; general constitution of the estates—not provincial estates; universal reason—mobility of everything individual. The *reason* of the people is as clever as its arrangements.'[28]

From all this it is evident that there are two conflicting forces at work here which are to be reconciled by means of Hegel's theory of cunning, his dialectics of freedom and necessity. On the one hand, there is the cunning of the government as opposed to the autonomous movement of the economy in modern civil society, and, on the other hand, there is the cunning of reason which itself becomes manifest in that movement, regulating the production, reproduction and the further advance of capitalist society.

We have already considered Hegel's views on the workings of this dialectic of freedom and necessity in the course of world history. We may refer the reader back to Hegel's ideas about the role of the tyrant in history, his necessary appearance and his no less necessary eclipse (p. 310ff.).

We have also seen that Hegel discerns a similar dialectic in the role played by great men, by the 'world-historical individuals' (cf. his remarks on Richelieu, p. 306). We should like to supplement our discussion there with a few quotations from the Jena Lectures which make the connection between the problem of freedom and necessity and the other question of necessity and contingency particularly clear. In one of the Lectures Hegel turns to a discussion of artistic genius. Openly satirical about the deification and mystification of the genius by the Romantics he gives a dispassionate account of the relationship between the activity of the individual genius and the movement of society and the life of the nation as a whole.

'Those who are called *geniuses* have acquired a particular skill by means of which they make the universal creations of the people into their own work, as others do with other things. What they produce is not their own invention, but the invention of the *entire* nation, or rather the *discovery*, that the nation has discovered its true essence. What really belongs to the artist as such is his formal activity, his particular skill in this mode of representation, and in this he was educated as part of the universal attainment of skill. He is like the man who finds himself among workers who are building a stone arch whose general structure is invisibly present as an idea. He so happens to be the last in line; when he puts his stone into place the arch supports itself. As he places his stone he sees that the whole edifice is an arch, says so and passes for the inventor.'[29]

Hegel's view is made even more explicit in another lecture written at the same time in which he discusses the role of prominent individuals in history, particularly in transitional periods.

'These self-possessed natures need do nothing but speak the word and the nations will flock to their support. The great minds who do this must, if they are to succeed, be *purified* of all the characteristics of the configuration which preceded them. If they wish to accomplish a work in *its* totality, they must grasp it with *their* totality. It may happen that they only *grasp* it by a corner and so advance it a little. But since nature wants the *whole*, it pushes them from the *pinnacle* to which they had climbed, and replaces them with others; and if these too are one-sided, there will be a succession of individuals until the whole work is finished. But if it is to be the work of *one* man, he must recognize the whole and so free himself from all limitations.'[30]

These passages do of course reveal the defects of Hegel's thought which will soon concern us more immediately. Chief among them is his wholesale mystification of the historical process, his hypostatization of a 'spirit' which acts as the conscious principle in which it is grounded. But ignoring this for the moment, we can see how dispassionately and dialectically Hegel analyses the role of the 'world-historical individual' in history, and we can admire the energetic manner in which he subordinates the outstanding personality to the exigencies of the objective tasks facing him, tasks arising from the objective circumstances of society itself. On the other hand, we may observe that Hegel is under no illusions about the element of chance in selecting those individuals who find themselves in a position to get to grips with major political or artistic dilemmas.

In this sphere too his lucidity enables him to anticipate some of the later ideas of historical materialism. Of course, Marx and Engels went far beyond Hegel in their materialist concretization of the problem of necessity and contingency, and it was only when they developed their really scientific language that Hegel's mystified constructs could finally be overcome. And of course we must remember to distinguish their contributions here from their later vulgarizers of the Second International who so over-emphasized the notion of necessity in history as utterly to eliminate the role of personality and of the activity of individuals in history, turning necessity into an automaton (for the use of opportunists) which functions without human agency. Lenin and Stalin have liberated historical materialism from this mechanical vulgarization and restored and extended the teachings of Marx and Engels in this respect too.

But even earlier Engels, in his old age, had been forced to conduct an ideological campaign against this mechanical vulgarization of history. Here is a passage from his letter to Heinz Starkenburg which not only corrects these false notions but also shows Hegel's contribution to the thought of historical materialism on this issue. Engels' argument begins with the subject of contingency and necessity and proceeds thus:

'This is where the so-called great men come in for treatment. That such and such a man and precisely that man arises at a particular time in a particular country is, of course, pure chance. But cut him out and there will be a demand for a substitute, and this substitute will be found, good or bad, but in the long run he will be found. That Napoleon, just that particular Corsican, should have been the military dictator whom the French Republic, exhausted by its own warfare, had rendered necessary was chance; but that, if a Napoleon had been lacking, another would have filled the place, is proved by the fact that the man was always found as soon as he became necessary: Caesar, Augustus, Cromwell, etc. While Marx discovered the materialist conception of history, Thierry, Mignet, Guizot and all the English historians up to 1850 are the proof that it was being striven for, and the discovery of the same conception by Morgan proves that the time was ripe for it and that it simply *had* to be discovered.'[31]

The decisive factor which prevented Hegel from making a concrete and accurate application of his philosophically correct view of freedom and necessity, contingency and necessity to the actual course of history is to be found in his ignorance of the class struggle as a motive force in society. Hegel's knowledge was undoubtedly vast and he was sufficiently critical and unprejudiced to be able to see isolated instances of class antagonisms in society. (We need refer only to his observations on the connection between poverty and the rise of factories, p. 331.) But his general view of history and society prevented him from grasping the importance of class antagonisms as a motive force, to say nothing of making any general inferences from their observed laws of motion.

Thus in Hegel's philosophy of history the particular states appear as unified and coherent individuals. He does of course realize that behind these individuals there are social processes at work. We may recall that he related the unity of France and the fragmentation of Germany to the different paths taken by feudalism in its period of disintegration. But these insights, accurate though they are, were not consistently applied and had no further consequences. The history of the world appeared essentially as a power struggle between 'unified' nations and states among themselves.

Hegel contemplates this struggle as dispassionately as he had contemplated the economic struggle of individuals in civil society. In *The Phenomenology of Mind* this appears as the internecine conflicts of the 'animal kingdom of the spirit' (*das geistige Tierreich*). This he analyses as the recurrence, indeed as the authentic form, of the state of nature which he sees as Hobbes' war of all against all. We shall see how the juridical control of economic affairs—which likewise consist of a *bellum omnium*

*contra omnes*—assumes an extreme, indeed an exaggerated importance in
Hegel's csocial philosophy, even though we must bear in mind that for
Hegel the idea of juridical control has a very different meaning from the
one it had for Kant and Fichte. But in Hegel's view once a nation or a
society has been formally constituted as a state, it ceases to be possible to
exercise control over the individual states.

In the Lectures of 1805–6 he puts the matter thus:

> 'The whole is an individual, a people that is directed against others.
> The restoration of the state of indifference between individuals, the
> *state of nature*—only here does it become *real*. This state of affairs is
> partly the peaceable existence of individuals independently of each
> other, sovereignty; and partly a union through treaties. But the trea-
> ties do not have the reality of real contracts; they are not an *existing*
> power, it is the individual people which represents the universal as an
> existing power. Hence they do not have the force of civil contracts;
> they are not binding if one party abrogates them. This is the eternal
> deception of concluding treaties, binding oneself and then nullifying
> one's obligation.'[32]

We shall see later on how crucial a part is played by war in the Jena
philosophy of history. Of course, here too, despite a Napoleonic overestimation of war, his customary dispassionate and historically grounded
view prevails. On the one hand, he takes issue with Kant's utopian conception of eternal peace, as we can see from the final remarks in the last
quotation. On the other hand, he is very far from being taken in by the
apologias of the various combatants. He is perfectly well aware of the use
made of the notions of offensive and defensive war. Each side claims to
be defending itself against the attack of the other. And at this level the
disagreement about who is in the right is incapable of resolution. In his
essay on the *German Constitution* Hegel observes:

> 'Each bases his claim on rights and accuses the other of violating those
> rights. . . . The public takes sides, each side claims to have right on its
> own side, and both are in the right and it is precisely the two rights
> that have come into conflict.'[33]

Hegel infers from this, consistently enough, that conflicts between
states are direct power struggles, in which God, the world-spirit, always
stands at the head of the big batallions. Hegel's realism here has been fas-
tened upon by the ideologists of the imperialist period (such as Meinecke
and Heller) to turn Hegel into a forerunner of the unthinking 'power
politics' promulgated by Treitschke. However, these gentlemen have
managed to overlook two inconvenient details. First, despite Hegel's ignorance of class struggles he never represents the power of a state as an
inexplicable gift of heaven, let alone the product of some 'genius' or

other. It is clear from the earlier contrast between France and Germany that Hegel regarded the immediate predominance of one or the other as just the surface of the problem: he was constantly concerned to discover the mediating factors, the objective social conditions underlying the immediate appearances. And later on, at the time of the shattering defeat of Prussia in the battles of Jena and Auerstedt in 1806, his sympathies may have lain with Napoleon, but this was no mere worship of the Emperor's 'superior force'; it was rather a sympathy for the social inheritance of the French Revolution combined with contempt for a Prussian state corrupted by its degenerate feudal traditions.

This one instance leads us to our second point. Meinecke, Heller and the others all forget that Hegel was the ideologist of a revolutionary age, the age of the revolutionary creation of the great nations of the modern world. Hegel rightly thought this process progressive. It took the form of a series of great wars which Hegel regarded as that state of nature in which the spirit emerges from the immediate dialectic of power struggles to attain the highest point in its history. This high point would be reached when the modern civil society of a great people finally constituted itself as a nation. That is to say, Hegel had grasped the main lines of the great problem of the age, and he also understood, and in this he showed great insight, how the dialectic necessarily makes its way through the seemingly fortuitous and incidental episodes of world history to arrive at its final goal.

However, the boundary of Hegel's view of history now becomes visible, since, on the one hand, he did not see anything beyond that point and, on the other hand, he himself remained enmeshed in the real contradictions surrounding the problem of German national unity. Hence of all the central issues which according to Lenin confronted the democratic revolution in Germany his system focused on just one area of unresolved contradiction.

But all this has nothing in common either historically or philosophically with Bismarck, let alone the 'power politics' of German Imperialism. Meinecke and Heller distort history in much the same way as the various groups of social-imperialist opportunists during the First World War. The latter appropriated the various statements by Marx and Engels about the progressive nature of national wars of liberation and applied them—quite unhistorically—to the imperialist World War with the intention of showing that it too was a 'just' national war worthy of their support. Of course, there are a number of obscurities, ambiguities and outright contradictions in Hegel which—if adroitly selected —will at least serve as a pretext for historical falsification, whereas in the case of Marx and Engels not even the pretext is there. But as the distortions of the ideas of the latter demonstrate, the validity of a pretext is by the way when an apologia of imperialism is what is really at stake.

The main thrust of Hegel's view of history, then, culminates in the concrete realm of human praxis; it aims at achieving a philosophical understanding of the real historical process that necessarily led to the establishment of modern civil society. This necessity arises from the actions of men, from passions and aspirations which, through the dialectics of freedom and necessity, produce other, higher and more universal effects than were originally intended or even contemplated. The concrete dialectic of freedom and necessity means, then, that these individual passions and self-interested aspirations are just as essential to the realization of history as their results are different and more than was originally intended and implicit in the immediate impulses of action. This whole system goes far beyond both the morality and the conception of history contained in subjective idealism. The movement of history according to Hegel is no 'infinite progress', but a concrete process of development; society and history are not the abstract aspirations of the even more abstract 'pure will'.

In a certain sense, Schelling anticipated Hegel's efforts to transcend the view of praxis and history found in subjective idealism. The principles of teleology as re-interpreted by Kant in the *Critique of Judgement* assisted Schelling to reach a new, coherent view of nature and history in their development. In the course of his reflections Schelling did indeed acquire a certain understanding of dialectics, since he glimpsed the fact that the sum of historical events is greater and on a higher plane than was intended by the men who participate in them. Schelling speaks of

'the assumed relation of freedom to a hidden necessity . . . by virtue of which men acting freely, yet against their own will, become the cause of something which they never desired, or conversely, something miscarries and is ruined even though they strove freely and with all the means at their disposal to bring it about.'[34]

But these intimations never lead to any real knowledge. The necessity of which he speaks is described as 'unconscious' in contrast to the conscious nature of freedom. This inflexibility goes so far that, having established the premise that the 'unconscious' is the principle of historical objectivity, he goes on to infer that 'it is simply impossible for anything objective to be produced consciously. . . .'[35] This abstract and unbending opposition between freedom and necessity, conscious and unconscious, eliminates all scope for a concrete dialectics of praxis. A mystical pseudo-dialectics is the most that can be achieved.

Thus on the one hand Schelling ends up in a mystical and irrational view of history, and, on the other hand, he remains firmly inside the framework of Kant's teleology, despite all his efforts to overcome Kant's subjectivity by means of his own specious objectivity. He does indeed sense that the old metaphysics were incapable of grasping the laws of history. He says of the concept of history that

> 'neither an absolutely lawless series of events nor another series entirely governed by law can deserve the name of history.'

But the bare hint of truth contained in this is at once nullified when he goes on to add:

> 'Theory and history are mutually exclusive. Man only has history because no theory can calculate in advance what he will do.'[36]

It is clear that Schelling's ideas lack precisely that quality which distinguishes Hegel's application of the dialectics of purposive action to history and which constitutes his greatness and his importance for later philosophers. It is, therefore, historically impermissible to deduce Hegel's philosophy of history and society from that of Schelling and to equate the ideas of the two men on the subject of freedom and necessity. It is possible and even likely that Schelling's view that history is the unconscious praxis of the absolute acted as a stimulus for Hegel. But it was never more than that. The essential moment of Hegel's philosophy of history is the dialectical unity of theory and practice, i.e. the very thing missing in Schelling who on this point never went beyond the dualism of Kant and Fichte.

The real connection between the two thinkers is in their limitations. In art Schelling discovered a unity of freedom and necessity, of conscious and unconscious production. By analogy with this—and with the aid of intellectual intuition he constructed a unity in the development of nature and history. The defect of the end-product is not so much the abstract mysticism in which it culminated, but the fact that he was never able to concretize or illuminate any given moment of history with its aid. And just here lies the strength of Hegel's system. But Hegel's system too culminates in a mystical chiaroscuro, and this is certainly an element which he shares with Schelling and which, as an idealist, he can never disown.

What is at stake here is the conception of history as a totality. For objective idealism, i.e. for both Hegel and Schelling, nature and history are the products of a 'spirit', and since this is so it follows that the old conception of teleology must inevitably recur, even though Hegel had eliminated it from his detailed discussions of society and history. For if history is an object which is guaranteed by a unified subject, if it is indeed the product of that subject's activity, then, for an objective idealist like Hegel, history itself must realize the purpose which the 'spirit' had posited as a goal from the outset. In consequence, for Hegel as for Schelling, the whole process is thereby transformed into a pseudo-movement: it returns to its starting-point, it is the realization of something that had always existed *a priori*.

Hegel has this to say about it in *The Phenomenology of Mind*:

'What has been said may also be expressed by saying that reason is purposive activity. The exaltation of so-called nature at the expense of thought misconceived, and more especially the rejection of external purposiveness, have brought the idea of purpose in general into disrepute. All the same, in the sense in which Aristotle, too, characterizes nature as purposive activity, purpose is the immediate, the undisturbed, the unmoved which is self-moving; as such it is subject. Its power of moving, taken abstractly, is its existence for itself, or pure negativity. The result is the same as the beginning solely because the beginning is purpose. Stated otherwise, what is actual and concrete is the same as its inner principle or notion simply because the immediate *qua* purpose contains within it the self or pure actuality.'[37]

Hegel fails to notice here that the consistent application of his own teleological principle leads him back into the old theological conception of teleology. His great philosophical achievement had been to take the concept of purpose down from Heaven, where the theologians had placed it, and bring it back to earth, to the reality of actual human action. His concept of teleology remained great, original and creative as long as it remained earthly. But by taking his ideas to their logical conclusion he destroys as an objective idealist, what he had laboriously built up as a dialectician. In this theological twist to his thought there is a lasting affinity between Hegel and Schelling which outlasts their disagreements.

But we must never lose sight of the fact that this affinity is an affinity imposed on them by the defects of their idealism. The difference between them is that before Hegel lost his way in the miasmas of idealism where a mystified demiurge carried on its 'activities', he made a great detour in the course of which he made innumerable fundamental dialectical discoveries. He then pushed forward to that frontier which no idealist can cross. This antithesis between system and method is rudimentary in Schelling and in time it gradually disappears altogether. For this reason what the historian of philosophy must emphasize is the differences between the two views of historical development.

NOTES

1  *Capital*, p. 170.
2  *A Contribution to a Critique of Political Economy. Introduction*, pp. 196–7.
3  *Dialectics of Nature*, p. 36.
4  Hobbes, *De Corpore*, English Works, ed. Molesworth, London 1839, Vol. I, p. 132.
5  Spinoza, *Ethic*, Part I Appendix, pp. 137–8.
6  Ibid., Part IV, p. 284.

7   *Erste Druckschriften*, p. 334f.
8   *Critique of Judgement*, trans. J. J. Bernard, London 1892, 75, pp. 312–13.
9   Ibid., 76, pp. 318–19.
10  Ibid., 77, p. 321.
11  *Dialectics of Nature*, pp. 277–8.
12  *Realphilosophie*, Vol. II, p. 198f. Cf. also Lasson, p. 422 and *Realphilosophie*, Vol. I, p. 220f.
13  *System des transzendentalen Idealismus*, *Werke*, Vol. II, p. 602.
14  *The German Ideology*, London 1965, p. 58.
15  Hegel's *Science of Logic*, trans. A. V. Miller, London 1969, p. 747.
16  Lenin, *Philosophical Notebooks*, pp. 189–90.
17  Hegel, *Science of Logic*, p. 740. Lenin, *Philosophical Notebooks*, pp. 188–9.
19  Hegel, op. cit., p. 821. Lenin, op. cit., pp. 215–16.
20  Lenin, op. cit., p. 216.
21  Ibid., p. 217.
22  Ibid., p. 212. G.L.'s italics.
23  Lasson, p. 330.
24  *Philosophy of Right*, trans Knox, § 189 Addition, p. 268.
25  *Anti-Dühring*, London 1969, p. 136.
26  *Realphilosophie*, Vol. II, p. 251.
27  Ibid., p. 262.
28  Ibid., p. 252.
29  Rosenkranz, p. 180.
30  Ibid., p. 189.
31  Letter to Starkenburg, 25 January 1894, in *Selected Works*, Vol. II, p. 458.
32  *Realphilosophie*, Vol. II, pp. 260ff.
33  Lasson, p. 99f.
34  *System des transzendentalen Idealismus*, *Werke*, Vol. III, p. 594.
35  Ibid., p. 613.
36  Ibid., p. 589.
37  *The Phenomenology of Mind*, p. 83.

# CHAPTER SEVEN

# The limitations of Hegel's economic thought

THE main line of Hegel's thought is an attempt to infer from man's relation to modern civil society all the categories of economics and sociology. He goes on to show how these in turn generate the objective laws
governing the interplay between man, nature and society, and how these
lead to contradictions whose elimination and re-appearance at a higher
level ultimately provides a map of the entire structure of society and
history.

Hegel's novel approach to the philosophical problems of human praxis
is strongly anti-fetishistic. His general dialectical view of the world as a
dynamic complex of contradictions leads him in his attitude to society to
regard all the objective categories of society and economics as dynamic
and contradictory relations between men. Thus his categories shed their
metaphysical inflexibility without having to sacrifice their objectivity.
Hegel's view of praxis always presupposes an interaction with objective
reality. The intensified activity of man and the progress of that activity to
higher and higher levels of achievement continually lead to new discoveries in the objective world which are then sucked into the overall
dialectical movement. The more ramified and complex the system of
human actions becomes, and the more necessary it is to struggle against
metaphysical dogmas and the fetishizing of the categories in which
human relations become objectified as self-created social institutions,
then the more the world of objective determinations will grow and
interact with human activity. In such circumstances the philosophical
tendency towards objectivity will flourish.

The main lines of Hegel's cognitive approach to society are now familiar to us. The question that concerns us now is: what are the limitations
of his method? And furthermore: how are those limitations connected
with his objective idealism? And finally: to what extent is that idealism
itself determined by Hegel's assessment of modern civil society, its origins and its worth? Here too we find ourselves confronted by highly
involved problems which interact in a by no means simple fashion. We
must investigate, on the one hand, the extent to which philosophical
idealism exerts an influence on the boundaries of Hegel's economic
views, and on the other, we must consider how far that idealism is rooted
in his own social position and the view of society arising from it.

The first essential point, one which will not have escaped the attentive reader, is that Hegel perceives civil society as a unified whole. This is undoubtedly a consequence of Germany's economic and social backwardness. The great class struggles in France and England at this period had the effect of forcing thinkers to dig deeply into the objective economic roots of class conflict, even though the classical economists were not yet in a position to realize the implications of this discovery for the antagonistic structure of class society. On the other hand, the immediate experience of these great class struggles led a whole series of thinkers, writers and politicians both in England and France to the more or less clear realization that class conflict was an objective reality. Indeed, roughly contemporary with Hegel's philosophy we may see at least the dawning awareness on the part of a number of people that the class conflicts of bourgeois society must eventually lead beyond the horizon of that society.

Hegel knew nothing of all this. It is true, as we have seen, that he perceived the antithesis of rich and poor in the modern world, not just as a matter of fact but as a necessary consequence of the development of society. (Factories and the resulting growth of poverty.) But it is interesting and also important that this insight had no repercussions for his economic and social attitudes. He neither attempted to relate it to Adam Smith's theory of value, nor did he see it as one of the driving forces of bourgeois society itself. The distinction between rich and poor remained partly a phenomenon which society simply had to learn to accept, and partly a disruptive element in the normal functioning of that society to mitigate whose worst effects was the task of government and state. Hence Hegel's excellent portrayal of the situation and even of the underlying laws which have produced it had no theoretical implications for his conception of the structure of society, let alone for his general philosophy.

The same is true of the entire methodology of Hegel's social philosophy so that Marx's criticism must be fully upheld when he remarks:

'It is moreover wrong to consider society as a single subject, for this is a speculative approach.'[1]

We have already seen that for Hegel the contradictions that determine the course of world history are the conflicts between rather than within nations. We have also been able to observe with what penetration he charted the changes in the social structure of particular nations and how ingeniously he made use of them to explain the progress of international conflicts. But he never thought of these internal changes with their immanent dialectic as the motor of world history.

That is to say, Hegel's philosophy is an idealism nourished on the economic base of the undeveloped class antagonisms of Germany. It would of course be an over-simplification if we were crudely to explain all the implications of Hegel's economic idealism in terms of his place in the social order. We have already noticed that the horizon of his philosophy extends far beyond the frontiers of Germany and that its essential features reflect less the contemporary state of Germany than the social and economic problems that arose on a European scale in the wake of the French Revolution and the Industrial Revolution in England. Nevertheless, it remains true that even these tended to reinforce Hegel's economic idealism. What I have in mind here is Hegel's exaggerated enthusiasm for the society of post-revolutionary France and above all the social and political changes that would be introduced, as he hoped, under the rule of Napoleon. Thanks to this Hegel's idealism, which was rooted in Germany, was further strengthened, for it was coloured by a sense of optimism, an enthusiasm, for the rebirth of the world, of a new configuration of the world-spirit whose consummation is reached in *The Phenomenology of Mind*. Without these exaggerated expectations, without these utopian hopes, the backwardness of Germany would quite certainly have had a very different impact on Hegel's philosophy.

Of course, we must not overlook one further social element at work in Germany which necessarily influenced Hegel's thought in this direction. Lenin has repeatedly pointed out that national unification was the central problem of the bourgeois revolution in Germany. We have seen how this played an important role in Hegel's intellectual and political development. Later on, it is true, he came increasingly to think of a Napoleonic solution to the problem of national unity, a problem which was connected in his mind with the elimination of the vestiges of feudalism and of the patch-work of petty states. But this should not be taken to suggest that the question of national unity ceased to occupy a prominent place in his thought and hence to reinforce his tendency to view society as a unified subject.

It is from here that we have to understand the birth of Hegel's doctrine of the state as the realization of 'reason': this is the vantage-point from which the state can appear as standing apart from the conflicts of civil society. (We shall soon see the effect of this upon the relations obtaining between civil society and the state.) The state can only be assigned such a role as this because Hegel believed that the nation could only become the embodiment of the concrete historical configurations of the spirit within the state. The history of the spirit does, of course, contain dialectical contradictions, indeed the entire course of world-history takes the form of conflicts and their repercussions. His view of world-history is of an unbroken series of conflicts in the course of which the flag of progress, the embodiment of the various stages of the world-spirit passes from one nation to the other. What we have in short is a sort of metempsychosis of the world-spirit in which the different nations have a unified configuration in which the world-spirit manifests itself at each particular stage of its journey.

There are two factors of interest here that must not be overlooked. First, within certain limits it is a legitimate procedure to try and define the 'character' of a nation. Only crude vulgarizers of Marxism fail to see this and strive to extinguish national characteristics by means of the doctrine of a succession of 'formations'. Because Marxism investigates the social origins of the uneven development in, let us say, France and England, because it recognizes that classes and class struggles must take different forms in different conditions, it is able to arrive at a more satisfactory understanding of national peculiarities than bourgeois thinkers and historians (Hegel included), who overlook the true forces at work and so arrive at more or less metaphysical views about national unity. So here, too, the radical transformation of a metaphysical problem into a dialectical one leads to a concretization of thought.

Second, we should not overlook the fact that the methodological endproduct of Hegel's philosophy of history is a necessary result, but it is one which obscures our view of the wealth of cross-currents present in his thought. We have seen some of these in our earlier discussions. And when we look at the account given in *The Phenomenology of Mind* of the way in which the spirit of Greece mutates into the spirit of Rome we can see that the process described by Hegel is essentially internal. This is above all the case in the *Phenomenology* where, as we might expect from its general approach, external events are played down, so that, for example, the destruction of the city-states in war and conquest (Macedonia, Rome) is not even mentioned. The dissolution of the Greek spirit is largely an internal process. The zenith and decline of Rome and the collapse of the *ancien régime* in France are also regarded in this manner in the *Phenomenology*. And by the time he came to the later *Philosophy of History* Hegel had accumulated such a wealth of information about society and culture that the tendency towards internal explanation was even more pronounced than in *The Phenomenology of Mind*.

But it is still only a counter-tendency which for all its importance never really gains the upper hand. The metaphysical unity of the spirit of the nation is a methodological necessity in Hegel's objective idealism. To dissolve that unity into the dynamic contradictions of antagonistic forces locked in conflict would indeed give rise to a very clear definition of national character, but since it would have no unified authority guaranteeing it, it would inevitably burst the confines of objective idealism. So cross-currents are undeniably present and sometimes they are extremely powerful. But they can only thrive within the framework of objective idealism. It is a significant fact that these tendencies and the greater concreteness of the historical analysis associated with them are most prominent wherever Hegel can by-pass the problem of the state. This happens, for instance, in the second part of the *Phenomenology* and in the *Aesthetics*.

The inability of these counter-tendencies to break through the idealist framework can be accounted for by referring to another no less contradictory aspect of his outlook: his resolute rejection of any thorough-going democracy, his failure to recognize the productive energies in the lower classes. We know of Hegel's views in this respect from his expressed opinions about the French Revolution, and we know too that they do not represent a defection from his youthful republicanism, but that they were an important element in his mental make-up right from the start. Nevertheless, his opinion about this question reflects back on his entire scheme of world-history, on his account of the development of antiquity and the Middle Ages. Now, of course, in contrast to his position in Berne, he does take cognizance of the slavery that existed in antiquity and he no longer underestimates the significance of slavery for the political life of the 'freemen' in the Greek city-states. We have also seen the weight given to 'servitude' and slavery in the development of human culture. But this is still a long way from saying that the antagonism between slaves and slave-owners, feudal lords and serfs played a major part in Hegel's dialectic of world history. Hegel's recognition of the productive energies of the 'mob' is confined to economics and this makes it easier for him to maintain the mystification of a unified spirit in the people and the state. This is an additional reason for the inability of counter-tendencies in his thought to make themselves felt.

It is easy enough to criticize Hegel now from our superior vantage-point. It is much more difficult to grasp the point that, given the economic, social and political situation in Germany at the time, a great and all-embracing philosophy such as Hegel's could not possibly have been created on radical-democratic foundations. Even the undemocratic perspective from which Hegel undertook to defend the idea of a progress through contradictions contains utopian overtones *vis-à-vis* the realities of Germany, a tendency to soar above the actual state of affairs. Fortunately, he does not simply vanish into the clouds, but, by leaving Germany behind him, he can base himself more surely on the world-historical processes taking place in France and England. Thus for all the idealist and utopian features of his thought, Hegel had his feet firmly planted on the ground of reality.

Following the defeat of the Babeuf conspiracy[2] and given the graveyard stillness of Germany, a radical democratic movement could not possibly have found support. Any such movement would have inevitably collapsed into subjective utopianism. The example of Hölderlin and Fichte shows perfectly what the result would have been. It is therefore not just a defect in Hegel if his ideas developed in an anti-democratic direction. We see the same trend in all the important figures in Germany at the time, and in Goethe above all. The contradictory strands in

German idealist dialectics enabled it to dissolve the metaphysical dogmas of the old materialism and at the same time, unconsciously, and somewhat in conflict with its own idealist programme, to incorporate powerful elements of an authentic materialism. But this could only occur in a situation which combined what was in Germany the least possible amount of utopianism with a concrete, uninhibited and quite unapologetic defence of progress in history. In the circumstances prevailing in Germany radical democracy could not be a creative feature of this realistic and dialectical view of reality, very much in contrast to Germany after the July Revolution or Russia in the 1850s and 1860s, when it became the basis for a comprehensive philosophy of history and society.

If we now turn to a closer examination of Hegel's Jena philosophy of society we may begin by noting two major flaws in it, both of which are closely connected with his economic idealism. First, the internal structure of society, its articulation into classes is not deduced from his economics. Second, the state and the government are not regarded for their part as the products of an internal economic and social dialectic of class conflict. These two defects could only be incorporated in the system because Hegel had abandoned his own highly original method of developing the higher categories from the lower ones by means of their internal contradictions (labour—division of labour; tools—machines, etc.) and instead had imposed an idealist construct from above.

In both cases it is impossible to overlook the tense inner struggle between the conflicting elements of his thought. Again and again he has an intimation of the right pattern, again and again he feels the need to work out the true, organic relationships. We may even go so far as to say that the dialectical deduction of the estates becomes increasingly 'economic'. The pinnacle of his purely idealistic philosophy was attained, as we shall shortly see, in Jena in his first attempt to construct a system. And the tendency towards an ever more concrete, more economic explanation of the social order does not by any means cease after Jena; on the contrary, it grows apace. We have already shown that the final and the sharpest formulation of the opposition between rich and poor was contained in *The Philosophy of Right* and this was no accident. For it was here that Adam Smith was joined by Ricardo as a guide in economic matters. And this tendency was strengthened still further in *The Philosophy of Right*. It is very characteristic of the way in which Hegel continued to develop and to cast old ideas aside that, following the July Revolution, in his very last essay, the pamphlet on the English Reform Bill (1831), he even came down in favour of the view that the old threefold division of the classes into nobility, burghers and peasantry no longer corresponded to the reality in most states.[3] It is true that, characteristically, he drew no general conclusions from this insight into a socio-economic reality. On the contrary, he still believed that if the government took the right steps, the existing structures could be maintained. But the mere fact that he so closely followed a development running counter to his basic scheme and that he had no hesitation in recording its implications, however much these went against his own views, testifies to the strength of the conflict within him. Of course, this very example shows that the contrary tendencies could never become the prevailing ones.

We can follow Hegel's gradual development towards a more realistic and economically based analysis of the estates structure in his Jena writings very precisely. The first statement of his social ideas, the *System of Ethics* marks the high point of his systematic idealism. It is no accident that this coincides with his most enthusiastic experimentation with Schelling's terminology. The growth of realism runs parallel to his gradual rejection of Schelling's conceptual world. As always, Hegel's starting-point is the people as a unified whole, that then articulates itself in the different estates in order finally to achieve a new synthesis. And we observe at once that in the process of arriving at this point Hegel betrays the higher dialectical insights he had already acquired. For his general practice was to start with a dynamic contradiction which he would resolve in that unity and contradiction characteristic of him, i.e. a resolution of the contradiction which followed from the dialectics of the matter itself to higher levels of contradiction and synthesis. Here, in contrast, the movement proceeds in the opposite direction: from unity via difference and back to unity. That being the case, it is inevitable that the synthesis should be of the Schellingian sort, i.e. that the contradictions should be wholly obliterated. However, the method is not entirely explicable in terms of Schelling's influence. It is rather an unavoidable consequence of the contradictions in Hegel's own view of society. We have already discussed the cross-currents in that view and we shall later see them at work in more detail. But we have also seen their ultimate inefficacy and our analysis of 'externalization' in *The Phenomenology of Mind* will show us that we are faced with a fundamental contradiction of Hegel's entire philosophy, one which he could never overcome without at the same time breaking free from the conceptual framework of objective idealism as such. As we know, this was simply not possible. Hegel's greatness lay in his ability to carve out great areas of experience where his more realistic impulses could be given a relatively free rein.

Hegel's development in Jena was one in which, within the overall conception of 'ethical life', objective, historical and economic aspects of life were given more and more emphasis at the expense of the merely moral. In the *System of Ethics* the importance of morality was still paramount. Proceeding from the unity of the people, Hegel deduces the different estates which are distinguished in terms of different stages of virtue. Hegel conducts this argument in this way:

'The people as an organic totality is the absolute indifference of all the determinate aspects of practical and ethical existence. Their phases are the form of identity, of indifference, then of difference, and finally of absolute, living indifference; and none of these phases is an abstraction, but all are reality. The concept of ethical life lies in its objectivity, in the annulment of individuality. . . . Ethical power is articulated within this perfect totality by the estates, and the principle of each is a determinate form of ethical existence. . . . Thus there is an estate of absolute free ethical existence, an estate of rectitude and an estate of unfree or natural ethical life.'[4]

The general progression from unity via difference and back to unity is clearly visable, as is the fact that the distinctions between the estates are distinctions in the unified ethical life of the people, a hierarchy of virtues in effect. The economic and social distinctions between the estates thus come to represent adequate fields of activity for these virtues.

Thus Hegel's argument proceeds from above to below, i.e. from the universal class to the class where a merely natural ethical existence holds sway, whereas the most mature outline of the social structure in Jena, the Lectures of 1805–6, advances in the opposite direction, from the 'concrete' labour of the peasant, via the increasing levels of abstraction in the middle classes, up to the highest universality of the upper class. It would be a mistake to see the distinction as something purely external or formal. For the road from below to above enshrines Hegel's impulse to greater realism, to a much more 'economic' view of the character of the different estates. And it is not just by chance that this more realistic and dialectical approach cannot be achieved with Schelling's conceptual system, even though it proved to be the perfect vehicle for the outline presented in the *System of Ethics*. The road from below to above is a prefiguration, an anticipation of the phenomenological method: the authentic Hegelian presentation of the nature of the spirit culminates in his view of it as a dialectical process of self-creation and self-discovery in the objects created. If the spirit is conceived as a result of a dialectical process it can only be presented in terms of a progression from below to above, whereas the deductive process from above to below has a profound affinity with Schelling's method of annulling contradictions in the static unity of intellectual intuition.

We have described the class structure outlined in the *System of Ethics* as essentially a hierarchy of virtues, but it is to be hoped that the reader will not be misled into thinking Hegel has drawn any nearer to an ethics on the lines of Kant and Fichte. For Hegel does not think of these virtues as abstract or formal in the least; they are by no means a mere 'ought' for a moral subjectivity. They are, on the contrary, the concrete totalities of social determinations within the concrete totality of society as a whole.

If we are to look back in history for models which anticipate Hegel here, we shall find them not in Kant and Fichte, but in the social philosophers of the Enlightenment, such as Montesquieu. Montesquieu's theory of the state makes a distinction between virtues and vices along socio-historical lines by arguing that under a monarchy the virtues which can and must have a positive social function are quite distinct from those which might have that effect in a republic. Hegel recognized the affinities between himself and Montesquieu quite clearly. In the essay on *Natural Law*, written a short while later, he remarked:

'It must be recognized how all the parts of the constitution and of the legislature, and how all the manifestations of ethical relations are utterly determined by the whole, and form an edifice in which no element whether structural or decorative existed *a priori*, but where each became what it is by virtue of the whole and remains subject to it. It is in this sense that *Montesquieu* based his immortal work on his idea of the individuality and the character of the nations. . . .'[5]

It is clear that the affinity is purely one of method, although, having said that, the parallel is far-reaching enough. And we see here, too, as in many other areas, that in his efforts to overcome the abstract character of subjective idealism Hegel has recourse to the methodological heritage of the great empiricists and realists of the Enlightenment.

Of course, this raises a new problem for him, a new contradiction in his conception of praxis. The social differentiation of morality was socio-historical fact for Montesquieu, one which he simply noted and analysed. Hegel, however, finds himself confronting the following dilemma: on the one hand, the concrete totality of socio-historical determinations (both in the objective realm of moral activity and in their subjective determinacy) is the method designed to overcome the more abstract subjectivity of the morality of Kant and Fichte. It is this concreteness, this socio-historical unity of the subjective and objective principles of morality that he opposes to the would-be sublimity of the abstract 'ought', the vacuous categorical imperative of Kant and Fichte. On the other hand, he finds it impossible to leave the matter there with moral values neatly assigned to particular places in the class structure. His road leads him into an impenetrable tangle of contradictions. For if his social philosophy were to culminate in the idea that the highest virtue, the highest level of consciousness attainable by each person, can only be that appropriate to his class, then he would be compelled to recognize that class antagonisms are the foundation of society—an idea which, as we have seen, necessarily lay beyond his horizon.

Moreover, simply to have asserted the fact of differentiation and to have left matters there would also have been inexcusably superficial. Society always constitutes an objective unity, albeit a dynamic, contradictory one, and Marx, Engels, Lenin and Stalin always placed the greatest emphasis on the implications of this for the formation of consciousness. Only in vulgar sociology do the individual classes constitute 'window-less monads'. For all sorts of reason then, Hegel was compelled both to regard the concrete differentiation of the virtues according to class as an essential principle of reality, and also to think of the principle as something that would be transcended in the higher unity. The contradictions flowing from this dilemma will frequently occupy our attention in our further discussions.

Hegel's analysis of the various classes remains basically stable even though he keeps refining on them, particularly as far as their economic characteristics are concerned. We shall therefore follow the account given in the Lectures of 1805–6, since that is the most developed one. On the other hand, his method of analysing the structure of society is more interesting. Hegel never again returned to that deduction from 'above' to which we have referred here. Obviously, his experiment with Schelling's conceptual system did not satisfy him.

The essay on *Natural Law* which followed close on the heels of the *System of Ethics* applied a radically different method: an historical one. Hegel takes the world of antiquity and its collapse as his starting-point and attempts to deduce from its development the three estates of modern society, of which he had already spoken in the earlier work. In many respects these historical observations are reminiscent of the philosophy of history of his earliest writings, but it is just at this point that we can see the extent of the change in his views.

Hegel's analysis concentrates on the first two estates. It is true that slavery does enter into his discussions of antiquity and the peasantry is occasionally mentioned also. But these are appendages which are not properly incorporated into the dialectic. What Hegel finds important is the opposition between freemen and bondsmen, and in antiquity, between the citizens of the *polis* and those whose task it is to provide material support for the freemen who live in politics and war. Thus the image of antiquity corresponds largely to the idea he had formed in his earliest youth. The only difference is that Hegel now depicts the material, economic foundations on which the freedom, the free political activity of the citizen of the *polis*, is based.

The account of the decline of antiquity also contains certain similarities to Hegel's earlier ideas. It is interesting to see that Gibbon is his historical source both now and then. Moreover, his general conclusions now are closely similar to his earlier ones, and in particular he attributes the decline of antiquity to the triumph of private life over public. The difference now is that, hitherto, Hegel had regarded this victory of the private only as something negative, as pure degeneration; whereas now he formulates the change in this way:

'With the loss of absolute ethics and the debasement of the class of nobles, the two previously existing separate classes have become equal. . . . The necessary triumph of the principle of formal unity and equality has done away with the true inner distinction between the classes. . . . The principle of universality and equality had to take possession of the whole in such a way as to replace the particular classes with a mixture of the two. Beneath the law of formal unity what has really happened is that this mixture has annulled the first class and made the second class into the sole class of the nation.'[6]

We see here the prototype of the philosophy of history contained in *The Phenomenology of Mind* where the decline of classical democracy under the Roman Empire becomes the foundation of the 'rule of law', the birth of the abstract juridical 'person'. Through the mediation of Christianity which now begins to make itself felt, this state of affairs gives rise to modern civil society, society based on the principle of individuality, the society of the bourgeois. Hegel regards this development as utterly inexorable. And even though this society ought not to achieve absolute supremacy, it must be allowed to grow to its fullest extent:

'This system of property and law which for the sake of singularity sacrifices the absolute and eternal in favour of the finite and formal, must be detached and separated off from the estate of nobles and constituted into an estate of its own where it may expand to its fullest extent . . . if this system must both develop itself and destroy that free ethical life wherever it mingles with its institutions and is not separated from them and their consequences, then it must be accepted consciously, its right should be acknowledged, it should be barred from the estate of nobles and assigned an estate, a realm of its own where it may establish itself and develop its own full activity through its own confusion and the abolition of that confusion.'[7]

This argument culminates in the proclamation of the economic dominion and the 'political nullity' of the *bourgeois* and it represents the clearest and frankest statement yet of Hegel's Jena philosophy of history. The profound contradictions that emerge from such a view of contemporary society are explored by Hegel in Chapter 8 which deals with 'Tragedy and Comedy in the realm of the ethical'. We shall postpone our own examination of these problems until then. For the time being we shall confine ourselves to a short description of Hegel's view of society. It is, to put it briefly, the social theory of the Napoleonic Age: it is the systematic expression of the illusions which Hegel cherished about the age. Their social import was roughly this: everything for the bourgeoisie in the economic sphere, but nothing for the bourgeoisie in the realm of politics and above all in the world-historical role of the nation, something which expresses itself primarily in war.

It is a very striking feature of the Jena period that war should be allotted such a crucial role. This had been prepared for as early as the essay on the *German Constitution*: the analysis of Germany's internal decay was designed to explain why the nation had become incapable of defending itself whereas the other mode of defeating feudalism had transformed France into a great military power. (We may recollect Hegel's early notes about the difference between the armies of the *ancien régime* and the Revolution, p. 44–5.) This emphasis on war is maintained throughout the Jena reflections on social philosophy.

It is only from this angle that we can begin to understand what Hegel meant by the 'class of nobles', the 'universal class'. This is the name given to the new, dominant military stratum that came to the fore in France after the Revolution and formed a new nobility under Napoleon. Rosenzweig and other more recent scholars of Hegel entirely distort the facts by imagining that Hegel has the traditional nobility in mind here. The dominance of singularity in modern society, the self-creation of the individual who has 'alienated' or 'externalized' himself cuts the ground from beneath the feet of the hereditary nobility. Hegel does speak, it is true, of a hereditary monarch in the Lectures of 1805–6, and he thinks of the person and family of the monarch as something 'natural', but he makes an exception for the monarch alone.

'*Other individuals have value only to the extent to which they are "externalized" and cultivated beings, as what they have made of themselves.*'[8]

This view is in line with the idea which pervades all the Jena writings that courage, the readiness to lay down one's life for one's country, is not just the highest of all virtues, but in practice the only one which can transcend particularity, the only one in which the concrete universality of the life of the nation can be realized in the single individual.

This conception of the first estate is buttressed by a philosophy of history which maintains that a constant, uninterrupted peace must lead to degeneration, trivialization and the collapse of civil society. In *The Phenomenology of Mind* we can find the most extreme formulation of this position:

'In order not to let [individuals] become rooted and settled in this isolation and thus break up the whole into fragments causing the common spirit to evaporate, government has from time to time to shake them to the very centre by war. By this means it confounds the order that has been established and arranged, and violates the right to independence, while the individuals (who, being absorbed therein, come adrift from the whole, though striving after inviolable *self-existence* and personal security), are made, by the task thus imposed on them by government, to feel the power of their lord and master, death. By thus breaking up the form of fixed stability, spirit guards the ethical order from sinking into merely natural existence, preserves the self of which it is conscious, and raises that self to the level of *freedom* and its own powers.'[9]

To grasp the real historical sources of this attitude it is sufficient to recall Marx's description of the Napoleonic era for this makes it quite clear that what Hegel did was to express the essence of that age in philosophical terms (together with all the misconceptions that were only to be expected from a man writing from the point of view of German idealism). Marx writes:

'Napoleon represented the last struggle of *revolutionary terrorism* against *civil society* and its policy, which was likewise established by the Revolution. Certainly Napoleon already understood the nature of the *modern state*; he recognized that it was based on the free development of civil society, on the free play of private interests, etc. He decided to acknowledge this basis and to protect it. He was not a visionary revolutionary. But Napoleon still regarded the state as an *end in itself*, and civil society only as a treasurer, a *subordinate* who was allowed to have no *will of his own*. He *practised* terrorism by substituting *permanent war* for *permanent revolution*. He satisfied to the full French national egoism, but he demanded in return the sacrifice of civil affairs, pleasure, wealth, etc., every time the political aim of conquest required it.'[10]

It is on foundations such as these that Hegel arrives at the final and most mature statement of his views on the structure of civil society in the Lectures of 1805–6. As we have already emphasized, the dialectical movement proceeds upwards from below, from the particular to the general. He attempts to depict the spirit in movement and to portray its structure as the product of that self-movement. The class structure is, as it were, a phenomenological process in the course of which spirit discovers itself. Within Hegel's Jena philosophy this is the most concrete and most emphatically economic analysis of the stratification of society into estates. The lacunae and fissures in his argument are correspondingly more overt here than anywhere. At the same time, we can also begin to see why Hegel's conception of ethics and its concrete manifestation in the class structure does not portend the final self-discovery of the spirit, but gives us instead the dialectical odyssey of spirit through society and the state. It is no accident that in these lectures we find for the first time that Hegel has introduced art, religion and philosophy as representing the highest phase of spirit, the phase he would later call absolute spirit. At least, the substance of this concept is already there, and also its problematic nature, even though the term is not yet employed.

The theoretical development of the estates and the subsequent advance of the spirit to the stage beyond is described by Hegel in these terms:

'Three things must now be demonstrated: First, the members of the whole, the hard external organization and its entrails, the powers they possess; second, the *outlook* of each estate, its self-consciousness, its *being* as pure knowing: immediate amputation from existence, the spirit's knowledge of its member as such, and *elevation* above it; the former, ethical life, the latter, morality. Third, religion. The first is spiritual nature at liberty; the second is its *knowledge* of itself as knowledge; the third, spirit knowing itself as absolute spirit, religion.—The estate and the spirit of the estate,—this determinate spirit is what actually develops from barbaric trust and labour on towards absolute spirit's knowledge of itself. It is at first the *life* of a people in general. From this it must struggle free. . . . The spirit which knows all reality and essence as itself contemplates itself, is its own object; or it is an existent organism. It forms its consciousness. It is as yet only true spirit, in itself. In every estate it has a distinct task, knowledge of its existence and activity in it, and a particular concept, knowledge of its essence. Both must partly separate and partly join together.'[11]

We can see here the problem of which we spoke earlier: the necessity for Hegel to rise above society, to establish the realm of absolute spirit in which the authentic self-discovery of mind would be consummated. Hegel is more or less clear in his mind about the complicated dialectics of this procedure. That he is well aware of the ramifications of the relation of the individual to modern civil society is shown by the fact that he builds the sphere of individual moral attitudes, the sphere of 'morality' into the social system (even though the movement of morality constantly aspires to a supra-social status) and assigns to morality a place in one sense above society, and in another sense below it (because of its abstract nature). (The dialectics of this are not finally worked out until the *Philosophy of Right*. Only there does it appear as the sphere of negation and difference which dialectically links the abstract system of mere 'right' with the concrete totality of the ethical life of the people.)

But even the most elaborate statement of this dialectic does not bring Hegel any nearer to a solution to the problem. In the later system, too, the absolute realm of art, religion and philosophy is placed higher than society, the realm of objective spirit. In the Lectures under discussion Hegel reveals one of the chief motives for this further progress of the spirit. As he has just informed us, spirit in a perfect society is still only spirit *in itself*. That is to say: it has divided up into its various moments (the estates). In themselves these form a unity; but this unity is not yet conscious of itself, i.e. it does not yet exist *for itself*; it has not yet consciously become incarnate in the consciousness of a single individual. The dialectic of morality and ethical life contains the imperative which insists that the individual moral consciousness (which must necessarily be abstract) can only find fulfilment when concretely incarnate in ethical life. (i.e. in the outlook of the estate to which the individual belongs by his own choice and achievement.) Hence a further progress beyond estates-consciousness, an estates-consciousness that preserves while it annuls, is possible for Hegel only in a religious form. On this point he writes as follows in the same Lectures:

'In religion everyone rises to a view of himself as a universal self. His nature, his *estate fades* like a dream, *like a distant island gleaming like a haze of mist on the edge of the horizon.* He is the equal of princes. His knowledge is of himself, as spirit; before God he is the equal of anyone. We see the externalization of his entire realm, his entire existing world—not the externalization which is only form, *culture* and whose content is once again the sensuous world, but the universal externalization of reality as a whole; this externalization restores reality to itself as something perfect.'[12]

In this passage we can plainly see one of the motifs that has become indispensable in Hegel's system as a result of the importance conferred on religion, and specifically on Christianity. It is no less plain that this motif is by no means religious in nature. The realization of a state in which spirit exists for itself, its elevation above the division of society into estates each with its own sharply distinct point of view, can only be annulled in the Hegelian sense, i.e. preserved at the same time as it is annulled, if a concept of complete equality can be discovered, with the aid of which spirit really can recognize itself. But (1) the inequality of wealth in capitalist society is an irremovable datum; it is indeed the economic foundation for that development of individuality which he considers the principle that renders the modern age superior to that of antiquity. (2) Hegel can have no conception of a state of affairs in which men might be truly equal. (3) his anti-democratic beliefs prevent him from sharing the illusions of the radical democrats at the time of the French Revolution. Finally, (4) he is willing to recognize the bourgeoisie as the representative class of the modern economic development, but he steadfastly refuses to adjudge them, their existence and consciousness, the crowning point of the entire history of man. For all these reasons no concept of equality remains available to Hegel but that of the equality of all men before God.

We shall later consider Hegel's tense and ambivalent relationship with Christianity at length in our discussion of the *Phenomenology*. At this point it was only necessary to draw attention to the important social impulse at work here. And in this context it is perhaps not without interest to note Napoleon's views on Christianity, for these contain definite parallels with Hegel's attitudes. Of course, the affinity operates at an abstract level: Napoleon was himself the leading figure in the great drama of the age; he put into action the deeds whose philosophical essence Hegel attempted to elucidate. For this reason, his attitude to Christianity could be expressed with a much more overt cynicism. It was enough for him to open the churches, to conclude a Concordat with the Pope, to have the Pope crown him Emperor and so on. At the same time he could freely express his own personal opinion about religion with the greatest cynicism. However, when Hegel attempted to reproduce the movement of history and the illusions it necessarily engenders, he was bound to take up a positive stance towards religion. Privately, there were indications enough that he also shared some of Napoleon's cynicism and these can be found not only in private utterances which we shall quote in their proper place, but also, if involuntarily, in his entire dialectical analysis of religion itself.

With all these reservations Napoleon's explicit views can undoubtedly throw light on Hegel's view of religion. He says:

'As far as I am concerned, I see in religion not the mystery of incarnation, but the mystery of the social order. It connects the idea of equality with Heaven and so prevents the rich from being slaughtered by the poor. . . . Society cannot survive without inequality of wealth, and inequality of wealth cannot endure without religion.'[13]

Hegel's Lectures of 1805–6 analyse the system of estates in a 'phenomenological' fashion. The estates represent what might be called the division of labour of objective spirit and they represent the different stages in the journey of spirit to its consciousness of itself. For this reason Hegel starts with the peasantry, since that is the class closest to a state of nature. We can see once again the high level of Hegel's understanding of economics in the fact that he looks for the essential distinction between the peasantry and the middle class in the different character of the work they perform. He contrasts the concrete labour of the peasant with the abstract labour involved in trade and industry and realizes that the explanation for this is that the peasant works to supply his own needs and not for the market. (Here, of course, we can again see how Hegel translates the ideas of the English economists into German. Since he has only read about farmers who pay ground-rent and produce for the market, and has never seen them in the flesh, he ignores their existence in his analysis.)

'The peasantry is, therefore the unindividuated trust that has its *individuality in that unconscious individual*, the earth. As a labourer the peasant does not perform abstract labour but instead he provides for most or all of his wants; in the same way his labour is only inwardly connected with his activity. The context of his purpose and its realization is the unconscious, nature; he ploughs, sows, but it is God who makes things prosper and provides the seasons and the trust that what he has put in the ground will grow of itself. The activity is subterranean.'[14]

Thus in Hegel's eyes the peasantry is the coarse and unconscious foundation of civil society. Just as he pays no heed to changes in the English peasantry, so too the solution to the peasant problem produced by the French Revolution apparently made no impression on him. He has eyes only for the retrograde peasantry of Germany.

This is all the more striking as his view of society requires that the peasantry should form the great mass of the army and we have already seen that he devoted much thought to the army and pondered in particular on the social roots of the superiority of the revolutionary and Napoleonic army. But his distrust of every mass movement from below obscured his vision. However bluntly he rebuts the claims of the surviving remnants of feudalism in Germany, however unreservedly he acknowledges the superiority of revolutionary France, the people never quite cease to be an aggregate of pre-revolutionary German philistines in his eyes. The army—whose significance for his theory of history and society we have seen—is no 'people in arms'; the middle class only makes material sacrifices in war, the peasants are mere cannon-fodder,—it is all as it was in the wars of the old feudal absolutism. The reflection of the German *misère* in his philosophy distorts his Napoleonic vision and reduces it to German philistinism.

In harmony with this view Hegel can see in a possible peasant uprising nothing but:

'a mad, blind, phenomenon . . . a flood which only destroys; at best it leaves a fertile marsh behind it, but otherwise it just recedes without achieving anything.'[15]

Raised above the peasantry is the estate of abstract labour, of trade and law, the bourgeoisie. We are already familiar with Hegel's analysis of its economic significance: it is the realm of contingency which attains necessity by developing its own autonomous laws. The German character of Hegel's social philosophy can be seen clearly in the chief feature of the outlook of this class: its rectitude. Evidently, Hegel was thinking of the German philistine rather than the English capitalist. We know from his account of the economic situation that the merchant is the highest representative of this class.

This is interesting and characteristic of his dominant phenomenological tendency to proceed from the lower to the higher and to derive the general from the particular: the middle class ends with the merchant and the account of the universal class begins with the man of affairs and advances via the scholar to its climatic point: the soldier. The method involves a progression from the particular to the general. Hegel says quite explicitly evidently referring to peasants and bourgeois:

> 'The lower classes or those whose object and consciousness lies in the particular.'[16]

He then accomplishes the transition in the following manner:

> 'The public class works for the state. The spirit has raised itself to the universal level in the *man of affairs*. But his labour is very divided, abstract, mechanical. It doubtless serves the universal immediately, but in a limited and fixed manner, which he cannot alter . . . He raises the determinate universal to knowledge of the universal . . . The spirit has raised him above his actual character [as man of affairs]. The authentic man of affairs is in part also a *scholar*.'[17]

Artificial though this is in parts, its superiority to the arguments of the *System of Ethics* is very plain. And if we do accept Hegel's premises, there really is a gradual development from the particular to the universal in which the crucial role is played by abstract labour, the unconscious self-transformation of every individual labour and every individual economic activity under capitalism into a social, universal activity. In short, if we accept his premises we may allow that there is a real understanding of the structure of modern civil society.

But this is true at best only to the stage of the man of affairs. The transition from there to the scholar is already artificial and strained. Hegel himself seems disinclined to regard the class of scholars as the social incarnation of true universality of thought, as the self-knowledge of objective spirit. He remarks dryly:

The scholar's prime concern is vanity of self.'[18] And from the scholar to the soldier there is no real transition at all: the soldier stands at the apex of society for a variety of reasons which we have already mentioned. But they have nothing to do with the economic, phenomenological movement from particular to universal.

We observe, then, that although Hegel has made the greatest efforts to provide an analysis of the estates-structure in economic terms, a not unimportant part of it is entirely spurious. The difficulties he encountered are only partly connected with those aspects of his view of society with which we are already familiar. There is a further facet of his economics that we must also consider briefly.

At issue is the decisive importance Hegel assigns to the juridical concept of 'recognition' within his economics. Thanks to this concept alone certain categories are elevated to the true dignity of economic categories; in other cases he establishes distinctions of no economic importance, but he lays great stress on them because they illustrate the principle of 'recognition' so vividly. Thus he makes an important distinction between possession and property:

'A possession contains the contradiction that a thing as such is universal and yet it exists as the possession of a single person. This contradiction is resolved by consciousness which posits it as the opposite of itself; when recognized, it is both single possession and something universal, for in this single possession all possess . . . My possession has acquired the form of consciousness; it is defined as my possession; but as *property* it pertains not just to me alone, but is universal.'[19]

Here we have an ingenious, almost scholastically tortuous argument to justify the juridical duplication of economic life. Hegel's aim is not just to reformulate economic categories in juridical terms, to raise them above mere economics in his conceptual scheme, but to quarry a new content from the juridical form. He proceeds in similar fashion to argue that a contract is a higher form of exchange.

'This knowledge is expressed in the *contract*. It is the same as exchange, but it is ideal exchange: (a) I give nothing away, I externalize nothing, I give nothing but my *word*, language, that I wish to externalize myself; (b) the other does likewise. This externalization of mine is also his will; he is satisfied if I give this to him, (c) It is also his externalization, it is our *common* will; my externalization is mediated by his. I only wish to externalize myself, because *he* wishes to externalize himself, because his negative becomes my positive. There is an *exchange* of declarations, not objects, but it is as valid as the exchange of objects. Both acknowledge the will of the other as such.—The will has returned to *its own concept*.'[20]

The over-valuation of juridical principles in the sphere of economics does not imply any approximation to the rather different over-estimation of the same thing in Kant and Fichte, even though the tendency is closely linked with the philosophical idealism common to them all. With Fichte, in particular, it is connected with his mistaken belief that until the rule of pure morality had arrived, the social life of man could be guided towards morality by laws and regulations. We know how Hegel ridiculed this idea. He always regarded the facts of society and economics as the true powers of life and it did not occur to him to violate them with some concept or other. For in his view the force and dignity of the concept manifests itself most clearly in these very facts of life as life itself has moulded them.

What drives Hegel in this direction are two motifs of philosophical idealism. First, we see here a general tendency of the whole age. In the course of some comments on civil society contemporary with the Feuerbach Theses, Marx talks about the origin of the modern state in the French Revolution:

'The self-conceit of the political sphere . . . all elements exist in duplicate form, as civic elements and (those of) the state.'[21]

This duplication which can be seen most strikingly in the doubling of man as *bourgeois* and as *citoyen*, occurs in Hegel as a division of economic categories into economic and juridical ones. But the great importance of this process, the central position occupied at times by 'recognition' is connected with the specific character of his entire philosophy.

We have already made mention of the category of 'externalization' in the context of Hegel's discussion of economic problems. A detailed analysis of the concept must be delayed until we come to the *Phenomenology*. All we can do here is to investigate 'recognition' in its relationship to the purely economic concept of 'externalization' of which it is a higher form. In the Lectures of 1805–6 where he discusses the transition from a state of nature to a state of law, he writes as follows:

> 'Right is the relation of the person in his behaviour towards others, it is the universal element of his free existence, or, in other words, the definition, limitation of his empty freedom. I have no need to excogitate this relation or limitation myself, for the object itself creates the right, i.e. the relation of *recognition*.—In the act of recognition, the self ceases to be a single thing; it becomes part of right in recognition, i.e. it ceases to be simply immediate existence. The object so recognized is recognized as immediately valid, thanks to *its existence*, but *this existence is produced by the concept*; it is existence recognized. Man necessarily recognizes and receives recognition. This necessity is his own, not that of our thought in opposition to the content. As recognition he is movement and precisely this movement annuls his natural state: he is recognition; the natural only *is*, it has nothing of the *spirit* about it.'[22]

These observations are very remarkable for the light they throw on the conflicting tendencies at work within him. Formally, they are highly objectivistic since they deduce all the determinations of right from the movement of the object itself, rather than from the nature of thought. Thought for Hegel in this passage is only the intellectual reflection of the movement of the real determinations in the object. The content of the same passage, however, tends in the opposite direction. The analysis of 'externalization' is momentous firstly because it is the first time in the history of philosophy that anyone has made the attempt to analyse what Marx would later call the fetishism of the commodity, and to use that analysis as a basis from which to explore society as a whole by dissolving the fetishized object-forms of society into a dynamic complex of relations between human beings. It is important, secondly, because Hegel is not unaware that the various forms of fetishization are not all on the same plane; he realizes that there is a hierarchy of fetishized objects, objects which are fetishes to a greater or lesser degree.

We have already seen this aspect of Hegel's thought at work when he describes such a hierarchy of ever higher forms of 'externalization' beginning with labour, the product of labour, exchange and trade, and finally ending in money. Even then the idealistic tendency to turn everything upside down was very much in evidence. Hegel sees, quite correctly, that trade and, above all, money are higher forms of 'externalization' than, e.g., simple production. Thus far he is in agreement with Marx's materialistic position. But whereas Marx regards the simplest form of fetishism, namely the commodity, as the key to the more complex and more highly fetishized forms of society, Hegel proceeds in the opposite direction. (In our detailed analysis of the *Phenomenology* we shall argue that the economic origin of Hegel's error here lies in his one-sided conception of labour, of man's economic activities.) In Hegel's eyes the 'externalization' of spirit and the ultimate retraction of that 'externalization' is the only road to the creation of reality by spirit and consequently also to the intellectual reproduction of that reality by cognition. For this reason the higher forms of fetishism are not higher in the sense that they are increasingly remote from the real object, i.e. that they are increasingly empty and hollow (cf. Marx on money). On the contrary, it is this process that converts them into authentically higher forms of 'externalization', namely pure forms of spirit, forms on the road back to spirit, forms which come closer to the revoking of 'externalization' by the spirit and the transformation of substance into subject, than the more primitive, more fundamental aspects of 'externalization' which are nearer to the material processes of economics.

This explains why it was methodologically necessary for Hegel to put law above economics. Whereas historical materialism regards the 'higher' fetishism of law as a proof of its secondary, derivative character, for Hegel the opposite is the case: the transformation of economic into juridical categories represents a higher, more spiritual form of 'externalization', a force closer to the realm of spirit. According to Hegel the recognized existence of law is actually created from the concept, whereas a merely economic object remains nearer to nature, at the level of unconscious being-in-itself. This argument is in a state of constant interaction with the view discussed earlier of the unity of the people in the state. Each reinforces the other and this helps to explain why those elements in Hegel which might have brought him to a true understanding of fetishism could never gain the upper hand, even though he often came close to it (as in his analysis of money, for instance, on p. 336, where he argues that it is both an actual thing and also the ego, or self, i.e. a relation between men).

This complex inner conflict which always ends with the victory of the mystifications of objective idealism, has consequences of two kinds. As Marx pointed out:

'. . . there is already latent in the *Phenomenology* as a germ, a potentiality, a secret, the *uncritical positivism* and the equally *uncritical idealism* of Hegel's later works—that philosophical dissolution and restoration of the existing empirical world.'[23]

From this defeat of realism two consequences follow: the first is the uncritical idealism which we have seen repeatedly, most recently in the inverted relationship of law and economics. The second is that Hegel simply introduces into his system crude empirical matter whose real social and philosophical universality he cannot discover, he incorporates it just as it is, and then 'deduces' its necessity by means of a pseudo-intellectual process of abstraction.

It is no accident that such categories are mostly described as 'natural'. Hegel himself senses that he has not really deduced them from the actual social reality and since he often has accurate and profound intuitions into the relation of society to its foundation in nature it is tempting to have recourse to nature in difficult cases and to mystify the inexplicable by calling it 'natural'. In his critique of Hegel's philosophy of right Marx keeps coming back to 'this inevitable lapse from empiricism into speculation and from speculation back to empiricism'. We quote the passage about the monarch because, as we have seen, the deduction of the hereditary monarchy from 'nature' was a prominent feature of the Lectures of 1805–6. Marx writes:

'In this way too the impression of *mystical profundity* is created. It is a vulgar truth that man was born; and that an existence posited by physical birth should become a social man, right up to the rank of citizen; through his birth man is all that he becomes. But it is very profound, it is really very striking that the idea of the state was immediately born, and that it gave birth to its empirical existence through the birth of the ruler. This idea has no new substance, all that is altered is the form of the old substance. It has acquired a philosophical form, a philosophical warrant.'[24]

When we look at Hegel's deductive argument about the hereditary monarch in the Lectures of 1805–6 in the light of this criticism we see how unerringly Marx has fixed on the spurious profundity in Hegel's 'uncritical positivism'. Hegel says of the monarch:

'The *free universal* is the point where individuality appears; the latter so free from the knowledge of all, is not constituted as individual by them, but as one extreme of government it is immediate and *natural*: it is the hereditary monarch. He is the firm immediate nodal point, binding all. . . . fluidity, he is immediate, *natural*. He alone is the *natural*, i.e. it is here that *nature has found refuge.* . . .'

Arguments of this sort can be found everywhere in Hegel and we shall have occasion to disentangle the rights and wrongs of his view of the 'natural'. For the time being we may confine ourselves to this example which has a particular interest for us over and above its general implications for his methodology as a whole. Up to now we have considered only one of the two flaws in Hegel's analysis of society to which we earlier made reference (p. 370), viz. his failure to relate the class-structure to the economy. We now find ourselves facing the second flaw: his failure to relate the class-structure to the government.

Hegel's philosophical analysis of the different classes progresses from the particular to the general. Once he has reached the universality of the upper class Hegel faces the problem of distinguishing between it and the government. Obviously, this is not just a philosophical or epistemological technicality. On the contrary, it is a question of the class character of society. And the internal conflict of opposing tendencies in his philosophy is mirrored very precisely in his hesitations on this issue. Of course, there is no question of Hegel's arriving at a real understanding of the class character of the state. This is precluded from the start by his view of the ultimate unity of society, which we have already discussed at length.

But even allowing for that we still discover in Hegel a dual tendency which reflects the objective contradiction in the Napoleonic solution to the problems of modern society posed by the French Revolution. Admittedly, this reflection is distorted by Hegel's special position as a German, and as one, moreover, who sets out to idealize that solution. On the one hand, he tends to identify the upper class (i.e. the Napoleonic military nobility) with the government and the state. This objectively expresses the character of Napoleon's military dictatorship and Hegel's enthusiastic support of the heroic glory of France created by Napoleon. On the other hand, Napoleonic government was not just a military dictatorship in the abstract, but one which came into being in the specific circumstances of post-revolutionary France, i.e. one which had the task of defending the ideas and values of the French Revolution, (its bourgeois heritage in short) against attempts to restore feudal absolutism and to advance the revolution in the direction of further democracy.

In the *System of Ethics* Hegel frankly expresses this contradiction. Writing about the government, he says:

'It appears to be the very first estate because it represents absolute potentiality to the others, the reality of absolute ethical existence and the truly intuited spirit of the others—while all the other estates remain in the realm of the particular. But it too is estate against estate, and there must be something higher still than it and its difference *vis-à-vis* the others. . . . The movement of the first estate as against the others is incorporated in the concept by the realization that both have reality, both are limited and the empirical freedom of each is annulled; this absolute preservation of all the estates must be the supreme government and it may not by definition be conferred on a single estate, since it is the identity of all. It must therefore comprise all those who have given up actual existence in an estate and who live simply in the sphere of the ideal, namely the elders and the priests, who are in fact one.[25]

Here too, then, nature must intervene like a *deus ex machina*. The elders and the priests (a mystified version of the Council of Elders in the Directory) are supposed to be raised above the antagonisms of the world of the particular solely by virtue of their age; this will suffice to enable them to achieve that degree of universality which even the first estate, as an estate against other estates, could not achieve. Obviously, Hegel is confronted with the same problem which he solves later on by affirming the claims of the hereditary monarch. And the method he employs is also the same: by a sort of intellectual legerdemain he transforms a simple fact of nature into a profound mystical truth.

We have repeatedly stressed that Hegel nowhere adopts Schelling's terminology so whole-heartedly as in the *System of Ethics*. The reason for Schelling's influence is quite plain here. For even though Hegel's concept of 'supersession' (*Aufhebung*), defined as the 'unity of unity and difference,' is vastly superior to Schelling's concept of 'identity' (*Indifferenz*), it could not be employed here. His own method, if applied consistently, would have led him in the direction of a real dialectical theory of class and of the position of the state *vis-à-vis* class conflict. For reasons which we have previously discussed, Hegel was not capable of this insight. Hence, for the relationship he is at present concerned to establish between the state and the government as opposed to the classes, Schelling's concept of identity is much more apt than Hegel's own concept of contradiction and its supersession. And if Hegel later dispenses with Schelling's terms, his analysis of this relationship always retains Schellingian overtones. We may say then that certain elements of Schelling's thought became permanent constituents of Hegel's system. However, this stands in need of qualification and if we adopt Engels' argument that Hegel's system and method are in contradiction with each other, we can say that the influence of Schelling is most marked wherever the system threatens to gain the upper hand, i.e. wherever Hegel is unable to draw the final consequences, both philosophical and social, from his method.

It must not be thought that we have provided a complete account of Hegel's view of the relations between the estates and the state. We have already pointed out, for example, that the hereditary monarch often plays a purely decorative role in the political system, and that Hegel fully recognizes the autonomous movement of civil society and is in favour of reducing the intervention of the state to its absolute minimum. But these remarks do not eliminate the contradictions we have described. They merely show that now one side of contemporary French history, and now the other *occupied the forefront of Hegel's attention. The recognition* of the economic necessities propelling civil society is part of his picture of the Napoleonic system which administered the inheritance of the French Revolution on behalf of the bourgeoisie, a system which Hegel regarded as the climatic moment of history, the contemporary incarnation of the world-spirit.

We may say in general that, when looking at Hegel's socio-philosophical theories at this time, it is always essential to go back to their actual French models which are then reflected—often in a mystified manner—in his ideas. This holds good not just for the elders and the priests but for his whole picture of the structure of the estates, and above all his definition of the universal class as a new military nobility on Napoleonic lines. The permanence of the impression left on Hegel by the Napoleonic constitution can be gauged by the fact that in his very last essay (on the English Reform Bill) he mentions the constitution Napoleon imposed on the Italians as a model for the present day and he does so at the very point where he discusses the problems posed for the estates-structure by the further development of capitalist society.[26]

We may sum up by saying that Hegel's theory of economics and society contains two diametrically opposed tendencies. On the one hand, there is the attempt to deduce the universal dialectically from the particular. This was most clearly manifest in his analysis of labour, the division of labour and tools, etc. It always reappears wherever Hegel can conduct his enquiry without having to be too much concerned about the problem of the state, or where he can draw conclusions of a general philosophical nature without directly referring to the state. Thus in the *Jena Logic* there is a highly interesting analysis of the concept of species arising from the dialectic of individuality as it emerges and functions in civil society.[27]

The tendencies we have described are anything but episodic. For the problem of modern capitalism, the economic role of the bourgeois, the modern individualism which thrives on the basis of this economic process—in a word the principles of capitalism as Hegel understood them are the very things which distinguish the modern age from antiquity. It is these principles that rendered antiquity obsolete and reduced it to a memory, something irrevocably past. They therefore constitute the climax of his Jena philosophy of history. Which in turn always remains fundamental to that of his later system.

Moreover, this philosophy of history is intimately connected with his generally philosophical interests, as could hardly be otherwise with a philosopher of Hegel's stature. We already know that the central problem of the *Phenomenology*, the principle with whose aid he finally leaves Schelling's dialectics behind him and appears before the public with his own, is the principle of 'externalization'. But at the same time our previous discussions have shown that the modern age and modern civil society represent a higher stage of history just because 'externalization' is more advanced than in the immediate social existence of antiquity. Hence the period of the greatest 'externalization' for Hegel must be the one in which what has been 'externalized' can be recovered by the spirit so that substance is entirely transformed into subject.

But as we have seen, Hegel's philosophy of history has yet another side: the detachment of the state and its world-historical functions from its economic base. Of course, connections are present, even economic ones, but instead of the real (if often incomplete) understanding of economic actualitities we find only a mystification of what was in itself the unreal view of the relation of the state to civil society that obtained under Napoleonic rule. According to this view the state is supposed to make use of civil society to accomplish its own ends which are independent of civil society. Civil society exists only to serve the state (the spirit), to make sacrifices for it. In return the state will protect civil society and guarantee its smooth functioning. The particular interests of civil society, of economic life are all subsumed in the state. They constitute partly the dark background against which the radiant figure of the spirit shines forth, partly they are the fragmented moments into which spirit is dialectically divided when it enters the empirical world in search of itself, when it 'externalizes' itself and then re-absorbs that 'externalized' reality within itself. We see then the dual tendencies in Hegel's philosophy that led to the concept of 'externalization', namely the real one and the mystified one. Their decisive battle for the control of Hegel's method will be treated at length in our discussion of *The Phenomenology of Mind*.

That these tendencies came into conflict in Hegel's own mind was, as we know, no accident. We have also seen the real source of their conflict in reality itself, namely in the reality of the Napoleonic state. However, the idealistic strains in Hegel's view of reality are intensified by the determinants of German society. In his criticism of Kant's philosophy, Marx, who regarded Kant as representing an intellectual reflection of the age of the French Revolution, described the specifically German distortions of French reality as they appeared in the work of the German philosopher. In Kant's practical reason Marx glimpsed the reflection of the actual material interests of the liberal bourgeoisie:

'Kant, therefore, separated this theoretical expression from the interests which it expressed; he made the materially motivated determinations of the will of the French bourgeois into *pure* determination of "*free will*", of the will in and for itself. . . .'

In this passage Marx supplies both the explanation of a social phenomenon and a criticism of Kantian philosophy; he goes on to describe the particular illusions that inevitably took hold of the minds of Germans in these circumstances:

'It is this position of the state which explains both the honest character of the civil servant that is found nowhere else, and all the illusions about the state which are current in Germany, as well as the apparent independence of German theoreticians in relation to the burghers —the seeming contradiction between the form in which these theoreticians express the interests of the burghers and these interests themselves.'[28]

Marx never simply put Kant and Hegel into the same category. This criticism, therefore, can only be applied to Hegel in so far as in Hegel too the general influence of the social situation can be detected. Marx repeatedly draws attention of such features of Hegel's thought in his detailed critique of the *Philosophy of Right*. In particular, he lays great emphasis on the retrograde character of German society which makes itself felt in Hegel's view of the role of the bureaucracy in society and the state. Of the greatest philosophical importance is the passage where he speaks of the 'imaginary universality' of the bureaucracy in Hegel's system and where he argues that Hegel's overall position is that the state and the government are not the representative bodies of civil society, but representative bodies against civil society.[29]

In these critical marginalia on the *Philosophy of Right* Marx emphasizes again and again that the contradictions in Hegel's philosophy are the reflections of actual social realities. If he subjects Hegel's mystifications to the most searching scrutiny he never does so in the belief that Hegel's ideas about society and the state are entirely arbitrary. He attacks him just because Hegel proposes an image of the modern world which is correct in many respects but in which Hegel does not pick out the really progressive elements. In consequence he finds himself driven increasingly to mystify the existing order. He writes, for example:

'Hegel is not to be blamed for depicting the modern state as it is but because he presents what is as the essence of the state. The claim that the rational is real is contradicted by *irrational reality* which is at every point the contrary of what it asserts and which asserts the contrary of what it really is.'[30]

This criticism of Hegel is in fact a concretization of his criticism of Hegel's 'uncritical positivism'. Because Hegel was unable to comprehend certain decisive tendencies in modern society, he was compelled to take the appearance for the reality and to ground this pseudo-reality philosophically with the aid of a spurious profundity and a specious show of dialectics. (In the *Philosophy of Right* Hegel's uncritical positivism was much more marked than in Jena. But we know from Marx's criticism that it was present even in the earlier period. Thus Marx's criticism may be applied to the social and political philosophy of the Jena period, with the one reservation which Marx himself insisted on.)

In the course of his critical discussion Marx broached the problem which constitutes one of the central defects of the entire Hegelian system: the problem of democracy. It is typical of the profundity of the young Marx's approach that he connected this with the problem of the general and the particular:

'Democracy is the truth of monarchy; monarchy is not the truth of democracy. Monarchy is necessarily democracy in contradiction with itself, an excrescence, the monarchical aspect is not a contradiction within democracy. Democracy can, monarchy cannot be conceived in its own terms. In democracy none of the aspects acquires any other meaning than the appropriate one. Each is actually only an aspect of the whole people. But in monarchy a part determines the character of the whole. The entire constitution must conform to a fixed point. Democracy is the generic constitution. Monarchy is a species and indeed a poor one. Democracy is "content and form". Monarchy *should* only be form, but it falsifies the content.

'In monarchy the whole, the people, is subsumed under one of its particular modes of existence, under political constitution. In democracy the *constitution itself* appears only as one determination, and indeed the self-determination of the people. In monarchy we have the people of the constitution; in democracy the constitution of the people. Democracy is the solution of the problem of all constitutions. In democracy the constitution is always based on its actual foundation, on *actual man* and the *actual people* not only *implicitly* and in its essence, but in its existence and its actuality. Here the constitution is man's and the people's *own* work. The constitution appears as what it is: the free product of man. One could say that in a certain sense this is also true of constitutional monarchy, but the specific difference in democracy is that here the *constitution* is only one particular moment of the people and that the *political constitution* in itself does not form the state.

'Hegel proceeds from the state and makes man into the state subjectivized. Democracy proceeds from man and makes the state into man objectivized.'[31]

When Marx describes democracy as a genus and monarchy as a poor species belonging to it, he is not so much indulging in abstraction as reproducing the abstractions of history which, in the course of many revolutions, has finally produced democracy as the perfected form of civil society. And when, only a few years later, Marx described democracy as the most favourable battleground upon which to struggle for socialism, and when he talked of the transformation of the bourgeois-democratic revolution into the proletarian revolution, he merely pointed to even higher forms of universality, realized by history itself. However, all the while the direction of his study of society remained constant and this is what enabled him to attack Hegel's social philosophy at its weakest point.

Since Hegel was not in a position to comprehend the movement towards democracy so magnificently inaugurated by the French Revolution, he simply had to abandon the possibility of arriving at the real generalizations that might have been deduced from history, from the dialectical interplay of its particular moments. On the one hand, he was compelled to invest particular moments with the false halo of a specious universality, and on the other he was seduced into crediting these 'universal' moments with an independent existence wrenching them from their socio-historical context. Then, having transformed them into fixed autonomous beings he subsumed under them all particular phenomena and all the specific manifestations of society and history.

Thus we are now in a position to see the philosophical implications of the two tendencies we have noted in Hegel's philosophy of society. The first tendency, namely the true and accurate cognition of actual dialectical processes, becomes the basis of a new dialectical logic. This deduces the general from the movement set up by the contradictions at the level of the particular and is led from one stage to the next by the annulment of these contradictions and the appearance of new, higher ones. The other tendency which leads directly to the idealistic hypostatization of pseudo-universals is forced to adopt the old metaphysical method of subsuming all particulars beneath the general. The conflict between these two tendencies reproduces itself in the *Logic* as a struggle between dialectics and speculation.

With this we have arrived back at one of the most crucial starting-points of classical German philosophy, namely at that celebrated section in the *Critique of Judgement* where Kant postulated an 'intellectus archetypus'. It will be recollected that he regarded it as an eternal frontier of the human understanding that the particular must be subsumed beneath the general. And the 'intellectus archetypus' therefore appeared to him as a purely hypothetical type of understanding which could advance from the particular to the general. Since it was hypothetical it could only serve as a 'regulative' and not as a 'constitutive' idea. The significance of this Kantian programme, we recall, was that, in the guise of delimiting human reason in general, it firmly and distinctly demarcated the limits of metaphysical thought. And the 'intellectus archetypus' was a programme for going beyond those limits, a programme for dialectics.

The paths of subjective and objective idealism diverge at the point where it has to be decided whether this programme can, or cannot, be carried out. For all subjective idealists the boundary here is absolute. To the subjective idealist the particular always appears contingent. It makes no difference whether the context is that of Fichte's rationalistic over-extension of the subject which causes all the particulars of empirical existence to pale into insignificance before its stern moral universality, or whether it results in Jacobi's worship of the particular from the standpoint of emotive irrationalism: in either case the upshot is the same and the limit set by Kant is not transcended.

Schelling was the first to make an advance with his 'intellectual intuition'. But here too the intention was better than the performance. He proclaimed the 'intellectus archetypus' to be an authentic mode of cognition, albeit one that was the monopoly of the artistic or philosophical genius. But this declaration achieves little of itself. And apart from its contribution to aesthetics Schelling's whole apparatus really gives very little idea of how the contingency of the particular can be annulled or how the general can be deduced from the particular. Even though he appears to have overcome the merely regulative status of the 'intellectus archetypus', in reality he does not get beyond the limits of metaphysical thought.

During the period in which he experimented most freely with Schellingian terms, Hegel made only the most sparing use of the phrase 'intellectual intuition' and he always constructed his arguments so as to rely on this new 'organ' as little as possible. We have seen the scale of Hegel's efforts to tear down the barriers between the general and the particular, and we have seen how genuinely philosophical his approach was, i.e. how closely concerned with life and the problem of generalizing about it. Hegel saw clearly that the element of contingency in particular could not simply be removed by decree, nor by the use of analogies as Schelling hoped.

In fact, in Hegel the annulment of contingency takes place on the assumption that it cannot be annulled. We are reminded here of his view of capitalist economics. It is a movement consisting of particular moments, subjective and objective, the peculiarities and faculties of individual people, their possessions, etc., all of which are irrevocably particular. Nevertheless, the universal, the economic law, necessarily emerges from the movements of these irreducibly contingent elements.

In these and other passages Hegel satisfies the conditions necessary for making a reality of the 'intellectus archetypus'. The Kantian prohibition turns out to be no more than the frontier of metaphysics. By taking the inner contradictions of metaphysics to extremes, by breaking up their immobile façade, by uncovering the concealed dynamic of the contradictions of the real world, Hegel not only points the way to dialectical thought, he also shows that it is not the private monopoly of privileged geniuses but a faculty inherent in all human thought which had been ossified by the habit of metaphysics.

The logical continuation of this road could only be the discovery of materialist dialectics, for this alone can reflect the dialectical movement of reality itself in such a manner as to do away with the Kantian prohibition altogether. But materialist dialectics and historical materialism necessarily go hand in hand. We have seen that the social preconditions of Hegel's philosophy forced it into an idealistic mould from the outset, and at the same time they set definitive limits to his understanding of the laws governing society and history, limits which only intensified the tendency towards idealism.

Thus Hegel's approach to dialectics had to be conducted on idealist lines. Its complex birth meant also that his objectivism too has a double aspect. On the one hand, it creates room for the manoeuvres of a real dialectic at a level of consciousness hitherto unknown. On the other hand, that same objectivism strengthens the idealism distorting and mystifying it still further.

Objective idealism requires an authority to guarantee its authenticity. As we have seen, the Hegelian 'spirit' is that authority and it fortifies those idealist tendencies which would hypostatize the universal as opposed to the particular and hence constantly force the dialectic back into metaphysics. This double aspect of objectivity is not simply the consequence of its so-called 'immanent' method. We have attempted to show how it springs from the socio-historical situation and was exacerbated further by Hegel's own position within it. Of course, once objective idealism came into existence, its methodological implications necessarily had an impact on tendencies that sprang directly from life itself. But here as everywhere society is the primary reality. And what we set out to show was how that specific social reality and the socially-conditioned understanding of that reality were recognizably reflected in the most complex categories of philosophy, however abstract and remote from them they appeared to be.

Engels has referred to this contradiction in Hegel as the contradiction between his method and his system. In his last years he attempted to induce younger Marxists to renew their acquaintance with Hegel, but he always warned them not to spend too much time on the arbitrary elements in the Hegelian system, and urged them instead to concentrate on the genuine dialectical movements it contained. The first approach would be simple enough and any schoolmaster could accomplish it, the second was vital for any Marxist. Marx too always had the same distinction in mind, even when he was most deeply immersed in bitter feuds with the representatives of Hegelianism. In *The Holy Family*, that great polemic in which he settles accounts with the Left-Hegelians, he ruthlessly exposes the 'mystery of speculative constructs', the false reasoning by means of which Hegel advances from the universal to the particular and the fallacies involved in Hegel's hypostatization of the universal *vis-à-vis* the particular. He mercilessly unmasks all the flaws in his arguments and the distortions of reality which spring from idealism of this sort. But at the same time Marx draws a sharp distinction between Hegel and the Hegelians who have acquired *only* his defects. He defines the difference between their dialectics and Hegel's in the following manner:

> 'Besides, Hegel very often gives a real presentation, a presentation of the *matter itself*, within his *speculative* presentation. This real development *within* speculative development misleads the reader into taking the speculative development as real and the real as speculative.'[32]

This additional distortion of Hegel was not just the work of his immediate disciples but was aggravated by later neo-Hegelians. If the real Hegelian dialectic is to be salvaged from the rubble and brought to life for the contemporary student then its internal contradictions have to be explained in terms of the problems which reveal their origins and social character most clearly: the problems of economics.

## NOTES

1   *A Contribution to the Critique of Political Economy*, p. 199.
2   The conspiracy against the Directory organized by Babeuf and the *Société des Egaux* had been fixed for 11 March 1796. Betrayed by a government spy within their ranks they were brought to trial. Babeuf and Durthé were sentenced to death and executed.—*Trans.*
3   Lasson, p. 305.
4   Lasson, pp. 464 and 471. It is generally recognized in the literature on Hegel that the *System of Ethics* was written in the years 1801–2 and that it therefore represents the first attempt at a written philosophical system. Lasson is alone in placing it later than the essay on *Natural Law*, i.e. in 1802–3. However, he is unable to adduce a single convincing argument in support of this view. Against his thesis is the fact that the influence of terminology derived from Schelling is much feebler in the essay on *Natural Law* than in the *System of Ethics*. Cf. Lasson, p. xxxiv.
5   Ibid., p. 406.
6   Ibid., p. 377.
7   Ibid., p. 378f.
8   *Realphilosophie*, Vol. II, p. 252.

9   *The Phenomenology of Mind*, p. 474.
10  *The Holy Family*, in Karl Marx, *Selected Writings in Sociology and Social Philosophy*, trans. T. B. Bottomore and M. Rubel, Penguin, Middlesex 1963, pp. 226–7.
11  *Realphilosophie*, Vol. II, p. 253.
12  Ibid., p. 267.
13  Quoted by Aulard, *Politische Geschichte der französischen Revolution*, München and Leipzig 1924, Vol. II, p. 614.
14  *Realphilosophie*, Vol. II, p. 254.
15  Ibid., p. 255.
16  Ibid., p. 253.
17  Ibid., p. 259f.
18  Ibid., p. 254.
19  Ibid., Vol. I, p. 240. Cf. also Lasson, p. 434.
20  Ibid., Vol. II, p. 218. Cf. also Lasson, pp. 438ff.
21  *The German Ideology*, p. 669.
22  *Realphilosophie*, Vol. II, p. 206.
23  *Economic and Philosophic Manuscripts*, pp. 175–6. G. L.'s italics.
24  MEGA, I, Vol. I, Part I, p. 446.
25  Lasson, p. 478f.
26  Ibid., p. 305. Napoleon divided the estates into *Possidenti, Dotti* and *Mercanti*.
27  *Jenenser Logik*. pp. 151ff.
28  *The German Ideology*, pp. 211–12.
29  MEGA, I, Vol. I, Part I, pp. 455 and 459.
30  Ibid., p. 476.
31  Ibid., p. 434. Marx's analysis here is particularly valuable since it is conducted from the point of view of revolutionary democracy, and not yet from a socialist standpoint.
32  *Die heilige Familie*, p. 168.

# CHAPTER EIGHT

# 'Tragedy in the realm of the ethical'

WHATEVER concrete problems we may have chosen for our starting-point, our studies have consistently led us back to the antithesis of materialist and idealist dialectics. But this very fact indicates that the antithesis only becomes manifest in its final form, in the purely epistemological antithesis of idealism and materialism. This final result is the climax of a great historical process: the organization of the revolutionary class of the proletariat as a class 'for itself' (Marx) in the midst of a general European revolutionary crisis. In this crisis the central task, the immediate goal, facing a number of very important states (such as Germany and Italy) was still the accomplishment of a bourgeois-democratic revolution. The campaign waged by the young Marx against Hegel and a Hegelianism in an advanced state of decomposition illustrates the clear connection between the emergence of materialist dialectics and the ideology of the new revolutionary class: the humanism of the proletariat.

This campaign implied a twofold annulment of bourgeois idealogy with all its contradictions. On the one hand, that ideology was subjected to criticism in the course of which materialist dialectics was able to solve a series of problems which the very ideologists of the preceding period had not been able to formulate properly, let alone solve. On the other hand, the new proletarian humanism embraced all the moments of the intellectual tradition which accurately reflected, or tended to reflect, the actual reality with all its contradictions. As in every authentic dialectical supersession the two elements of annulment and preservation go together; the third moment of dialectical supersession: elevation to a higher plane, can take place only on the basis of the unity of these two.

Earlier on (p. 352) we quoted Lenin's statement that Marx had followed Hegel's lead. In the historical context of the origins of dialectical materialism this may be taken as referring to the way in which proletarian humanism grew out of the last great crisis of bourgeois thought, just as the class struggle of the proletariat itself grew gradually out of the struggles of the exploited and oppressed for liberation. As Lenin put it there is no Chinese wall between the bourgeois democratic and the proletarian revolution and the proletarian revolution has developed slowly, painfully and uncertainly from the struggles for liberation conducted by the oppressed throughout history. The particular contradictions of the last great period of crisis in the ideological development of bourgeois society (1789–1848) is in every sense the ideological starting-point, the point at which the new world-view of the revolutionary proletariat really can take its cue from the bourgeoisie.

Hegel's objective idealism is the philosophical apex of this phase of bourgeois thought. It is its climax in the double sense that it represents the philosophical synthesis of thousands of years of human development and, indissolubly connected with that is the fact that it comprehends the contradictory movement of that development, with all its unsolved and insoluble contradictions, all at their highest level. Hegel's unique position in this period rests on the fact that for the first time in human history the *contradictory nature of existence itself* was consciously made the central preoccupation of philosophy.

The objective and increasingly insoluble problems of contemporary reality can be found in the works of all the eminent ideologists of the period. A whole series of concrete contradictions is even set forth in more truthful, realistic terms by these thinkers than by Hegel himself. For these thinkers, however, the contradictions are only present objectively, in themselves. As Marx puts it, they all seek the truth 'amid the "manure" of contradictions',[1] they frankly declare their findings, but contradictoriness as such does not reveal itself to them as the foundation of objective existence. (Fourier is the only outstanding thinker of the period, apart from Hegel, to divine the central position of contradictoriness as such.) Thus the growing awareness of the insoluble contradictions of history, which culminate in the contradictions of capitalism, drives thinkers like Saint-Simon, Fourier, and Owen beyond the criticism of capitalism to the point where they call for a new form of society which will really solve the problems they discern; in short, it drives them to socialism.

Ricardo, the last and most consistent of the systematizers of capitalist economics focuses on the development of the material forces of production as the foundation of human progress with an incisiveness hitherto unknown. Nevertheless, although on the surface Ricardo's system seems entirely coherent, although he himself defends the most barbarous and inhuman consequences of capitalist production against romantic sentimentality in every form, because it alone will lead to the advancement of mankind, the internal contradictions in bourgeois culture are plainly revealed in his work. And these contradictions point not only to the time when the dominant role of the bourgeoisie will come to an end, but they also illuminate the ambiguous and problematic role of the bourgeoisie in a process initiated by itself and on which its own material prosperity and dominant position was based.

It is not our intention here to speak of the contradictions in Ricardo's theory of value, contradictions which enabled the first ideologists of the proletariat who emerged at the time of the disintegration of his school to

draw socialist conclusions from his theories. We need only refer to the
ambiguity of Ricardo's attitude towards the contribution of the bourgeoisie in increasing the material forces of production, an ambiguity
which Marx defined as follows:

> 'He wants *production for the sake of production* and this with *good reason*.
> To assert, as sentimental opponents of Ricardo's did, that production
> as such is not the object, is to forget that production for its own sake
> means nothing but the development of human productive forces, in
> other words the *development of the richness of human nature as an end in
> itself.* . . . Apart from the barrenness of such edifying reflections, they
> reveal a failure to understand the fact that, although at first the devel-
> opment of the capacities of the *human* species takes place at the cost of
> the majority of human individuals and even classes, in the end it
> breaks through this contradiction and coincides with the develop-
> ment of the individual; the higher development of individuality is
> thus only achieved by a historical process during which individuals
> are sacrificed. . . . Thus Ricardo's ruthlessness was not only *scientifi-
> cally honest* but also a *scientific* necessity from his point of view. But be-
> cause of this it is also quite immaterial to him whether the advance of
> the productive forces slays landed property or workers. . . . Ricardo's
> conception is on the whole, in the interests of the *industrial bourgeoisie*,
> only *because*, and *in so far as*, their interests coincide with that of pro-
> duction or the productive development of human labour. Where the
> bourgeoisie comes into conflict with this, he is just as *ruthless* towards
> it as he is at other times towards the proletariat and the aristocracy.'[2]

Balzac, the great realist of the age, creates in his *Human Comedy* a compendium of the tragic, tragi-comic and comic contradictions growing
out of the soil of bourgeois society and manifesting themselves in the relations between men. The vast scale of Balzac's work constitutes a gigan-
tic fresco on which the 'animal kingdom of the spirit' of capitalism is
depicted in all its monstrosity, with its contradictions, its victims, and its
heroic and futile struggles against its own inhumanity. Ricardo and
Balzac were no socialists, indeed they were declared opponents of socialism. But both Ricardo's objective economic analysis and Balzac's literary
mimesis of the world of capitalism point to the necessity for a new world
no less vividly than Fourier's satirical criticism of capitalism.

Goethe and Hegel stand on the threshold of the last great and tragic
blossoming of bourgeois idology. *Wilhelm Meister* and *Faust, The
Phenomenology of Mind* and the *Encyclopaedia* form one part of the monu-
mental achievement in which the last creative energies of the bourgeoisie
are gathered together to give intellectual or literary expression to their
own tragically contradictory situation. In the works of Goethe and
Hegel the reflection of the heroic period of the bourgeois age is even

more clearly visible than in Balzac, for whom the age appears as no more than a glorious prelude to the final and terrible victory of the prose of the capitalist epoch. The young Hegel, in particular, remains under the immediate influence of the heroism and the heroic illusions of the transition period—right up to the end of the heroic age and the fall of Napoleon.

'But unheroic as bourgeois society is, it nevertheless took heroism, sacrifice, terror, civil war and battles of the nations to bring it into being.'[3]

The young Hegel, in particular, is not prepared to ignore the heroism of the rise of the bourgeoisie because of its later development. Or in other words: he refuses to acknowledge that all the heroism served only to turn the capitalist into the ruler of the world.

The true idealist contradiction in Hegel's early thought is that he who had discovered the new teleology of human activity was neither able nor willing to perceive the tragic teleology of his own age. He inverts the relationship of ends to means. Whereas in reality all the heroic efforts of the French people, the deeds of all the great heroes from Marat to Napoleon only resulted in the establishment of capitalism on the ruins of feudalism, Hegel is concerned to formulate a philosophy of history that shows how the unleashing of the forces of production by capitalism and the rise of a triumphant bourgeois society will provide the basis for a new heroic age, a new glorious era of human culture.

Hegel's idealistic error, his inversion of the true state of society nevertheless contains a profound humanist truth, a profound, if also contradictory, criticism of capitalism. For it is clear that if he cannot declare himself satisfied that the entire history of mankind with all its struggles and sacrifices, took place with the sole purpose of finally placing mankind in the capitalist interests of men like Nucingen, Tailleffer and Keller, if he regarded their dominion as a real degradation of mankind as a whole, and if he constructed a heroic utopia to show men the way out of the terrible impasse in which they found themselves, then this utopia must be construed as a very definite protest against capitalism. And objectively, without his knowing or willing it himself, this protest must point beyond the horizon of capitalism no less surely than do Ricardo's economic analyses or the literary works of the legitimist and royalist Balzac.

Hegel would be a lesser philosopher, a sentimental utopian Romantic, if he had carried through his protest to its logical conclusion. His achievement, the seminal importance of his work rests precisely on his inconsistency, on the fact that he too, like Ricardo, sought, and partly found the truth 'amid the manure of contradictions'. And when we consider Hegel's critique of capitalist culture we must never allow ourselves to forget that the inevitability and the progressive nature of capitalism form the starting-point and the methodological core of his philosophy of history.

And by no means in a narrow 'economic' sense. His entire philosophy of culture rests on the idea that to modern civil society goes the credit of producing that individuality in which the superiority of modern man over classical man in every sphere of human culture can be said to consist. In Hegel's view modern individuality is no natural product, it is nothing 'organic' as the Romantics imagined when they rigidly contrasted the 'organic' individual with the fragmenting and destructive effects of capitalism. On the contrary, it is for him the necessary result of the development of society, or, in philosophical terms, it is the inevitable result of the progressive 'self-externalization' of man, a process which reached its height in modern civil society. Thus this contradiction in Hegel's philosophy of culture has nothing in common with the anti-capitalism of the Romantics. It goes much deeper than that; it consists of the affirmation of the necessity and progressiveness of the forces that led to capitalism, with all their dire consequences to which, as we have seen in his description of poverty and wealth, he never closes his eyes; and at the same time, there is an impassioned struggle against the degradation and deformation of man brought about by capitalism with an equally compelling necessity.

The contradictions that we see in Hegel amount to the dialectical sequel to the criticism of the capitalist division of labour and their cultural implications that we have found in the great English economists of the Enlightenment, and in Ferguson and Adam Smith in particular. The cult of antiquity from the Renaissance to the Napoleonic age and the elevation of this cult to an ideal are founded on the objective impossibility of solving this contradiction of capitalist development. All the utopias which set out to realize or revitalize antiquity, whether politically, culturally or artistically, are premised on the hope of overcoming that great contradiction of the modern world: the destruction of man through the development of his productive energies.

Ricardo's greatness as an economist lies in the fact that he steadfastly ignored this contradiction; that is to say, he duly recorded all the facts of the matter, while holding fast to the hope that the progressive development of the material forces of production would eventually sweep all the contradictions away. And this is in fact true; Ricardo was quite right. However, it will be true only under socialism, not under capitalism,—and that was where Ricardo was historically wrong. But it is very clear that in the absence of this error his thought would never have generated the power that it in fact possessed and which enabled it to influence a future which of course was necessarily hidden from him.

Hegel approaches this contradiction from the opposite end, from the problems of culture. But this does not alter the fact that a comparable amalgam of truth and error is to be found in his philosophy. The superiority of antiquity over modern society is the precise expression of this contradiction which Ferguson has aptly formulated as follows:

'If the pretentions to equal justice and freedom should terminate in rendering every class equally servile and mercenary, we make a nation of helots, and have no free citizens.'[4]

This is also the point of view of the young Hegel. And as we have seen, his important contribution from the time of the Frankfurt crisis was to insist that antiquity had gone for ever, that it had ceased to be a model for modern man and that with the *development* of forces of production by capitalism human history had reached its peak. And he maintained all this despite his veneration of antiquity and his certainty that capitalism is what it is. The tragic contradiction lying at the heart of this development is Hegel's awareness of the nullity of its central figure: the nullity of the bourgeois.

'Tragedy in the realm of the ethical' is the title Hegel gave to a brief and extremely obscure section in the essay on *Natural Law*, following directly after the discussions we have mentioned, dealing with the inevitability of capitalist society and its progressive nature *vis-à-vis* antiquity. In highly condensed form Hegel sets forth a summary of the contradiction we have discussed. As he presents it here, it appears as a permanent antithesis in human history, i.e. to a certain extent it is dehistoricized, even though he sharply differentiates between his ancient and modern solutions.

These arguments are among the most obscure in the entire corpus of his early writings. The exaggerated idealism is all too patently obvious. And above all as we have said, a specific modern conflict is rendered permanent. The 'duplication' of man as 'bourgeois' and 'citoyen' appears as a tragic collision of spirit with itself, eternally posed only to be eternally annulled. In order to eternalize life-as-bourgeois i.e. private life, Hegel mystifies it by describing it as 'nature', the 'lower world'. Whereas man's aspect as citizen becomes the 'light' eternally triumphing over the 'lower world', but eternally chained to it. Thus 'dual nature' of the spirit, this eternal creation and abolition of the contradiction is what constitutes the 'tragedy in the realm of the ethical'.

'This is nothing but a performance of the tragedy in the realm of the ethical which the Absolute puts on for its own benefit so that it is eternally born anew into the objective world and in this form it submits to suffering and death, only to rise again in all its glory from the ashes. The divine assuming this shape and this objectivity has a dual nature, and its life is the absolute identity of these natures.'[5]

Despite the tragedy, and indeed by virtue of it, Hegel must and will find a solution. It is not only the conflict which is eternal, the abolition of conflict is no less permanent. The culmination of objective idealism in the identical subject—object represents on the one hand the mystificatory, intellectualized annulment of (insoluble) contradictions. On the other hand, the very structure of his philosophy, which cannot dispense with the identical subject—object, presses forward in its own right towards the same solution: in the spirit all the contradictions must be annulled, even though we know that Hegel was more interested in the process of annulment than the final state in which all has been annulled.

We are already familiar with the social implications of this annulment: it is the 'taming' of the economy by the state (an operation that took a variety of historical forms), its subordination to the interests of a fully-developed, socialized humanity. According to Hegel the 'tragedy in the realm of the ethical' unfolds in a variety of historical forms. The beautiful solution achieved by the civilization of antiquity had to perish. For his own age Hegel lived in hopes that 'the great teacher of constitutional law in Paris' would discover a novel solution.[6] In this capitalism appears as the material foundation, the servant of the new heroic age. These illusions about Napoleon merge here with the idealist dialectic to form a curious organic synthesis, a synthesis which concludes Hegel's early development. We have seen how the collapse of his hope that a revival of classical society was possible triggered off a crisis in Frankfurt. His new hopes find their most moving expression in *The Phenomenology of Mind* and their collapse following the defeat of Napoleon was succeeded by a profound resignation in which he realistically came to terms with the prose of capitalism, whose triumph had now become definitive. Nevertheless, although this contradiction had apparently been resolved, it continued to perplex him and it remained the central problem of Hegel's philosophical inquiries into culture under capitalism.

The discussion of tragedy in the essay on *Natural Law* is supplemented by a brief look at the comic solution to the same problem. Here, too, we find different solutions for antiquity and the modern world; here, too, we find the radiant beauty of antiquity and its tragic end, while the prosaic definition and solution of the conflicts of the modern world through comedy is the task of the present. Against the backdrop of the deeds of the world-spirit, the 'comedy in the realm of the ethical' becomes manifest in the petty absurdities of the banal conflicts of civil life, especially when these are contrasted with the earnestness and the self-importance with which they are pursued.

> 'Contrasted with this there is the *other comedy* [i.e. as distinct from the *Divine Comedy*] whose dénouments have no destiny or authentic struggle because ethical nature itself feels too constrained. Its conflicts unfold not playfully but by means of complications that seem serious

to those involved although comic to the spectators. Their resolutions are sought in an affectation of character and absolute principle which constantly finds itself disappointed and let down.[7]

It is easy to carp at the tortuous and mystificatory idealism of arguments such as these, but it is more important to ask what lies behind them. Above all, there is a critique of the political impotence of the German bourgeoisie which is extended to include the bourgeoisie as such. We have seen how this point of view grew out of Hegel's hopes and expectations of Napoleonic rule and his very pertinent criticism of conditions in Germany; we have seen likewise how his blank incomprehension of the problems of democracy and of the political and cultural potential of mass movements set limits to his insight.

But for all his limitations here he does put his finger on one aspect of bourgeois society which will only become obvious later on in the nineteenth century: the failure of the bourgeoisie, the German bourgeoisie in particular, to use its dominant economic position to obtain the political power it deserved. This is a matter to which Engels drew attention in 1870:

> 'It is a peculiar feature of the bourgeoisie in which it is unlike all previous ruling classes: there is a turning-point in its development after which every increase in its power, in its capital above all, only serves to make it more and more incapable of wielding political authority.'[8]

This remark which refers immediately to the German bourgeoisie is itself formulated so as to apply to the bourgeoisie in general. In an essay on historical materialism he makes this generalization more explicit still:

> 'It seems a law of historical development that the bourgeoisie can in no European country get hold of political power—at least for any length of time—in the same exclusive way in which the feudal aristocracy kept hold of it during the Middle Ages.'[9]

Naturally, there could be no question of any such insight in Hegel, since Engels' statement was made in the full awareness of the growing strength of the proletariat, while Hegel knew nothing of class struggle between the bourgeoisie and the proletariat and its political and cultural consequences. Nevertheless Hegel did observe the 'political nullity' of the bourgeoisie, and this, together with his awareness of their growing economic power and the generally progressive nature of that power, shows that he had an intuitive insight into the future position of the bourgeoisie in modern society.

We have already mentioned one notably idealistic element in Hegel's discussion of 'tragedy in the realm of the ethical', namely his treatment of a specific modern problem as if it were an eternal human conflict. But even this exaggeration contains a grain of truth since it anticipates a genuine conflict between the real potential of mankind and the limitations placed upon it by the economic activities of class society as such. For the human race as a whole work has undoubtedly been the foundation of progress; and at that level of generality Hegel sees no contradiction. The contradiction only starts when we examine the progress of the individual in the various class societies. It then turns out that the great human and cultural advances of history, looked at from the point of view of the individuals involved in them, stand in contradiction to the subjugation of man to economic activities and to the division of labour.

In the heyday of antiquity the strict division between what Hegel would call the 'lower world' of economic labour carried out by slaves and the high culture of the freemen who exploited that economic base was one of the factors that placed classical culture in such a seductive light. Of course, honest thinkers could only succumb to this as long as they remained blind to the true facts of the situation. We have already referred to Ferguson's remark which envisaged not the general emancipation of humanity following the abolition of the division between freemen and slaves, but the transformation of all men into helots, i.e. the general debasement of all the talents and abilities of man, of human personality in fact, as a result of the extension of economic activity to all the members of society. Hegel, who, as we have repeatedly emphasized, was disinclined to indulge in romantic sentimentality and who never underestimated the importance and the progressive nature of capitalism, nevertheless stood firmly opposed to the cultural value placed on economic activity both by the classical economists and their disciples and critics.

In his historic analysis of Adam Smith Marx gives a detailed account of the great debate that echoed through the whole of Europe, on Smith's distinction between productive and unproductive labour, a debate in which the economic idealogists of the Directory and the Consulate (Garnier) and the Empire (Ferrier and Ganilh) played a prominent part. Like the bourgeoisie in general during its revolutionary phase, Smith regarded all non-economic activities as the incidental expenses of production which must be reduced to the absolute minimum in the interests of the increased development of productive forces. (The affinity with the views of Ricardo referred to above is evident.)

In line with this all the great economists tended to equate the various forms of unproductive labour with each other and they advanced their views with the frankness and the cynical aplomb of true revolutionaries. For instance, Marx quotes the following statement in Adam Smith:

'They are the servants of the public, and are maintained by a part of the annual produce of the industry of other people. . . . In the same class must be ranked . . . churchmen, lawyers, physicians, men of letters of all kinds; players, buffoons, musicians, opera-singers, opera-dancers, etc.'

Marx comments:

'This is the language of the still revolutionary bourgeoisie which has not yet subjected to itself the whole of society, the state, etc. All these illustrious and time-honoured occupations—sovereign, judge, officer, priest, etc.,—with all the old ideological professions to which they give rise, their men of letters, their teachers and priests, are *from an economic standpoint* put on the same level as the swarm of their own lackeys and jesters maintained by the bourgeoisie and by idle wealth —the landed nobility and idle capitalists. They are mere servants of the public, just as the others are their servants. They live on the produce of other people's industry, therefore they must be reduced to the smallest possible number.'[10]

The substance of this clear revolutionary standpoint is contained in Ricardo's later exhortation to develop the forces of production whatever the cost. It is modified once the ideologists of the bourgeoisie have acquired power, or at least a decisive influence on the government, usually on the basis of significant compromises. This is the beginning of that 'educated' outlook which attempts to justify all the activities the bourgeoisie finds useful or desirable by extending the concept of productivity to them, i.e. by regarding the labour involved in them as somehow productive in an economic sense. For this attitude in which we can see the clean and strict principles of classical economies being transformed into an apologia for the bourgeoisie, Marx has unrelieved contempt. He quotes this statement by Nassau Senior:

'According to Smith, the lawgiver of the Hebrews was an unproductive labourer.'

And he comments:

'Was it Moses of Egypt or Moses Mendelssohn? Moses would have been very grateful to Mr. Senior for calling him a "productive labourer" in the Smithian sense. These people are so dominated by their fixed bourgeois ideas that they would think they were insulting Aristotle or Julius Caesar if they called them "unproductive labourers". Aristotle and Caesar would have regarded even the title "labourers" as an insult.'[11]

Hegel's view seems to be directed against both Smith and his detractors. In reality there is only a gulf between him and these 'educated' apologists of the bourgeoisie. It did not occur to him for a moment to justify the existence of the universal class by describing its members as productive workers in some figurative sense of the term. On the contrary, in all the writings where he is concerned to define the different estates he emphasized that the 'universal class' is economically inactive and lives on the fruits of the labours of the second and third estates. In fact it can only be held to be a universal class in Hegel's eyes because it is unproductive.

Now, when Hegel distributes all the light on the side of unproductive activities and the shadows on the side of the bourgeoisie, he poses a problem that did not even occur to Smith and Ricardo, since they, and especially Ricardo, had their attention focused above all on the development of productive forces and the consequent advancement of humanity. (This is not to imply that either of them was blind to the human and cultural consequences of e.g. the capitalist division of labour. On the contrary, both men saw the problems very clearly and Smith especially who was not a disciple of Ferguson devoted much thought to them. But all this was secondary in their eyes to the great question of the development of the material forces of production.)

The hard core of Hegel's conception of 'tragedy in the realm of the ethical' is that he is wholeheartedly in agreement with Adam Smith's view that the development of the material forces of production is progressive and necessary, even in respect to culture since, as we have repeatedly maintained, the higher, more developed and spiritual form of individuality of the modern world goes hand in hand with the growth in the productive forces. He is as forceful as Smith and Ricardo in his strictures on the complaints of the Romantics about the modern world and he heaps scorn on their sentimentality which fixes on particulars while ignoring the overall situation. But at the same time, he also sees—and this brings him closer to the interests and preoccupations of Balzac and Fourier—that the type of man produced by this material advance in and through capitalism is the practical negation of everything great, significant and sublime that humanity had created in the course of its history up to then. The contradiction of two necessarily connected phenomena, the indissoluble bond between progress and the debasement of mankind, the purchase of progress at the cost of that debasement—that is the heart of the 'tragedy in the realm of the ethical'.

Thus Hegel articulates one of the great contradictions of capitalist society (and with certain reservations, of all class societies). The opaque, mystificatory form and the illusory solution of the Jena period should not blind us to the fact that Hegel has hit upon a crucial contradiction in the history of bourgeois society, a contradiction that the founders of Marxism always acknowledged and which only the Menshevik opportunists and the vulgar sociology that followed them continually obscured in their eagerness to kowtow to the bourgeoisie.

Maxim Gorki gave his view of the question in the speech he made at the Writers' Congress in Moscow in 1934:

'We have every reason to hope that when one day the history of culture is written by Marxists, it will be revealed that the *creative contribution of the bourgeoisie to culture has been greatly exaggerated*. . . . The bourgeoisie is not favourably inclined towards cultural creativity, nor has it ever been—if we think of creativity as something larger than the uninterrupted growth of external material comforts and luxuries. The culture of capitalism—what is it but a system of measures taken to ensure the physical and moral expansion of the bourgeoisie and the strengthening of its hold over people, mineral wealth and the forces of nature throughout the entire world?'[12]

What Gorki asserts confirms what Marx repeatedly said of the role of the bourgeoisie in the culture of the modern world. It is interesting to note that in such statements Marx frequently refers to the culture of antiquity as an appropriate standard by which to judge the shabby inhumanity, the base hypocrisy of bourgeois ideologists and to see them in their true light. Thus in one passage he talks of the illusions of classical poets and philosophers who had hoped that technical inventions and the mechanization of labour would lead to the liberation of mankind, and he adds:

'Oh those heathens! They understood, as the learned Bastiat, and before him the still wiser MacCulloch have discovered, nothing of political economy and Christianity. They did not, for example, comprehend that machinery is the surest means of lengthening the working-day. They perhaps excused the slavery of one on the ground that it was a means to the full development of the other. But to preach the slavery of the masses, in order that a few crude and half-educated parvenus might become "eminent spinners", "extensive sausage-makers" and "influential shoe-black dealers", to do this they lacked the bump of Christianity.'[13]

This annihilating criticism of the inhumanity and the anti-cultural nature of capitalism was anticipated by the major ideologists of what we described as the last great crisis of bourgeois development. In the case of Fourier, of course, the transition from the critique of capitalism to the advocacy of socialism is an important factor and one which adds clarity and incisiveness to his criticism. At the moment when the vision of a socialist society is added to the perspective of the dissolution of the economic and cultural contradictions of capitalism, the movement of those contradictions can itself be seen in a new light. Nevertheless, anyone who takes the trouble to compare the novels of Balzac with Fourier's

criticism will be astonished to see how closely the conservative novelist
parallels the utopian socialist.

Goethe and Hegel not only belong to an earlier, less well-developed
stage in the growth of capitalism, but they also lived in Germany, where
its contradictions were much less clearly manifest. Nevertheless, the
great works of Goethe constantly reveal these contradictions, directly
criticize them and put forward opposing models (sometimes of a utopian
variety).

As an abstract thinker, Hegel was in a much more difficult position
than Goethe or Balzac. It could not satisfy him simply to portray the contradictions of capitalism and the anti-cultural phenomena that come to
light in the midst of economic progress in terms of particular human
individuals and types. On the contrary, he was compelled to abstract
from experience and frame the contradictions at the highest possible
level of generality, to see them as philosophical contradictions of life
itself. Because of the social situation in which he found himself, and
which we have described, he could not progress beyond the point of arti-
culating the problems, indeed his method induced him to construct specious, mystificatory solutions for dilemmas that had proved intractable.
But all that notwithstanding, the contradictions of capitalist culture are
as clearly expressed in his thought as in the works of the other major
poets and philosophers who together with him make up the last great age
of bourgeois culture.

However, we have by no means exhausted the philosophical profundities of 'tragedy in the realm of the ethical'. Hitherto we have confined
ourselves chiefly to the substance of the contradictions explored by
Hegel and have paid no heed to the particular ways in which he mystifies
them. But if we now turn our attention to this we shall see, firstly, that
the formal aspects of his argument are by no means purely formal and
that they are bound up for good or ill with the substantive problems of
his view of society and his philosophy in general. Secondly, we have
observed frequently that Hegel's mystifications are rarely quite simple in
nature. No doubt, they are often just idealistic evasions of a problem
which Hegel finds insoluble for social or philosophical reasons. In very
many cases, however, these mystifications or pseudo-solutions or false
dilemmas are closely, if deviously, connected with problems which he
could not indeed resolve but which he could illuminate in a stimulating
and profound manner, often glimpsing a solution he could not quite
reach. In all these cases it is vital to distinguish the false depth from the
true, for often it is hard to keep them apart in Hegel.

The particular manifestation of mystification in 'Tragedy in the realm
of the ethical' is its view of a struggle between the 'light' aspects of
human existence with the 'dark' forces of the 'lower world'. In illustration of these terms Hegel himself refers to the *Oresteia* of Aeschylus

where the battle between light and darkness is fought out by Apollo and the Eumenides, and the indecisive end of the tragedy with its propitiation of the avenging Furies is meant to show that in history, too, neither of the two principles can be finally defeated and destroyed; on the contrary, the eternal renewal of the conflict between them *is* the tragedy in the realm of the ethical. This consists, as Hegel says, in the fact that:

> 'ethical nature, in order not to become inextricably enmeshed in its inorganic part, divides itself off from it and stands opposed to it as to its fate; but then through recognizing it in the course of the struggle, it becomes reconciled to the divine essence which is the union of the two.'[14]

The 'lower world' manifests itself in a variety of ways. Above all in the family, which according to Hegel is the 'highest totality of which nature is capable.' It goes without saying that his aim is not to deny the social character of love, marriage and the family. But he is concerned, and rightly so, to repudiate e.g. Kant's barbarous view of marriage in which all its natural aspects together with the cultural and spiritual values it generates are extinguished, and in which, as a consequence, the physical side of love is reduced to an arbitrary contract regulating the use of organs and faculties. In contrast to this Hegel constructs a complex dialectic of natural and the social determinants that convincingly demonstrates the superiority of objective over subjective idealism. But the problem of the family has another aspect for Hegel, one which combines profound intuitions about its real historical co-ordinates with the limitations inherent in his historical and philosophical horizon.

Hegel had no more idea of the nature of tribal society than any other scholar of his time. He believed, however, and rightly so, that the state must have been preceded by a stateless society. Hegel fixes on the family of the 'lower world', with its close ties with nature, and makes it the embodiment of spirit in this primitive, stateless society. In *The Phenomenology of Mind* he gives an admirable and comprehensive analysis of these two stages of society in his discussion of the tragic conflict in the *Antigone* of Sophocles. In a sense he anticipates the discussion of the *Oresteia* by Bachofen and Engels.

The difference between them is that Bachofen, writing much later and, of course, from within the limits of his own view of history, hit upon the problem of matriarchy, and that Engels was able to clarify the mystifications in his view with the aid of Morgan's discoveries and provide them with a materialist explanation. We repeat: Hegel had no conception of tribal society or matriarchal systems. His notion of a society without a state is unhistorical since he bases it on the family, a much later phenomenon. This error is one he shares with his age.

However, his discussion of the *Antigone* gains greatly in stature and

anticipates these future discoveries, thanks to his extraordinarily im-
partial analysis of the historical rights and wrongs of the tragic conflict
and his demonstration of the dialectical 'rightness' of the opposing sides.
He can see the historical justification of Creon's point of view and the
necessity underlying it: the inevitable triumph of the state. At the same
time he can recognize the ethical superiority of *Antigone* and the state of
society for which she speaks. This impartiality not only results in a brilliant analysis; it also expresses that contradictory view of progress to
which Engels draws attention in his own reflections on the break-up of
tribal society. What is striking about Hegel's view of the *Antigone* is the
way in which the two poles of the contradiction are maintained in a tense
unity: on the one hand, there is the recognition that tribal society stands
higher morally and humanly than the class societies that succeed it, and
that the collapse of tribal society was brought about by the release of base
and evil human impulses. On the other hand, there is the equally powerful conviction that this collapse was inevitable and that it signified a definite historical advance. And even though the entire discussion was
clarified immeasurably by the later discoveries of Bachofen, Morgan and
finally Engels, it should not be forgotten that Hegel's abstract and in certain crucial respects, wrong-headed recognition of the contradictory
nature of the rise of the state nevertheless forms the basis of his war between the light powers of the gods and the powers of the 'lower world'.

A further feature of the 'lower world' is already known to us: it is the
'incalculable power' of a cohesive economic system. We have seen that
Hegel repeatedly succumbed to the illusion that the economy could be
tamed by the intervention of the state. But his correct understanding of
definite antagonistic trends in the capitalist economy led him to the conclusion that if these antagonisms were allowed too much scope they
might easily lead to the collapse of society.

> 'In that event great wealth, which is indissolubly connected with the
> direst poverty—since through division labour becomes universal and
> objective on both sides—produces on the one hand in ideal universa-
> lity and on the other in reality and mechanically. And this purely
> quantitative, inorganic quality of labour, where all is isolated right
> down to the concept, is the worst form of barbarism. The first charac-
> teristic of the class of traders, its capacity for an organically absolute
> intuition and respect for something divine, (which admittedly is
> external to it) disappears, and bestial contempt for all higher values
> takes its place. Absence of wisdom, the purely universal, the mass of
> wealth—that is the sum of existence; and the bond uniting the whole
> people, the ethical, vanishes and the people is dissolved.'[15]

This makes it quite clear why Hegel regarded the entire realm of economics as one of the powers of the 'lower world' against which the God of

Light of civilization and the state had to struggle continuously.

In these and other manifestations of the 'natural' the 'lower world' in society we can see Hegel's 'uncritical positivism' at work, a tendency we have already criticized in the appropriate place. However, there are other and more important features of the 'lower world'. If we hark back to what Hegel said about work and the tools of work it will be remembered that spirit, conscious human activity was put higher than mere nature, and that through spirit nature was brought under the control of conscious human activity. At the same time, however, the objectivity of nature did not cease to exist, it was not eliminated by spirit but continued to act on and interact with society. And it is a very important feature of Hegel's supersession of subjective idealism that he does not impose abstractions upon nature but integrates it in society through this concrete dialectic.

This introduces conflicts of the most varied sort into his philosophy. It forces him to acknowledge the authentic existence, the autonomy of the powers of the 'lower world'. Hegel is the first thinker in Germany to acknowledge that economic life is governed by laws of its own, and for all his illusions about the mitigating influence of the state he never conceives of state intervention in the form of abstract regulations which would do vilence to the nature of the economy or attempt, as Fichte does, to do away with the laws of capitalism by a simple fiat. But just because he does call for a concrete process of interaction, admittedly in an abstract and mystificatory manner, the real social basis for 'tragedy in the realm of the ethical' is created. This in turn is due to Hegel's recognition of the blind, elemental character of the capitalist economy.

Thus in the 'tragedy in the realm of the ethical' we find a continuous tragic struggle between the forces of 'externalization' (civilization, the state—light) and those of nature (the immediate and elemental—the 'lower world'), a struggle whose chief characteristic in Hegel's eyes is the dialectical interplay between the opposing forces. For, on the one hand, the essence of social progress, i.e., the triumph of civilization over nature, is no once-and-for-all matter, nor is it a smooth 'infinite progress', but a victory arising from a conflict which is always being renewed and always fought with increasing violence. On the other hand, civilization can never gain an absolutely decisive victory. For Hegel's humanism postulates the whole man in a state of integrity. The climax of 'externalization' is the turning-point where 'externalization' is revoked, re-absorbed into the subject and annulled. Without this constantly renewed struggle with the forces of the 'lower world' man would lose all contact with nature, with the elemental forces of existence and would degenerate into an abstraction, a machine.

The dialectical interplay between the different moments must also be considered from the other side, from the point of view of civilization, the

state, the gods of light. We have seen how for Hegel the essence of the
state, its independence and domination of civil society was embodied in
the military caste, the necessary apex of the universal class. And at this
juncture the 'lower world', the elemental re-appears with a new lease of
life, just when it had seemed to be utterly defeated.

We have already discussed that aspect of Hegel's theory according to
which the state of nature re-emerges in the relations between independent states. We have seen how he considered every attempt to enforce
legal sanctions as merely provisional, and he saw that international trea-
ties would endure only as long as they coincided with the real interests,
the real power relations and the real shifts in power among the states concerned. Hegel has a very realistic view of the relations between juridical
control and social realities, unlike his illusions about the rule of law
within the state. (And even here, as we have noted in the case of his interpretation of the collapse of feudalism and the French Revolution,
these illusions are not unlimited.)

Thus it is only in its relations with civil society that the state can function as a true god of light. By realizing its own existence it enters the
realm of the 'lower world' and is engulfed by the elemental powers of
necessity. Moreover, it is from the elemental collision between states, the
unavoidable reappearance of the state of nature that the real meaning of
history is born. Schiller's aphorism: 'Universal history is universal
judgement', provides a motto for the entire drama. And to the extent
that it does so, we may regard the realm of history ultimately as a victory
for the god of light. But it is evident, nevertheless, that the 'tragedy in
the realm of the ethical' acted out 'below' is reproduced 'above'
throughout the entire process of world history.

The reappearance of this fundamental contradiction at a higher level
has an interesting precedent in his analysis of the 'universal class', at the
apex of which stands the warrior, an analysis of such moment that we
must pause to consider it briefly. We are already familiar with one
aspect of it: the military caste appears as the very epitome of the state,
of the 'light' side of man.

But there is also another side to the matter, almost diametrically
opposed to the first side and it is stated most clearly in the *System of
Ethics*. This contains a chapter with the title 'The Negative or Freedom
or Crime'. In this chapter Hegel develops a number of principles which
he later gathers together as the several strands of his view of the social
and historical role of evil. He begins with a series of concrete examples
of negation as seen in the historical representatives of 'natural destruction' such as Ghengis Khan and Tamburlane.

'The fanaticism of destruction is outwardly invincible, because it is absolutely elemental, having taken the form of nature; for the differentiated and the determinate must succumb to the undifferentiated and the indeterminate. But like all that is negative, it contains within itself its own negation.'

It would be striking and interesting enough if Hegel had contented himself with deducing modern war from this vantage-point. But his actual argument is more interesting still. In what follows he goes on to discuss individual acts of criminality within a society already constituted. He speaks of robbery and theft, of crimes against honour, and he makes it especially clear that they signify the re-establishment of a state of nature. From there he proceeds to discuss murder, revenge and duelling, ending up in war as the state of nature reinstated.[16]

In the later Lectures the logical deduction of the military caste is explained in a manner wholly consonant with this.

'War and the class of soldiers are . . . the actual sacrifice of the self, the danger of death for the individual, the contemplation of his abstract immediate negativity, which is also his immediate positive self—(for *crime* is necessarily implicit in the concept of law dealing with right and force)—so that each person as this individual makes himself into absolute power, regards himself as absolutely free, real and for himself as opposed to some other which is universal negativity. In war this is granted to him; it is crime *on behalf of the universal interest*, its purpose is the maintenance of the whole against the enemy who would destroy it.'

Here we have the succinct summary of the earlier argument: war is crime on behalf of the universal interest. Hegel goes on to underscore heavily this universal interest to which war is subject, a moral necessity that goes hand in hand with his realistic view of history. For in the course of the argument he demonstrates the modern character of war, i.e. he shows how socialization and 'externalization' permeate even war, and this shows once again that his military caste has nothing in common with a cult of the nobility or the romantic glorification of chivalry. He continues:

'This "externalization" must have this abstract form, it must be unindividuated, death must be coldly meted out and received, not as in the pitched battle where the individual looks his enemy in the eye and kills him in an upsurge of hatred, but death must be given and received emptily, *impersonally*, from amidst the powder fumes.'[17]

It might appear as if, by interpolating 'externalization' in its modern form, Hegel was attempting to annul the natural, elemental, 'lower worldly' aspects of war, so as to remove his warrior, notwithstanding his earlier arguments, from the control of these powers and to present him as the real apex of the state, of the citoyen, as the protagonist of the god of light. This aspect is undoubtedly present but as a whole the argument is more complex and contradictory. For his intention is by no means to suggest that negation, crime, is simply the immediate, elemental and natural, something starkly opposed to the social without any possible interaction. But the contrary is the case: as we have seen the path leading from Tamburlane to the modern soldier is one of 'externalization', of socialization. And this is true also of the intermediate types of individual crime. They too contain stages of 'externalization'. Indeed, Hegel regards evil as the climax of 'externalization' though in a form in which it can be transformed into its opposite. It is not for nothing that the section under discussion should also have included the word 'freedom' in the title. He concludes, by way of summary:

> 'Evil—individuality which has entered wholly into itself and is therefore entirely "externalized". It is a self that has abandoned its own existence and knows another world as its own. In actuality only this "externalization" becomes manifest.'[18]

Thus we can see how the obscure contradictions treated in 'Tragedy in the realm of the ethical' provide the intellectual foundations of one of the crucial problems in his entire philosophy of history. Engels, in his critical comments on Feuerbach's moral views, emphasized the superiority of precisely this aspect of Hegel's thought over that of Feuerbach:

> 'With Hegel evil is the form in which the motive force of historical development presents itself. This contains the twofold meaning that, on the one hand, each new advance necessarily appears as a sacrilege against things hallowed, as a rebellion against conditions, though old and moribund, yet sanctified by custom; and that, on the other hand, it is precisely the wicked passions of man—greed and lust for power —which, since the emergence of class antagonisms, serve as levers of historical development—a fact of which the history of feudalism and of the bourgeoisie, for example, constitutes a single continual proof.'[19]

Hegel's bourgeois commentators constantly waver between two extremes. Before it became fashionable to praise him as 'the greatest irrationalist' in the history of philosophy, it was not uncommon for him to be criticized for being 'panlogical', i.e. all too harmonious. Above all, at the time when the superficial pessimism of Schopenhauer and Eduard von Hartmann was in vogue, it was customary to condemn Hegel for ignoring the darker sides of human existence. A knowledge of his real philosophy shows that he had nothing in common either with the superficial optimism of a direct apologia of bourgeois society, or with the equally superficial pessimism of an indirect apologia.

On the contrary, he stands in a line of great philosophers who from the beginnings of bourgeois society have insisted that the progress of man is inseparably intertwined with the worst impulses of human nature, with 'greed and lust for power'. In this sense Hegel's philosophy is the direct continuation of Hobbes and Mandeville, with the important difference that what in their case had been a spontaneous dialectic, a descriptive presentation of the contradictory nature of human progress, had become in his works a conscious dialectic, a philosophy of contradiction. Marx always saw Hegel's philosophy in just this context. After reading Darwin he wrote to Engels saying:

> 'It is remarkable how Darwin can examine the world of plants and animals and discover there his own English society with its division of labour, competition, the opening up of new markets, "inventions", and Malthus' "struggle for existence". It is Hobbes' *bellum omnium contra omnes* and reminds one of Hegel in the *Phenomenology* where· bourgeois society appears as the "animal kingdom of the spirit", whereas in Darwin the animal kingdom appears as bourgeois society.'[20]

Here again we find the same ambiguity in Hegel's theory of contradiction which we have already noted. On the one hand—and that is Hegel's greatness—he is utterly frank in his presentation of the contradictions he finds and the impossibility of resolving them. The 'tragedy in the realm of the ethical' is nothing but the great tragedy of the contradictory path of human progress in the history of class societies—a great and real tragedy; for the extremes of the elements in conflict are both valid and in the wrong.

Hence although Hegel also analyses 'comedy in the realm of the ethical' it is the tragedy that is the closer to reality.

> 'Comedy separates the two zones of the ethical so that each exists for itself. In one antagonisms and the finite appear as a shadow without substance, while in the other the absolute is a delusion. However,. the authentic and absolute relationship is that the one is manifest in all earnestness in the other, and that each enters bodily into relationship with the other so that together they constitute fate in all its earnestness for each other. Thus the absolute relationship is to be found in tragedy.'[21]

Since Hegel could not look beyond the confines of class society in general, and bourgeois society in particular, his commitment to tragedy bears testimony to his utter integrity as a thinker: he recognized the contradictions of progress within class society as irremediable.

But even this is not the whole story. From the moment that these contradictions entered his mind at the time of the Frankfurt crisis, the tendency towards their 'reconciliation' began to develop. And from Frankfurt to the late Berlin period it was not only present but it constantly grew in strength. It would be easy to condemn this tendency as something merely negative, as a simple accommodation to the civil society of his day. No doubt, such conformist elements are implicit in his concept of 'reconciliation'; we have repeatedly drawn attention to the distorting effects of its triumph over indissoluble contradictions in his philosophy of society.

Hegel himself, however, often had the opposite feeling: the realization that the contradictions were insoluble was more important than their 'reconciliation'. Thus, in the passage just quoted, the task Hegel assigns to comedy is identical with what he elsewhere regards as the key to the contradictions of civil society: viz., the separation of the spheres of the *bourgeois* and the *citoyen*, the primacy of the public realm of the state over the private realm of civil society. And if he now arrives at the conclusion that the absolute relationship is to be discovered in tragedy where this separation does not take place, where the opposed sides contend with each other to the point where both are destroyed, then the implied criticism of his own concept of 'reconciliation' is plain to see.

At the same time, it would be superficial to urge that Hegel would have been all the greater if he had never taken up the concept of 'reconciliation'. For the real, dialectical analysis of human progress and its contradictions can only be undertaken from a point of view dominated by a belief in the ultimate victory of progress, despite all the contradictions. Only the perspective of a classless society can provide a view of the tragedies to be encountered *en route* without succumbing to the temptations of a pessimistic romanticism. For this reason we must place Fourier's social criticism higher than Hegel's.

If this perspective is not available to a thinker—and we have seen that it could not be available to Hegel—then there are only two possibilities open to anyone who has a clear view of the contradictions. Either he will hold fast to the contradictions, in which case he will end up as a romantic pessimist. Or he will keep his faith, despite everything, that progress is inevitable, however many tragedies lie along the road. In that case his faith must be embodied in one or other of the mystifications of false consciousness.

The greatness of the age in which Hegel lived and worked is manifest in many ways; one of them is that there is scarcely any possible problem and solution which did not find an advocate to argue it out at the highest level. This is certainly true of our first-mentioned possibility of holding fast to contradictions regarded as irreconcilable. The advocate of this position was the outstanding philosopher of Romanticism in Germany, Solger, a man whom Hegel held in the highest esteem for his integrity and his intellectual prowess.

In Solger the problem we are discussing appears in a much more mystified form than in Hegel himself. He formulates the contradiction as one between the absolute and its incarnation in the empirical world. Turning back to the introductory words of Hegel's 'Tragedy in the realm of the ethical' we recollect that according to him, the absolute 'is eternally born anew into the objective world'. We can see Solger concerned with the same problem in a more abstract form (for all that he is directly concerned with it as a problem in the philosophy of art). In the concluding paragraphs of his principal work on aesthetics he says of the relation of the absolute to its incarnation in the empirical world:

> '. . . and sorrow without end must take hold of us when we see that which is most glorious doomed to destruction by the necessity of an earthly existence. And yet we cannot put the blame anywhere but upon the perfect thing itself as it is revealed to us in time; for that which is merely of the earth, when we only perceive it, holds together through its links with other things and as part of an unending process of birth and death. Now this transitional moment in which the idea necessarily annihilates itself must be the true seat of art.'[21]

We cannot pause to discuss the aberrations that this conception of contradictoriness led Solger into for all his ability and integrity. Suffice it to say that it enabled him to provide the most profound, and most dialectical explanation of the mistaken and distorted concept of 'Romantic irony' so that notwithstanding his greater philosophical gifts he ended up by going the way of the Schellings and Schlegels. And this is no accident, just as it is no accident that Hegel's attempt to reconcile the inexorably tragic course of human progress led to such a rich and concrete account of history and society, while Solger's retention of tragic contradiction led only to abstract mystification.

This last contrast offers a pointer to the internal contradictions in Hegel's concept of 'reconciliation'. On the one hand, it presents an idealistic mystification of irreconcilable contradictions. On the other hand, this very fact points to Hegel's underlying realism, his commitment to the concrete social realities of his age, his profound understanding of the actual life of man in society, his aspiration to see the contradictions in human progress where they are actually fought out in the arena of economic life. Only because of this love of reality and his profound commitment to it could the concrete richness of the Hegelian dialectic come into being. And if his system culminates in 'reconciliation', this only shows that, as long as the horizon of class society is closed off, human progress even in the realm of the mind, of philosophy, is compelled to take detours through the labyrinths of what Engels called 'false consciousness'.

NOTES 1   *Theories of Surplus Value*, Part III, p. 84.

   2   Ibid., Vol. II, pp. 117–18.

   3   Marx, *The Eighteenth Brumaire of Louis Napoleon*, *Selected Works*, I, p. 226.

   4   Adam Ferguson, *An Essay on the History of Civil Society*, Edinburgh 1966, p. 186.

   5   Lasson, p. 380.

   6   Hegel to Niethammer, 29 August 1807, *Briefe von und an Hegel*, Leipzig 1887, p. 130.

   7   Lasson, p. 383.

   8   Preface to the Second Edition of *The Peasant War in Germany*, Berlin 1951, p. 13f.

   9   Introduction to the English Edition of *Socialism: Utopian and Scientific, Selected Works*, Vol. II, p. 102.

 10   *Theories of Surplus Value*, Vol. I, pp. 300–1.

 11   Ibid., p. 287.

 12   Gorki, *Über Literatur*, Moscow 1937, p. 448.

 13   *Capital*, Vol. I, pp. 408–9.

 14   Lasson, p. 381.

 15   Ibid., p. 492.

 16   Lasson, p. 458f.

 17   *Realphilosophie*, Vol. II, p. 261f.

 18   Ibid., p. 258.

 19   *Feuerbach*, in Marx/Engels, *Selected Works*, Vol. II, pp. 345–6. We have concerned ourselves here only with the second half of Engels' arguments. We may remind the reader, therefore, that Hegel's analysis of the *Antigone* and the origins of the state, his observations on revolution and tyranny are all part of the same complex of the part played by evil in history.

 20   To Engels, 18 June 1862, MEGA II, Vol. 3, p. 77f.

 21   Lasson, p. 384.

 22   Solger, *Erwin*, Berlin 1815, Vol. II, p. 277. Hegel frequently drew attention to the importance of Solger's philosophy, e.g. in the *Aesthetics* (ed. Glockner), Vol. I, p. 105 and also in an extended essay on Solger's posthumous writings, *Sämtliche Werke*, Vol. XX, ed. Glockner, pp. 132ff.

# PART IV

# The Breach with Schelling and
*The Phenomenology of Mind* (Jena 1803–1807)

# CHAPTER ONE

# The growing estrangement between Schelling and Hegel up to the final breach

OUR previous discussions have made it plain that, while Hegel and Schelling joined forces in an attack on subjective idealism, they were by no means at one on all questions of philosophy. Differences of opinion did not make their appearance during their collaboration and up to 1803, the year of Schelling's departure for Würzburg. They can only be discovered by a thorough scrutiny of the writings of the two men, and this, as we have seen, is no easy task since this was the period when Hegel was experimenting with Schelling's conceptual system. Not until the Lectures of 1805–6 do we find that Hegel has freed himself from Schelling's terminology.

When Hegel finally disengaged his own philosophical approach and language, he launched a polemic against Schelling's followers and disciples, and also against Schelling himself, a polemic that was conducted with increasing acerbity as time went on. For this transitional phase we are able to draw on Hegel's Notebook, the dating of which we have already discussed (p. 254f.). Furthermore, we can also refer to the lecture fragments from the last years in Jena. These fragments, which Rosenkranz has published with the title *Didactic Modification of the System*, are of great importance.[1]

If we wish to understand the disagreement that arose between Hegel and Schelling we must not be misled by the framework of our own analysis which made it necessary to follow Hegel's development step by step, while invoking Schelling's philosophy only as a foil or as the object of Hegel's criticism. This may well have created the impression that Schelling's thought remained static at this period and that Hegel's final criticism, his blunt rejection of Schelling's philosophy in 1807, implied a denial of the Schelling with whom he had joined forces in 1801 in an attack on subjective idealism.

It is not possible for us to give an account of Schelling's inner development here.[2] All we can do here is to indicate briefly the main phases of his thought during the period under discussion. As we know, the point of departure for Hegel's collaboration with him was his *System of Transcendental Idealism* (1800). His next work, *Presentation of My System of Philosophy*, was the one closest to Hegelian thought and provides evidence of Schelling's efforts to appropriate the principles of

Hegel's dialectics. But we very soon perceive the emergence of quite opposite principles in Schelling. These become manifest partly in his growing tendency to make arbitrary constructs in the philosophy of nature and partly in the increasing weight he places on aesthetics—a result of grounding 'intellectual intuition' in aesthetics. This tendency was already apparent in his first system but it now brought him into closer proximity to the Romantics' cult of genius. A further tendency diametrically opposed to Hegel is to be found in his growing receptivity to mystical ideas which likewise had their roots in the Romantic movement which had glorified the theosophy and nature philosophy of Jacob Böhme. This increased proximity to Romantic ideas at first went no further than a mystical Platonism, in the Jena dialogue *Bruno* of 1802. But no sooner had he arrived in Würzburg than he published a new work, *Philosophy and Religion* (1804) in which his now thoroughly religious mysticism was frankly asserted. This work is of the first importance for an understanding of his development since it already contained the seeds of the purely reactionary philosophy of his later years. Thus Schelling had turned away from the principles they had shared, from the common attempt to extend the dialectics of objective idealism in a progressive sense, even before Hegel embarked on his attack. Objectively, the parting of the ways had come with the publication of the last-named work of Schelling's. Schelling's other major publications during the last part of his stay in Jena include the *Lectures on the Methods of Academic Study* (1802) and the *Philosophy of Art* (1802–3). They define the intermediate stages of Schelling's progress towards religious mysticism, although it is only fair to remark that the *Philosophy of Art* in particular contains a vast amount of valuable material and is one of Schelling's greatest achievements. Thus if we now turn our attention to Hegel's increasingly forthright criticism of Schelling we must pay due heed to the fact that this reflects not only Hegel's development, but Schelling's own development in the opposite direction. Furthermore, in our discussion of their controversy we must bear in mind that we have no documentary evidence and no recorded statement by Hegel relating to a number of questions on which their disagreement was obviously at its greatest. Moreover, we are not thinking here of fortuitous gaps in our knowledge, but of the fundamental divergence in method between Hegel's attack on the subjective idealism of Kant, Jacobi and Fichte, and the manner in which he later criticized Schelling. As we have seen, the attack on subjective idealism was comprehensive. It began with the most general problems concerning the nature of philosophy and went on to quite specific issues of moral philosophy and the philosophy of law and society. In contrast to this, his criticism of Schelling, even in his private notebooks takes issue only with the central problems of philosophical method. If we compare the Jena publications of Hegel and Schelling—and we shall quote a few more examples of their most characteristic ideas—it will be plain to everyone that their opinions had already diverged greatly at that period. But it is precisely on such objective disagreements that we are left in the dark. Whether and to what extent they were aired in conversation is not known to us, and Hegel himself does not make the slightest allusion to conversations of that sort in his private diaries.

In these differences of approach, in this restriction to the fundamental questions of philosophical method, we can see how greatly Hegel had gained in assurance since the days of the debate with Fichte. At that time he was concerned to extend his method systematically and to apply it to the various spheres of knowledge (society, history, nature). This process took place in and through the campaign against subjective idealism By now, however, the task of self-clarification was complete. He was no longer interested in demonstrating the superiority of his method by exposing his opponent's weaknesses and his own strengths by testing it out on all sorts of concrete issues. A further factor was that while moral and political philosophy had constituted an important part of the philosophy of subjective idealism they were marginal in Schelling's system. At stake now were the great central methodological questions raised by objective idealism. It is obviously Hegel's view that if these were settled then all was settled as far as philosophy was concerned.

Nevertheless, it is important to quote one or two passages from Schelling which have no direct bearing on Hegel's criticisms, but which are rendered necessary by our own approach. We have shown in some detail the close connections between Hegel's views on history, economics and society, and his philosophical views, and how the latter arose out of the former and acquired their specific philosohhical form through them. It is obvious that similar connections, if in a much modified form, must have been present also in Schelling—as indeed in every other philosopher. Obviously it cannot be our task to establish these connections in Schelling's thought—that must be left to the Schelling specialists. But it is of interest to give just one or two examples which make it clear that the disagreement with Hegel was not just confined to the questions of philosophical method on which Hegel concentrated, but that it extended to all the problems of the philosophy of history and society. It is important to stress this for the additional reason that the more recent bourgeois literature on Hegel makes it easier to blur the distinctions between the dialectical methods of Hegel and Schelling by completely trivializing the differences of opinion on these other questions. (This process can be seen at its worst in Heller, but it is a standing feature of the more recent literature on Hegel.)

Let us just glance at Schelling's views on society in Jena. His *Lectures on the Methods of Academic Study* must obviously include something about the problems of history and society. What he does is to make a purely formal equation in which he transforms the harmony of necessity and freedom into 'stages of being' (*Potenzen*) of the real and the ideal. The upshot is that this unity is embodied, in real terms, in the perfect state and, at the level of the ideal, in the church. This pair of opposites is then formally related to antiquity and the modern world, thus revealing Schelling's fundamental inability to grasp the specific character of modern civil society:

> 'That so-called civil freedom has produced only the saddest mixture of freedom and slavery, but not the absolute and hence free existence of the one or the other.'[3]

On the surface what we have here is Schelling's total failure to understand those problems of modern civil society and its economy that were so vital to the development of Hegel's philosophical system. But behind his incomprehension we may detect other tendencies when we look at his views about the Enlightenment, the Revolution and the tasks of philosophy *vis-à-vis* both. He reviles the Enlightenment for its 'dearth of ideas' and refers to it as the philosophy of common sense. This he defines as

> 'the understanding instructed in lofty and vacuous reasoning by a false and superficial culture.'

The victory of that understanding is a disaster, according to Schelling:

> 'The elevation of the common understanding to the position of judge in matters of the reason, leads necessarily to ochlocracy in the realm of science and sooner or later this ends with the general uprising of the mob.'

According to Schelling another dangerous conception of philosophy attempts to orientate it towards the useful. The task of philosophy is to wage war incessantly on all such tendencies:

> 'If anything at all is able to offer some resistance to the approaching flood in which more and more visibly high and low have been commingled, ever since the mob began to write and every plebeian elevates himself to the rank of judge, it is philosophy whose natural motto is: *odi profanum vulgus et arceo*.'[4]

These quotations could be multiplied with ease. We believe, however, that the position is perfectly clear: on the one hand, Hegel never took the trouble to attack views of this sort as expressed by Schelling; on the other hand, anyone who has followed Hegel's development in Jena will be aware that Hegel's views are diametrically opposed to those expressed here.

Of course, in the period leading up to the *Phenomenology* there is an extensive series of satirical passages attacking the reactionary Romanticism of the Schelling school, and also of Schelling himself. In particular, Hegel criticizes their flirtation with mystical and religious concepts, the denigration of the understanding in philosophy, the playing with forms and the barbaric confusion of feeling and understanding. Here are some of Hegel's observations on these matters:

'Just as there was a cult of the genius in literature, so now we seem to have a similar *cult of philosophical genius*. They mix some carbon, oxygen, nitrogen and hydrogen together, wrap it up in paper which contains some writing about polarity, give it a wooden pigtail of vanity and shoot it off like a rocket—and then they they have depicted the empyrean. There we have Görres and Wagner. The crudest empiricism mixed with formalistic ideas about matter and polarities, adorned with senseless analogies and *intoxicated aperçus*.'[5]

In lectures written at the same time Hegel attacks mysticism, which he finds even worse.

'There is indeed a poor *middle thing* standing between feeling and *science*, a speculative feeling, or an idea which cannot free itself from feeling and imagination, but which is no longer just feeling and imagination.'[6]

And he goes so far in his contempt for would-be profundity that he noted down this aphorism:

'Whatever has a deep *meaning*, is worthless for that very reason.'[7]

But for all this Hegel makes a clear distinction, especially in his lectures, between Schelling's supporters and Schelling himself. We have seen that Hegel always respected Schelling's historical achievement of taking the first steps in objective idealism. At this period he was obviously of the opinion that Schelling was still on the right road and that he was still open to logical argument. Even the letter accompanying a presentation copy of *The Phenomenology of Mind* only contained criticism of Schelling's followers and not of Schelling himself. And as the reader will recollect, this was at a time when Schelling was making experiments in magic with a divining rod, experiments which Hegel viewed with extreme scepticism for all the politeness and restraint in which he couched his letters on the subject. He made up for this by the open mockery with which he treated the Schelling school in his lectures. He warns his listeners to beware of the magniloquent, orotund language of the school, for, he says,

'the secret will one day be revealed that *behind the imposing façade of expression, very vulgar thoughts lay hidden* . . . I cannot introduce you . . .

to the profundities of this philosophy, for it has none, and I say this lest
*you be imposed upon* and deceived into believing that there must be
some sense in these ornate and weighty words. . . . In actual fact this
formalism can be acquired in half an hour. For example, instead of
saying something is *long*, say it has length, and that this length is *magnetism*; instead of *broad*, say it has *breadth* and that it is *electricity*; instead
of *thick*, corporeal, say that is enters the *third dimension*; instead of *pointed*, say that it is the *pole of contraction*; and instead of saying, the fish is
long, say it belongs in the scheme of magnetism, etc.[8]

But these are just preliminary skirmishes. On the essential issues,
however, Hegel did not spare Schelling, for all that he respected him and
he still believed he was not irrevocably lost. Hegel directed his attack at
the central pillars of Schelling's philosophy.

Chief among these is the problem of whether knowledge of the absolute can be achieved and by what means. That there can be such knowledge was common ground between Hegel and Schelling, and this was
what they had fought for against subjective idealism. The point at issue,
then, was how to acquire such knowledge. As we know, 'intellectual intuition' was the means preferred by Schelling. The stronger his aesthetic
and later his religious preoccupations became, the more *immediate* this
knowledge became. Thus in *Philosophy and Religion* he asserts that

'it is only called intuition because the soul which is one and the same
as the absolute, can have none but an *immediate* relationship with it.'[9]

Now the immediacy of 'intellectual intuition' has two very important
consequences. In the first place, it is placed in blunt opposition to 'ordinary' conceptual modes of cognition. The fact that both art and religion
are the exclusive 'organs' by which to perceive the absolute underscores
Schelling's tendency to drive a wedge between normal thought and cognition of the absolute. This yearning to have done with thought, with
understanding and reason is what constantly calls forth Hegel's mockery,
and it is easy to see his indignation with this self-important mystical irrationalism. Thus we find the following passage in his Notebook:

'If the absolute, while out for a stroll, should slip and fall from its own
proper sphere into the water, then it will become a fish, an organic,
living thing. And if it were to slip and fall into the realm of *pure
thought*—for even pure thought is supposed not to be its proper realm
—then it would come blundering in, a wicked, finite thing, which
one would be too ashamed to mention, if it weren't one's job, since
for once it cannot be denied that an actual logic is present. Water is
such a cold, wicked element, and yet life thrives in it. Is thought such
an inferior element? Must the absolute really be so badly off in it and
behave so badly in it?'[10]

In the implied contempt felt for the understanding Hegel detects a fear of the understanding as something barbaric. He therefore places the aristocratic philosophy of irrationalism on the same plane as ordinary illiteracy.

'The barbaarian is astonished when he hears that the square on the hypotenuse is equal to the sum of the squares on the other two sides. He thinks it could really be otherwise, draws away from the understanding in fear, and prefers to hold fast to his intuitions. *Reason without understanding is nothing, but understanding in the absence of reason is still something.* The understanding cannot be dispensed with.'[11]

Hegel never tires of repeating that truth, knowledge of the world as it really is, knowledge of the absolute, is only to be gained by advancing along the road from immediate intuition via understanding and reason. Anyone who really strives for knowledge should not allow himself to be deterred by the apparent abstraction, the apparent barrenness and poverty of conceptual thought as opposed to the immediate vitality of intuition, for only if he passes along the road described above will he discover that the correctly defined concept comes from life and returns to life.

'The individual well knows the truth of his individuality which precisely prescribes the course of his existence, but consciousness of life in general is something he expects from philosophy. Here his hopes appear to be shattered when, instead of the richness of life, mere concepts appear, and instead of the wealth of the immediate world, the most dessicated abstractions. But the concept is itself the *mediator between oneself and life* since it teaches us to discover life in it, and itself in life. Of course, this is a matter of which science must convince itself.'[12]

In these passages the polemic against Schelling is quite evident. But in addition to them there is a whole series of statements from the period leading up to the *Phenomenology* in which Hegel directly or indirectly attacks Schelling's cognitive method, without mentioning Schelling but in such a way as to leave no doubt that it is the premises underlying Schelling's position that are being undermined. This can be seen above all from the way in which Hegel strives—the more energetically as time goes on—to subordinate art and religion to philosophy as modes of cognizing the absolute, and to deny that they are adequate to the task on their own. Since art was the point at which the identity of subject and object was most patently made manifest in Schelling's view, such passages may undoubtedly be held to contain an indirect attack on his theory of 'intellectual intuition'. This polemic even influences Hegel's own intellectual style. From this point on art always remains the most immediate and hence the lowest form of apprehension of the absolute. However, in his later works, and starting in *The Phenomenology of Mind*, Hegel emphasizes that despite the inadequacy of art, its *content* remains absolute truth. In the Lectures of 1805–6 his animus against Schelling's philosophy is such that he concentrates almost entirely on the inadequacies of art as a cognitive instrument. He refers to art as

> 'an Indian Bacchus which is no clear, self-knowing spirit. . . . It is therefore an element inadequate for spirit. Hence art can only give its configurations a limited spirit. . . . This finite medium contemplation, cannot encompass infinity. It is only an *intended* infinity . . . it is only *intended*, not *true* representation. The necessity, the shape of *thought* is not contained in it. Beauty is the veil that conceals the truth, rather than what presents it.'[13]

We repeat, Hegel corrected this one-sided view by the time he came to write the *Phenomenology*. And we have only quoted it to show the reader how far his dislike of Schelling's 'intellectual intuition' would take him in this transitional period.

Hegel's passion throughout this polemic is to be explained by the fact that 'intellectual intuition' was not just a particular cognitive mode, but something which had the most far-reaching consequences for the entire system of philosophy, for an understanding of the relations of man to the truth and to the absolute. This brings us to the second important consequence of Schelling's view of the absolute. 'Intellectual intuition' goes hand in hand with an aristocratic theory of knowledge. Schelling repeatedly argues that authentic philosophical truth, knowledge of the absolute, is attainable only by a few chosen people, by geniuses. One part of philosophy, the most important part, simply could not be acquired by learning:

> 'However, this very principle of the antinomy of the absolute and of merely finite forms, the conviction that in philosophy art and production can no more be separated than form and content in poetry, demonstrates that the dialectic too has a side from which it cannot be *learnt*, and that it too is founded upon the productive faculty, no less than what might be called, in the original sense of the word, the element of poetry in philosophy.'[14]

The connection between this theory of knowledge and Schelling's views on society, on the Enlightenment and Revolution, which we have already quoted, is obvious. His aristocratic theory of knowledge is designed to create an unbridgeable gulf between the 'chosen' and the mob, just like the gulf the Restoration attempted to create in the realm of politics. Thus Hegel's passionate tone is based, on the one hand, on his determination to liberate philosophy from every sort of irrational mystification and self-important obscurity; on the other hand, it has its roots in politics. Modern society as Hegel understands it and as it emerged from the French Revolution exists not only objectively and in itself, but also subjectively and for itself, it is the incarnation of the world-spirit. And that means that the self-discovery of the spirit in the modern state and modern society must not only be objectively true in itself, but it must be knowledge available to every individual. In his lectures Hegel makes this idea quite explicit:

'It should briefly be noted that, as the *science of reason*, philosophy is of its very nature, by virtue of its general mode of existence, available *for all*. Not all can attain to it, but that is not in question, any more than *that few people become princes*. That some men are placed higher than others is a *scandal* only if it is claimed that they are *creatures of another kind* and that nature had created them so.'[15]

Thus the connection between Hegel's theory of knowledge and his general political attitudes is evident. It also provides additional proof that Hegel's universal class could not possibly have reference to the hereditary feudal nobility. Furthermore, it is plain that the purely philosophical disagreement between Hegel and Schelling had its roots in profound social and political differences of opinion.

Hegel's repudiation of the predestined genius did not go beyond the recognition that the knowledge of the absolute is *possible* for all, and that every individual *can* acquire it. Actually to do so requires significant intellectual labour, in Hegel's view. Nevertheless, one of the outstanding tasks of philosophy was to develop a methodology which would facilitate this task. In his private notebooks Hegel proposed this programme:

'The partition between the terminology of philosophy and ordinary consciousness has still to be broken through.'[16]

It is this programme that Hegel carried out in the *Phenomenology*. In the Preface to that work Hegel states:

'Science on its side requires the individual self-consciousness to have risen into this high ether, in order to be able to live with science, and in science, and really to feel alive there. Conversely the individual has the right to demand that science shall hold the ladder to help him get at least as far as this position, shall show him that he was in himself this ground to stand on. His right rests on his absolute independence, which he knows he possesses in every type and phase of knowledge; for in every phase, whether recognized by science or not, and whatever be the content, his right as an individual is the absolute and final form, i.e. he is the *immediate certainty of self* and thereby is unconditioned being, were this expression preferred.'[17]

The entire *Phenomenology* is dedicated to the fulfilment of this programme. And even in this preliminary statement there is a peremptory rejection of Schelling's philosophy of immediacy. And directly following this passage we find the celebrated criticism of Schelling's 'intellectual intuition' which is referred to as

'the sort of ecstatic enthusiasm which starts straight off with absolute knowledge, as if shot out of a pistol, and makes short work of other points of view simply by explaining that it is to take no notice of them.'[18]

This criticism represents a sharpening of the distinction, long familiar to us, between the dialectics of Hegel and Schelling. The disagreement turned on the nature of contradiction and supersession. We have already discussed it on a number of occasions. We have seen how Schelling is concerned to reconcile the contradictions in such a way that no element of contradiction survives, whereas Hegel's concept of the identity of opposites is that of both identity and non-identity. This implies that contradictions are not extinguished in the unity, nor do moments or parts lose themselves in the absolute, but instead they are superseded in the well-known Hegelian use of the concept, i.e. they are annulled, preserved and elevated to a higher level.

Now in the Preface to the *Phenomenology* what Hegel reproaches Schelling with is precisely this obliteration of the various moments in the absolute. He criticizes Schelling for causing to be swallowed up in the empty gulf of the absolute:

'To pit this single assertion, that "in the absolute all is one" against the organized whole of determinate and complete knowledge, or of knowledge which at least aims at and demands complete development—to give out its absolute as the night in which, as we say, all cows are black—that is the very *naïveté* of emptiness of knowledge.'[19]

And Hegel goes on to give a thorough analysis of immediacy, which he combats from the vantage-point of his own belief that man is the product of his own activity and so can only reach his real existence at the end and not at the starting-point of the process. This transformation of existence into activity also annuls Schelling's rigid antithesis of positive and negative

'True reality is merely this process of *reinstating* self-identity, of reflecting into its own self in and from its other, and is not an *original and primal* unity as such, not an *immediate* unity as such. It is the process of its own becoming, the circle which presupposes its end as its purpose, and has its end for its beginning; it becomes concrete and actual only by being carried out, and by the end it involves.'[20]

It is not without interest to pause here and look back at the discussion of a few years previous to this between Schelling and Fichte. At that time Fichte reproached Schelling with introducing distinctions, and what was worse, quantitative distinctions, into the absolute.
He wrote to Schelling:

'I can define the difference between us in a few words.—According to you, I maintain that the absolute exists in the form of quantitative distinctions. This is indeed what *you* maintain; and it is *just for that reason* that I find your system mistaken. . . . That is just what Spinoza does, and every other type of dogmatism. . . . The absolute would not be the absolute if it could exist in any form whatsoever.'[21]

This remark makes the bond between Kant and Fichte absolutely plain. Although the Fichtean Ego is an attempt to overcome the Kantian Thing-in-itself, it shares at least one thing with it: the absence of qualities of any kind. Fichte does indeed claim to achieve a sort of self-knowledge of the Ego through his own version of 'intellectual intuition'. But since he denies his absolute every kind of quality, determination or modification, this self-knowledge is evidently illusory. Formally indeed Fichte repudiates Kant's idea that the Thing-in-itself cannot be known, by saying that something can be known; but what it is that is known, its *content*, he does not say and so this knowledge remains as empty as Kant's renunciation of knowledge of the absolute.

In comparison Schelling's objective idealism represents a great step forward, since according to him all sorts of concrete, recognizable attributes and determinations are to be conferred on the absolute. That is to say, he is moving towards the view that knowledge of the absolute should be knowledge of objective reality. (We recollect Hegel's later criticism of the Thing-in-itself. It was precisely the relation he established between thing and attribute that was to prove so fruitful for the theory of knowledge.) The philosophical importance of the common struggle waged by Schelling and Hegel in those first years in Jena lay in their refusal to accept the vacuous and self-defeating abstractness of Fichte's view of absolute knowledge and their resolve to invest it instead with a wealth of determinations. Thus the first stage of the argument hinged on whether absolute knowledge had recognizable determinations or not. Schelling and Hegel were in total agreement that it could and did. The disagreements between them, and they already existed, referred on the one hand to the way in which this knowledge could be acquired, and on the other hand, to the nature of such knowledge. It is easy to understand that at this stage the divergences of opinion receded before the need to defeat the common enemy.

Thus Hegel's criticism of Schelling assumes that this battle has now been won; the new disagreement moves on a higher plane than the earlier argument. It is interesting to see Hegel taking up Fichte's argument about quantitative determinations in the absolute. But he does so from quite a different angle: what appeared to Fichte as going beyond the bounds of knowledge appears to Hegel as an abstraction, a failure to gain sufficiently concrete knowledge of the absolute.[22] Rosenkranz summarizes one passage from Hegel's lectures of 1805–6 as follows:

'He spoke publicly of *Schelling*, referred with great warmth to his great achievements, but criticized the merely *quantitative* distinction of division in the absolute; this he said meant all was indifferent, a mere predominance of one factor or another so that there was no true distinction.'[23]

This restriction of the distinctions in the absolute is one of the sources of Schelling's formalism. He cannot possibly incorporate the richness of life, of objective reality within his concept of the absolute. He must therefore content himself with inane arguments such as, e.g. , the idea that nature represents the predominance of the real over the ideal. Obviously, formalistic pronouncements of this sort can never do justice to the movement of objective reality. It is not fortuitous that, following the criticism of Schelling just referred to, Hegel goes on to reproach Schelling for his lack of dialectics.

If we now look back at Hegel's criticism of Schelling we can see that all his methodological objections cluster around one great point: that Schelling's use of their common concept of the absolute fails to do justice to the richness and vitality of the real world. His critique of Schelling's formalism becomes concretized in the *Phenomenology* in the following requirements of philosophical method:

'*A table of contents* is all that [the schematic] understanding gives, the *content* itself it does not furnish at all. If the specific determination (say even one like magnetism) is one that in itself is concrete or actual, it all the same gets degraded into something lifeless and inert, since it is merely predicated of another existing entity, and not known as an imminent living principle of this existence; nor is there any comprehension of how in this entity its intrinsic and peculiar way of expressing and producing itself takes effect. This, the very kernel of the matter, formal understanding leaves to others to add later on. Instead of making its way into the inherent content of the matter in hand, understanding always takes a survey of the whole, assumes a position above the particular existence about which it is speaking, i.e. it does not see it at all. True scientific knowledge, on the contrary, demands abandonment to the very life of the object, or, which means the same thing, claims to have before it the inner necessity controlling the object, and to express this only.'[24]

Here we can see the real philosophical connection between Hegel's dialectic and that sympathy for the empiricists which we have frequently observed during the Jena period. Hegel regards the correspondence between existing reality and the conclusions reached by a philosophy as a decisive criterion for the correctness of the philosophy concerned. In a diary entry from the Jena period he gives a survey of the rapid succession of philosophical systems. The relation of each system to empirical reality is evidently the decisive factor hastening or retarding its downfall:

'*Science*. Whether a person possesses it or not is something of which he can assure himself and others. Whether it is true or not is decided by those around him, the contemporary world and then posterity, after the former has already bestowed its praise. Yet as civilization has advanced, consciousness has risen so far, the barbarian slowness to comprehend has become so much smoother and swifter that a few years suffice to bring about that *posterity*. *Kant's* philosophy has long since been judged and found wanting, whereas *Wolff's* system lasted 50 years and more. *Fichte's* philosophy has been placed even more quickly and the essence of Schelling's thought will soon be revealed. Its sentence is almost upon us since many already understand it. But these philosophies succumbed less to proof than to empirical experience which showed us how far they could take us. They blindly educate their supporters, but the texture becomes thinner and thinner until they are surprised by its transparency. It has melted like ice, slipped through the fingers like quicksilver before they knew what had happened. They have simply lost their grip on it and anyone who looks at the hand that proffered so much wisdom sees only that the hand is empty and scornfully goes his way.'[25]

The objective idealism of Schelling and Hegel has this common feature that the category of the whole, of totality, plays a decisive part. But today, when the most reactionary philosophy of all plays totality off against causality, erecting it into a bulwark of obscurantism (as in the works of Spann) it is vital to take a closer look at Hegel's conception of totality and to show that it has nothing in common with these reactionary positions, indeed that in the debate with Schelling the reactionary elements in the latter's conception of totality are criticized and overcome.

We have already drawn attention to the importance of the element of preservation in Hegel's conception of supersession. This is very evident in his analysis of the relations between the parts and the whole. Here we see once again the high esteem in which Hegel holds the specialist knowledge of the particular sciences. His dialectics does not set out to negate them, to erect a philosophy quite separate from them. It aims rather to preserve their real significance and to place them within an overall context of knowledge. It is for this reason that he writes the following in his Notebook:

> 'Bad reflection is the fear of immersing oneself in the subject-matter; it always goes beyond it and returns to itself. As Laplace says, the analyst follows where his calculations lead him and so he loses sight of the task, i.e. the overall view, the whole on which the parts all depend. And it is not just the dependence of the parts on the whole which is important, but also that each moment, independently of the whole, is the whole—and this is what immersion in the subject-matter involves.'[26]

Only when we realize this can we appreciate the freedom of Hegel's concept of totality from reactionary features. In the Phenomenology he states his position quite unambiguously:

> 'The truth is the whole. The whole, however, is merely the essential nature reaching its completeness through the process of its own development. Of the absolute it must be said that it is essentially a result, that only at the end is it what it is in very truth; and just in that consists its nature, which is to be actual, subject or self-becoming, self-development. Should it appear contradictory to say that the absolute has to be conceived essentially as a result, a little consideration will set this appearance of contradiction in its true light. The beginning, the principle, or the absolute, as at first or immediately expressed, is merely the universal.'[27]

This abstract universal is the immediate knowledge of Schelling's 'intellectual intuition'. In the passage immediately following this quotation Hegel illustrates its emptiness by remarking that the phrase 'all animals' cannot pass for zoology. We have now seen that Hegel regards independent research into all the empirical sciences as indispensable for philosophy. But this is not to say that philosophy is no more than a collection of factual knowledge; its task rather is to articulate their interconnections. So that when Hegel emphasizes the philosophical significance of mediation what he is doing is to establish the same relationship between the parts and the whole on the formal, philosophical side, that he has earlier defined in terms of content and subject-matter. For this reason, Hegel supplements the definition of truth as the whole, as the result and end of the process, with a definition of mediation and reflection:

'For mediation is nothing but self-identity working itself out through an active self-directed process; or, in other words, it is reflection into self, the aspect in which the ego is for itself, objective to itself. It is pure negativity, or, reduced to its utmost abstraction, the process of *bare and simple becoming*. . . . We misconceive therefore the nature of reason if we exclude reflection or mediation from ultimate truth, and do not take it to be a positive moment of the absolute. It is reflection which constitutes truth the final result, and yet at the same time does away with the contrast between result and the process of arriving at it. For this process is likewise simple, and therefore not distinct from the form of truth, which consists in appearing as simple in the result; it is indeed just this restoration and return to simplicity.'[28]

In our discussion of Hegel's Jena period we spoke at length about Hegel's positive attitude towards what he called philosophical reflection and we showed then that Schelling's misconception of the principle led to a quite different philosophical outlook. For this reason Hegel, looking back at this period in his lectures, remarks that Schelling's refutation of subjective idealism took place without philosophical consciousness of its implications. Schelling, Hegel says by way of conclusion,

'postulates the speculative idea quite generally *without any development* and then proceeds at once to its embodiment in the philosophy of nature.'[29]

These diametrically opposed ideas about knowledge of the absolute reflect diametrically opposed views of the course of history. We have earlier quoted statements by Schelling about the philosophy of the En-lightenment, the French Revolution and modern civil society. Hegel's opinions on all these subjects have been explored in detail. No extended argument is required to show that Schelling's rejection of the Enlight-enment and his negative view of reflection in the cognition of the absol-ute are but the two sides of the same coin. And the same may be said of the relation between his other opinions about society and history, on the one hand, and his philosophical positions, on the other. Whereas the development of Hegel's dialectic went hand in hand with the growth of his historical consciousness, Schelling's attachment to the immediacies of 'intellectual intuition' resulted in an increasingly anti-historical posture.

This contrast between the two calls for special emphasis today when bourgeois scholars increasingly take the view that historicism was the product of Romanticism and the philosophy of the Restoration. Even if Hegel is graciously allowed the title of historicist, thus modifying Ranke's stern judgement, this is only permitted at the cost of assimi-lating Hegel to the so-called historicism of the Romantics. But in what does Schelling's celebrated historicism consist? In his one-sided and

exaggerated emphasis on continuity in history—along the lines of the
ideological opponents of the French Revolution. So one-sided is he that
all the so-called disruptions of that continuity (and this includes the Reformation as well as the French Revolution itself) are held to be purely
negative; they are regarded as mere disturbances in the smooth evolution
of history. Such assumptions could only result in a reactionary pseudo-
historicism and it is no wonder that Fascists such as Mehlis have become
great admirers of Schelling's philosophy of history.

Hegel's view of history, in contrast to this, shows the uneven progress
of man through conflicts and contradictions and as the result of his own
activity. The unity of the process is the unity of continuity and discontinuity, i.e. revolutions are for Hegel an integrating moment of this
uneven but progressive movement. In his theory of history and his praxis
as a historian he followed the tradition of the Enlightenment (Gibbon,
Montesquieu, Voltaire, Rousseau, Herder and Forster among others)
and through his new consciousness of the contradictions in history he
raised it to a new level. He thus inaugurated the historicism of the last
great phase of bourgeois idealogy, the phase which spans the works of
the great French historians and extends to the discovery of class conflict
in history and to historical materialism, while Schelling's view of history
is one of the sources upon which the reactionary Romantic pseudo-
historicism of the nineteenth century drew for inspiration.

This concludes our survey of the principal methodological differences
between Schelling and Hegel at the time of the breach between them.
We must now go on to discuss another essential question which is raised
by the divergence of Hegel's views not only from those of Schelling but
from those of all the philosophers and thinkers of the age of classical
idealism. We refer to Hegel's creation of a *dialectical logic*. The finished
product, of course, lies beyond the scope of this study, since the *Logic*
was completed in Nuremberg years after the *Phenomenology* was written. But the methodological problem is already present in Jena as a crucial issue, indeed as the apex of his conceptual system. It is well known
that the *Phenomenology* was published as the first part of a philosophical
system and that the *Logic* was to be its sequel. This unity must have been
apparent in Hegel's lectures in Jena. Rosenkranz writing about them,
remarks,

> 'Hegel's abstract of the whole which he made as an aide-mémoire to
> delivery, is still extant. He established continuity between the
> *Phenomenology* and the *Logic* by regarding the former as an intro-
> duction to the latter and by advancing from the concept of absolute
> knowledge directly to that of existence.'[30]

Once one is accustomed to the thought that the dialectical method is the great achievement of classical German Idealism and that Hegel's *Logic* is its greatest monument, then it may come as something of a surprise to learn that the demand for a dialectical logic and or the transformation of logic into dialectics was Hegel's own personal achievement and that he stands out in altogether dramatic contrast to his predecessors. Objectively, of course, there were very powerful trends towards dialectics. The so-called Transcendental Philosophy of Kant, Fichte and Schelling is shot through with dialectical tendencies. But in the minds of Kant, Fichte and Schelling this Transcendental Philosophy is thought of as existing *alongside* logic. The dialectical problems are dealt with there, while the old formal logic lived out its venerated or despised existence unchanged side by side with the newly emerging science.

Of course, it is not possible for us to analyse all the implications of the attitudes towards logic held by Kant, Fichte and Schelling. It must suffice if we illustrate the state of affairs at the time when Hegel was working on the *Phenomenology* by quoting some of the characteristic statements of his predecessors, mainly to demonstrate that they did not think of the problem of dialectical logic as one that needed attention.

In the Preface to the second edition of the *Critique of Pure Reason* Kant discusses the problem of logic. He states that since Aristotle logic has not been required to retrace a single step, nor indeed has it advanced a single step, unless we care to count certain external and needless improvements affecting its elegance rather than its certainty. In logic as in the other branches of philosophy Kant is concerned to draw dividing lines between its various aspects as clearly and firmly as possible. He comes to this view of the nature of strict, formal logic:

> 'The sphere of logic is quite precisely delimited; its sole concern is to give an exhaustive exposition and a strict proof of the formal rules of all thought, whether it be *a priori* or empirical, whatever be its origin or its object, and whatever hindrances, accidental, or natural, it may encounter in our minds.
>
> 'That logic should have been thus successful is an advantage which it owes entirely to its limitations, whereby it is justified in abstracting—indeed, it is under obligation to do so—from all objects of knowledge and their differences, leaving the understanding nothing to deal with save itself and its form.'[31]

The Transcendental Philosophy which, according to Kant, is concerned with the objects of the world must leave this safe territory. This leads Kant to a situation in which he makes all sorts of contributions to dialectical logic without ever becoming aware of the existence of a problem, without ever noticing that formal logic must be transformed into dialectical logic if the logical problems of objective reality, of the world of objects and relations, are to be satisfactorily solved.

The confusion which Kant thus introduced and which neither Fichte nor Schelling saw for what it was invested the whole of the Transcendental Philosophy with a certain vagueness and ambivalence. On the one hand, it was clearly not a 'logic' since it was concerned with objects and their relations, but, on the other hand, it was unlike all other special sciences concerned with objective reality since it focused on objects and object-relations in general, and on the premises upon which they were 'posited'. This turned the Transcendental Philosophy into an apparently infinite and elastic thing. Looked at from this angle, the supersession of Kant by Fichte, and of Fichte by Schelling, always takes the form of a broader interpretation of the nature and method of Transcendental Philosophy, an interpretation which is then presented as the authentic and only true meaning of the science. From the other side, however, Kant in his debate with Fichte, and Fichte in his debate with Schelling, held on to the original concept of Transcendental Philosophy and so each attacked his predecessor or successor from a vantage-point whose ultimate principles and frontiers were indefinable from the outset, since a definition would only be possible if the relationship between logic and dialectics could be clarified.

It is this lack of clarity in the ultimate principles of the philosophy which makes these discussions so incomprehensible to the modern reader. A further puzzling consequence is that time and again one or other of the disputants makes a 'sudden' appeal to the logic which is otherwise ignored. A very typical example of this can be found in Fichte's polemic against Schelling's impermissible extension of Transcendental Philosophy to cover the problems of a philosophy of nature. In a letter to Schelling, he writes:

> 'A philosophy of nature may indeed proceed from an already existing concept of nature: but in a comprehensive system of knowledge this concept and its philosophy can only be inferred from an absolute by the law of finite reason. However, an idealism which could tolerate a realism co-existing with it would be worthless: or if it were anything it would have to be a universal formal logic.'[32]

Thus confronted by the first signs of a dialectics of nature Fichte could see nothing but the old dilemma: either he must retain the dialectics of the *Theory of Science* in which case nature would be treated as a 'small province of consciousness', or he will be forced to admit a formal logic which can be used as the philosophical foundation of an empirical natural science.

If we turn to Schelling's attitude to the problem, what is most striking is how little he understood of Hegel's central ideas even at the time of their closest collaboration. In the *Lectures on the Method of Acedemic study* Schelling broaches the topic of the relations between dialectics and logic and it is obvious that what he has in mind here is the dialectical logic that Hegel was just beginning to develop. How little he understood of it becomes obvious from his discussion. We have earlier quoted his thesis that the dialectic has an aspect which cannot be learned but which is accessible only to the genius, the philosophical 'initiate'.

> 'Such a dialectic does not yet exist. If it were to set out merely the forms of finite reality in their relations to the absolute, it would be a form of scientific scepticism: even Kant's transcendental logic cannot be called that.'

It is very clear from this how Schelling envisaged the nature and significance of the logic that Hegel had obviously already conceived: as the dialectical dissolution of all finite concepts, a procedure which would lead to the abolition of rational knowledge and thence to the leap into immediate knowledge, 'intellectual intuition'. The allusion to Kant's transcendental dialectic is surely not fortuitous. In the antinomies of the transcendental dialectic Kant dissolved all absolute knowledge of the principles governing the phenomenal world into nothing, he laid the philosophical foundations for the theory that things-in-themselves were unknowable—so as to open the way to attain the absolute with the aid of 'practical reason' and faith. Schelling rejects Kant's solution here as half-hearted and partial.

Typically, however, he somehow contemplates a similar solution himself. For the task of dialectical logic is to found a 'scientific scepticism', i.e. the repetition of the Kantian antinomies at a higher level. This 'scientific scepticism' will pave the way not for subjective faith, but for the objective intuition of the absolute. But the collapse of the world as something knowable and with it of the method of cognition retains the framework of Kantian dualism, albeit in a modified form. In Kant the two aspects of the dualism were knowledge of the phenomenal world and subjective faith in the absolute; in Schelling they are the self-annihilation of knowledge derived from the understanding and the supra-rational self-contemplation of the identical subject-object. The sphere of intuition is raised far above any imaginable category of the understanding—how could there be a logic to fit it, a logic concerned with the ultimate principles of human knowledge? The abolition of contradictions, the new theory of contradiction is in Schelling's eyes not the kernel of the new philosophy but merely a 'propaedeutic' overture to it. (This makes clear just how far Schelling's rejection of the categories of reflection had taken him.) It follows inexorably from this that for Schelling the only logic to survive alongside his sceptical dialectic is the old formal logic. The latter is a purely empirical science, the former, as in Fichte, just a part of a universal Transcendental Philosophy.[33]

These quotations from the writings of Hegel's most important predecessors make it quite plain that they neither saw nor understood anything of the specific problems connected with dialectical logic. What
Hegel, and he alone, perceived was that the existing content of even the
most abstract categories makes it possible to discern and portray them in
movement; that in consequence the absence of content in traditional
formal logic is merely a borderline case, just as repose is only a borderline
case of movement; that therefore all the problems of both objective reality and man's subjective knowledge form the subject-matter of this logic
and, finally, that only in and through this logic could the problems encountered by classical German idealism in its efforts to overcome
metaphysics be finally resolved. These things were Hegel's exclusive intellectual property and before him they were not even formulated as
problems, let alone solved.

It would be a rewarding and interesting task to follow the gradual
emergence of these ideas to the point where they finally crystallized into
a definite programme. There can be no doubt that there are many signs
of such an approach in the first part of his stay in Jena, above all in the
doctoral theses and in parts of the *Jena Logic*. But the polemical activities
of this first period and his hunger for information about the most varied
branches of human knowledge (it was in this period that he acquired his
very solid grounding in the natural sciences) prevented him from elaborating his views in any systematic fashion. Only his later preparations for
the construction of a philosophical system brought a final clarification of
the central task of philosophy. This programme is made fully explicit in
the *Phenomenology* as is the relationship of the *Phenomenology* to dialectical
logic as contained in the idea that the latter is an introduction to philosophy proper.

We limit ourselves here to quoting Hegel's own statement of his programme in the *Phenomenology*. In the Preface he declares logic to be identical with speculative philosophy.[34] This assertion is then concretized in
the following way:

'Philosophy, on the contrary, does not deal with a determination that
is non-essential, but with a determination so far as it is an essential
factor. The abstract or unreal is not its element and content, but the
*real*, what is self-establishing, has life within itself, existence in its very
concept. It is this process that creates its own movements in its course
and goes through them all; and the whole of this movement constitutes . . . its truth. . . . It might well seem necessary to state at the
outset the chief points in connection with the *method* of this process,
the way in which science operates. Its nature, however, is to be found
in what has already been said, while the proper exposition of it is the
special business of logic, or rather is logic itself. For the method is

nothing else than the structure of the whole in its pure and essential form.'[35]

Here then Hegel explicitly defines logic as the essence of philosophy in which the philosophical method informing the entire edifice and the order of all its substantive categories are contained within an overall process. The idea that logic is the authentic philosophy is both the premise, the continuation and the consummation of *The Phenomenology of Mind*, which constitutes an introduction to it. A little later in the Preface Hegel concretizes the method of logic and its relation to phenomenology i.e. to the content of its objects, still further.

'Thus, then, it is the very nature of *understanding* to be a process; and being a process it is *rationality*. In the nature of existence as thus described—to be its own *concept* and *being* in one—consists *logical necessity* in general. This alone is what is rational, the rhythm of the organic whole: it is as much knowledge of content as that content is concept and essential nature. In other words, this alone is the sphere and element of speculative thought . . . This nature of scientific method, which consists partly in being inseparable from the content, and partly in determining the rhythm of its movement by its own agency, finds, as we mentioned before, its peculiar systematic expression in speculative philosophy.'[36]

Thus *The Phenomenology of Mind* is conceived as an introduction to this speculative philosophy whose essence we now see to be identical with that of dialectical logic. Of course, the *Phenomenology* is an introduction of a peculiar sort. In what follows we shall describe its method in detail, but its fundamental idea has already become plain from what has been said: its aim is to chart the course to be taken by ordinary consciousness if it is to raise itself to the heights of philosophical consciousness. If then, according to Schelling, access to authentic philosophy is the privilege of an elite which is precipitated into an immediate knowledge of the absolute thanks to an act of 'intellectual intuition', according to Hegel, we find both that the absolute itself is objectively a process and its product, and that the acquisition of subjective human reason, the vantage-point from which the absolute can be attained, is likewise a process and its product.

Just as this introduction differs qualitatively from all previous introductions to philosophy, so too the relation of its content to philosophy diverges radically from previous definitions. Earlier introductions were either purely formal so that the actual content was provided in the philosophy proper, or, as in Schelling, the philosophy put forward contents that were radically different from the 'profane', finite knowledge that had gone before.

In Hegel's eyes, however, philosophy is always and everywhere the same: it is always the expression of the essential contents of reality in their dialectical self-movement. It follows that the introduction to philosophy must comprehend *exactly the same* contents as philosophy itself. Thus to scale the heights of philosophy with the aid of the ladder which Hegel had, in his own words, provided in the *Phenomenology*, meant to digest mentally the contents of reality at the various stages of human consciousness in its long march upwards towards the absolute. And even though these contents re-appear at different stages in a modified form, they remain the same as those with which objective philosophy, dialectical logic, has to concern itself. Furthermore, the various stages of consciousness which, in the *Phenomenology*, are manifested as 'configurations of consciousness', have nothing fortuitous about either their nature or the order in which they make their appearance. When the positions they represent are generalized they have the same contents as philosophy itself, only their sequence differs from the order in dialectical logic. But since the reality underlying both the *Phenomenology* and the *Logic* is the same, the contents of each must necessarily match up in the last analysis, albeit in a complex, irregular and unmechanical way. Thus the path to philosophy in Hegel runs through philosophy itself.

In the concluding pages of the *Phenomenology* Hegel describes this process himself:

'While in *The Phenomenology of Mind* each moment is the distinction of knowledge and truth, and is the process in which that distinction is cancelled and transcended, science [i.e. logic—G.L.] does not contain this distinction and supersession of distinction. Rather, since each notion has the form of the concept, it unites the objective form of truth and the knowing self in an immediate unity. Each individual moment does not appear as the process of passing back and forward from consciousness or figurative (imaginative) thought to self-consciousness and conversely: on the contrary, the pure shape, liberated from the condition of being an appearance in mere consciousness—the pure concept with its further development,—depends solely on its pure *characteristic nature.* Conversely, again, there corresponds to every abstract moment of science a mode in which mind as a whole makes its appearance. [i.e. the phenomenological mode.—G.L.] As the mind that actually exists is not richer than it [i.e. science] so, too, mind in its actual content is not poorer. To know the pure concepts of science in the form in which they are modes or shapes of consciousness—this constitutes the aspect of their reality, according to which their essential element, the concept, appearing there in its *simple* mediating activity as thinking, breaks up and separates the moments of this mediation and exhibits them to itself in accordance with their immanent opposition.'[37]

It is abundantly clear, then, that the method of the *Phenomenology* evolves out of Hegel's attack on Schelling's philosophy. Of course, its implications go far beyond the controversy that occasioned them and have a validity of their own. At the same time, the polemical parts of this, the final product of the Jena period could easily bear the title: *Difference between the Hegelian and the Schellingian System of Philosophy*. With the *Phenomenology* the dramatic process of differentiation within classical German Idealism comes to an end: the era of Hegelian philosophy had begun.

Our discussions up to this point have attempted to clarify the profoundly original nature of Hegel's method in *The Phenomenology of Mind*. If we have done this successfully then all the philological quibbles of bourgeois scholars with their frantic and pedantic search for the 'forerunners' of the *Phenomenology* will require no further demolition. And if it were merly a matter of the philological games played by idle scholars we could indeed leave the matter there. However, as matters stand, these philological labours are just a part of a larger campaign to make the idea of classical German Idealism as a coherent unity plausible. And this in turn implies denying the uniqueness of the Hegelian dialectic, which after all is the predecessor of dialectical materialism, and attempting to reduce it either to the level of Kantian agnosticism or of the irrationalism of the Romantics. In the face of efforts such as these, the emphasis on the methodological originality of *The Phenomenology of Mind* is not without a certain historical significance.

Later on, for those readers who may be interested in the details, we shall provide a note of the essential data concerning the so-called antecedents of Hegel. On the point of principle, however, all that need be said is that the idea of the *Phenomenology* was in the air. The wide range of motifs drawn together in the *Phenomenology* and which we shall examine in due course, were not the arbitrary inventions of Hegel, but were very definite problems of the age.

But it is one thing for a number of thinkers to be concerned with the same problems and another to establish whether their various questions and answers can be said to have exercised a determining influence. And it is only the latter that we dispute. Ever since Kant, the idea of dialectical relations had been in the air, and yet as we have seen, Hegel was the first to put the problem on a scientific basis.

There is a similar situation in regard to the problems of the *Phenomenology* itself. There are two general areas of interest here. On the one hand, the dialectics of the categories of the understanding and their mutual supersession in Kant necessarily raised the question of what path led to that dialectic and from there to knowledge of the absolute. On the other hand, the constant growth of a sense of history and of historical

knowledge led to the need for a view of history as a unified process leading up to the present and above all for a map charting the unified and
necessary development of human thought and of philosophy. (Winckel-
mann, Herder and Schiller are the men whose work in the history of art
and literature prefigured developments in the history of philosophy.) All
these are the general tendencies of the age which, it is scarcely necessary
to say, had the most varied influence on *The Phenomenology of Mind*. But
that is by no means to admit that these very fragmentary and episodic
writings before Hegel had any influence on the *particular* method of the
*Phenomenology* and it simply will not do to take up some highly con-
jectural connections and affinities so as to make all sorts of dubious inferences about how the history of this period of philosophy should be
treated now.

The most recent attempt of this kind is that of Hoffmeister[38] who sets
out to build a bridge between the 'Ages of Reason' in Schelling's *System
of Transcendental Idealism* and the *Phenomenology*. His argument lacks all
cogency. From the point of view of form, because Schelling constantly confuses the subjective (phenomenological) and the objective
(logical) sides of the problem, whereas the *Phenomenology* is concerned
above all with the consistent methodological elaboration of the subjective side; and because Schelling does not even develop his idea to its logical conclusion since his 'Ages' come to an end just where Hegel begins:
at the philosophy of praxis. And his argument fails from the point of
view of content, because all the problems arising from the relation between human praxis (labour) and the growth of consciousness are
wholly absent. Of course, there are passages in Kant that point in the
same direction. *The Critique of Pure Reason* ends with a fragmentary section entitled 'The History of Pure Reason'[39] But it contains only isolated
suggestions for a scheme of the history of philosophy in which the historical element is emphasized least, since he is more interested in producing a typology of the various possible responses to the crucial problems
of philosophy.

From the other side, Kroner sets out to prove Fichte's claims to be
regarded as a forerunner.[40] Fichte does indeed speak at one point of a
'pragmatic history' of the spirit.[41] But a closer examination reveals that,
even more than in Schelling, this is just an isolated idea from which
Fichte nowhere draws any significant methodological conclusions. It is
undeniable that ideas of this sort have their roots in the same tendencies
and problems of the age that influenced the *Phenomenology*, but this has
nothing to do with 'influences' in any specific sense.

Worthy of more serious attention, on the other hand, are certain ideas
in the works of Goethe and Schiller. In a letter to Schiller of 24 January
1798, Goethe describes how his work on the theory of colours has given
him some important new ideas.

'When the series of mental events which in fact go to make up the history of the sciences are spread out before us, we cease to laugh at the idea of writing a history *a priori*: for everything is in fact developed from the human mind as it moves backwards and forwards, from nature as it now advances and now holds back.'

In view of the profound affinity existing between Goethe and Hegel in other respects such a meeting of minds is undoubtedly of interest. Even more important are certain of Schiller's ideas expressed in the *Philosophical Letters*. For this is the only case in which a forerunner of Hegel is in a certain sense acknowledged as such. In its last part Schiller's work contains a number of philosophical poems from one of which Hegel quotes freely in the final passage of the *Phenomenology*.

'aus dem Kelche dieses Geisterreiches
schäumt ihm seine Unendlichkeit.'[42]

But even the ideas scattered through the *Philosophical Letters* which do have affinities with Hegel are only really interesting from the point of view of Schiller's own development, of his earnest and often successful efforts to free himself from the limitations of Kant's subjective idealism. As the 'prehistory' of the *Phenomenology* they add very little to our understanding of Hegel.

## NOTES

1 Rosenkranz, pp. 178ff. The fragments published here cannot be dated with any precision, but since a number of them are identical with the Lectures of 1803–4 and 1805–6 as published by Hoffmeister we are surely fully justified in assigning the whole collection to that period. It would of course be interesting to give a precise date to each fragment and this would enable us to follow Hegel's estrangement from Schelling step by step, but this is of secondary importance for our present discussions.

2 The reader may be referred to my book, *The Destruction of Reason*, Chapter 2, Berlin 1954. *Werke*, Vol. I, pp. 84–269.

3 Schelling, *Werke*, Vol. V, p. 314.

4 Ibid., pp. 258ff.

5 Rosenkranz, p. 539.

6 Ibid., p. 182.

7 Ibid., p. 544.

8 Ibid., p. 184f.

9 *Werke*, Vol. VI, p. 23.

10 Rosenkranz, p. 540.

11 Ibid., p. 546. G.L.'s italics.

12 Ibid., p. 182.

13  *Realphilosophie*, Vol. II, p. 265.

14  *Werke*, Vol. V, p. 267.

15  Rosenkrauz, p. 186.

16  Ibid., p. 552.

17  *The Phenomenology of Mind*, pp. 86–7.

18  Ibid., p. 89.

19  Ibid., p. 79.

20  Ibid., p. 80–1.

21  Fichte to Schelling, 15 October 1801, op. cit., Vol. II, p. 341.

22  It is just not possible to refute in detail all the senseless arguments put forward by bourgeois historians of philosophy about this phase in Hegel's development. But we should at least mention one theory that has been popularized in recent years to the effect that Hegel's repudiation of Schelling's objective idealism involved a return of a sort to Fichte or even Kant. Here, where Hegel returns to the crucial argument in the old debate between Fichte and Schelling, it must be plain to every reader that although the issue is the same, Hegel criticizes Schelling *for the opposite reason*.

23  Rosenkranz, p. 201.

24  *Phenomenology*, p. 112.

25  Rosenkranz, p. 544.

26  Ibid., p. 548.

27  *Phenomenology*, pp. 81–2.

28  Ibid., pp. 82–3.

29  Rosenkranz, p. 188f.

30  Ibid., p. 214. This manuscript which Rosenkranz had at his disposal has since been lost.

31  *Critique of Pure Reason*, trans. N. Kemp Smith, London 1950, p. 18.

32  Fichte to Schelling, 31 May 1801, op. cit., Vol. II, p. 327.

33  *Werke*, Vol. V, p. 269f.

34  *Phenomenology of Mind*, p. 97.

35  Ibid., pp. 105–6.

36  Ibid., p. 115.

37  Ibid., pp. 805–6.

38  *Einleitung zur Realphilosophie*, Vol. I, p. 91.

39  Kant, op. cit., pp. 666ff.

40  Kroker, op. cit., Vol. I, pp. 147 and 372f.

41  *Werke*, Vol. III, p. 415.

42      The chalice of this realm of spirits
        Foams forth to God his own infinitude

Hegel's political opinions and his approach to history in the period of *The Phenomenology of Mind*

WE have seen how the central problem of Hegel's later philosophy was already announced programmatically in *The Phenomenology of Mind*. The *Phenomenology* marks the close of the preparatory phase of the Hegelian system; with its publication the fully-developed personality of Hegel stands before us in its world-historical significance. Nevertheless, it would be going too far simply to identify the Hegel of the *Phenomenology* with the progenitor of the later system. Between the two, great events in the external world intervene, events to which Hegel responds passionately and from the centre of his being, and which consequently cannot pass away without leaving their traces in his work. It is not possible for us to examine these changes since they affect the entire structure of his philosophy and involve the revision of important categories. In what follows we shall be able to touch on a few of the issues, but only in so far as they enable us to clarify certain aspects of the *Phenomenology*.

On the other hand, we must also insist that it would be false to open up a great chasm between the *Phenomenology* and the later work. The fact that in the *Encyclopaedia* the chapter on phenomenology is much reduced in importance when set alongside *The Phenomenology of Mind* in the context of the Jena system, does not justify such a conclusion. Especially since we know that, in his last years, Hegel was engaged on preparing a new edition of the *Phenomenology*. Naturally, we would only be able to draw conclusions about his later attitude towards it if it had in fact been published. Unfortunately that was not the case. Our knowledge of his development, however, does allow us to assert that he continued to adhere to the idea of dialectical unity as the 'identity of identity and non-identity'. The particular nature of this development, the relations between its various stages and the great events of the contemporary world, are tasks that remain for Marxist scholars once the vast available material has been assimilated.

For bourgeois students of Hegel the *Phenomenology* is an unpalatable, even uncanny work. Various 'ingenious' hypotheses have been devised to obliterate its specific character. We do not intend to importune the reader with these various arbitrary theories, but will content ourselves with mentioning just one example as a warning: the latest theory of the noted Hegel scholar Th. Haering concerning the origins of the *Phenomenology*. According to him the *Phenomenology* is nothing but an improvisation.

'This strongly suggests that it did not really occur to him to write a full-scale introduction until *after* the publisher's contract was signed and even after the first part of the MS had been delivered.'

And since Haering really can show from Hegel's letters that there were delays in delivering the manuscript to the printers he ventures the 'ingenious' hypothesis that Hegel had quickly improvised the second half of the work, hastily assembling it·from earlier manuscripts and old lecture notes. From this account of its origin Haering draws the conclusion that the *Phenomenology* represented 'a merely provisional' stage. In essence it is no more than

'a character study (*Wesensschau*) of the spirit in an almost Husserlian sense.'[1]

It is not too hard to discover why a Fascist like Haering should have striven to depreciate the *Phenomenology* in this way. Haym, the old, national-liberal biographer of Hegel, let the cat out of the bag years ago, though of course without knowledge of the particular problems under discussion here. His discussion of the *Phenomenology* ends in an indignant stream of abuse at Hegel for his unpatriotic attitude at the time of the Prussian catastrophe, at the great defeat at Jena in 1806. After Jena Hegel had celebrated Napoleon's victory over the Prussians as the victory of civilization over feudal barbarism. Of course, Haym's conclusions are not at all limited to the *Phenomenology*, in fact they are extended to apply to his entire philosophy. He discerns an 'aesthetic' element in Hegel which causes him to turn away from life, to do violence to it, and this is compared very unfavourably with Fichte's upright patriotism:

'He cast dusty metaphysics aside and his manly voice uttered a clarion call arousing the torpid consciousness of the nation from its slumbers.'[2]

Of course, the fact that this awakening meant the end of Fichte's career as a philosopher of European significance, the fact that as a philosopher he fell a tragic victim to the insoluble contradictions of contemporary Germany worried Haym not at all. After all his biography of Hegel was written at that turning-point of history when the German bourgeoisie had become fully determined to liquidate its old liberal traditions and utterly to subordinate the idea of 'freedom' to that of 'unity', and in a word to capitulate entirely to what Engels called the 'Bonapartist monarchy' of the Hohenzollerns under the leadership of Bismarck.[3]

The outstanding German Marxist, Franz Mehring has provided the best description of the complex situation in Germany at the time of the battle of Jena. He makes an illuminating comparison between the battle of Jena and the storming of the Bastille in Paris and argues very convincingly that the collapse of the feudal monarchies in France and Germany had very different consequences in the two countries because of the different manner of their downfall.[4] In particular this was the moment when the trends of which we have been speaking came into existence, it was the time when the movement to liquidate the vestiges of feudalism in Germany parted company from the movement to achieve national unity and to free Germany from the domination of France. In this historical parting of the ways the Romantics placed themselves on the side of national liberation under the leadership of Austria and Prussia and since the latter became increasingly reactionary, especially after the fall of Napoleon, the Romantics lapsed for the most part into the worst sort of obscurantism. (It was the insoluble contradictions arising from this situation that were the ruin of Fichte as a philosopher.) The most outstanding Germans of the day, Goethe and Hegel, became supporters of Napoleon; they hoped he would bring destruction to the remnants of feudalism in Germany and they thereby cut themselves off from the sympathies of the great mass of the people, especially in North Germany.

The reverence felt by Goethe and Hegel for Napoleon is too well known and too well authenticated to be entirely denied even by German nationalist historians. But even here they try to confuse the issue by representing it as part of an abstract cult of genius in general. (This was especially true of the literature on Goethe produced during the Age of Imperialism from Nietzsche to Gundolf.) What concerns us is the concrete political meaning of Hegel's attitude towards Napoleon. For reasons that require no explanation when considering the general state of affairs in Germany we find it expressed less in his published works than in his private letters. Indeed, he spoke really openly only to his proven friend, the philosopher Niethammer.

In his letters to Niethammer his political views emerge quite unambiguously. We need only cite a few major statements, for these will suffice to make it perfectly clear to the reader that Hegel's admiration for Napoleon had none of the marks of an abstract worship of genius in general—and, as we know from his ideas about the role of great men in history, such a posture was quite alien to him. On the contrary, it was concerned entirely with Napoleon as the man destined to make the heritage of the French Revolution a practical reality in Germany. In a word, we may say that throughout the entire period up to the fall of Napoleon, and even beyond that, Hegel *consistently supported the policy of the Confederation of the Rhine*.

The letter to Niethammer in which he described his immediate feelings after learning of the battle of Jena is well known. We quote it only because the other letters belong to the period after the completion of the *Phenomenology* and our aim is to show that there was a consistent pattern in Hegel's views from his approval of Napoleon's coup d'état of the 18th Brumaire to the essay on *Natural Law* and on to the fall of Napoleon. Our point, then, is that the political mood and the appraisal of the present age contained in the *Phenomenology* was an organic component of this development. On 13 October 1806 he wrote:

> 'The Emperor—this world soul—I saw riding through the city to a review of his troops; it is indeed a wonderful feeling to see such an individual, who concentrated here in a single point, riding on a horse, reaches out over the world and dominates it. . . . Of course, a more favourable prognosis for the Prussians was not really possible, but even so, to make such progress between Thursday and Monday was something that only this extraordinary man could have achieved, and it is not possible not to admire him.'[5]

In subsequent letters the concrete political content is much more explicit. On 29 August 1807 he wrote to Niethammer:

> 'The German teachers of constitutional law are still busy turning out a plethora of writings on the concept of sovereignty and the meaning of the Federal Constitution. Meanwhile the great teacher of constitutional law is sitting in Paris.'

He goes on to speak of disputes between the rulers and the Estates in a number of Federal states and then says:

> 'When the Estates in Württemberg were dissolved Napoleon said to Grimm, the Württemberg Minister; "I made your master a sovereign, not a despot." The German rulers have not yet understood the concept of a free monarchy, nor have they tried it in practice—Napoleon will have to organize all that.—The changes he will make will come as a surprise in certain quarters.'[6]

And on 13 October 1807, he writes in the same vein:

> 'The final decision does not yet seem to have been reached in Paris. When it does come, there are a number of pointers which suggest that it will go beyond the external division of territory and affect internal organization too, to the advantage of the peoples.'[7]

And he writes similarly on 11 February 1808, in connection with the introduction of the Code Napoléon into Germany:

'The importance of the Code, however, is nothing as compared with the hope it gives rise to that even the other parts of the French or Westphalian constitution might be introduced.—It will hardly take place voluntarily, nor from the realization of its merits—for where can that be found? It will only come to pass if it is the will of Heaven, i.e. of the French Emperor, and if the contemporary characteristic *modalities of centralization* and organisation disappear which embody neither justice nor the will of the people but only the arbitrary caprice and the casuistry of an individual.'[8]

It is thus perfectly clear that during this period Hegel was not only in agreement with the policy of the Confederation of the Rhine, but also that on every single question he expected a progressive solution from Napoleon and from the vigorous pressure he would bring to bear on the German rulers. The only point on which he diverges from Napoleon is on the issue of complete administrative centralization. And even here his letters indicate that he thought improvement would come from an internal evolution of the Napoleonic system itself. Thus this single caveat does not allow us to infer any larger hostility towards the Napoleonic regime.

It is consistent with this that Hegel regarded the German War of Liberation against Napoleon with scepticism, and that he hoped for and expected a victory for the Emperor right to the very end. The fall of Napoleon appeared to him to be a tragedy of universal dimensions and his letters are full of the bitterest criticism of the mediocrity which had triumphed. It was a long time before Hegel could bring himself to accept the new order and he continued to live in hope that the world-spirit would take a great leap and drive the triumphant fleas and vermin to the devil. It is only gradually that his 'reconciliation' with the existing state of affairs in Germany began to become reality but it is not possible for us to describe the various phases of that development in the present study.[9] It would be a mistake to interpret Hegel's anger and contempt for the mediocrity of the ruling strata of the Restoration in terms of the Romantic antithesis between the lonely genius and a universal human mediocrity. This sort of criticism of the age may also be found in the works of the French realists, in Balzac and especially in Stendhal. But even apart from that the political significance of Hegel's contempt is made quite explicit in the letters. For example, in the letter we have just quoted he makes fun of the people who are looking forward to a revival of the good old days and refers in particular to the mood in Nuremberg where he was living at the time and where people hoped that the Restoration would bring back the old 'independence' (*Reichsunmittelbarkeit*) of Nuremberg in which it owed allegiance to none but the Empire itself.

We have described Hegel's reactions in such detail because they are closely bound up with a number of important problems in the *Phenomenology*: above all, that of the historical view of the present, and following from that, of the nature of philosophy in the present so understood. In brief, Hegel's position was that after the great crisis of the French Revolution in the Napoleonic regime a new epoch was about to dawn. His philosophy was to be its intellectual expression. The specific value that Hegel puts on his own philosophy is that it is the philosophical synthesis of the *birth* of this *new* historical epoch.

Rosenkranz has published the words with which Hegel concluded his lectures on phenomenology in the autumn of 1806:

> 'This, Gentlemen, is speculative philosophy as far as I have been able to construct it. Look upon it as the beginnings of the philosophy which you will carry forward. We find ourselves in an important epoch in world history, in a ferment, when spirit has taken a leap forward, where it has sloughed off its old form and is acquiring a new one. The whole mass of existing ideas and concepts, the very bonds of the world have fallen apart and dissolved like a dream. A new product of the spirit is being prepared. The chief task of philosophy is to welcome it and grant it recognition, while others, impotently resisting, cling to the past and the majority unconsciously constitute the masses in which it manifests itself. Recognizing it as the eternal, it falls to philosophy to pay it reverence.'[10]

In the programmatic sections of the Preface to the *Phenomenology* this view is expressed even more strongly. He supplements it by explaining that of necessity the philosophy which expresses this new configuration of the spirit will have an abstract form in the first instance. For it has not yet developed in reality, in history; it has not yet divided up into a rich manifold of different elements. This connection between time and philosophy is the lasting foundation of Hegel's conception of the history of human thought. For that very reason it is vital to realize that when he wrote the *Phenomenology* he conceived it as the intellectual form of a *newly-born* configuration of world history, whereas, as we shall see, his view of the relation of his philosophy to world history undergoes a radical change later on, even though he does not deviate from the same general principles. The great importance of this question for his philosophical development makes it necessary to quote his arguments in detail:

> 'For the rest it is not difficult to see that our epoch is a time of birth, and a period of transition. The spirit of man has broken with the old order of things hitherto prevailing, and with the old ways of thinking, and is in the mind to let them all sink into the depths of the past and to set about its own transformation. It is indeed never at rest, but

carried along the stream of progress ever onward. But it is here as in case of the birth of a child; after a long period of nutrition in silence, the continuity of the gradual growth in size, of quantitative change, is suddenly cut short by the first breath drawn—there is a break in the process, a qualititative change—and the child is born. In like manner the spirit of the time, growing slowly and quietly ripe for the new form it is to assume, disintegrates one fragment after another of the structure of its previous *world*. That it is tottering to its fall is indicated only by symptoms here and there. Frivolity and again ennui, which are spreading in the established order of things, the undefined foreboding of something unknown—all these betoken that there is something else approaching. This gradual crumbling into pieces, which did not alter the general look and aspect of the whole, is interrupted by the sunrise, which, in a flash and at a single stroke, brings to view the form and structure of the new world.

'But this new world is perfectly realized just as little as the newborn child; and it is essential to bear this in mind. It comes onto the stage to begin with in its immediacy, in its bare generality. A building is not finished when its foundation is laid; and just as little is the attainment of a general notion of a whole the whole itself. When we want to see an oak with all its vigour of trunk its spreading branches, and mass of foliage, we are not satisfied to be shown an acorn instead. In the same way science, the crowning glory of the spiritual world, is not found complete in its initial stages. The beginning of the new spirit is the outcome of a widespread revolution in manifold forms of spiritual culture; it is the reward which comes after a chequered and devious course of development, and after much struggle and effort. It is a whole which, after running its course and laying bare all its content, returns again to itself; it is the resultant *abstract concept* of the whole. But the actual realization of this abstract whole is only found when those previous shapes and forms, which are now reduced to ideal moments of the whole, are developed anew again, but developed and shaped within this new medium, and with the meaning they have thereby acquired.

'While the new world makes its first appearance merely in general outline, merely as a whole lying concealed and hidden within a *bare abstraction*, the wealth of the bygone life, on the other hand, is still consciously present in recollection. Consciousness misses in the new form the detailed expanse of content; but still more the developed expression of form by which distinctions are definitely determined and arranged in their precise relations. Without this last feature science has no general *intelligibility*, and has the appearance of being an esoteric possession of a few individuals. .'. . Only what is perfectly determinate in form is at the same time exoteric, comprehensible, and capable of being learned and possessed by everybody.'[11]

We repeat: it is not possible to give an account, even in outline, of Hegel's later development. However, it is sufficient for our purposes if we quote the very explicit statements contained in the Preface of 1820 to the *Philosophy of Right* about the relation of philosophy of the age, by way of contrast with the Preface to the *Phenomenology*. Whereas Hegel had thought of the *Phenomenology* as a guide to a *completely new* world, he later gives an *entirely opposed picture* of the relation between his philosophy and the present, even though he is operating from the same general methodological base.

'One word more about giving instruction as to what the world ought to be. Philosophy in any case always comes on the scene too late to give it. As the *thought* of the world, it appears only when actuality is already there cut and dried after its process of formation has been completed. The teaching of the concept, which is also history's inescapable lesson, is that it is only when actuality is mature that the ideal first appears over against the real and that the ideal apprehends this same real world in its substance and builds it up for itself into the shape of an intellectual realm. When philosophy paints its grey in grey, then has a shape of life grown old. By philosophy's grey in grey it cannot be rejuvenated but only understood. The owl of Minerva spreads its wings only with the falling of dusk.'[12]

The extraordinary vividness with which Hegel expresses his ideas in each passage points up the contrast in his views even more sharply. In the first case he speaks of the dawn, in the second, of the dusk; the *birth* of a new epoch in the first case, the end of an era of human history in the second. Since there are no moods in Hegel's philosophy it will be evident that we are confronted by two totally different views of modern history.

Hegel's new periodization of the modern world can be easily defined and documented. His general historical perspective did not change after Jena. His conception of Greece and Rome remained much as it had been then, except for his much more extensive knowledge of the Orient, a development which did not introduce any methodological change. In fact this is something that had already begun in Frankfurt and we shall see him devoting a significant chapter of the *Phenomenology* to the oriental religions. Another permanent feature is the short shrift given to medieval history. Only in the *Aesthetics* and the *Philosophy of Religion* is it given a greater importance and in the former case, there is a marked tendency to regard the really world-historical values of art as the products of the Renaissance rather than the Middle Ages proper. Hence the heavy emphasis on the 'romantic' age of art does not imply any concession to the Romantics' glorification of the Middle Ages.

The really incisive change in his later philosophy of history affects his view of the modern world: in Jena the French Revolution and its super-session (in all three senses) by Napoleon was the decisive turning-point. It had provided the historical foundation for the picture he gives of the philosophical situation of the present and the indispensable tasks of a modern scientific system. However, in his later lectures on the philo-sophy of history we find that the place formerly assigned to the French Revolution and Napoleon has now been given to the *Reformation*.

Let us briefly review his most important statements about this new periodization. He describes the Renaissance of the arts and sciences, the discovery of America and of the route to the Indies as a '*dawn* . . . which follows after lengthy storms and for the first time again proclaims a fine day.' The utterly revolutionary event of the age, however, is the Reformation:

> 'This reconciliation of church and state took place *without mediation.* We have, as yet, no reconstruction of the state, of the legal system, etc., for the essential principles of law had yet to be discovered. The laws of freedom had first to be developed into a system of what is right in and for itself. Spirit does not appear in such perfection at once; after the Reformation it confined itself at first to immediate changes, such as the secularization of the monasteries, bishoprics, etc. The reconciliation between God and the world took place in abstract form at first and had not yet expanded into the system of an ethical world.'[13]

In our view, the similarity between Hegel's approach here and in the *Phenomenology* is very striking: both insist on the abstract undeveloped nature of a new idea, and its one-sided concentration on one essential point where a break-through is possible. But for such a consistent and historically concrete thinker as Hegel there must be qualitative distinc-tion between a situation in which an idea has only reached the level of bare abstraction in Hegel's own day, and one in which his philosophy comes into being three hundred years after the world-historical turn-ing-point whose effects have since penetrated every aspect of man's life and thought. The conception of philosophy as the 'owl of Minerva' is just the necessary consequence of his later view of the modern world as having begun with the Reformation and which in his own words has as its sole task to shape the whole world in accordance with the principle embodied in it.

Of course, even in the later philosophy of history the French Revol-ution is evaluated very positively. Even though Hegel's account of it is very well known and much quoted, we must refer to it yet again if only because an analysis of it and Hegel's further elucidations make it quite clear that the esteem in which he holds the Revolution does not modify

the ideas we have just been examining: that the modern world began
with the Reformation and that all subsequent events are but the development and concretization of that major turning-point and cannot produce
anything radically new.

'Never since the sun stood in the firmament and the planets revolved
around it had man been seen to stand himself on his head, i.e. on
thought, and construct reality in accordance with that. Anaxagoras
had been the first to say that *nous* rules the world; but only now did
man come to recognize that thought should rule spiritual reality. This
was a glorious dawn. All thinking beings joined in celebrating the
age. A sublime emotion ruled, an enthusiasm of the spirit overwhelmed the world *as if only then had* the deity been truly reconciled
with it.'[14]

We have italicized these words to draw the reader's attention to a certain stylistic reservation implicit in them. Hegel seems to hint that men
lived in the enthusiastic, subjective faith that they were about to bring
about a new turning-point in history—but that objectively, this turning
had already been taken in the Reformation. For if we scrutinize the *content* of the new age it can be identified with what Hegel had said about
the Reformation. Of course, when analysing particular passages from
Hegel's lectures we are continually hampered by the fact that we do not
know precisely when Hegel said what he did. His pupils have assembled
these books partly from Hegel's own summaries and partly from lecture
notes taken by his audience. In the case of the latter, the dates are known
exactly, but they did not establish the dates of his own summaries. So
what they have done is to create unified texts from materials very widely
separated in time, without concerning themselves overmuch if ten or
twenty years lay between one statement and the next. As long as we
remain ignorant of the various strata incorporated in these lectures we
must proceed with extreme caution in deducing anything from them
about Hegel's development.

However, our task is not to establish an exact chronological progress
of his subsequent views. We shall indeed attempt to show later on that he
developed in a particular direction, basing ourselves on texts whose dates
are indisputable, and we shall find our view completely vindicated. But
for the time being it is enough if we just show the *general contrast* obtaining between his periodization of history in Jena and after the fall of
Napoleon. And for that there are enough passages in the lectures on the
*Philosophy of History* even if they cannot be dated with any precision.

The principal thesis of the Lectures on the *Philosophy of History* is that a
socio-political upheaval of the sort that resulted in the French Revolution was only possible and necessary in countries where the Reformation had failed to carry the day. Hegel states this proposition quite

unequivocally. His starting-point is the fact that the French Revolution triggered off a movement in the Latin countries where Catholicism was the prevailing religion. This movement was not brought to a halt and waves of reaction and further revolution followed in relatively quick succession. The source of all this unrest lay, according to Hegel, in the fact that these nations had remained Catholic.

> 'Thus liberalism traversed the Latin world as an abstraction emanating from France; but religious subjection held that world in the fetters of political servitude. For it is a false principle that the shackles which bind right and freedom can be broken without the emancipation of the conscience, that there can be a Revolution without a Reformation.'[15]

And it is quite in harmony with this view that when Hegel lists the factors that contributed to the outbreak of the French Revolution he adduces as the last and decisive cause,

> 'The fact that the government was Catholic, and that therefore the concept of freedom, the rationality of the laws, was not absolutely binding, since the religious conscience and the sense of the sacred were separated from them.'[16]

And by way of contrast Hegel explains why there was no revolution in Germany along the lines of the upheaval in France, and why indeed one was not even strictly necessary:

> 'In Germany secular society as a whole had already been improved by the Reformation . . . To that extent the principle of thought had already been reconciled. Moreover, the Protestant world was convinced that the reconciliation that had already been achieved itself contained the principle for a future elaboration of law.'[17]

Thus in Hegel's later philosophy of history revolutions on the French pattern represent vain efforts to achieve through secular means, the reconciliation of reason with reality, that had already been brought about in Germany by the Reformation.

In harmony with these ideas is the greater emphasis Hegel now places on the particular positive religions, an emphasis they never possessed in the Jena period. We shall discuss the methodological and historical significance of religion in the *Phenomenology* in due course; what needs to be said here is that in that work Hegel only speaks of religion in general, or at most of Christianity. In Jena Hegel is very little concerned with the differences between Catholicism and Protestantism (to say nothing of Lutheranism and Calvinism, which are given a certain prominence later on). He does not indeed neglect them entirely, but they certainly do not have the importance they will acquire in later years.[18]

In Hegel's later philosophy of history he is no longer concerned just with Christianity, but precisely with the concrete distinctions between Catholicism and the various forms of Protestantism. Without going into his later development in any detail, an impossible undertaking in this context, we nevertheless would like to show that the general thesis we have been discussing to the effect that the Reformation was the turning-point of the modern world and that the division of modern Europe into Catholic and Protestant determined its later political and social destiny, took hold of him in Berlin and hardened out as the years went on. In the first edition of the *Encyclopaedia* (Heidelberg 1817) there is as yet no trace of the idea. By the time the *Philosophy of Right* the first major work of the Berlin period, was published in 1820, it had already become explicit. He speaks there of the relation of the Reformation to the emergence of the modern political state.

> 'Hence so far from its being or its having been a misfortune for the state that the church is disunited, it is *only as a result of that disunion* that the state has been able to reach its appointed end as a self-consciously rational and ethical organization.'[19]

The idea is given even greater prominence in the second edition of the *Encyclopaedia* (1827). In the course of an attack on the catholicizing philosophers of the Restoration, he observes:

> 'Logically enough, Catholicism has been and still is loudly praised as the religion which best assures the security of governments. And indeed this is true of those governments whose security depends on institutions founded on the unfreedom of the spirit which ought ethically and by right to be free, i.e. institutions based on injustice, moral corruption and barbarism.'

And in the third edition of 1830 he adds the following explanatory remark:

> 'These governments do not realize, however, that they possess a terrible power of fanaticism which only does not turn against themselves as long as, and on the condition that, they remain in thrall to injustice and immorality. But in the spirit a different power is at hand . . . the wisdom about what in the real world is right and reasonable in and for itself.'[20]

These few quotations make it quite clear that there is a constant development at work here, one which probably had its beginning in Berlin.

An evaluation of this period lies beyond the scope of the present study, and on such a slender basis it would inevitably be cursory. A real analysis of that 'reconciliation' with reality which characterized the Berlin period above all must be left for a thorough Marxist investigation of

Hegel's later development. We would merely reiterate the point we have already made: that in his later years Hegel came much closer to accepting contemporary German actuality than he had during the period when he had hoped for radical change in Germany as a consequence of Napoleon's policies in the Confederation of the Rhine. And it will be necessary to digest and weigh up all the available material in order to determine where and how this greater realism represents a step forward in his grasp of objective reality, and where and how it involved an intensification of his 'uncritical positivism'. Both tendencies are present in his later works; the problem is to depict their conflict and to assess the price that he had to pay for his final and most mature systematic expression of his ideas.

However, without going into any details or attempting any evaluation ourselves, it is important to counter one misunderstanding: even though his view of history represented a move to the right in comparison with his position in Jena, even though it involved him in a greater acceptance of German society as it was, the 'owl of Minerva' never became the carrion-crow of reaction under the Restoration.

There have been times when this was precisely the reproach levelled at Hegel by liberal critics, and now, of course, Fascists and semi-Fascists praise him for it. The only hard fact is that throughout the entire period Hegel was implacably opposed to German liberalism. But in the first place, this opposition needs to be looked at very carefully, for we can only judge whether Hegel's attitude was reactionary in every case once we have really established the reactionary or progressive nature of various tendencies in the age itself. For example, in the constitutional crisis in Württemberg in 1815–16 Hegel campaigned vigorously against the defenders of the ancient rights of the Estates and came out in favour of a revision of the constitution 'from above'. However, if we read what he actually said it turns out that it was the conservative side of the 'ancient rights' which he criticized and that he scornfully held up to their defenders the great example of the French nation which had abolished the 'ancient rights' of feudalism. And, secondly, we must not overlook the fact that in the *Philosophy of Right* his most violent and bitter polemics were directed at the ideologists of the Restoration, Savigny and Haller. Therefore, it would be a mistake to take the problem of assessing Hegel's later political views too lightly, for every superficial judgement plays into the hands of reactionary attempts to distort and falsify his ideas.

Nor should we be misled by the increased emphasis on the positive religions in his later philosophy of history into drawing over-hasty conclusions about his own religious beliefs, even though it is certainly true that religion was more important to the older than to the younger Hegel. His attitude towards religion was always highly ambiguous and even contradictory, as both his right-wing detractors and his left-wing supporters have recognized. It would be pointless to describe at length the attacks made on him by religious reactionaries. One quotation from Friedrich Schlegel after his conversion to Catholicism should be enough to convey the bitterness aroused by Hegel's 'philosophy of negation':

> 'Hegel's system of negation would be one shade worse than the atheism or the *idolatry of Ego and self* of Fichte: it is a genuine idolatry of the spirit of negation and hence an actual philosophical Satanism.'[21]

Nor did Hegel's left-wing supporters put a higher estimate on his positive relationship with religion. The great poet Heinrich Heine, who, according to Engels, was for a long time the only man who understood the revolutionary character of Hegel's dialectic, was also the first to make a sharp distinction between his exoteric proclamation of religion as absolute spirit and his esoteric atheism. For Heine, who had been a personal student of Hegel's it was self-evident that the exoteric philosophy was merely an act of conformity with the political realities of the day. In the course of a discussion of atheism he writes as follows:

> 'I stood behind the maestro as he composed it [the music of atheism—G.L.] of course he did so in very obscure and abstruse signs so that not everyone could decipher them—I sometimes saw him anxiously looking over his shoulder, for fear that he had been understood. . . . When once I expressed disapproval of his assertion "everything which exists, is rational" he gave a strange smile and said that one might equally say "everything which is rational, must exist". . . . It was not until much later that I understood why he had argued in the *Philosophy of History* that Christianity was an advance if only because it taught of a God who had died, while pagan gods were immortal. What progress it would be, then, if we could say that God had never existed at all!'[22]

The authenticity of this conversation with Hegel has often been questioned by bourgeois scholarship. For our purposes it · is irrelevant whether a conversation on exactly these lines ever took place. What is important is that this is how radical intellectuals in the Thirties and Forties interpreted Hegel's attitude towards religion. This was true not just of Heine, but of the whole radical wing of the Young Hegelians. Bruno Bauer's *Trumpet of the Last Judgement* is an ingeniously assembled anthology of quotations from Hegel which point politically towards revolution and religiously towards atheism.

Typical of the Jena period, however, is that the 'esoteric' aspect of his attitude towards religion is more or less openly expressed. In the fragment of a lecture published by Rosenkranz we find this statement:

'Religion is supposed to present us with the truth, but in the eyes of our culture faith has utterly passed away. Reason has gained in strength and with it the requirement that we do not believe the truth, but know it; that we do not just intuit it, but comprehend it. The individual well knows the truth of his individuality which precisely prescribes the course of his existence, but consciousness of life in general is something he expects from philosophy.'[23]

Hegel's 'esoteric' view of religion is much more explicit in the Notebook which contains a number of derisive witticisms about the fact that religion is a thing of the past. Here is one of them:

'In Swabia when something is long since past people say of it: it is so long ago that it isn't true. And we may say that Christ died so long ago for our sins that it isn't true.'[24]

Even more revealing is another passage where Hegel expresses his well-known and much-quoted *mot* that a party can be said to have vitality once it is divided. If we look at the way Hegel applies this aphorism both to religion and the Enlightenment his position becomes clear enough. In the Notebook he writes:

'A *party* exists when it becomes internally disunited. So with Protestantism, whose differences are to dissolve in attempts at unification —a proof that it no longer exists. For in disunity the internal difference constitutes itself as reality. When Protestantism came into being all the schisms in Catholicism had ceased to exist.—Now the truth of Christianity is always being proved; it is not clear for whose benefit, since the Turks are no longer imminent.'[25]

In the *Phenomenology* the same idea is applied to the Enlightenment and the different strands within it. Just as it had been used to show that the Christian religions had lost their vitality in the modern world, so now it is used to prove the vitality of the Enlightenment:

'One party proves itself to be victorious by the fact that it breaks up into two parties; for in that fact it shows it possesses within it the principle it combats, and consequently shows it has abolished the one-sidedness with which it formerly made its appearance. . . . So that the schism that arises in one party, and seems a misfortune, demonstrates rather its good fortune.'[26]

We shall attempt to give a full account of Hegel's real conception of religion in its proper place in our discussion of the *Phenomenology of Mind*. At this point it was only necessary to establish that the ambiguity we have noted was not exclusively the mark of the Jena period but was something that, with various modifications, characterized his entire de-velopment. On the other hand, it was also important to show that it ap-peared much more openly and explicitly in Jena than later on when his preoccupation with the positive religions became greater. The duality of an esoteric and exoteric conception of religion characteristic of Jena pro-vides still further justification for our earlier quotation of Napoleon's openly cynical views about religion as a parallel to Hegel's own. (p. 380). Of course, this parallel is far from exhausting the whole complex problem, but it undoubtedly throws light on one element in it.

NOTES

1   Haering, *Die Entstehungsgeschichte der Phänomenologie des Geistes*, in *Verhandlungen des dritten Hegelkongresses* (1933), Haarlem–Tübingen 1934, pp. 126, 130 and 137.

2   Haym, op. cit., pp. 258ff.

3   A detailed account of the development of the German bourgeoisie and its ideological consequence can be found in my essay 'Karl Marx und F. Th. Vischer', in *Beiträge zur Geschichte der Ästhetik*, Berlin 1954.

4   Mehring, *Gesammelte Schriften und Aufsätze*, Berlin 1930, Vol. III, pp. 374ff.

5   *Briefe von und an Hegel*, Leipzig 1887, p. 68.

6   Ibid., p. 130.

7   Ibid., p. 135.

8   Ibid., p. 158f.

9   For Hegel's response to the fall of Napoleon cf. above all the letter to Niethammer on 29 April 1814, ibid., p. 371f.

10  Rosenkranz, p. 214f.

11  *The Phenomenology of Mind*, pp. 75–6. It is remarkable that in Hegel's view all the problems of the *Phenomenology* centre on the historical fact that his task is to articulate the philosophical signifi-cance of a wholly new epoch in world history. Even the esoteric quality which in its Schellingian form the *Phenomenology* is designed to supersede appears as a necessary product of this uni-versal conjuncture. This historical explanation of Schelling's philosophy is not intended to diminish the force of Hegel's attack on it.

12  *Philosophy of Right*, pp. 12–13.

13  Ibid., p. 510.

14  Ibid., p. 535f. G.L.'s italics.

15  Ibid., p. 542.

16  Ibid., p. 535. Cf. also his statements about the Restoration and the July monarchy, ibid., p. 540f.

17  Ibid., p. 533.

18　The contrast between Catholicism and Protestantism most frequently met with in Jena is that Catholicism is regarded as an aesthetic faith, as 'beautiful religion' whereas Protestantism is seen as the religion that presides over the emergence of the world of prose. This has led modern scholars to advance the idea that in Jena Hegel had Romantic sympathies with Catholicism. Here, too, we find Hegel's thoughts distorted and misunderstood. The passage where Hegel discussed the difference in the greatest detail is in one of the Rosenkranz fragments. Here he does indeed characterize Catholicism as a 'beautiful religion', but Protestantism is said to be a manifestation of the steady growth of 'externalization', as a symptom of the crisis that will culminate in the return to the spirit of that which has been 'externalized'. From what we have seen of Hegel's view of this process, of its historical causes and its philosophical consequences, it is evident that this places Protestantism on a higher plane than Catholicism and that here, as everywhere else, he stands in sharp opposition to the Romantics. The fragment in question probably stems from the first period in Jena and in it Hegel looks to a new, a third religion to solve the conflict. It is plain that it represents a much more rudimentary stage of his thought than the *Phenomenology*, but even so its content is the exact opposite of that Romantic reversion to Catholicism that became manifest so early in e.g. Novalis, cf. Rosenkranz, p. 139ff.

19　*Philosophy of Right*, p. 174.

20　*Encyclopaedia*, ed. Lasson, Leipzig 1923, p. 466f.

21　F. Schlegel, *Philosophische Vorlesungen*, Bonn 1837, Vol. II, p. 497.

22　Heine's *Werke*, ed. Elster, Vol. IV, p. 148f. There are other observations along the same lines in the *Confessions*, Vol. VI, pp. 46ff.

23　Rosenkranz, p. 182. Very similar is the passage in the *Difference* where Hegel says that in the modern world religion can only claim a place by the side of culture. *Erste Druckschriften*, p. 15. We shall also encounter such views in the *Phenomenology*.

24　Ibid., p. 541.

25　Ibid., p. 537f.

26　*The Phenomenology of Mind*, op. cit., p. 591.

# CHAPTER THREE

# A synoptic view of the structure of *The Phenomenology of Mind*

## INTRODUCTION

THE method used in the *Phenomenology* rests on a synthesis of the systematic and historical approach. The underlying assumption is the conviction that there is a profound bond connecting the logical deduction of the various categories, their dialectical series, and the historical evolution of man. However, in order to understand Hegel's historicism correctly, in order to comprehend his radical historicization of philosophy we must constantly bear in mind two aspects of his method which make Hegel become, in this respect too, a forerunner of historical materialism. Furthermore, both aspects stand in such sharp contradiction to the modern philosophy of the bourgeoisie in its declining phase that bourgeois commentators have utterly failed to comprehend them, and indeed for the most part have simply overlooked them.

The first aspect is that for Hegel *only spirit as a whole* has a real history. He stands at the opposite pole to modern specialized histories of specific ideological disciplines such as law, art, literature and the like. And even when in his later period he himself comes to deal with a single specialized aspect of ideology, such as aesthetics, we find him giving the evolution of spirit as a whole, albeit with particular reference to the place of art. The whole idea is made perfectly explicit in the *Phenomenology*:

'It is only spirit in its entirety that is in time, and the configurations assumed, which are specific embodiments of the whole of spirit as such, present themselves in a sequence one after the other. For it is only the whole which properly has reality, and hence the form of pure freedom relatively to anything else, the form which takes expression as time. But the moments of the whole, consciousness, self-consciousness, reason and spirit, have, because they are moments, no existence separate from one another.'[1]

If we consider the real content and the real implications of Hegel's method for a historical view of the evolution of man its affinities with the view Marx advanced in *The German Ideology* are very striking (setting aside the general idealistic framework of Hegel's system for the moment):

> 'Morality, religion, metaphysics, all the rest of ideology and their corresponding forms of consciousness, thus no longer retain the semblance of independence. They have no history, no development; but men, developing their material intercourse, alter, along with this their real existence, their thinking and the products of their thinking.'[2]

Of course, passages such as this one where Marx and Hegel undoubtedly have a similar approach also high-light the fundamental antithesis separating them. They make it particularly clear just how necessary it was to translate Hegel's idealistic dialectic into a materialistic one. Marx's action in putting the spirit 'back on its feet', in asserting the priority of the means of production over ideology did not simply mean putting pluses for minuses; it meant a thorough revision of all the substantive and ideological moments of history. But for all that it would be an error to overlook the fact that Hegel's approach to history flows in the direction of historical materialism.

The second important aspect of Hegel's method is that he sets out to comprehend everything produced in the course of human history as the product of this history to be explained in terms of its roots in it. But this historical approach to the movements and products of history does not entail a historical relativism. In the most varied spheres of human activity throughout the course of history absolute truths have been discovered. Their emergence is always historically conditioned, but even the most detailed knowledge of their origins can never exhaustively account for their nature in all its richness. Hegel's historicism has nothing in common with the historical relativism that runs into the sands of mysticism, the relativism that we can see in the reactionary philosophy of history from Ranke to Spengler. This is a problem to which we shall return in the course of our discussion of absolute spirit.

Hegel's historicism determines both the method and the structure of *The Phenomenology of Mind*. What we find there is that history and system are constantly separated and joined together again by means of a particular method, a method which bourgeois interpreters of the *Phenomenology* have never been able to comprehend. The bluntest and frankest statement of incapacity is to be found in Haym. His impressions—for they cannot be given a more dignified name—are summed up in this way:

> 'History in the *Phenomenology* is a history emancipated from the rule of chronology. Sometimes the sequence of world history becomes the thread by means of which the dialectic crawls from one psychological configuration to the next. . . . At other times, the motif of dialectical progress is logical or psychological, and formations remote from each

other are suddenly juxtaposed in obedience to this order, while others
which condition each other historically are wrenched apart. One is
equally baffled whichever strand one tries to hold on to. In a word,
the *Phenomenology* is a *psychology confused and thrown into disarray by history, and a history hopelessly fragmented by psychology.*[3]

This ingenuous statement of his perplexity is quite disarmingly sympathetic when set beside the 'profound' or 'ingenious' explanatory
schemes put forward by more recent commentators.

Friedrich Engels has provided us with very clear guide-lines for
understanding the *Phenomenology*. He says that

> 'one may call it a parallel of the embryology and the paleontology of
> the mind, a development of individual consciousness through its dif-
> ferent stages, set in the form of an abbreviated reproduction of the
> stages through which the consciousness of man has passed in the
> course of history.'[4]

It is certainly no accident that it fell to Engels to provide such a clear and
succinct formulation of the fundamental method of the *Phenomenology*,
nor that he should have done so in a way which linked Hegel's method
with the much later application of the theory of evolution to the natural
world, a development necessarily unknown to Hegel himself. The perplexity of bourgeois scholars is due in part to their general hostility to
theories of evolution in both nature and society and this leads them to
wage a reactionary campaign against them and to obscure their merits,
all of which prevents them from recognizing those features of Hegel's
work in which he magnificently anticipates later developments of this
sort.

And yet there is no lack of perfectly clear programmatic statements on
Hegel's part. We have seen from his quarrel with Schelling that the project he had set himself in the *Phenomenology* was to provide ordinary consciousness with a ladder with which to ascend to the standpoint of
philosophy. Moreover, this is to be understood not abstractly but concretely and historically: the road which each individual must traverse is
at the same time the road of human evolution in general; it is the abbreviated synthesis of all the experience of the human race and as such it may
stand for the historical process itself. What is thought of as an arbitrary
selection of the historical moments acting as signposts along this road is
no more than a reflection of the fact that the individual's conscious
acquisition of the experience of the species is necessarily an *abbreviated*
process which confines itself to the nodal points of the line of development. Of course, this abbreviation is purely relative: the simple and abstract appropriation of conclusions could not lead to the authentic
acquisition of the species-experience of mankind and its evolution. If

Aristotle formulated the great truth that man is a 'political animal', it was left to Hegel to concretize it in the *Phenomenology* by adding that he was also 'an historical animal'. The relationship between the experience of the individual and the species is formulated by Hegel in the Preface to the *Phenomenology* and in view of its cardinal importance for an understanding of the work as a whole we find it essential to quote the passage at length:

'The task of conducting the individual mind from its unscientific standpoint to that of science had to be taken in its general sense; we had to contemplate the formative development of the universal individual, of self-conscious spirit. . . . The individual whose substance is mind at the higher level, passes through these past forms, much in the way that one who takes up a higher science goes through those preparatory forms of knowledge, which he has long made his own, in order to call up their content before him; he brings back the recollection of them without stopping to fix his interest upon them. The particular individual, so far as content is concerned, has also to go through the stages through which the general mind has passed, but as configurations once assumed by mind and now laid aside, as stages of a road which has been worked over and levelled out. . . . This bygone mode of existence has already become an acquired possession of the general mind, which constitutes the substance of the individual, and by thus appearing externally to him, furnishes his inorganic nature. In this respect culture of development of mind, regarded from the side of the individual, consists in his acquiring what lies at his hand ready for him, in making its inorganic nature organic to himself, and taking possession of it for himself. Looked at, however, from the side of universal mind *qua* general spiritual substance, culture means nothing else than that this substance gives itself its own self-consciousness, brings about its own inherent process and its own reflection into self.

'Science lays before us the morphogenetic process of this cultural development in all its detailed fullness and necessity, and at the same time shows it to be something that has already sunk into the mind as a moment of its being and become a possession of mind. The goal to be reached is the mind's insight into what knowing is. Impatience asks for the impossible, wants to reach the goal without the means of getting there. The length of the journey has to be borne with, for every moment is necessary; and again we must halt at every stage, for each is itself a complete individual form, and is fully and finally considered only so far as its determinate character is taken and dealt with as a rounded and concrete whole, or only so far as the whole is looked at in the light of the special and peculiar character which this determination gives it. Because the substance of individual mind, nay, more, because the world-spirit itself, has had the patience to go through these forms in the long stretch of time's extent, and to take upon itself the prodigious labour of the world's history, where it bodied forth in each form the entire content of itself, as each is capable of presenting it; and because by nothing less could that all-pervading mind ever manage to become conscious of what itself is—for that reason, the individual mind, in the nature of the case, cannot expect by less toil to grasp what its own substance contains. All the same, its task has meanwhile been made much lighter, because this has historically been *implicitly* accomplished, the content is one where reality is already cancelled for spiritual possibilities, where immediacy has been overcome and brought under the control of reflection, the various forms and shapes have been already reduced to their intellectual abbreviations, to determinations of thought pure and simple.'5

What Hegel is concerned with in *The Phenomenology of Mind*, then, is the acquisition by the individual of the experience of the species. Considered from this angle it is not so hard to comprehend its overall structure, as might appear at first. The chaotic mingling of history and system does not in fact exist; the two are carefully related in accordance with strict methodological principles.

One further point stands in need of explanation: why is it that the entire course of history has to be traversed *three times*? The various aspects of history that are treated do not occur arbitrarily, as has often been thought; in fact they occur in their correct historical sequence, which, however, is repeated three times in the course of the work. It is important to realize that this is not just a whim, a quirk of Hegel's mind, but the necessary consequence of his conception of the task confronting him.

We shall state the position baldly and abstractly for the present, leaving a more detailed account to our treatment of the particular sections. There is no mystery about the threefold repetition of the course of history: it simply means that Hegel has divided the process in which the individual acquires the historical experience of the species into different stages.

His point of departure is necessarily the ordinary natural consciousness of the individual. For the ordinary individual society in all its forms manifests itself as an established *datum*, existing quite independently of himself. As the individual works his way individually from the immediate perception of objective reality to the point where its rationality is discerned, he traverses all the phases of man's history up to the present. However, he is *not yet* conscious of them as history, but as a sequence of different human destinies. What the acquisition of rationality means to the individual consciousness is that he gradually comes to perceive that the real character of society and history is something created by men together.

With this realization the conscious individual enters the second cycle. He now recognizes history as *real*, society and its development ceases to be a lifeless thing or an uncanny destiny; it is the product of activity, of human praxis. But considered as the bald statement of the first stage of the journey such a recognition is empty and abstract. The individual consciousness must therefore traverse the entire road *again*. Thus the second phase repeats the entire course of history from its beginnings up to the present—*real* history in its concrete social totality.

Having thus achieved an understanding of what history really is the individual now arrives at the stage of absolute knowledge. From this supreme eminence consciousness *looks back* over the panorama of history. By recognizing, gathering together and ordering those moments of absolute truth by means of which spirit has achieved an adequate knowledge of itself, consciousness arrives, in Hegel's view, at an understanding of the laws *governing the movement* of history, in short of the dialectics of reality.

The dialectic which merely determined the course of history objectively at the first two stages, becomes manifest as the possession of consciousness, as knowledge, at the third stage. But this knowledge too is not just a fixed product, an abstract formulation cut off from the road which led up to it. For this reason the historical survey in the third stage once again recapitulates the past *in its entirety*. Thus the course of history is repeated for the third time. However, on this occasion we no longer find the *actual* series of events, but a summary of mankind's efforts to comprehend reality. Art, religion and philosophy are for Hegel the three great instruments by which man cognizes the world, by which he comprehends the dialectical movement informing both human consciousness and objective reality in all their aspects.

This, in the crudest outline, is the basic structure of *The Phenomenology of Mind*. After what we have said it will not have to be repeated that bourgeois scholars have never even noticed it. Today, of course, Haym's view that the *Phenomenology* is merely chaotic has long since been abandoned. But the various 'orders' they have constructed rival the chaos that raged in his mind. It would be unrewarding to consider them in detail.

In contrast to them, we must point out that the structure we have discerned corresponds in all essentials to the arrangement Marx proposed in the form of a table of contents in the *Economic and Philosophic Manuscripts*, though of course he was not concerned at the time to provide it with any sort of rationale.[6]

The problems arising from the most important moments in Hegel's elaboration of his general principle will have to be considered in the course of our analysis of the particular sections. But we must remark here that our discussion will necessarily be confined to these crucial moments, and in fact to those factors which are connected either directly or indirectly with the basic problem of the present work. The reader should not expect a detailed commentary on *The Phenomenology of Mind* as a whole.

To distinguish the various stages from each other we have decided to make use of the concepts Hegel employed later on in the *Encyclopaedia,* where he spoke of 'subjective', 'objective' and 'absolute' spirit. The reader should bear in mind that these concepts only approximate to the stages of the *Phenomenology.* Hegel does indeed make frequent use of them in Jena, but their definitive incorporation into the system is the product of a later development. However that may be, even though Hegel did not explicitly sanction the use of these terms as a conceptual framework, we think that, with this reservation, they do facilitate an analysis of the internal structure of the *Phenomenology.*

For the purpose of this survey, then, we suggest the following division of the *Phenomenology:*

A  *Subjective spirit:* Chapters I–V: Consciousness, Self-Consciousness, Reason.

B  *Objective spirit:* Chapter VI: Spirit.

C  *Absolute spirit:* Chapters VII–VIII: Religion, Absolute Knowledge.

A  *Subjective Spirit*

Hegel presents here the evolution of individual consciousness from its lowest form, the merely immediate perception of the world, right up to the highest categories of reason as these appear in individual consciousness. What is common to the different kinds of consciousness manifested is that it is everywhere confronted by an already established, alien world (nature and society). By coming into conflict with this world, and interacting with it, consciousness gradually ascends to its higher forms. In another context we quoted Feuerbach's materialist criticism of this way of relating the individual to objective reality, and above all to nature (p. 282f.). His criticism accurately defines the limitations of Hegel's idealist approach, and shows in particular that Hegel has inverted the relation of the individual consciousness to nature.

Considerably more complex is his relation to society. In the final chapter of this study we shall attempt a detailed critique of Hegel's concept of 'externalization' which will reveal, among other things, the deformations introduced into his conception of the objective nature of societal categories by his idealist approach. But since our previous discussions have already thrown some light on specific aspects of 'externalization' we may anticipate our later conclusions by observing that his theory does indeed contain a whole series of insights into man's relations with society, with social praxis.

In Hegel's view the individual consciousness stands opposed to an unknown objective reality. This appears to be fixed and alien because the determinations and mediations which are what make objective social reality and the role of individual consciousness in it what they are, have not yet crossed the threshold of consciousness. *Implicitly (an sich)*, however, they are already present and effectual.

The theoretical and practical activity of individual consciousness consists in the acquisition of these determinations. In a long, strife-torn historical process the individual advances from consciousness to self-consciousness and from there to reason, transforming substance into subject as he goes. In the last part of the *Phenomenology* Hegel gives a description of the whole process, showing how the subject gradually wrests its content from substance, an idealistic formulation which yet contains the extremely materialistic idea that the development and the vitality of consciousness depend on the extent to which it is able to reflect objective reality.

In this context Hegel explains the distinction between the bonds linking the categories in objective logic and in the picture given of the relations between consciousness and reality in the *Phenomenology*. In the *Logic* the particular moments are deduced separately and their totality yields the concrete totality of the system. In the case of the *Phenomenology*, however, consciousness confronts reality as a whole. This reality is, to begin with, abstract and uncomprehended, and the substantive and structural wealth of its moments is only revealed in the course of a lengthy process, the same process which causes the equally abstract individual consciousness to become more concrete. Hegel outlines the main theme of this process as follows:

'To begin with, therefore, it is only the *abstract moments* that belong to *self*-consciousness concerning the substance. But since these moments are pure activities and must move forward by their very nature, self-consciousness enriches itself until it has torn from consciousness the entire substance, and absorbed into itself the entire structure of the substance with all its constituent elements. Since this negative attitude towards objectivity is positive as well, establishes and fixes the content, it goes on till it has produced these elements out of itself and thereby reinstated them once more as objects of consciousness. In the *concept*, knowing itself as concept, the *moments* thus make their appearance prior to the whole in its *complete* fulfilment; the movement of these moments is the process by which the whole comes into being. In *consciousness*, on the other hand, the whole—but not as comprehended conceptually—is prior to the moments.[7]

From this it follows that the gradual development of consciousness is not the real movement of spirit in and for itself, but just its phenomenal form, a semblance, albeit a necessary one grounded in the nature of spirit itself. As we have emphasized, the objective determinations of reality are effectively present, but for consciousness actively developing itself they are still unknown and hence fixed, alien things. Thus a movement is initiated within a 'false consciousness', the supersession of one configuration of 'false consciousness' by another. However, since objective categories of the development of society are at work behind this movement, and since they objectively constitute the societal activity of individuals who nevertheless remain in ignorance of them, it becomes evident that this process will tend to transform false consciousness into true consciousness, i.e. individuals will gradually become aware of the social character of their activity and of society as the total product of their activity.

A unique feature of Hegel's mode of presentation in the *Phenomenology* is that the reader is constantly made aware of the connections between the subjective and objective categories, connections which remain hidden from the various 'configurations of consciousness'. In the context of a particularly outstanding instance Hegel defines the general situation as follows:

> '*We* who trace the process, see the preceding movement, therefore, as in opposition to the new form, because the latter has essentially arisen from it, and the moment whence the new form comes is necessary for it. The new mode, however, looks on that moment as something *simply met with*, since it has no consciousness of its *origin*, and takes its real essence to consist rather in being independent, in *being for itself*, or negatively disposed toward this positive, implicit, immanent content.[8]

The difficulties presented by the first part of the *Phenomenology* stem in great measure from Hegel's two-sided treatment. On the one hand, he merely presents 'configurations of consciousness', i.e. he shows again and again how the external structure of the world, and its independent movement appear from the standpoint of the different stages of individual consciousness. The point of departure is always the individual consciousness, his view of reality, his action on the basis of that view and the movement of that stage of consciousness implicit in it. Immediately—and this immediacy is an important part of Hegel's meaning—it appears as if the movement we are examining in which one 'configuration of consciousness' makes way dialectically for another, higher, more profoundly subjective one, is a movement determined solely by the dialectics of consciousness. The great phases of this journey from consciousness to self-consciousness and on to reason evolve *immediately* within the consciousness of the individual.

On the other hand, this dialectic is just a part, a moment of the overall dialectical movement. However, this movement goes on *behind the back* of the various 'configurations of consciousness'. Hegel is no Kantian and so, unlike Kant, he does not equate the forms of subjective consciousness with the forms and laws of objective reality (which for Kant was the only cognizable phenomenal world). The fact that in the *Phenomenology*, particularly in the first part, he treats all the categories of the objective world in their organic relation to consciousness, i.e. the fact that the categories are introduced to us in the order and the context in which they are more or less adequately grasped and digested by consciousness,—is the necessary method of the work. Only in this way can consciousness be introduced into philosophy and induced to begin the ascent towards the philosophical viewpoint.

But not for a moment do the objective categories of reality cease to exist and to have their effect. But at this stage they form a mute or even hostile background, always on the move but never comprehended by the 'configurations of consciousness'. They are present and active *in themselves*, but only in themselves, not for the consciousness of the immediate subjects of the given stage of the spirit. Spirit has not yet recognized itself as spirit in man.

This duality is the methodological consequence of the abstraction from which the *Phenomenology* begins; it does not imply a dualistic vision of the world. But naturally, it is reflected in his mode of presentation where, however, it is present only for the 'configurations of consciousness', and not for the reader. When, in the passage just quoted, Hegel remarks that the crucial connections between subjectivity and objectivity are veiled from the 'configurations of consciousness', but accessible *to us*, he means to the philosophical reader who observes the evolution of the human race from a higher vantage-point.

This duality results in a persistent ambivalence between the immediate subjectivity of the 'configurations of consciousness' and the implicit objectivity of the laws whose workings they cannot penetrate, a continuous oscillation between these two opposed points of view. The difficulties of comprehension thus arise above all from the method of the *Phenomenology* itself. The work does not contain the objective history of reality (which is to be found in the *Encyclopaedia* and in his specialist studies such as the *Philosophy of History*), but the history of mankind's experiences as a species as enacted in individual consciousness. Thus the objective categories do indeed obey their own objective laws, but the manner of their appearance is dictated by their relations with consciousness.

Behind this methodological abstraction a much more important and seminal idea can be discerned, namely that the relation between species and individual is a highly complex dialectical process, and that the individual plays an incalculable and indispensable role in the creation of the species and in the evolution of its experiences. It is true that Hegel's narrowing of his focus to the individual consciousness is a methodological abstraction; it is true that the individual's belief that he can construct his own reality on his own, by virtue of his own activity, is a self-deception whose tragic breakdown forms the theme of the first part of the *Phenomenology*. Nevertheless, the part played by individual consciousness in the overall objective life of the species is not just a delusion, but an indispensable element in the process.

By insisting on the objectivity of the ceaseless activities of actual existence Hegel overcomes the subjective idealism worked out by Kant and Fichte. By holding fast to the crucial importance of the individual, of individual consciousness, he overcomes the mechanical conception of the species operating in the old materialism, including that of Feuerbach. To understand Hegel's true achievement here it is necessary to remind ourselves of Marx's criticism of Feuerbach in the 6th Thesis:

> 'Essence, therefore, can be comprehended only as "species" (*Gattung*), as an internal dumb generality which *naturally* unites the many individuals.'[9]

The value of Hegel's conception is that for him there is no merely *natural* union, but instead union is a phase in the general process of 'externalization'.

We may summarize our account of the difficulties inherent in this first part of the *Phenomenology* by saying that the consciousness of the individual moves within a reality 'externalized' by human activity itself, but has not yet realized that the objectivity of that reality is the product of his own act of 'externalization'. What Hegel does in this first part is to lead the individual to the threshold of that realization and beyond.

As individual consciousness evolves to higher and higher stages (from consciousness to self-consciousness to reason) the more it finds itself caught up in tragic conflict with that 'externalized' reality. And it is from within these tragic conflicts that spirit, which hitherto had existed merely *in itself* (the unity of objectivity and subjectivity in the experience and praxis of the human race), becomes transformed into spirit existing *for itself*, knowing itself for what it is.

From this point of view the connection between history and the growth of consciousness is seen to be necessary in yet another sense. When Hegel thinks of his age as the point in history when spirit can revoke and absorb back into itself that completed process of 'externalization', this idealist mode of thought (which we shall criticize in due course) obscures the true insight that modern capitalist society has produced a greater sum of 'externalization' than all previous societies. And the tragic conflicts between the individual consciousness and the objective social realities which fill the last parts of this section express a very real tendency: human individuality as we understand it today is in reality no product of nature; it is the result of a socio-historical process that has been going on for thousands of years and which has reached its culmination in modern civil society.

Thus all Hegel's arguments about the evolution of individual consciousness at this level must be seen in the light of this dialectic. Only then will the objectively necessary appearance which assumes independent shape in the mind of the individual who makes an immediate response to it be dissolved, and become instead an integral part of the experience of the human race. Hegel discusses this dialectic in these terms:

'The conception of this individuality, as it takes itself as such to be all reality, is in the first instance a mere *result*: its own movement and reality are not yet set forth; it is here in its *immediacy* as something *purely and simply implicit*. . . . This *limitation cannot*, however, *limit the* action of consciousness, for this consists in the present stage in thorough and complete *relation of itself to itself*: relation to what is other than itself, which its limitation would involve, is now overcome. . . . This determinate original *nature* of consciousness, in which it finds itself freely and wholly, appears as the immediate and only proper *content* of the purpose of the individual. That content is indeed a *definite* content, but is only content so far as we take the *implicit nature* in isolation. In truth, however, it is reality permeated by individuality; actuality in the way consciousness *qua* individual contains this within itself. . . .'[10]

A comprehensive account of the different stations along this road would be the task of a general commentary on *The Phenomenology of Mind* but cannot possibly be undertaken here. We have to confine ourselves to the analysis of certain essential moments, above all those which have a bearing on our problem of Hegel's relations with bourgeois society. The most important turning-point of the first section, the role of work in the emergence of human self-consciousness has already been treated in our discussion of the chapter on Master and Servant (p. 326f.).

The point we stressed there was that the growth of self-consciousness is bound up with work, i.e. the line of development passes via the servant who toils rather than the master who is idle. But mere labour, both in a society based on slavery and in the dissolution of that society as experienced in the collapse of the Roman Empire, was at first an abstract activity. In the sections on Stoicism, Scepticism and the Unhappy Consciousness (early Christianity) Hegel depicts various forms of this developing consciousness in all of which he discerns abstraction, the failure to comprehend the nature of reality, of human activity. Of the ideology of the Unhappy Consciousness he writes as follows:

'Consciousness of life, of its existence and action, is merely pain and sorrow over this existence and activity; for therein consciousness finds only consciousness of its opposite as its essence—and of its own nothingness . . . Its thinking as such is no more than the discordant clang of ringing bells, or a cloud of warm incense, a kind of thinking in terms of music, that does not get the length of concepts, which would be the sole, immanent, objective mode of thought. This boundless pure, inward feeling comes to have indeed its object; but this object does not make its appearance in conceptual form, and therefore comes on the scene as something external and foreign. . . . Consciousness, therefore, can only come upon the *grave* of its life.[11] . . . Since it does not *in its own view* have that certainty, its inner life really remains still a shattered certainty of itself; that confirmation of its own existence which it would receive through work and enjoyment, is, therefore, just as *tottering and insecure*; in other words, it must consciously nullify this certification of its own being, so as to find therein confirmation indeed, but confirmation only of what it is *for* itself, viz. of its disunion. Actual reality . . . is, from the point of view of this consciousness, no longer *in itself something null and void*, something merely to be destroyed and consumed (like Stoicism and Scepticism); but rather something like that consciousness itself, a *reality broken in sunder* . . .'[12]

The line of historical development in this part of the *Phenomenology* is difficult to grasp because, although historical events and epochs appear in the correct order and exert the influence to be expected from their place in world-history, they yet manifest themselves in a form determined by the way they are mirrored in the consciousness of the individual. Hence, what strikes us most about this section is Hegel's treatment of two great crises in human history. The first, the end of the classical world and the rise of Christianity, has already been briefly described. The difficulties of understanding presented by these chapters can only be clarified in the sections on 'Objective' and 'Absolute' Spirit when the objective social and historical events underlying these modes of consciousness will have been made explicit, enabling us to integrate this stage of consciousness into the general dialectical pattern of the development of mankind. But even here it is clear, as we have seen long since, that Christianity provides the general ideological foundation for the modern age. The short account we have given of the Unhappy Consciousness demonstrates that Christianity can fulfil this function because the 'externalization' of the individual, his emancipation from the 'natural' bonds of a primitive society, operates at a higher level than the philosophies of antiquity which provided an ideological accompaniment to the break-up of the classical world. For in Hegel's view they all suffered from the defect that their reaction was purely negative and abstract, and was less well equipped to accommodate the new forms of 'externalization'.

The second crisis of the individual consciousness is acted out in modern bourgeois society at the time of its birth and after. We must here omit the intervening chapters between these two crises in which Hegel is concerned with the conquest by consciousness of the external world of nature. In the second crisis we encounter all the social and moral problems whose substance is known to us from his polemics against the positions of subjective idealism. We must refer the reader back to these in order that our discussions should not become too extended and we shall confine ourselves here to the purely phenomenological implications. What is at stake, then, is the tension between the individual and the social reality in which he finds himself, a reality which, as we have seen, appears to him as an enigmatic, uncomprehended necessity, alien to his praxis and, in extreme tragic instances, inimically disposed to his aspirations.

> 'Consciousness, therefore, through the experience in which its truth ought to have come to light, has instead become to itself a dark riddle; the consequences of its deeds are to it not really its own deeds. What happens to it is found to be not the experience of what it *inherently* is; the transition is not a mere alteration in form of the same content and essential nature, presented now as content and true reality of consciousness, thereafter as object or *intuitively perceived* essence of itself. The *abstract necessity* thus gets the significance of the merely negative uncomprehended *power of universality*, on which individuality is broken in pieces.'[13]

Hegel then goes on to describe various forms of purely individual reactions towards reality, the different stages of purely individual consciousness: 'pleasure' which inevitably collides with necessity and is broken by it; the 'law of the heart' in which the subjective individual prescribes laws for the whole of mankind on the basis of his own conviction, only to discover that different individuals live according to 'laws of the heart' which propose different and frequently incompatible ends. And lastly, at a higher level, there is 'virtue' which sets out to reform the world according to exalted moral standards, but is made to realize that the objective necessities of 'the way of the world' (*Weltlauf*) are utterly unconcerned about the subjective prescriptions of individual morality.

In all these struggles and conflicts the particular 'configurations of consciousness' witness the disappointment of their aspirations, the destruction at the hands of an unknown power, an alien reality, of all that their consciousness enjoins upon them as necessary. Only the detached observer is able to see the forces at work in what seem to be purely individual philosophical tragedies.

> 'The *purely particular* activity and business of the individual refer to

needs which he has a part of nature, i.e. as a *mere existent particular*. That even these, its commonest functions, do not come to nothing, but have reality, is brought about by the universal sustaining medium, the *might* of the entire nation.'[14]

Once again we cannot pause to go into details. The principle to be emphasized is that the individual consciousness becomes implicated in a series of tragic conflicts and that very slowly and gradually the realization that his own subjectivity is connected with the unknown, merely implicit existence of objective social reality is painfully drummed into him. The principle at work in this process of education is visible in the preceding quotation: the individual is bound to society by his needs, by their gratification and by the labour which creates the conditions for their gratification. Once again it is characteristic of the structure of Hegel's philosophy that the sublime tragedies to which subjectivity succumbs are often enacted in rarefied ideological regions and that they often articulate profound moral problems; but it is no less true that problems which could never break out of the sphere of tragic conflict between alien and incompatible principles, can be resolved by the economic activities of men in society. And this resolution is valid philosophically, for the individual consciousness of the *Phenomenology*. The man who works, then, is, to use a Goethean term which is not far removed from Hegel's dialectic, the *Urphänomen*, the primal reality of the identical subject–object, the substance that becomes subject, the 'externalization' which is reintegrated into the subject. The social reality implicit in all human praxis comes closest to a transformation into an explicit conscious reality in the satisfaction of needs through work.

This systematic nexus is matched by an historical one: by the fact that the merely subjective consciousness of the individual is overcome in capitalist society through economic activity. The tragic catastrophes that befall the individual consciousness are described by Hegel in the section entitled 'The realization of rational self-consciousness through itself'.[15] As the real power of implicit social existence becomes more and more apparent we find ourselves coming closer and closer to capitalist society, to what Hegel refers to as 'the animal kingdom of the spirit'. This is the highest stage attainable by the individual as 'individuality which takes itself to be real in and for itself', before its actual supersession.

This realization of the individual is vouchsafed by the social nature of work:

'The *labour* of the individual for his own wants is just as much a satisfaction of those of others as of himself, and the satisfaction of his own he attains only by the labour of others.

'As the individual in his *own particular* work *ipso facto* accomplishes *unconsciously* a *universal* work, so again he also performs the universal task as his *conscious* object. The whole becomes *in its entirety* his work, for which he sacrifices himself, and precisely by that means receives back his own self from it.'[16]

If we think back to Hegel's economic views throughout the Jena period we shall find nothing new or surprising in this passage. The philosophical supersession of the individual consciousness which is dependent only on itself and imprisoned in the narrow world of its own subjectivity is achieved by an understanding of the economic activity of man in modern civil society. That is to say, Hegel achieves it by drawing all the inferences from Adam Smith's economics that were open to him at that time. The standpoint to which the individual is to be brought is, of course, the unity of the individual and the social both subjectively and objectively. This unity is implicit in man's own economic praxis, i.e. in his ordinary daily work. The only problem is to ensure that he becomes fully conscious of the objective determinants of his own activity.

It is symptomatic both of the social and philosophical origins of Hegel's thought and for the fundamental principles informing the *Phenomenology* that the 'configuration of consciousness' that finally effects the decisive movement of the spirit is 'self-interest' (*Eigennutz*). Hegel here builds on the tradition of the social philosophy of the Enlightenment from Hobbes to Helvétius, and above all Adam Smith. The autonomy and the power of individuality—the very principle which displayed the superiority of modern society over that of antiquity—finds expression here in the fact that, on the one hand, self-interest constitutes the immediate reality and the subjective validation of individual consciousness, and on the other hand, without either knowing or wishing it, it is the primary motor of modern civil society.

In later years Hegel described the contrast between classical and modern society in a highly ideological manner:

'The development of particularity to self-subsistence is the moment which appeared in the ancient world as an invasion of ethical corruption and as the ultimate cause of that world's downfall.'[17]

Hegel then goes on to define Christianity as the essential distinguishing principle between the ancient and the modern worlds. In the *Phenomenology* the entire argument is more palpable and down to earth. He explains the dialectics of self-interest and in particular that false consciousness which persuades the individual to live in accordance with the principles of self-interest while in reality his selfish actions are necessarily connected with the labours of others and so flow into the stream of social, socially useful species-activity of mankind.

'If it (individuality) acts selfishly, it does not know what it is doing; and if it insists that all men act selfishly, it merely asserts that all men are unaware as to what action is.'[18]

However, the fact that the man who thinks he is acting selfishly is under an illusion does not imply the negation or even the diminution of self-interested action, of the role and importance of individual praxis in society. Just here, where the *Phenomenology* is about to emerge from the stage of subjectivity, where Hegel has emphatically argued that the implicit social nature of individuality is the truth concealed by the self-deception of the individual consciousness, he now insists on the in-alienable *social* purport of human individuality. And he locates this social significance, moreover, not in a stylized world of moral sublimity as Kant and Fichte might have done, but in the selfish immediacy of the ordinary reality of the capitalist world. The vitality and the living move-ment of human society depends according to this disciple of Adam Smith on the self-interested actions of individuals.

> 'Thus, then, *the struggle, the activity of individuality is inherently an end in itself; the use of powers, the play of their outward manifestations*—that is what gives them life: otherwise they would be lifeless, potential and merely implicit. The inherent implicit nature is not an abstract uni-versal without existence and never carried into effect; it is itself im-mediately this actual present and this living actuality of the process of individuality.'[19]

The essential moment of this dialectic is the gradual annulment of sub-jective activity in its immediacy, and with that go the immediacies of individual consciousness: its 'externalization' and its consciousness of that 'externalized' reality as a field of activity for individuality which is both an alienation and, inseparably from that, the foundation, content and determinate existence of individuality. This 'externalization' is ac-complished by man's devotion to his real concerns (*die Sache selbst*) by investing and externalizing his labour in those concerns, which we are not to think of merely as an object of the external world (transformed by labour), but as a nodal point of social interests, a focus of individual aspirations, a point where the subjective is transformed into the objec-tive.

It is through such complex cross-fertilizations, such an impenetrable network of human actions and of the concerns in which these actions are incorporated that the autonomous and dynamic unity of the whole comes into being. Its totality and unity remains hidden from those who act within it. As Marx said, 'They know it not, but they do it.'[20] However, their actions not only increase the objectivity of these re-lations, but they also strengthen their reflection in men's minds, even though at this stage Hegel does not attempt to go beyond the assump-tions and prerequisites of the real, conscious appropriation of social praxis in all its objectivity. He now gives this definition of the relation of individual consciousness to the whole:

'The *whole* is the moving process of permeating individuality with the universal. In that this consciousness finds this whole, however, to be merely the *simple* ultimate nature and thus the abstraction of his *real concerns* (*die Sache selbst*), the moments of this whole appear as distinct outside that object and outside one another. As a single whole it is only exhaustively exhibited by the process of alternately exposing its elements to view and keeping them within itself.'[21]

That is to say, by the processes of the capitalist commodity-relation.

In the frequently difficult and obscure account of the relation of the 'struggle and activity of individuality' and his 'real concerns' it must always be borne in mind that this real concern embraces the commodity in both its aspects: its natural objectivity as thing and its social objectivity as commodity. The individual regards it, on the one hand, as the product of his own activity, the aim and end of that activity, and on the other hand, as a means of satisfying his wants. And thanks to both these aspects he enters into the most varied relations with other individuals and consequently with the living movement of society as a whole.

Thus arises the dialectic by means of which man is raised above the plane of subjectivity to that of the social universal in the course of his own individual labour, through the medium of economic exchange. This argument is one familiar to us from Hegel's earlier works in Jena.

'It [human consciousness] is not concerned with the matter in hand as "fact" in the sense of this its own *particular* fact, but as fact *qua* fact, *qua* something universal, which is for all. . . . Those, however, who regard themselves as, or profess to be, deceived by this interference from others wanted really themselves to deceive in the same way. They give out their efforts and doings as something only for themselves, in which they merely have *themselves* and their *own nature* in view. But since they do something, and thus express their nature, bring themselves to the light of day, they directly contradict by their deed the pretence of wanting to exclude the daylight, i.e. to exclude the publicity of universal consciousness, and participation by everyone. Actualization is, on the contrary, an exposing of one's universal element, where it comes to be and has to be *"fact"* for everyone.'[22]

In this way the dialectic of labour, of human activity and social praxis in general is integrated into the dialectic of the commodity and subordinated to it. For Hegel saw quite clearly that the mere activity of work was not a sufficient basis upon which to construct the complex edifice of objective social realities. If he wished to show how human relations provide a foundation for the institutions of modern civil society, it was essential for the simple 'externalization' involved in the mere activity of work to give way to a more complex form, more profoundly imbued with the fetishism of capitalism. (Where Hegel does wrong in his analysis of the capitalist form of 'externalization' and the concrete consequences of his errors will be discussed in the last chapter in conjunction with Marx's critique of his theory of 'externalization'.)

For the time being we must content ourselves with the conclusions to which Hegel was led by this dialectic of 'externalized' object-forms, by the dynamic contradictions between man's activity, his relations to other men and his relation to the objects of his activity and those which satisfy his needs. He summarizes these conclusions in this way:

'Consciousness finds both sides to be equally essential moments, and thereby learns what the *nature of the "fact of the matter"*, his real concern, is, viz., that it is neither merely "fact", which is opposed to action in general and to individual action, nor action which is opposed to permanence and is the *genus* independent of these moments as its *species*. Rather it is an essential reality whose *existence* means the *action* of the *single* individual and of all individuals, and whose action is immediately *for others*, or is a *"fact"*, and is only "fact" in the sense of an *action of each and all*—the essential reality which is the essence of all beings, which is *spiritual essence*. Consciousness learns that no one of these moments is *subject*, but rather gets dissolved in the *universal objectified intent*. The moments of individuality which were taken as subject one after another by this unreflective incoherent stage of consciousness, coalesce and concentrate into simple individuality, which *qua this*, is no less immediately universal. The real concern thereby . . . loses the characteristic of lifeless abstract universality: it is substance permeated by individuality: it is subject, wherein is individuality just as much *qua* individual, or *qua this*, as *qua all* individuals: and it is the universal, which has an *existence* only as being this action of each and all, and gets an actual reality in that *this* consciousness knows it to be its own individual reality, and the reality of all.'[23]

This clarification makes possible the supersession of individual consciousness and its integration within objective social reality. Subjective spirit becomes objective spirit. Hegel concludes his first section with two further chapters on 'Reason as law-giver' and 'Reason as test of laws'.[24] Both contain incisive criticism of the philosophies of Kant and Fichte as the highest expression of that stage of consciousness in which the general attitude of subjective consciousness to objective reality does not go beyond that immediacy in which the world of objects must necessarily appear to be alien or even hostile. Since we are familiar with the burden of Hegel's strictures on Kant and Fichte there is no need for us to rehearse them once more.

Nor need we be surprised by Hegel's method of taking issue at some length with arguments that have just been superseded by his analysis of work and the commodity-relation. It is nothing new. On the one hand, we have seen how he regards Kant and Fichte as the consummate philosophical expression of that general historical crisis which manifested itself in the French Revolution. On the other hand, we are familiar with that idealistic side of Hegel which caused him to regard the 'higher', more 'spiritual' forms of 'externalization', those further removed from the immediate commodity-relation, as somehow closer to the culminating act of self-dissolution and supersession than the economic '*Urphänomen*' of 'externalization' itself.

This idealistic emphasis is something which we have already encountered in his views on economics where he accorded higher status to the concept of 'recognition' than to the categories of economics. It repeats itself here in the *Phenomenology* at this crucial point. The real turning-point and transition to 'objective' spirit is located not in the dialectics of capitalist society, but in the philosophies of Kant and Fichte, so that the relation between economics and philosophy is inverted here, just as earlier on the relation between juridical and economic concepts was reversed. When we come to judge the entire argument it is obvious that this idealism cannot be simply passed over without criticism. But it cannot be allowed to obscure the prodigious merits of the argument as it stands: its insistence that the dialectics of economic activity lead the individual to recognize his own social nature.

## B  *Objective Spirit*

Hegel has thus brought the consciousness of the individual to the stage where he is in a position to understand his own history, the history of the human race, in its reality. It is therefore comprehensible, indeed absolutely essential, that he should now recapitulate the actual course of history from this new, hard-won vantage-point.

Of course, he now does so in quite a different way. History had previously provided a shadowy, enigmatic backcloth for the phenomenological unfolding of the consciousness of the individual. Now, however, it appears as a coherent rational order. Objectively, the course of history remains the same; objectively, its governing laws are unchanged; objectively, neither the relation of the individual to the socio-historical totality, nor the role of his 'efforts and doings' in it have altered.

But we already know that the method of the *Phenomenology* requires all the categories to be arranged in reference to the development of the subject. A higher level of subjectivity, therefore, implies that they too will acquire a new reality: the nature of the 'configurations' that now become manifest and which embody mankind's generic experience, has radically altered. This renders it essential to present this higher stage of generic experience in its historical sequence, i.e. to run through the entire historical development of consciousness once again.

We thus find ourselves in the midst of history as it *actually* happened, while the first run-through, although of course 'historical', did *not yet* allow the genuine Hegelian categories of history to emerge in their fullness. Hegel himself stresses the qualitative difference between the two stages. In his preliminary remarks to the introduction of the new 'configurations', he says:

> 'The distinction between these and those that have gone before consists in their being real spiritual individualities (*Geister*), actualities proper, and instead of being forms merely of consciousness, they are forms of a world.'[25]

In his analysis of the world of antiquity Hegel makes this distinction clearer, though it must be borne in mind that his concretization of the 'form of a world' applies here to antiquity, and not to this entire stage of consciousness. Nevertheless, we believe that his arguments here do throw more light on the distinction between the two kinds of forms:

> 'The universal elements of the ethical life are thus the (ethical) substance *qua* universal, and that substance *qua* particular consciousness. Their universal actuality is the nation and the family. . . . Here in this content of the ethical world we see attained those purposes which the previous insubstantial modes of conscious life set before them. What reason apprehended only as an object has become self-consciousness, and what self-consciousness merely contained within is here explicit true reality. What observation knew—an *object given externally and picked up*, and one in the constitution of which the subject knowing had no share—is here a given ethical condition, a custom found lying ready at hand, but a reality which is at the same time the deed and product of the subject finding it.'[26]

And Hegel goes on to give a detailed criticism of a number of the 'configurations of consciousness' already described, by representing each stage in turn as the 'truth' of the preceding one (to use the term employed in the *Logic*).

Thus what we are confronted with here is the real history of mankind, but here too, in accordance with the particular objectives of the *Phenomenology*, history is not spread out before us in extenso. Instead Hegel concentrates on the great crises and turning-points in human history and in the history of man's consciousness. Hence we find this section subdivided as follows:

'1. *Objective Spirit: the ethical order.*' (The society of antiquity and its dissolution.)

'2. *Spirit in self-estrangement*: the discipline of culture.' (The rise of civil society, the ideological crisis in the Enlightenment and the world-crisis of the French Revolution.)

'3. *Spirit certain of itself*: Morality.' (Hegel's utopian dream of a Germany under the dominion of Napoleon. The poetry and philosophy of German Classicism as the supreme ideological achievement of the Napoleonic Age, the solution to the universal crisis.)

We have arrived at Hegel's mature statement of the problem that has preoccupied him centrally ever since his crisis in Frankfurt: the rise of modern civil society. It consisted in showing, on the one hand, how the necessary dissolution of the society of antiquity came about, and on the other hand, how the contradictory forms of civil society came to constitute a higher stage of human development arising out of this dissolution. Lastly, he had to show how in his view the contradictions of civil society might be 'reconciled'. Here too we are confronted by a series of problems and solutions already familiar to us from his earlier works. We shall not dwell on the features already known to us, but shall focus instead on those elements that are particularly characteristic of the *Phenomenology* and which represent an advance on his earlier work.

As far as the latter is concerned, the dialectics of 'externalization' are of prime importance. Even though we have seen various sides of Hegel's preoccupation with this concept it is only in the *Phenomenology* that it becomes the chief pillar supporting the entire edifice of the dialectic. In line with this the argument of this Section recapitulates that of Section A in a modified form and at a higher level. In that Section he had started with the immediate relation of consciousness to a wholly alien world of objects and he carried it through right up to the dawning realization that this societal world of objects has its foundation in 'externalization'. In the present Section, too, the path traversed proceeds from immediacy to the completed process of 'externalization'.

But both mean something quite different, viz. something objective. Immediacy here is the objective relation between classical man and the commonwealth of the democratic city-states. Hence the dialectical dissolution of immediacy, the road towards complete 'externalization' in capitalist society is no longer primarily a process affecting consciousness. On the contrary, it is the objective collapse of the social formations which constituted the city-states of antiquity, the complex, uneven development that led via Rome and the Middle Ages to the emergence of modern civil society. Hegel announces this programme also in the introductory remarks to this Section. He treats the world of the Greeks as the true incarnation of ethical life, while at the same time he sees the necessity for the collapse of that world to make room for the higher, more 'externalized' world of modern civil society:

'Spirit so far as it is the *immediate truth*, is the *ethical life* of a *nation*:—the individual, which is a world. It has to advance to the consciousness of what it is immediately; it has to abandon and transcend the beautiful simplicity of ethical life, and get to a knowledge of itself by passing through a series of stages and forms.'[27]

Hegel's description of the beautiful, unmediated ethical life of the Greeks, both here and in Section C, is one of his greatest achievements as a writer. But since we are already thoroughly conversant with Hegel's view of antiquity and the problems arising from it we need not repeat them here. All we need do is to comment briefly on the fall of the ancient world and in particular on the phenomenal forms of the spirit by means of which Hegel depicts the rise of the already 'externalized' individuality existing in the Roman Empire. This not only brings us closer to the argument of the *Phenomenology* but is particularly well adapted to provide us with concrete examples clarifying the distinction between the first stage, 'subjective spirit', and the present 'objective' stage.

We recollect that, in the former, the dialectic of Master and Servant engendered the 'configurations of consciousness' of Stoic and Sceptical philosophy and later of the Unhappy Consciousness (Christianity). Hegel now depicts the same process from the objective social angle. Greek society had been defined as one of unmediated ethical life. We also remember the dialectic between individual and society that sprang from it: a beautiful and harmonious development of man resulting from the immediate harmony between man and society, a development, however, in which human personality existed as yet only in itself, implicitly i.e. immediately, in a non-externalized form. Every development of the personality must have a disintegrating impact on that society (as we have seen in our discussion of the problem of self-interest).

In Hegel's view of history, then, the collapse of classical society gives birth to the Roman Empire: unmediated ethical life is succeeded by a system of abstract law. The fact that law should be the decisive factor in this development towards greater objectivity will not come as a surprise to us after what we have seen of his social views. And here, especially, where Hegel sets out to depict the first and therefore the simplest and most abstract form of 'externalization', it is only natural that the juridical should become its epitome, only unfolding gradually into a rich system of concrete moments through the development of the economy in modern capitalism.

Hegel gives this description of the resulting social order and of the new externalized subject necessarily emerging within it:

'The universal being thus split up into the atomic units of a sheer plurality of individuals, this inoperative, lifeless spirit is a principle of *equality* in which *all* count for as much as *each*. i.e. have the significance of *persons*. . . . We saw the powers and forms of the ethical world in the bare necessity of mere *destiny*. This power of the ethical world is the substance turning itself back into its ultimate and simple nature. But that absolute being turned back into itself, that very necessity of characterless destiny, is nothing else than the *Ego* of self-consciousness.'[28]

This new order is Roman society, the rule of the abstract right:

> 'To be so *acknowledged* is its [i.e. the Ego's] substantiality; but this is *abstract universality*, because its content is this *rigid self*, not the self dissolved in the substance. Personality, then, has here risen out of the life and activity of the ethical substance. It is the condition in which the independence of consciousness has *actual concrete validity*.'[29]

Now it is very interesting to see how Hegel now returns to the corresponding 'configurations of consciousness' of Section A: Stoicism and Scepticism. (Even more interesting is the fact that the Unhappy Consciousness is not even mentioned.) Hegel's account here is quite unambiguous and requires no lengthy explanations. Only one point need be made, viz. that Hegel underlines the homology existing between these ideological forms and the dominance of Roman Law (i.e. the social order of the Roman Empire), emphasizing that the latter represents reality and the former a merely subjective response to that reality:

> 'What in Stoicism was *implicit* merely in *an abstract way* is now an *explicit concrete world*. . . . By its flight from *actuality* it attained merely the idea of independence: it is absolutely subjective, exists solely *for itself*, in that it does not link its being to anything that exists, but is prepared to give up every kind of existence, and places its essential meaning in the unity of mere thinking. In the same manner, the "right" of a "person" is not linked to a richer or more powerful existence of the individual *qua* individual, nor again connected with a universal living spirit, but, rather, is attached to the mere unit of its abstract reality, or to that unit *qua* self-consciousness in general.'[30]

This homologous structure becomes even more apparent in Hegel's treatment of Scepticism where he establishes a parallel with the necessarily formal condition of law. For here he shows that lying behind both is another, more real power, that of the forces moving society as a whole, and that both are but expressions of a world-order dissolving under the impact of the negative action of what later would become the constitutive elements of modern civil society. As yet these do not form an independent, coherent system of man's 'externalized' relations with other men; they appear therefore as the manifestations of an unknown, contingent and capricious social power.

'For what passes for the absolute essential reality is self-consciousness in the sense of the *bare empty unit* of the person. As against this empty universality, the substance has the form of what supplies the *filling* and the *content*; and this content is now left completely detached and disconnected; for the spirit which kept it in subjection and held it together in its unity, is no longer present. The empty unit of the person, is, therefore, as regards its *reality*, an accidental existence, a contingent insubstantial process and activity that comes to no durable subsistence. Just as was the case in Scepticism, the formalism of "right" is, thus, by its very conception, without special content; it finds at its hand the fact of "possession", a fact subsisting in multiplicity, and imprints thereon the abstract universality, by which it is called *"property"*—the same sort of abstraction as Scepticism made use of. But while the reality so determined is in Scepticism called a mere appearance, "mere semblance" and has a merely negative value, in the case of right it has a positive significance. . . . Both are the same *abstract universal*. The actual content, the *proper value* of what is "mine"—whether it be an external possession, or again inner riches or poverty of mind and character—is not contained in this empty form and does not concern it. The content belongs, therefore, to a *peculiar specific power*, which is something different from the formal universal, is chance and caprice. Consciousness of right, therefore, even in the very process of making its claim good, experiences the loss of its own reality, discovers its complete lack of inherent substantiality; and to describe an individual as a "person" is to use an expression of contempt.'[31]

And Hegel goes on to show how the increasingly private nature of life, the transformation of all men into abstract legal persons, into 'bourgeois' wholly taken up with economic life, goes hand in hand with the decay of public life of every sort and with the growing despotism of the Roman Emperors. Arguments such as these, already familiar to us from the essay on *Natural Law*, are summed up here with a brief description of the typical despot, the 'lord of the world'.

Thus we are concerned here with 'externalization' in its first primitive and abstract form. Hegel's view of the Roman Empire as an abstract forerunner of modern capitalism and his cursory treatment of the Middle Ages as a mere episode of only incidental importance for the development of the human spirit is, and will remain, a permanent feature of his periodization of history. This is because, in accordance with his scheme, man's societal existence cannot be anything 'natural' or immediate. The beautiful incarnation of such a natural immediacy in Greek democracy, therefore, contains within it the seeds of its own destruction. The subject must steadily increase its own externalization, estrangement, since it continually enters into new, richer social relations and since its labour, its individual efforts and activities turn it into the identical subject–object of these social relations. The entire process gradually advances to the point at which the wealth of social determinations, the coherence and independence of the modern economic system reaches its peak and the individual then recognizes himself as the identical subject–object of social praxis.

Hegel's description of this process provides the finest example of the general philosophical method the *Phenomenology*: the forcible appropriation by the subject of the wealth of substance (cf. p. 472f.). It is here that we find those quintessential determinations which Marx repeatedly shows lying concealed in Hegel's mystified analysis of alienation. For here Hegel takes leave of his view of nature as the mere externalization of spirit, as what Feuerbach has shown to be a purely idealistic inversion of the true state of affairs (cf. p. 282f.). Nor is there any sign here, except towards the end, of the religious and mystificatory side of his theory of 'externalization', viz. its reintegration into the subject, the abolition of the object-world along with 'externalization'. Here then the 'externalization' of the human subject appears as the social activity of the human race thanks to which a self-created objective society comes into being drawing its vital energy from the social activity of the subject, grows steadily in complexity, richness and scope, so that eventually it displaces what had been lifeless substance and occupies it on behalf of the subject. In a word, by wholly estranging itself, the subject recognizes itself in theory and practice to be identical with the substance.

Only from this vantage-point does Hegel's periodization of world history make sense, only from here does its (relative) justification become apparent as a view which focuses entirely on the origins and growth of modern civil society. We have already observed that Hegel swiftly passes over the Middle Ages. He briefly remarks on the relations of the feudal nobility to the mediaeval monarch. He is much more interested in the decline of the feudal system and here, as in the pamphlet on the *German Constitution*, he clearly thinks of the fall of feudalism in France and the emergence of absolute monarchy as paradigmatic.

And in general, the whole of the *Phenomenology* is oriented on French history in a quite remarkable way. Apart from Greece and Rome whose essential character is discussed at length in this Section only France is given comparable treatment and it is evident that he thinks of France as representative of the entire modern development of philosophy. Thus from the collapse of feudalism to the French Revolution the *Phenomenology* does not leave French soil. And even in the sphere of ideological conflict only French sources are considered: the struggle between the Enlightenment and the religious tradition is confined wholly to France and French experience and the same holds good for the social and political struggles of the period. The only writer to be quoted in this Section, although he is not in fact mentioned by name, is Diderot.

The phenomenological form in which the internal struggles within French absolutism are fought out is the dialectical conflict between wealth and the power of the state. Hegel shows how once-independent vassals degenerate into sycophantic courtiers and how the 'noble consciousness' of the feudal lords (another echo of Montesquieu) had been translated into mere flattery of the monarch. This process involves, at the same time, the transformation of the 'state-power' into 'wealth', the very thing to which, at an earlier stage, it had been implacably opposed and alien.

In short, what we have here, couched in the peculiar form of the *Phenomenology* is the gradual bourgeoisification of absolute monarchy. And it is absolutely typical of Hegel that the road taken by the spirit in its journey towards self-consciousness passes over bourgeois 'wealth' and not the absolute 'state-power', just as earlier on the transition from a state of nature to civilization had been effected by the labour of the servant. Here, then, it is not the 'noble consciousness' of feudalism that leads the subject to conscious existence for itself, or that accomplishes the transformation of substance into subject. It is not the 'state-power' that incorporates the real historically progressive estrangement, on the contrary,

'Wealth has within it from the first the aspect of existence for itself.'[32]

The decisive ideological content of this transformation is the conflict between the Enlightenment and religion. In order to gain an insight into Hegel's historical view here we must begin by remarking that according to him the Enlightenment arose out of the contradictions within the absolute monarchy in the process of bourgeoisification and that the end of that conflict is to be found, on the economic plane, in the flowering of capitalist society, and politically, in the French Revolution.

Now as to the conflict between Enlightenment and religion, what is most striking is the poor figure cut by 'belief' (which is the name given here to religion as a 'form of the world'). True substance, genuine wealth of thought is found only in the Enlightenment. There is, it is true, a criticism of Enlightenment, familiar to us from Frankfurt, in which he protests against the insinuation that religion is no more than a conscious deception of the people. However, his protest is made not in the name of religion and its truth, but in that of historicism, i.e. of the historical necessity of certain ideological formations at certain stages of human history.

'When the general question has been raised, *whether it is permissible to delude a people*, the answer, as a fact, was bound to be that the question is pointless, because it is impossible to deceive a people in this matter. Brass instead of gold, counterfeit instead of genuine coin may doubtless have swindled individuals many a time; lots of people have stuck to it that a battle lost was a battle won; and lies of all sorts about things of sense and particular events have been plausible for a time; but in the knowledge of that inmost reality where consciousness finds the direct *certainty of its own self*, the idea of delusion is entirely baseless.'[33]

How little this redounds to the advantage of religion is revealed by another remark, shortly before this one, in which Hegel almost anticipates Feuerbach's critique of religion:

'It is precisely this which Enlightenment rightly declares belief to be, when Enlightenment says that the absolute reality professed by belief is a being that comes from belief's own consciousness, is its own thought, something produced from and by consciousness. Enlightenment, consequently, explains and declares it to be error, to be a made-up invention about the very same thing as Enlightenment itself is.'[34]

Of much greater significance is the actual development of Enlightenment itself. We have already seen in Hegel's earlier Jena writings that he regards the Enlightenment as the symptom of that great crisis which culminated later in the French Revolution. The *Phenomenology* goes further and gives a much clearer and more detailed picture of that crisis. The restratification of society that takes place according to Hegel with the transformation of feudalism into absolute monarchy and in the process of bourgeoisification, is depicted here as a succession of different and at first sight antithetical configurations. From these Hegel distils the essence of the processes at work: the shaking of all the foundations of existing moral certitudes, of existing forms of ethical life in society, the gradual erosion of these forms and their transformation into their opposites.

We have earlier drawn attention to some of these changes, e.g. the transformation of the feudal nobility into a court aristocracy, the infiltration of all the organs and institutions of the state by the power of money in the hands of the middle class. Thus the erosion of ethical values in this transitional phase is expressed in phenomenological terms by the fusion of the 'noble' and the 'base' consciousness, i.e. by making it possible for the philosophical reader to witness the dialectical marriage of these types of moral position.

As the most highly developed mental product of this transitional phase, the 'disintegrated consciousness' epitomizes the general relativism. This 'consciousness' no longer thinks of the 'configurations' and the socio-moral processes they represent as an endless procession, each flowing into the next, but instead it understands what is really happening. It thinks of the process as the drama of its own disintegration culminating in itself: the consciousness of the dialectic process viewed as the process achieving an awareness of itself.

> 'The language expressing the condition of disintegration, wherein spiritual life is rent asunder, is, however, the perfect form of utterance for this entire realm of spiritual culture and development, of the formative process of moulding self-consciousness (*Bildung*), and is the spirit in which it most truly exists. This self-consciousness, which finds befitting the rebellion that repudiates its own repudiation, is *eo ipso* absolute self-identity in absolute disintegration, the pure activity of mediating pure self-consciousness with itself. . . . What exists *as a self on its own account* has for its object its *own self-existence*, which is object in the sense of an absolute *other*, and yet at the same time directly in the form of *itself*—itself in the sense of an other, not as if this had another content, for the content is the same self in the form of an absolute opposite, with an existence completely all its own and indifferent. We have, then, here the spirit of this real world of formative culture, conscious of its own nature as it truly is, and conscious of its ultimate and *essential principle* (*Begriff*).'[35]

The basic ideas expressed here are not entirely new to us. Hegel had spoken as early as *The Difference* of culture as a world of disintegration and at the same time as a necessary crisis preliminary to the emergence of true philosophy. Moreover, Hegel has repeatedly maintained that a thorough-going scepticism, a consistent awareness of the way objects and concepts relativize each other so that no authentic reality remains —nevertheless still contains its own element of truth, an element that can lead to a dialectical understanding of the dynamic unity of opposites.

These ideas are now incorporated in the general socio-philosophical scheme of 'externalization'. As the process of 'externalization' moves towards its climax all the immediate bonds of human society are dissolved, they lose their natural coherence, their immediate self-sufficiency, and are caught up in the maelstrom of emergent capitalism, whose essence is 'externalization'. 'Externalization', however, is not an external process, impinging on the subject from the outside without really affecting it. In its more primitive forms it is accomplished unconsciously. Its consequences overwhelm consciousness to which they appear as an alien, uncomprehended fate. In its highest form of development, however, as embodied in the disintegrated consciousness, whose very essence lies in its self-knowledge, the subject attains an insight into the objective movement which had brought this externalized reality about, and with it the disintegrated consciousness.

A few years before the writing of *The Phenomenology of Mind*, Goethe had discovered the manuscript of Diderot's uniquely original dialogue *Le Neveu de Rameau* which he translated into German and published with his own annotations. Once again the affinities between Goethe and Hegel are evident in the way in which Hegel seized upon this work, and was in fact one of the first to recognize its literary, intellectual and social merits. It cannot be by mere chance that Diderot's dialogue is the only modern work to be quoted in the *Phenomenology*.

And in one very important respect Hegel's insight goes further than Goethe's. In his eyes it is not just a masterpiece that epitomizes the age in exemplary fashion, but the expression of the Enlightenment at the moment when the *dialectic* consciously emerges. As we know, the philosophical significance of 'externalization' for Hegel is that it alone can express the particular form of dialectics that has dominated his thought ever since his period in Frankfurt. And at the very moment when he was concerned to disengage his own dialectic from that of Fichte and Schelling he came across Diderot's dialogue, a work in which he could discern a genuinely like-minded thinker. (It may be remarked in passing that Marx and Engels endorsed Hegel's valuation of *Le Neveu de Rameau*; Engels considered it together with Rousseau's *Discourse on Inequality* as the first great modern essay in dialectics.)

What is particularly important about the Diderot essay is that the dialectic is not the product of abstract philosophical considerations, but that it grows naturally from the actual moral problems of the day. It thus becomes an apt text to prove Hegel's fundamention that, as the possession of subjective consciousness, the dialectic is also the product of social consciousness, and not just the result of abstract philosophizing. Although, as we shall later see, philosophy is the highest expression of human thought, it is no part of its task to invent new knowledge; its original and proper function is to order and clarify what the social process has created in such a manner that its highest laws, the dialectic, can emerge in a clear and undistorted form.

Diderot's dialogue is made the centre-piece of Hegel's exposition of the Enlightenment because it illustrates so perfectly his idea that the self-knowledge of the socio-moral process arises necessarily as a dialectic in consciousness, and that it does so, moreover not as a philosophy but as an insight of life itself. Hegel's summary of Diderot's work and his own comments on it are of such outstanding importance and form such a crucial turning-point in the phenomenological development of human consciousness that we must quote them at length. The nature of this turning-point will have become clear from what we have said already and from other quotations from Hegel: hitherto the phenomenological 'configurations' were the objects of an objective dialectic; now the dialectic has become subjective, the 'externalized' subject has become conscious of the entire dialectic of 'externalization':

> 'This type of spiritual life is the absolute and universal inversion of reality and thought, their entire estrangement the one from the other; it is *pure culture*. What is found out in this sphere is that neither the *concrete realities*, state-power and wealth, nor their determinate *conceptions*, good and bad, nor the consciousness of good and bad (the consciousness that is noble and the consciousness that is base) possess real truth; it is found that all these moments are inverted and transmuted the one into the other, and each is the opposite of itself.

> 'The universal power, which is the *substance*, when it gains a spiritual nature peculiarly its own through the principle of individuality, accepts the possession of a self of its own merely as a name by which it is described, and, even in being *actual* power, is really so powerless as to have to sacrifice itself. But this self-less reality given over to others, this self that is turned into a thing, is in fact the return of the reality into itself; it is a *self-existence that is there for its own sake*, it is the existence of spirit.

> 'The *principles* belonging to these realities, the thoughts of *good* and *bad*, are similarly transmuted and reversed in this process; what is characterized as good is bad, and vice versa. The consciousness of each of these moments by itself, the conscious types judged as noble and base—these are rather in their real truth similarly the reverse of what these specific forms intend to be; nobility is base and repudiated, just as what is repudiated as base turns round into the nobleness that characterizes the most highly-developed form of free self-consciousness.

> 'Looked at formally, everything is likewise in its *external* aspects the reverse of what it is internally *for itself*; and again it is not really and in truth what it is for itself, but something else than it wants to be; its existence on its own account is, strictly speaking, the loss of self, and alienation of self is really self-preservation.

> 'The state of affairs brought about here, then, is that all moments execute justice on one another all round, each is just as much in a condition of inherent self-alienation as it moulds itself into its opposite, and in this way reverses the nature of that opposite.

> 'Spirit truly objective, however, is just this unity of absolutely separate moments, and in fact comes into existence as the common ground, the mediating agency, just through the *independent reality* of these *self-less* extremes. Its existence consists in universal talk and depreciatory judgement rending and tearing everything. . . . This judging and talking is, therefore, the real truth, which cannot be got over, while it overpowers everything—it is that which in this real world is *alone truly of importance*. Each part of this world comes to find

there its spirit expressed, or gets to be spoken of with *esprit* and finds said of it what it is.

'The honest soul [metaphysical thought in the sphere of morality—G.L.] takes each moment as a permanent and essential fact, and is the uncultivated thoughtless condition that does not think and does not know that it is likewise doing the very inverse. The distraught and disintegrated soul is, however, aware of inversion, it is in fact a consciousness of absolute inversion: the conceptual principle predominates there, brings together into a single unity the thoughts that lie far apart in the case of the honest soul, and the language conveying its meaning is, therefore, full of esprit and wit.'[36]

It was necessary to quote this passage at such length because it signifies the point in Hegel's history of man's generic experience at which the dialectic appears in full view. And it is of the greatest importance for our understanding of Hegel's philosophy of history that the appearance of the dialectic is not a function of life in general but the product of the capitalist 'externalization' and alienation of social and personal life, i.e. self-consciousness can only come to itself and can only see itself as a part of objective reality in this alienation.

A further point of interest is that Hegel locates the emergence of dialectical consciousness in the literature and philosophy of the Enlightenment. Of course, the dialectic he discerns there is not quite its perfected form. A careful reading of the passage just quoted reveals that it does contain the moment in which opposed determinations are inverted the one into the other, but that there is no dialectical synthesis. The opposites continuously break down and merge with each other, thus exposing the nullity of all metaphysical notions about the solidity and permanence of the object-world, of the abstract identity of objects with themselves. But this continuous process of inversion has no direction; it is a perpetuum mobile.

For this reason we may say that the aspect of capitalism that stands in the forefront of attention today has been much more successfully defined here from the standpoint of social morality than in those passages where Hegel brings about a 'reconciliation' of opposites. On the other hand, it is no less obvious—and we have already seen the problem discussed in 'Tragedy in the realm of the ethical'—that a dialectic which contains no progressive impulse, no tendency towards a higher evolution, would be incapable of generating a history of mankind. This situation gives rise to a contradiction in Hegel's thought to which we shall return.

Here, however, we are not concerned just with the emergence of dialectical consciousness in general, but with the question of which concrete social context favoured its appearance, which ideological conflicts facilitated the break-through. And we must repeat that, on the one hand, Hegel regards the entire period as an important transitional crisis in man's history, indeed as the most decisive crisis of all. And on the other hand, the dialectic of the 'disintegrated consciousness' is not simply the expression of that crisis, but also a decisive weapon of the human spirit in its fight against 'belief'.

In this context Hegel lays great emphasis on the irresistible force of this idea. The whole section echoes with the victory of Enlightenment over religion. 'Belief' is driven relentlessly from positions it has occupied for thousands of years and the dialectic of the immanent movement of terrestrial objects, of the relations of man to society, of human consciousness to the things in which human praxis is articulated—all this rushes to fill the ideological gap abandoned by religion.

> 'Belief has by this means lost the content which furnished its filling, and collapses into an inarticulate state where the spirit works and weaves within itself. Belief is banished from its own Kingdom; this kingdom is sacked and plundered, since the waking consciousness has forcibly taken to itself every distinction and expansion of it and claimed every one of its parts for earth, and returned them to the earth that owns them.'[37]

Of course, Hegel does express certain reservations, but these refer to the later part of his argument, to the sphere of 'absolute spirit' where, as we shall see, religion acquires a quite different function. Thus Hegel's present reservations about the irresistible triumph of Enlightenment over belief are merely preparatory to the dialectical move to the next stage. Here, in the chaos from which the new spirit is born, in which the perfected 'externalization' of the spirit leads it to the discovery of itself, the inexorable advance of Enlightenment is in Hegel's eyes, an historically necessary and progressive fact.

The following chapter in this section bears the title 'The Truth of Enlightenment'.[38] This truth, or, in Hegel's general usage, this higher stage of the dialectical development, is capitalist society in all its glory. We have already encountered it in Section A of the *Phenomenology*. There, viewed from the standpoint of individual consciousness, it had appeared as the 'animal kingdom of the spirit', the world of self-interest. At the same time, unbeknown to the individual subject, the implicit dynamic already contains the universal social implications of the efforts and activities of the individual, of the self-interested subject. Here, in contrast, corresponding to the higher plane of human development, the objective context is quite explicit, though of course it is never separated from the evolution of consciousness. For this reason, the real substance of 'externalization' is fully objective: '*Thought* is *thinghood*, or *thinghood* is *thought'.*[39] Hegel's concept of alienation has now been fully explicated. It is important to state this to prevent confusion about Section C, for we shall see there that the culmination of absolute spirit in 'absolute knowledge' does not represent any *material* advance on the present stage.

Thus the greatest abstraction coincides with the greatest alienation: the essence of capitalist society. By raising the earlier concept of merely subjective self-interest to a higher, more objective level, he systematizes fundamental conceptions of the social philosophy of the Enlightenment: he revives the Enlightenment's theories of utility or exploitation in a form which has already become dialectical for the subject.

It is very interesting to see how Hegel takes the dialectic we have just seen at work in the sphere of moral philosophy and extends and objectivizes it, transforming it into the dialectical law governing the movement of capitalist society, at the same time, he uses it to deduce the theory of 'utility'. His starting-point is that perpetuum mobile of the dialectic that we have already depicted.

'This simple motion of rotating on its own axis is bound to resolve itself into separate moments, because it is itself only motion by distinguishing its own moments. . . . The process which thus puts itself *outside* that *unity* thereby constitutes, however, the shifting change—a change *that does not return into itself*—of the moments of *being-in-itself*, of *being-for-another*, and of *being-for-self*: it is actual reality in the way this is object for the concrete consciousness of pure insight—viz. utility.

'Bad as utility may look to belief or sentimentality, or even to the abstraction that calls itself speculation, and deals with the *inherent nature* in fixed isolation; yet it is that in which pure insight finds its realization and is itself the *object* for itself, an object which insight now no longer repudiates, and which, too, it does not consider as the void or the pure beyond. For pure insight, as we saw, is the living concept itself, the self-same pure personality, distinguishing itself within itself in such a way that each of the distinguished elements is itself pure concept, i.e. is *eo ipso* not distinct; it is simple undifferentiated pure self-consciousness, which is *for itself* as well as *in itself* within an immediate unity.'[40]

With these words Hegel depicts the relations between men in capitalism showing it to be the most 'externalized' and therefore the most progressive form of human development and the form best adapted to the spirit. In this view capitalist society is the perpetuum mobile, swinging backwards and forwards between thing and self. Each man, caught up in a continuous pendulum-movement for himself and for others, is simultaneously both. And the perpetual motion of capitalism, the real paradigm of this stage of the Hegelian dialectic, can only be sustained as long as this movement is maintained, i.e. as long as men continue to accomplish something of objective use, while subjectively pursuing their own selfish interests.

How very concerned Hegel was to translate the concepts of capitalism into the language of dialectics can be seen from an examination of the highly abstract inferences he draws from the analysis of utility we have just quoted. In formal terms he is discussing quite abstract relations between being-in-itself, being-for-another and being-for-self. But if we look a little deeper, we see that his true subject is the phenomenological dialectic of the commodity-relation, and that he is investigating both its objective nature and its subjective implications in its relation to the consciousness of man in capitalist society.

'Its *being-in-itself* is therefore not fixed and permanent, but at once ceases, in its distinction, to be something distinctive. A being of that kind, however, which is immediately without support and cannot stand of itself, has no being *in itself*, no inherent existence, it is essentially *for something else*, which is the power that consumes and absorbs it. But this second moment, opposed to that first one, disappears just as immediately as the first; or, rather, *qua being merely for some other*, it is the very process of *disappearing*, and there is thus affirmed being that has *turned back into itself, being for itself*.

'This nature of pure insight in thus *unfolding and making explicit its moments*, in other words insight *qua object*, finds expression in the useful, the profitable. What is useful is a thing, something that *subsists in itself*; this being-in-itself is at the same time only a pure moment: it is in consequence absolutely *for something else*, but is equally for another merely as it is in itself: these opposite moments have returned into the indivisible unity of being-for-self.'[41]

The dialectic of the commodity is then the kernel of what is meant by the dialectical unity of thing and self. The subject—object duality of utility expresses for Hegel the movement of human praxis in which and through which the objectification of man and the subjectivization and socialization of things is accomplished. The theory of utility borrowed from the Enlightenment signifies the highest intellectual understanding attainable at this stage. It is adequate knowledge and hence indicates that the self-knowledge of the spirit has been achieved. But it is not the ultimate destiny of knowledge, for it knows only its actual state, and not the whole movement leading up to it and beyond:

'In the useful, pure insight thus possesses as its *object* its own peculiar concept in the *pure* moments constituting its nature; it is the consciousness of this *metaphysical* principle, but not yet its *conceptual* comprehension, it has not yet itself reached the *unity of being* and *concept*.'[42]

In the limitations of Hegel's view here we again find ourselves confronted by a basic problem of the Hegelian dialectic, viz. of the absolute necessity of going beyond the mere self-recognition of capitalist society. This necessity invariably entails either the commitment to some sort of utopianism or an attempt to achieve an accommodation, a 'reconciliation'. That is to say, Hegel is forced into either uncritical idealism or uncritical positivism.

But just because of these manifold and intractable complexities it is of the greatest importance to underline just what has been achieved at this stage of the evolution and self-appropriation of the spirit. We have seen what is involved from the side of consciousness in this discussion of Enlightenment. In the concluding observations of the chapter now under discussion, Hegel approaches the problem from the side of existence. He confirms that what had been lacking in the previous stages of the *Phenomenology* was the world, terrestrial reality. In this sense a fully realized and evolved capitalist society signifies something quite new in history.

> 'What is thus wanting is reached in the fact of utility so far as pure insight is thereby a concrete actual consciousness satisfied within itself. This objectivity now constitutes its *world*, and is become the final and true outcome of the entire previous world, ideal as well as real. . . . The useful is the object so far as self-consciousness sees through it, and *individual certainty* of self finds its enjoyment (its *self-existence*) in it; self-consciousness *sees into* it in this manner, and this insight contains the *true* essence of the object (which consists in being something seen through, in other words, in being for *an other*). This insight is thus itself *true knowledge*; and self-consciousness directly finds in this attitude universal certainty of itself as well, has its *pure consciousness* in this attitude, in which *truth* as well as immediateness and *reality* are united. Both worlds are reconciled and heaven is transplanted to the earth below.'[43]

Thus the reality of capitalism corresponds in Hegel's view to the dialectical insight that was first articulated as the self-knowledge of man as a social being in the Enlightenment. The truth and reality of both movements, the social and the ideological, are the sources of that indomitable force with which they invade and take possession of the worlds of reality and thought. But the irresistible progress of the human spirit to the pinnacle of its development, to that extreme of 'externalization' leading to the reintegration into the subject of that which has been 'externalized', is embodied in a third 'form of the world', the highest and the most extreme form yet: the French Revolution and the Terror of 1793. Here too Hegel emphasizes the ineluctable necessity of this movement. According to him capitalism and Enlightenment must give way to the highest form of 'externalization', 'absolute freedom' must come into being and begin its triumphal march through the world.

> 'This undivided substance of absolute freedom puts itself on the throne of the world, without any power being able to offer effectual resistance.'[44]

Hegel's understanding of the French Revolution has now been sufficiently explored and requires no further investigation on our part. We shall just summarize some of its most important aspects. First, Hegel emphasizes here too that the French Revolution introduced a caesura into world history after which none of the old configurations could survive or return in their old shape:

> 'All these determinate elements disappear with the disaster and ruin that overtake the self in the state of absolute freedom.'[45]

The new world now rising up from the ruins of the old is its authentic Hegelian supersession. Secondly, 'absolute freedom' is the Jacobin Terror and its arrival is a world-historical necessity in the *Phenomenology* too: it is the final stage of 'externalization', the point at which the 'externalized' world can be rintegrated in the subject.

> 'Absolute freedom has thus squared and balanced the self-opposition of universal and single will. The self-alienated type of mind, driven to the acme of its opposition, where pure volition and the purely volitional agent are still kept distinct, reduces that opposition to a transparent form, and therein finds itself.'[46]

But the 'reconciliation' with reality made possible by the 'tyranny' of the Jacobin Terror and Robespierre's role as 'Theseus' represents in actual fact a reconciliation with bourgeois society. That is to say, just as in the earlier Lectures, Hegel rejects those features of 'absolute freedom' that go beyond the destruction of lingering feudal institutions and precipitate the liberation of all the forces of bourgeois society. Hegel describes 'absolute freedom' as 'a complete interpenetration of self-consciousness and the subject' but adds the following crucial rider:

> 'an interpenetration in which self-consciousness, which has experienced the force of its universal nature operating negatively upon it, would try to know and find itself not as this particular self-consciousness but only as universal, and hence, too, would be able to endure the objective reality of universal spirit, a reality, excluding self-consciousness *qua* particular.'[47]

Despite the stylistic obscurity of this passage it is clear enough that by the particular we must understand the maintenance and liberation of capitalist society, while the universal refers to the transformation of formal, social equality before the law into an authentic social equality. We have seen from other passages that Hegel was perfectly well aware of the actual inequalities existing in bourgeois society on the foundation of that very equality of law established by the French Revolution and that it was precisely this realistically viewed state of capitalist society that he welcomed as progressive, while rejecting as 'empty talk' any action that went further than the abolition of feudal privileges or that set out to promote the creation of real freedom (cf. p. 311). For this reason the 'tumult' of 'absolute freedom' would 'be appeased' and be succeeded by the perfected, fully reconciled form of bourgeois society.

With this we observe the re-emergence of the problem which we have already discussed in detail in 'Tragedy in the realm of the ethical'. Now, however, it has been somewhat modified in the light of the changed situation in world politics and partly also by the rather different methodology of the present work. To take the political situation first, the *Phenomenology* was effectively completed by the time the battle of Jena was fought, but Austerlitz and other actions of the Napoleonic Empire had been accomplished so that the impact of Jena on Hegel may be taken not as precipitating a change in his ideas, but merely as confirming views formed earlier on. And it is in line with them that the final part of the section on 'objective spirit' was written, and above all the description of German affairs contained in it.

Hegel's political outlook in this period is documented in his letters to Niethammer. In one of them, written shortly after the fall of Napoleon, Hegel referred to his analysis of the dialectical transition from the French Revolution to the existing state of affairs in Germany arguing that he had anticipated future developments. The passage follows immediately after the one just quoted in which he spoke of the positive and irreversible effects of 'absolute freedom':

'Just as the realm of the real and actual world passes over into that of belief and insight, absolute freedom leaves its self-destructive sphere of reality, and passes over into another land of self-conscious spirit, where in this unreality freedom is taken to be and is accepted as the truth. In the thought of this truth spirit refreshes and revives itself (so far as spirit is *thought* and remains so), and knows this being which self-consciousness involves (viz. thought) to be the complete and entire essence of everything. The new form and mode of experience that now arises is that of the *moral life of spirit*.'[48]

The chapter on Morality (Spirit certain of itself)[49] represents, then, Hegel's utopian vision of a Napoleonic Germany. It is noteworthy how lacking in content this chapter is compared to the preceding ones. Essentially it rehearses in systematic form the Jena critique of the moral

theories of Kant, Fichte and Jacobi. Obviously our disappointment is
not due to the fact that he just systematizes his general ideas about the
philosophy of history. He does that also in the chapters on antiquity and
the French Revolution. But the latter are nevertheless full of quintessential material because they contain an important and original account of
certain major themes in the socio-historical development of man. Here,
however, where Hegel ought to present his view of the dawning era in
world history which he had proclaimed in his Jena Lectures, the era destined to fulfil the moral life of the spirit and to be embodied in a Germany liberated and unified by Napoleon—here he can offer only critical
and negative remarks to the effect that this new age will overcome the
internal contradictions in the moral doctrines of Kant, Fichte and Jacobi.

In his earlier analysis of their positions he had appealed to the ethical
nature of society as an antidote to the abstract dogmas of subjective idealism in its various forms. Thus he had convincingly refuted Jacobi (pp.
294ff.) by pointing to the harmony between individual morality and
the ethics of society that had obtained in Greece. However, this avenue
no longer remained open to him in the context of the *Phenomenology*,
since he would have to demonstrate this harmony in the case of a society
where no such harmony existed as yet. That a liberated Germany would
in fact embody the form of capitalism which would exhibit the right relation between ethical life and the state, i.e. that it would present the
modern analogue to Greek civilization that Hegel had propounded in
'Tragedy in the realm of the ethical'—that is one of Hegel's convictions,
but it is abstract, it lacks all social content and hence remains a mere
postulate without any philosophical substance either.

Hegel's resignation, his descent to a mere imperative, an 'ought',
absent elsewhere in his work, is most in evidence in the concluding parts
of the chapter where the actual content of this society turns out to be the
'absolute spirit' as incorporated in religion. The 'absolute spirit' signals
the first appearance of that affirmation of a reality that has discovered
itself, of that 'reconciliation' towards which the entire philosophy of
history was leading up.

> 'The reconciling affirmation, the "yes", with which both Egos desist
> from their *existence* in opposition, is the *existence of the Ego* expanded
> into a duality, an Ego which remains therein one and identical with
> itself, and possesses the certainty of itself in its complete relin-
> quishment and its opposite: it is God appearing in the midst of those
> who know themselves in the form of pure knowledge.'[50]

Hegel's general philosophical position has always been that the 'objective spirit' must be transcended by 'absolute spirit' (cf. our account of the
estates and religion, p. 379). But elsewhere he never fails to give a real
description of the social contradictions that can only be resolved in this

ultimate synthesis and supersession *before* proceeding to that 'reconciliation'. Here, however, the positive side, the social content of reconciliation, is left vacant and thought leaps *directly and without mediations* from the preparatory stages of social morality straight into the sphere of 'absolute spirit'.

This is the distinction between Hegel's philosophy of history in the Napoleonic period and his later phase which we have already treated at length from another angle (p. 456f.). The reconciliation of the later Hegel was consummated with a slightly utopian but essentially *realistic* view of society: that of the Prussia of the 1820s and 1830s. Here, however, the 'reconciliation' is *wholly utopian* in character. It is typical of Hegel's integrity that he prefers to leave vacant in thought a place that was vacant in reality, rather than to fill it with figments of the imagination. On the other hand, the later form of 'reconciliation' derives superior strength from its greater economic and social content (even though this strength was purchased, as we saw, by a reinforcement of Hegel's 'uncritical positivism').

This particular development of German history and of Hegel's place in it strengthens the mystificatory aspects of 'absolute spirit'. We now see the sporadic appearance in his philosophy of history and society of that division into esoteric and exoteric which we discovered in his philosophy of religion (cf. p. 462f.). Needless to say, in both cases there are complex factors at work, an intertwining of both tendencies, and, at worst, a discreet silence or a circumspect formulation of certain ideas in his published writings; but there is no question of a rigid division between his private and public utterances.

It was inevitable that the 'absolute spirit' should be so prominent a part of the content of Hegel's theory of society, since, in the circumstances, there was no other possible role that a realist like Hegel could have assigned to Germany. In the *Phenomenology*, as we have seen, this takes the form of the empty utopia of the 'moral life of the spirit'.

After the fall of Napoleon this tendency sometimes became so powerful that the appearance in history of the German nation was confined entirely to the role of the incarnation of 'absolute spirit', as the mouthpiece of philosophy. For example, in his inaugural lecture in Heidelberg Hegel said:

> 'Nature has entrusted us [i.e. the Germans—G.L.] with the more exalted mission of acting as the guardians of this sacred flame . . . just as in earlier times the world-spirit reserved the highest consciousness for the Jewish nation so that it might arise from among them as a new spirit.'[51]

It is easy to see that such an extreme flight from historical reality, from the contemporary significance of philosophy, could not last long, and in

Berlin this extreme adherence to absolute spirit was succeeded by the
final 'reconciliation' with which we are already familiar.

Within this current of thought, however, there is an esoteric tendency. For the Hegel of this transitional period absolute knowledge was
not only and not always a merely conceptual statement of how far history had progressed and what laws determine its progress. It also had an
'esoteric' sub-current in which he hoped that a revolution of reality
would be brought about or at any rate accelerated by a revolution of the
world of thought. Thus in the Napoleonic era he wrote to Niethammer
in these terms (28 October 1808):

> 'I become more convinced every day that theoretical work accom-
> plishes more than practical. Once the realm of ideas has been revol-
> utionized, reality cannot hold out.'[52]

And the letters written directly after the fall of Napoleon were on the
same lines and even more emphatic.

Of course, this belief had a different import at different times. At the
time of the Confederation of the Rhine it simply meant an adherence to
those aspects of Napoleon's policy that Hegel approved of. In that case a
revolution in the realm of German ideas referred simply to the liquidation of feudalism. In the transitional period between the fall of Napoleon
and Hegel's new Prussia-orientated philosophy of history, this 'esoteric'
tendency became increasingly utopian: it lived in the hope that, notwithstanding the patent triumph of the reaction, the world-spirit would
once again resolve to advance, even though from where Hegel was
standing there were no forces in sight that could have accomplished such
a movement. The new, Berlin version of the relation of philosophy to
history as summed up in the conception of the 'owl of Minerva' was less
compatible with such an 'esoteric' undercurrent of revolution. Nevertheless, the remarks attributed to Hegel by Heine about the real interpretation of the identity of the 'real' and the 'rational' suggests that
even in Hegel's last period such ideas were not wholly in abeyance.

The absence of any real content in Hegel's treatment of the development of society in the final and crucial chapter of this Section, makes it
perfectly clear that it was objectively impossible for him to resolve the
contradictions of capitalist society which he discerned in 'Tragedy in the
realm of the ethical'. Once he had provided a profound and central
analysis of the movement of history, in terms of contradictions which
continuously reproduce themselves, once he had given an account of the
Enlightenment, of the economy of capitalist society and of the French
Revolution, Hegel was not able to go further and propose a definite
social form in which to clothe his 'reconciliation'.

Nevertheless, this positive form is a necessity for his system, both from
the point of view of his conception of the position and significance of

Germany in his historical scheme, and from the standpoint of his general philosophy of society which could not allow him simply to pause in the midst of a dialectic such as the one represented by Diderot's *Le Neveu de Rameau*. This twofold compulsion was not able, however, to yield any new social content. Hegel could only indicate the place where a new form should stand in his system; the form, itself, remained insubstantial and shadowy, a mere transition to 'absolute spirit'. We have stressed Hegel's intellectual integrity, his decision rather to leave a gap than to fill it with an ingenious construct. This honesty endows the otherwise rather empty chapter with an important historical truth: the social backwardness, the political inanity and nullity of German life at this period really was the historical foundation for the birth of 'absolute spirit' or rather for its actual living model, the classical literature and philosophy of Germany.

C  *Absolute Spirit*
We have seen how in the final chapter of the Section on Objective Spirit the real movement of history was brought to a standstill. The third, highest stage in which consciousness passes through the course of history from the beginnings up to the present for the last time, is in a sense *not real* history any more. That is to say, we are no longer concerned with the emergence of 'forms of the world', nor with their sequence and origins. Spirit has realized itself objectively and so consciousness too must have reached a point corresponding to that development of the spirit.

Having come this far, Hegel now conducts a *retrospective* survey of history up to the present. In Section A real history had been enacted, as it were, behind the backs of the 'configurations of consciousness', so that the latter regarded themselves as the finished product of an unknown process and viewed their conflicts with the outside world as abstract contradictions between absolute subjectivity and absolute objectivity. In Section B the 'forms of the world' were the actors in the drama of worldhistory in which spirit moved from one form to the next on its journey of self-discovery. At this stage the different forms always experienced this process as a dramatic struggle in the present, regardless of whether they were victorious or defeated. Now, in Section C, the great epic of worldhistory is narrated as a continuous process. Our use of the distinction between drama as present and epic as past, as formulated by Goethe and Schiller, is something more than a simile in the present case. For it gives us a real insight into the distinction between Sections B and C of the *Phenomenology*. We can only understand Hegel's ideas about the absolute spirit if we realize that we are surveying in retrospect an evolution of the spirit now at an end, because an understanding of the deepest laws governing that evolution is only possible in retrospect and 'post festum'.

Hegel himself repeatedly advocated this method of approaching the

*Phenomenology*. Thus when talking of classical works of art he emphasized the distinction between their meaning for their contemporaries and
the meaning they have for us now looking back:

> 'So too it is not their living world that Fate preserves and gives us
> with these works of ancient art, not the spring and summer of that
> ethical life in which they bloomed and ripened, but the veiled re-
> membrance alone of all this reality . . . so too the spirit of the fate
> which presents us with those works of art, is more than the ethical life
> realized in that nation. For it is the *inwardizing in us*, in the form of
> conscious memory, (*Er-Innerung*), of the spirit which in them was
> manifested in a still *external* way. . . .'[53]

And in the concluding remarks on absolute knowledge this idea is again
given great emphasis:

> 'But recollection (*Er-Innerung*) has conserved that experience, and is
> the inner being, and, in fact, the higher form of the substance. While,
> then, this phase of spirit begins all over again its formative develop-
> ment, [i.e. the *Phenomenology* is succeeded by the *Logic*—G.L.], ap-
> parently starting solely from itself, yet at the same time it commences
> at a higher level. The realm of spirits developed in this way, and
> assuming definite shape in existence, constitutes a succession, where
> one detaches and sets loose the other, and each takes over from its pre-
> decessor the empire of the spiritual world.'[54]

It is consistent with this concept of *Er-Innerung* [i.e. internalization and
recollection] that no new content should emerge at this point. World-
history itself has completed the process in which spirit discovers itself in
the objective reality of society. All the contents available to absolute
knowledge, to philosophy, arise not from philosophy itself, but from
reality; they are produced by the historical process of the self-positing of
the spirit. The novelty at this stage is that the laws and the interconnections that have accompanied and determined the struggles of history but
which had hitherto not been recognized by the heroes in the drama, now
enter their consciousness and are illuminated by the light of absolute
knowledge.

In his treatment of religion, a theme that occupies a strategic position
in this development, Hegel discusses the methodology of this Section. In
particular, he sets out the relation of religion to the 'configurations of
consciousness' and the 'forms of the world':

> 'Thus, if consciousness, self-consciousness, reason and spirit belong to
> self-knowing spirit in general, in a similar way the *specific* shapes,
> which self-knowing spirit assumes, appropriate and adopt the distinc-
> tive forms which were specially developed in the case of each of the

stages—consciousness, self-consciousness, reason and spirit. The *determinate* form assumed in a given case by religion, appropriates, from among the forms belonging to each of its moments, the one adapted to it, and makes this its actual spirit.'[55]

The material which spirit has worked through historically is now rearranged:

'In this way the arrangement now assumed by the forms and shapes which have thus far appeared, is different from the way they appeared in their own order. On this point we may note shortly at the outset what is necessary. In the series we considered, each moment, exhaustively elaborating its entire content, evolved and formed itself into a single whole within its own peculiar principle. And knowledge was the inner depth, or the spirit, wherein the moments, having no subsistence of their own, possessed their substance. This substance, however, has now at length made its appearance. . . . Thus while the previous linear series in its advance marked the retrogressive steps in it by knots, but thence went forward again in one linear stretch, it is now, as it were, broken at these knots, these universal moments, and falls asunder into many lines, which, being bound together into a single bundle, combine at the same time symmetrically, so that the similar distinctions, in which each separately took shape within its own sphere, meet together.' And Hegel adds that 'these distinctions are to be taken to mean essentially and only moments of the process of development, not parts.'[56]

Thus familiar historical material is reorganized in order to explore its internal laws. Hence Hegel's approach is now partly historical, partly systematic, instead of purely historical.

We have emphasized the distinction between Sections B and C, but before proceeding to our discussion of the principal consequences arising from the change in approach it is as well to observe that these distinctions should not be adhered to pedantically. That is to say, it is not the case that the spirit now operates on a lifeless body of material, sorting and arranging it in the effort to deduce general laws, ignoring its historical aspects.

On the contrary, there are two movements in this Section. First, as we have noted, Hegel's treatment is partly systematic, partly historical, and not just abstractly systematic. That is to say, the patterns discerned are the patterns of a historical sequence and they find their expression in the unfolding of historical events. Thus Hegel is neither ahistorical nor supra-historical, but instead he provides a *recapitulation* of the entire process from his present vantage-point. Second—and we shall return to this later—this Section contains a subjective, phenomenological movement: the evolution of consciousness towards absolute knowledge, passing through art and religion on the way. So the recapitulation of the history of mankind is at the same time man's conscious struggle to achieve his highest development, to attain an adequate understanding of the world in the science of philosophy. It will be remembered that in his polemic against Schelling Hegel spoke of handing a ladder to the man of ordinary consciousness for him to make the ascent to the standpoint of philosophy. We are concerned here with the last and highest step in that ladder.

We have frequently pointed out in the course of our discussions that 'absolute spirit' is the true haven of Hegel's tendencies towards idealistic mystification and we shall have occasion to return to this theme. But it would be quite mistaken to see the 'absolute spirit' as nothing but mystification. This was fashionable when positivism was the rule in bourgeois ideology and the heritage of the most superficial positivism lives on in our vulgar sociology.

The method of vulgar sociology is built on the belief that an historical phenomenon is adequately explained once its social origins have been uncovered. (We cannot concern ourselves here with its superficial and distorted view of what constitutes social origin.) But let us not forget that although the vulgar sociologists claim to defend historical materialism against idealism, historical materialism in fact opposes their view on principle. Marx, Engels, Lenin and Stalin never imagined that the substance, the truth-content of a scientific theory could be assessed in terms of its social origins. Even if we were to lay bare all the social factors underlying the revolution in astronomy carried out in the fifteenth and sixteenth centuries by Copernicus, Galileo and Kepler in the greatest detail and with the greatest subtlety, this would still not constitute an answer to the truth-value of the new astronomy, nor would it explain whether and to what extent the new theories correctly reflected the objective realities of nature.

Marx was quite clear about the distinction as we can see from a comment made about works of art. After making a profound analysis of the social conditions in which the Homeric epics were written he remarks:

> 'The difficulty we are confronted with is not, however, that of understanding how Greek art and epic poetry are associated with certain forms of development. The difficulty is that they still give us aesthetic pleasure and are in certain respects regarded as a standard and unattainable ideal.'[57]

And in *Materialism and Empirio-Criticism* and his *Philosophical Notebooks* Lenin provides the foundations for a dialectical approach to the objectivity of knowledge.

But it is of the greatest importance to understand that Hegel's conception of 'absolute spirit' represents a step in the direction of such objectivity. In the seventeenth and eighteenth centuries philosophers frequently thought of objectivity and historicity as virtually opposed and created a rigid, undialectical antithesis between the objectivity of knowledge and the historical origins of all the institutions of human society and the formations of human thought. Now one of Hegel's most important innovations was his introduction of a true historicism. His efforts were directed towards comprehending all the manifestations of society, including philosophical knowledge, as the products of a unified, progressive historical process, in which every institution, every work of art and every idea can be seen as the creation of the age in which it came into being.

This thorough-going historicism would simply have finished up in relativism if Hegel had stopped there. If his system was to lay claim to objective knowledge, and above all to the proper foundations of objective knowledge, he would have to emphasize the other side.

This is precisely what he does in the Section on 'Absolute spirit'. The manifestations of man's evolution belong in the sphere of 'absolute spirit' by virtue of their objective truth-content. The historical configurations of objective spirit rise and fall with the rise and fall of the historical conditions which determine their existence. But throughout the entire process man never ceases to conquer terrain hitherto unknown. And the discoveries made in this way are not simply reabsorbed into the historical continuum, but so far as they are authentic contributions to man's understanding of reality, they preserve an existence over and above the historical moment that has given them birth. In this sense they form part of 'absolute spirit'. From this point of view it is possible to understand what Hegel meant when he said that 'absolute spirit' introduces no new moments of its own but only those thrown up by history and these are presented in a new arrangement. For the actual historical impact of e.g. a theory is not identical with its truth-content. Hegel realizes that the two aspects require a different treatment. The first belongs in the realm of 'objective spirit', the second in that of 'absolute spirit'.

The simultaneous division and union of objective and absolute spirit is at the same time a step forward in comparison with the mechanistic view of historical progress held by the majority of his predecessors. Before Hegel historians had not only made a sharp distinction between history and objective truth, but also there had been a widespread tendency to think of history in terms of a linear development, gradually moving upward. Thanks to the dialectical unity of objective and absolute spirit (which also contains a dialectical separation and opposition) it is possible for Hegel to register irregularities in history, i.e. advances that contain retrograde moments, retrograde developments that in certain circumstances can provide the impetus for a new advance. It goes without saying, that many important thinkers had noticed these irregularities in history and even drew attention to them. (An obvious example is the way the Enlightenment used classical civilization as a yardstick by which to measure and criticize the division of labour under capitalism.) But the Hegelian dialectic was the first major attempt to elaborate a general method whereby such contradictions can be not just recorded but comprehended and integrated into an overall view of history. (In this sense only Vico can be said to have anticipated Hegel.)

The retrospective approach used in Section C of the *Phenomenology* has a further important methodological implication. Marx has pointed out that lower forms of existence can only be understood from already existing higher ones. The tendencies at work in history only reveal their full significance when the higher product towards which they are advancing has become reality. In this section of the *Phenomenology*, then, Hegel attempts to look back over the history of man's efforts to comprehend the world from the standpoint of the most advanced methodology available, the dialectic. The tendencies towards dialectics which have been present and active in history, whether conscious or unconscious (and for the most part they were unconscious), are now to be gathered together into a unified process leading up to the present and highest manifestation of dialectical thought.

Hegel distinguishes three great stages in the evolution of consciousness: art, religion and philosophy. We shall later have occasion to speak of the idealistic distortions resulting from the position assigned here to religion. At present, however, it is more important to draw attention to a far-reaching and highly original insight. He not only realizes that the rational and the right has often appeared in irrational and mistaken guises; he also regarded it as the task of the historian to uncover and explicate the inherent 'reason of history' implicit in every phenomenon, every development, however, irrational it might appear.

And looking even further afield, Hegel was very far removed from the narrow-mindedness that later entered academic circles, where it still thrives, and that consists in the refusal to acknowledge the value of important discoveries unless they appear in the form of an official scholastic discipline with the appropriate philosophical label. On the contrary, Hegel is of the opinion that mankind in the course of its evolution has sought to appropriate reality by a large variety of methods. He is at pains, therefore, to portray the various stages of that evolution in accordance with what actually happened and refuses to allow himself to be confined by the narrow preconceptions of the different specialisms. Energetic though he was in his attacks on those of his contemporaries who refused to submit themselves to the strict discipline of philosophy, indulging instead in philosophical belles-lettres, he was yet perfectly well aware that e.g. the great works of art, the Homeric epics, Greek tragedy and comedy, Shakespeare, Diderot or Goethe all represent major stages in man's intellectual conquest of reality, and that their high aesthetic value forms an integral part of that achievement. We have seen how Hegel objected to Schelling's exaggerated view of the importance of art and how he refused to allow art to be canonized as the authentic medium by which to obtain knowledge of the absolute. But his dislike of such procedures did not lead to a narrowing of his own view.

From this standpoint 'absolute spirit' encompasses Hegel's efforts to organize the conquest of reality by mankind into a large, complex and uneven process in which philosophy has to set aside all preconceptions and devote itself to defining and evaluating the particular stages in accordance with their material, historical and dialectical significance.

The path of 'absolute spirit' through art, religion and on to philosophy has yet another implication, one in which the specific issues raised by the Hegelian dialectic find expression. Absolute knowledge, Hegel's designation for the highest stage of human knowledge, has a definite idealistic significance: the reintegration of 'externalized' reality into the subject, i.e. the total supersession of the objective world. Our final criticism of this theory must be postponed until the last chapter of this study. But we must anticipate here by raising a number of methodological questions closely connected with the problem. The description of the actual historical process we gave in Section B led only as far as the completion of the process of 'externalization'. We have seen that the Enlightenment, capitalism and the French Revolution formed the climax of the journey towards the abolition of every sort of natural immediacy and the realization of 'externalization'.

But we saw too that Hegel's attempt to anchor that retrospective process in social reality right from the start was defeated by his own integrity. In the Hegelian scheme the 'moral life of the spirit' should be the point at which movement enters into actual social life. The scheme remained skeletal, i.e. Hegel points to the place where 'externalized' reality was to have been reintegrated in the subject, but the place remains vacant in his account. We shall see that this failure has profound social causes, over and above the historical position of Germany which we have already considered, and that only a concrete conception of a condition of society which would offer a real solution to the contradictions of capitalism can also hope to discover a way to resolve the problem of 'externalization'. In Hegel, however, what we find is a falsely posed problem, a pseudo-problem, and so he is unable to resolve the issues whose real implications he can nevertheless intuit.

What we must hold on to for the present, however, is that Hegel's attempt to reintegrate 'externalized' reality takes the form of the abolition of the objective world. The greater one's understanding of the world, in Hegel's view, the more pronounced this tendency becomes. This theme influences the other aspect of 'absolute spirit'. We have seen how positive and fruitful it was to step back from the immediate contemplation of history. Here, however, this distance from history is transformed into the attempt to abolish reality's character as real, to transmute objectivity into something posited by the subject and into an identity of subject and object, in short to complete the transformation of substance into subject. This not only conditions the whole sphere of absolute spirit, but it also determines its structure and the order in which its components make their appearance. The Hegelian sequence: art, religion and philosophy is dictated essentially by the extent to which each stage can express this supersession of the world of objects.

Here, too, Hegel remains true to the methodology proposed in the introduction to this Section. Absolute spirit introduces no really new knowledge about the actual evolution of history; it sets out only to clarify the products of that evolution. For this reason Hegel refers back to the conclusions familiar to us from his account of the Enlightenment and capitalism:

> '*The thing is Ego*. In point of fact, thing is transcended in this infinite judgement. The thing is nothing in itself; it only has significance in relation, only *through the Ego* and its *reference* to the Ego. This moment came before consciousness in pure insight and enlightenment. Things are simply and solely *useful*, and only to be considered from the point of view of their utility.'[58]

This was the point reached, it will be remembered, in the discussion of the Enlightenment, and thus far it expresses what is right and justifiable in Hegel's supersession of 'externalization': viz. the dissolving of all fixed objectivity into dialectical processes (even though Hegel necessarily rests this on the idealistic premise that without a subject no such complex of objective processes is possible). Knowledge of the essential connections at this stage of 'externalization', however, can only be found through a rigorous attention to social processes and the elucidation of essential moments in these processes results from the interaction between subject and object, the dissolving of the fetishized institutions of society into the dynamic and contradictory relations between people.

We know, however, that Hegel could not rest content with his account of 'externalization' and its supersession. He had to go further and in doing so he embraced a purely mystified view of the supersession of the objective world. Recalling what he had said about the highest stage of objective spirit, that of morality, he says:

> 'The *trained and cultivated* self-consciousness which has traversed the region of spirit in self-alienation, has by giving up itself, produced the thing as itself; it retains itself, therefore, still in the thing, and knows the thing to have no independence, in other words, knows that the thing has *essentially* and solely a *relative existence*. Or again—to give

complete expression to the *relationship*, i.e. to what here alone constitutes the nature of the object—the thing stands for something that is *self-existent*; sense-certainty (sense experience) is announced as absolute truth; but this *self-existence* is itself declared to be a moment which merely disappears, and passes into its opposite, into a being at the mercy of an "other". . . . In so far as the moral consciousness, in its view of the world, lets *existence* drop out of the self, it just as truly takes this existence back into itself.'[59]

Hegel clearly designates the moral consciousness as the form which completes the transition to absolute spirit and this is in effect its principal task. He thus provides retroactive confirmation of what we have already observed, namely that no new social knowledge emerges in the moral consciousness. Morality stands at the beginning of the process by which alienation or 'externalization' is reversed: it is the start of 'internalization'. By means of this etymological breakdown of the word *Erinnerung* (recollection) into *Er-Innerung* (internalization) Hegel gives it a further dimension. That is to say, he is not concerned with a mere recollection, an act by means of which a process now past is recapitulated in the human memory (or in the mystificatory memory of the spirit). But something which is 'internal' is to be emphasized at the expense of 'externalization'. 'Internalization' is the expression denoting the reversal of the process of 'externalization' by the subject. This, then, is the ultimate reason why there can be no new knowledge at this stage. According to Hegel, spirit has created the real objects of the world in the process of 'externalization'. It is only logical for the reverse process of 'internalization' to be nothing other than the supersession of the forms of objective reality so created, and their reintegration into the subject.

The highest stage of spirit in the *Phenomenology* is designated absolute knowledge as opposed to religion because it alone clearly and unambiguously expresses this principle, whereas religion, as we shall see, still retains a certain element of objectivity and hence is unsuited to provide the complete realization of the identical subject–object. On the relations between these two stages Hegel observes:

'Thus, then, what was in religion *content*, or a way of imagining an *other*, is here [in absolute knowledge—G.L.] the *action proper of the self*. . . . What we have done here, in addition, is simply to *gather together* the particular moments, each of which in principle exhibits the life of spirit in its entirety, and again to secure the concept in the form of the concept, whose content was disclosed in these moments, and which had already presented itself in the form of a mode or *configuration of consciousness.*'[60]

Turning now to an analysis of the most important problems raised by this whole argument we should begin by referring to a number of features relating to the differences between this Section and the previous one. Hegel is deceiving himself if he believes that nothing else is present here but the twofold movement of the recollection and the internalization of the objects of reality already created. Since this reverse movement, this supersession of 'externalization' is not an internal movement of objective reality at all, but merely something he has invented in order to bring his philosophy to a conclusion, and to solve certain idealistic and hence intractable difficulties in his dialectic, new problems of content must arise, problems which will for the most part be exposed as historical and systematic distortions of knowledge acquired earlier on. Though we must hasten to add that a philosopher of Hegel's stature will not fail to extract significant truths even from such unpromising material.

In the first place, it must be noted that the place of religion is now the very opposite of what it had been in Section B. There it had played a very minor role compared to the Enlightenment. Here, however, the importance of the Enlightenment is greatly diminished and religion is assigned a central function in the development of man's conscious life. This is evident from the fact that art becomes a sub-division of religion. The art of antiquity, for example, is treated under the heading of 'Religion in the form of art'.[61] Even more striking is the shift of emphasis in the history of the modern world. By making religion, i.e. Christianity, the centre-point of his thought a whole new view of history emerges, quite the reverse of what we found in Section B.

This contrast between the two Sections exposes that antagonistic, contradictory principle in Hegel's dialectic which we have frequently mentioned and to which we shall return in our discussion of the problems of religion. Before doing that, however, there are a number of observations to be made. First, it is very revealing that Hegel's 'esoteric' view of religion comes to the fore when his intention is to give an account of the actual course of history, i.e. in Section B. Second, it is indicative of the contradictory tendencies in Hegel's conception of 'externalization' that the problem of nature is almost wholly ignored in Section B, which is devoted entirely to social and historical problems. The problems of the philosophy of naure, and especially those arising from the relation of the individual consciousness to the contents and the objective forms of nature are given a prominent role in Section A. They then re-emerge in Section C so that they too, like the problems of society, may be reintegrated in the subject. This shows the dual nature of the idea of 'externalization' very clearly: in its really seminal aspects it refers to the social activities of man; in its idealistic generality it is extended to embrace all objective reality without exception. And while he can describe the process of 'externalization' in society in terms which are concrete, finely graded and of central importance, his statements about the 'externaliza-tion' of nature are mystificatory and merely assertive.

Furthermore, we may observe that Hegel fails to carry through his principle to its logical conclusion, but that this very inconsistency proves his greatness as an historian and a philosopher. We shall return to his treatment of the Enlightenment in Section C and its role in the emerg-ence of the dialectic. But we may point out now that in his description of classical art, he attaches the greatest importance to the anti-religious, en-lightened features of Greek comedy and tragedy. Needless to say, both in Hegel's account and in reality, these tendencies were directed against Greek conceptions of God and the forms of religion prevalent in Greece. Nevertheless, it is symptomatic of Hegel's 'esoteric' philosophy of his-tory that there is scarcely a single climactic form of the ideological pro-cess in which he fails to detect such enlightened, anti-religious features.

We may illustrate this from a few brief comments on the nature of tragedy and comedy:

> 'This destiny completes the depopulation of Heaven—of that unthinking blending of individuality and ultimate being—a blending whereby the action of this absolute being appears as something inco-herent, contingent, unworthy of itself. . . . The expulsion of such unreal insubstantial ideas, which was demanded by the philosophers of antiquity, thus already has its beginning in tragedy in gen-eral. . . .'[62]

And in similar vein, but even more trenchantly, on comedy:

> '*Comedy* has, then, first of all the aspect that actual self-consciousness represents itself as the fate of the gods. These elemental beings are, *qua universal* moments, no definite self, and are not real. They are, indeed, endowed with the form of individuality, but this is in their case merely put on, and does not really and truly belong to them. The real self has no such abstract moment as its substance and content. The sub-ject, therefore, is raised above such a moment, as it would be above a particular quality, and when clothed with this mask gives utterance to the irony of such a property trying to be something on its own account.'[63]

Lastly, we must draw attention to one further peculiarity of Section C. It is the only occasion in the *Phenomenology* when Hegel makes reference to the history of the Orient. It is true that Section A presented the so-called state of nature and the transition from that to civilization. However, this path led to the ancient form of slavery in the chapter on Master and Servant. Section B then commences real history with the Greek democracies. Here in Section C, where religious history appears as the highest expression of history, as man's profoundest struggle to acquire an understanding of the world and its laws, Hegel thinks he has the right to revert to those epochs which had been omitted from his real historical account. These pre-historical periods are also important to Hegel for another reason: in the oriental religions the mystified relations between man and nature, both organic and inorganic, play an important part so that Hegel can make use of them to exemplify the first attempts to reintegrate the world of natural objects in the subject as part of his general theory of the supersession of objective reality.

Thus at this the highest level, the history of the spirit is the history of religion—as is later true of Feuerbach as well. But Hegel's treatment of it stands in glaring contrast to Feuerbach's in every respect. On the one hand, Hegel is far less inclined than his great materialist successor to restrict himself to his religious subject-matter; and the earlier Sections contain a history of the secular world notable for the profundity and the wealth of its ideas. On the other hand, Feuerbach's history of religion is in effect a materialist exposure, whereas Hegel's amounts to the vindication of religion both in history and in philosophy, notwithstanding the depreciation of religion in the preceding Sections.

This double movement in Hegel's philosophy, this negation and reinstatement of religion, was first observed and criticized by Feuerbach. His objections do not refer to the *Phenomenology* but to the Hegelian system as a whole; but they do apply to those aspects of Hegel with which we are concerned. His chief point, that Hegel first negates and then reinstates Christian theology, undoubtedly applies to Section C of the *Phenomenology*, particularly if we bear in mind the conclusions reached in Section B. Feuerbach writes:

> 'Matter is indeed posited in God, i.e. posited as God, and to posit matter as God is to say in effect: there is no God. That is to say, it amounts to the negation of theology and the recognition of the truth of materialism. But at the same time, the truth of theology is still assumed. Atheism, the negation of theology is thus negated once more, i.e. theology is re-established by philosophy. God is *God* in that he supersedes matter, the negation of God. And according to Hegel, only the negation of the negation is true affirmation. So finally we are where we were at the beginning—in the bosom of Christian theology.'[64]

Of course, there is still criticism of religion even in the sphere of 'internalization', the retraction of 'externalization', indeed criticism constitutes one of the chief features of the Section. For Hegel wishes to advance from the incomplete, merely mental supersession of the objective world to its complete negation in the realm of the concept, of philosophy. But his criticism is the very opposite of a materialist criticism. He starts from the assumption that the essential contents of the dialectical self-discovery of the spirit are contained in religion, i.e. that religion correctly carries out the process of reintegrating the 'externalized' world and indeed that the positive aspects of the dialectical synthesis, the element of 'reconciliation', are to be found primarily in religion. On the other hand, however, he maintains that these elements of the true dialectic can only be inadequately realized in the context of religion.

Hence, according to Hegel, philosophy is essentially critical of religion. But this criticism, unlike Feuerbach's, does not set out to undermine the entire edifice of religious ideas by reducing the truths distorted by religion to their true status. Hegel's criticism of religion represents rather the preservation, the perpetuation, of all the tenets of religion while criticizing the form in which they appear, the figurative or pictorial *ideas* in which they are embodied. Naturally this criticism cannot but have repercussions on the content of religion some of which is effectively rejected, but the overall effect is, as Feuerbach maintains, to reinstate both religion and theology.

The ambiguity of Hegel's position *vis-à-vis* religion is fully revealed in this Section of the *Phenomenology*. Religion in his view is only an intermediate stage in the spirit's Odyssey of self-discovery, but following the main line of the argument, it is an indispensable one. As the Hegelian 'configurations' progress, as they must, towards 'reconciliation', they must inevitably strive towards religion. The importance of religion here is partly that the substance of history that forms the content of absolute knowledge can be influenced by religion in the direction of that reintegration of the 'externalized' world in the subject, and partly that the forms of religion contain the most important categories of dialectical synthesis (even though in an incomplete and unsatisfactory form).

It is characteristic of the ambiguity of his position that despite the main trend prescribed by crucial elements of his idealism, real, irreligious tendencies make themselves felt even here. He expressly mentions two paths leading to the dialectic and asserts that the form of dialectic we encountered in the Enlightenment takes precedence phenomenologically over the religious dialectic and that its mode of self-existence is superior in his eyes.

> 'This reconciliation of consciousness with self-consciousness thus proves to be brought about in a double-sided way: in the one case, in the religious mind, in the other case, in consciousness itself as such. They are distinguished *inter se* by the fact that the one is this reconciliation in the form of *implicit immanence*, the other in the form of *explicit self-existence*. In the order in which the modes or shapes of consciousness came before us, consciousness has reached the individual moments of that order, and also their unification, long before ever religion gave its object the shape of actual self-consciousness.'[65]

These observations would suggest that religion is superfluous. If, as Hegel had already demonstrated for the Enlightenment, human consciousness had attained a clear subjective insight into the dialectical contradictions of existence and thought, i.e. if dialectic had come into being in the form of existence-for-self *before* religion had made its appearance in his argument, then it would seem that Hegel had no real need of an intermediate religious stage at all.

We have already drawn attention to the various factors which prevent Hegel from taking this argument to its logical conclusion. First, the idealist conception of the identical subject–object requires the utter negation of the objective world. The dialectic described here, however, can only go so far as transforming the objective character of things into processes; it lacks the mystificatory climax of idealism. Second,—and this is crucial—owing to the historical limits of his horizons, Hegel finds himself on the horns of a dilemma whose two alternatives he finds himself unable to accept, and this forces him to embark on a search for a third and higher solution. We have already explained the two sides of the dilemma: to remain at the level of the dialectic we have been speaking of would lead to a romantic scepticism about the development of society, viz. it would force Hegel to content himself with the mere statement that reality was contradictory. This would lead him to a position close to that held by e.g. Sismondi. However, if an 'immanent' 'reconciliation' of these contradictions is sought and found, it would have to be on Benthamite lines. It is no accident that the real fulfilment of the dialectic, the 'Heaven upon earth' of which Hegel speaks, is the world of 'utility'. (The prerevolutionary members of the Enlightenment, such as Helvétius, were able to escape this logic by virtue of their historical situation: the 'principle of utility' in their case consisted of demanding the destruction of the remains of feudalism and the introduction of bourgeois society. It did not, however, commit them to the support of a fully-developed and hegemonic capitalism.)

Consequently, Hegel found himself confronted by a dilemma which Marx declared to be insoluble in the bourgeois context. Speaking of the different effects wrought by individuality Marx notes that it is the cause both of undeveloped forms of society and also of capitalism. He thus applies a particular analysis to the problem which comes very close to Hegel's dilemma. He observes:

'It is as ridiculous to wish to return to that primitive abundance as it is to believe in the continuing necessity of its complete depletion. The bourgeois view has never got beyond opposition to this romantic outlook and thus will be accompanied by it, as a legitimate antithesis, right up to its blessed end.'[66]

For reasons known to us, the third and real solution, i.e. the possibility of a socialist society, could not be available to Hegel. He consistently rejected romantic solutions and his views of society and the state similarly precluded Benthamite answers. Thus Hegel was compelled not just by the general idealistic strain in his thought—to go beyond this type of dialectic in search of further possibilities.

For an idealist the religious path is always close at hand. Our last quotation of Hegel's views, however, shows that what he was looking for was a synthesis of both paths, of both kinds of dialectic. Such an enterprise could not possibly end in a satisfactory unified result. This very search conducted amidst the 'manure of contradictions', and the ambiguous view of religion resulting from it, is what determines in equal measure the achievement and the failure of his creation of the dialectic. The impulse towards religion leads to the specifically Hegelian form of the dialectic: an immediacy to be superseded—externalization'—reintegration of 'externalization' in the subject. In the process his critique of religion develops into the very opposite of Feuerbach's materialist criticism: he does not reduce the mystified content of religion to its 'human' basis (as does Feuerbach), or to its foundation in history and society and so dissolve it. On the contrary, it is this very content that Hegel preserves and even mystifies still further. As we shall see: his criticism is directed simply and solely against the form in which this content became manifest, i.e. against the pictorial representation (*Vorstellung*) which according to Hegel failed to do justice to the content.

We have described in detail the social forces impelling Hegel towards idealism. We now see how this idealism discovers itself in the myths of religion and how it can only realize its own essence by superseding them in the sense of preserving them. This truth of religion is the dialectic of alienation, of 'externalization' and its antidote 'internalization'. Here alone can be discovered what Hegel found wanting in the dialectics of 'culture' in the Enlightenment: the synthetic unity, the 'reconciliation', the supersession of the objective world. The myths of religion and of Christianity in particular, are thus mystified by Hegel in the sense that he detects in them the prototypes of his own dialectic, the dialectical triad, 'externalization' and its revocation etc. And this he elevates to the real truth of religion. Hence religion provides Hegel—in appearance at least —with a historical reality, a historical movement from which these dynamic forms of thought and reality may be alleged to have sprung.

This is the ultimate form of Hegel's ambiguous view of religion. On the one hand, the historical religion is both a historical movement and also the form of consciousness which embodies the highest relationship between man and his self-created socio-historical environment. To make this relationship a reality, all the myths of religion must be reinterpreted in terms of the Hegelian dialectic. Hegel discusses in turn the creation of the world, God's relation to man, the Trinity, the death of the Redeemer etc., showing how each of them exhibits the basic categories of his own system. On the other hand, this mystification is the point of departure for his own criticism. It expresses itself in two ways. First, these religious categories seem to be insufficiently human, i.e. the mythical projection of the human into the divine by religion, extended and exaggerated still further by Hegel himself, obscures the nature of man in whom and in whose consciousness Hegel discerns the key to all mysteries. Religion, in Hegel's view, ought to demonstrate the identity of the human and the divine; but it only does so imperfectly and as he criticizes it he overlooks the fact that it was he who had taken the mystification to its furthest extreme. Second, and in sharp contradiction to the previous position, Hegel finds that what religion teaches and what religious communion represents is still too 'earthly', too 'externalized', too objective for his liking. In religion and in the faith of community of believers, the concept has not yet discovered itself as concept.

In our view it is not necessary to give a detailed analysis of Hegel's interpretation of Christian dogmas, or rather, of this injection of Hegelian categories into Christian theology, nor of his criticism (which consists in essence of the failure of religion to provide a satisfactory mythical framework for the Hegelian dialectic). It is enough if we quote a few passages to exemplify Hegel's interpretation of Christianity and to show how he proceeds from interpretation to criticism. E.g. he presents the dialectical transition of abstract spirit into reality much in the way in which he later argues the transition from logic to the philosophy of nature in the *Encyclopaedia*. He imputes this meaning to the Christian myths and gives the following interpretation and criticism:

> 'Merely eternal or abstract spirit, then, becomes an *other* to itself: it enters existence, and, in the first instance, enters *immediate existence*. It *creates* a world. This "creation" is the word which pictorial thought (*Vorstellung*) uses to convey the *concept* of itself in its absolute movement; or to express the fact that the simple which has been expressed as absolute, or pure thought, just because it is abstract, is really the negative, and hence opposed to itself, the *other* of itself.'[67]

And here is his interpretation of the death of Christ:

> 'That which belongs to the sphere of *pictorial thought*—viz. that absolute spirit presents the nature of spirit in its existence, *qua individual* or rather *qua particular*,—is thus here transferred to self-consciousness itself, to the knowledge which maintains itself in its *otherness*. This self-consciousness does not therefore really *die*, as the *particular person*

[i.e. Christ] is pictorially imagined to have *really* died; its particularity expires in its universality, i.e. in its *knowledge*, which is essential being reconciling itself with itself. . . . When the death of the mediator is grasped by the self, this means the supersession of his *factuality*, of his *particular independent existence*: this *particular* self-existence has become universal self-consciousness.'[68]

Thus Hegel's objections to religion are founded on his contention that these dialectical relations, these 'ultimate mysteries' of the Hegelian dialectic—which have been smuggled into religion by Hegel himself—are inadequately expressed in pictorial form. Here is one instance of this at work:

'But the *pictorial* thought of the religious communion is not this *conceptual* thinking; it has the content without its necessity; and instead of the form of the·concept it brings into the realm of pure consciousness the natural relations of Father and Son. Since it thus, even when thinking, proceeds by way of *figurative ideas*, absolute being is indeed revealed to it, but the moments of this being, owing to this synthetic pictorial thinking, partly fall of themselves apart from one another . . . while, partly again, this figurative thinking retreats from the pure object it deals with, and takes up a merely external relation towards it. The object is externally revealed to it from an alien source, and in this thought of spirit it does not recognize its own self, does not recognize the nature of pure self-consciousness.'[69]

Hegel's ambivalent frame of mind is well reflected in the fact that he both criticizes the discrepancy between the figurative language of religion and the concept, while at the same time he thinks of it as merely a formal problem arising from the difficulty of making ultimate, decisive truths manifest and does not think of the distortions of religion as having any content of importance. At an earlier stage of his argument, before the relation of figurative language to religion had become pressing, he makes this characteristically earthy comment on the question of content:

'The purer the concept itself is, the more silly an idea does it become, if its content does not take the shape of a concept, but of a merely pictorial presentation or idea . . . and the *ignorance* on the part of this consciousness as to what it really says, is the same kind of connection of higher and lower which, in the case of the living being, nature naively expresses when it combines the organ of its highest fulfilment, the organ of generation, with the organ of urination.'[70]

Spirit, then, must transcend religion. In the religious communion the identical subject–object has not yet been attained.

'This spiritual communion is not also consciously aware what it is; it is spiritual self-consciousness, which is not object to itself as this self-consciousness, or does not develop into clear consciousness of itself. Rather, so far as it is consciousness, it has before it those picture-thoughts which were considered. . . . Since this unity of essential being and self has been *inherently* brought about, consciousness has this *idea* also of its reconciliation, but in the form of an imaginative idea. It obtains satisfaction by attaching, in an *external* way, to its pure negativity the positive significance of the unity of itself with essential being. Its satisfaction thus itself remains hampered with the opposition of a beyond. Its own peculiar reconciliation therefore enters its consciousness as something *remote*, something far away in the *future*, just as the reconciliation, which the other *self* achieved [i.e. Christ—G.L.], appears as away in the distance of the *past*. . . . Its reconciliation, therefore, is in its heart, but still with its conscious life sundered in twain and its actual reality shattered.[71]

Thus a true reconciliation, a true supersession can take place only in absolute knowledge. Here we see Hegel's ambiguous attitude towards religion at its most extreme. On the one hand, he smuggles the contents of his dialectic into Christianity—thus granting it salvation through speculation. On the other hand, this speculative salvation negates religion as such, destroying it as religion.

This is the vindication of Feuerbach's criticism that Hegel's philosophy is an amalgam of atheistic and theological tendencies. And indeed it is not just atheistic-minded thinkers who have drawn attention to this aspect of Hegel, either criticizing it for its half-heartedness, like Feuerbach, or, like Heine and Bruno Bauer, carefully separating the 'esoteric atheism' from the exoteric Christianity—and we should add that there can be no doubt that Feuerbach is nearer the mark. But apart from such thinkers there is not a single important reactionary religious philosopher who has accepted Hegel's theory or who could see in it the authentic philosophical expression of the religious essence of Christianity. We have already quoted a remark by Friedrich Schlegel, a convert to Catholicism, who regarded Hegel's dialectic as even worse than atheism, indeed as a form of Satanism. A thinker to be taken rather more seriously is the Danish philosopher of the 1840s, Søren Kierkegaard, who has been a major influence on the irrationalist philosophy of existentialism in modern times. Kierkegaard devoted whole books to the refutation of Hegel's religious ideas. For us they have only symptomatic importance as providing confirmation, from the enemy, as it were, of Hegel's ambiguous position.

What is noteworthy about Kierkegaard's polemic is that it begins at the point where religion is deemed to be a moment of absolute spirit, i.e. where it is held to participate, albeit imperfectly according to Hegel, in the dialectical objectivity of philosophy. Hegel had attempted the 'rescue' of Christianity, as we have seen, by demonstrating that its myths objectively contain the highest forms of the absolute dialectic. Kierkegaard attacks this objectivism as being diametrically opposed to the nature of Christianity:

'If, then, Christianity is essentially something objective, then it is important for the observer to be objective; but if Christianity is essentially subjective, then it is a mistake for the observer to be objective. . . . If the speculative thinker is also a believer, (and this too is claimed), then he must have realized long since, that speculation can never have the same importance for him as faith. Precisely as a believer he is infinitely concerned about his own salvation and in his faith he is certain of it. (NB as certain as one can be as a believer, i.e. not once and for all, but daily, with the certainty of a faith inseparable from an undying, passionate interest.) And he will not erect his eternal bliss on his speculation, rather will he mistrust his speculation, lest it seduce him and lure him away from the certainty of faith (which contains the infinite dialectic of uncertainty at every moment) into the indifference of objective knowledge. These are the simple dialectical facts of the matter. Thus if he says that he erects his eternal bliss on the foundation of his speculation, he is the comic victim of contradiction, for in its objectivity speculation is utterly indifferent to his and my and your eternal bliss, whereas that bliss lies in the rapidly vanishing feeling of self that has taken such efforts to acquire. And at the same time he lies, giving himself out as a believer. . . . But for the man of speculation the question of his own personal eternal bliss cannot even arise, just because his task is to remove himself further and further from himself and to become objective, to vanish from himself and become the contemplative force of speculation.'[72]

We have given so much space to Kierkegaard's objections to Hegel because his position exposes Hegel's modern irrationalist interpreters better than any polemic. But, even more importantly, it reveals the existence of two divergent currents in modern idealism, both of which are concerned to bring about a revival of religion, but in radically opposed ways. It should be emphasized that both currents flow *within* idealism and that both should be combated in equal measure. But it would be a mistake to confuse them with each other and to overlook the social and philosophical distinctions between them.

Kierkegaard stands for the irrationalist revival of religion as a philosophy of life, a tendency that had manifested itself in Germany while Hegel was in Jena in Schleiermacher's *Discourses on Religion*, a work which Hegel had attacked in the course of his polemic against subjective idealism. This view of religion is based on an agnostic subjective idealism; it perceives that the old forms of religion are incompatible with the contents and methods of modern science and consequently it sets out to demarcate a sphere of subjectivity in which religion may flourish, in which religion may be assured of a continued existence as an elemental, inalienable manifestation of human subjectivity which for these thinkers was identical with human nature. Schleiermacher, and even Kierkegaard, imagined that it was possible to combine this mystical irrationalism with the subjectivist elements of Protestant theology. Their more recent successors, say from Simmel to Heidegger, renounce any such theological garniture and attempt to preserve religion only as a subjective life-form of man in general. Nevertheless, the basic agnostic and irrationalist emphasis remains constant, and in Heidegger, its latest and most consistent advocate, it reaches its climax in utter despair, in the outright denial that any objective knowledge can exist or be of value. (Similar tendencies appeared earlier in Klages.)[73]

Hegel's revival of religion, the culmination of his idealist philosophy in religion and theology has a different character and origin. As we have seen, it is objectivist. It establishes no hard and fast line between the knowledge of objective reality and itself; on the contrary, the value of religion in Hegel's eyes is precisely that it allows the highest objective categories of the dialectic to be expressed and even though the form in which it does this is inadequate, it nevertheless represents the penultimate stage before arriving at absolute knowledge.

These contrary tendencies naturally have differing origins. The revival of religion by Schleiermacher and Kierkegaard is an essentially modern phenomenon even though it may be traced back to earlier, rather differently constituted irrationalist philosophies of life, such as Jacobi's from whom it has borrowed a number of features. (The affinity between Schleiermacher and Jacobi was pointed out by Hegel in *Faith and Knowledge*.) It becomes the direct predecessor of the irrationalist currents that ultimately flow into the reactionary extremes of Fascist 'theories of myth'. Hegel's philosophy of religion, however, is the last philosophical manifestation of the *German* Enlightenment.

Our analysis has shown that wherever Hegel's ideas have been truly great and original they have been found to lie apart from the mainstream of German history. We have shown that wherever he was forced to take his German predecessors as a reference point he consistently broke through the limits imposed by Kantian problems and solutions, and that it was above all this that distinguished him from Fichte and Schelling who never escaped from that magic circle. Nevertheless, wherever the ideological consequences of the social condition of Germany set limits to Hegel's ideas, we find him falling heir to the Kantian tradition. In the case of his philosophy of religion this is not without its tragi-comic overtones. It will be remembered with what scorn Hegel had treated Kant's re-introduction of religion as the proper sphere for the realization of the postulates of practical reason (p. 19f.). Ironically, in his own philosophy of religion, Hegel now revives the Kantian salvage-operation—though on the higher level of objective idealism.

The affinity of method between the two lies in the circumstance that neither version of idealism is able to do justice to the dialectics of objective reality. This failure, which springs from the social condition of Germany of which idealism is the philosophical expression, now becomes obscured and concealed within the overall system. In Kant's case the denial that things-in-themselves can be known was complemented by his insistence on the absolute validity of the moral imperatives in 'practical reason'. The religion of reason provided a pseudo-objective realm in which these postulates might flourish, a realm of his own invention: Kant constructed an imaginary religious sphere so as to provide his moral postulates with a firm hold on reality. Hegel overcame this dualism both in the realm of epistemology (the knowability of the thing-in-itself) and in the relation of theory to practice (work and teleology). But this does not mean that he solved the problem of the ultimate objectivity of his dialectical categories. The principle of 'reconciliation', the actual transformation of substance into subject, the revoking of 'externalization', the supersession of the objective world in the identity of subject and object —none of this is to be found in reality itself. The development of religion in what we have seen to be a mystified form opens up the possibility of a new pseudo-reality and pseudo-objectivity on Kantian lines: a realm of historical development, the development of the human consciousness in which the categories of Hegelian thought themselves appear as moments of the movement of reality.

The German Enlightenment, unlike that of France or England, was never able to mount a resolute or radical attack on religion. Thanks to the backwardness of German society, it was always looking for a reconciliation between religion and the principles of reason, and strove to emasculate ordinary religion, reinterpreting it in accordance with its own principles, harmonizing it with the constantly changing conceptions of what constituted reason. In *this* sense, then, Hegel's philosophy of religion may be regarded as the continuation of Kant's and of the German Enlightenment in general.

Thus Hegel's philosophy of religion in all its ambiguity and inconsistency is part of the larger pattern of the German Enlightenment. It is not surprising, then, that it could dominate the intellectual scene only as long as economic forces did not accentuate internal class conflicts. In the 1840s when the struggles leading to bourgeois revolution became acute, Hegelian philosophy was forced to give up its position as mediator in the conflict between materialism, on the one hand, and romantic irrationalism, on the other. The fact that the dissolution of the Hegelian school

began with dissension on the subject of religion, leading on the one side
to reactionary dogmatism and on the other to the materialist criticism of
Hegel's position by Feuerbach, is anything but fortuitous—and the same
may be said of the summoning of Schelling to Berlin in 1843 to seal the
fate of Hegelianism as the official philosophy of the Prussian state.

From that time on Hegel's philosophy of religion ceased to play any
significant ideological role. It was utterly overtaken by events. Not just
in the sense that the progressive element in German ideology had superseded it; even the religious reaction was unable to establish contact with
Hegel's *real* philosophy of religion. Of course, this is the very aspect of
Hegel that modern neo-Hegelians seize upon. Their falsifications are of
many different varieties, but their level of philosophical argument is so
abysmal that debate with them is unrewarding. The above-mentioned
Kierkegaard-Heidegger reinterpretation of Hegel's philosophy which
brings it into line with modern irrationalism, is an extreme instance.
Kroner's view that Hegel is the 'greatest irrationalist' is merely an eclec-
tic variant of the same position, of this extreme modernist falsification of
Hegel, this adaptation to the ideological requirements of the Fascist
movement which was remoulding German philosophy in its own image.
Equally unworthy of discussion is Lasson's 'theory' of the Protestant
Hegel, whose works from the Berne fragments right up to his last writings are allegedly imbued with Protestant religiosity, for such a view
stands in glaring contradiction to all the known facts.

To point to the affinities between the positions of Kant and Hegel on
the philosophy of religion, their common origins in the failings and limitations of the German Enlightenment, does not of course imply that their
views were identical. We have already drawn attention to the chief
differences between them. What they amount to is that Hegel's ambivalence in this area is even more marked than that of Kant, which for
all its essential reservations remains within the framework of an enlightened deism.

Hegel's philosophy, notwithstanding all his protests, is overwhelm-
ingly pantheistic. The powerful impact of Spinoza on the thought of
the German Enlightenment at the end of the eighteenth century, beginning with Lessing, Herder and the young Goethe, called a general pantheistic trend into being. Within this trend there were varying
proportions of materialism. The advantage of pantheism was that it
gave German idealists the opportunity to analyse objective reality, both
nature and society, in a scientific manner, i.e. according to their own
immanent laws; it enabled them to reject out of hand all appeals to
another world, while permitting them to construct a general system in
which their idealist principles could achieve their necessary philosophical consummation in God. Hegel himself was always bitterly
opposed to descriptions of himself as a pantheist even though, as we

have seen from his critique of religion in the *Phenomenology*, its inadequacy in his eyes lay in the fact that in pantheism the dialectical forms do not manifest themselves as the laws of movement of the world, of the identical subject–object, but that they still retain the pictorial form of otherworldliness.

His ambiguity on the religious question expresses his reluctance to accept that this otherworldliness is the very essence of religion, i.e. he is concerned both to annul and to preserve religion. He will not see that a God who fulfils all the Hegelian requirements will cease to be the God of religion or theology. We are reminded here of Schopenhauer's *mot* that pantheism is the polite form of atheism, a polite stratagem for bowing God out of the universe. The irreducible ambiguity of classical German idealism, and of Hegel above all, is that they attempt to reconcile the irreconcilable: they deny that God created the world and that he rules over it, while at the same time they wish to salvage for philosophy certain religious conceptions inseparable from Him.

This peculiarity is not confined to Hegel. But since it was Hegel who raised the dialectic to its highest level, in this period, the contradictions arising from it are more glaring and irreconcilable than in other thinkers. It would be a mistake to think of them simply as the expression of Hegel's political accommodation to the retrograde condition of Germany. Characteristically, Marx consistently rejected such a view and always sought to explain the contradictions that led to it. This was his position right from the start, as early, in fact, as the *Dissertation* of 1840. Here, too, it becomes evident how Hegel's limitations are bound up with the limitations of German idealism in general.

Kant in his day had pointed to scepticism and dogmatism as the great dangers threatening philosophical thought and in his philosophy he explored the possibility of a third way that would avoid the pitfalls of the other two. The modern reader has no difficulty in seeing that this third way could only be the dialectical way, for this alone avoids the denial of objective truth (scepticism), striking a correct dialectical balance between the relative and the absolute. Similarly, it rejects philosophies which simply decree objective truths that cannot be scientifically based, i.e. it rejects every variety of pseudo-objectivity, pseudo-absoluteness (dogmatism). We know, from Hegel's criticism, if not from elsewhere, that Kant failed in his attempt. We know too how far Hegel advanced in his efforts to overcome the antinomies involved, in particular, his attempted definition of the correct dialectical balance between relative and absolute. Nevertheless, what he does ultimately is to reproduce the same dilemma at a very high level, without being able to arrive at a fully satisfactory solution.

The moment corresponding to scepticism at a level higher than that envisaged by Kant is that pattern in which the dialectic simply causes

opposites to synthesize aimlessly, without direction, without higher development; it is the pattern we have witnessed in the *Phenomenology* as
the dialectic of 'existence-for-self', the dialectics of Enlightenment.
Earlier on, in our discussion of 'Tragedy in the realm of the ethical' we
saw that the limitations of that dialectic were imposed by Hegel's inability to discern the direction that would be taken by the dialectical
contradictions that he had so perceptively observed in capitalism. Had he
consistently followed this argument through to its conclusion this stasis
would have led to a dialectical nihilism along the lines of Solger's. From
this standpoint we can understand why Schelling strives to connect scepticism with dialectics. Hegel, it is true, does not countenance scepticism,
but only

> 'the bacchanalian revel where not a member is sober; and where
> every member no sooner becomes detached than it *eo ipso* collapses
> straightaway.'[74]

It is in short the undirected flow of a stream of contradictions which are
constantly being broken up and reformed. From this angle it is finally
possible wholly to understand why Hegel locates this dialectic in the
'disintegrated consciousness', and why he thinks of the Enlightenment as
a crisis of the spirit.

This dialectic need not necessarily take romantic forms, as it does in
Solger. It is the dialectic propounded by Mephistopheles in Goethe's
*Faust*:

'Faust:            Who then are you?
Mephistopheles: Part of a good that would
                   Alone work evil, but engenders good.
Faust:            What  hidden  meaning  in  this
                   riddle lies?
Mephistopheles: The spirit I that endlessly denies.
                   And rightly too; for all that comes to birth
                   Is fit for overthrow as nothing worth;
                   Wherefore the world were better sterilized.'[75]

It is obvious that this diabolic philosophy comes fairly close to the
Hegelian version of the function of evil in history. More importantly,
Goethe too was unable to resolve the contradictions here. It is evident
that Faust, and with him Goethe, does not share Mephisto's 'dialectical scepticism', but it is no less clear (though for reasons of space we
cannot go into the matter here) that Goethe can only arrive at a positive solution in *Faust* at the level of myth.

This is a method of which we have seen all too much in the parts
of the *Phenomenology* that deal with religion. But Hegel's heroic
achievement in struggling for the dialectical truth amidst the 'manure

of contradictions' can be seen in the restraint with which, in his philosophical battles with Kant, Fichte and Schelling, he postpones the act of making a dogmatic decree to the last possible moment, developing the dialectical truth as far as possible from the internal movement of the contradictions in reality itself. In order to achieve this fully Hegel would have had to be able to see where the contradictions of capitalism, the 'bacchanalian revel', were leading. But he did not and could not have done so. He understood capitalism as the highest 'configuration' of the historical process to date; what would come after could only be vaguely formulated with the aid of empty idealist constructs. In this sense, we may apply to him what Marx said about the view of history to be found in classical economics:

'Thus there has been history, but there no longer is any.'[76]

This simple proclamation of the concluding positive truth of the system is a product of the social conditions in which and from which the Hegelian dialectic came into being. Its philosophical implications, however, are very complex. It has immediate consequences for his social and historical philosophy, but over and above that it has repercussions in the furthest and most abstract reaches of philosophy: in the problem of the criterion of truth. The older materialism rightly insisted on the criterion of correspondence between objective reality and man's view of it, on the correct reflection of an external world independent of consciousness. The limitation of this view, as Lenin has shown, was that it was unable to discover and hence articulate in philosophical terms, the dialectic involved in that process of reflection.

German idealism intervenes at precisely this moment. It finds itself confronted by the problem of the criterion of truth, a problem it is unable to solve. The question it cannot answer is: *with what* does a statement have to agree in order to be recognized as true? Kant now has to pay for his inconsistency in his approach to dialectics by finding himself compelled to fall back on formal logic as a guarantee of the criterion of truth: truth is to be found in the internal logical consistency of a proposition with itself. Of course, Kant makes other attempts to deal with the problem. But we have seen how at all decisive points he was compelled to have recourse to the apparently apodictic security of formal logic. This was particularly obvious in his failure to discover any other criterion with which to validate the categorical imperative. Hegel's criticism of the inadequacies and the defects of his arguments will be remembered from his discussion of the Kantian example of the deposit (p. 293ff.).

Objective idealism had necessarily to go in search of new criteria. Schelling discovered them in a revised form of the Platonic Idea: the criterion of truth would consist in a correspondence with these Ideas, since philosophical propositions and works of art, etc., are nothing but the reflections of these Ideas in the consciousness of man. What we have here, then, is a mystically inverted materialism; objective reality is mystified and translated into Platonic Ideas so that these in turn shall furnish a criterion of the truth. Despite these mystifications Schelling's *Philosophy of Art* contains vestiges of the epistemology of materialism as these have survived unconsciously in Schelling's mind, so that his book does mark a significant advance in aesthetics. But as early as his dialogue, *Bruno*, the mysticism gains the upper hand and leads straight to his later religious mysticism. His notion of 'intellectual intuition' as a 'quality of genius' vouchsafed to a few chosen people intensified the dogmatic and mystical tendencies in his thought.

Hegel's dialectical logic goes much further than the ideas of his predecessors. However, his advance is really no more than a postponement of the problem, enabling him to apply a theory of reflection on particular issues of epistemology, a theory to which his own premises do not entitle him. He can thus solve these particular problems only to find the whole dilemma recurring at the end of his system in a more acute form than ever. Hegel's logic shows on the one hand that the objects which seem to be so fixed and rigid are in reality processes, and, on the other hand, it regards the objective nature of the objects as products of 'externalization' on the part of the subject. Both do away with the Kantian problem of the thing-in-itself, the problem of the relation of an object to its attribute, whereas Fichte had hoped to eliminate it by decree and Schelling had attempted to achieve the same solution by the opposite decree. Now, by defining objects as alienations, 'externalizations' of the spirit, Hegel finds it possible simply to apply the theory of reflection to empirical reality without admitting it. Every thought can be compared to the corresponding reality—and the criterion is one that holds good on particular issues—even though this reality is viewed as not being really independent of consciousness, but as the product of the 'externalization' of a subject that is on a higher plane than individual consciousness. And since the process of 'externalization' is dialectical, Hegel's unintended and unconscious application of the materialist criteria of true knowledge sometimes advances his position beyond that of the old materialists themselves.

The difficulty arises only in connection with knowledge as a whole. Hegel emphasizes that knowledge is a process, that the absolute itself is a result of the overall process. But he obviously requires a criterion by which to gauge the truth of our knowledge of the overall process. And it is at this point that we can see how the highest concepts of the Hegelian dialectic in all their abstruse mysticism, nevertheless spring necessarily from his own premises. For if the objectivity of the world of objects is the product of a provisional disunity in the identical subject–object, then, inevitably, the criterion of the validity of the total process can lie only in the demonstration that subject and object are identical, in the self-realization of the identical subject–object. If, however, the starting-point of the spirit must be an identity on which the whole argument must be premised, and if the process itself consists in the creation of objects through 'externalization', then it is absolutely necessary for Hegel to close the circle by positing a recovery of that original identity of subject and object in the form of the retraction of 'externalization', the transformation of substance into subject and the annulment of objective reality as such.

Thus Hegel's dialectic has a prodigious advantage over other theories of knowledge in classical German idealism. For long stretches it can function with a theory of knowledge as a reflection of reality, which although illicitly acquired, nevertheless gains great scope for a comprehensive understanding of the external world and for the elaboration of the essential determinants of knowledge.

But it is no more than that. As far as the problem of knowledge in general is concerned Hegel can only offer the same sort of mystified and mystifying answers as his predecessors to the question *with what* an object of cognition should agree. We have repeatedly claimed that in certain decisive areas Hegel could not advance further than Schelling and this is undoubtedly true of the final stage, the apogee of his philosophy. Despite Hegel's ambiguous attitude towards religion itself, the limits of his theory of knowledge—whose social base has, we hope, now become sufficiently clear—strengthens and hardens out the religious and theological tendencies in his thought. For ultimately the pull of the forces governing society must carry the day.

'The *religious reflex* of the real world,' Marx observes, 'can in any case only then finally vanish, when the practical relations of everyday life offer to man none but perfectly intelligible and reasonable relations with regard to fellow men and to nature. The life-process of society, which is based on the process of material production, does not strip off its mystical veil until it is treated as production by freely associated men, and is consciously regulated by them in accordance with a settled plan.'[77]

## NOTES

1 *The Phenomenology of Mind*, p. 689.
2 *The German Ideology*, p. 38.
3 Haym, op. cit., p. 243.
4 *Feuerbach*, in Marx/Engels, *Selected Works*, Vol. II, p. 330.
5 *The Phenomenology of Mind*, pp. 89–91. The general context makes it quite clear that what concerns Hegel here is the relationship between the experience of the individual and the historical experience

of the species. He refers here to the individual as 'incomplete mind, a concrete shape in whose existence, taken as a whole, one determinate characteristic predominates, while the others are found only in blurred outline', ibid., p. 89. And in earlier discussions of the relation of individual to species he refers to the latter on one occasion as 'the supreme being' (*Jena Logic*, p. 158). There can be no doubt, then, that the modern reader may everywhere read 'species' for 'mind' or 'spirit' (*Geist*).

6    Op. cit., pp. 173–4.
7    *The Phenomenology of Mind*, pp. 799–800.
8    Ibid., p. 392.
9    *The German Ideology*, p. 661.
10    *The Phenomenology of Mind*, pp. 419–20.
11    This passage refers to the struggles of the Crusaders to recover the tomb of Christ.—*Trans.*
12    Ibid., pp. 252, 257, 258 and 259.
13    Ibid., p. 388.
14    Ibid., pp. 376–7.
15    Ibid., pp. 373–412.
16    Ibid., p. 377.
17    *Philosophy of Right*, p. 123.
18    *The Phenomenology of Mind*, p. 411.
19    Ibid., pp. 411–12.
20    *Capital*, Vol. I, p. 74.
21    *The Phenomenology of Mind*, p. 435.
22    Ibid., pp. 436–7.
23    Ibid., pp. 437–8.
24    Ibid., pp. 439–45 and 446–53.
25    Ibid., p. 460.
26    Ibid., p. 479.
27    Ibid., p. 460.
28    Ibid., p. 501.
29    Ibid., pp. 501–2.
30    Ibid., p. 502.
31    Ibid., pp. 503–4.
32    Ibid., p. 536. The reader will recollect the earlier definition of money as Ego, self. *Realphilosophie*, Vol. II, p. 257.
33    Ibid., p. 570.
34    Ibid., p. 567.
35    Ibid., pp. 540–1.
36    Ibid., pp. 541–3.
37    Ibid., p. 588.
38    Ibid., pp. 590–8.
39    Ibid., p. 594.

40   Ibid., pp. 594–5.
41   Ibid., p. 595.
42   Ibid., p. 596. Marx had a clear view of the Enlightenment principle of utility. Cf. *The German Ideology*, p. 460 et seq. Marx goes on to give an outline of the history of the theory from Hobbes to Bentham.
43   Ibid., pp. 597–8.
44   Ibid., p. 601.
45   Ibid., p. 608. Thus the 'tranquil' state of the world following the French Revolution does not imply a restoration, a return to the ancien régime. This is of great importance for Hegel's assessment of the German situation since Hegel constantly protests that his conception is not applicable to conditions in Germany. Thus in a marginal note in the Lectures of 1805–6 he comments: '*Guarantee* against arbitrary rule. General constitution of the estates—not local estates (*Landstände*)' i.e. not the form in which the estates existed in Germany at the time. *Realphilosophie*, Vol. II, p. 252.
46   Ibid., p. 451.
47   Ibid., p. 607.
48   Ibid., p. 610. The passage is quoted in a letter to Niethammer on 29 April 1814, op. cit., p. 372. It is of interest to note that he there underlined the phrase 'into another land', adding in brackets 'It was one *country* in particular that I had in mind.'
49   Ibid., pp. 611–79.
50   Ibid., p. 679.
51   *History of Philosophy*, Vol. I, ed. Glockner, p. 20.
52   Briefe von und an Hegel, p. 194.
53   *The Phenomenology of Mind*, pp. 753–4.
54   Ibid., p. 808.
55   Ibid., pp. 690–1.
56   Ibid., pp. 691–2.
57   *A Contribution to the Critique of Political Economy*, p. 217.
58   *The Phenomenology of Mind*, p. 792.
59   Ibid., p. 792.
60   Ibid., p. 797.
61   Ibid., pp. 709–49.
62   Ibid., p. 743.
63   Ibid., p. 745.
64   L. Feuerbach, *Grundsätze der Philosophie der Zukunft*, § 21, Works, op. cit., Vol. II, p. 301.
65   *The Phenomenology of Mind*, pp. 793–4.
66   *Grundrisse*, trans. D. McLellan, London 1971, p. 71.
67   *The Phenomenology of Mind*, pp. 769–70.
68   Ibid., p. 781.

69   Ibid., pp. 767–8.

70   Ibid., p. 372.

71   Ibid., pp. 783–4.

72   S. A. Kierkegaard, *Gesammelte Werke*, Jena 1910, Vol. VI, pp. 146ff.
Kierkegaard's radical rejection from an irrationalist point of view
does not deter modern scholars of Hegel in their attempts to make a
synthesis of the two thinkers and to interpret the *Phenomenology*
from a Kierkegaardian/Heideggerian standpoint. Apart from a
number of Germans (e.g. Karl Löwith), Jean Wahl has devoted a
whole book to this enterprise: *Le malheur de la conscience dans la philosophie de Hegel*, Paris 1929. Wahl's Kierkegaardism shows itself in
the fact that he places the Unhappy Consciousness at the very centre
of the *Phenomenology*. Either he does not or cannot see that it is one of
the 'configurations' of subjective, individual consciousness to which
the religion of Section C does occasionally refer back, as it does to
other earlier 'configurations of consciousness', but that in all essentials it proceeds in the opposite direction and, as we have seen,
regards the myths of religion as the repository of the objective categories of the dialectic. It is instructive, therefore, to contrast
Kierkegaard's own words with those of his modern admirers and
followers. We find the same situation as the one Lenin found when
he confronted the confused and over-circumspect utterances of
modern solipsists with the straightforward language of the old reactionary philosopher Berkeley. Kierkegaard, too, is a reactionary in
every sense but he has not yet degenerated into the eclecticism of his
modern successor; he speaks his mind openly and makes no attempt
to reconcile incompatible opposites.—On Kierkegaard's philosophy cf. my book: *The Destruction of Reason*, Berlin 1954, chap. 2, in
*Werke*, Vol. IX, pp. 219–69.

73   On Klages, cf. *The Destruction of Reason*, chap. 4.

74   *The Phenomenology of Mind*, p. 105.

75   *Faust*, trans. P. Wayne, Penguin 1951, p. 75.

76   *The Poverty of Philosophy*, London and Moscow, n.d., p. 135.

77   *Capital*, Vol. I, pp. 79–80.

# 'Entäusserung' ('externalization') as the central philosophical concept of The Phenomenology of Mind

BEFORE turning to a detailed analysis of the concept of 'externalization' it may be as well to recapitulate briefly the growth of the problem and the history of the concept in Hegel's works. It will be remembered that in his republican phase in Berne the term 'positivity' was used to describe an institution or a complex of ideas standing opposed in lifeless objectivity to the subjectivity, and above all the praxis of man. Even at that early date 'positivity' was used to define the specific character of modern society. At that time, however, Hegel contrasted it rigidly with the 'non-positive' age of Greek democracy. His philosophy of history culminated in the revolutionary hope that the revival of antiquity in and through the French Revolution would lead to a new era of freedom, and the true hegemony of man, an era without 'positivity'.

The disappointment of these hopes which triggered off the Frankfurt crisis in his thought brought in its wake a more historical and dialectical conception of 'positivity'. Modern institutions were no longer hopelessly 'positive' from the very outset, but instead Hegel became increasingly interested in discovering in detail just how something became 'positive', how the relations between man's social praxis and the institutions of society originate, how they decline and how they are transformed in the course of history. This greater concreteness went hand in hand with his study of the intellectual implications of English economic theory, with his deepening interest in the economic problems of capitalism and his growing insight into them. And we have seen also how Hegel gradually began to formulate his own specific concept of dialectics in the course of his own intellectual crisis. The further the process advanced and the more mature Hegel's own philosophy became, the more the concept of 'positivity' receded into the background. It never disappeared entirely, but, increasingly, it came to be used in the sense in which lawyers and theologians speak of positive law 'or positive theology. The philosophical generality of the Berne and Frankfurt periods vanished. Typically, however, the word 'positive' embodied in Hegel's philosophy could not allow the great age of an institution to be used to justify its further existence. For many years after the Jena period Hegel continued to treat this sort of 'positivity' as the lifeless detritus of history, to be cleared away as soon as possible.

Thus the maturing and deepening of Hegel's philosophy only eliminated the concept of 'positivity', not the problem to which it had referred in Frankfurt, namely the dialectical relation of the praxis of man in society to the objects he has created. It is not necessary to rehearse here the results of our analysis either of the social content or the philosophical terminology of Hegel's Jena period. In the course of his uninterrupted experimentation with terminology, what emerged more and more clearly was that the primal immediacy, the natural, has to be overcome and is overcome in the social praxis of man. It is replaced by a system of institutions created by man in the course of his own labours and endeavours., These labours not only create the institutions of society; they also transform the human subject since they annul his original immediacy, alienating the subject from itself.

In the course of his debate firstly with subjective idealism and later with objective idealism in its Schellingian form, Hegel developed a new terminology with which to describe these novel ideas and to translate into the general language of philosophy the social phenomena that he had come to understand in his study of history and economics. In this way concepts such as 'mediation' and 'reflection' acquired their specifically Hegelian significance. Likewise, the abstract theory of contradictions and their unity, first formulated in Frankfurt, evolved into the mature theory of the movement of contradictions and their supersession. In the course of this development the terms *Entäusserung* (externalization) and *Entfremdung* (alienation) came to occupy a central position in the Hegelian system. It is difficult to establish the exact chronology here. We noted that the Lectures of 1803–4 still operated to a great extent with Schelling's terminology. In the Lectures of 1805–6 the term *Entäusserung* occurs repeatedly, but is by no means dominant, although in both lecture courses, particularly the later ones, very many of the social and philosophical problems which become the problems of 'externalization' in the *Phenomenology*, are already present and given the sort of treatment they receive later, but without being gathered together under the general heading of 'externalization'. Not until the *Phenomenology* do we find the new conceptual system fully worked out and applied.

In themselves there is nothing novel about the terms *Entäusserung* and *Entfremdung*. They are simply German translations of the English word 'alienation'. This was used in works on economic theory to betoken the sale of a commodity, and in works on natural law to refer to the loss of an aboriginal freedom, the handing-over or alienation of freedom to the society which came into being as a result of a social contract. Philosophically, the term *Entäusserung* was first used, to the best of my knowledge, by Fichte for whom it meant both that the positing of an object implied an externalization or alienation of the subject and that the object was to be thought of as an 'externalized' act of reason.[1]

The same problem but with a different terminology turns up in the early works of Schelling. We quote his comments on it since they testify both to his flair for discerning new problems and to his extremism, his tendency to exaggerate his own dialectical insights until they suddenly harden out into sterile dogmas, very much in contrast to Hegel. Schelling uses the term 'to condition' (*bedingen*) to describe what Hegel will later call 'externalization'.

> 'To *condition* is the name we give to the action by virtue of which something becomes a *thing*; *conditioned (bedingt)* is what has become a thing *(Ding)*. And this makes clear at the same time that no thing can be posited *as a thing by itself*, i.e. an unconditioned thing (*ein unbedingtes Ding*) is a contradiction. For that which is *unconditioned* is something which has not been and cannot be made into a thing.'[2]

There can be no doubt that Schelling is touching upon the same problem with which Hegel had been so profoundly preoccupied. In contrast to Hegel, Schelling easily hits upon an elegant and ingenious solution which 'only' suffers from the slight defect that it opens up a yawning abyss between praxis and the object, thus rendering the entire problem intractable for Schelling himself. However, since these terminological experiments are merely episodes as far as Fichte and Schelling are concerned, episodes which exert no lasting influence on the problems with which they were most deeply concerned, there is no reason to deny Hegel the credit of having developed an original conceptual system in the *Phenomenology*, notwithstanding the use made of certain elements by his predecessors.

In the *Phenomenology* the term 'externalization' is deployed at a very high level of philosophical generality. It has flown far above its original use in economics and social theory. Nevertheless, it is possible to establish with some precision the various meanings given to it by Hegel and which derive from its original use as well as its later philosophical accretions.

We may in fact distinguish three stages in the Hegelian concept of 'externalization'. (1) It refers firstly to the complex subject–object relation inseparably bound up with all work and all human activity of an economic or social kind. What is involved here is the problem of the objectivity of society, of its development, of the laws governing that development, all this in the general context of the idea that men make their own history themselves. History, then, is regarded as a complex dialectical evolution of the human race, a process rich in contradictions and interactions, propelled by the praxis of socialized individuals. Hegel's achievement in establishing the dialectical relations between subjectivity and objectivity represents a prodigious step forward. On the one hand, it is a great advance on the old materialists who had been unable to reconcile the importance of subjective human praxis with the objectivity of what were largely thought of as 'natural' laws of society (e.g. the climate) and so were unable to move beyond the antinomies resulting from an exaggerated emphasis on one or other of these 'natural' phenomena. On the other hand, it is also a great advance on Kant and Fichte in whose writings necessity and objectivity constitute a world in themselves utterly alien to and different from freedom and praxis. As we have seen, Schelling made efforts to go a step further in his objective-idealist phase but his innovations turned out to be no more than obscure premonitions which were put forward in a declamatory rather than true philosophical manner.

(2) Secondly, there is the specifically capitalist form of 'externalization', i.e. what Marx would later call 'fetishism'. Naturally, Hegel has no clear insight into what is involved here, if only because his view of the economic base of class conflict does not go beyond an empirical division into rich and poor, and this is not sufficient for him to deduce any significant theoretical conclusions. But he undoubtedly has intimations of the problems arising from the fetishization of objects in capitalist society, and it must be stated that in this respect he stands alone in classical German idealism. Needless to say, the absence of a grounding in economic theory leads him constantly to confuse this class of 'externalized' social objectivity with the first, i.e. he regards many things as the products of social work, of human praxis in general, which are in actuality only the fetish-forms of objectivity specific to capitalism, and vice versa. Despite this defect which is one of the central foci of Marx's criticism there are undoubtedly powerful tendencies in Hegel to explain the fetishized objectivity of socio-economic formations in terms of the social relations between men.

Here, too, idealism leads Hegel badly astray and in the process of reducing social formations to human relations he frequently overlooks the mediating role of things. Frequently, but not invariably. This particular form of idealism occurs, to the best of my knowledge, earlier in Hegel than elsewhere, although it is not uncommon in early attempts to explain fetishized forms of objectivity. It becomes prominent, for example, in the break-up of the Ricardo School. Marx comments on it in his discussion of Hodgskin:

> 'The whole objective world, the "world of commodities", vanishes here as a mere aspect, as the merely passing activity, constantly performed anew, of socially producing men. Compare this "idealism" with the crude, material fetishism into which the Ricardian theory develops in the writings "of this incredible cobbler", MacCulloch, where not only the difference between man and animal disappears but even the difference between a living organism and an inanimate

object. And then let them say that as against the lofty idealism of bourgeois political economy, the proletarian opposition has been preaching a crude materialism directed exclusively towards the satisfaction of coarse appetites.'³

Of course, the profound differences between Hodgskin and Hegel should not be overlooked. Hodgskin is able to draw socialist conclusions from Ricardo's theory of value, albeit confused and contradictory ones. Hegel, as we saw, had not even understood all the problems and contradictions in Adam Smith's theories at the time when he was working on the *Phenomenology*. There can be no question of him deriving socialist ideas from there. And it goes without saying that Hodgskin is and had to be a good deal clearer and more penetrating than Hegel on all such questions. Nevertheless, there is no gain saying that Hegel's thoughts were moving powerfully in this direction and that he was the only thinker concerned to deduce philosophical conclusions from these economic facts.

(3) Thirdly, there is a broad philosophical extension of the concept 'externalization' which then comes to be synonymous with 'thinghood' or objectivity. This is the form in which the history of objectivity is portrayed: objectivity as a dialectical moment in the journey of the identical subject–object on its way back to itself via 'externalization'. Hegel says:

> 'The mind's immediate existence, *conscious life*, has two aspects
> —cognition and objectivity which is opposed to or negative of the
> subjective function of knowing. Since it is in the medium of consciousness that mind is developed and brings out its various moments,
> this opposition between the factors of conscious life is found at each
> stage in the evolution of mind, and all the various moments appear as
> modes or forms of consciousness. The scientific statement of the
> course of this development is a science of the *experience* through which
> consciousness passes; the substance and its process are considered as the
> object of consciousness. Consciousness knows and comprehends
> nothing but what falls within its experience; for what is found in experience is merely spiritual substance, and, moreover, *object* of itself.
> Mind, however, becomes object, for it consists in the process of becoming an *other to itself*, i.e. an *object for its own self*, and in transcending
> this otherness.'⁴

The essential tendencies of the mystification involved in the retraction of 'externalization' are already familiar to us. But we know too that by thinking of 'externalization' as a process and by regarding the absolute, the identical subject-object, as the end-product of that process, he opened up entirely new terrain in which to explore the implications of the essential dialectical determinations of objective reality 'so that, ultimately, the Hegelian system represents merely a materialism idealistically turned upside down in method and content.'[5]

It would be a grave error to take Engels' statement to imply that one had merely to turn Hegel the right, i.e. the materialist, way up again. Our investigations have shown that, on the contrary, quite crucial problems have been distorted by the idealist method and that in the treatment of individual issues, important insights continually rub shoulders with idealist distortions, sometimes even in the same sentence. It would also be wrong to focus on the large area opened up to analysis which we have emphasized for the sake of simplicity and clarity, as if all were well on the journey towards the absolute and the idealist mystifications intervened only at the very end. We believe that our earlier concrete analyses have shown such ideas to be misconceived. Here, we must confine ourselves to a statement of the most important problems.

The false equation of 'externalization' and 'thinghood' or objectivity leads Hegel to make quite false distinctions in his definition of nature and society and his attempt to distinguish between them. According to his view both nature and history are 'externalizations' of the spirit. But nature is an eternal externalization, its movement is a pseudo-movement, a movement of the subject; in Hegel's theory nature has no real history.

'This last form into which spirit passes, *nature*, is its living immediate process of development. Nature—spirit divested of self (externalized)—is, in its actual existence, nothing but this eternal process of abandoning its (nature's) own independent *subsistence*, and the movement which reinstates subject.'[6]

In contrast to this, 'externalization' in the social praxis of the human race, i.e. in history, is an 'externalization' of the spirit in time, that is to say, there is a real process of becoming and real history. Of course, in the end, as we shall see, even this turns out to be a pseudo-movement, despite Hegel's intentions. About this form of 'externalization', Hegel writes as follows:

'The other aspect, however, in which spirit comes into being, *history*, is the process of becoming in terms of knowledge, a *conscious self-mediating process*—spirit externalized and emptied into time. But this form of externalization is, similarly, the emptying of itself by itself; the negative is negative of itself. This way of becoming presents a slow procession and succession of spiritual shapes, a gallery of pictures, each of which is endowed with the entire wealth of spirit, and moves so slowly just for the reason that the self has to permeate and assimilate all this wealth of its substance. Since its accomplishment consists in spirit knowing *what it is*, in fully *comprehending* its substance, this knowledge means its *concentrating itself on itself (Insichgehen)*, a state in which spirit leaves its external existence behind and gives its embodiment over to recollection (*Erinnerung*).[7]

The immediate methodological implications of the distinction between the form assumed by 'externalization' in nature and history is
something we have already observed in the *Phenomenology*. In Section B
where Hegel focuses on real history, the problems of nature are as good
as non-existent. They are treated only in Sections A and C, and in the
latter, above all, Hegel's view of the objectivity of nature contributes in
no small measure to the mystifications of the problems of dialectics. But
over and above that, it spells the end of any real interaction between
nature and society, as well as the history of nature during the development of society. As a disciple of the Enlightenment Hegel is by no means
ignorant of the relations between nature and society and of those social
developments determined by natural conditions (such as the climate). In
his later philosophy of history these problems reappear, but only as part
of the general introduction to history on the substance of which they do
not really impinge.

Even more revealing is the fact that, great dialectician of history
though he was, he does not even mention the historical development of
nature itself, despite Kant's great discoveries in the field of cosmogony
(which, incidentally, remained quite without influence on Kant's own
philosophical system and failed to historicize his own view of nature).
Nor did the important efforts of some others of his contemporaries,
above all Goethe, to introduce the notion of development into the
organic world influence him in this direction.

There is, of course, a development of a sort in Hegel's philosophy of
nature, but it is precisely not historical: it does not unfold in time. Tem-
poral development is reserved by him for history in the narrower sense,
for the history of human society. This is not to deny the existence of contrary tendencies in his work. But they never get beyond the initial stages
whereupon they break off abruptly. In the *Jena Logic*, for example, there
is an incipient analysis of the earth in evolutionary terms as the theatre of
human history. However, the idea that there has been history, but there
is none any more, then makes its appearance with a vengeance: according to Hegel by the time human history is launched, the history of the
earth is completed and has ceased utterly to develop further. And even
while it was still developing the picture Hegel gives of it is highly contradictory. We quote his final summary since this is typical of the whole:

'The present moment reached by the earth in its cycle is one of immo-
bility, it has emerged from its process; in this moment it really is the
whole, and the character of determinate existence has been stamped
on it, a determinate existence, however, which endures, since it is
removed from time. . . . The earth, then, as this totality, represents
this image of process without the process itself. . . . The living process

of the earth is present only in its elements, not in its totality. . . . For this content, then, the process is something in the past; to infuse life into it through time and to represent the moments of its formation as a sequence, does not impinge upon its content.[8]

Since all of Hegel's statements on this theme are full of contradictions and since we have always found important dialectical and historical discoveries concealed beneath his mystifications it will not come as a surprise to learn that his over-sharp distinction between 'externalization', i.e. objectivity, in nature and in history also has its positive side, and that here too Hegel is on the track of important discoveries. His aim is to clarify the particular character of human existence and he is condemned to do so in an age when the thinkers closest to him in the field of the dialectics of objective idealism (Schelling and Goethe) were excessively preoccupied with nature. It was an age in which the ideas of such men were taken up and exaggerated and developed into a romantic, mystical cult of nature philosophy which threatened to engulf all efforts to achieve a really concrete analysis of the historical development of society in an all-consuming formalist mysticism of the 'eternal' and the 'natural'.

In circumstances such as these it is easy to understand how Hegel came to make such an abrupt distinction between nature and history, and even to make a moral issue of the superiority of spirit over nature. There is a very interesting statement to that effect in the Jena Lectures:

'In actual fact the individual spirit can depend on the energy of his own character and can assert his individuality, regardless of nature. His negative attitude towards nature although it differs from himself, scorns its power and in this scorn he holds nature at arm's length, preserving his freedom. And in fact the individual is only great and free in proportion to the extent of this contempt for nature.'[9]

This extreme expression of Hegel's position should not blind us to the fact that he is speaking here of the individual man who acts and that therefore his observations here do not cancel out or in any sense contradict his polemic against the violation of nature at the hands of the subjective idealism of Fichte.

Marx was fully appreciative of Hegel's attitude here, one which frequently recurs in his later works. Lafargue reports that Marx often quoted the following remark of Hegel's with approval:

'Even the criminal thought of a malefactor has more grandeur and nobility than the wonders of the heavens.'[10]

The aim of such paradoxical formulations is to make a sharp distinction between specific sides of man's social evolution and evolution in nature. And even if Hegel did not take the evolution of nature into account he nevertheless touched upon a fundamental determination of the evolution of society: the idea that men make their own history. Marx too endorses this distinction between the two forms of history, though of course within the context of a true appreciation of their objectivity and unity. Thus, for example, after talking of Darwin's idea of Nature's Technology he calls for a critical history of human technology:

'And would not such a history be easier to compile, since, as Vico says, human history differs from natural history in this, that we have made the former, but not the latter?'[11]

This side of human history was correctly intuited by Hegel, as by Vico, even though he failed to recognize, and hence mystified, the other side, the history of nature.

To recognize and to give Hegel the credit for having both constructed a rich and in many respects valid picture of human history and also for having discovered many of the essential determinations of historiography, is not to deny the distortions introduced by the mystificatory aspects of 'externalization'. Here, too, through his conception of the whole Hegel cancels out what he had so laboriously, thoroughly and ingeniously built up in the course of his analysis of the parts. We have already mentioned that the historical process as a whole has a definite goal, one which takes the form of its own self-annulment, its own return into the identical subject–object. Similarly, we have seen that Hegel thinks of history in general as an 'externalization' of spirit into time. Hence the reintegration of history in the absolute subject implies the annulment of time, which in its turn is the consequence of the annulment of objectivity. It is not the case that the dialectical process of history is suspended between two mystical points, with the beginning and end of time defined in terms of religious categories of the creation, etc. In Hegel's scheme, the beginning and end of the historical process coincide, i.e. the end of history is prefigured in its beginning. What we have here, then, is the same negation of a brilliant conception by an unbounded, all-engulfing process of generalization as we found in our discussion of Hegel's teleological ideas. He is quite explicit about this aspect of his historical scheme:

'But this substance, which is spirit, is the *development* of itself explicitly to what it is *inherently and implicitly*; and only as this process of reflecting itself into itself is it essentially and in truth *spirit*. It is inherently the movement which is the process of knowledge—the transforming of that *inherent nature* into *explicitness*, of *substance* into *subject*, of the object of *consciousness* into the object of *self-consciousness*, i.e. into an object that is at the same time transcended—in other words into the *concept*. This transforming process is a cycle that returns into itself, a cycle that presupposes its beginning, and reaches its beginning only at its end.'[12]

This end, however, is absolute spirit at its peak, as absolute knowledge, as philosophy. History is reduced to a process which is acted out in reality but which reaches its consummation, the goal immanent in it, the nature implicitly contained in it from the very beginning, only in philosophy, in a post-festum commentary on the path leading up to it. This idea is of such overwhelming significance for the view of history in the *Phenomenology* that it occupies a central position in the conclusion of the entire work:

> 'But *recollection (Er-innerung)* has conserved that experience, and is the inner being, and, in fact, the higher form of the substance. While, then, this phase of spirit begins all over again its formative development, apparently starting solely from itself, yet at the same time it commences at a higher level. The realm of spirits developed in this way, and assuming definite shape in existence, constitutes a succession, where one detaches and sets loose the other, and each takes over from its predecessor the empire of the spiritual world. The goal of the process is the revelation of the depth of spiritual life, and this is the *absolute concept*. This revelation consequently means superseding its "depth", is its "extension" or *spatial* embodiment, the negation of this inwardly self-centred ego—a negativity which is its self-relinquishment, its externalization, or its substance: and this revelation is also its *temporal* embodiment, in that this externalization in its very nature relinquishes (externalizes) itself, and so exists at once in its spatial "extension" as well as in its "depth" or the self. The *goal*, which is absolute knowledge or spirit knowing itself as spirit, finds its pathway in the recollection of spiritual forms as they are in themselves and as they accomplish the organization of their spiritual kingdom. Their conservation, looked at from the side of their free existence appearing in the form of contingency, is *history*; looked at from the side of their intellectually comprehended organization, it is the *science of the ways in which knowledge appears*. Both together, or history comprehended *(begriffen)*, form at once the recollection and the Golgotha of absolute spirit, the reality, the truth, the certainty of its throne, without which it were lifeless, solitary, and alone. Only
>
> > The chalice of this realm of spirits
> > Foams forth to God His own Infinitude.'[13]

This amounts to the self-annulment of history. History is transformed into the mere realization of a goal inherent in its subject, its spirit from the very outset. At the same time, its immanent reality is also annulled: history does not contain its own real autonomous laws of motion, but on the contrary, the latter only really exist and come into their own in the science that comprehends and annuls history, i.e. in absolute knowledge. But this annuls the whole scheme of history elaborated by objective idealism. The spirit which is supposed to make history and whose very essence is supposed to be the fact that it is the actual driving force, the motor of history, ends up by turning history into a mere simulacrum, as Marx has argued in *The Holy Family*:

> 'Hegel is . . . inconsistent . . . because according to him the absolute spirit makes history only in *appearance*. For as the absolute spirit becomes *conscious* of itself as the creative world-spirit only in the philosopher and *post festum*, its making of history exists only in the consciousness, in the opinion and conception of the philosopher, i.e. in the speculative imagination.'[14]

All this—and we have drawn attention only to the most essential points—is the necessary consequence of Hegel's concept of 'externalization'. It is at this point that the young Marx's great criticism of Hegel's central dilemma intervenes in the debate. This criticism is one of the crucial texts in the process of turning the idealist dialectic into a materialist one and in the criticism of Hegelian idealism. At the same time it is a *locus classicus* establishing continuity between the dialectical heritage and the new science of dialectical materialism.

In the *Economic and Philosophic Manuscripts* of 1844 Marx provides a comprehensive and systematic criticism of the Hegelian dialectic.[15] This criticism has two methodological characteristics of interest to us.

(1) In the first place, it concentrates on *The Phenomenology of Mind*, and within this, on Hegel's conception of 'externalization' and its supersession. This emphasis, meaningful in itself, can also be explained by reference to the polemical needs of the period, since the subjectivization of Hegelian philosophy carried out by the Young Hegelians, Bruno Bauer and Max Stirner in particular, was based largely on the *Phenomenology* and extends its mystification into realms not dreamt of by Hegel. The philosophical annihilation of this Left-Hegelianism was an important premise both of the new science of dialectical materialism and also of the theoretical and practical programme of the workers' party then in the process of formation. Marx's arguments here, then, are in a sense preparatory to the *Communist Manifesto*.

On the other hand, as we shall see, the critique of Hegel's concept of 'externalization' forms an important element of Feuerbach's criticism of Hegel and hence of the great shift from idealism to materialism that took place in Germany in the 1840s. Feuerbach's criticism is a concentrate of the virtues as well as the defects and limitations of Feuerbach's materialism. Marx's critique of Hegel's 'externalization' shows him entering into possession of the Feuerbachian heritage and at the same time we see him transcending the old materialism dialectically and leaving it behind.

(2) The second important characteristic of Marx's critique is that for the first time in Germany since Hegel himself it combines economic and philosophical perspectives in its treatment of the problems of society and philosophy. Needless to say, this functions at an incomparably higher level in Marx than in Hegel, and this is as true of the philosophical as of the economic aspect. Philosophically, as we know, the problem is the replacement of idealist by materialist dialectics. The critique of idealism here is based on a much greater knowledge of economics than was available to Hegel. Marx's economic observations already contain a *socialist critique* of the ideas of the classics of economic theory. (The brilliant essay of the young Engels in the *Deutsch–Französische Jahrbücher* had already appeared a little earlier.) And it is only this socialist criticism of capitalist economics and its scientific formulation in the works of the classics of economic theory that makes it possible to discover the real dialectical movement in the actual life of the economy, in the economic praxis of man. The rapid progress made by the young Marx and Engels in their study of the real dialectics of economic life soon laid the foundations for the criticism of the ideas which had sought to grasp that life: the classics of economic theory, on the one hand, and Hegel, on the other.

Thus Marx's emphasis on 'externalization' as the central concept of the *Phenomenology* and of idealist dialectics in general was not the result of an arbitrary decision. Hegel's inspired guess on the basis of very incomplete knowledge of economics enabled him to see that 'externalization', alienation, was a fundamental fact of life and *for that reason* he put it in the centre of philosophy. Marx's critique of Hegel proceeds from a more profound and accurate grasp of the *economic realities*. That is to say, it was first necessary to gain an understanding of the fundamental facts of economics on the basis of a socialist critique of the alienation of labour under capitalism before it became possible to assess the rights and wrongs, the essential truths and the mystifications of Hegel's interpretation of them.

The one-sidedness of Feuerbach's criticism of Hegel is due in great measure to the fact that he analysed and overcame Hegel's 'externalization' only in its ultimate philosophical consequences. He had no conception whatever of the process that led from reality itself to the philosophical conception and that threw up such a contradictory reflection in his philosophy. That is to say, he had no inkling of the connections between economics and philosophy. Hence his criticism remained one-sided, incomplete and abstract. Hence, too, despite his materialist opposition to Hegel's idealism, he was not really able to overcome the limitations and defects of Hegel's thought, for these ultimately were social and not philosophical; as we shall see they were closely bound up with the nature of bourgeois society.

The bond between economics and philosophy is, then, a profound necessity: it is the precondition of any real refutation of Hegel's idealist dialectic and for any further advance. For that reason it would be superficial to imagine that Marx's concern with Hegel begins only in the last portion of the Manuscript which contains the critique of the *Phenomenology*. The four preceding sections on economics, which do not expressly concern themselves with Hegel at all, are nevertheless the foundation on which that criticism is built: they provide the economic clarification of the real nature of alienation. We shall quote only a few of Marx's salient definitions. Marx takes as his point of departure the real facts of capitalist economics. He rejects every type of economic Robinsonade out of hand. For the latter explain the division of labour, exchange, etc., just as theology explains the origin of evil by means of the Fall, i.e. by assuming the existence of the very thing whose origins it is supposed to explain. On the basis of an analysis of the actual facts of capitalist economics Marx gives this definition of alienation as it is created in the labour process:

'This fact expresses merely that the object which labour produces—labour's product—confronts it as *something alien*, as a *power independent* of the producer. The product of labour is labour which has been embodied in an object, which has become material: it is the *objectification* of labour. Labour's realization is its objectification. In the sphere of political economy this realization of labour appears as *loss of realization* for the workers; objectification as *loss of the object* and *bondage to it*; appropriation as *alienation*, as *externalization*. . . . All these consequences result from the fact that the worker is related to the *product of his labour* as to an *alien* object.'[16]

Hegel is not even mentioned here by name and no philosophical inference is drawn from this economic analysis. But even a cursory glance is enough to reveal that these apparently descriptive remarks in fact contain a fundamental critique of Hegel's philosophy. For alienation is sharply distinguished from objective reality, from objectification in the act of labour. The latter is a characteristic of work in general and of the relation of human praxis to the objects of the external world; the former is a consequence of the social division of labour under capitalism, of the emergence of the so-called free worker who has to work with the means of production belonging to another and for whom, therefore, these means of production as well as his own product exist as an independent, alien power.

Now when we examine the process of labour itself, this fundamental aspect of capitalist society appears to be doubly intensified and concentrated in the person of the worker. Marx emphasizes here above all,

'the fact that labour is *external* to the worker, i.e. it does not belong to his essential being; that in his work, therefore, he does not affirm himself but denies himself, does not feel content but unhappy, does not develop freely his physical and mental energy but mortifies his body and ruins his mind. The worker therefore only feels himself outside his work, and in his work feels outside himself. He is at home when he is not working, and when he is working he is not at home.'

This results in the inversion of all human values:

'What is animal becomes human and what is human becomes animal. Certainly, eating, drinking, procreating, etc., are also genuinely human functions. But abstractly taken, separated from the sphere of all other human activity and turned into sole and ultimate ends, they are animal functions.[17]

In this way alienation permeates the entire subjective and objective reality of human life. Objectively, the product of labour appears as an alien thing ruling over man; subjectively, the process of labour is a self-alienation corresponding to the alienation of the thing described above.

From these premises, all of which without exception are the product of a close examination of economic realities, he comes to the following conclusions about the relation of the individual to the species in capitalist society:

'In alienating from man (1) nature, and (2) himself, his own active functions, his life activity, alienated labour alienates the *species* from man. . . . Firstly, it alienates the life of the species and individual life, and secondly it makes individual life in its abstract form the purpose of the life of the species, likewise in its abstract and alienated form.'[18]

It is obvious that such insights into the alienation of labour with all its human and social consequences could only be obtained through a socialist criticism of capitalism. This circumstance enables us to appreciate the full implications of Marx's statement that Hegel does indeed stand on the heights of classical economic theory and that he has a genuine understanding of work as the process by which man creates himself, but that he has no insight into the negative aspects of work in capitalist society since he only considers its positive sides. Marx's whole criticism of the fundamental concepts of the *Phenomenology* is based on this assertion: since Hegel does not see the negative aspects of work, he becomes guilty of false distinctions and false syntheses, of the mystifications of idealism. The discovery of the true dialectics of labour in capitalist society is the precondition for a materialist critique of the philosophy which developed a one-sided view of labour and made it into the foundation of a general philosophy of the evolution of the human race.

We have already referred to Marx's comment that Hegel's philosophy contains a tendency towards an 'uncritical idealism'. This 'uncritical idealism' is expressed—and here we are already poised at the centre of the critique of the *Phenomenology*—in Hegel's view of what philosophy is. Hegel speaks of 'externalization' and its annulment by philosophy. He does not suspect, however, that the philosophy which is supposed to annul 'externalization' is itself an egregious instance of 'externalization':

'. . . the philosophic mind is nothing but the alienated mind of the world thinking within its self-estrangement—i.e., comprehending itself abstractly. *Logic* (mind's *coin of the realm*, the speculative or *thought-value* of man and nature—their essence grown totally indifferent to all real determinateness, and hence their unreal essence) is *externalized thinking*, and therefore thinking which abstracts from real man: *abstract* thinking.'[19]

Hegel does not perceive this and by failing to notice that alienated thought is alienated and by regarding it, indeed, as the very instrument by which alienation can be annulled, he succumbs to an uncritical idealism and turns the true pattern of alienation on its head. Consistently with this, Hegelian idealism identifies man with his self-consciousness.

'All alienation of human essence is therefore *nothing but alienation of self-consciousness*. The alienation of self-consciousness is not regarded as an *expression* of the *real* alienation of the human being—its expression reflected in the realm of knowledge and thought. Instead, the *real* alienation—that which appears real—is according to its *innermost*, hidden nature (a nature first brought to light by philosophy) nothing but the *manifestation* of the estrangement of the real essence of man, of *self-consciousness*. The science which comprehends this is therefore called *Phenomenology*. All reappropriation of the alienated objective essence appears, therefore, as a process of incorporation into self-consciousness: The man who takes hold of his essential being is *merely* the self-consciousness which takes hold of objective essences. Return of the object into the self is therefore the reappropriation of the object.'[20]

Marx's critical comments show succinctly how the false identification of man and self-consciousness necessarily springs from a false view of alienation in society. On the subjective side, there is the mistaken identification of man and self-consciousness demonstrated and criticized by Marx; on the objective side, there is the equation of alienation and objectification in general.

In his discussion of economics Marx, drawing on his knowledge of the empirical evidence, distinguishes sharply between objectification in work in general and the alienation of subject and object in the *capitalist form* of work. Armed with this distinction he can expose Hegel's erroneous equation. He proffers the following criticism of the methodological foundations of the *Phenomenology*:

> 'It is not the fact that the human being *objectifies himself inhumanly*, in opposition to himself, but the fact that he *objectifies himself* in *distinction* from and in *opposition* to abstract thinking, that constitutes the essence of the alienation and the thing to be superseded.'[21]

Hegel's false problem, with which we are now thoroughly familiar from our discussion of the *Phenomenology* and its antecedents, is followed by the equally false culmination of his philosophy in the annulment of objectivity:

> 'The task, therefore, is to surmount the *object of consciousness. Objectivity* as such is regarded as an *alienated* human relationship which does not correspond to the *essence of man*, to self-consciousness. The *reappropriation* of the objective essence of man, begotten in the form of alienation as something alien, therefore not only as the annulment of *alienation*, but of *objectivity* as well. Man, that is to say, is regarded as a *non-objective, spiritual* being.'[22]

We can see quite clearly here how the false idealist problem with its equally false idealist solution springs necessarily from Hegel's no less necessarily one-sided and incomplete interpretation of capitalist society. It is no less clear that this, the highest form of idealist dialectics, can only be wholly superseded if and when a socialist critique of capitalist economics has been rendered practicable by the emergent possibility of a real annulment of capitalist alienation.

Marx now goes on to oppose a materialist theory of objectivity to the idealist theory of the annulment of objectivity. It must be noted right away, and we shall return to it later, that Marx's materialist theory explains both capitalist alienation and its annulment and for that reason is in a position to give a more complete and comprehensive refutation of Hegel's idealism than was Feuerbach. Since Feuerbach had paid no heed to this social problem he failed to register the valid aspects of the Hegelian theory and furthermore he fell into the same errors as Hegel himself, though starting from an opposed point of view. The quintessence of Marx's materialist theory of objectivity is as follows:

> 'Whenever real, corporeal *man*, man with his feet firmly on the solid ground, man exhaling and inhaling all the forces of nature, *establishes* his real, objective *essential powers* as alien objects by his externalization, it is not the *act of positing* which is the subject in this process: it is the subjectivity of *objective* essential powers, whose action, therefore, must also be something *objective*. An objective being acts objectively,

and he would not act objectively if the objective did not reside in the very nature of his being. He creates or establishes only *objects, because* he is established by objects—because at bottom he is *nature*. In the act of establishing, therefore, this objective being does not fall from his state of "pure activity" into a *creating of the object*; on the contrary, his *objective* product only confirms his *objective* activity, establishing his activity as the activity of an objective, natural being. . . . *To be* objective, natural and sensuous, and at the same time to have object nature and sense outside oneself, or oneself to be object, nature and sense for a third party, is one and the same thing. . . . An unobjective being is a nullity—an *un-being*."[23]

Thus Marx's materialist criticism of Hegel's idealism is based on his account of the real premises of human thought and human praxis, as opposed to the alleged absence of premises in absolute idealism. The comparison also exposes the real premises of absolute idealism. In this sense, too, then, materialist dialectics are the truth of objective idealism. They not only annihilate it critically, but also deduce the source of its mistakes and use this discovery to clear the way for its real supersession, i.e. to an annulment which also conserves its essential and valid insights. By opposing the real premises of philosophy, the real facts of existence (of nature, economics and history) to the mystified premises of objective idealism, and by inferring the correct philosophical conclusions from the accurate dialectical reflection of these facts, Marx reveals that both the 'uncritical idealism' and the 'uncritical positivism' of Hegel are the necessary consequence of his social existence. It then becomes plain 'of its own accord' how and why Hegel was able to work within the framework of these idealist mystifications and to make so many discoveries not just about economics and history but also about the dialectical laws of objective reality in general; it becomes plain, in short, how Hegelian dialectics were able to serve as the immediate prototype of materialist dialectics. The decisive factor, as we have observed, was that Hegel thought of work as the self-creating process of man, of the human species.

It is on the basis of this recognition that Marx formulates his most penetrating criticism, focusing unerringly on the points at which Hegel's insights are distorted by the mystical form in which they appear. We have already quoted Marx's criticism that the course of history is really only an apparent movement in Hegel. Our point then was that the annulment of objectivity in absolute knowledge had the consequence that the Hegelian 'bearer' of history, the absolute spirit, did not really make history as Hegel imagined, but only seemed to do so. Proceeding from the criticism of Hegel's theory of objectivity Marx now mounts a frontal attack on the mystifications in the entire theory of a 'bearer' of history, which is itself the foundation of the idealist mystification of history itself.

> 'This process must have a bearer, a subject. But the subject first emerges as a result. This result—the subject knowing itelf as absolute self-consciousness—is therefore *God—absolute spirit—the self-knowing and self-manifesting idea*. Real man and real nature become mere predicates—symbols of this esoteric, unreal man and of this unreal nature. Subject and predicate are therefore related to each other in absolute reversal—a *mystical subject–object* or a *subjectivity reaching beyond the object*—the *absolute subject* as a *process*, as *subject alienating itself* and returning from alienation into itself, but at the same time retracting this alienation into itself, and the subject as this process; a pure *restless* revolving within itself.[24]

Real history, according to Hegel, is thus made to depend on an abstract, imaginary, mystificatory 'bearer' which, it goes without saying, can only 'make' history in an abstract, imaginary, mystificatory fashion. The real process, the real determinants of the process can only, as it were, sneak in through the back door. The fact that they dominate the particular, concrete stages of history is what creates that contradictory image which we have now analysed at length.

More than a decade later, Marx returns to the same question, no longer in the context of a critique of the *Phenomenology*, but instead as part of a comprehensive assessment of the philosophical foundations of Hegel's idealism as a whole. In the great Introduction to the *Contribution to the Critique of Political Economy* Marx analyses the various complementary and interconnected modes of reflecting, of coming to grips with objective reality, and in the course of his discussion he compares the real, materialist approach with Hegelian illusions:

> 'The concrete concept is concrete because it is a synthesis of many definitions, thus representing the unity of diverse aspects. It appears, therefore, in reasoning as a summing-up, a result, and not as the starting-point, although it is the real point of origin, and thus also the point of origin of perception and imagination. The first procedure attenuates meaningful images to abstract definitions, the second leads from abstract definitions by way of reasoning to the reproduction of the concrete situation. Hegel accordingly conceived the illusory idea that the real world is the result of thinking which causes its own synthesis, its own deepening and its own movement; whereas the method of advancing from the abstract to the concrete is simply the way in which thinking assimilates the concrete and reproduces it as a concrete mental category. This is, however, by no means the process of evolution of the concrete world itself.'[25]

This then is Marx's critique of Hegel in its maturest form.

This comprehensive analysis of Hegel's conception of alienation makes it possible for Marx to provide a materialist critique of that other fundamental concept, supersession. Once again, it is important to bear in mind that when Marx subjects idealist dialectics to criticism and transcends it critically, importing its valuable elements into materialist dialectics, he is *exclusively* concerned with idealism in its Hegelian form. Thus in the problem under discussion Marx utterly ignores Schelling's definition of 'supersession': the destruction of the annulled determinations, their annihilation through their elevation into the absolute. Nor does he so much as mention the Kantian variant of agnostic antinomy. Marx regards Hegelian dialectics as the complete and definitive answer to all earlier versions. Accordingly it is with the Hegelian conception that he takes issue, i.e. with that highest form of 'supersession' in which the annulled determinations are not simply negated but also conserved at a higher level, a 'supersession' in which otherness is not annihilated in the absolute but finds its existence and its relative justification respected. Hegel's definition of 'externalization', unlike that of Schelling, has a positive connotation since it creates objectivity and it is this that Marx takes as his point of departure, taking it as read that the discussions of Hegel with his predecessors had been resolved in Hegel's favour. Marx goes on to examine the defects of Hegel's version of 'supersession' and comes to this conclusion:

'On the other hand, says Hegel, there is here at the same time this other moment, that consciousness has just as much annulled and re-absorbed this externalization and objectivity, being thus *at home* in its *other-being as such*.

'In this discussion are brought together all the illusions of speculation.

'*First of all*, consciousness, self-consciousness is *at home in its other being as such*. . . . This implies for one thing that consciousness (knowing as knowing, thinking as thinking) pretends to be directly the other of itself—to be the world of sense, the real world, life. . . . This aspect is contained herein, inasmuch as mere consciousness takes offense not at alienated objectivity, but at *objectivity as such*.

'*Secondly*, this implies that self-conscious man, in so far as he has recognized and annulled and superseded the spiritual world (or his world's spiritual, general mode of being) as self-alienation, nevertheless again confirms this in its alienated shape and passes it off as his true mode of being—re-establishes it, and pretends to be *at home in his other-being as such*. Thus, for instance, after annulling and superseding religion, after recognizing religion to be a product of self-alienation, he yet finds confirmation of himself in *religion as religion*. Here is the root of Hegel's false positivism, or of his merely apparent criticism:

this is what Feuerbach designated as the positing, negating and re-establishing of religion or theology—but it has to be grasped in more general terms. Thus reason is at home in unreason as unreason. The man who has recognized that he is leading an alienated life in politics, law, etc., is leading his true human life in this alienated life as such. Self-affirmation, in *contradiction* with itself—in contradiction both with the knowledge of and with the essential being of the object—is thus true *knowledge* and *life*.

'There can therefore no longer be any question of an act of accommodation on Hegel's part *vis-à-vis* religion, the state, etc., since this lie is the lie of his principle.'[26]

Here, then, we have the profoundest criticism precisely of Hegel's most positive and significant ideas. Marx exposes the ultimate philosophical implications of Hegel's position vis-à-vis capitalist society in so far as these are reflected in the abstract problems arising from the dialectical structure of his philosophy. We have ourselves drawn attention to some of these contradictions and have shown how they have their roots in the society of his age, as well as in his attitude towards it. Now we see the purely philosophical consequences to which these social contradictions had to lead and did lead in actual fact. Now, too, we can see that all criticism of Hegel's ambiguous stance on problems of religion, the state, etc., that was based on a dualism between his esoteric and exoteric philosophy was bound to miss the central problems. This is so regardless of the fact that subjectively, as we saw, Hegel was from time to time not unaware of such a cleavage in his thought; for the contradictions, the problematic nature of his philosophy, reach into the very centre even of his exoteric ideas. Of course, it is and will remain for the student of the history of philosophy to establish where, when and how in particular questions Hegel made any concessions to the society of his day. But any such historical analysis must make it quite clear that whatever answers it comes up with, will not touch the central issue of the problematic nature of the Hegelian dialectic.[27]

The profundity of Marx's criticism is apparent from the way in which it moves from the problems of actual life to the most abstract questions of the Hegelian dialectics, solves them finally in terms of dialectical materialism and then moves on at once, finding an immediate connection with the problems of real life. What we are concerned with here is the central problem of the whole philosophy of Hegel, what Engels called the contradiction between method and system.

This contradiction embraces further contradictory attitudes on the question of human progress and, specifically, on the question of the position of capitalism in history in general, and in German history in particular. The question of supersession is on the one hand one of the ultimate and most abstract components of the dialectic, but on the other hand it is of the greatest importance for his philosophy of history and society. The mixture of progressive and reactionary tendencies in Hegel crystallizes out in the contradictions contained in the dialectical process of supersession, contradictions which have been analysed and criticized by Marx in the passages just quoted.

The socialist critique of 'externalization' has exposed the real alienation contained in the capitalist form of work, an alienation that has to be annulled in reality. Expressing this critique in general philosophical terms, we see that since the Hegelian concept of 'externalization' implies that consciousness is at home in its other-being as such, it *eo ipso* contains an important reactionary element, a vindication of what exists even if it has been overcome historically. The fact that Hegel also exhibits the opposite tendency and repeatedly follows it up simply confirms the accuracy of Marx's and Engels' diagnosis of an indissoluble contradiction between system and method.

This contradiction and the tendencies contained within it played a crucial role in the great ideological debates of the 1840s which prepared the ground for democratic revolution. What we find there are two different interpretations of Hegel's views, both of which lead to political passivity, to the non-comprehension of the concrete problems of the democratic revolution and beyond that—in theory—of revolution in general. The general significance of these problems far exceeds the importance of the debates of the 1840s, for the misconceptions we are concerned with are rooted in capitalism and it is only their intellectual form that is determined by the arguments surrounding Hegel's view of dialectical supersession. The first of these views is the direct continuation of Hegelian idealism; it involves the further subjectivization, the exaggeration of Hegel's idealistic misconceptions by the Young Hegelians. The other tendency arises from the epistemologically correct but abstract and one-sided critique of Hegel's supersession by Feuerbach himself.

Let us begin with the first position. Since, according to Hegel, 'externalization' is ultimately the 'externalization' of consciousness, it ought to be superseded *exclusively* by consciousness, *within* consciousness. In Hegel himself the identity of absolute knowledge and the philosopher who possesses it remained in the half-light. His objectivism prevented him from making this identity into a simple personal union. But the tendency was nevertheless implicit in his position. Once again it was Heinrich Heine who with irony and self-irony took the matter to its logical conclusion:

> 'I was never an abstract thinker and I accepted the synthesis of Hegel's doctrine without questioning it, since its consequences flattered my conceit. I was young and proud and it pleased my vanity when I

learned from Hegel that the God residing in Heaven was not God, as
my grandmother imagined, but that I living here on earth, was He.'[28]

What Heine said ironically was taken up in Bruno Bauer's *Philosophy
of Self-Consciousness* and turned into a philosophical and political doctrine which exercised a dangerous and pernicious influence on the left-
wing German intelligentsia, as well as on the emergent proletarian party
(via the detour of 'True Socialism').

If we examine Marx's penetrating criticism of Bauer's view in *The
Holy Family*, we can see how it grows directly out of his criticism of
Hegel's view of 'supersession'. We should note, however, that Bauer's
intellectual arrogance, his overweening contempt for the action of the
masses in history is something that has grown out of Hegel's philosophy
and his view of history, but it appears in Bauer without Hegel's important progressive and realistic tendencies and instead it takes Hegel's idealism to an extreme of subjectivity. Marx discusses Bauer's views in these
terms:

> 'The enemies of progress *outside* the mass are precisely those *products* of
> *self-debasement, self-rejection* and *self-alienation* of the *mass* which have
> been endowed with independent being and a life of their *own*, The
> mass therefore rises against its own deficiency when it rises against the
> independently existing *products* of its *self-debasement* just as man, turn-
> ing against the existence of God, turns against his *own religiosity*. But as
> those practical self-alienations of the mass exist in the real world in an
> external way, the mass must fight them in an *external* way. It must by
> no means consider these products of its self-alienation as mere *ideal*
> fancies, mere *externalizations of self-consciousness*, and must not wish to
> abolish *material* alienation by a purely *inward spiritual* action. As early
> as 1789 Loustalot's journal gave the motto:
>
> > The great appear great in our eyes
> > Only because we kneel.
> > Let us rise!
>
> 'But to rise it is not enough to do so *in thought* and to leave hanging
> over our *real sensual* head the *real palpable* yoke that cannot be subti-
> lized away with ideas. Yet Absolute Criticism has at least learnt from
> Hegel's *Phenomenology* the art of changing *real objective* chains that
> exist *outside me* into *mere ideal*, mere *subjective* chains existing *in me*, and
> thus to change all *exterior* palpable struggles into pure struggles of
> thought.'[29]

It is not necessary to provide further evidence in support of the proposition that Bauer's ideology grows out of Hegel's 'externalization' and
its supersession. Nor of the political danger inherent in such views, to say

nothing of the persistence of the ideology of passivity among an arrogant intelligentsia in capitalist societies, an ideology which endures to this day, though of course it has long ceased to base itself on Hegelian philosophy. But Hegelianism does lend itself to such use, as we can see not just from the history of the 1840s but also—and in particularly extreme and grotesque forms—in the neo-Hegelianism of the Imperialist age.

To turn to the second form, viz. Feuerbach's critique of the Hegelian dialectic, it is important to consider Marx's attitude. Marx thinks that what was important and original in Feuerbach's analysis was that he showed how Hegel's supersession in fact entailed the reinstatement of what had been superseded. We have already quoted the crucial passage from his critique in another context (p. 518f.) Marx praised Feuerbach for proving that Hegel's philosophy amounted to a reinstatement of religion. Furthermore, he admired Feuerbach's advance to a true materialism and, lastly, his critique of supersession, of the negation of negation. We shall confine ourselves to this latter point. Feuerbach was right

'in opposing to the negation of the negation, which claims to be the absolute positive, the self-supporting positive, positively based on itself.'[30]

This positive represents the priority of existence over consciousness. According to Feuerbach the process of supersession in Hegel's dialectic inverts the relation of existence to consciousness. He goes on to show how this idealist inversion leads to the reinstatement of religion by philosophy. Marx summarizes Feuerbach's position in this way:

'Feuerbach thus conceives the negation of the negation *only* as a contradiction of philosophy with itself—as the philosophy which affirms theology (the transcendental, etc.) after having denied it and which it therefore affirms in opposition to itself.'[31]

Marx accepts this, the materialist side of Feuerbach's criticism, but he immediately qualifies his praise by pointing out its one-sidedness. This consists, on the one hand, in the fact that Feuerbach treats 'externalization' purely as a philosophical problem so that he too sticks fast in abstraction (cf. Marx's and Engels' later criticism of the abstractness of Feuerbach's 'man'). On the other hand, Feuerbach's materialist view of reality is not dialectical so that he overlooks Hegel's real insights because of their idealist form and so rejects the whole of Hegel's dialectic, the good along with the bad. Thus as Marx emphasizes in the last quotation, Feuerbach can only see the weaknesses of Hegel's idealism in the negation of the negation, 'which he directly and immediately confronts with the position of sense-certainty based on itself'.

Feuerbach's self-imposed restriction to epistemology is the source of his abstractness; the direct, conscious exclusion of all mediations does away with Hegel's dialectics as well as his idealism. This is why Feuerbach ignores the most important and crucial determinations of Hegel's philosophy. Marx adds:

'But because Hegel has conceived the negation of the negation, from the point of view of the positive relation inherent in it, as the true and only positive, and from the point of view of the negative relation inherent in it as the only true act and self-realizing act of all being, he has only found the *abstract, logical, speculative* expression for the movement of history; which is not yet the *real* history of man—of man as a given subject, but only man's *act of creation*—the story of man's origin.'[32]

Thus the socialist criticism of capitalism discerns in Hegel's *Phenomenology* some of the essential and correct definitions of the process that Marx was later to call the 'pre-history' of mankind. Feuerbach, however, is no less imprisoned within the horizon of the bourgeoisie than Hegel, albeit from a very different standpoint, and so he can only deal with Hegel's thought in terms of an absolute Either/Or. In his account of the *Phenomenology*, Marx refers to a number of passages where Hegel correctly understood certain specific features of the 'pre-history' of mankind. And he shows, further, that although the concepts of alienation and supersession are distorted by idealism and given a reactionary colouring in Hegel, they are not utterly false, as Feuerbach believed, but are a one-sided reflection of reality, deformed and inhibited by the capitalist perspective, whose correct intuitions, however, were worthy of preservation:

'The *Phenomenology* is, therefore, a hidden and mystifying criticism—still to itself obscure; but inasmuch as it grasps steadily man's *alienation*, even though man only appears in the shape of mind, there lie concealed in it *all* the elements of criticism, already *prepared* and *elaborated* in a manner often rising far above the Hegelian standpoint. The Unhappy Consciousness, the Honest Consciousness, the struggle of the Noble and Base Consciousness, etc. etc.,—these separate sections contain, but as yet in an alienated form, the *critical* elements of whole spheres such as religion, the state, civil life, etc.'[33]

Thus Marx's really comprehensive criticism of Hegel's dialectic grows into a criticism of Feuerbach's one-sided and myopic judgement of Hegel, and that leads to a criticism of Feuerbach's metaphysical materialism and of his rejection of dialectics. The point of interest to us is that in the debates of the 1840s the Feuerbachian critique of Hegel's idealism had very dangerous political repercussions. For although Feuerbach's critique of the negation of the negation is based on the immediate sensuousness of material life, he is unable to grasp the dialectical movement within that material life. As Marx points out in the *Theses on Feuerbach* he is unable to comprehend sensuousness in its practical implications.

'The chief defect of all hitherto existing materialism (that of Feuerbach included) is that the thing, reality, sensuousness, is conceived only in the form of the *object or of contemplation*, but not as *sensuous human activity, practice*, not subjectively. Hence, in contradistinction to materialism, the *active* side was developed abstractly by idealism—which of course does not know real, sensuous activity as such. Feuerbach wants sensuous objects, really distinct from the thought objects, but he does not conceive human activity itself as *objective* activity. Hence, in *Das Wesen des Christenthums*, he regards the theoretical attitude as the only genuine human attitude, while practice is conceived and fixed only in its dirty-Jewish manifestation. Hence he does not grasp the significance of "revolutionary", of "practical-critical" activity.'[34]

This makes it very clear that the analysis of economic concepts, the precise distinction between objectivity and alienation in human praxis prepared the ground for a critique not only of Hegel's idealism but also of Feuerbach's mechanical materialism.

It is important to give a brief account of the implications of Feuerbach's position in the ideological and political struggles of the 1840s. Engels has provided a clear definition (and trenchant criticism) of the crucial aspect of Feuerbach's stance vis-à-vis the real world. He quotes the following passage from Feuerbach's *Philosophy of the Future*:

'Existence is not a general concept which can be separated from things. . . . Existence is the positing of essence. *My essence is my existence.* . . . Even language identifies existence and essence. Only in human life is existence divorced from essence—*but only in exceptional, unhappy cases*; it happens that a person's essence is not in the place where he exists, but just because of this division his soul is not truly in the place where the body really is. *You are* there only where your heart is! But all things—*apart from abnormal cases*—are glad to be in the place where they are, and are glad to be what they are.'[35]

Engels then delivers the following scathing commentary on this passage, drawing out the necessary political implications, implications certainly unwelcome to Feuerbach who subjectively was a sincere revolutionary democrat, but which flow inevitably from his liquidation of the Hegelian dialectic, from the elimination of all mediating determinations and relations, from his return to immediacy—all of which reflects the fact that he was unable to overcome his built-in preconceptions and look the economic and social realities of capitalism squarely in the face. Objectively, as Engels shows, his blindness on this score could have the effect of turning him into apologist for reactionary conditions.

'A fine panegyric upon the existing state of things. Exceptional cases
and a few abnormal cases apart, when you are seven years old you are
glad to become a door-keeper in a coal-mine and to remain alone in
the dark for fourteen hours a day, and because it is your existence,
therefore it is also your essence. . . . It is your "essence" to be subservient to a branch of labour.'[36]

Engels' criticism helps to explain why the radical and sometimes even
socialist intellectuals of the 1840s who looked to Feuerbach to provide
them with a philosophical foundation for their political radicalism, were
as unsuccessful as those who attempted to use Hegel for the same purposes. A close examination of Feuerbach's position would reveal that
such conscious or unconscious apologias for the existing order of things
on the basis of the immediate philosophical identity of existence and
essence have—*mutatis mutandis*—continued to play a part in the defence
of reactionary conditions and still do so today long after Feuerbach and
quite independently of him.

It was necessary to point to the political consequences of the ideological conflicts of the 1840s to make it clear how Marx's criticism of
Hegel's idealist dialectics grows out of the socialist critique of capitalism
and into the preparatory phase of the 1848 Revolution, and beyond that
to all the democratic and proletarian revolutions of the future. The internal movement of Marx's criticism shows how wrong it would be to
consider these problems purely as problems of philosophy even in Hegel.
Not the least of Feuerbach's defects is that his approach to Hegel was
confined to the purely epistemological and philosophical plane while the
dialectical interaction of such problems with the problems of society, of
man's social and economic praxis, were as good as non-existent for him.
The superiority of Hegel's philosophy over Feuerbach's (in a certain
sense, in certain areas)—despite his idealism—is precisely that Hegel did
strive, if often in vain, to make these connections the basis of his dialectics. It is for this reason that his dialectics is a watershed in the history of
philosophy: it is the highest form of idealist dialectics and so of bourgeois
philosophy in general and hence it is the mediating link capable of form-
ing a *direct* connection with dialectical materialism.

Lenin was not able to consult the Marxian Manuscripts which we have
now discussed at length and so could not know of the connections established there between economics and dialectics in the course of his critique of Hegel. Nevertheless, he had a clear view of what these
connections entailed. We have already quoted his comment that there
was a *direct* link between Marx and Hegel (p. 352). His remark insists on
a point that was wholly neglected during the period of the Second International even though Marx and Engels lost no opportunity—in prefaces,

comments and letters, etc.—to draw attention to the importance of Hegel and to urge the study of his philosophy as an indispensable prerequisite for the understanding dialectical materialism. These exhortations were utterly ignored by the most important and honest theoreticians of the period. Not even Plekhanov who, unlike Mehring and Lafargue, had made an intensive study of Hegel, had the least idea of the connections, the profound methodological links between economics and dialectics.

Following Marx, Lenin was the first to re-establish them. It would be a gross over-simplification to imagine that Lenin's critical commentary of Hegel's *Logic* should be confined to epistemology in the narrower sense. Even when he is talking about problems of knowledge Lenin is always concerned, as we saw in his remarks on teleology, with the great, universal perspectives of Marxism. In his critical comments on Hegel, therefore, he continually returns to this decisive question.

We shall illustrate this briefly, confining ourselves to a few of Lenin's most important statements:

> 'It is impossible completely to understand Marx's *Capital*, and especially its first chapter, without having thoroughly studied and understood the *whole* of Hegel's *Logic*. Consequently, half a century later none of the Marxists understood Marx!!'[37]

And elsewhere:

> 'If Marx did not leave behind him a *Logic* (with a capital letter), he did leave the *logic* of *Capital*, and this ought to be utilized to the full in this question [i.e. the question of dialectics—G.L.]. In *Capital*, Marx applied to a single science logic, dialectics and the theory of knowledge of materialism (three words are not needed: it is one and the same thing) which has taken everything valuable in Hegel and developed it further.'[38]

These comments are to be found, characteristically enough, in the midst of Lenin's analysis of the plan of Hegel's dialectics and they are followed, no less characteristically, by his observations on Marx's dialectical application of the categories of economics in *Capital*. Lenin thus demonstrates, as Marx had done before him, how philosophical problems are to be tackled and solved in dialectical materialism. The 'Lenin period' of philosophical development initiated by Stalin ought to extend these methods to every aspect of philosophy so that philosophical praxis will finally be able to eradicate the traditions of the Second International.

The 'Lenin period' of philosophy must also devote itself to the problems of history, it goes without saying. The present study was designed to make a contribution to this aspect. It aimed to explore the impact of the contradictions of capitalist society on the highest expression of bour-geois philosophy, on Hegel's idealist dialectics. We hoped to show this connection in all its social and philosophical complexity, and in particu-lar to reveal how the origins and development of the dialectic were in-fluenced by the intellectual reflection of these contradictions in the classical economic theory of England and by their actual explosion in the French Revolution. Moreover, we have been concerned to show the ef-fects—for good and evil—that resulted from the circumstance that these French and English events, both real and ideological, were brought to-gether into a dialectical method and an idealist system in the mind of a man living in the socially and economically backward nation of Germany.

Only this approach has enabled us to treat the relation between Hegel and his predecessors in a manner that could dispense with the schematic method, the violations and factual distortions current in bourgeois histo-ries of philosophy, traces of which are not uncommon in the treatment of such questions by Marxists. We believe that we have been able to show that both Hegel's independence of his important contemporaries and forerunners and also his involuntary agreement with them are to be ex-plained in terms of these problems of the nature of society.

This is not merely an historical question, not merely an issue of importance to the so-called Hegel scholars (even though they have become important and topical in consequence of the recent Fascist and Fascistoid distortions of history). An understanding of the real causes of the greatness and the limitations of the Hegelian dialectic also results in the clarification of the relation of Marx to Hegel, and the concretization of the historical heritage of Hegelianism as critically sifted and preserved in Marxism. For if one thing is clear, it is that Marx was always con-cerned with the *real* Hegel. In the midst of his polemics he always makes a clear distinction between Hegel with all his limitations, and whatever his disciples and followers have made of him. Between Marx's criticism and our age there lies almost a century whose 'achievement' in this respect consists in the distortion of our image of the real Hegel, a distortion which up to now has not been made good in any Marxist study of Hegel or any attempt to excavate the real Hegel from the rubble. The ideas with which even the majority of philosophically educated readers ap-proach Hegel are, even without their knowing it, profoundly influenced by these bourgeois falsifications. And the far-reaching implications of the critical comments of Marx, Engels, Lenin and Stalin can only be properly understood and utilized if we know the *real* object of their criti-cism, i.e. if we know the *real* Hegel.

Only in the context of this situation can the *philosophical* significance of Hegel's economic studies and ideas become fully apparent. Contradic-tory and imperfect though Hegel's views may have been, and we have analysed the contradictions inherent in them at length, it is undoubtedly no accident that the man who completed the edifice of idealist dialectics was the *only* philosopher of the age to have made a *serious* attempt to get to grips with the economic structure of capitalist society. Rather is it the case that the *specific* form of dialectics evolved by him grew out of his preoccupation with the problems of capitalism and of economics.

We repeat: the mere form of a unity of opposites, of contradictions, can be found everywhere in the modern era from Nicholas of Cusa and Giordano Bruno onwards. But as far as the *decisive* questions of dialectics are concerned, even Schelling's philosophy, the most highly developed philosophy of dialectics before Hegel, does not really advance matters further than they. The specifically Hegelian categories, whose emergence and problematic nature we have studied, were the first to elaborate the essential determinations to the point where the materialist dialectics of Marx could take over—criticizing Hegel and turning him the right way up, but nevertheless taking up *directly* where he had left off. The unique importance of Marx's critique of Hegel consists in the fact that it locates the achievement and the limitations of his dialectics in the accuracy and the defects of his grasp of the contradictions and the laws of motion of capitalist society and its economics.

Only from this vantage-point can Hegel's historical achievement be seen for what it is. Every thinker is, as Hegel remarks, the child of his age; as such he takes up where his predecessors left off. But if we wish to establish the greatness and the achievement of a thinker we must enquire how far he was dependent on his predecessors for the methods and the substance of his thought and how far he was able to test them against reality and develop them further, in short, we must determine to what extent his thought is based on reality and to what extent he remains bound by the philosophical traditions and horizons of his predecessors.

This is the qualitative distinction between Fichte and Schelling on the one hand and Hegel on the other (to say nothing of the lesser thinkers of the age, who, however, are themselves real giants when put by the side of the so-called 'great' minds of contemporary bourgeois philosophy). Obviously, the philosophies of Fichte and Schelling were determined by objective social reality, both in their assumptions and in their general lines. Philosophically speaking, however, they remain imprisoned within the framework of Kantianism, and even though Schelling, for instance, takes the step from subjective to objective idealism he remains unable to break out of that framework; all he can do is try new combinations within it, and although he declares his intentions of going beyond Kant, his real advance is proclaimed and asserted rather than genuinely realized in philosophical terms.

Hegel is the only philosopher of the period following Kant to make a truly original approach to the problems of the age. We have explored his early beginnings in detail and have seen how all the problems of dialectics grew out of his reflections on the two great world-historical facts of the age: the French Revolution and the Industrial Revolution in England. Only in the course of the concrete elaboration of his system did Hegel begin to take issue with his predecessors. Moreover, right from the start, his preoccupation with them was critical, bursting the framework of the Kantian system. Similarities with his forerunners can be found only occasionally, where the social condition of Germany forced his thought into narrow-minded and even philistine channels.

Historically, only one figure may be placed on a par with Hegel: Goethe. It is not just a coincidence that the preparatory stages of the *Phenomenology* provide evidence of a long and detailed preoccupation with Goethe's *Faust*. Both works express a similar aspiration: to provide an encyclopaedic account of the development of the mankind to the point reached in the present, and to portray that development in its immanent movement, in terms of its own laws. It was not for nothing that Pushkin referred to *Faust* as an 'Iliad of the modern world' and Schelling's witty description of his philosophy of spirit as the homecoming of spirit, as an 'Odyssey of the spirit' is an epithet better applied to the *Phenomenology* than to any work of Schelling's.

Goethe and Hegel lived at the beginning of the last great tragic period of bourgeois development. Both could see the insoluble contradictions of bourgeois society opening up on the horizon, both could see how history was creating an abyss between the individual and the species. Their greatness lay, on the one hand, in their fearless confrontation of these contradictions and in their efforts to express them at the highest level of philosophy or poetry. On the other hand, they both lived at the beginning of the period so that both were able—though not always without artificiality or inconsistency—to create lasting images of the generic experience of mankind and the development of man's generic consciousness, images which were comprehensive and large in scope, yet penetrating and true in detail. In this respect, *Wilhelm Meister* and *Faust* are documents of man's development which are just as immortal as the *Phenomenology*, the *Logic* and the *Encyclopaedia*. Of course, these profound affinities should not blind us to their differences: Goethe was much more at home in nature than was Hegel, he was closer to materialism, but equally he was unable to respond to some of Hegel's most important dialectical discoveries. A detailed history of the epoch would have to deal fully with these differences. They are of the greatest importance since only when they have been clarified will it be possible to obtain a really clear picture of the internal contradictions in the progressive currents of the period.

For our purposes, however, it is enough to establish the parallel between the two men. We do not need to chart in detail the complex dialectic that made Goethe's treatment of the problems of capitalist society partly more realistic and perceptive about the future, partly less dialectical and less sensitive to contradictions than Hegel's. It is enough for us to point out that fundamental to them both was the principle of human labour as the key to the self-creation of man. This idea appears as early as the Prometheus Fragment of the young Goethe, though not yet in a consciously economic form and—revealingly, from the point of view of the differences between Goethe and Hegel—with a marked anti-religious bias. In Goethe's greatest works, however, the self-creation of man through work is closely connected with the relation of man to capitalist society and ends in a humanist critique of capitalism. This critique does not lose sight of the idea of human progress for a single instant and so prefers to move 'amidst the manure of the contradictions' than to make concessions to any reactionary romanticism. It would be ridiculous and pedantic to attempt to draw any mechanical parallels between Goethe's literary works and the philosophy of Hegel. But the road on which Goethe discovers his *Faust* or *Wilhelm Meister* is, broadly speaking, the same as that of the spirit in Hegel's *Phenomenology*.[39]

## NOTES

1  For the first meaning cf. *Die Grundlagen der gesamten Wissenschaftslehre*, 1794, *Werke*, Vol. I, p. 360; for the second cf. *Darstellung der Wissenschaftslehre*, 1801, ibid., Vol. IV, p. 73.
2  *Werke*, Vol. I, p. 166.
3  *Theories of Surplus Value*, Vol. III, p. 267.
4  *The Phenomenology of Mind*, p. 96.
5  Engels, *Feuerbach*, in *Selected Works*, Vol. II, p. 336.
6  *The Phenomenology of Mind*, p. 807.
7  Ibid., p. 807.
8  *Jena Logic*, pp. 320ff.
9  Rosenkranz, p. 187.
10  *Reminiscences of Marx and Engels*, Moscow, n.d., p. 76.
11  *Capital*, Vol. I, p. 372.
12  *The Phenomenology of Mind*, p. 801.
13  Ibid., p. 808. The verse at the end is a free adaptation of the concluding lines of Schiller's poem *Friendship* and also the poem *God* from the *Philosophical Letters*.
14  *The Holy Family*, pp. 115–16.
15  On what follows cf. my study: 'Zur philosophischen Entwicklung des jungen Marx', in *Deutsche Zeitschrift für Philosophie*, No. 2/II /1954.
16  *Economic and Philosophic Manuscripts of 1844*, p. 108.
17  Ibid., pp. 110–11.
18  Ibid., pp. 112–13.

19   Ibid., p. 174.
20   Ibid., pp. 178–9.
21   Ibid., p. 175.
22   Ibid., p. 178.
23   Ibid., pp. 180–2.
24   Ibid., p. 188.
25   *Contribution to the Critique of Political Economy*, p. 206.
26   *Economic and Philosophic Manuscripts of 1844*, pp. 184–5.
27   In my article 'Zur philosophischen Entwicklung des jungen Marx',
     *Deutsche Zeitschrift für Philosophie*, No. 2/II/1954, I have shown that
     Marx consistently rejected the Young-Hegelian distinction be-
     tween Hegel's esoteric and exoteric line from his *Dissertation* on, and
     that he regarded attempts to explain away the exoteric line in terms
     of an accommodation to society as superficial.
28   *Werke*, Vol. VI, p. 48.
29   *The Holy Family*, p. 111.
30   *Economic and Philosophic Manuscripts of 1844*, p. 172.
31   Ibid., p. 172.
32   Ibid., p. 173.
33   Ibid., p. 176.
34   *The German Ideology*, p. 659.
35   *Werke*, Vol. II, p. 311.
36   *The German Ideology*, p. 675.
37   Lenin, *Philosophical Notebooks*, p. 180.
38   Ibid., p. 319.
39   I have discussed the parallels between *Faust* and the *Phenomenology* at
     length in my book, *Goethe and his Age*, London 1968, pp. 157–255.

# Appendix: the text of the fragment in French attributed to Hegel

The text of Hegel's French fragment: [see p. 44–5]

'Dans la monarchie le peuple ne fut une puissance active, que pour le moment du combat. Comme une armée soldée il devoit garder les rangs non seulement dans le feu du combat même, mais aussitôt après la victoire rentrer dans une parfaite obéissance. Notre expérience est accoutumée, de voir une masse d'hommes armés entrer, au mot d'ordre, dans une furie reglée du carnage et dans les loteries de mort et de vie, et sur un même mot rentrer dans le calme. On le demanda la même chose d'un peuple, qui s'est armé lui-même. Le mot d'ordre étoit la liberté, l'ennemie la tyrannie, le commandement en chef une constitution, la subordination l'obéissance envers ses réprésantants. Mais il y a bien de la différence entre la passivité de la subordination militaire et la fougue d'une insurrection; entre l'obéissance à l'ordre d'un général et la flamme de l'enthousiasme que la liberté fond par toutes les veines d'un être vivant. C'est cette flamme sacrée, qui tendoit tous les nerfs, c'est pour elle, pour jouir d'elle, qu'ils s'étoient tendus. Ces efforts sont les jouissances de la liberté et Vous voulez, qu'elle renonce à elles; ces occupations, cette activité pour la chose publique, cet intérêt est *l'agent*, et Vous voulez que le peuple s'élance encore à l'inaction, à l'ennui?'

# Index